October 15–16, 2016
Tokyo, Japan

I0038032

Association for Computing Machinery

Advancing Computing as a Science & Profession

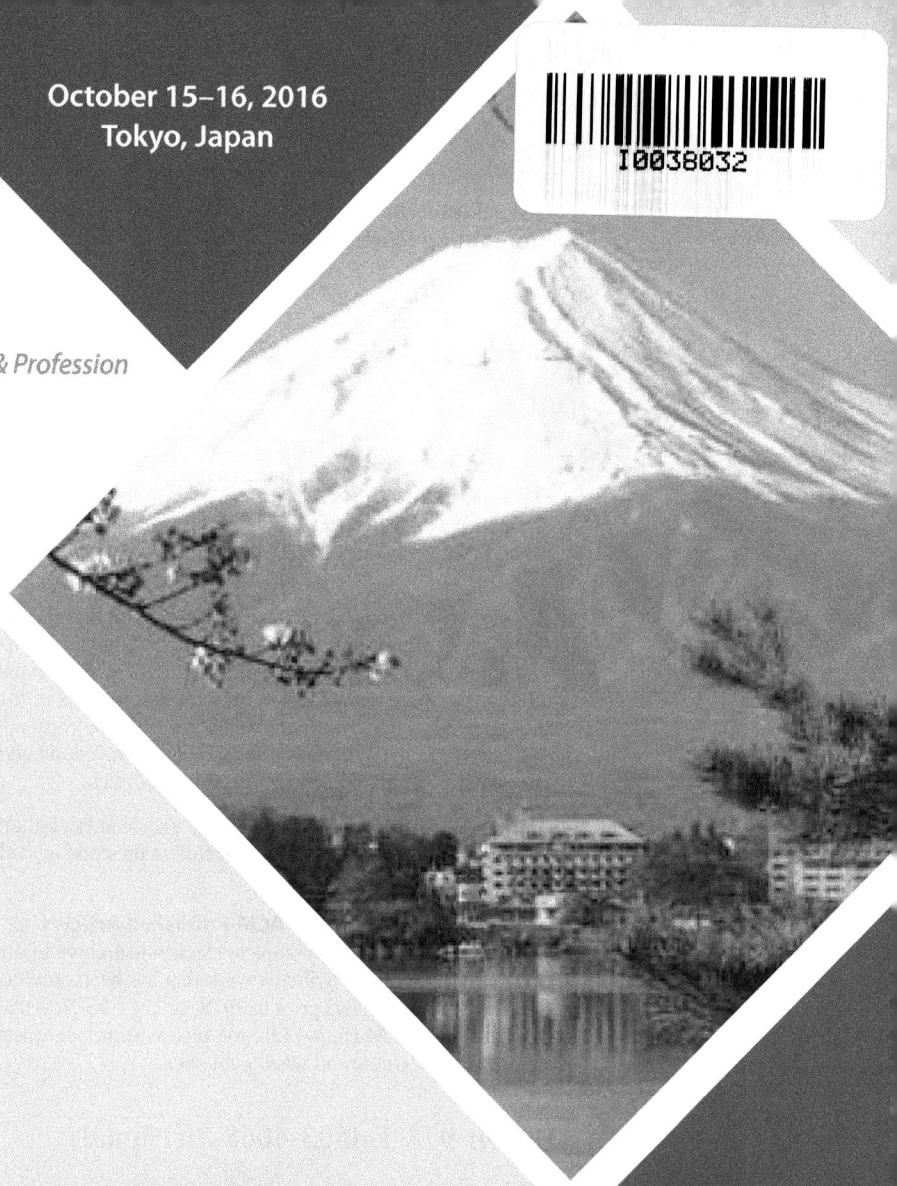

SUI'16

Proceedings of the 2016 Symposium on
Spatial User Interaction

Sponsored by:
ACM SIGCHI, ACM SIGGRAPH, and VRSJ SIG-MR

Supported by:
NS Solutions Corporation, Google, Tateisi Science and Technology Foundation,
The Institute of Image Information and Television Engineers,
The Japan Society of Artificial Intelligence, Human Interface Society,
The Robotics Society of Japan, The Virtual Reality Society of Japan,
The Institute of Electronics, Information and Communication Engineers,
& Information Processing Society of Japan

Association for
Computing Machinery

Advancing Computing as a Science & Profession

The Association for Computing Machinery
2 Penn Plaza, Suite 701
New York, New York 10121-0701

ISBN: 978-1-4503-4068-7 (Digital)

ISBN: 978-1-4503-4685-6 (Print)

Additional copies may be ordered prepaid from:

ACM Order Department
PO Box 30777
New York, NY 10087-0777, USA

Phone: 1-800-342-6626 (USA and Canada)
+1-212-626-0500 (Global)
Fax: +1-212-944-1318
E-mail: acmhelp@acm.org
Hours of Operation: 8:30 am – 4:30 pm ET

Printed in the USA

SUI 2016 Welcome Message

It is our great pleasure to welcome you to the fourth ACM Symposium on Spatial User Interaction. This event focuses on the user interface challenges that appear when users interact in the space where the flat, two-dimensional, digital world meets the volumetric, physical, three-dimensional (3D) space we live in. The symposium considers both spatial input as well as output, with an emphasis on the issues around the interaction between humans and systems. Due to the advances in 3D technologies, spatial interaction is now more relevant than ever. Powerful graphics engines and high-resolution screens are now ubiquitous in everyday devices, such as tablets and mobile phones. Moreover, new forms of input, such as multi-touch, finger and body tracking technologies are now easily available, and more and more commercial 3D systems with spatial interaction capabilities exist, many priced at the consumer level. However, the challenges, limitations, and advantages of leveraging this third dimension in human-computer interfaces are still not yet fully understood. These questions will only become more relevant as these emerging technologies continue to cross the barrier towards wide adoption.

This year, SUI received 77 submissions, the highest number since its inception. Submissions came from numerous countries including Australia, Canada, China, France, Germany, India, Israel, Japan, Korea, Saudi Arabia, Switzerland, and the United States, making SUI a truly international conference. Reviews were conducted by a similarly international team of 25 program committee members, all experts in their respective areas of spatial UIs. Three submissions were reviewed by the program chairs and rejected outright without further review due to being off topic for SUI. All other submissions received at least four reviews, two by program committee members and two by external reviewers recruited by the program committee. We employed double-blind reviewing: only the program chairs and primary reviewers were aware of the identity of authors of submissions they reviewed. The review process yielded 20 accepted papers (13 full papers, and 7 short papers) for an overall acceptance rate of 26% (or 25% for full papers, 29% for short papers). Five research demonstrations and 26 posters were also accepted for presentation at the Symposium. A unique feature of SUI 2016 is that the demonstrations will also be presented at the co-located ACM UIST 2016; furthermore, the five best SUI papers will also be presented as posters at UIST. Shahram Izadi (perceptiveIO Inc.) will deliver the Symposium keynote.

Organizing SUI 2016 was a team effort. We would like to thank the authors for providing the technical content of the program, along with the members of the international program committee and the external reviewers. We would like to thank all members of the organizing committee of SUI, consisting of 25 members. We thank the sponsoring organizations, the ACM Special Interest Groups on Graphics and Human-Computer Interaction (SIGGRAPH, SIGCHI) for co-sponsoring this event together with The Virtual Reality Society of Japan's Special Interest Group on Mixed Reality (VRSJ SIG-MR). We would also like to thank the general and local arrangement chairs of ACM UIST 2016 for their support. Last, but not least, we are grateful to Google Inc. NS Solutions and Tateisi Science and Technology Foundation for providing financial support for SUI.

We hope that you will find our program interesting, and that SUI 2016 will inspire you to discuss and share ideas with other researchers and practitioners of spatial user interaction from institutions around the world.

SUI 2016 General Chair
Christian Sandor

SUI 2016 Program Chairs
Robert Teather, Evan Suma, Kyle Johnsen

Table of Contents

Session: Applications & Technology
Session Chair: Daisuke Iwai *(Osaka University)*

Session: Input Device & Usability
Session Chair: Wolfgang Stuerzlinger *(Simon Fraser University)*

Panel
Session Chair: Aitor Rovira *(Nara Institute of Science and Technology)*

Demonstrations

Posters

SUI 2016 Symposium Organization

General Chair: Christian Sandor *(Nara Institute of Science and Technology, Japan)*

Program Chairs: Robert Teather *(Carleton University, Canada)*
Evan Suma *(University of Southern California, USA)*
Kyle Johnsen *(University Of Georgia, USA)*

Poster & Demo Chairs Gerd Bruder *(University of Central Florida, USA)*
Daisuke Iwai *(Osaka University, Japan)*

Local Arrangement Chairs Goshiro Yamamoto *(Kyoto University, Japan)*
Takuji Narumi *(University of Tokyo, Japan)*

Web Chairs: Norihiko Kawai *(Nara Institute of Science and Technology, Japan)*
Yoshinari Nishiki *(Nara Institute of Science and Technology, Japan)*

Publicity Chairs: Yuta Itoh *(Munich University of Technology, Germany)*
Maki Sugimoto *(Keio University, Japan)*
Francisco Ortega *(Florida International Univeristy, USA)*

Publication Chair: Kazuki Takashima *(Tohoku University, Japan)*

Award Chair: Steven Feiner *(Columbia University, USA)*

Finance Chair: Sei Ikeda *(Ritsumeikan University, Japan)*

Sponsorship Chair: Nobuchika Sakata *(Osaka University, Japan)*

Tourism Chair: Sebastien Duval *(Travel Stand, Japan)*

Registration Chair: Sho Sakurai *(University of Tokyo, Japan)*

Panel Chair: Aitor Rovira *(Nara Institute of Science and Technology, Japan)*

AV Chair: Parinya Punpongsanon *(Osaka University, Japan)*

Advisor: Hirokazu Kato *(Nara Institute of Science and Technology, Japan)*

Steering Committee: Frank Steinicke *(University of Hamburg, Germany)*
Wolfgang Stuerzlinger *(Simon Fraser University, Canada)*
Evan Suma *(University of Southern California, USA)*

External reviewers (continued): Benjamin Nuernberger, Jason Orlosky, Kasim Ozacar, Wai-Man Pang, Tabitha Peck, Simon Perrault, Anthony Perritano, Nate Phillips, Katrin Plaumann, Parinya Punpongsanon, Hrishikesh Rao, Alberto Raposo, Bernhard Riecke, Anne Roudaut, Nobuchika Sakata, Francesca Samsel, Anthony Scavarelli, Aaron Scherzinger, David Schroeder, Stela Seo, Marcos Serrano, Silva do Monte Lima, Paulo João, James Tompkin, Laura Trutoiu, Umair ul Hassan, Khrystyna Vasylevska, Zachary Wartell, Benjamin Weyers, Mark Whiting, Mary Whitton, Andrea Won, Paweł Woźniak, Keiko Yamamoto, Goshiro Yamamoto, Shota Yamanaka, Asim Yantac, Kian Meng Yap, Hui-Shyong Yeo, Sang Ho Yoon, James Young, Kening Zhu, David Zielinski, Angela Zoss

SUI 2016 Sponsors & Supporters

Sponsors:

Association for Computing Machinery

ACM**SIGGRAPH**

SIGCHI

SigMR

Industry Supporters

NS Solutions

Google

Grant Supporter

Tateisi Science and Technology Foundation

Academic Supporters

ITE

JSAI

Human Interface Society

RSJ

THE VIRTUAL REALITY SOCIETY OF JAPAN

EiC

IPSJ

The Reality of Mixed Reality

Shahram Izadi
perceptiveIO, Inc
San Francisco, CA, USA
shahram@perceptiveio.com

ABSTRACT

Since Ivan Sutherland's Sword of Damocles, researchers have been pushing to make augmented, virtual and mixed reality, a reality. In recent years, these technologies have exploded onto the grand stage, with many devices on the consumer market, with no apparent slowing down in terms of demand. However, whilst excitement and thirst for mixed reality technologies is at a high, there are still many challenges in making such technologies a reality for everyday consumers. In this talk, I will outline some of these challenges -- some technical, some experiential, almost all social -- and discuss how one of the key factors of taking mixed reality to the next level is around enhancing the way humans can ultimately interact and communicate. As part of this I will outline why real-time 3D capture, reconstruction and understanding of humans and the world around us is the key technology enabler in making this form of mixed reality truly ubiquitous.

Keywords

Mixed reality.

BIOGRAPHY

Shahram Izadi is CTO and co-founder of perceptiveIO a new bay area research and development lab specializing in real-time computer vision and machine learning techniques for mixed reality and interaction. Previously he was a partner researcher and research manager at Microsoft Research (Redmond) for 11 years where he led the interactive 3D technologies (I3D) group. This was an extremely multi-discipline group, which straddles many boundaries including human-computer interaction, augmented reality, applied computer vision and graphics, electronics, signal processing, and optics.

His research focuses on building new technologies and systems that blur the boundaries between real and virtual interaction. This typically involves building new types of depth cameras, sensors or displays; creating practical algorithms and techniques for these types of novel technologies; as well as designing new user experiences that are enabled through this technical research.

Previously he spent time at Xerox PARC before. Prior to that, he obtained his PhD at the Mixed Reality Lab from the University of Nottingham, United Kingdom, in 2004. In 2009, he made the TR35, an annual list published by MIT Technology Review magazine, naming the world's top 35 innovators under the age of 35 as well as a Microsoft Next award in 2012.

He has published over 120 research papers (see DBLP & Scholar), and over 120 patents.

His work has led to products such as the Microsoft Touch Mouse, Kinect for Windows, Kinect Fusion, and most recently HoloLens and Holoportation.

SUI'16, October 15-16, 2016, Tokyo, Japan
ACM 978-1-4503-4068-7/16/10.
http://dx.doi.org/10.1145/2983310.2983311

Interacting with Maps on Optical Head-Mounted Displays

David Rudi
ETH Zürich, Chair of
Geoinformation Engineering
Stefano-Franscini-Platz 5
Zürich, Switzerland
davidrudi@ethz.ch

Ioannis Giannopoulos
ETH Zürich, Chair of
Geoinformation Engineering
Stefano-Franscini-Platz 5
Zürich, Switzerland
igiannopoulos@ethz.ch

Peter Kiefer
ETH Zürich, Chair of
Geoinformation Engineering
Stefano-Franscini-Platz 5
Zürich, Switzerland
pekiefer@ethz.ch

Christian Peier
ETH Zürich, Chair of
Geoinformation Engineering
Stefano-Franscini-Platz 5
Zürich, Switzerland
chpeier@gmail.com

Martin Raubal
ETH Zürich, Chair of
Geoinformation Engineering
Stefano-Franscini-Platz 5
Zürich, Switzerland
mraubal@ethz.ch

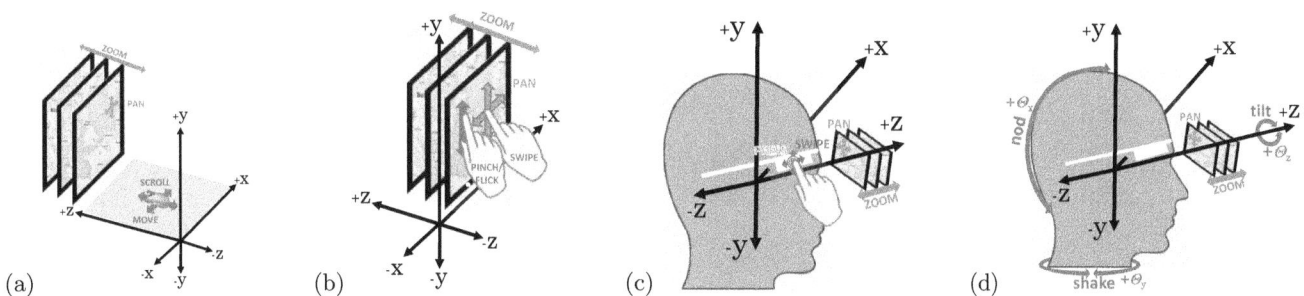

Figure 1: A depiction of how control inputs (e.g., moving the mouse along the x-axis to the left or right) correspond to map interactions (i.e., moving the map along the same axis/in the same direction) for: (a) mouse controls, (b) touch controls, (c) haptic controls on OHMD, (d) head controls on OHMD. (a) and (b) are adapted from [18].

ABSTRACT

This paper explores the design space for interacting with maps on Optical (See-Through) Head-Mounted Displays (OHMDs). The resulting interactions were evaluated in a comprehensive experiment involving 31 participants. More precisely, novel head-based interactions were compared with well-known haptic interactions on an OHMD regarding efficiency, effectiveness, user experience and perceived cognitive workload. The tasks involved navigating on maps by panning, zooming, and both panning and zooming. The results suggest that interaction methods exploiting congruent spatial relationships, i.e., mappings between the same axis in the control and display space, outperform others. In particular, the head-based interactions incorporating such mappings, significantly outperformed the haptic interactions for tasks involving panning, and combined tasks of panning and zooming.

Keywords

Interaction Design; Optical Head-Mounted Display; Maps

1. INTRODUCTION

The market for wearables, such as OHMDs is rapidly growing, and constantly new interaction modalities are introduced. Nonetheless, many limitations still exist. A common limitation of OHMDs is a restricted surface for haptic inputs, resulting from amongst others, weight restrictions and ergonomic design guidelines. This limitation is especially cumbersome in situations where users wish to navigate in large information spaces [24]. For example, consider a surveyor who is taking measurements and simultaneously has to interact with a map of her surroundings. In that case, a limited interaction surface or even the use of hands is bothersome.

To overcome the limitations of OHMDs, some researchers extended the interaction modalities (i.e., how to interact) using the built-in OHMD-hardware by, e.g., adding gesture-recognition [17]. Others added hardware, such as eye trackers [13], while a number of researchers focused on extending the interaction methods (i.e., how to use the modalities) by, e.g., using the user's head-movement [26].

In this work, we focus on those two types of input which are already available on most OHMDs on the market: head-based gestures and touch interactions. We systematically explore the design space for interacting with these two types of input in large information spaces on OHMDs, such as maps. Both the head-based gestures and the touch interactions are performed in space. In particular, we argue that the congruency of the spatial movements (required for the interactions) with their mapping to the display space is decisive for their adequateness. Moreover, we introduce a novel design that allows for a better user performance while navigating on maps displayed on OHMDs using head-based gestures.

We developed a prototypical client for Google Glass supporting the Web Map Service (WMS) standard[1] and conducted a user study with 31 participants. Cartographic maps, amongst others, are documents containing a rich amount of information, requiring users to navigate using pan and zoom interactions [1, 24]. Considering that we live in a mobile information society, where people extensively use mobile maps and navigation services, there is a need to explore appropriate interaction methods with these [10]. This paper makes the following contributions concerning the navigation on maps using OHMDs:

- The exploration of the design space for the navigation on maps on OHMDs, following a method proposed by MacKenzie for interactions with desktops and tablets [18].

- A novel design for interactions with maps on OHMDs, based on head gestures with the aim to avoid unintentional interactions.

- The comparison of the novel head-based with the haptic interactions, with regard to efficiency (task completion time), effectiveness (error rate), user experience (UEQ), and perceived cognitive workload (raw NasaTLX) for tasks involving navigation on maps, i.e. panning, zooming and combinations thereof.

The remainder of this paper is structured as follows: sections 2 and 3 describe the existing research and evaluate the design space for map navigation on desktops and tablets, as well as OHMDs. Then, in section 4 we introduce our hypotheses and methodology. The results are presented in section 5 and discussed in section 6. Finally, the conclusions and future work are given in section 7.

2. RELATED WORK

This section reviews the interaction methods (i.e., input controls) for OHMDs that have been explored in previous research. Furthermore, section 2.2 explains the methodological approach proposed by [18] upon which we base our exploration of the design space in Section 3.

2.1 Interaction Methods for OHMDs

Head Mounted Displays (HMDs) are displays that are worn on the head and exist in many different variations [3]. They are usually categorized into optical see-through HMDs (OHMDs), video see-through HMDs or opaque ones. Information is either presented in front of one (monocular) or both eyes (binocular). The study in this paper is conducted using Google Glass [25], which is categorized as a monocular OHMD.

2.1.1 Haptic- and Other Interaction Methods

To circumvent the limited haptic interaction space, OHMDs were enhanced with external input devices, such as large external touch pads or a belt [19, 6].

Furthermore, several state-of-the art OHMDs provide alternatives to the haptic methods, such as external smartphones for controlling the OHMD remotely, or hand gesture recognition capabilities. The latter has been evaluated in detail [15] and extended by introducing input modalities that use different body parts for gesture recognition, such as the face [22] or feet [17].

Even though these methods provide a wide range of interaction possibilities, they all involve the use of extraneous body parts. This implies that they are very visible in public [26], and not suitable for users with disabilities [19] or in situations where users cannot involve the respective body parts in the task at hand. Some of these alternatives require the use of an additional device, which usually implies additional weight, costs and maintenance effort.

2.1.2 Hands-Free Interaction Methods

There has been extensive research on the use of voice as an interaction method for OHMDs, e.g., to perform game control tasks [26], to navigate between instructions [28] and to evaluate their use for people with disabilities [20]. However, it was found that voice commands have performance issues and are less favored interaction methods in public.

Head-based gestures were explored for simple interactions with mobile devices (e.g., scrolling [21]) or displays (e.g., point of view changes in games [5]). Concerning OHMDs, head-based gestures were for instance used to determine user activities (in combination with eye gestures) [12], for game control tasks [26], to select elements in physical spaces [27] and to evaluate smart spaces interactions [15]. Similar to voice commands, head-based gestures have the drawback of being visible in public and can result in fatigue.

Another approach to hands-free interaction with OHMDs is based on using gaze as an input method [11, 13]. While using gaze as an interaction method is promising, the currently available OHMDs can only detect blinks, but not fixations or saccades[2].

Regarding the previously described advantages and disadvantages of the various interaction methods, we decided to focus on the possibilities of using head-based gestures for interacting with OHMDs and compared our approach with the built-in capabilities of OHMDs using haptic inputs. A further reason for this decision is the fact that this type of interaction can also be used in scenarios where, e.g., the use of hands is not possible.

2.2 Spatial Control-Display Relationships

MacKenzie describes the *control-display relationship* as one that attributes to "how a controller property maps to a display property" (p. 75) and separates between *spatial*, *dynamic* and *physical relationships* (or "- mappings") [18]. *Spatial relationships* represent mappings from movements of the controller in space to movements on the display, e.g., the mapping from a mouse to a cursor. To systematically examine the relationships in more detail, he introduces (arbitrarily chosen) labels for the axes of a 3D Cartesian coor-

---

[1]A WMS is a web service providing (geographically referenced) map images, generated by a server using data from a Geographic Information System (GIS) database. See also http://www.opengeospatial.org/standards/wms

[2]The recently introduced HoloLens (https://www.microsoft.com/microsoft-hololens/en-us) is an exception, but has not yet surpassed the development state.

dinate space, i.e., the degrees of freedom (DOF) (see Figure 1). Table 1 visualizes these mappings, by showing how control inputs map to display outputs. For example, the first row shows that moving the mouse along the x-axis, moves the cursor (a map) along the same axis on a display.

spatially congruent mappings, i.e., a mapping between the same axes in the control and display space. These mappings pose natural relationships (as opposed to learned relationships) and thus result in a better user experience.

Cartographic maps can be considered 2D (or even 3D) representations of spatial phenomena [23]. They commonly follow the metaphor of viewing a certain extent of a space from a top-down perspective. To solve a task, a user is required to change this limited extent, either by moving it (panning) or by (de-) magnifying a specific part to the full extent (zooming). Both panning and zooming are considered to be the most important map interactions [8].

The spatial relationship between a mouse and a cursor easily translates to panning a map. A movement of the mouse along the x-axis (i.e., left or right) can be related to moving a map extent along the same axis (congruent), while moving the mouse along the z-axis (i.e., forwards or backwards) corresponds to moving the map along the y-axis (i.e., up or down) (see Figure 1). Zooming can be described as the movement along a virtual z-axis of a display, where each zoom-extent is a different layer. The mouse-wheel is commonly used as the control input when zooming and scrolling the wheel forwards or backwards along the z-axis results in movements along the same axis (see Figure 1 (a) and Table 1 ("Mouse")).

The mouse-display relationship can be extended to touch displays as depicted in Figure 1 (b) and Table 1 ("Touch"). That is, the controller is a user's touch input and the display a touch display, such as a tablet. Touch displays allow a fully congruent mapping for panning, i.e., moving the finger along the x-axis or y-axis (i.e., the z-axis, when the display is lying flat) results in a movement along the same axis for the map. As for zooming, the touch display's multi-touch capabilities allow users to flick or pinch with two fingers (moving them into opposite directions) to respectively zoom in or out. The control input by flicking or pinching takes place on a plane perpendicular to the z-axis (i.e., along the x-axis, the y-axis, or a combination of both).

Next to the ones described above, desktops and tablets have other hard controls, such as mouse-clicks and tapping. A thorough description of those and their spatial relationships can be found in [18]. For maps on OHMDs, a detailed evaluation of the spatial relationships is missing and is therefore evaluated in the next section for head-based gestures and touch interactions.

3. SPATIAL RELATIONSHIPS FOR MAPS ON OHMDS

Next to the interaction methods being explored in ongoing research, an analysis of the specifications of OHMDs on the market showed that they all support head-based inputs and most support touch inputs. For the studies conducted in this research Google Glass was used, which supports both. Hence, the spatial relationships that hold true for head and haptic gestures concerning panning and zooming on an OHMD are evaluated.

For pan interactions, movements of the map extent along

Table 1: Visualization of how inputs along a control axis, map onto a display axis (adapted from [18]).

DOF	Panning		Zooming	
---	Control	Display	Control	Display
	Controller: Mouse			
x				
y				
z				
	Controller: Touch			
x				
y				
z				

Table 2: An overview of the spatial relationships evaluated in this paper between touch and head control inputs with an OHMD for both pan and zoom.

DOF	Panning		Zooming	
---	Control	Display	Control	Display
	Controller: Touch			
x		right/left	z^t_{press}	
y	$P^t_{up/down}$	up/down	$z^t_{up/down}$	
z	$P^t_{forth/back}$		$z^t_{forth/back}$	out/in
	Controller: Head			
x		right/left		
y		up/down		
z				out/in
$\Theta(x)$	P^h_{nod}		z^h_{nod}	
$\Theta(y)$	P^h_{shake}			
$\Theta(z)$				

the x- and y-axis need to be covered by two corresponding inputs of the controller. Zoom interactions require a control input for movements along the z-axis, while combinations of pan and zoom need a mapping for all axes.

Touch pads of OHMDs commonly provide 2.5 DOF for inputs. That is, swiping forwards or backwards along the z-axis, sliding upwards or downwards along the y-axis and tapping or pressing on the x-axis (see Figure 1 (c)). All of these inputs can be extended by considering the use of one or more fingers or (except for the x-axis) multi-touch gestures such as flicking or pinching.

The built-in gyroscope and accelerometers of OHMDs allow a distinction between six DOF for head-based gesture inputs. On the one hand, a user can move her head along the three axes (3 DOF), i.e., do "head slides" along the axes while standing still. On the other hand, a user can turn her head to the left or right around the y-axis (shake), look up or down around the x-axis (nod) and tilt it to the left or right around the z-axis (tilt) (see Figure 1 (d)).

3.1 Design Space

This section analyzes the design space. That is, spatial relationships are evaluated concerning potential map movements, for zoom-, pan- and mixed tasks. We justify which mappings were chosen to be included in the user study (see section 4.5) and provide an overview of the corresponding spatial relationships in Table 2.

For an easy and clear evaluation of the design space the following abbreviations are used: a large letter represents the map interaction, "$\mathbf{Z}$" for zooming and "$\mathbf{P}$" for panning; a small superscript letter represents the modality, "$\mathbf{h}$" for head and "$\mathbf{t}$" for touch; finally in subscript the modality is described, e.g., "$\mathbf{press}$" for pressing the finger against the touch pad.

Panning, touch (P^t). The x-axis can be used for panning, either by considering subsequent taps (e.g., 1 tap = up, 2 taps = down) or different numbers of fingers that press against the touch pad (e.g., 1 finger = up, 2 fingers = down). However, simultaneously using up to 4 fingers (i.e., for 4 directions) would require a large interaction space, contradicting the common OHMD design restrictions. Additionally, our pilot study showed that excessive tapping led to displacements of the OHMD. Combinations of control inputs of pressing on the x-axis with swipes along the y- or z-axis were dismissed due to the anticipated higher workload resulting from the degree changes. Furthermore, the pilot study did not show any indication that swiping with a different number of fingers results in measurable performance differences. Finally, both flicking and pinching were abandoned, due to the limited space along the y-axis.

Consequently, the only remaining axes to be combined were the y- and z-axis, which were used with single finger inputs as $\mathbf{P}^t_{\text{up/down, forth/back}}$ (see Table 2 rows 2 and 3 under "Panning"). There is no consensus on the directionality of the input in the literature [14, 4], i.e., whether swiping forward on the touch pad of the OHMD corresponds to panning left or right on the map. In this work backward (forward) swipes are associated with pans to left (right) as suggested in [4].

Panning, head (P^h). The analysis of the design space for head-based gestures out-ruled the use of x, y and z, because "head slides" turned out to be difficult to perform and are difficult to differentiate from rotations (technically). While head "rotations" around all axes can be associated with either one of the pan movements, some variants were excluded based on the experiences from the pilot study. That is, "tilting" in general, "nodding" for left/right pans and "shaking" for up/down pans.

Hence, $\mathbf{P}^h_{\text{nod, shake}}$ (see Table 2 rows 7 and 8 under "Panning") was evaluated by congruently mapping pan directions according to the head movement, i.e., moving the head upwards (nodding) is mapped onto panning the map upwards. Note, that even though mapping "nodding" onto the y-axis does not appear congruent at first, it actually is, because a nodding user is looking up and down along an "invisible" y-axis.

Zooming, touch (Z^t). In contrast to panning, the x-axis can be used for zooming. While tapping was still excluded due to the inherent displacement of the OHMD, using different numbers of fingers that press and hold was a valid alternative. More precisely, based on our experience from the pilot study, $\mathbf{Z}^t_{\text{press}}$ (see Table 2 row 1 under "Zooming") was evaluated as the combination of pressing with two fingers to zoom-in and three to zoom-out.

Both the y- and z-axis can be used for zoom interactions. Regular swipes along these axes are denoted as $\mathbf{Z}^t_{\text{up/down}}$ and $\mathbf{Z}^t_{\text{forth/back}}$ (see Table 2 rows 2 and 3 under "Zooming"). With regard to directionality, forward/backward swipes along the z-axis were interpreted as a zoom out/in interactions and upward/downward swipes as zooming out/in.

Zooming, head (Z^h). The axes x, y and z were excluded for zooming with the same argumentation as for panning. Furthermore, "tilting" and "shaking" were excluded for zooming, due to their lack of intuitiveness. Thus, $\mathbf{Z}^h_{\text{nod}}$ (see Table 2 row 7 under "Zooming")was evaluated and head-up (down) gestures were associated with zooming out (in).

Finally, combinations of haptic interactions and head-based gestures (e.g., swipe up = pan up and head left = pan left) for both panning and zooming were not evaluated, to avoid mode changes within a single interaction.

Panning and Zooming. Given the selected zoom and pan interactions, the design space for combinations thereof is large. However, combining $\mathbf{Z}^t_{\text{up/down}}$ or $\mathbf{Z}^t_{\text{forth/back}}$ with $\mathbf{P}^t_{\text{up/down, forth/back}}$, as well as $\mathbf{Z}^h_{\text{nod}}$ with $\mathbf{P}^h_{\text{nod, shake}}$ is not possible due to ambiguities.

Furthermore, the remaining combinations of $\mathbf{Z}^h_{\text{nod}}$ with $\mathbf{P}^t_{\text{up/down, forth/back}}$ and both $\mathbf{Z}^t_{\text{up/down}}$ and $\mathbf{Z}^t_{\text{forth/back}}$ with $\mathbf{P}^h_{\text{nod, shake}}$ were skipped in favor of comparing $\mathbf{P}^h_{\text{nod, shake}}$ with $\mathbf{P}^t_{\text{up/down, forth/back}}$ using the only zoom input that can be combined with both, i.e., $\mathbf{Z}^t_{\text{press}}$.

Thus, in this paper, the combinations ($\mathbf{P}^h_{\text{nod, shake}}$, $\mathbf{Z}^t_{\text{press}}$) and ($\mathbf{P}^t_{\text{up/down, forth/back}}$, $\mathbf{Z}^t_{\text{press}}$) are evaluated.

4. METHODOLOGY

In this section we first explain the overall study design, including the dependent and independent variables and present our hypotheses. Afterwards, we give an overview of the study, including information of the participants and the setup, i.e., the hardware and software. Next, we elaborate on how we realized the novel head-based gestures and explain the study procedure in detail. That is, the lessons learned from the pilot study, how we advanced for the main study, as well as a detailed explanation about the tasks involved.

4.1 Study Design and Hypotheses

A within subject design was employed for the experiment with the interaction method as the independent variable and effectiveness, efficiency, user experience and perceived cognitive workload as dependent variables.

More precisely, effectiveness was measured by the number of errors made. That is, each zoom or pan step that did not get closer to a target zoom level (i.e., the difference of the current zoom and the target zoom is increasing) or location (i.e., increasing euclidean distance) was counted as an error. However, errors did not accumulate for consecutive incorrect steps, i.e., moving farther away from the target twice was still counted as one error[3]. Efficiency was measured by the task completion time, while user experience as well as perceived cognitive workload were measured using standardized questionnaires (UEQ [16] and NASA TLX [9]).

With regard to the independent variables, users were given three different tasks:

- The first task involved zooming and had four conditions: $\mathbf{Z}^h_{\text{nod}}$, $\mathbf{Z}^t_{\text{press}}$, $\mathbf{Z}^t_{\text{up/down}}$ and $\mathbf{Z}^t_{\text{forth/back}}$.

- The second task required users to pan and had two conditions $\mathbf{P}^h_{\text{nod, shake}}$ and $\mathbf{P}^t_{\text{up/down, forth/back}}$.

- The final, third task was a combination of panning and zooming and had two conditions ($\mathbf{P}^h_{\text{nod, shake}}$, $\mathbf{Z}^t_{\text{press}}$) and ($\mathbf{P}^t_{\text{up/down, forth/back}}$, $\mathbf{Z}^t_{\text{press}}$).

---

[3]This was introduced to account for sensory imprecision.

To avoid a learning effect we used a counterbalanced design (balanced latin square) (see subsection 4.5.3 for details).

Considering the spatial mappings of the interaction methods and the assumption that congruent mappings between a control input and the display have a higher level of intuitiveness, the following **hypotheses** were made:

H1. For the panning task, the interaction method $\mathbf{P}^h_{\text{nod, shake}}$ performs best with regard to the given dependent variables.

H2. For the zooming task, the interaction method $\mathbf{Z}^t_{\text{forth/back}}$ performs best with regard to the given dependent variables.

H3. For the combination of panning and zooming, the interaction method $(\mathbf{P}^h_{\text{nod, shake}}, \mathbf{Z}^t_{\text{press}})$ performs best with regard to the given dependent variables.

4.2 Participants

In total 31 participants (18 males) were recruited for the experiment. The participants had a mean age of 30 years *(SD = 11)*. On average, the participants were using digital maps more than once per week and except for 5 participants, they had never used an OHMD before.

4.3 Setup

The room lighting was slightly dimmed to allow for a better contrast between the Google Glass display and the white wall participants were facing during task execution. A monitor was placed to the participants' right-hand side on which participants read questionnaires and instructions before and between the tasks.

The hardware setup consisted of a Google Glass[4] (OS version: XE22) paired with a smartphone (Google Galaxy Nexus 2 (I9250), OS version: 4.2.1). The paired smartphone allowed us to observe participants remotely throughout the study and supplied the Google Glass with internet access.

The software setup included the WMS client, which loaded and displayed (study specific) maps and allowed participants to interact with them (see section 4.4 below). The application had a logging mechanism that stored each zoom or pan interaction made by the users with its time of occurrence.

The questionnaires and instructions were created using the Collector Application[5].

4.4 Implementation of Interaction Methods

Evaluating possible implementations for head-based gestures revealed that users had difficulties controlling their input. Users found it particularly difficult to identify the moment a head-based gesture results in a reaction from the application. To overcome these limitations, we introduced a novel approach for implementing head-based gestures. That is, for $\mathbf{Z}^h_{\text{nod}}$ the user was provided a dot representing her current head orientation, as well as two horizontal bars at the top and bottom area of the display (see Figure 2 (a)). Thus, whenever the user moved her head up or down (i.e., nods) the dot moved accordingly. As long as the dot was within

---

[4]The touch pad of Google Glass has a width of 8cm and a height of 1.1cm.

[5]http://www.survalyzer.ch

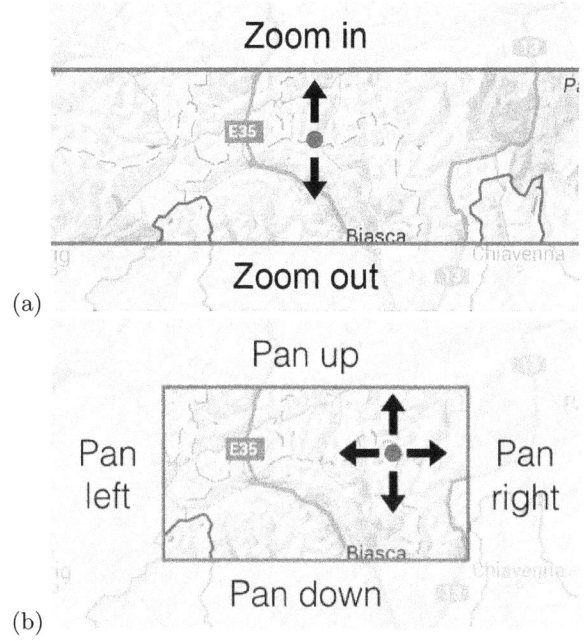

(a)

(b)

Figure 2: The user's current head orientation (red dot) in relation to the amount of rotation required for an interaction (red lines) was displayed for interaction methods (a) $\mathbf{Z}^h_{\text{nod}}$ and (b) $\mathbf{P}^h_{\text{nod, shake}}$. The arrows and text were not visible on the screen.[7]

the bars, the map did not move, i.e., zoom (or pan). However, as soon as the dot surpassed either one, the app started zooming. A single zoom was realized as (de)magnifying the current pane by a factor of two, every 400ms as determined in the pilot study. Moreover, if users moved the red dot to the far edge of the screen a zoom-in or -out happened every 200ms.

$\mathbf{P}^h_{\text{nod, shake}}$ provided the user a dot and a rectangle (see Figure 2 (b)). As for $\mathbf{Z}^h_{\text{nod}}$, the dot moved according to the users nodding (up or down) or shaking (left or right) and panning began when the dot surpassed the borders of the rectangle. A pan interaction implied moving the pane by 1/8 of its overall width in the given head direction every 400ms. When the dot was moved to the edge of the pane, the panning took place every 200ms, too.

Touch interactions were identified by the number of units surpassed during a continuous swipe. A zoom occurred, when swipes surpassed 150 units (of 1366) for $\mathbf{Z}^t_{\text{forth/back}}$ and 30 units (of 187) for $\mathbf{Z}^t_{\text{up/down}}$. As for $\mathbf{P}^t_{\text{up/down, forth/back}}$, swipes in both directions exceeding 30 units were considered a pan. For $\mathbf{Z}^t_{\text{press}}$, a zoom occurred every 400ms.

4.5 Procedure

4.5.1 Pilot Study

A pilot study with three participants was conducted in order to ensure that the study procedure would be flawless, as well as to receive feedback on the interaction methods. As a result, we dismissed tapping as input control, due to displacement of the glasses. Furthermore, we chose to use

---

[7]Map data ©2016 Google

a single finger for swiping inputs, because there were no measurable differences between the number of fingers. After looking into the different head inputs, we chose the given head rotations to be most suitable as control inputs, due to the lower fatigue compared to actual movements and based on their technical feasibility. Finally, we chose the number of fingers for $\mathbf{Z}^t_{press}$ giving the interaction the highest stability and the step sizes (times and units) for zooming and panning, which the pilot study participants perceived to be the most convenient.

4.5.2 Main Study

While participants were sitting in the office, they received a brief introduction to the overall experiment and were asked to fill out a questionnaire assessing demographics and experience information (regarding OHMDs and digital maps). Google Glass and its mechanisms were explained and participants had time to adjust the prism to ensure that the edges of the screen were visible.

Each task was introduced in general and with an example instruction. A task consisted of several instructions. Participants were asked to execute instructions as fast as possible. Before solving a task with an interaction method, the method was explained, and a 30 second training phase was granted. A task was successful when participants completed all instructions, i.e., reaching a given location and zoom level. A task was aborted, if the time surpassed 180 seconds (for Task 1 and 2) or 240 seconds (for Task 3).

Each instruction requires users to repeat an interaction a different number of times. The frequency was chosen as to avoid fatigue, but to provide meaningful data. Furthermore, to avoid learning effects, the order of the instructions was changed between interaction methods. Finally, we chose the order of the tasks based on the number of axes involved.

After completing a task with an interaction method, the participant was asked to fill out the UEQ questionnaire [16] and the "Raw" Nasa TLX [9].

4.5.3 Tasks

Task 1 - Zooming. A total of 4 instructions had to be executed, performing a sequence of alternating zoom in and -out interactions starting and ending at zoom level 1. A typical instruction was of the form *"Please zoom in, until you see the label of the countries, for example, Switzerland"*.

Task 2 - Panning. In a total of 7 instructions, participants had to pan to a specific target location denoted by a white letter in a yellow pentagon. To know whether the correct map extent was reached, a small yellow rectangle was included. The target location was reached, when the pentagon was inside the rectangle (see Figure 3). A typical instruction was of the form *"Pan left, until location A is in the yellow box"*.

Task 3 - Panning and Zooming. Participants were asked to navigate to a specific target location by zooming and panning. This task included a total of 10 instructions, consisting of 3 zoom and 7 pan instructions. The procedure for those instructions was the same as for task 1 and 2, but included the yellow box for both panning and zooming. As an example, an instruction sequence of panning followed by zooming, was of the form *"Pan left, until the country label "CH" is in the yellow box"* followed by *"Zoom in, until location A is in the yellow box"*.

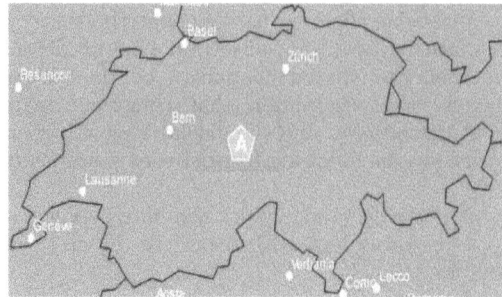

Figure 3: Map shown for the navigation tasks on the OHMD. In this example, the task is finished since the target position (A) is inside the yellow rectangle.

5. RESULTS

In this section we present the experimental results for the zooming, panning and their combination (see independent variables, section 4.1) with regard to efficiency, effectiveness, user experience (UX) and perceived cognitive workload (TLX).

5.1 Zooming

To evaluate the zooming task with four test conditions we applied the Friedman test to identify any statistical significance and the Wilcoxon signed-rank test for a pairwise comparison of the test conditions along with the Bonferroni correction [2], to weigh out the multiple comparison problem.

5.1.1 Effectiveness and Efficiency

Effectiveness. There was a significant difference over all interaction methods ($\chi^2 = 16.875$, $p < .05$). However, there were no significant differences between $\mathbf{Z}^h_{nod}$ and $\mathbf{Z}^t_{up/down}$, $\mathbf{Z}^h_{nod}$ and $\mathbf{Z}^t_{press}$, or $\mathbf{Z}^t_{up/down}$ and $\mathbf{Z}^t_{press}$. All other methods showed pairwise significant differences (see Table 3). The most effective zoom interaction method in terms of average number of errors was $\mathbf{Z}^t_{forth/back}$ with a mean of *1.13* errors *(SD = 1.76)*. The least effective one was $\mathbf{Z}^t_{press}$ with a mean of *4.65* errors *(SD = 5.096)* (see Figure 4).

Efficiency. There was a statistically significant difference over all interaction methods ($\chi^2 = 33.387$, $p < .05$). However, there were no significant differences between $\mathbf{Z}^t_{forth/back}$ and $\mathbf{Z}^t_{up/down}$ or between $\mathbf{Z}^h_{nod}$ and $\mathbf{Z}^t_{press}$ (after a Bonferroni correction). All other interaction methods showed pairwise significant differences (see Table 3). The most efficient zoom interaction in terms of average completion time was $\mathbf{Z}^t_{up/down}$ with a mean of *17.1* seconds *(SD = 6.9)*. The least efficient one was $\mathbf{Z}^t_{press}$ with a mean of *33.9* seconds *(SD = 18.2)*.

5.1.2 User Experience and Workload

UX. We will abbreviate the UX scales as follows: Attractiveness = **AT**, Perspicuity = **PE**, Efficiency = **EF**, Dependability = **DP**, Stimulation = **ST** and Novelty = **NV**. Furthermore, for the UX only the results for the UX-AT scale are described in detail, since it represents the overall impression of the method.

There was a significant difference over all interaction methods for all UX scales ($\chi^2 > 15$, $p < .001$). For the

Table 3: Inferential statistics on effectiveness (top) and efficiency (bottom). Z values in bold, when $p < .012$ (Bonferroni adjusted), i.e., indicating significant differences.

Method	Z^h_{nod}	$Z^t_{forth/back}$	$Z^t_{up/down}$
$Z^t_{forth/back}$	**-2.656**	-	-
$Z^t_{up/down}$	-0.186	**-3.225**	-
Z^t_{press}	-1.277	**-3.396**	-1.213

Method	Z^h_{nod}	$Z^t_{forth/back}$	$Z^t_{up/down}$
$Z^t_{forth/back}$	**-3.763**	-	-
$Z^t_{up/down}$	**-3.116**	-0.607	-
Z^t_{press}	-2.391	**-4.017**	**-4.507**

Table 4: The inferential statistics on the UX scales for the zoom methods. The Z values are given in bold, when $p < .012$ (Bonferroni adjusted), i.e., there was a significant difference.

Method	Z^h_{nod}		$Z^t_{forth/back}$		$Z^t_{up/down}$	
$Z^t_{forth/back}$	**-3.955**^{AT}	**-3.334**^{PE}	–	–	–	–
	-4.271^{EF}	**-4.159**^{DP}	–	–	–	–
	-2.054ST	**-3.695**^{NV}	–	–	–	–
$Z^t_{up/down}$	**-3.150**^{AT}	-2.102^{PE}	-2.049^{AT}	-0.986^{PE}	–	–
	-3.451^{EF}	-1.830^{DP}	-1.250^{EF}	**-3.183**^{DP}	–	–
	-2.471ST	**-3.667**^{NV}	-1.171ST	-0.592^{NV}	–	–
Z^t_{press}	-0.125^{AT}	-0.626^{PE}	**-3.982**^{AT}	**-3.736**^{PE}	**-3.121**^{AT}	**-2.657**^{PE}
	-0.858^{EF}	-2.009^{DP}	**-3.791**^{EF}	**-4.630**^{DP}	**-3.631**^{EF}	**-3.355**^{DP}
	-2.398ST	**-3.183**^{NV}	-1.760ST	**-3.039**^{NV}	-1.498ST	**-2.782**^{NV}

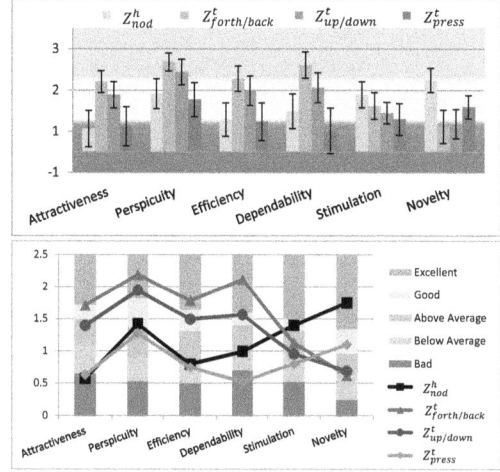

Figure 5: The UX scale (top) and benchmark (bottom) of the zoom methods.

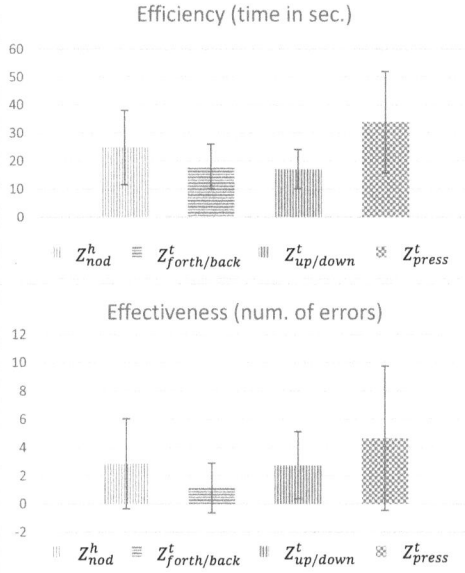

Figure 4: The efficiency (top) and effectiveness (bottom) of the zoom methods, measured as the average task completion time in seconds (SD as error bars).

UX-AT scale, there were no significant differences between $\mathbf{Z}^t_{forth/back}$ and $\mathbf{Z}^t_{up/down}$, as well as between $\mathbf{Z}^h_{nod}$ and $\mathbf{Z}^t_{press}$. All other methods showed a pairwise significant difference with regard to UX-AT (see Table 4). The highest overall UX-AT value was that of $\mathbf{Z}^t_{forth/back}$ with a value of *1.71* *(SD = .75)*, while $\mathbf{Z}^h_{nod}$ had the lowest value with .57 *(SD = 1.24)* (see Figure 5).

TLX. We will abbreviate the TLX components as follows: Mental Demand = **MD**, Physical Demand = **PD**, Temporal Demand = **TD**, Performance = **OP**, Effort = **EF**, Frustration = **FR** and **OV** for the overall workload (sum of components). Furthermore, for the TLX only the results for the TLX-OV component are described in detail, since it represents the overall perceived workload.

There was a significant difference over all interaction methods for all components $(\chi^2 > 16, p < .001)$ except for TLX-TD $(\chi^2 = 5.581, p < .134)$ (see Table 5). However, for the TLX-OV there were no significant differences between $\mathbf{Z}^t_{forth/back}$ and $\mathbf{Z}^t_{up/down}$, or $\mathbf{Z}^h_{nod}$ and $\mathbf{Z}^t_{press}$. All other meth-

Table 5: The inferential statistics on the TLX (top) and TLX-OV (bottom) for the zoom methods. The Z values are given in bold, when $p < .012$ (Bonferroni adjusted), i.e., there was a significant difference.

Method	Z^h_{nod}		$Z^t_{forth/back}$		$Z^t_{up/down}$	
$Z^t_{forth/back}$	**-3.451**^{MD}	**-4.008**^{PD}	–	–	–	–
	-0.792^{TD}	**-2.920**^{OP}	–	–	–	–
	-2.919^{EF}	**-3.312**^{FR}	–	–	–	–
$Z^t_{up/down}$	-2.483^{MD}	**-4.000**^{PD}	-1.654^{MD}	-0.525^{PD}	–	–
	-2.200^{TD}	-2.103^{OP}	-1.913^{TD}	-0.771^{OP}	–	–
	-2.607^{EF}	**-2.997**^{FR}	-0.824^{EF}	-0.343^{FR}	–	–
Z^t_{press}	-0.542^{MD}	**-3.384**^{PD}	**-3.055**^{MD}	-2.029^{PD}	-2.147^{MD}	-2.277^{PD}
	-0.635^{TD}	-1.152^{OP}	-0.128^{TD}	**-3.515**^{OP}	-2.284^{TD}	**-3.604**^{OP}
	-0.308^{EF}	-0.653^{FR}	**-3.193**^{EF}	**-3.143**^{FR}	**-2.779**^{EF}	**-3.144**^{FR}

Method	Z^h_{nod}	$Z^t_{forth/back}$	$Z^t_{up/down}$
$Z^t_{forth/back}$	**-4.087**	-	-
$Z^t_{up/down}$	**-3.940**	-0.154	-
Z^t_{press}	-0.588	**-3.685**	**-3.632**

ods showed a pairwise significant difference with regard to TLX-OV. The highest TLX-OV value was that of $\mathbf{Z}^h_{nod}$ with a mean of 36 *(SD = 18.13)*, while $\mathbf{Z}^t_{forth/back}$ had the lowest value with a mean of 20.87 *(SD = 13.40)* (see Figure 6).

5.2 Panning

For panning we applied the Wilcoxon signed-rank test, since we had only two test conditions.

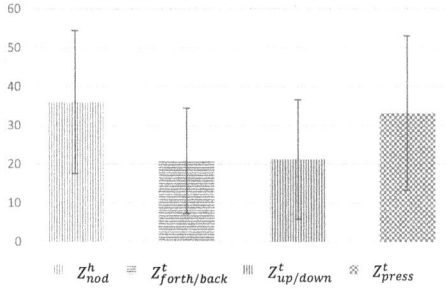

Figure 6: The results of the TLX-OV for the zoom methods (SD as error bars).

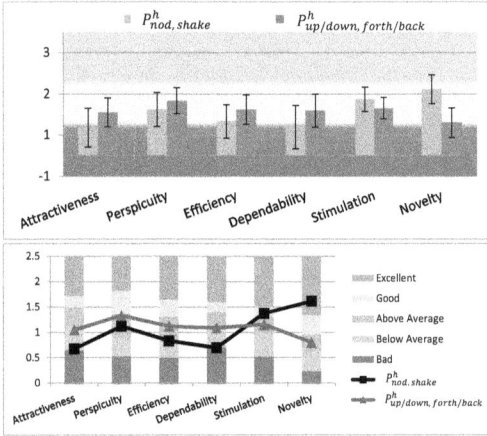

Figure 7: The UX scales (top) and benchmark (bottom) of the pan methods.

5.2.1 Effectiveness and Efficiency

Effectiveness. There was a significant difference between the interaction methods $(Z = -2.582, p < .05)$. The more effective pan interaction method was $\mathbf{P}^h_{\text{nod, shake}}$ with a mean of *12.6* errors *(SD = 18.37)*, while $\mathbf{P}^t_{\text{up/down, forth/back}}$ resulted in a mean of *25* errors *(SD = 20.69)*.

Efficiency. There was no significant difference between the interaction methods $(Z = -1.920, p = .055)$. $\mathbf{P}^t_{\text{up/down, forth/back}}$ had a mean completion time of *56* seconds *(SD = 28.2)*, while $\mathbf{P}^h_{\text{nod, shake}}$ resulted in a mean of *72.3* seconds *(SD = 39.2)*.

5.2.2 User Experience and Workload

UX. There were no significant differences over the two interaction methods for all UX scales except for UX-NV $(Z = -3.240, p < .05)$. The higher UX-AT scale value was that of the interaction method $\mathbf{P}^t_{\text{up/down, forth/back}}$ with a value of *1.05 (SD = 1.00)*, while $\mathbf{P}^t_{\text{up/down, forth/back}}$ had the lower value with *0.68 (SD = 1.35)* (see Figure 7).

TLX. There were no significant differences over the two interaction methods for all TLX components except for TLX-PD $(Z = -2.078, p < .05)$. The higher TLX-OV component value was that of the interaction method $\mathbf{P}^h_{\text{nod, shake}}$ with a mean of *39.48 (SD = 22.55)*, while $\mathbf{P}^t_{\text{up/down, forth/back}}$ had the lower value with a mean of *35.10 (SD = 18.95)*.

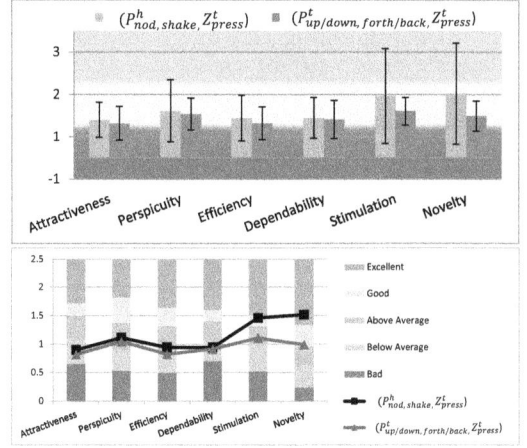

Figure 8: The UX scales (top) and benchmark (bottom) of the pan and zoom methods.

5.3 Panning and Zooming

For the combined tasks of panning and zooming, we applied the Wilcoxon signed-rank test, because there were only two test conditions.

5.3.1 Effectiveness and Efficiency

Effectiveness. There was a significant difference between the interaction methods $(Z = -3.832, p < .05)$. $(\mathbf{P}^h_{\text{nod, shake}}, \mathbf{Z}^t_{\text{press}})$ had a mean of *12.50* errors *(SD = 13.74)*, while $(\mathbf{P}^t_{\text{up/down, forth/back}}, \mathbf{Z}^t_{\text{press}})$ had a mean of *26* errors *(SD = 28.50)*.

Efficiency. There was no significant difference between the interaction methods $(Z = -.921, p = .357)$. $(\mathbf{P}^t_{\text{up/down, forth/back}}, \mathbf{Z}^t_{\text{press}})$ had a mean completion time of *94.18* seconds *(SD = 42.48)*, while $(\mathbf{P}^h_{\text{nod, shake}}, \mathbf{Z}^t_{\text{press}})$ had a mean of *104.50* seconds *(SD = 52.77)*.

5.3.2 User Experience and Workload

UX. There was a significant difference over the two interaction methods for the UX scales UX-ST $(Z = -2.225, p < .05)$ and UX-NV $(Z = -3.023, p < .05)$. The higher UX-AT scale was that of the interaction method $(\mathbf{P}^h_{\text{nod, shake}}, \mathbf{Z}^t_{\text{press}})$ with a value of *0.90 (SD = 1.37)*, while $(\mathbf{P}^t_{\text{up/down, forth/back}}, \mathbf{Z}^t_{\text{press}})$ had the lower value with *0.82 (SD = 1.15)* (see Figure 8).

TLX. There was no significant difference over the two interaction methods for all TLX components. The higher TLX-OV component value was that of the interaction method $(\mathbf{P}^t_{\text{up/down, forth/back}}, \mathbf{Z}^t_{\text{press}})$ with a mean of *37.74 (SD = 18.38)*, while $(\mathbf{P}^h_{\text{nod, shake}}, \mathbf{Z}^t_{\text{press}})$ had the lower score with a mean of *37.13 (SD = 19.97)*.

6. DISCUSSION

Hypotheses **H1** and **H2** were confirmed, while **H3** was partially confirmed. First, the results confirmed that $\mathbf{P}^h_{\text{nod, shake}}$ was significantly more effective than $\mathbf{P}^t_{\text{up/down, forth/back}}$, while there were no significant differences concerning efficiency, user experience and perceived cognitive workload (**H1**). Second, $\mathbf{Z}^t_{\text{forth/back}}$ was the significantly most effective zoom interaction method. Furthermore, except for when being compared to $\mathbf{Z}^t_{\text{up/down}}$, it was the significantly most efficient interaction, had the significantly highest user experience and lowest perceived cognitive workload. Finally, $(\mathbf{P}^h_{\text{nod, shake}}, \mathbf{Z}^t_{\text{press}})$ was significantly more effective, but there was no significant difference compared to $(\mathbf{P}^t_{\text{up/down, forth/back}}, \mathbf{Z}^t_{\text{press}})$ otherwise.

Thus, the results reflected the assumption that interaction methods with congruent spatial mappings are able to outperform others independent of the interaction modality. That is, no matter whether head-based or haptic interactions are used.

The results also indicate that familiarity with the input method correlates with performance. That is, the more common haptic input methods performed significantly better than the less common head-based gestures. This can be observed when comparing $\mathbf{Z}^t_{\text{up/down}}$ with $\mathbf{Z}^h_{\text{nod}}$, where $\mathbf{Z}^t_{\text{up/down}}$ performed significantly better for all DVs and both can be considered as input modalities along the y-axis.

We observed high SD values in our data, which can be explained by extreme outliers. These were not excluded from evaluation, in order to truly reflect difficulties with the interaction methods. In particular, we identified two possible causes for the deviations. First, some participants appear to have had particular difficulties with a specific zoom method resulting in bad efficiency and effectiveness values. For example, one participant had a completion time of 81.56 seconds and 15 errors for $\mathbf{Z}^h_{\text{nod}}$. Considering the average completion time of 24.84 seconds and average number of errors of 2.84, this demonstrates the extremity of these outliers. We observed similar effects for $\mathbf{Z}^t_{\text{press}}$. The second reason for these outliers is our abort-condition, i.e., we stopped the experiment after 180 seconds, e.g., when participants claimed or we realized they are not able to complete the experiment, because they "got lost" on the map or simply could not cope with the interaction method. For example, we had 3 such observations for the efficiency measurements of $\mathbf{P}^h_{\text{nod, shake}}$ and 1 for $\mathbf{P}^t_{\text{up/down, forth/back}}$.

Finally, such an extensive comparison has many possible sources for confounding variables. However, we narrowed those down by analyzing the design space, conducting a pilot study and choosing the same parameters for the interaction methods whenever possible. It should be noted, that the aim of this paper was not to find the optimal settings for either one of the inputs, but to explore the potential of the novel head-based approaches.

Limitations As explained in section 3.1, we did not implement and evaluate all possible interaction methods that were identified in the design space, amongst others, because they contradicted with the assumption of congruent mappings. Furthermore, the explored design space was limited to basic gestures, such as swipes and refrained from evaluating gesture patterns on the touch pad.

Furthermore, we only tested the setup with one OHMD, i.e. Google Glass, but we investigated the specifications of different OHMDs and found that our input modalities were provided by the majority of them. Even though some do not provide a touch pad for interaction input, they all allowed for inputs based on head-based gestures.

We decided to have a 30 second introductory session with each new interaction method and further chose to have 5 seconds between each of the instructions. These intervals could have been chosen differently, but their usefulness was determined during the pilot study. We did not receive any feedback indicating the need for additional time.

For zooming and panning, we predefined the movement direction (e.g. "zoom in") and required the participants to reflect on their actions, by asking them to perform an action until they see a specific label (or it is centered within the yellow rectangle). This approach was chosen for several reasons. First, restricting the direction and destination allowed for comparability. By letting all participants, for example, zoom in until they see the label "Paris", we ensure that they perform the same actions. Additionally, we know how many actions they should perform to reach the label. Thus, the results for task completion time and error rate can be compared. Second, asking participants to look for a particular label ensures a more realistic setup, where a user is actually looking for a particular piece of information.

The study was conducted under lab conditions and the results for user experience and perceived cognitive workload might have been different if the experiment were conducted in an outdoor environment, as discussed in [26]. We refrained from letting participants stand, because the combination with the arm movements required for haptic inputs might have led to earlier physical exhaustion and lower user experience ratings. However, efficiency and effectiveness results would not have been influenced, because, for the given interaction methods (using a touch pad and head movements), they are less dependent on the surrounding environment.

The choice of the step sizes for the zoom interactions is a potential source for improvement, especially for $\mathbf{Z}^h_{\text{nod}}$ and $\mathbf{Z}^t_{\text{press}}$. Those values were chosen based on the pilot study, but alternative solutions are thinkable, such as an adjustable zoom speed.

Finally, choosing the sequence of the tasks based on the number of axes involved, might result in order effects, since some of the interaction methods for panning were already used for zooming.

7. CONCLUSIONS AND FUTURE WORK

This paper explored the design space for map interaction methods on OHMDs. After a thorough analysis, novel head-based and common haptic interaction methods were selected and compared with regard to panning, zooming, as well as the combination of panning and zooming on maps.

In a study with 31 participants, the selected interaction methods were evaluated concerning effectiveness, efficiency, user experience and perceived cognitive workload. We were able to demonstrate that congruent mappings outperform others. More precisely, for panning interactions, head-based gestures were competitive, since they were able to congruently map control inputs onto the display. As for the zooming interactions, even though our approach was outperformed by the more common haptic interactions, it still showed potential for improvement.

In consequence, the head-based interaction methods introduced in this paper are suitable in scenarios where users want to navigate on an OHMD, but cannot use their hands or other bodily extremities except the head, e.g., due to disabilities or because their current activity does not allow for it. An example could be a plumber looking at a plan of the pipes in a house while fixing one. Many more examples can be thought of, e.g., the use by airplane engineers, car mechanics, etc.

Based on this study's results, evaluating the combinations of $\mathbf{P}^h_{\text{nod, shake}}$ with $\mathbf{Z}^t_{\text{forth/back}}$ and $\mathbf{Z}^t_{\text{up/down}}$, as well as

$\mathbf{P}^t_{\text{up/down, forth/back}}$ with $\mathbf{Z}^h_{\text{nod}}$, would give us further valuable insights on the impact of congruent spatial mappings on the performance for interacting with OHMDs. Furthermore, to fully evaluate the potential of our novel head-based interaction methods, it is necessary to conduct a longitudinal study.

Finally, the possibility to integrate Eye Tracking capabilities [13] into OHMDs, holds the potential for many new interaction methods. For example, extending the mixed interaction methods with the approach introduced by [7], i.e. using markers to emphasize regions on a display that were previously consulted for a given task, might allow for enhanced user orientation and more coherent user experience.

8. REFERENCES

[1] B. B. Bederson, J. D. Hollan, K. Perlin, J. Meyer, D. Bacon, and G. Furnas. Pad++: A zoomable graphical sketchpad for exploring alternate interface physics. *Journal of Visual Languages & Computing*, 7(1):3–32, March 1996.

[2] J. M. Bland and D. G. Altman. Multiple significance tests: the bonferroni method. *Bmj*, 310(6973):170, 1995.

[3] O. Cakmakci and J. Rolland. Head-worn displays: A review. *J. Display Technol.*, 2(3):199–216, 2006.

[4] J. Chen and R. W. Proctor. Up or down: Directional stimulus-response compatibility and natural scrolling. In *Proceedings of the Human Factors and Ergonomics Society Annual Meeting*, pages 1381–1385. SAGE Publications, 2012.

[5] S. Christian, J. Alves, A. Ferreira, D. Jesus, R. Freitas, and N. Vieira. Volcano salvation: Interaction through gesture and head tracking. In *CHI*, pages 297–300. ACM, 2014.

[6] D. Dobbelstein, P. Hock, and E. Rukzio. Belt: An unobtrusive touch input device for head-worn displays. In *CHI*, pages 2135–2138. ACM, 2015.

[7] I. Giannopoulos, P. Kiefer, and M. Raubal. Geogazemarks: Providing gaze history for the orientation on small display maps. In *ICMI*, pages 165–172. ACM, 2012.

[8] M. Harrower and B. Sheesley. Designing better map interfaces: A framework for panning and zooming. *Transactions in GIS*, 9(2):77–89, 2005.

[9] S. G. Hart and L. E. Staveland. Development of NASA-TLX (Task Load Index): Results of empirical and theoretical research. In *Human Mental Workload*, pages 139–183. North-Holland, 1988.

[10] S. C. Hirtle and M. Raubal. Many to many mobile maps. In *Cognitive and Linguistic Aspects of Geographic Space*, pages 141–157. Springer, 2013.

[11] H. Hua, X. Hu, and C. Gao. A high-resolution optical see-through head-mounted display with eyetracking capability. *Opt. Express*, 21(25):30993–30998, 2013.

[12] S. Ishimaru, K. Kunze, K. Kise, J. Weppner, A. Dengel, P. Lukowicz, and A. Bulling. In the blink of an eye: Combining head motion and eye blink frequency for activity recognition with google glass. In *AH*, pages 15:1–15:4. ACM, 2014.

[13] S. Jalaliniya, D. Mardanbegi, I. Sintos, and D. G. Garcia. Eyedroid: An open source mobile gaze tracker

on android for eyewear computers. In *PETMEI*, pages 873–879. ACM, 2015.

[14] J. A. Johnson. A comparison of user interfaces for panning on a touch-controlled display. In *CHI*, pages 218–225. ACM, 1995.

[15] B. Kollee, S. Kratz, and A. Dunnigan. Exploring gestural interaction in smart spaces using head mounted devices with ego-centric sensing. In *SUI*, pages 40–49, 2014.

[16] B. Laugwitz, T. Held, and M. Schrepp. Construction and evaluation of a user experience questionnaire. In *HCI and Usability for Education and Work*, pages 63–76. Springer Berlin Heidelberg, 2008.

[17] Z. Lv, A. Halawani, S. Feng, S. Ur Réhman, and H. Li. Touch-less interactive augmented reality game on vision-based wearable device. *Personal Ubiquitous Comput.*, 19(3-4):551–567, 2015.

[18] I. S. MacKenzie. *Human-computer interaction: An empirical research perspective*. Newnes, 2012.

[19] M. Malu and L. Findlater. Personalized, wearable control of a head-mounted display for users with upper body motor impairments. In *CHI*, pages 221–230. ACM, 2015.

[20] R. McNaney, J. Vines, D. Roggen, M. Balaam, P. Zhang, I. Poliakov, and P. Olivier. Exploring the acceptability of google glass as an everyday assistive device for people with parkinson's. In *CHI*, pages 2551–2554. ACM, 2014.

[21] M. F. Roig-Maimó, J. Varona Gómez, and C. Manresa-Yee. Face me! head-tracker interface evaluation on mobile devices. In *CHI*, pages 1573–1578. ACM, 2015.

[22] M. Serrano, B. M. Ens, and P. P. Irani. Exploring the use of hand-to-face input for interacting with head-worn displays. In *CHI*, pages 3181–3190. ACM, 2014.

[23] T. A. Slocum, R. B. McMaster, F. C. Kessler, and H. H. Howard. *Thematic cartography and geovisualization*. Pearson Prentice Hall Upper Saddle River, NJ, 2009.

[24] M. Spindler and R. Dachselt. Paperlens: Advanced magic lens interaction above the tabletop. In *Proceedings of the ACM International Conference on Interactive Tabletops and Surfaces*, pages 7:1–7:1. ACM, 2009.

[25] T. Starner. Project glass: An extension of the self. *Pervasive Computing, IEEE*, 12(2):14–16, 2013.

[26] Y.-C. Tung, C.-Y. Hsu, H.-Y. Wang, S. Chyou, J.-W. Lin, P.-J. Wu, A. Valstar, and M. Y. Chen. User-defined game input for smart glasses in public space. In *CHI*, pages 3327–3336. ACM, 2015.

[27] B. Zhang, Y.-H. Chen, C. Tuna, A. Dave, Y. Li, E. Lee, and B. Hartmann. Hobs: Head orientation-based selection in physical spaces. In *SUI*, pages 17–25. ACM, 2014.

[28] X. S. Zheng, C. Foucault, P. Matos da Silva, S. Dasari, T. Yang, and S. Goose. Eye-wearable technology for machine maintenance: Effects of display position and hands-free operation. In *CHI*, pages 2125–2134. ACM, 2015.

Touching the Sphere: Leveraging Joint-Centered Kinespheres for Spatial User Interaction

Paul Lubos, Gerd Bruder, Oscar Ariza, Frank Steinicke
Human-Computer Interaction, Department of Informatics, Universität Hamburg
{lubos,bruder,ariza,steinicke}@informatik.uni-hamburg.de

ABSTRACT

Designing spatial user interfaces for virtual reality (VR) applications that are intuitive, comfortable and easy to use while at the same time providing high task performance is a challenging task. This challenge is even harder to solve since perception and action in immersive virtual environments differ significantly from the real world, causing natural user interfaces to elicit a dissociation of perceptual and motor space as well as levels of discomfort and fatigue unknown in the real world. In this paper, we present and evaluate the novel method to leverage *joint-centered kinespheres* for interactive spatial applications. We introduce kinespheres within arm's reach that envelope the reachable space for each joint such as shoulder, elbow or wrist, thus defining 3D interactive volumes with the boundaries given by 2D manifolds. We present a Fitts' Law experiment in which we evaluated the spatial touch performance on the inside and on the boundary of the main joint-centered kinespheres. Moreover, we present a confirmatory experiment in which we compared joint-centered interaction with traditional spatial head-centered menus. Finally, we discuss the advantages and limitations of placing interactive graphical elements relative to joint positions and, in particular, on the boundaries of kinespheres.

Categories and Subject Descriptors

H.5.2 [**Information Interfaces and Presentation**]: User Interfaces–Input Devices and Strategies, Evaluation / Methodology; I.3.7 [**Computer Graphics**]: Three-Dimensional Graphics and Realism–Virtual Reality

Keywords

Spatial user interfaces; 3D touch interaction; kinespheres; virtual environments; head-mounted displays

1. INTRODUCTION

The recent developments in the field of virtual reality (VR) and augmented reality (AR) head-mounted displays (HMDs) such as the Oculus Rift, HTC VIVE, Meta or Hololens have received much

SUI '16, October 15-16, 2016, Tokyo, Japan
© 2016 ACM. ISBN 978-1-4503-4068-7/16/10... $15.00
DOI: `http://dx.doi.org/10.1145/2983310.2985753`

public interest and praise for their design, tracking and visual quality. However, they also received much critique for their spatial interaction and, in particular, for how they handled interaction with 3D graphical user interfaces (GUIs). By combining HMDs with depth sensors such as the Leap Motion it has become possible to leverage direct hand input for spatial interaction, as also seen in the Meta and Hololens. User interfaces based on direct hand interaction, however, received less user acceptance than expected, such that Oculus and HTC even abandoned it in favor of hand-held controllers. While portions of the challenge lie on the hardware side with still limited tracking ranges and accuracy, it has become necessary to revisit spatial menu designs and to develop methods to improve the user acceptance of free-hand spatial user interfaces by considering the human factors of 3D mid-air interaction [33].

In this paper, we revisit mid-air interaction based on the simple observation that for the human jointed arm structure the reachable space from each joint is naturally limited. We refer to such an interactive volume of space around the center of a user's kinematic joint as a *joint-centered kinesphere*. While traditional head-centered menus are by design placed within arm's reach in front of the user, it is seldomly the case that they can be reached without requiring movements of the shoulder joint and as a result inducing high levels of fatigue over time [10]. Moreover, most traditional menus are not matched to each user's arm length but rather use population means, which means that for some users the menus are placed closer to their maximal reachable arm distance than for others. Requirements for the visual placement and size of spatial GUI elements for good visibility and high interaction performance have been extensively researched [5, 29], but their optimal location in the kinematic chain has received less attention.

To evaluate the optimal placement of menus in the scope of joint-centered kinespheres, we conducted an experiment in which we collected quantitative and qualitative data on usability and selection performance between interaction targets located at different distances on such kinespheres with a Fitts' Law task. The results support the notion that the efficiency of selections in spatial menus within arm's reach can be improved by placing interactive elements on joint-centered kinespheres at certain distances, in particular at the maximal reachable distance. We confirm the practical usability of joint-centered menus in an experiment by comparing them against traditional head-centered GUIs. We discuss the advantages and limitations of this method focusing on differences in the length of the kinematic chain for kinespheres centered around the shoulder, elbow or wrist joint.

In this paper we provide the following contributions:

- we evaluate the placement of interactive elements in joint-centered kinespheres with a view on usability and touch performance, and

- we present a joint-centered user interface and compare user acceptance against head-centered menus.

The remainder of this paper is structured as follows: Section 2 presents an overview of related work. Section 3 introduces the concept of joint-centered kinespheres. In Section 4 we describe the experiment that we conducted to evaluate the placement of interactive elements for 3D touch interaction in joint-centered kinespheres. Section 5 describes the confirmatory study that we performed comparing joint-centered and head-centered menus. Section 6 concludes the paper and discusses vistas for future work.

2. RELATED WORK

3D user interfaces and spatial interaction has been in the focus of many research groups over the last decades. According to Mine et al. [35], direct 3D interaction leads to significantly higher performance than manipulation of objects at a distance from the user's hand. Most results from similar studies agree that optimal performance may be achieved when visual and motor spaces are superimposed or coupled closely within arm's reach [12, 25, 43]. In contrast, interaction techniques offering the possibility to interact with distant objects by decoupling the virtual hand from the user's real hand pose include the Go-Go technique [37] and HOMER [6], which work by nonlinear scaling of hand positions within arm's reach, approaching infinity in the virtual environment (VE) when approaching the maximal reachable distance in the real world.

However, it is still an open research question, how the position of virtual target objects located within arm's reach may affect interaction performance [29, 30]. Direct 3D interaction in HMD environments is subject to perceptual limitations, e. g., the accommodation-convergence mismatch, ghosting or double vision, which can result in strong misperception effects [8, 9, 11]. Depending on the location of virtual objects, users may be unable to discriminate interrelations between objects or they may perceive distances to objects to be smaller or larger than they are geometrically [28, 30]. Consistently, evaluations of 3D selection performance found that users made most errors along the view direction due to incorrectly judged distances of virtual objects [29]. Such distortions do not appear in the real world and are likely caused by limitations of current technology to correctly reproduce depth cues from the real world in a perfect way [44]. Internal representations of the 3D space are influenced and updated by both visual as well as motor input, which may affect interaction performance [41, 45].

Various interaction techniques have been proposed to improve upon traditional 2D menus anchored on an arbitrary plane in 3D space. For instance, Li et al. [26] propose using the orientation of a mobile device held with outstretched arms for menu control. Shoemaker et al. [40] propose using a user's personal space to display menus at a comfortably reachable position on large displays. Ens et al. [14] propose a personal cockpit with menu items placed on a sphere centered around the user's point of view. Also, Gerber and Bechmann [16] center their Spin Menu around a user's wrist.

Selection Performance

3D selections by touching or grasping objects with a user's hands can be split up into two phases, the *ballistic* phase and the *correction* phase [27]. The ballistic phase consists of focusing on the target object and bringing the hand in the proximity of the goal by using proprioceptive motor control. After that, visual feedback is used in the correction phase in order to incrementally reduce the distance from the hand to the goal.

For such selections, Fitts' Law predicts the movement time $MT \in \mathbb{R}^+$ for a given target distance $D \in \mathbb{R}^+$ and target size

$W \in \mathbb{R}^+$ [13, 15, 31, 32]. They are brought together in a log term, which describes the difficulty of the task overall with $MT = a + b \cdot log_2(D / W + 1)$. The values $a \in \mathbb{R}^+$ and $b \in \mathbb{R}^+$ can be empirically derived for different setups. The *index of difficulty* (ID) is given by the log term and indicates overall task difficulty; smaller or/and farther targets result in increased difficulty, whereas larger or/and closer targets provide a decreased ID. The formula has been extended in order to get effective measures. The error rate is adjusted to 4% by resizing targets to their effective width $W_e \in \mathbb{R}^+$. This adjustment is supported by an international standard [21]. By calculating the average of the measured movement distances, $D_e \in \mathbb{R}^+$ can be determined. With that, the effective throughput can be computed as a useful combination of speed and accuracy: $TP = log_2(D_e / W_e + 1) / MT$.

Wingrave and Bowman, as well as Murata and Iwase showed that Fitts' Law also holds when pointing in VEs [46, 36]. They observed that D was related to the amplitude of the movement, and W to the visual size of the target. Poupyrev et al. [38] defined the size of an object W according to the vertical and horizontal angles that the object occupies in the user's field of view (FOV). Similarly, Kopper et al. [24] propose a modification of Fitts' Law as a model for human performance in distal pointing tasks. Their model is based on angular amplitude and angular width as they argue that, contrary to classic 2D Fitts' Law tasks, the objects are floating in 3D space and the sizes and distances depend on the user's position, which can be solved by using angular measurements. Ha and Woo [19] adopted Fitts' Law for tangible AR environments with virtual hand metaphors by using the model established by Grossman et al. [17], which however was based on 3D objects arranged on a 2D plane.

3. JOINT-CENTERED INTERACTION

In this section we describe the motivation and rationale of joint-centered interaction, as well as the single components.

3.1 Kinespheres

Figure 1 illustrates the kinespheres at the maximal reachable distance for three joints typically involved in 3D mid-air interaction. According to the biomechanics and human factors literature, when assuming that a joint (e. g., wrist, elbow or shoulder) is rested and the remaining joints are stretched, the user's fingertip will be approximately on a partial sphere centered on the joint [34, 39]. Finger positions close to a kinesphere are usually regarded as easily reachable and comfortable, whereas it is harder to reach the mid region of a kinesphere closer to the center joint. This fact has been utilized in previous research using joint angles and hyperplanes [18, 22].

3.2 Kinematic Chain

We refer to the term kinematic chain as a series of links connected by joints, or more specifically, a human's arm from the shoulder joint to a fingertip. Previous studies have shown that interaction higher up the kinematic chain is less accurate and and causes higher energy expenditure if the corresponding muscle groups are used, and more accurate and less fatiguing further down [3, 39]. Optimally, a physical support at a joint as low as possible in the kinematic chain allows users to relax muscle groups higher in the kinematic chain, reducing exertion and increasing comfort. In contrast, traditional head-centered spatial menus are placed within arm's reach in front of the user's eyes, requiring movements of the entire kinematic chain.

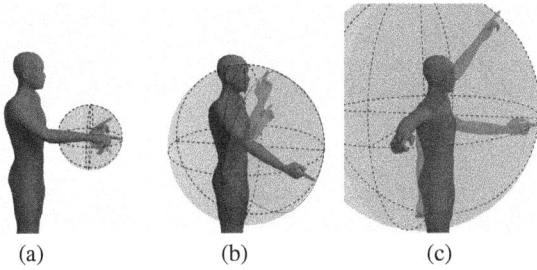

Figure 1: Illustrations showing the joint-centered kinespheres around (a) the wrist joint, (b) the elbow joint, and (c) the shoulder joint for a standing user for 3D mid-air interaction. If the user is seated or uses an arm rest the comfort is increased while the corresponding kinespheres are reduced. The reachable area on the kinesphere is shown in green.

3.3 Boundary

The boundary of a joint-centered kinesphere defines a 2D manifold in 3D space that, conceptually, reduces the interaction complexity of touch gestures in terms of the degrees of freedom (DOF) of arm movements from three to two since the finger's distance from the joint is clamped to its maximum and does not have to be controlled consciously. Since large overshooting and undershooting are not possible as long as the corresponding kinematic chain is stretched, selection performance can be described by Fitts' Law in 2D during the correction phase, using visual perception only to correct for lateral offsets from the target.

2D GUI elements may be placed anywhere on the accessible part of a kinesphere, i.e., on the opposite side from the user's head, while ensuring visibility and low muscle exertion. Arranging 2D GUI elements or widgets at the maximal reachable distance, e.g., from the shoulder, elbow or wrist, might thus provide advantages in performance based on Fitts' Law over placing them anywhere else within arm's reach. Moreover, in contrast to pointing techniques, this approach has the advantage of maintaining the superimposed perceptual and motor spaces as well as direct interaction with the graphical elements, since they are located within arm's reach. However, we have to consider that fully-stretched kinematic chains are regarded as less comfortable than slightly relaxed joints. Thus, though placing menus slightly inwards from the boundary may lose the advantages described above, it may lead to higher user acceptance.

3.4 Implementation

For joint-centered menus we align the touch-enabled 2D GUI elements in a local coordinate system around the center joint which is limited by the maximal reachable distance and the biomechanics described above. With respect to the kinematic chain we have implemented joint-centered 2D GUIs around the following joints:

1. *Shoulder joint* is a ball-and-socket joint providing the largest kinesphere (see Figure 1(c)). With a stretched elbow and wrist such that upper arm, forearm and index finger are colinear, the user can select targets on the kinesphere.

2. *Elbow joint* is the synovial hinge joint proving the second largest kinesphere (see Figure 1(b)). Assuming a stretched wrist such that forearm and index finger are colinear, the user can select targets on the kinesphere.

3. *Wrist joint* that bridges the hand to the forearm proving the smallest kinesphere in our implementation (see Figure 1(a)).

With the stretched index finger the user can select targets displayed on the surface of the kinesphere.

In our implementation the application can choose whether the shoulder, elbow or wrist kinespheres are used to present a joint-centered menu. Informal testing also included various other joints of the human body at finger level, legs, trunk and back. As the center of our kinesphere, we always chose the joint furthest down in the kinematic chain if they are rested using a physical support in the workspace. For instance, when a user is seated in an office chair, they can place their wrist or elbow on the arm rest and the interface elements are centered around the respective joint (see Figure 2). Alternatively, without physical support a kinesphere is chosen to minimize occlusion of the environment and proximity to affected targets while maximizing user preference and selection accuracy as discussed in Section 4.

Interaction with the joint-centered GUI elements is implemented following the literature based on the three components [1, 5]:

1. *Indication of target object* by touching,

2. *Confirmation of selection*, e.g., with a touch or flip gesture with the dominant or non-dominant hand, voice command or timed response, and

3. *Feedback* generated by the system.

The joint-centered kinespheres described in this paper contribute mainly to the first component. Interaction designers may combine the joint-centered approach to indicate target objects with any of the confirmation and feedback methods presented in the literature as desired.

Overall, this describes the conceptual part of joint-centered approaches. We implemented the ideas using the Unity engine and a PPT active IR optical tracking system. More information about the hardware and the implementation is described in Sections 4 and 5.

4. EXPERIMENT

We conducted a Fitts' Law experiment to evaluate selection performance of GUI elements within arm's reach focusing on the relationships between joint, distance, performance, comfort and user acceptance.

4.1 Participants

20 participants (5 female and 15 male, ages $20 - 36$, $M = 26.1$) took part in the experiment. The participants were members or students of the local department of computer science, who obtained class credit for their participation. All of our participants had normal or corrected-to-normal vision. Seven participants wore glasses and one participant wore contact lenses during the experiment. None of our participants reported a disorder of equilibrium or a motor disorder such as an impaired hand-eye coordination. One of our participants reported a color blindness; no other vision disorders have been reported. 10 participants had participated in an experiment involving HMDs before. 18 participants were right-handed and 2 were left-handed. We measured the interpupillary distances (IPDs) of our participants before the experiment using the measurement tool of the Oculus Rift configuration utility. The IPDs of our participants ranged between $6.2 - 7.2$cm ($M = 6.5$cm, $SD = 0.2$cm). We used the IPD of each participant to provide a correct perspective and stereoscopic rendering on the HMD. We measured each participant's maximal reaching distance from joint to fingertip for the shoulder joint ($M = 0.726$m, $SD = 0.055$m), for the elbow joint ($M = 0.423$m, $SD = 0.036$m),

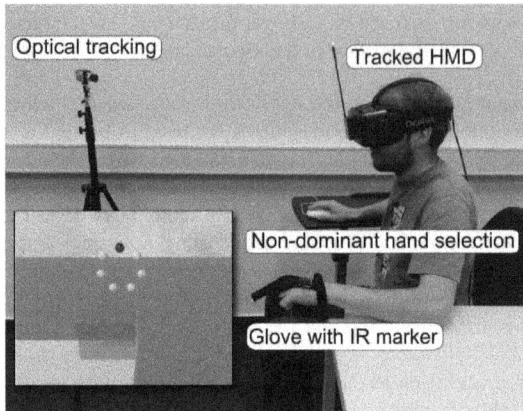

Figure 2: Experiment setup: Participant with a tracked Oculus Rift HMD and glove; the inset shows the participant's view of the VE.

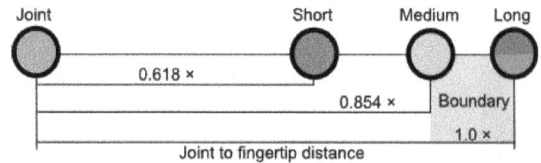

Figure 3: Evaluated distances: Taking into account the joint position and the position of the user's fingertip in a comfortably stretched pose, this illustration shows the distances tested in the experiment as detailed in Section 4.3.

and for the wrist joint ($M = 0.195$m, $SD = 0.027$m). We confirmed each participant's ability to perceive binocular depth before the experiment via stereograms. 17 participants had prior experience with 3D stereoscopic display (cinema, games etc.). The total time per participant, including pre-questionnaires, instructions, experiment, breaks, post-questionnaires, and debriefing, was 1 hour. Participants wore the HMD for approximately $45 - 50$ minutes. They were encouraged to take regular breaks between trials in order to rest their arm.

4.2 Material

As illustrated in Figure 2, participants were instructed to sit in an upright position facing towards the cameras of the optical tracking system. The experiment was conducted with the user wearing an Oculus Rift (Developer Kit 2) HMD with an attached active infrared (IR) target. Additionally, we attached an IR target to the index finger of the participant's dominant hand (see Figure 2). The targets were tracked by an optical WorldViz Precision Position Tracking (PPT X4) system with sub-millimeter precision, which was chosen to offer maximal precision for the Fitts' Law task. The visual stimulus displayed during the experiment showed a 3D scene, which was rendered with the Unity3D engine with an Intel computer with a Core i7 3.4 GHz CPU and an Nvidia Geoffrey GTX780TI. The Oculus Rift DK2 offers a nominal diagonal FOV of approximately 100 degrees at a resolution of 1920×1080 pixels (960×1080 for each eye).

4.3 Methods

The targets in the experiment were represented by spheres. All target spheres for one trial were always visible and colored white, except for the current target. The current target sphere was colored red when the marker was outside, and green when the marker was inside to give the participants a visual cue about selection performance. The spheres were highlighted in the order specified by the ISO 9241-9 standard for Fitts' Law evaluations [21]. As illustrated in the inset of Figure 2, each trial consisted of an arrangement of 7 target spheres, forming a circle with each sphere at the same distance to the participant's joint.

In the experiment we used a within-subjects repeated measures 3 (joints) $\times$ 4 (distances) $\times$ 4 (index of difficulties) $\times$ 3 (repetitions) full-factorial design. As described before, we considered the shoulder, elbow and wrist joints. As Figure 3 illustrates, we considered three distances (with j being the distance between the joint

and the finger in a comfortably stretched pose: $0.618 \times j \cong$ short, $0.854 \times j \cong$ medium, $1.0 \times j \cong$ long) in the experiment, which were chosen using the knowledge that the distances between a human's joints can be approximated with the golden ratio [34]. The fourth distance condition denotes the boundary technique. When touching an object at the maximal reachable distance it might be advantageous in practical scenarios to include a tolerance range to account for slight overshooting or undershooting in depth (cf. Section 2), hence in this technique we considered a range stretching from $[0.854, 1] \times j$. We evaluated the ecologically viable IDs 2, 2.5, 3 and 3.5. All conditions were tested three times and their order was fully randomized. We included 38 training trial (one for each condition), which were excluded from the analysis.

Before the experiment, all participants filled out an informed consent form and received instructions on how to perform the task. Furthermore, they filled out the simulator sickness questionnaire (SSQ) [23] immediately before and after the experiment, the Slater-Usoh-Steed (SUS) presence questionnaire [42], and a demographic questionnaire. We further observed the behavior of the participants during the experiment, and debriefed the participants after the experiment.

4.4 Results

We analyzed the results with repeated-measure ANOVAs and multiple pairwise comparisons with Bonferroni's correction at the 5% significance level. We confirmed the assumptions of the ANOVA for the experiment data. A Shapiro-Wilk test did not indicate that the assumption of normality had been violated. Degrees of freedom were corrected using Greenhouse-Geisser estimates of sphericity when Mauchly's test indicated that the assumption of sphericity had been violated.

4.4.1 Selection Performance

Figure 4(a) shows the mean time elapsed until a participant selected a target object for each condition in the experiment. Table 1 shows the results of the statistical analysis.

Figure 4(b) shows the mean error distances, i. e., the Euclidean distance between the participant's fingertip and the center of the target sphere when a participant selected the target object for each condition in the experiment. Table 2 shows the results of the statistical analysis.

Figure 4(c) show the mean error rate between the times when the participant's fingertip was within or outside of the target sphere when a participant selected the target object, for each condition in the experiment. Table 3 shows the results of the statistical analysis.

Figure 4(d) shows the mean effective throughput for each condition in the experiment. Table 4 shows the results of the statistical analysis.

4.4.2 Questionnaires

Asked to rate their level of comfort during the joint conditions

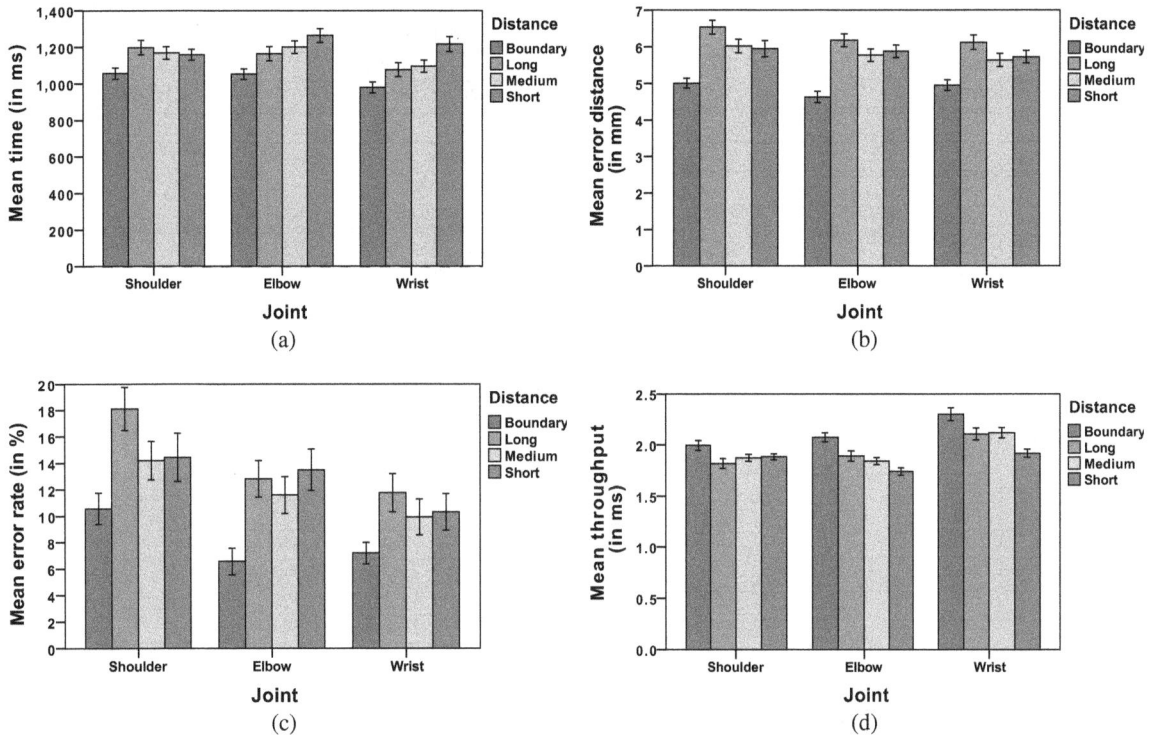

Figure 4: Results for Fitts' Law trials with the joint on the horizontal axis and pooled results on the vertical axis for (a) movement times, (b) error distances, (c) error rate and (d) effective throughput. The error bars show the standard error. Red bars show the results for the short distance, yellow for medium distance, green for long distance, and blue for the boundary technique.

joint	M	SD	F	p	η_p^2
wrist	1093ms	202ms	(2, 38)		
elbow	1171ms	203ms	=	< .001	.26
shoulder	1146ms	195ms	6.56		
Post-hoc					p
wrist–elbow					< .001
wrist–shoulder					.18
elbow–shoulder					.79
distance	M	SD	F	p	η_p^2
short	1214ms	193ms	(3, 57)		
medium	1155ms	172ms	=	< .001	.67
long	1146ms	236ms	38.30		
boundary	1030ms	186ms			
Post-hoc					p
medium–long					.99
others					< .05
ID	M	SD	F	p	η_p^2
2	861ms	144ms	(1.41, 26.7)		
2.5	1028ms	184ms	=	< .001	.95
3	1230ms	205ms	375.89		
3.5	1426ms	247ms			
Post-hoc					p
all					< .001

Table 1: Statistical analysis for the movement time

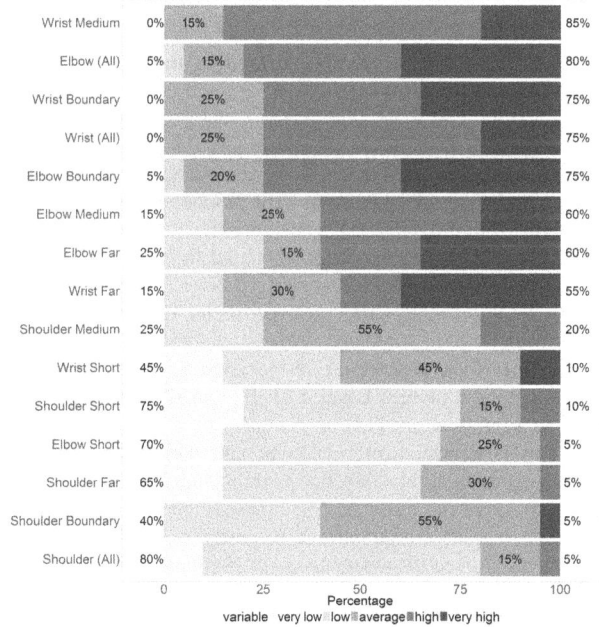

Figure 5: The results showing the subjective comfort ratings (x), and the joint and distance condition (y).

with 5-point Likert scales (0 = very low, 4 = very high) (see Figure 5).

We further asked the participants for each joint condition

joint	M	SD	F	p	η_p^2
wrist	5.6mm	1.0mm	(2, 38)		
elbow	5.6mm	1.0ms	=	.075	.13
shoulder	5.9mm	1.2mm	2.78		

Post-hoc					p
all					> .05

distance	M	SD	F	p	η_p^2
short	5.9mm	1.2mm	(1.93, 36.57)		
medium	5.8mm	1.1mm	=	< .001	.75
long	6.3mm	1.1mm	55.8		
boundary	4.9mm	.9mm			

Post-hoc					p
short–medium					.99
short–long					.05
others					< .001

ID	M	SD	F	p	η_p^2
2	6.7mm	1.0mm	(3, 57)		
2.5	4.8mm	1.0mm	=	< .001	.9
3	6.4mm	1.2mm	165.14		
3.5	4.9mm	1.0mm			

Post-hoc					p
2.5–3.5					.99
others					< .001

Table 2: Statistical analysis for the error distance

joint	M	SD	F	p	η_p^2
wrist	9.8%	9.1%	(2, 38)		
elbow	11.9%	9.1%	=	< .001	.36
shoulder	14.3%	11.3%	10.85		

Post-hoc					p
wrist–elbow					.33
wrist–shoulder					< .001
elbow–shoulder					< .05

distance	M	SD	F	p	η_p^2
short	12.8%	11.5%	(2.22, 42.11)		
medium	11.9%	10.2%	=	< .001	.42
long	14.2%	10.6%	13.47		
boundary	8.1%	7.0%			

Post-hoc					p
short–medium					.99
short–long					.99
others					< .05

ID	M	SD	F	p	η_p^2
2	7.4%	7.4%	(1.74, 32.99)		
2.5	11.7%	10.3%	=	< .001	.6
3	11.1%	10.3%	27.95		
3.5	16.8%	11.8%			

Post-hoc					p
2.5–3					.99
others					< .001

Table 3: Statistical analysis for the error rate

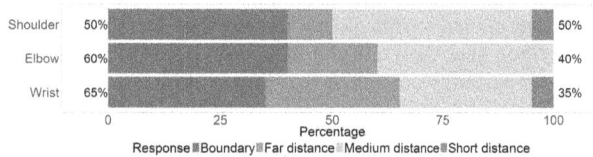

Figure 6: The user preference regarding the evaluated distances (x), and the joint (y).

which distance they preferred with the alternatives boundary, long, medium and short (see Figure 6). The responses show that most participants preferred the boundary technique and medium distance, followed by the long distance, but not the short distance.

We measured a mean SSQ score of 15.15 ($SD = 17.77$) before and 26.18 ($SD = 29.67$) after the experiment. The results indicate a typical increase in simulator sickness symptoms with an HMD over the time of the experiment. The mean SUS score for the sense of feeling present in the VE was 4.57 ($SD = .97$), which indicates a high sense of presence [42].

We further collected informal comments during the debriefing after the experiment. Notably, one participant explained the preference of the wrist condition by, *"My arm was too heavy for keeping it up in the air with the shoulder-based interface."* Another participant stated, *"I liked the wrist condition; similar to a mouse."*

4.5 Discussion

Overall, the results show that the interaction performance highly depended on the placement of targets within arm's reach. In the following, we discuss the findings focused on the kinematic chain and kinespheres and summarize the main ones as practical guidelines.

4.5.1 Kinematic Chain

We found the significantly highest effective throughput for the wrist joint condition, whereas we found lower effective through-

puts for the elbow and shoulder conditions, between which the results showed no significant difference. There are multiple possible explanations of this effect. First, from a biomechanical point of view a longer kinematic chain leads to more weight and inertia while requiring more muscle exertion and might thus have caused longer movement times [34, 39]. Moreover, the presence of a physical support by means of an elbow or a wrist cushion might have reduced fatigue and hand tremors by shortening the kinematic chain [18, 30]. Additionally, we have to consider that the wrist condition was similar to using a mouse and might have benefited from this similarity.

4.5.2 Placement in Kinespheres

As expected, the practically-inspired *boundary technique* with the short tolerance range near the maximal reachable distance showed the overall significantly lowest errors, shortest movement times, and consequently highest effective throughput. This result might be explained by the reduction from 3 DOF to 2 DOF due to the stretched-out kinematic chains and short tolerance range, which additionally eliminated errors along the depth axis over the similar long distance condition.

While we expected an overall high performance for the *long distance* condition second only to the boundary technique due to the matching stretched-out kinematic chains, our results instead show performance that is very similar to the medium distance condition. Hence, we further analyzed the distribution of errors in the joint-centered kinespheres. With stretched-out limbs we observed mean selection errors of -1.76mm ($SD = 1.43$mm) for the shoulder condition, -2.97mm ($SD = 1.48$mm) for the elbow condition, and -2.83mm ($SD = 1.40$mm) for the wrist condition as measured from the center of the kinesphere to the target. The negative values might be explained by the participants calibrating their hand position with a truly outstretched arm, while they later drew

joint	M	SD	F	p	η_p^2
wrist	2.11bps	.38bps	$(1.4, 26.51)$		
elbow	1.89bps	.29bps	$=$	$< .001$	.57
shoulder	1.89bps	.26bps	25.31		

Post-hoc					p
wrist–elbow					$< .001$
wrist–shoulder					$< .001$
elbow–shoulder					.99

distance	M	SD	F	p	η_p^2
short	1.85bps	.21bps	$(1.5, 28.57)$		
medium	1.95bps	.25bps	$=$	$< .001$	.39
long	1.94bps	.4bps	12.15		
boundary	2.12bps	.39bps			

Post-hoc					p
short–long					.93
medium–long					.99
others					$< .05$

ID	M	SD	F	p	η_p^2
2	2.05bps	.32bps	$(1.98, 37.61)$		
2.5	1.95bps	.34bps	$=$	$< .001$	.4
3	1.98bps	.29bps	12.43		
3.5	1.87bps	.28bps			

Post-hoc					p
2–2.5					$< .01$
2–3.5					$< .01$
3–3.5					$< .01$
others					$> .05$

Table 4: Statistical analysis for the throughput

their arm back a few millimeters into a more comfortable pose. Without this systematic undershoot in depth it appears that the long distance condition would have, indeed, resulted in higher performance. However, most participants indicated the boundary technique or the medium distance condition as their preference while estimating the long distance (without boundary) and the short distance as least comfortable.

4.5.3 Guidelines

We found the highest performance for the wrist joint using the boundary technique, which we recommend for practitioners in the field of spatial user interfaces. However, overall performance and user acceptance also showed that placing menus at the medium tested distance is an ecologically viable alternative. We do not recommend placing menus near the long or short tested distances. We found similar performance for the elbow and shoulder conditions, but user preference based on estimated comfort clearly shows that the shoulder joint should be ruled out in practical applications.

5. CONFIRMATORY STUDY

In this section we present a confirmatory study in which we compared a traditional head-centered menu with a joint-centered menu that we designed based on the results of the first experiment. The menus were compared in a practical interior design application. While direct interaction is a great choice for many applications in spatial user interfaces, interior design is merely one of them. The concept of joint-centered user interfaces is applicable for any applications with context changes and tasks which require menus and which can benefit from direct interaction. These could be applications involving planning, construction, design, entertainment or smart environments. In this case, the example of interior design

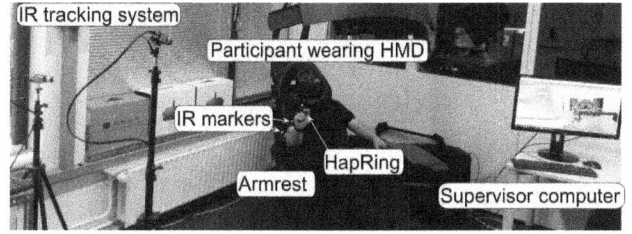

Figure 7: Illustration of the confirmatory study setup.

Figure 8: The virtual room for the confirmatory study.

was picked because it offers many opportunities to offer the user a selection of multiple items.

5.1 Participants

20 participants (2 female, 18 male, ages 19–44, $M = 27.6$) took part in the experiment. The participants were students or experts from computer science or human-computer interaction, and one journalist. Most participants had normal or corrected-to-normal vision (10 no correction, 7 glasses, 3 lenses, 1 with strong eye dominance, 1 with dyschromatopsia (red-green color weakness) and strong eye dominance and astigmatism). 14 of the participants took part in a study with an HMD before. All participants were right-handed. 18 participants reported at least some experience with computer games. The total time per participant was approximately 30 minutes.

5.2 Material

The experiment setup is illustrated in Figure 7. Participants were seated in an MWE Lab Emperor Chair 1510 and wore an Oculus Rift CV HMD on their head, IR markers on their wrist and elbow and a haptic ring input device on their index finger (similar to [2]). The IR markers and the ring were tracked in 3 DOF using an optical WorldViz PPT X4 tracking system with sub-millimeter precision. Additionally, the ring includes an inertial measurement unit, which allows for 6 DOF tracking of the user's index finger. The living room shown in the virtual scene was rendered in Unity3D on an Intel computer with a Core i7 4 GHz CPU, 16 GB RAM and an Nvidia GeForce GTX 980. The Oculus Rift CV offers a resolution of 1200×1080 per eye and approximately 94H×93V degrees FOV for both eyes. The in-house implemented interior design application is illustrated in Figure 8.

5.3 Methods

Half of the participants started with the joint-centered user interface (JCUI) and afterwards completed the second part of the experiment with the head-centered user interface (HCUI), and vice versa. The tasks for the participants were, first, to familiarize themselves with the spatial user interface, toggling the light by pointing at it and pressing the button on the input device, then moving a table by pointing at it, pressing a button and then pointing to the target location and pressing the button to confirm the position. Afterwards, the participants were instructed to change the wall, ceiling and floor materials by pointing at them, respectively, and then touching

19

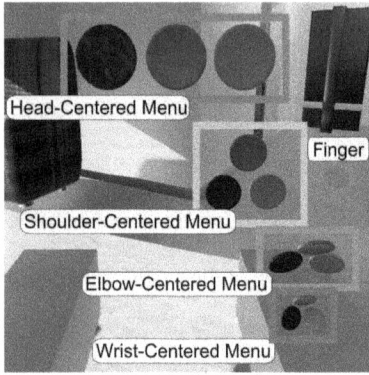

Figure 9: The menus that participants would see with annotations. Maximally one menu was visible at a time.

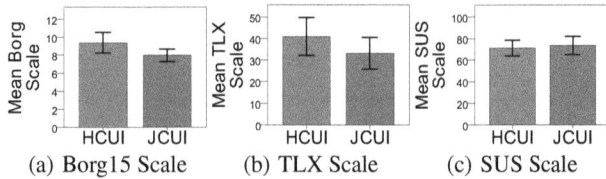

(a) Borg15 Scale   (b) TLX Scale   (c) SUS Scale

Figure 10: Results of the confirmatory study.

one of the appearing menu buttons of their choice. The appearing menus were either positioned centered around the head, in the head-centered condition, or one of the three joints, in the joint-centered condition, depending on whether the participants were resting their wrist, elbow, or nothing (shoulder) as shown in Figure 9. Next, the participants had to move the couch and then change its color. For this they had to point at the couch, press a button, touch a context button (move or color), and then either move it or color it as described above. We positioned the menus and determined input based on the *boundary technique* described in Section 4.3.

After the experiment, the participants had to complete different questionnaires comparing the conditions. As a measure of usability, we used the simple usability scale [7]. Additionally the participants had to complete a NASA TLX [20] and a Borg15 Scale [4] to measure the task difficulty and physical exertion. Afterwards, the participants were asked to provide subjective feedback and answer questions regarding the demographics in a questionnaire.

5.4 Results

Questionnaire	M	SD	$T(19)$	p	d_{Cohen}
SUS JCUI	73.625	18.308	.373	.713	.373
SUS HCUI	71.25	15.822			
TLX JCUI	33.16	15.740	-1.538	.14	-.344
TLX HCUI	40.91	18.854			
Borg15 JCUI	8	1.522	-2.463	<.05	-.551
Borg15 HCUI	9.4	2.458			

Table 5: Statistical analysis for the confirmatory study

The results were analyzed with a paired-samples t-test for each of the three main questionnaires and are shown in Figure 10 and Table 5.

Additionally, we analyzed the subjective feedback to the questions whether participants liked the joint-centered approach (15

positive), whether they liked head-centered interfaces (12 positive), whether joint-centered interfaces could be applied in other domains also (16 positive), which technique was less tiring (15 joint-centered), and which technique was more fun (11 joint-centered, 5 indifferent).

5.5 Discussion

Overall, the feedback was very positive concerning the joint-centered menu, and the results from the Borg15 Scale show that it is estimated as significantly less tiring than head-centered menus. Our results did not show significant differences for the SUS and NASA TLX usability questionnaires.

5.5.1 Improvements

We received qualitative feedback and suggestions for improvement, which we plan to incorporate in the next iteration of the design. For instance, the tracking of the different joints with IR markers occasionally caused an unintended switch of the interface to another joint, which we aim to resolve using improved skeletal sensors. Moreover, our participants remarked that the level of fatigue during the few minutes with the interface in the experiment was still tolerable using either head-centered or joint-centered menus, but they estimated that their preference would be clearly shifted towards joint-centered interfaces during longer use. Also, as two participants commented, the joint-centered menu is positioned around the user's arm, which is not necessarily always within the user's FOV, but due to the matching perceptual and motor space it might be possible to interact even without vision, potentially supported by (vibro-)tactile feedback (cf. [2]).

5.5.2 Implications

Our results imply multiple advantages of presenting 2D GUIs on joint-centered kinespheres instead of traditional head-centered GUIs:

- Physical support, if available, can be used to rest joints without the need to lift the arm up for GUI interaction.

- Users can move the GUI closer to their eyes if need be to increase accuracy and precision during interaction [29, 30].

- Matching joint-centered perceptual and motor spaces support motor training and may even be used for GUI selections without vision for experienced users.

- Joint-centered menus located at the maximal reachable distance ensure that false positives of unintended selections, when moving the hands casually within arm's reach, are highly unlikely.

- Using the boundary technique that combines the positioning of menus on kinespheres with a small tolerance area can significantly improve interaction performance.

6. CONCLUSION

In this paper we presented and evaluated joint-centered kinespheres for efficient and comfortable spatial interaction in virtual and augmented reality. We performed a Fitts' Law experiment, which showed that the interaction performance largely depends on the placement of menus along the kinematic chain and within the kinespheres centered around the shoulder, elbow or wrist joint. In particular, the effective throughput was highest for the wrist joint and menus that were placed on the boundary of the kinesphere with a small tolerance region for touch input. Based on the results, we implemented a joint-centered user interface and compared it to a traditional head-centered user interface in an in-house developed interior planning application. We discussed our observations and presented practical guidelines for how to leverage joint-centered kinespheres for the design of menus for spatial user interfaces.

There are several possible paths to extend and to adapt the method of joint-centered spatial user interfaces. For instance, kinespheres could be applied at finger level, but also at the legs, trunk or back to incorporate further modalities. Moreover, placing interactive objects on joint-centered kinespheres may require a new class of optimized widgets or layered menu structures. Furthermore, since we observed both high efficiency and high comfort in the wrist boundary condition in our experiment, following up on this path may lead towards spatial user interfaces for productive long-time use. While joint-centered user interfaces provide an efficient solution for long term direct interaction, future work could offer a comparison with indirect interaction methods to place the joint-centered user interfaces in the wide field of spatial user interfaces.

Acknowledgments

This work was partly supported by grants from the Deutsche Forschungsgemeinschaft.

7. REFERENCES

[1] F. Argelaguet and C. Andujar. A survey of 3D object selection techniques for virtual environments. *Computers & Graphics*, 37(3):121–136, 2013.

[2] O. J. Ariza Nunez, P. Lubos, and F. Steinicke. Hapring: A wearable haptic device for 3D interaction. In S. Diefenbach, N. Henze, and M. Pielot, editors, *Proc. of Mensch und Computer*, pages 421–424. De Gruyter Oldenbourg, 2015.

[3] R. Balakrishnan and I. S. MacKenzie. Performance differences in the fingers, wrist, and forearm in computer input control. In *Proc. of ACM CHI*, CHI '97, pages 303–310. ACM, 1997.

[4] G. Borg. Psychophysical bases of perceived exertion. *Medicine and science in sports and exercise*, 14(5):377, 1982.

[5] D. Bowman. *Interaction Techniques for Common Tasks in Immersive Virtual Environments: Design, Evaluation, and Application*. PhD thesis, Georgia Institute of Technology, 1999.

[6] D. Bowman and L. Hodges. An Evaluation of Techniques for Grabbing and Manipulating Remote Objects in Immersive Virtual Environments. In *ACM SIGGRAPH i3D*, pages 35–38, 1997.

[7] J. Brooke et al. Sus-a quick and dirty usability scale. *Usability evaluation in industry*, 189(194):4–7, 1996.

[8] G. Bruder, F. Steinicke, and W. Stuerzlinger. Effects of visual conflicts on 3D selection task performance in stereoscopic display environments. In *Proc. of IEEE 3DUI*, pages 115–118, 2013.

[9] G. Bruder, F. Steinicke, and W. Stuerzlinger. Touching the Void Revisited: Analyses of Touch Behavior On and Above Tabletop Surfaces. *Proc. of INTERACT*, 8117:278–296, 2013.

[10] S. Card, J. Mackinlay, and G. Robertson. A morphological analysis of the design space of input devices. *ACM Transactions on Information Systems (TOIS)*, 9(2):99–122, 1991.

[11] L.-W. Chan, H.-S. Kao, M. Y. Chen, M.-S. Lee, J. Hsu, and Y.-P. Hung. Touching the void: Direct-touch interaction for intangible displays. In *Proc. of ACM CHI*, pages 2625–2634, 2010.

[12] J. Djajadiningrat. *Cubby: what you see is where you act. Interlacing the display and manipulation spaces*. PhD thesis, Industrial Design Engineering, Delft University of Technology, 1998.

[13] A. Dvorkin, R. Kenyon, and E. Keshner. Reaching within a dynamic virtual environment. *Journal of NeuroEngineering and Rehabilitation*, 4(23), 2007.

[14] B. M. Ens, R. Finnegan, and P. P. Irani. The Personal Cockpit: A Spatial Interface for Effective Task Switching on Head-worn Displays. In *Proc. of ACM CHI*, CHI '14, pages 3171–3180. ACM, 2014.

[15] P. Fitts. The Information Capacity of the Human Motor System in Controlling the Amplitude of Movement. *Journal of Experimental Psychology: General*, 47(6):381–391, 1954.

[16] D. Gerber and D. Bechmann. The Spin Menu: A Menu System for Virtual Environments. In *Proc. of IEEE VR*, VR '05, pages 271–272. IEEE Computer Society, 2005.

[17] T. Grossman and R. Balakrishnan. The design and evaluation of selection techniques for 3d volumetric displays. In *Proc. of ACM UIST*, pages 3–12, 2006.

[18] D. Guinness, A. Jude, G. Poor, and A. Dover. Models for rested touchless gestural interaction. In *Proc. of ACM SUI*, pages 34–43, 2015.

[19] T. Ha and W. Woo. An empirical evaluation of virtual hand techniques for 3d object manipulation in a tangible augmented reality environment. In *Proc. of IEEE 3DUI*, pages 91–98, 2010.

[20] S. G. Hart. NASA-task load index (NASA-TLX) 20 years later. In *Proc. of Human Factors and Ergonomics Society Annual Meeting*, pages 904–908, 2006.

[21] International Organization for Standardization. *ISO/DIS 9241-9 Ergonomic requirements for office work with visual display terminals (VDTs) - Part 9: Requirements for non-keyboard input devices*, 2000.

[22] A. Jude, G. Poor, and D. Guinness. Personal Space: User Defined Gesture Space for GUI Interaction. In *Proc. of ACM CHI*, pages 1615–1620, 2014.

[23] R. Kennedy, N. Lane, K. Berbaum, and M. Lilienthal. Simulator Sickness Questionnaire: An Enhanced Method for Quantifying Simulator Sickness. *The International Journal of Aviation Psychology*, 3(3):203–220, 1993.

[24] R. Kopper, D. A. Bowman, M. G. Silva, and R. P. McMahan. A human motor behavior model for distal pointing tasks. *International Journal of Human-Computer Studies (IJHCS)*, 68(10):603–615, 2010.

[25] D. Lemmerman and J. LaViola Jr. Effects of Interaction-Display Offset on User Performance in Surround screen virtual environments. In *Proc. of IEEE VR*, pages 303–304, 2007.

[26] F. C. Y. Li, D. Dearman, and K. N. Truong. Virtual Shelves: Interactions with Orientation Aware Devices. In *Proc. of ACM UIST*, UIST '09, pages 125–128. ACM, 2009.

[27] G. Liu, R. Chua, and J. T. Enns. Attention for perception and action: task interference for action planning, but not for online control. *Experimental Brain Research*, 185:709–717, 2008.

[28] J. Loomis and J. Knapp. Visual Perception of Egocentric

Distance in Real and Virtual Environments. In L. Hettinger and M. Haas, editors, *Virtual and Adaptive Environments*, pages 21–46. Erlbaum, 2003.

[29] P. Lubos, G. Bruder, and F. Steinicke. Analysis of Direct Selection in Head-Mounted Display Environments. In *Proc. of IEEE 3DUI*, pages 1–8, 2014.

[30] P. Lubos, G. Bruder, and F. Steinicke. Influence of Comfort on 3D Selection Task Performance in Immersive Desktop Setups. *Journal of Virtual Reality and Broadcasting (JVRB)*, 12(2), 2015.

[31] C. MacKenzie, R. Marteniuka, C. Dugasa, D. Liskea, and B. Eickmeiera. Three-dimensional movement trajectories in Fitts' task: Implications for control. *The Quarterly Journal of Experimental Psychology A*, 34(4):629–647, 1987.

[32] I. MacKenzie and P. Isokoski. Fitts throughput and the speed-accuracy tradeoff. In *Proc. of ACM CHI*, pages 1633–1636, 2008.

[33] S. Mann. *Intelligent Image Processing*. John Wiley and Sons, 2001.

[34] J. McLester and P. S. Pierre. *Applied Biomechanics: Concepts and Connections*. Cengage Learning, 2007.

[35] M. Mine, F. B. Jr, and C. Sequin. Moving Objects in Space: Exploiting Proprioception in Virtual-Environment interaction. In *Proc. of ACM SIGGRAPH*, pages 19–26, 1997.

[36] A. Murata and H. Iwase. Extending Fitts' Law to a three-dimensional pointing task. *Human Movement Science*, 20:791–805, 2001.

[37] I. Poupyrev, M. Billinghurst, S. Weghorst, and T. Ichikawa. The Go-Go Interaction Technique: Non-Linear Mapping for Direct Manipulation in VR. In *Proc. of ACM UIST*, pages 79–80, 1996.

[38] I. Poupyrev, S. Weghorst, M. Billinghurst, and T. Ichikawa. A framework and testbed for studying manipulation techniques for immersive vr. In *Proc. of ACM VRST*, pages 21–28, 1997.

[39] M. Sanders and E. McCormick. *Human Factors in Engineering and Design*. McGRAW-HILL Book Company, 1987.

[40] G. Shoemaker, T. Tsukitani, Y. Kitamura, and K. S. Booth. Two-Part Models Capture the Impact of Gain on Pointing Performance. *ACM Trans. Comput.-Hum. Interact.*, 19(4):28:1–28:34, Dec. 2012.

[41] J. A. Thomson. Is continuous visual monitoring necessary in visually guided locomotion? *Journal Experimental Psychology Human Perception Performance*, 9(3):427–443, 1983.

[42] M. Usoh, E. Catena, S. Arman, and M. Slater. Using Presence Questionaires in Reality. *Presence: Teleoperators & Virtual Environments*, 9(5):497–503, 1999.

[43] Y. Wang and C. MacKenzie. Effects of orientation disparity between haptic and graphic displays of objects in virtual environments. *Proc. of INTERACT*, 99:391–398, 1999.

[44] P. Willemsen, M. Colton, S. Creem-Regehr, and W. Thompson. The Effects of Head-Mounted Display Mechanical Properties and Field-of-View on Distance Judgments in Virtual Environments. *ACM Transactions on Applied Perception (TAP)*, 2(6):1–14, 2009.

[45] P. Willemsen, A. Gooch, W. Thompson, and S. Creem-Regehr. Effects of Stereo Viewing Conditions on Distance Perception in Virtual Environments. *Presence: Teleoperators & Virtual Environments*, 17(1):91–101, 2008.

[46] C. Wingrave and D. Bowman. Baseline factors for raycasting selection. In *Proc. of HCI International*, pages 1–10, 2005.

Optimising Free Hand Selection in Large Displays by Adapting to User's Physical Movements

Xiaolong Lou[1]

Andol X. Li[1]

Ren Peng[1]

Preben Hansen[2]

[1]Department of digital media, College of computer science and technologies, Zhejiang University, 38 Zheda road, Hangzhou China P.R. 310027

{dragondlx68, axli, pengren}@zju.edu.cn

[2]Department of Computer and Systems Sciences (DSV), Stockholm University, Sweden

preben@dsv.su.se

ABSTRACT

Advance in motion sensing technologies such as Microsoft Kinect and ASUS Xtion has enabled users to select targets on a large display through natural hand gestures. In such interaction, the users move left and right to navigate the display, and they frequently adjust body proximity against the display thus to switch between overall views and focus views. These physical movements benefit information navigation, interaction modality switch, and user interface adaptation. But in more specific context of free hand selection in large displays, the effect of physical movements is less systematically investigated. To explore the potential of physical movements in free hand selection, a physical movements-adapted technique is developed and evaluated. The results show that the new technique has significant improvements in both selection efficiency and accuracy, the more difficult selection task the more obvious improvement in accuracy. Additionally, the new technique is preferred to the baseline of *pointer acceleration* (PA) technique by participants.

Keywords

Large displays; free hand selection; selection efficiency; selection accuracy; physical movement

1. INTRODUCTION

Given the fast development of motion-sensing and large display technologies in the last decade, free hand gestures are used in interaction with large displays, and this has become an increasingly prevalent interaction method in wide domains and applications [1; 19]. Unlike touching- or mouse- based interaction, free hand operation is another form of interaction method preferred by users, which not only provide naturalness of interaction but also is independent to specific hardware devices. The independence smoothens transition from distant operation to up close touch [7], and makes interaction position more flexible [26]. Despite these merits, free hand gestures are poor at locating and selecting distal targets on large displays [8]. For example, users have to move cursors across a much longer distance (i.e. amplitude) than that in normal-sized desktop monitors. As a result, slow and inaccurate performances are achieved when selecting distal targets on a large display with traditional mouse-style selection techniques [8]. Furthermore, free hand selection confronts limited camera resolutions and unstable gesture motion recognition accuracy, which further weakens its abilities of small target approaching [15].

A number of studies have been conducted to remedy the weakness of free hand gestures in the interaction with large displays. For example, *dual-precision* (DP) techniques were applied and these satisfied both efficiency and precision in mid-air pointing on the large display [19]. The DP techniques comprise two precision modes, a coarse mode that can quickly approach the vicinity of the target, and a precise mode to focus on the small targets. Users are flexible to switch between two modes through manipulating a hand-held device. In addition, user's bimanual operations are also explored to realise the DP technique: the non-dominant hand engages in coarse moving while the dominant hand is used for precise action [18]. Another notable technique *pointer acceleration* (PA) [6] is often used in current interaction devices and systems. In this technique, the control-to-display (CD) gain, which refers to the ratio between cursor movement and input side's displacement, is dynamically adapted based on the velocity of input movements. That is, when the input side moves at a high velocity, the CD gain turns to a large value, which then helps to traverse a large span of distance; but when the input velocity slows down, the CD gain turns to a small value, which is suitable to precisely select small targets.

In addition to gestural movements, users' standing positions are subject to freedom of body movement and thus are dynamically changing. The body movements are driven by complicated motor behaviours, which lead to a practical impact on free hand operation [17]. These motor behaviours are utilised to provide assistance in spatial interaction. For example, in the context of *ambient displays* and *proxemic interaction* [3; 25], user's orientation and proximity toward displays are captured to adjust interaction modalities and information density on the display. However, in general free hand selection, user's physical movements such as moving left or right and stepping forward or backward in front of large display, are rarely considered as an important influence factor of free hand selection.

In this paper, therefore, we explore the effects of user's physical body movements in free hand selection, and we proposed a physical movement-adapted technique. The technique provides two levels of optimisations in horizontal and depth directions, respectively. In the horizontal direction, it senses user's left/right body movements to gain cursor's coarse movement in horizontal direction. In the depth direction, user's head-to-display distance is used to dynamically adjust CD gains, either approach closer to decrease CD gain or step farther to promote CD gain. Our new technique is not proposed as an independent technique that aims to compete

SUI '16, October 15-16, 2016, Tokyo, Japan
© 2016 ACM. ISBN 978-1-4503-4068-7/16/10...$15.00
DOI: http://dx.doi.org/10.1145/2983310.2985754

with other interaction techniques. Rather, it is studied as if a technique that can be implemented to automatically adapt to existing free hand pointing and selection systems, and as so it can be integrated into other selection techniques in order to support efficient and precise selection operations.

2. RELATED WORK
2.1 Free Hand Selection in Large Displays

As mentioned earlier, depth and motion sensing technologies have emerged into various applications [27]. Among these applications, free hand selection of targets on user interface is the most fundamental operation command that are familiar to users. Thus in this paper, selection tasks are designed to simulate the basic operation in interaction with large displays.

In large display environment, free hand selection shows various advantages to other interaction approaches. First, large-sized displays have larger visual fields than that of traditional desktop monitors, and as a result, users have to stand in a far distance for overall views of large displays, but in a closer distance for detail views [13]. Such dynamic distance adjustments can be naturally addressed through free hand selection. Second, free hand selection does not require specific input devices or platforms, because all interactions are done through natural gestures [19]. This is of particular usefulness, for example, in public spaces such as airport, because providing specifically designed input device for users in such scenario is unaffordable in terms of economy and interaction.

Free hand gestures are not a one-for-all solution in the interaction with large displays, as the usability disadvantages are pointed out in previous studies. For example, hand gestures are inefficient and inaccurate to reach distal and detail information items [8]. These problems are mostly incurred by weak recognition accuracy of motions [15], flexible hand gestures [19] and unmatched sizes between display and input sides [1].

To optimise free hand selection in the interaction of large displays, previous studies propose a collection of methods that have practical effects on specific aspects of free hand selection. For example, in body-centric interaction, interface areas that are covered by user's body shadows are made reachable. Users step closer or farther toward the display to change the size of reachable area [23; 24]. In tabletops, [4] proposed *pointable* technique to reach distal targets, which sensed fingers' pointing directions to get targets focused. *Laser pointing* is a widely used method in remote selection, but which is often criticised for its inaccuracy [9]. To remedy the inaccuracy problem, dual-mode techniques that combine absolute laser pointing and relative cursor control are developed, and results demonstrate higher efficiency and precision when selecting small targets [26]. In addition, target assistance techniques are applied to optimise laser pointing. For example, in [5], stickiness and gravity attributes are added to targets, thus the targets can be more easily selected with less possible miss of cursors. In the mobile contexts, a wrist-worn gloveless sensor is used to recover 3D pose of the user's hand, thus to accurately recognise hand postures and related commands [16]. A recent research utilises an arm-mounted Myo device to capture hand motions, thus to implement precise pointing and clicking in remote large displays [12]. Other methods such as [22] and [20] adopt user's bimanual operations (e.g. left hand for zoom and rotation while right hand for selection) to realise more precise interaction in air, which improve the usability when accessing distal targets.

From shadow reaching to dual-mode pointing, previous techniques primarily take use of user's bodily and input features to optimise

selection in remote displays. However, factors such as user's horizontal movements and proximity towards display are less concerned in this situation. To further understand the effect of physical movements on free hand selection, more related work are reviewed in following section.

2.2 Physical Movements

Adopting free hand interaction means users are allowed to move body gestures and positions in the interaction space. The physical body movements provide important spatial clues, such as user's orientation, distances against screens, proximity towards the other users, moving direction and velocity [3].

User's physical movements and other spatial factors affect task performance in large displays. For example, in navigating large information spaces, user's physical navigation results decrease virtual navigation and promote task performance [2]. In navigating large-scale virtual environment, physical movement is found to improve user's cognitive map in context, which results better navigation performance [21]. In laser pointing task, the distance between user and display is pointed out to influence pointing accuracy [14; 19].

Given physical movement's influence on cognitive learning and navigation, they are utilised to optimise interactions in varied situations. In *proxemic interaction* and *ambient interface*, physical dynamics such as user's orientation, proximities toward displays and other users, are sensed to automatically adjust user interface on displays [3; 25]. Similarly, the distance between user and display is captured to decide what interaction modality is applied, which assures that user can select targets on the display by a more suitable interaction method at any distance [7; 11]. In body-centric interaction, interface areas that are occupied by user's body shadows are accessible regions, users adjust shadow size by adjusting distance towards the large display [24]. Another technique integrates user's position, orientation, and distance to user interface to realise zoom in, zoom out and navigation on large displays, thus users can more efficiently and accurately focus on specific content of visualization [13].

Like navigation in large-scale visualisation, in free hand selection tasks, users spontaneously perform physical movements to satisfy different accessibility and precision requirements. They move left or right to horizontally navigate on interface, and step forward or backward to either focus on a detail region of display or get an overall view of whole display. These physical movements, however, are less explored to optimise free hand selection. In order to investigate the physical movements' effects on optimising free hand selection in large displays, a physical movement-adaptive technique is developed. A comparative selection experiment was conducted to evaluate the technique, in terms of both selection efficiency and accuracy.

3. PHYSICAL MOVEMENT-ADAPTED TECHNIQUE
3.1 Baseline Technique

Pointer acceleration (PA) technique is selected as the baseline technique in this paper. It dynamically adjusts the CD gain according to the velocity of user's hand movements, based on the principle that the faster the input movement, the further away the cursor should go [6]. We achieved dynamic CD gains ($CD_{velocity}$ in equation 1) based on the algorithm in [19] (in section 4.2), with maximum and minimum CD gains (CD_{max} and CD_{min}), lower and upper bounds of hand velocity (V_{max} and V_{min}), and other function parameters adjusted according to the span of user's hand velocity and actual configurations (i.e. physical size of display and interactive space) in our study. Figure 1 illustrates the correlation between hand velocity and CD gain in baseline PA technique. Pilot evaluation was conducted, and results demonstrated that participants could complete selection task effectively with this baseline PA technique.

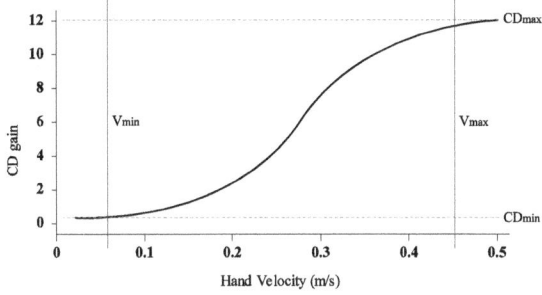

Figure 1. Transfer function of Control – Display gain in baseline PA technique (V_{max}= 0.45m/s, V_{min}= 0.06m/s, CD_{max}= 12.0, $CD_{min} = 0.2$).

3.2 New Technique

The new proposed physical movement-adapted technique is an optimised solution on the basis of PA technique. Except for the fundamental PA technique, the new technique incorporates another two adaptions based on user's physical movements. First, it senses user's horizontal movements to gain cursor's horizontal movement in a large span. For example, when the user moving towards left to reach a distal target on the same side, the cursor's moving span in left direction is gained, thus can quickly reach the vicinity of the target (Figure 2a). Second, it obtains the distance between user and display and then generates a dynamic selection precision. At a close distance, a precise pointing mode is mapped to the cursor movement, but a coarse pointing mode is mapped at a far distance (Figure 2b). All these two adaptions are realised by changing CD gain.

In our implementation, user's head joint is tracked to get the horizontal movement and distance information. In horizontal adaption, user's movements in left and right directions are used to amplify cursor's movement in large scale. To decide the mapping relation between user's motions and amplification in cursor's movement, we initially used a simple user's 2D position-based mapping, which captures user's positions in sensor's perspective to determine cursor's coordinates on the display. But results from the pilot evaluation showed such mapping was either inefficient to operate or difficult to control the cursor, and it was criticised for restriction in user's position. Finally, we designed a moving speed-based amplification method, which translated user's moving speed to an amplified speed with a constant CD gain ($CD_{constant}$ in equation 1). Through pilot test, we selected a gain of 2.5, which made it convenient to move the cursor from one side of the display to the other side, but did not introduce additional difficulties in controlling the cursor. Additionally, we defined a moving speed of 200mm/s as the threshold speed, which was used to recognise when to activate or prohibit the horizontal adaption. If user's moving speed is faster than the threshold, the horizontal adaption is activated and its effect is accumulated to the cursor's velocity. Combining velocity-based adaption with horizontal adaption, the cursor's velocity is represented as follows:

$$V_{cursor} = V_{hand} \times CD_{velocity} + V_{body} \times CD_{constant} \quad (1)$$

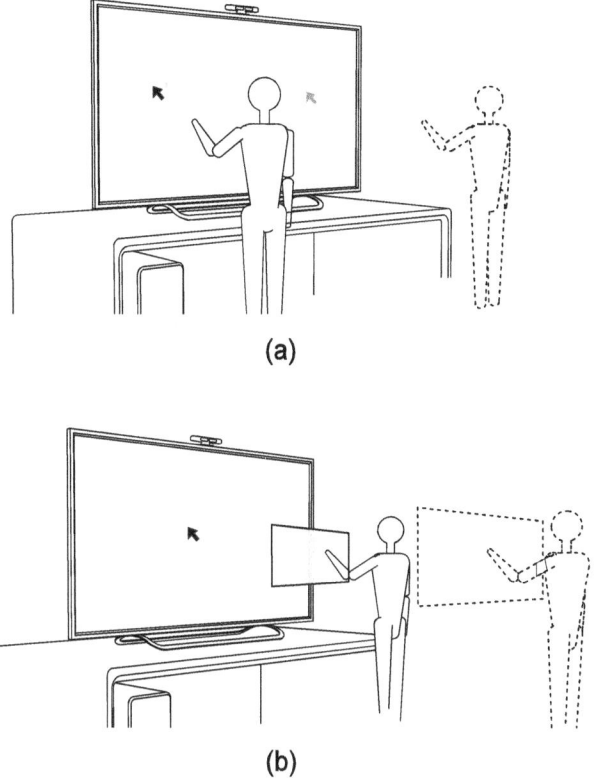

(a)

(b)

Figure 2. Physical movement adaptions: (a) amplified movement in horizontal direction; (b) dynamic input precision by changing distance towards display.

In distance adaption, user's head proximity towards display is used to adjust the input precision. The closer distances users stand at, the higher input precision is adapted. To deploy this precision adaption, we introduced a scale factor ($S_{distance}$ in equation 2) to dynamically adjust the cursor's movement scale. We designed a linear function of distance to generate dynamic scale levels (equation 3). Considering the depth camera's available distance, we limited the distance between 800mm (D_{min} in equation 3) and 3200mm (D_{max} in equation 3) in this study. The middle distance 2000mm corresponds to the scale of 1.0, it represents the distance adaption has no effect at the distance of 2000mm (D_{middle} in equation 3). When standing at a distance closer than D_{middle}, the cursor's movement span becomes smaller by multiplying a scale ratio that is smaller than 1.0. In contrast, the cursor's movement span becomes larger at a distance farther than D_{middle}. By pilot test, we selected a smallest scale ratio of 0.2 (S_{min} in equation 3), which is corresponded to the D_{min}. And selected the top scale ratio of 2.2 (S_{max} in equation 3), which is corresponded to the D_{max}. Given an actual distance (D_{actual}), the equation of cursor's velocity is adjusted to:

$$V_{cursor} = \left(V_{hand} \times CD_{velocity} + V_{body} \times CD_{constant}\right) \times S_{distance} \quad (2)$$

$$Where \quad S_{distance} = \frac{(S_{max} - S_{min}) \times (D_{actual} - D_{min})}{D_{max} - D_{min}} + S_{min} \quad (3)$$

4. HYPOTHESES DEVELOPMENT

Unlike other selection assistance techniques that either introduce either additional devices and configurations (e.g. motion tracking system, handheld touch screen) or complex operation commands (e.g. bimanual operation), technique proposed in this paper involves less additional operations, all optimising adaptions are conducted automatically by program, thus we raise hypothesis 1 and 2 as follows:

H1: Compared with the baseline of pointer acceleration technique, the new technique has higher selection efficiency and accuracy;

H2: The physical movement-based adaption has less influence on operation, thus it has the same user preference as the baseline technique;

In addition, the new technique largely relies on user's physical movements. When selecting different sized targets at different distances, user performs different levels of physical movements. For example, when selecting large targets in small amplitude (i.e. movement distance between targets), user can complete the selection efficiently without performing physical movements. But in selecting small targets in large amplitude, physical movements are more frequent. Given the differences, we raise hypothesis 3 as follows:

H3: In different target width and amplitude conditions, the new technique has different levels of gains on selection: in large amplitude, the gains are achieved in selection efficiency; in small target width, the gains are achieved in selection accuracy.

5. METHODS

The objective of this study is to evaluate the optimising effects in free hand selection brought by the physical movement-adapted technique. The same velocity-based PA method is used in the new and baseline techniques. These two techniques were compared in terms of selection efficiency, accuracy and user evaluation.

5.1 Participants

The study recruited 12 volunteered participants (5 females), aged 22 to 30 (M = 24.5, SD = 4.90). The participants are employees and undergraduate students from local companies and universities, they are all right-handed with normal or correct-to-normal eyesight, and without body impairments. The participants were familiar with remote interactions in large display environment, for example, using Wii controller to play video games on large screens.

5.2 Apparatus

The experiment was conducted in a laboratory that equipped with a 70-inch large display, workstations and tables. The display is a 1560mm × 877.5mm flat screen, with a resolution of 3840 × 2160. The screen was connected to a workstation (Windows 7, 32 GB memory, and 4.0 GHz Intel 32-core processor) and it displayed task programmes from the workstation. An ASUS Xtion Pro Depth/RGB camera was used to track the participants' head joints, it was mounted on the middle top of the large screen. The participants were allowed to move within the space in front of the screen, which ranged from 800mm to 3200mm.

5.3 Task and Procedure

To simulate selection tasks, a multi-directional selection interface was designed. To configure varied levels of selection difficulties, inconsistent target width and amplitude were introduced. Taking account of the experiment variables in [26] and the actual sizes of screen in the study, we selected the values of width as 72, 24, and 8 mm. All participants were confirmed to be able to see these

targets. The values of amplitude were 670 and 1340 mm. The Fitts' index of difficulty (ID) of our selection tasks ranged from 3.37 to 7.75 bits.

The tasks were in a Fitts reciprocal pointing style [10]. The tasks consist of acquiring circular targets (three width conditions) in two distance conditions. Targets were presented in 10 (in 1340mm distance) or 12 (in 670mm distance) possible locations, they were arranged in a circle in the centre of the display. Figure 3 illustrates the selection tasks.

In each trial, a random start location (an unfilled circle) was firstly displayed. The participant moved the cursor to the start location to show a target (a black filled circle) which was symmetric to the start location from the centre of the display showed (Figure 4). The participant moved the cursor inside the target zone and sustained 500 milliseconds to complete one selection trial. Then, the target disappeared and a subsequent location was showed, signalling the start of a new trial. During this procedure, the interval from one target displayed (i.e. the cursor reached the start location) to it was touched by the cursor was defined as the *selection time*. When acquiring the target, if the cursor moved away from the target zone without sustaining 500 milliseconds, it represented one *selection error*. If more than one time of error occurred in a trial, only one error was counted. After the participant completed 60 times of selection, the interface exited, the *selection time* for each selection and the total *selection error* counting were automatically recorded and stored in a log file.

Following the tasks, participants were asked to evaluate the tasks and two techniques, in terms of mental effort, accuracy, speed, perceived fatigue, comfort, and overall easiness on 5-point Likert scales. Then, participants were asked to give comments on two techniques.

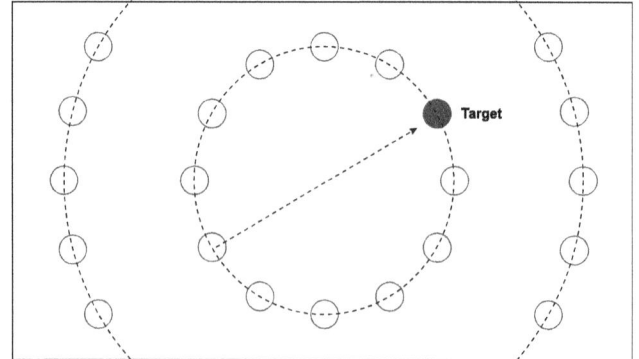

Figure 3. Selection task.

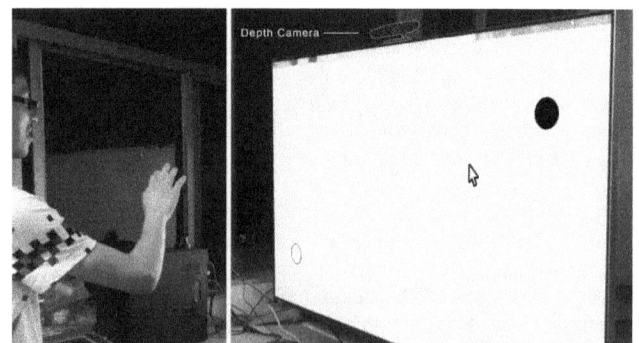

Figure 4. Study scenario: distance between the start location and the target is the amplitude.

5.4 Design

A 2×3×2 repeated measures within-participant factorial design was used. The factors were:

- *Technique: physical movement-adapted technique, baseline technique;*

- *Width: 72 mm (180 pixels), 24 mm (60 pixels), and 8 mm (20 pixels);*

- *Amplitude: 1340 mm (3300 pixels), 670 mm (1650 pixels).*

For each participant, we grouped trials into 12 blocks of 60 trials, one block per combination of Technique, Width, and Amplitude. In each block, each location had the same times to be highlighted as target, either 5 times (in small amplitude) or 6 times (in large amplitude). The presentation order for technique, width, amplitude, and target location was counterbalanced using a Latin square.

Each time when a new Technique began, participants were allowed to have practice trials until they told they had sufficient confidence in operation. Finally, we collected 2 technique × 3 width × 2 amplitude × 12 participants = 144 task logs. Each log file contained 60 *selection time* and one *selection error* counting.

6. ANALYSIS

We found there existed some overlong selection time, which were 3 times larger than mean values. These data were caused when participants moving their hands too fast or extending hands outside the perspective of the camera, which resulted in occasional losing track of hand. In order to ensure the validity, these error data were excluded. Finally, 968 (11.2%) trials were removed from the total 8640 trials.

We analysed the data with multiway ANOVAs, and performed Turkey HSD post-hoc tests for pairwise comparisons. We verified there had no significant effect of technique presentation order, which indicates that a within-participants design is reasonable. All results below are significant at the $p < 0.05$ level.

6.1 Selection Time

There was a significant effect for Technique on selection time ($F_{1, 11} = 19.47$, $P < 0.001$), with mean values of 1497 and 1597

milliseconds for the new physical movement-adapted and baseline techniques respectively. Table 1 shows the mean selection time results in different combinations of amplitude and width. In addition, there was a significant effect on selection time for amplitude ($F_{1, 11} = 464.25$, $p < 0.001$), width ($F_{2, 22} = 362.92$, $p < 0.001$), technique × width ($F_{2, 22} = 44.82$, $p < 0.001$) and technique × amplitude ($F_{2, 22} = 17.08$, $p = 0.002$).

Table 1. Selection time results in different conditions

Amplitude	Width	Technique	Selection Time (ms)	
			Mean	SD
1340mm	72mm	P.M. - Adapted	976.73	85.53
		Baseline	1425.02	145.87
1340mm	24mm	P.M. - Adapted	1599.99	214.43
		Baseline	1745.41	167.59
1340mm	8mm	P.M. - Adapted	2320.49	110.79
		Baseline	2232.73	135.21
670mm	72mm	P.M. - Adapted	798.41	76.39
		Baseline	1094.26	147.31
670mm	24mm	P.M. - Adapted	1294.23	213.31
		Baseline	1289.44	215.33
670mm	8mm	P.M. - Adapted	1992.69	112.29
		Baseline	1795.75	97.72

Figure 5 revealed the interactions between technique and width, and between technique and amplitude. Post hoc multiple means comparison tests revealed the physical movement-adapted technique had significantly shorter selection time compared to the baseline technique in large amplitude condition (by 168.65 millisecond, $p < 0.05$), but had less advantage in small amplitude (Figure 5a). This suggested that amplitude factor had a significant effect on the new technique's effectiveness, the larger amplitude the more noticeable gains on selection efficiency the new technique had.

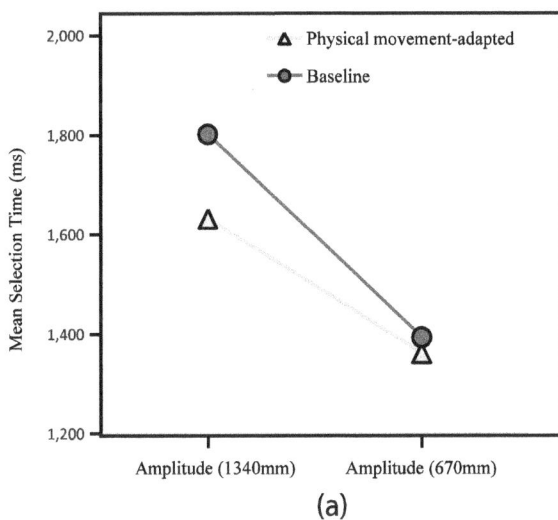

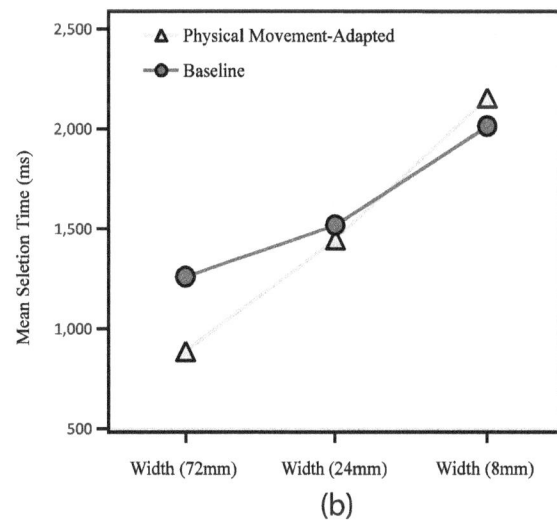

Figure 5. Interactions between technique and amplitude, and between technique and width on selection time.

The new technique had significantly shorter selection time for large width (by 372.07 millisecond, $p < 0.05$), whereas it had a shorter selection time for small width (by 142.35 millisecond, $p < 0.05$) (Figure 5b). This indicated that target width factor had a strong influence on the new technique's function. In large width, the new technique optimised selection efficiency significantly; but in small width, the new technique performed inefficiency in comparison to the baseline technique. This was believed to be caused by the scale effect in distance adaption, which made the cursor moving less efficient. In overall, the new technique showed noticeable advantages in selection efficiency in the combinations of width and amplitude.

6.2 Selection Error Rate

There was a significant effect on selection error rate for technique ($F_{1, 11} = 35.589$, $p < 0.001$). As expected, the new technique had an optimising effect on selection accuracy. The new technique had a mean error rate of 7.692 % (SD = 0.330) while the baseline one had a mean error rate of 11.617 % (SD = 0.485). Table 2 showed more detailed error rate results in different combinations of technique, amplitude and width.

Table 2. Selection error rate results in different conditions

Amplitude	Width	Technique	Selection Error Rate (%)	
			Mean	SD
1340mm	72mm	P.M. - Adapted	5.64	1.22
		Baseline	5.17	0.45
1340mm	24mm	P.M. - Adapted	7.84	1.42
		Baseline	10.99	1.94
1340mm	8mm	P.M. - Adapted	12.21	2.45
		Baseline	19.89	3.32
670mm	72mm	P.M. - Adapted	4.94	1.10
		Baseline	5.71	1.70
670mm	24mm	P.M. - Adapted	5.94	1.41
		Baseline	10.56	2.25
670mm	8mm	P.M. - Adapted	9.58	3.42
		Baseline	17.37	5.04

Unsurprisingly, there was a significant effect on selection error rate for target width ($F_{2, 22} = 147.767$, $p < 0.001$), the larger width the higher selection error rate. And there was a significant effect for amplitude ($F_{1, 11} = 15.225$, $p < 0.001$). In 670 mm amplitude, the new and the baseline techniques had error rates of 6.82 % and 11.21 %, respectively; in 1340mm amplitude, two techniques had

error rates of 8.56 % and 12.02 %, respectively. We suspected this was caused by the velocity adaption of PA technique: in larger amplitude, participants performed faster hand movement, which generated more frequency of occasional selection error.

There was a significant interaction between technique and width on selection error rate ($F_{2, 22} = 17.786$, $p < 0.001$). Multiple means comparison tests showed the new technique had less difference in error rate for 72 mm width, but had significantly lower error rate for 24 mm (new technique: 6.89 %; baseline technique: 10.77 %; $p < 0.05$) and 8 mm width (new technique: 10.89 %; baseline technique: 18.63 %; $p < 0.05$) (Figure 6).

There was no significant interaction between technique and amplitude on selection error rate. It indicated that physical movement-based adaption posed less influence on selection error rate in different amplitude conditions.

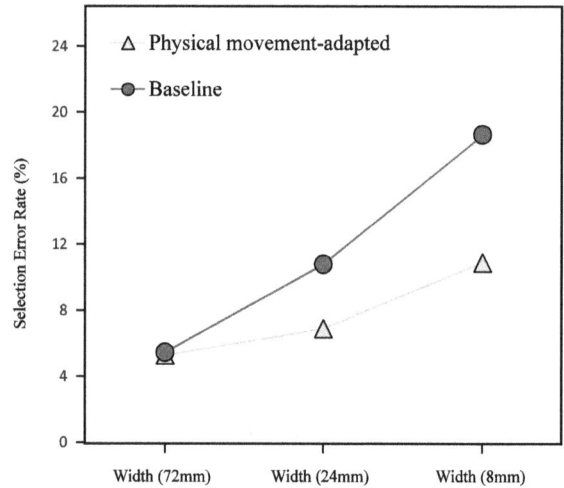

Figure 6. Interaction between technique and width on selection error rate.

6.3 User Evaluation and Feedback

Finally and yet importantly, we compared participants' subjective evaluations on the new and the baseline techniques (Table 3). Pearson χ^2 test was used to analyse the evaluation data. The results showed that there was a significant effect on accuracy and speed, and overall preference (all $p < 0.05$). 5 participants graded the new technique as accurate or upper (very accurate), while all 12 participants graded the baseline technique as accurate or below (normal, not accurate, coarse). For speed scale, 4 participants graded 'very fast' while the remainders graded 'fast' for the new

Table 3. Subjective evaluation results on two techniques

	Technique	Strongly Disagree	-		Strongly Agree		Mean score
		1	2	3	4	5	
Need much **Mental Effort**	P.M. - Adapted	2	3	4	2	1	2.75
	Baseline	3	2	4	2	1	2.67
It is **Accurate**	P.M. - Adapted	0	2	5	4	1	3.33
	Baseline	1	5	6	0	0	2.42
It is **Speedy**	P.M. - Adapted	0	0	0	8	4	4.33
	Baseline	0	0	5	6	1	3.67
Easy to cause **Fatigue**	P.M. - Adapted	2	1	5	2	2	3.08
	Baseline	2	0	7	2	1	3.00
It is **Comfortable** to use	P.M. - Adapted	0	1	4	4	3	3.75
	Baseline	0	0	5	5	2	3.75
Overall easy in use	P.M. - Adapted	0	2	4	3	3	3.58
	Baseline	0	2	3	4	3	3.67

technique; for the baseline technique, however, 1 participant graded 'very fast', 6 participants graded 'fast' and the others graded 'normal'. These findings indicate that participants are satisfied with new technique's gains in selection efficiency and accuracy.

But in scale items of mental effort, perceived fatigue, comfort in use and overall easiness, there was less significant evaluation difference between two techniques, this result is consistent with our expectation that physical movements in horizontal and depth directions are user's spontaneous behaviours in spatial interaction, thus has less significant effect on operation complexity and difficulty. Finally, 8 participants preferred the new technique overall, other 4 participants showed no preference bias toward two techniques.

Participants' comments confirmed the results. The participants commented on the new technique that was more adaptive to their operate actions. One of participants rated the new technique positively due to the high efficiency and naturalness, he commented *'I only need to move left or right one step to quickly get periphery targets on the display'*. Other participants pointed out that precision adaption in depth direction was particularly useful in selecting faraway and small targets.

7. RESULTS

The abovementioned analysis results revealed that new technique had significant influence on both selection time and error rate. The physical movement-adapted technique was found to be faster and more accurate in comparison to the baseline technique, thus hypothesis 1 (**H1**) is supported.

In the respect of selection time, significant interaction effects were found between technique and width, and between technique and amplitude. The new technique was found to have more obvious advantages in selection time for larger amplitude and width. In the respect of error rate, significant interaction effect between technique and width showed that the smaller target width, the more obvious optimisation new technique had in selection accuracy. Hypothesis 3 (**H3**) is supported.

Our new technique was developed on the basis of baseline technique, without adding additional operation command. User evaluation results showed participants could perceive the adaption of the new technique. Our new technique was preferred by participants to the baseline technique, in particular in efficiency and accuracy. Therefore, hypothesis 2 (**H2**) is denied.

8. DISCUSSION

The findings of the study show the optimising effects of physical movement-based adaption on free hand selection in large displays. In varied selection difficulty indexes, multiple levels of optimising effect were found in selection time and accuracy. For example, in the term of selection time, the larger amplitude and larger target width, the more obvious advantages the new technique has. While in the term of selection error rate, the new technique has the most significant optimising effect for the smallest width.

The findings gained in this study are generally consistent with previous research, as that user's physical movements, such as moving left and right, have a promoting effect on task performance in large interactive space [2]. And user's horizontal movement and proximities towards display can be adapted to develop more suitable visualisation on the large display [13]. As an exploratory study, the paper also supplies new insights into how spatial factors such as users' positions and distances against display can be utilised to promote free hand selection efficiency and accuracy in large display environment.

Implications about physical movement adaption and PA technique are provided. First, physical movement adaption has double-edged effects on free hand selection efficiency and accuracy. Although the new technique performs a generally positive effect on selection performance, its adaption has negative influences on some conditions. For example, when selecting small targets, users naturally approach their hands closer toward the display, such distance adaption makes the cursor's movement span smaller, which further makes distant selection less efficient. Second, study results showed that PA technique becomes more error-prone in large amplitude. This is because users move their hands more quickly when selecting faraway targets, velocity-adapted amplification in PA technique makes it more difficult to focus on small targets.

The findings, as well as practical implications drawn previously, are helpful for interface designers and interaction engineers capitalise users' spatial factors and their practical effects in large display-based interactions. For example, when designing user interfaces for a large display that has the whole screen area viewable and reachable, too small target size should be forbidden, as small-sized user interface elements drive users to stand at a close distance. When designing user interfaces for wall-sized displays (e.g. 5m in width), users' horizontal movement can be used to assist selecting periphery targets. But bodily motion has a weak precision in control, thus a small mapping ratio between interface and body movements is reasonable. In addition, the study revealed that amplitude has a negative influence on selection accuracy, in particular in selecting small targets. When designing high precision-required user interfaces such as rich information visualisations, too large distance between targets should be avoided.

The significance of this paper is not limited to presenting an optimised technique for free hand selection in the interaction with large displays, but also provides generalising understandings of physical movement's effects on free hand interaction. In our new technique, physical movement-adapted optimisation is added to the baseline PA technique without introducing any other configurations and operation commands. Results show that the integration of movement adaption significantly promotes selection efficiency and accuracy, but impose less negative influence on operation. This indicates physical movement-adapted method can integrate well with other selection techniques. Except for the most widely used PA technique, more techniques can benefit from this method.

Limitations of this study are noted. For example, the new technique is proposed for optimising selection efficiency of faraway targets, whereas it is limited by the display size in the experiment. Larger amplitude is difficult to simulate, thus the new technique's deeper potentials are still unrevealed and we plan to further investigate the new technique's optimising effects in future work. In this study, we implemented horizontal adaption algorithms with a constant CD gain and distance adaption algorithm with a simple linear function, other factors such as bodily movement speed are not ever explored in adaption function. In following work, we plan to have a further investigation of user's physical movements in free hand selection tasks and design a more reasonable adaption algorithm to achieve larger improvements in free hand selection. In addition, more user's behavioural dynamics such as head orientation and bimanual operation are expected to be used to promote selection performance, they are all planned in our future study.

9. CONCLUSIONS

In this paper, we propose a physical movement-adapted technique to promote the efficiency and precision of free hand selection in large displays. In particular, we design a comparative study to investigate the effectiveness of the new technique. The results reveal that (i) the new technique has optimising effects in both selection efficiency and accuracy; (ii) in more difficult selection tasks, the new technique's adaptions have more obvious optimisation in accuracy; (iii) the new technique has equal operation complexity and easiness to the baseline PA technique, but its optimising effects are widely accepted and it is preferred by users. Based on these findings, we summarise optimising effects of the new technique, and conclude generalising implications for future development of large display-related user interface and free hand interaction technique.

10. ACKNOWLEDGMENTS

The authors thank all participants who took part in the study and contributed feedbacks. This research was supported by the funding of Zhejiang Provincial Natural Science Funding (LQ15F020002) and China Knowledge Centre for Engineering Science and Technology (CKCEST-2014-3-2).

11. REFERENCES

[1] Ardito, C., Buono, P., Costabile, M.F., and Desolda, G. 2015. Interaction with Large Displays: A Survey. *ACM Computing Surveys*. 47, 3, 1-38.

[2] Ball, R., North, C., and Bowman, D.A. 2007. Move to improve: promoting physical navigation to increase user performance with large displays. In *Proceedings of the SIGCHI Conference on Human Factors in Computing Systems* (San Jose, California, USA, 2007). CHI '07. ACM, New York, NY, 191-200.

[3] Ballendat, T., Marquardt, N., and Greenberg, S. 2010. Proxemic interaction: designing for a proximity and orientation-aware environment. In *Proceedings of the ACM International Conference on Interactive Tabletops and Surfaces* (Pittsburgh, PA, USA, 2010). ITS '10. ACM, New York, NY, 121-130.

[4] Banerjee, A., Burstyn, J., Girouard, A., and Vertegaal, R. 2011. Pointable: an in-air pointing technique to manipulate out-of-reach targets on tabletops. In *Proceedings of the ACM International Conference on Interactive Tabletops and Surfaces* (Kobe, Japan, 2011). ITS '11. ACM, New York, NY, 11-20.

[5] Bateman, S., Mandryk, R.L., Gutwin, C., and Xiao, R. 2013. Analysis and comparison of target assistance techniques for relative ray-cast pointing. *International Journal of Human-Computer Studies*. 71, 5, 511-532.

[6] Casiez, G. and Roussel, N. 2011. No more bricolage!: methods and tools to characterize, replicate and compare pointing transfer functions. In *Proceedings of the 24th annual ACM symposium on User interface software and technology* (Santa Barbara, CA, USA, 2011). UIST '11. ACM, New York, NY, 603-614.

[7] Clark, A., Dünser, A., Billinghurst, M., Piumsomboon, T., and Altimira, D. 2011. Seamless interaction in space. In *Proceedings of the 23rd Australian Computer-Human Interaction Conference* (Canberra, Australia, 2011). OzCHI '11. ACM, New York, NY, 88-97.

[8] Czerwinski, M., Robertson, G., Meyers, B., Smith, G., Robbins, D., and Tan, D. 2006. Large display research overview. In *CHI '06 Extended Abstracts on Human Factors in Computing Systems*. ACM, New York, NY, 69-74.

[9] Dan R. Olsen, J. and Nielsen, T. 2001. Laser pointer interaction. In *Proceedings of the SIGCHI Conference on Human Factors in Computing Systems* (Seattle, Washington, USA, 2001). CHI '01. ACM, New York, NY, 17-22.

[10] Fitts, P.M. 1954. The information capacity of the human motor system in controlling the amplitude of movement. *Journal of experimental psychology*. 121, 3, 381-391.

[11] Garzotto, F., Gelsomini, M., Mangano, R., Oliveto, L., and Valoriani, M. 2014. From desktop to touchless interfaces: a model based approach. In *Proceedings of the 2014 International Working Conference on Advanced Visual Interfaces* (Como, Italy, 2014). AVI '14. ACM, New York, NY, 261-264.

[12] Haque, F., Nancel, M., and Vogel, D. 2015. Myopoint: Pointing and Clicking Using Forearm Mounted Electromyography and Inertial Motion Sensors. In *Proceedings of the 33rd Annual ACM Conference on Human Factors in Computing Systems* (Seoul, Republic of Korea, 2015). CHI '15. ACM, New York, NY, 3653-3656.

[13] Jakobsen, M.R., Haile, Y. S., Knudsen, S., and Hornbaek, K. 2013. Information Visualization and Proxemics: Design Opportunities and Empirical Findings. *IEEE Transactions on Visualization and Computer Graphics*. 19, 12, 2386-2395.

[14] Jota, R., Pereira, J.M., and Jorge, J.A. 2009. A comparative study of interaction metaphors for large-scale displays. In *Proceedings of the CHI '09 Extended Abstracts on Human Factors in Computing Systems* (Boston, MA, USA, 2009). ACM, New York, NY, 4135-4140.

[15] Jungong, H., Ling, S., Dong, X., and Shotton, J. 2013. Enhanced Computer Vision with Microsoft Kinect Sensor: A Review. *IEEE Transactions on Cybernetics*. 43, 5, 1318-1334.

[16] Kim, D., Hilliges, O., Izadi, S., Butler, A.D., Chen, J., Oikonomidis, I., and Olivier, P. 2012. Digits: freehand 3D interactions anywhere using a wrist-worn gloveless sensor. In *Proceedings of the 25th annual ACM symposium on User interface software and technology*. ACM, New York, NY, 167-176.

[17] Kopper, R., Bowman, D. A., Silva, M. G., and Mcmahan, R. P. 2010. A human motor behavior model for distal pointing tasks. *International Journal of Human-Computer Studies*. 68,10, 603-615.

[18] Malik, S., Ranjan, A., and Balakrishnan, R. 2005. Interacting with large displays from a distance with vision-tracked multi-finger gestural input. In *Proceedings of the 18th annual ACM symposium on User interface software and technology* (Seattle, WA, USA, 2005). ACM, New York, NY, 43-52.

[19] Nancel, M., Pietriga, E., Chapuis, O., and Beaudouin-Lafon, M. 2015. Mid-Air Pointing on Ultra-Walls. *ACM Transactions on Computer-Human Interaction*. 22, 5, 885-889.

[20] Nancel, M., Wagner, J., Pietriga, E., Chapuis, O., and Mackay, W. 2011. Mid-air pan-and-zoom on wall-sized displays. In *Proceedings of the SIGCHI Conference on*

Human Factors in Computing Systems (Vancouver, BC, Canada, 2011). CHI '11. ACM, New York, NY, 177-186.

[21] Ruddle, R.A., Volkova, E., and Bülthoff, H.H. 2011. Walking improves your cognitive map in environments that are large-scale and large in extent. *ACM Transactions on Computer-Human Interaction*. 18, 2, 445-470.

[22] Schwaller, M., Brunner, S., and Lalanne, D. 2013. Two Handed Mid-Air Gestural HCI: Point + Command. In *International Conference on Human-Computer Interaction* (Las Vegas, NV, USA, 2013). HCII '13. Springer, Berlin, Heidelberg, 388-397.

[23] Shoemaker, G., Tang, A., and Booth, K.S. 2007. Shadow reaching: a new perspective on interaction for large displays. In *Proceedings of the 20th annual ACM symposium on User interface software and technology* (Newport, Rhode Island, USA, 2007). UIST '07. ACM, New York, NY, 53-56.

[24] Shoemaker, G., Tsukitani, T., Kitamura, Y., and Booth, K.S. 2010. Body-centric interaction techniques for very large wall displays. In *Proceedings of the Proceedings of the 6th Nordic Conference on Human-Computer Interaction: Extending Boundaries* (Reykjavik, Iceland, 2010). ACM, New York, NY, 463-472.

[25] Vogel, D. and Balakrishnan, R. 2004. Interactive public ambient displays: transitioning from implicit to explicit, public to personal, interaction with multiple users. In *Proceedings of the Proceedings of the 17th annual ACM symposium on User interface software and technology* (Santa Fe, NM, USA, 2004). UIST '04. ACM, New York, NY, 137-146.

[26] Vogel, D. and Balakrishnan, R. 2005. Distant freehand pointing and clicking on very large, high resolution displays. In *Proceedings of the 18th annual ACM symposium on User interface software and technology* (Seattle, WA, USA, 2005). UIST '05. ACM, New York, NY, 33-42.

[27] Zhengyou, Z. 2012. Microsoft Kinect Sensor and Its Effect. *IEEE multimedia*. 19, 2, 4-10.

Locomotion in Virtual Reality
for Individuals with Autism Spectrum Disorder

Evren Bozgeyikli
University of South Florida
evren@mail.usf.edu

Andrew Raij
University of Central Florida
raij@ucf.edu

Srinivas Katkoori
University of South Florida
katkoori@mail.usf.edu

Rajiv Dubey
University of South Florida
dubey@usf.edu

ABSTRACT

Virtual reality (VR) has been used as an effective tool for training individuals with autism spectrum disorder (ASD). Recently there have been an increase in the number of applications developed for this purpose. One of the most important aspects of these applications is locomotion, which is an essential form of human computer interaction. Locomotion in VR has a direct effect on many aspects of user experience such as enjoyment, frustration, tiredness, motion sickness and presence. There have been many locomotion techniques proposed for VR. Most of them were designed and evaluated for neurotypical users. On the other hand, for individuals with ASD there isn't any study to our knowledge that focuses on locomotion techniques and their evaluation. In this study, eight locomotion techniques were implemented in an immersive virtual reality test environment. These eight VR locomotion techniques may be categorized as follows: three commonly used locomotion techniques (redirected walking, walk-in-place and joystick controller), two unexplored locomotion techniques (stepper machine and point & teleport) and three locomotion techniques that were selected and designed for individuals with ASD based on their common characteristics (flying, flapping and trackball controller). A user study was performed with 12 high functioning individuals with ASD. Results indicated that joystick and point & teleport techniques provided the most comfortable use for individuals with ASD, followed by walk in place and trackball. On the other hand, flying and hand flapping did not provide comfortable use for individuals with ASD.

Keywords
Locomotion; Virtual Reality; Human Computer Interaction; Autism

1. INTRODUCTION

Autism spectrum disorder (ASD) is a form of developmental disability which may cause behavioral, social and communication difficulties. Currently there are more than 3.5M individuals with ASD only in the United States [4]. According to the Centers for Disease Control and Prevention, the identified prevalence of ASD was 1 in 68 births in the United States in 2012, which shows an increase of almost 120% since 2000 [5]. Because of social and communication differences, individuals with ASD often have difficulties in getting employed and sustainability. 34.9% of young (aged 19-23) individuals with ASD neither have a job nor received a postsecondary education [39]. It was also reported by the same study that the employment rate for individuals with ASD is significantly lower than the employment rates for individuals with other forms of disabilities such as learning disabilities, mental retardation and speech/language impairment.

Virtual reality (VR) is a powerful tool for training and rehabilitation since it offers safety, real time feedback, structured training, repetition, customization of scenarios and reduced transportation costs to real work places. However, little research has been performed on applying VR to training and rehabilitation of individuals with ASD. With the new generation head mounted displays such as Oculus Rift [31] and HTC Vive [15], the affordability and the availability of the VR technology improved significantly. Many applications are being developed for neurotypical users as well as individuals with ASD. For these applications to provide maximum benefit to their audience, all components need to be well designed. Human computer interaction is an important aspect of VR applications that may have a direct impact on user experience. Locomotion is one of the most commonly used and important interaction components of virtual reality. Locomotion is defined as travel in a virtual environment which is controlled by self-propulsion [14]. Almost every VR application requires some sort of travel in the virtual environment. Locomotion technique may have an effect on user experience [44]. A wrong choice or design of locomotion technique may limit the benefits offered by the application. Hence, it is important to choose a locomotion technique that is well suited for the targeted audience and the context of the application.

Since the early days of virtual reality, many different locomotion techniques have been developed and studied. However, almost all of these studies were designed for and studied on neurotypical users. No locomotion study to our knowledge focused on individuals with ASD. This paper addresses this gap in the literature by evaluating eight different locomotion techniques with 12 high functioning individuals with ASD. Analysis of the results implied the choice of the following for the future VR applications targeting high functioning individuals with ASD: joystick for controller based interaction, point & teleport for gesture based interaction, point & teleport for gesture based interaction, walk in place for exercise aimed interaction in small tracked areas, and redirected walking for exercise aimed interaction in small tracked areas. Locomotion that is triggered with continuous hand gestures and automatic movement turned out to be practices that should be avoided in VR applications targeting individuals with ASD.

SUI '16, October 15-16, 2016, Tokyo, Japan.
© 2016 ACM. ISBN 978-1-4503-4068-7/16/10...$15.00.
DOI: http://dx.doi.org/10.1145/2983310.2985763

2. RELATED WORK

Many different locomotion techniques have been designed and developed for neurotypical users. One of the studies compared flying technique with real walking and walk-in-place techniques [48]. The results showed that flying technique was inferior as compared to the other techniques in terms of realism and sense of presence. Furthermore, real walking received the best scores for naturalness as compared to the flying and walk-in-place techniques. Another study examined the virtual walking trajectories for different controllers; joystick, joypad and keyboard [6]. The results showed that the conformity of the continuous controllers (joystick and joypad) to the real walking trajectories were higher than the binary controllers (keyboard). Another study compared the joystick controller with real walking in a CAVE environment with HMD for perceptual-motor coordination tasks [13]. The locomotion speed was found to be different with the different locomotion techniques; joystick controller resulted in higher locomotion speed than walking. Another study compared real walking with joystick locomotion and real rotation with joystick [33]. The results were similar in terms of task performance for real walking and real rotation with joystick locomotion techniques.

Locomotion techniques were also compared based on different cognitive criteria for neurotypical users. As the results for learning tasks that were performed in complex maze environments were compared, virtual locomotion techniques received similar scores as the real walking [46]. Another study compared flying, real walking and joystick controller techniques [52]. Real walking turned out to be better than the two other techniques in terms of understanding the application.

While similar studies that evaluate different locomotion techniques do not exist for individuals with ASD, many VR training and rehabilitation applications have been built for this population. These VR applications that target individuals with ASD utilized either real walking or standard controllers such as gamepads, joysticks or keyboards. Real walking was used in different forms; some studies used electromagnetic tracking in a CAVE environment [10, 51], some studies used Microsoft Kinect for tracking and TV [1, 12] or projection [32] for display. In all of these previous studies, real walking was used in a tracked area of limited size. No algorithms were utilized to keep the users in the tracked area (such as in the redirected walking) and thus movement in the virtual world was limited by the size of the tracked physical area. Some applications targeting individuals with ASD used standard controllers instead. In some studies, a HMD was used with a gamepad [2] or joystick [45]. Other studies used TV displays with mouse [38], keyboard [19, 20], both mouse and keyboard [45] or joystick [28]. However, these studies mainly focused on the effectiveness of VR in training individuals with ASD and did not evaluate or consider the effects of the locomotion techniques on user experience. Fornasari et al. studied the differences between children with autism and neurotypically developed children in terms of navigation in a computer based virtual environment [11]. In the study, navigation was performed with mouse. The researchers found no differences between the two groups for the exploration with a goal; however, found that children with autism spent less time for the free exploration task.

3. LOCOMOTION TECHNIQUES

In this study, eight locomotion techniques were implemented and evaluated with high functioning individuals with ASD. These techniques involve three commonly used VR locomotion techniques, two locomotion techniques that hadn't been explored deeply in the literature, and three locomotion techniques that were

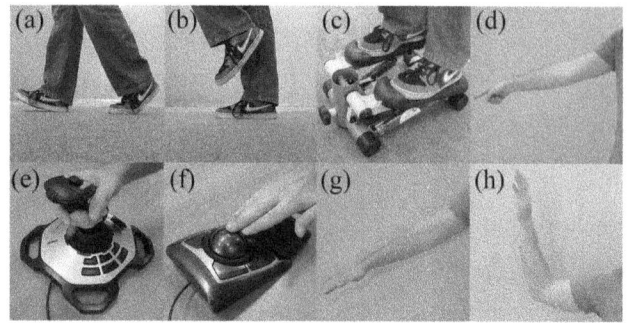

Figure 1. Representative photos of the locomotion techniques used in the study: (a) redirected walking, (b) walk-in-place, (c) stepper machine, (d) point & teleport, (e) joystick, (f) trackball, (g) hand flapping, and (h) flying.

selected and designed specifically for individuals with ASD considering their characteristics (Figure 1). Speed of the locomotion in all of the eight techniques were kept as similar to each other as possible for the sake of obtaining comparable results. For example, the locomotion speed of the flying method was equal to the locomotion speed of the joystick as the joystick was pushed to its physical limit. The size of the tracked area was 8ft by 8ft.

3.1 Commonly Used Locomotion Techniques

Three commonly used locomotion techniques were implemented and evaluated in this study: redirected walking, walk-in-place and joystick control.

3.1.1 Redirected Walking

It is usually considered ideal to use real walking for locomotion in virtual environments, but real walking may not be suitable for virtual environments that are larger than the tracked area in the real world. In these cases, some modifications need to be made in order to overcome the physical limitation of the tracked area. One solutions may be using virtual environments that are not larger than the tracked physical area, but this approach puts a limitation on the design of virtual training applications. Another approach may be using algorithmic modifications that enable real walking by directing the user so that they do not step outside of the tracked physical area. Redirected walking [35] is one of the most widely used techniques for this purpose. It manipulates the visual cues of the users to keep them in the tracked physical area. These manipulations are performed by applying varying gains to the user's displacement data (position and orientation). These gains can be translational, rotational, and curvature. With the gains applied, the virtual translational or rotational speed could be lower or higher than the real translational or rotational speed. Furthermore, virtual environment may be slightly rotated to direct the users to walk in circles while they think that they walk straight. Redirected walking alone does not provide a total remedy for the physical limitation of the tracked area. If the user comes close to the edge of the tracked area, some form of warning or manipulation needs to be done in order to forward them towards the center of the tracked area. For this purpose, Williams at al. proposed three different methods called "freeze backup", "freeze-turn" and "2:1-turn" [49]. Freeze backup and freeze-turn methods stopped the application as the user approached to the edge of the tracked area and asked the user to move backwards or make a 180 degree turn. 2:1-turn method asked the user to make a full rotation and applied a doubled virtual rotational speed while the user rotated. Another repositioning method was proposed by Peck et al. [34]. They used virtual distracters to get the user's attention and direct them towards the center of the tracked area. The authors reported that this method helped in avoiding interruptions which may result in breaks in the presence and degrade the user experience.

In this study, redirected walking locomotion technique was implemented with dynamic translational, rotational, and curvature gains. These gains were applied continuously with dynamically changed values based on user's position and direction in the tracked area. A virtual wall was used for repositioning the users towards the center of the tracked area. Once the user reached to the edge of the tracked physical area, a virtual wall popped up from the ground. In that case, the user needed to walk around the virtual wall, during which the user was redirected and hence was kept inside the tracked area.

3.1.2 Walk-in-Place

As opposed to real walking, some VR locomotion techniques were designed to be controlled with body gestures. One of the most popular gesture based locomotion techniques - walk-in-place - uses the marching gesture to be performed in the same place without moving forward or backward [40]. Walk-in-place gesture is described as one of the closest gestures to real walking [44]. Walk-in-place is found to be cost effective [9], easy to learn [42], and providing proprioceptive feedback to the users [41]. In walk-in-place, locomotion direction can be defined by the direction of the head, the torso or the feet [29]. Walking speed can be controlled using step frequency, step height or leaning [3, 22]. In this study, walking speed is controlled with the frequency of the steps. The length of one step is assumed to be 1.64ft and the user needed to step in every 0.7 seconds for a continuous movement. The locomotion direction was controlled with the head direction of the user.

3.1.3 Joystick

Many VR applications use standard controllers such as joysticks, joypads or touchpads. These controllers are low cost, easy to implement and easy to use since many users are familiar with these controllers from their daily lives. In this study, a Logitech Extreme 3D Pro Joystick [25] was used to control locomotion. When the joystick was pushed forward, the locomotion was performed in the user's head direction. Turning could be done either pushing the joystick sideways or rotating the head.

3.2 Unexplored Locomotion Techniques

Two locomotion techniques that were implemented and evaluated in this study have not been deeply explored in the literature previously. These techniques are stepper machine and point & teleport.

3.2.1 Stepper Machine

Some locomotion techniques use special devices to control the locomotion and keep the users in a secure place. Omni-directional treadmills were designed and developed for this purpose [7, 16, 37]. These treadmills sense walking in any direction and keep the user at the center. Another approach was to create a low friction surface with ball bearings and place them on a concave surface [18, 47]. The design of this device made it possible to walk without a displacement in the real world. There were also some experimental devices such as human size hamster balls [27] or robotic tiles [17]. These devices provided locomotion in virtual environments but they were large and expensive, hence were not found to be convenient for an affordable training application.

In this study a cheaper alternative - stepper machine - was used as a VR locomotion device. Although it is affordable and it provides proprioceptive feedback, there is not much research done on the usability of stepper machine in VR locomotion. Matthies et al. used

stepper machine with a microcontroller [26]. As it was compared with balance board and joystick, stepper machine received the highest scores for enjoyment and immersion. Nilsson et al. compared stepper machine, Wii Balance Board, keyboard and mouse in a virtual skiing game [30]. The results indicated that the stepper machine was found to be the most enjoyable and the second easiest to use. In our study, the movement of the stepper machine was tracked by an optical motion tracking system with the use of a reflective marker. The stepping movement on the machine was transferred to the virtual world as locomotion by means of a marker that was attached on the pedal. The locomotion direction was defined by the user's head direction. An additional automatic rotation feature was triggered if the head was rotated more than 45 degrees. This way, the virtual environment could be rotated around the user so that the user did not need to turn their heads back while their body faced forward.

3.2.2 Point & Teleport

Locomotion techniques mentioned so far required continuous input for locomotion. Some techniques may use instantaneous input instead. One example is point & teleport technique. With this technique, the users point to wherever they want to be in the virtual world, and the virtual viewpoint is instantaneously teleported to that position. The triggering can be done with a gesture or a controller. In this study, no additional controllers were used, teleportation was done with the pointing gesture. The teleportation was triggered when the user pointed to the same position on the ground for two seconds. When the user kept their arms lowered, the teleportation became inactive, so that they could stay at the same position as long as they wanted. A virtual ring on the ground and a virtual laser beam that was cast from the hand of the user towards the pointed location were used as visual cues. The users could point anywhere on the ground without a distance limitation. However, the users could not point the obstacles or the surrounding virtual walls.

3.3 ASD Specific Locomotion Techniques

The techniques mentioned so far have been designed for and evaluated with the neurotypical users in the literature. For individuals with autism, there is no study to our knowledge that has focused on the design or evaluation of VR locomotion techniques. Although we believe that some of these well-established locomotion techniques would cater for individuals with ASD as well as the neurotypical individuals, we wanted to design new locomotion techniques and alter the existing locomotion techniques considering the characteristics of individuals with ASD. In this study, the following three additional locomotion techniques were designed and implemented: flying, hand flapping and trackball control. To design these locomotion techniques for individuals with ASD, the research team collaborated with ASD experts - professional job coaches. Job coaches work with individuals with ASD on a daily basis to understand their needs and unique abilities, and match them to appropriate vocations. Job coaches gave significant input throughout the design process of these three locomotion techniques.

3.3.1 Flying

Individuals with ASD may not handle extensive cognitive load well, especially when paired with other tasks to perform. Hence, flying was selected as a locomotion technique to be suitable for individuals with autism. Flying is one of the simplest locomotion techniques. It gets an input from the user to move the viewpoint in the virtual environment [36]. The input can be either continuous to keep moving or instantaneous to start or stop the movement. For the input, a controller button or a body gesture can be used. In our study, in order to avoid the cognitive load of an additional controller, a hand raising gesture was selected for triggering the automatic locomotion in virtual environment. The same gesture was used to stop the locomotion as well. To reduce the physical load, raising the hand up to the shoulder level was defined as the trigger threshold. Hand raising gesture was selected because of its resemblance of indicating that an action is needed to be done such as raising hand to request an action. The walking speed was constant with 0.8m/s.

3.3.2 Hand Flapping
Individuals with autism commonly engage in self-stimulating (stimming) behaviors such as flapping arms and hands or rocking [8]. These movements are observed to provide soothing for them. Hence, the hand flapping technique was designed in which the hand flapping movement was used for the locomotion. The flapping motion was kept independent from the position of the hand. It could be performed wherever was more comfortable for the user such as near the hips, near the shoulder or in front of the torso. As long as the user flipped their hand, the viewpoint in the virtual environment was moved. This technique was thought to provide the users soothing and help in practicing controlling the unintentional stimming behaviors since the user needed to stop the stimming to stop moving in the virtual world.

3.3.3 Trackball
Individuals with autism are commonly characterized to be fascinated by or obsessed with spinning objects, such as wheels of toys or washing machines [8]. For that reason, a new locomotion alternative was designed in this study with a Kensington Expert Trackball [21] controller. This controller has a smooth surfaced large ball that can be span in any direction. The spinning of the ball controlled the locomotion in the virtual environment. Forward spinning resulted in forward movement and side spinning (left/right) controlled the rotation. The user needed to keep spinning to move the virtual world viewpoint. One rotation of the ball provided a movement of one step in the virtual world. The user could spin the ball fast or slow, resulting in more or less rotation, and more or less movement in the virtual world respectively.

4. EXPERIMENT
An immersive virtual reality experiment was designed and implemented to evaluate the eight different locomotion techniques with individuals with ASD.

4.1 Experiment Design
A within-subjects experiment was designed with the independent variable of locomotion technique having eight levels: redirected walking, walk-in-place, joystick control, stepper machine, point & teleport, flying, hand flapping and trackball control. All of these eight locomotion techniques were tried by all users with a randomly assigned order. Counterbalancing was applied to have a distribution close to equal for all combinations of ordering. For each technique, the locomotion direction was defined as the head direction and the head rotation could be used for rotating the virtual viewpoint. For the controller based techniques, the virtual rotation could be controlled via the controller and/or the head rotation. All applicable techniques (point & teleport, hand flapping and flying) were implemented to work with either left hand or right hand to cater for both right handed and left handed users.

4.2 Virtual Avatar
The user was represented with two hand and two feet models in the virtual environment. The users were able to see these virtual hands and feet in the virtual environment, which moved according to their real hand and foot movement. The reason for this was to give feedback on their position and orientation. For an accurate representation, marker sets were attached to the hands and the feet of the user. The physical space that user's body occupied in the virtual environment was defined as a vertical capsule with a 0.5m diameter that was placed at the weighted center of the user's two feet and the head.

4.3 Virtual Environment
To evaluate the eight locomotion techniques, a simple yet realistic looking outdoor virtual environment with 16m by 16m dimensions was designed. The virtual environment was restricted on all sides with virtual walls of 2.2m height. The users initially appeared in the center of the virtual environment. They were free to move inside the virtual environment but they could not go beyond the virtual walls. The virtual environment was designed plain to avoid exerting additional cognitive load to the users, overwhelming or distracting them (Figure 2). A simple, relaxing outdoor sound was played in low volume to increase the immersion. A basic ambient light was used along with low intensity directional lights to create a good visibility from all sides of the virtual environment.

4.4 Objective
The users were asked to go to ten destination points with each locomotion technique. Once arrived to a destination point, the users needed to wait inside until the marking objects around them disappeared. The disappearance of the marking objects was done after three continuous seconds starting when the user stepped inside the destination point area. The clearance of the destination points was not designed to be instantaneous since user's control on stopping the locomotion technique was also desired to be observed and evaluated. The objective of the experiment was kept as simple as possible to be able to evaluate the user experience on locomotion techniques without the additional effects that may come from different factors.

After the sixth destination point, 21 obstacles in the form of cylindrical roman pillars appeared in the virtual world. Each obstacle was of 0.4m diameter and 2.4m height and was 1.77m away from the neighboring obstacle, which gave enough space to the user to move around them. The reason behind these obstacles was to observe and evaluate the user's control on making turns with the locomotion techniques. The users were supposed to go to the destination points without colliding with the obstacles. Without the obstacles, the users could reach to the destination points with movements close to straight lines. The placement of the obstacles and the destination points were designed so that the users required to make turns to avoid collision with the obstacles. The positions of the pillars were identical across all trials.

4.5 Destination Points
The destination points were marked with a circle on the ground having 1.2m diameter, a semi-transparent cylinder with 2m height and 1.2m diameter, and a 3D arrow above the cylinder oscillating in the y-axis to point to the destination point (Figure 2). All these objects were designed to be easily seen and identified even from the longest distance in the virtual environment. The marker objects were designed in orange to be easily visible. Once the user gets inside the destination point area, the objects immediately turned to green to give feedback to the user. If the user stayed inside the destination point area, the color of the objects gradually turned to blue. If the user left the area, the color turned back to orange. For each technique, a different set of destination points were used to eliminate any possible learning effect that might be caused by memorization. The set of destinations points of each technique

were the same for all participants; however, the placement of the destination points was kept similar in terms of distance and rotation. The first destination point appeared 2 meters away from the user. After the first one, each new destination point appeared 4 meters away from the previous one. Furthermore, each destination point required $180° \pm 30°$ turns to be reached after the previous one.

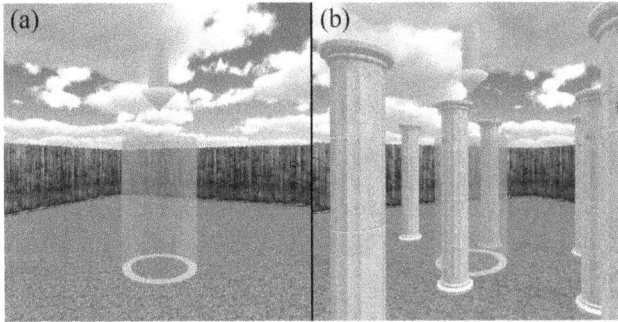

Figure 2. Virtual environment and destination points (a) without, (b) with obstacles.

4.6 System

The PC used for the user study had an AMD FX-8150 3.61Ghz Eight-Core CPU, an AMD FirePro W600 GPU, and a 16GB memory. The motion tracking was performed with twelve OptiTrack V100R2 cameras. The tracking space was 8ft by 8ft. A high resolution VR2200 head mounted display was used for viewing the virtual world. MotionTrack software was used to track five marker sets: one for head tracking (placed on the HMD), the other four mostly used for the hands and the feet. For the stepper machine, one of the hand marker sets was used to track the movement of the stepper machine. For the point & teleport, non-dominant hand marker set was attached to the shoulder of the dominant hand to accurately track the user's pointing direction. All implementation was done using Unity game engine and C# codes.

4.7 Participants

12 individuals who were diagnosed with high functioning autism participated in the study (9 male, 3 female). All participants were older than 18 years old with ages ranging from 18 to 41 with a mean age of 23.9 (SD = 5.99). 8 participants' dominant side was right and 4 participants' dominant side was left. Most of the participants (11 out of 12) had no prior VR experience while only 1 participant had minimal prior VR experience.

4.8 Procedure

The participants arrived at the research laboratory. They read and signed the IRB approved consent form and filled out a demographics questionnaire. Then, research staff explained the VR system and their objective in the experiment to the participants. The destination points, color changing dynamics of the destination point visibility elements and the obstacles that appear after the sixth destination point were explained to the participants. They were requested to try not hitting the obstacles. Then, research staff helped the participants to wear the HMD, and hand and feet marker bands for motion tracking. The experiment then started. Participants tried one of the randomly assigned eight locomotion techniques. When they completed all 10 destination points with the assigned locomotion technique, a user experience survey was given to the participants for evaluation of the tried technique. After all of the locomotion techniques were tried, an overall survey was given to the participants that requested them to rank the locomotion techniques according to their preference. The experiment lasted around one hour per participant, with 3 minutes of VR exposure

followed by 5 minute breaks to fill out the surveys for each locomotion technique. Experiment sessions were video and audio recorded and are kept confidential.

4.9 Hypotheses

Following null hypotheses were constructed: $H_{1,0}$: All locomotion techniques will result in similar performance in terms of average time to reach to the destination points. $H_{2,0}$: All locomotion techniques will result in similar ranking scores.

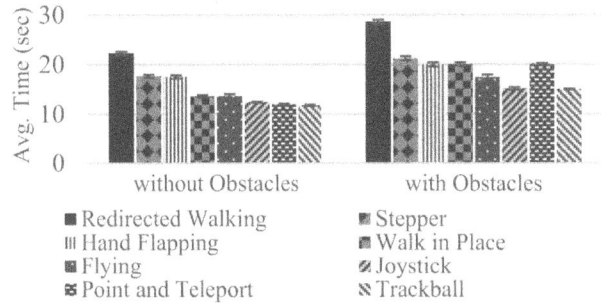

Figure 3. Average time to reach to the destination points without and with obstacles for eight locomotion techniques.

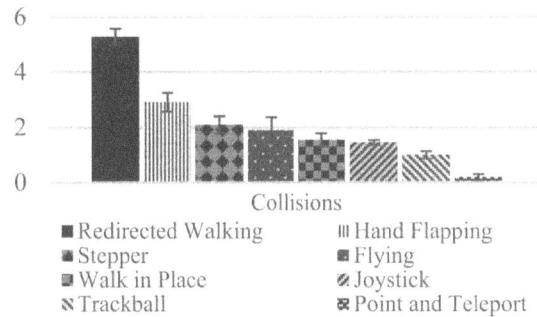

Figure 4. Total number of collisions.

4.10 Measurements and Surveys

During the user study, timestamps for clearing each destination point and collision with obstacles, and virtual locomotion paths of each user was stored for each locomotion technique. After the completion of each technique trial, the users were asked to fill out a survey about their experience with that locomotion technique. The questions included the following aspects: ease of understanding, ease of operating, required effort, tiredness, being in control, enjoyment, being overwhelmed and frustrated; questions about motion sickness and presence. The survey was constructed as modified a version of Loewenthal's core elements of the gaming experience questionnaire [24], Pensacola Diagnostic Criteria survey on motion sickness [23] and Witmer and Singer's questionnaire on presence [50].

After completing the testing of all eight locomotion techniques, the users were asked to rank the eight techniques according to their preference by placing the representative photos of the locomotion techniques on a paper with blank spots. This ranking technique was utilized to decrease the cognitive effort required to rank eight locomotion techniques, with the recommendation of the professional job coaches of individuals with ASD.

5. RESULTS

5.1 Data Results

We analyzed the data of the time it took for the users to reach to the destination points in two groups according to the presence of

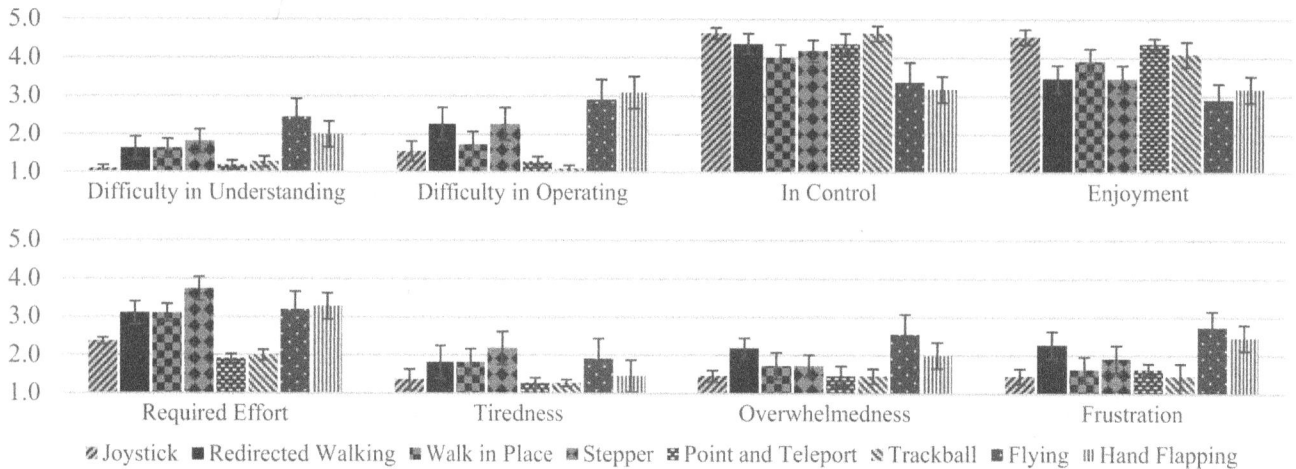

Figure 5: Survey results for the eight locomotion techniques.

obstacles in the virtual world. The results are presented in Figure 3 (error bars in all of the charts represent standard error of the mean). As one way ANOVA with repeated measures was performed, significant difference was found in the time to reach to the destination points for both of these cases: $F(7, 4) = 6.54$, $p = 0.005$ for without obstacles case, and $F(7, 4) = 8.72$, $p = 0.0004$ for with obstacles case. Mauchly's sphericity test failed and Greenhouse-Geisser correction was done for both cases. As paired t-tests were performed, for without obstacles case, the largest significant mean difference was between redirected walking and point & teleport (μ difference = 11.29, $p = 0.016$), and the smallest significant mean difference was between walk-in-place and trackball (μ difference = 10.265*, $p = 0.008$). For with obstacles case, the largest significant mean difference was between redirected walking and joystick (μ difference = 13.303*, $p = 0.0009$), and the smallest significant mean difference was between walk in place and flying (μ difference = 2.922*, $p = 0.039$).

Number of collisions with the static obstacles in the virtual environment were also analyzed (Figure 4). Additional dynamic obstacles of the redirected walking technique in the form of pop-up walls aiming to keep the users inside the tracked area were not included in this analysis. One way ANOVA with repeated measures yielded statistically significant difference between the techniques: $F(7, 4) = 7.94$, $p = 0.001$, Mauchly's sphericity test failed and Greenhouse-Geisser correction was done. The largest significant mean difference in the paired t-tests was between redirected walking and point & teleport (μ difference = 4.778*, $p = 0.0019$), and the smallest significant mean difference was between walk in place and trackball (μ difference = 0.778*, $p = 0.043$).

5.2 Survey Results

Usability part of the survey included questions on eight categories: difficulty in understanding the locomotion method, difficulty in operating the method, feeling of being in control while using the method, required effort to use the method, feeling of tiredness the method caused, feeling of enjoyment the method caused, feeling of being overwhelmed the method caused and feeling of frustration the method caused. The questions had answers on a 5 point Likert scale (1: not at all, 5: very much). Results of these categories are presented in Figure 5. One-way ANOVA with repeated measures analysis was performed for each category yielding the results that are presented in Table 1. All categories other than tiredness and overwhelmedness resulted in statistically significant difference. Results of the paired t-tests that yielded the largest and the smallest significant mean differences are presented in Table 2.

There were also questions on motion sickness and presence. These questions had answers on a 4 point Likert scale (0: none, 3: major). Results for these two categories are presented in Figure 6. One way ANOVA with repeated measures revealed that there wasn't any significant difference between the techniques for motion sickness ($F(7, 4) = 0.95$, $p = 0.43$) and presence ($F(7, 4) = 1.4$, $p = 0.259$). Mauchly's sphericity test failed and Greenhouse-Geisser correction was done for both motion sickness and presence data.

After the testing, participants were requested to rank the locomotion techniques according to their preference. Results for preference ranking are presented in Figure 7. One way ANOVA with repeated measures resulted in significant difference for the preference results ($F(7, 4) = 3.82$, $p = 0.001$, sphericity assumed). Then, paired t-tests were performed to find out differences between the technique pair combinations. The largest significant mean difference was found to be between joystick and flying (μ difference = 3.333*, $p = 0.00007$), and the smallest significant mean difference was found to be between joystick and trackball (μ difference = 1.333*, $p = 0.025$).

Table 1. One-way ANOVA results for usability survey data.

	Correction	df	df Err.	F	Sig.
Difficulty in Understanding	Greenhouse-Geisser	3.301	33.013	3.007	0.040
Difficulty in Operating	Sphericity Assumed	7.000	70.000	5.784	0.000
In Control	Greenhouse-Geisser	3.126	31.262	4.499	0.009
Enjoyment	Sphericity Assumed	7.000	70.000	4.354	0.000
Required Effort	Sphericity Assumed	7.000	70.000	5.068	0.000
Tiredness	Greenhouse-Geisser	2.691	26.908	2.208	0.116
Overwhelmed-ness	Greenhouse-Geisser	2.518	25.178	2.548	0.087
Frustration	Greenhouse-Geisser	3.269	32.687	3.043	0.039

5.3 Participant Comments

Participants were encouraged to share their comments, suggestions, likes and dislikes about any aspect of the experiment on the surveys. Some of these comments are shared in this subsection. Joystick received many positive comments from the participants: User 22: "Joystick is what my favorite tech is and it's perfect for walking in virtual world." User 25: "Awesome!" Many participants made positive comments for point & teleport as well: User 7: "I do enjoy the technology used." User 22: "Teleport is really the way to walk." User 25: "I wanna buy this game." User 26: "It's teleporting! It was really cool!" Trackball received mostly positive comments: User 7: "I liked that it was super easy. I want to play this one again." User 8: "It was very fun. Rolling it was like moving around on an office chair." User 22: "Very interesting indeed." User 26: "I liked that when you're trying to walk and turn all you had to do is use your hand." One user on the other hand, made a negative statement about trackball: User 24: "It was a bit difficult to move the ball to keep walking all the time." Redirected walking received mixed comments from the users: User 8: "I liked it a lot. It was fast changing and challenging in a positive way." User 22: "I liked walking in virtual world, it was so interesting." User 23: "It was good to really walk." User 26: "I liked it since it felt like I was really in the game. User 22: "I walk fast in real world yet I can't control my speed in virtual world." User 25: "It was close to the edge and a bit confusing." Stepper machine also received mixed comments from the participants: User 16: "I liked it the most because it made me to exert the most effort." User 25: "I wanna do it again!" User 22: "It wasn't so easy to do stepping machine in virtual world." User 26: "I liked that one but it felt a bit tiring at the back of my legs." Walk in place also got mixed comments from the users: User 24: "It was realistic." User 25: It helped to keep me in the center and I liked it." User 28: "Really interesting concept." User 26: "I didn't like this method because it was like real walking but not so." Hand flapping received mostly negative comments: User 22: "Hand flapping for walking is harder than I thought." User 23: "It was a bit hard to use flapping." User 24: It was a little hard to control." User 26: "It was not so realistic to use hand flapping for walking." User 25: It was comfortable." Flying also received mostly negative comments from the participants: User 14: "It was completely frustrating." User 22: "It's hard to control it." User 25: "I didn't like this one."

6. DISCUSSION

6.1 Summary of the Results

Time to Reach to the Destination Points: It took less time to reach to the destination points with joystick and trackball independent of the presence of obstacles in the virtual world, in alignment with [11]. Point & teleport provided short times without the presence of obstacles whereas providing long times with the presence of obstacles, hence the null hypothesis $H_{1,0}$ was rejected. We interpret the reason behind this as multiple teleportations needed to move around the obstacles requiring waiting times for the activation of the teleportation. Redirected walking yielded the longest times to reach to the destination points for both with obstacles and without obstacles cases. We interpret the reason behind this as the additional time it took for the participants to overcome the dynamic obstacles that appeared when the users got close to the edges of the tracked area.

Collisions: Point & teleport, trackball and joystick resulted in the least amount of collisions with static obstacles whereas redirected walking resulting in the most. We interpret this as the point & teleport, trackball and joystick providing more control to the users whereas redirected walking providing the least. Gains that were applied in redirected walking may have caused exaggerated movements resulting in unintentional hits to obstacles.

Survey Metrics: Flying resulted in the most difficulty in understanding whereas joystick, point & teleport and trackball provided the least difficulty, in alignment with [46]. Hand flapping and flying were the most difficult to operate whereas trackball, point & teleport and joystick were the least difficult to operate. Joystick and trackball shared the feeling of most being in control whereas flying and hand flapping provided the least feeling of

being in control. Joystick, point & teleport and trackball provided high level of enjoyment whereas flying and hand flapping provided significantly lower levels of enjoyment. Stepper machine resulted in the most required effort whereas point & teleport and trackball resulted in the least. Tiredness and overwhelmedness wasn't significantly different for all of the techniques. Flying, hand flapping and redirected walking caused the most frustration whereas joystick and trackball and causing the least. Low results for flying was in alignment with [42]. There wasn't any significant difference between the locomotion techniques in terms of motion sickness and presence, in alignment with [40, 42].

User Preference: Participants preferred joystick and point & teleport the most, that was followed by walk in place and trackball. Flying and hand flapping were preferred the least. The null hypothesis $H_{2,0}$ was also rejected.

Table 2. The largest and the smallest significant mean differences from paired t-test results of usability survey data.

		μ Diff.	Std. Err.	Sig.
Difficulty in Understanding				
Flying	Joystick	1.364*	0.509	0.023
Hand Flapping	Point & Teleport	0.818*	0.296	0.020
Difficulty in Operating				
Flying	Point & Teleport	1.636*	0.527	0.011
Redirected Walk.	Trackball	1.182*	0.483	0.034
Stepper	Trackball	1.182*	0.464	0.029
In Control				
Joystick	Hand Flapping	1.455*	0.366	0.003
Trackball	Hand Flapping	1.455*	0.366	0.003
Walk in Place	Hand Flapping	0.818*	0.182	0.001
Enjoyment				
Joystick	Flying	1.636*	0.453	0.005
Point & Teleport	Redirected Walk.	0.909*	0.315	0.016
Point & Teleport	Stepper	0.909*	0.285	0.010
Required Effort				
Stepper	Point & Teleport	1.818*	0.377	0.001
Walk in Place	Joystick	0.727*	0.304	0.038
Frustration				
Flying	Joystick	1.273*	0.407	0.011
Flying	Trackball	1.273*	0.449	0.018
Flying	Stepper	0.818*	0.325	0.031
Hand Flapping	Point & Teleport	0.818*	0.325	0.031

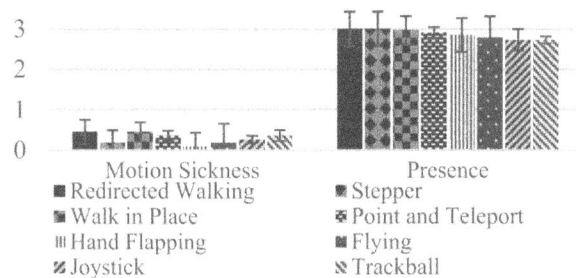

Figure 6. Motion sickness and presence scores.

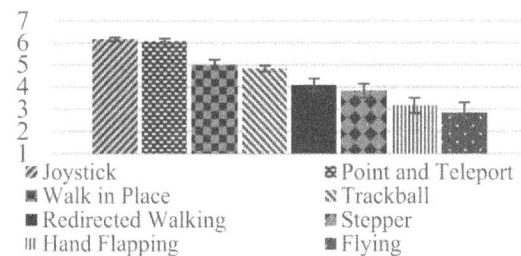

Figure 7. Weighted averages of the preference ranking data.

6.2 Implications of the Results

Analysis of the results, observations throughout the user study sessions and comments from the participants shaped our interpretation on the implication of the results. For virtual reality applications targeting high functioning individuals with ASD, we recommend using joystick, point & teleport, redirected walking or walk in place under different circumstances.

Joystick: Users liked the feeling of being in control, the simplicity of use and the translation of movement into the virtual world (pushing forward to go forward). Its reminding of video games and familiarity may be another positive factor for joystick, considering that individuals with ASD feel more comfortable using familiar objects. Although most of our participants didn't have any prior VR experience, more than half of them mentioned that they frequently played video games in real life. We recommend that in VR applications where accuracy of the control is important, joystick can be used for locomotion.

Point & Teleport: This technique created excitement in our participants. Many users made positive statements such as *'Wow'*, *'So cool'* when only heard its name or when we explained them how the technique worked. We interpret that affinity of individuals with ASD to technology may have contributed to this. Since teleportation is a term reminding of technology, users may have felt sympathy for this technique. Beyond this, we observed that they were comfortable in using this technique and embraced it very quickly as well. Pointing to where they wanted to be in the virtual world provided a simple form of representation. However, point & teleport may not be applicable in virtual environments that contain many elements that the user needs to move around. In VR applications with vast environments that require long travel distances, we recommend using point & teleport for high functioning individuals with ASD.

Redirected Walking: It may result in long times to reach to the destination points when implemented on smaller tracked areas. The reason behind this is that in smaller tracked areas, there will be more frequent appearances of the dynamic obstacles that are used for directing users towards the center of the tracked area. These additional obstacles will yield longer travel times since the users need to overcome them by walking around. Hence, in applications in which time to complete the tasks is important, we do not recommend using redirected walking in smaller tracked areas. However, if there is a large tracked area around 40m by 40m as recommended by the literature [43], redirected walking can be used in applications that encourage exercise for high functioning individuals with ASD.

Walk in Place: It turned out to be a good alternative to redirected walking. Since it urged the users to stay in the same place, the size of the tracked area did not impose a limitation. The users were quick to grasp the concept. Hence, we recommend using walk in place in applications that encourage exercising for high functioning individuals with ASD however size of the tracked area is small. Stepper machine gave the users a similar experience with walk in place however did not provide additional comfort or ease of use. Hence, we recommend selecting walk in place over stepper machine for high functioning individuals with ASD.

Other Techniques: In our study, locomotion that required continuous input from the hands or feet did not provide convenient use for the participants. For flying, which required the users to release their hands after triggering the movement by raising it up, it was difficult for users with ASD to put their hands down in the idle pose. They tended to keep their hands close to their chests while waiting, which resulted in unintentional movements and problems in deactivation. Hence, we suggest that incorporating relaxed hand pose into gesture controlling for individuals with ASD may not work well. Another hand gesture controlled locomotion, hand flapping also didn't provide comfortable use. We observed that some users had difficulty in keeping their hands still while waiting for the destination points to disappear, which caused unintentional movements. Some users did the hand flapping motion with their hands around their chest level but tried to touch their bodies with their hands after stopping doing the flapping motion. This made the virtual viewpoint move more since moving the hand back to touch the body for the idle pose elongated the flapping motion, causing overshoots. We recommend that gesture design for locomotion should give individuals with ASD concrete poses (such as putting their hands on the body or making a specific gesture). More abstract concepts such as releasing the hands and stopping making the flapping motion did not work in our study.

To sum up, for high functioning individuals with ASD, in VR applications with motion tracking, we do not recommend using locomotion that is triggered or maintained with continuous movement of the hands. Instead, controller based locomotion (such as joystick) or locomotion with instantaneous hand gesture control (such as point & teleport) would be more suitable for high functioning individuals with ASD. In applications with the aim of physical activity, redirected walking can be used in large tracked areas and walk in place can be used in smaller tracked areas.

6.3 Limitations

It should be noted that this study focused on the high functioning individuals with ASD. Since Autism is a spectrum based disorder, individuals on the different sides of the spectrum may have different needs and characteristics. Hence, the results of this study may not be applicable to the medium and low functioning populations with ASD. Number of participants in this study was 12 high functioning individuals with ASD. Although this number is not as high as it was desired by the authors to be able to see statistical differences with high power, it should be noted that finding participants belonging to special populations is more difficult than finding typical participants. The number of participants in this study was aligned with the previous studies that focused on this area [1, 2, 10] however, we still think that the low number of participants is a limitation of this study. Redirected walking was implemented on an 8ft x 8ft tracked area in this study, which is considered smaller as compared to the large tracked areas recommended in the previous studies on redirected walking [30]. The main concern of the previous studies while recommending large tracked areas was the motion sickness that would be induced by the large gains that are needed to be applied in smaller areas. In our study, although there wasn't any significant difference between the locomotion techniques in terms of motion sickness, redirected walking received a relatively higher score. Hence, the small tracked area is considered as a limitation of the study. A final limitation is some differences imposed by the different locomotion techniques such as possible differences in the time to complete the trials due to the adjustable locomotion speed with some techniques (redirected walking, walk in place, stepper machine, point & teleport, trackball and hand flapping) and the constant maximum locomotion speed with some techniques (joystick and flying).

7. CONCLUSION and FUTURE WORK

In this study, eight VR locomotion techniques were implemented and evaluated with high functioning individuals with ASD. These techniques were: redirected walking, walk-in-place, joystick, stepper machine, point & teleport, flying, hand flapping, and trackball controller. The locomotion techniques were implemented in an immersive VR environment and a user study was performed with 12 high functioning individuals with ASD. Results indicated that for high functioning individuals with ASD; joystick, point & teleport, redirected walking and walk in place are suitable VR locomotion alternatives whereas continuous hand gesture based (such as hand flapping) and automatic movement based locomotion techniques (such as flying) are not convenient for them. Future work will consist of evaluating different versions of the locomotion techniques that resulted in high preference scores in this study, such as point & teleport with controller, point & teleport with non-linear paths, wireless hand held joystick and redirected walking in large tracked areas. The aim of these evaluations will be providing more comfortable VR experiences for individuals with ASD. Evaluating these VR locomotion techniques with low and medium functioning individuals with ASD would also be important. Moreover, a comparison study between high-functioning individuals with ASD and neurotypical individuals is planned as future work, with the goal of clarifying the similarities and differences between the abilities of the two groups for VR system designers.

8. REFERENCES

[1] Bartoli, L., Corradi, C., Garzotto, F., and Valoriani, M. 2013. Exploring motion-based touchless games for autistic children's learning. In *Proceedings of the 12th International Conference on Interaction Design and Children*, ACM, 102-111.

[2] Bernardes, M., Barros, F., Simoes, M., and Castelo-Branco, M. 2015. A serious game with virtual reality for travel training with Autism Spectrum Disorder. In *International Conference on Virtual Rehabilitation Proceedings (ICVR)*, 127-128.

[3] Bruno, L., Pereira, J., and Jorge, J. 2013. A New Approach to Walking in Place. In *IFIP Conference on Human-Computer Interaction*, Springer Berlin Heidelberg, 370-387.

[4] Buescher, A. S., Cidav, Z., Knapp, M., and Mandell, D. S. 2014. Costs of autism spectrum disorders in the United Kingdom and the United States. *JAMA Pediatrics*, 168 (8), 721-728.

[5] Christensen, D. L. 2016. Prevalence and characteristics of autism spectrum disorder among children aged 8 years—autism and developmental disabilities monitoring network, 11 sites, United States, *MMWR. Surveillance Summaries*, 65.

[6] Cirio, G., Olivier, A., Marchal, M., and Pettre, J. 2013. Kinematic Evaluation of Virtual Walking Trajectories. *IEEE Transactions on Visualization and Computer Graphics*, 19 (4), 671-680.

[7] Darken, R. P., Cockayne, W. R., and Carmein, D. 1997. The omni-directional treadmill: a locomotion device for virtual worlds. In *Proceedings of the 10th annual ACM symposium on User interface software and technology*, ACM, Banff, Alberta, Canada, 213-221.

[8] Dodd, S. 2005. Understanding autism. Elsevier Australia, Marrickville, N.S.W.

[9] Feasel, J., Whitton, M. C., and Wendt, J. D. 2008. LLCM-WIP: Low-Latency, Continuous-Motion Walking-in-Place. In *IEEE Symposium on 3D User Interfaces*, 97-104.

[10] Finkelstein, S., Nickel, A., Barnes, T., and Suma, E. A. 2010. Astrojumper: motivating children with autism to exercise using a VR game. *CHI '10 Extended Abstracts on Human Factors in Computing Systems*, ACM, Atlanta, Georgia, USA, 4189-4194.

[11] Fornasari, L., Chittaro, L., Ieronutti, L., Cottini, L., Dassi, S., Cremaschi, S., Molteni, M., Fabbro, F., and Brambilla, P. 2013. Navigation and exploration of an urban virtual environment by children with autism spectrum disorder compared to children with typical development. *Research in Autism Spectrum Disorders*, 7 (8), 956-965.

[12] Garzotto, F., Gelsomini, M., Oliveto, L., and Valoriani, M. 2014. Motion-based touchless interaction for ASD children: a case study. In *Proceedings of the 2014 International Working Conference on Advanced Visual Interfaces*, ACM, 117-120.

[13] Grechkin, T. Y., Plumert, J. M., and Kearney, J. K. 2014. Dynamic Affordances in Embodied Interactive Systems: The Role of Display and Mode of Locomotion. *IEEE Transactions on Visualization and Computer Graphics*, 20 (4), 596-605.

[14] Hale, K. S. and Stanney, K. M. 2014. Handbook of virtual environments: Design, implementation, and applications. CRC Press.

[15] HTC, Vive. 2016. Retrieved April 15, 2016 from https://www.htcvive.com/.

[16] Iwata, H. 1999. The Torus Treadmill: realizing locomotion in VEs. *IEEE Computer Graphics and Applications*, 19 (6), 30-35.

[17] Iwata, H., Yano, H., Fukushima, H., and Noma, H. 2005. CirculaFloor [locomotion interface]. *IEEE Computer Graphics and Applications*, 25 (1), 64-67.

[18] Jiung-Yao, H. 2003. An omnidirectional stroll-based virtual reality interface and its application on overhead crane training. *IEEE Transactions on Multimedia*, 5 (1), 39-51.

[19] Josman, N., Ben-Chaim, H. M., Friedrich, S., and Weiss, P. L. 2008. Effectiveness of virtual reality for teaching street-crossing skills to children and adolescents with autism. *International Journal on Disability and Human Development*, 7 (1), 49-56.

[20] Kandalaft, M. R., Didehbani, N., Krawczyk, D. C., Allen, T. T., and Chapman, S. B. 2013. Virtual Reality Social Cognition Training for Young Adults with High-Functioning Autism. *Journal of Autism and Developmental Disorders*, 43 (1), 34-44.

[21] Kensington, Trackball. 2016. Retrieved April 15, 2016 from http://www.kensington.com/us/us/4493/k64325/expert-mousespan-classregsymspan-wired-trackball.

[22] Langbehn, E., Eichler, T., Ghose, S., von Luck, K., Bruder, G., and Steinicke, F. 2015. Evaluation of an Omnidirectional Walking-in-Place User Interface with Virtual Locomotion Speed Scaled by Forward Leaning Angle. In *Proceedings of the GI Workshop on Virtual and Augmented Reality (GI VR/AR)*, 149-160.

[23] Lawson, B. D., Graeber, D. A., Mead, A. M., and Muth, E. 2002. Signs and symptoms of human syndromes associated with synthetic experiences. *Handbook of virtual environments: Design, implementation, and applications*, 589-618.

[24] Loewenthal, K. M. 2001. An introduction to psychological tests and scales. Psychology Press.

[25] Logitech Extreme 3D Pro Joystick. 2016. Retrieved April 15, 2016 from http://gaming.logitech.com/en-us/product/extreme-3d-pro-joystick.

[26] Matthies, D. J. C., Manke, F., Müller, F., Makri, C., Anthes, C., and Kranzlmüller, D. 2014. VR-Stepper: A Do-It-Yourself Game Interface For Locomotion In Virtual Environments. *arXiv preprint arXiv:1407.3948*.

[27] Medina, E., Fruland, R., and Weghorst, S. 2008. Virtusphere: Walking in a Human Size VR "Hamster Ball". In *Proceedings of the Human Factors and Ergonomics Society Annual Meeting*, 52 (27), 2102-2106.

[28] Mitchell, P., Parsons, S., and Leonard, A. 2007. Using virtual environments for teaching social understanding to 6 adolescents with autistic spectrum disorders. *Journal of autism and developmental disorders*, 37 (3), 589-600.

[29] Nilsson, N. C., Serafin, S., Laursen, M. H., Pedersen, K. S., Sikstrom, E., and Nordahl, R. 2013. Tapping-In-Place: Increasing the naturalness of immersive walking-in-place locomotion through novel gestural input. In *IEEE Symposium on 3D User Interfaces (3DUI)*, 31-38.

[30] Nilsson, N. C., Serafin, S., and Nordahl, R. 2015. Comparisons of Two Commercial and Two Low-cost Interfaces for Virtual Skiing. *PsychNology Journal*, 13 (1), 57-74.

[31] Oculus, Rift. 2016. Retrieved April 15, 2016 from https://www.oculus.com/.

[32] Parés, N., Carreras, A., Durany, J., Ferrer, J., Freixa, P., Gómez, D., Kruglanski, O., Parés, R., Ribas, J. I., and Soler, M. 2006. Starting research in interaction design with visuals for low-functioning children in the autistic spectrum: A protocol. *Cyberpsychology & Behavior*, 9 (2), 218-223.

[33] Peck, T. C., Fuchs, H., and Whitton, M. C. 2011. An evaluation of navigational ability comparing Redirected Free Exploration with Distractors to Walking-in-Place and joystick locomotion interfaces. In *2011 IEEE Virtual Reality Conference (VR)*, 55-62.

[34] Peck, T. C., Fuchs, H., and Whitton, M. C. 2010. Improved Redirection with Distractors: A large-scale-real-walking locomotion interface and its effect on navigation in virtual environments. In *2010 IEEE Virtual Reality Conference (VR)*, 35-38.

[35] Razzaque, S., Kohn, Z., and Whitton, M. C. 2001. Redirected Walking, University of North Carolina at Chapel Hill.

[36] Robinett, W. and Holloway, R. 1992. Implementation of flying, scaling and grabbing in virtual worlds. In *Proceedings of the 1992 symposium on Interactive 3D graphics*, ACM, Cambridge, Massachusetts, USA, 189-192.

[37] Schwaiger, M., Thummel, T., and Ulbrich, H. 2007. Cyberwalk: An advanced prototype of a belt array platform. In *IEEE International Workshop on Haptic, Audio and Visual Environments and Games*, 50-55.

[38] Self, T., Scudder, R. R., Weheba, G., and Crumrine, D. 2007. A virtual approach to teaching safety skills to children with autism spectrum disorder. *Topics in Language Disorders*, 27 (3), 242-253.

[39] Shattuck, P. T., Narendorf, S. C., Cooper, B., Sterzing, P. R., Wagner, M., and Taylor, J. L. 2012. Postsecondary education and employment among youth with an autism spectrum disorder. *Pediatrics*, peds. 2011-2864.

[40] Slater, M., Steed, A., and Usoh, M. 1995. The virtual treadmill: a naturalistic metaphor for navigation in immersive virtual environments *Virtual Environments' 95*, Springer Vienna, 135-148.

[41] Slater, M., Usoh, M., and Steed, A. 1994. Steps and ladders in virtual reality. In *Proceedings of the ACM Conference on Virtual Reality Software and Technology*, 45-54.

[42] Slater, M., Usoh, M., and Steed, A. 1995. Taking steps: the influence of a walking technique on presence in virtual reality. *ACM Transactions on Computer-Human Interaction (TOCHI)*, 2 (3), 201-219.

[43] Steinicke, F., Bruder, G., Jerald, J., Frenz, H., and Lappe, M. 2010. Estimation of Detection Thresholds for Redirected Walking Techniques. *IEEE Transactions on Visualization and Computer Graphics*, 16 (1), 17-27.

[44] Steinicke, F., Visell, Y., Campos, J., and Lcuyer, A. 2013. Human Walking in Virtual Environments: Perception, Technology, and Applications.

[45] Strickland, D. C., McAllister, D., Coles, C. D., and Osborne, S. 2007. An evolution of virtual reality training designs for children with autism and fetal alcohol spectrum disorders. *Topics in language disorders*, 27 (3), 226.

[46] Suma, E. A., Finkelstein, S. L., Reid, M., Babu, S. V., Ulinski, A. C., and Hodges, L. F. 2010. Evaluation of the Cognitive Effects of Travel Technique in Complex Real and Virtual Environments. *IEEE Transactions on Visualization and Computer Graphics*, 16 (4), 690-702.

[47] Suryajaya, M., Lambert, T., and Fowler, C. 2009. Camera-based OBDP locomotion system. In *Proceedings of the 16th ACM Symposium on Virtual Reality Software and Technology*, ACM, 31-34.

[48] Usoh, M., Arthur, K., Whitton, M. C., Bastos, R., Steed, A., Slater, M., and Brooks Jr, F. P. 1999. Walking > walking-in-place > flying, in virtual environments. In *Proceedings of the 26th annual conference on Computer graphics and interactive techniques*, ACM Press/Addison-Wesley Publishing Co., 359-364.

[49] Williams, B., Narasimham, G., Rump, B., McNamara, T. P., Carr, T. H., Rieser, J., and Bodenheimer, B. 2007. Exploring large virtual environments with an HMD when physical space is limited. In *Proceedings of the 4th symposium on Applied perception in graphics and visualization*, ACM, 41-48.

[50] Witmer, B. G. and Singer, M. J. 1998. Measuring Presence in Virtual Environments: A Presence Questionnaire. *Presence: Teleoperators and virtual environments*, 7 (3), 225-240.

[51] Yiyu, C., Chia, N. K. H., Thalmann, D., Kee, N. K. N., Jianmin, Z., and Thalmann, N. M. 2013. Design and development of a virtual dolphinarium for children with autism. *IEEE transactions on neural systems and rehabilitation engineering*, 21 (2), 208-217.

[52] Zanbaka, C., Babu, S., Xiao, D., Ulinski, A., Hodges, L. F., and Lok, B. 2004. Effects of travel technique on cognition in virtual environments. In *Proceedings of IEEE Virtual Reality*, IEEE, 149-286.

A Non-grounded and Encountered-type Haptic Display Using a Drone

Kotaro Yamaguchi
Graduate School of Information Science and Technology, Osaka University, 1-5 Yamadaoka, Suita, Osaka 565-0871, Japan
yamaguchi.koutarou @lab.ime.cmc.osaka-u.ac.jp

Ginga Kato
Graduate School of Information Science and Technology, Osaka University, 1-5 Yamadaoka, Suita, Osaka 565-0871, Japan
katou.ginga @lab.ime.cmc.osaka-u.ac.jp

Yoshihiro Kuroda
Graduate School of Engineering Science, Osaka University, 1-3 Machikaneyama, Toyonaka, 560-8531, Japana
ykuroda@bpe.es.osaka-u.ac.jp

Kiyoshi Kiyokawa
Cybermedia Center, Osaka University, 1-32 Machikaneyama, Toyonaka, Osaka 560-0043, Japan
kiyo@ime.cmc.osaka-u.ac.jp

Haruo Takemura
Cybermedia Center, Osaka University, 1-32 Machikaneyama, Toyonaka, Osaka 560-0043, Japan
takemura@ime.cmc.osaka-u.ac.jp

ABSTRACT

Encountered-type haptic displays recreate realistic haptic sensations by producing physical surfaces on demand for a user to explore directly with his or her bare hands. However, conventional encountered-type devices are fixated in the environment thus the working volume is limited. To address the limitation, we investigate the potential of an unmanned aerial vehicle (drone) as a flying motion base for a non-grounded encountered-type haptic device. As a lightweight end-effector, we use a piece of paper hung from the drone to represent the reaction force. Though the paper is limp, the shape of paper is held stable by the strong airflow induced by the drone itself. We conduct two experiments to evaluate the prototype system. First experiment evaluates the reaction force presentation by measuring the contact pressure between the user and the end-effector. Second experiment evaluates the usefulness of the system through a user study in which participants were asked to draw a straight line on a virtual wall represented by the device.

Keywords

virtual reality; haptic display; encountered-type device; non-grounded-type; unmanned aerial vehicle

SUI '16, October 15-16, 2016, Tokyo, Japan

© 2016 ACM. ISBN 978-1-4503-4068-7/16/10. . . $15.00

DOI: http://dx.doi.org/10.1145/2983310.2985746

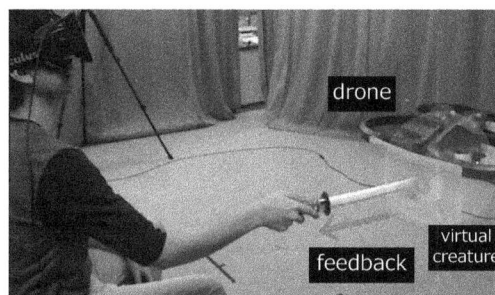

(a)

(b)

Figure 1: An example of haptic feedback by our device in (a) the real and (b) virtual environments.

1. INTRODUCTION

Haptic feedback systems can be classified into three types according to their mechanical grounding configuration; the *wearing* type, the *grip* type and the *target* type. The *wearing* type haptic devices represent reaction force by attaching the device to the body of the user. The *grip* type haptic devices perform as a haptic display by getting the user to grip the tool-shaped devices such as a pen. *Target* type haptic devices represent the target surface by changing the shape, material properties, or/and location of the display itself. The *wearing* type and *grip* type haptic devices may cause the sense of incongruity in presence and the burden because these devices are always in contact with the body of the user. On the other hand, with the *target* type haptic devices, the user rarely feels a burden. However, it is difficult to present a virtual object in the real world with an arbitrary shape, material and position.

One of the approaches to realize a *target* type haptic device is called encountered-type. Encountered-type haptic displays present haptic feedback by moving the end-effector to the surface of the virtual object which the user is going to touch. Encountered-type haptic devices have an advantage that the user doesn't feel the contact force unless the user touch a virtual object because the devices themselves move. However, there is a disadvantage that the work space is limited because conventional encountered-type haptic devices need to be grounded.

We intend to develop a novel encountered-type haptic device that does not limit a work space. In this study, we propose an attachment of a light-weight flat object to an unmanned aerial vehicle (drone) and a force generation mechanism using its own airflow that would realize the non-grounded encountered-type haptic display. Figure 1 shows an example of haptic feedback by our haptic device in the real environment (RE, (a)) and a virtual environment (VE, (b)).

2. RELATED WORK

In this section, we will introduce the conventional grounded type haptic displays and some important studies. In addition, we will also introduce a work support device using a drone. When haptic devices apply forces to a user to represent the sensation of external force, the reaction force is also generated. Most conventional haptic devices are grounded to the environment to resist the reaction force from the user. However, the grounded haptic displays have a disadvantage of a limited work space due to the fixed position of the device. Therefore, in recent years, numerous non-grounded haptic devices have been developed[1][2]. Rekimoto et al. developed Traxion, which represents a virtual force by controlling an asymmetric waveform of vibration with an electromagnetic coil supported by leaf springs[3]. The size of Traxion is 7.5 mm × 35.0 mm × 5.0mm and the weight is 5.2 g. Yoshie et al. developed a device performing nongrounded torque display using a gyro effect[4]. When the force to change the rotation axis is applied to a disk that rotates at a high speed, the force in the direction perpendicular to the applied force is generated in the rotation axis. These devices can display a virtual force or an actual torque with a large work space. However, they cannot display actual translation forces.

Even in the case of no contact with a virtual object, most haptic devices excluding encountered-type devices cannot avoid displaying forces, because a part of the haptic display, e.g. an end-effector, is grasped or worn by the user. In contrast, an encountered-type haptic device realizes an ideal non-contact state, because no force arises unless a user touches a virtual object[5][6]. When the user is going to touch the object, the device moves toward the position of the virtual object surface in a forestalling manner so that a

force is displayed to the user upon actual touch. Yokokoji et al. developed the trajectory planning system with the encountered-type haptic device to represent multiple virtual objects in the three-dimensional space[7][8].Yafune et al. proposed displaying a couple of virtual objects at the same time using an encountered-type haptic device[9]. The above-mentioned conventional encountered-type haptic devices are grounded in space. Therefore, the work space of those devices is limited.

A drone is an unmanned aerial vehicle that can fly and move by a remote control. It is attractive not only for aerial photography and transport, but also for an interaction media with a human. Some devices using a drone have been developed to support a user's work. Agrawal et al. developed a drone to assist a daily life of a person in a room[10]. A table attached to the top surface of the drone supports writing text, and the drone's bottom surface controls illumination in a room. Weise et al. used a commercial head mounted display (HMD), Oculus Rift, to enable the user to control the drone remotely from the first person view [11]. The user can watch the remote scene captured by the camera attached to the drone through the HMD, and can operate a drone using a controller. These studies focus on positioning and the operability of the drone.

We focus on developing an encountered-type haptic display using a drone. The non-grounded mechanism may display a limited force in magnitude due to a lack of fixation. However, we address this issue by taking advantage of the drone's own strong airflow to represent the reaction force from a virtual object such as a virtual creature illustrated in Fig. 1.

3. DRONE-BASED NON-GROUNDED HAPTIC DISPLAY

A light-weight flat object is attached to a drone as an end-effector, as shown in Fig. 2(a). The reaction force is displayed parallel to the ground when a user touches the end-effector with a grasping object, as shown in Fig. 2(b). The strong airflow induced by the drone itself enables to display force even with a light-weight and flexible object, e.g. a sheet of paper. Then, the user can feel the contact from the virtual object.

When the user is going to touch the virtual wall, the proposed haptic display moves towards the corresponding position in a forestalling manner and displays the reaction force to the user upon actual touch. In our system, a user touches a virtual object with a grasping object (see Fig. 1(a) and Fig. 3) for safety. With a safer drone design, it is possible to directly touch the end-effector. The system requires the position and orientation information of the haptic display and that of the grasping object. In the current implementation, a motion capture system is used to acquire these information, and to synchronize their positions in VE. The process flow is as follows:

1. Acquire the positions of the drone and the grasping object from a motion capture system.

2. Update their positions in VE.

3. Estimate the contact position on the virtual wall where the virtual grasping object might touch.

4. Move the drone to the corresponding estimated position in RE. The user receives the reaction force when

(a)

(b)

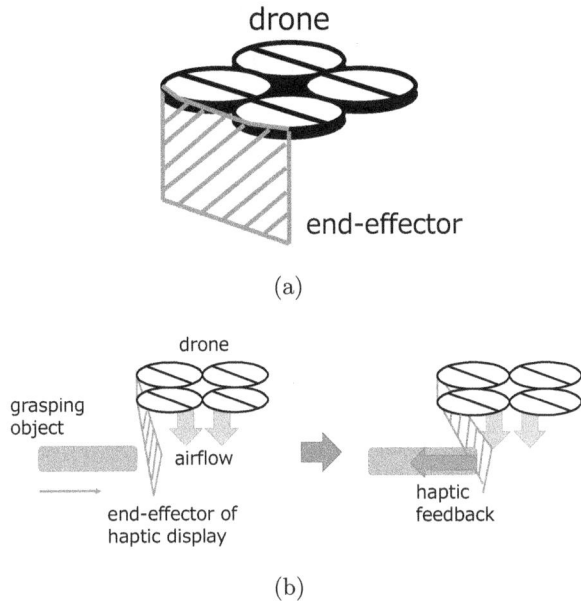

Figure 2: Design and a principle of our haptic display: (a) an end-effector attached to a drone, (b) force display using drone's own airflow.

the collision between the grasping object and the end-effector of the drone occurs.

AR Drone 2.0 by Parrot is used for the drone in the proposed device. Unity 4 by Unity Technologies is used to construct the VE and control the drone. The stereo images of VE are sent to the HMD device, Oculus Rift DK1 by Oculus VR, through Oculus Unity Integration. The positions of the drone and the grasping object are measured by the motion capture system, Motive and OptiTrack by NaturalPoint. The measured positions are broadcasted to local hosts, and are transmitted to Unity. The system controls the drone position using a Unity project, RiftDrone [11].

4. MEASUREMENT

We investigated whether or not the proposed haptic device can produce a perceptible force to a user. Specifically, the effect of the drone's airflow is examined because the proposed mechanism uses the airflow to display the reaction force.

Triaxial force sensor MFS20-025 by Nippon Liniax was used to measure the force. Its maximum measurable force is 50 N. The obtained signal was amplified 20 times with an inversion amplification circuit because the range of the measured force is less than 1.0 N. The amplified signal was converted to digital signal and recorded in PC. The force sensor was attached to the grasping object. The drone is controlled at a fixed position and the experimenter (one of the authors) pushes the end-effector of the proposed haptic device with the grasping object. The pushing distance was about 100 mm in depth from the initial surface position of the end-effector. The force perpendicular to the surface of the end-effector was measured at 100 Hz for a short period. The force was measured with and without the presence of the airflow. In the case of latter, the drone was not flying

Table 1: Average and standard deviation of the measured forces with and without airflow

airflow	average (N)	standard deviation
ON	1.18×10^{-1}	3.6×10^{-2}
OFF	3.6×10^{-2}	1.3×10^{-2}

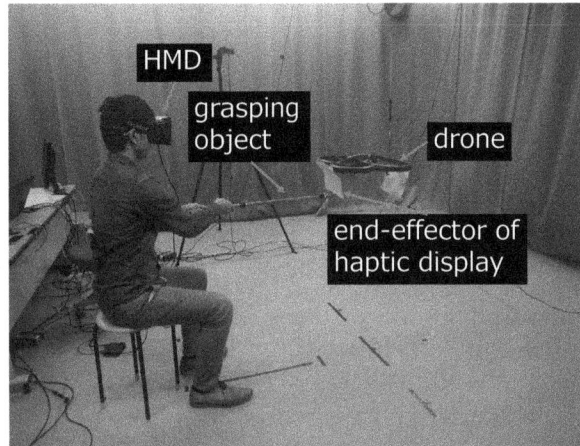

Figure 3: Experimental setup.

and placed on a tripod. We performed the pushing task 10 times in each condition.

For calibration, the average of 100 consecutive samples was set as a baseline before each trial. A moving average filter with a span of 5 samples was applied to the measured data. Table 1 shows the average forces of the 10 trials. The result shows that the measured reaction force by the airflow induced by the proposed haptic device is 0.118 ± 0.036 N, which is weak but well perceptible. In contrast, the measured force without the airflow is 0.036 ± 0.012 N which is too weak to perceive. A one-tailed t-test found that the force with the presence of airflow was significantly greater than the force without the airflow (t(11)=6.80, p≪0.001).

5. SUBJECTIVE STUDY

5.1 Experimental conditions

We investigated whether or not a user can stably draw a straight line in midair using the proposed haptic display. Four participants were recruited (all right-handed male, M= 24.0, SD=2.16) to take part in the experiment. They wore the HMD and held the grasping object. They were requested to move the grasping object following a marker on a horizontal straight line of 1 m in length drawn on a virtual wall which was presented about 1 m in front of the user. The marker was moving at a constant speed (10 cm/sec) from left to right, or from right to left. In a session they repeated this line drawing task 10 times for each direction in a randomized order, and they repeated the session twice, with and without the proposed haptic display in a randomized order. The position and orientation of the grasping object are reflected at 60 frames per second in VE, and its tip position is used to draw a line on the virtual wall. These positions were recorded at 10 times a second for analysis.

45

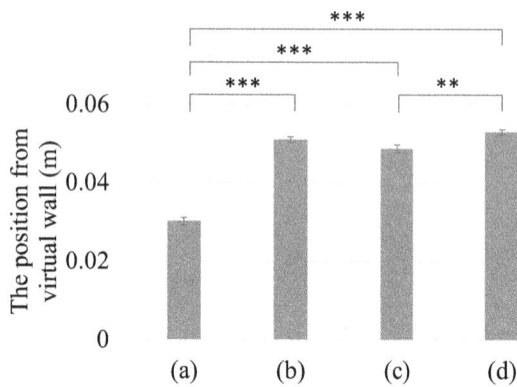

Figure 4: Average and standard error of deviation of the tip of the grasping object from the surface of the virtual wall; rightward lines with (a) and without (b) the haptic display, leftward lines with (c) and without (d) the haptic display. (**: p<0.01, ***: p<0.001)

5.2 Results and Discussions

Figure 4 shows the average and standard error of the deviation of the tip of the grasping object from the surface of the virtual wall for each of four combinations of conditions. A two-way ANOVA found the main effects of both the haptic display condition ($F(1,15996)=215.18$, $p \ll 0.001$) and the line direction ($F(1,15996)=143.58$, $p \ll 0.001$). A post-hoc analysis using Bonferroni correction revealed that the haptic display was helpful in drawing a straight line in midair regardless of the direction (rightward, $p \ll 0.001$, leftward, $p<0.01$). Also found was that rightward lines were far more accurate than leftward ($p \ll 0.001$) when the haptic display was used. This is presumably because drawing a rightward line is more natural considering our writing skills and the fact that all the participants were right-handed, thus the physical support of the tool tip on the virtual wall was more helpful. In the case of drawing a leftward line, it was probably difficult even with the physical support. It is also worth noting that the precision of positioning the drone was insufficient which may also have contributed to the amount of deviation when the haptic display was used.

6. CONCLUSIONS

In this study, we investigated the potential of an unmanned aerial vehicle (drone) as a flying motion base for a non-grounded encountered-type haptic device. We proposed a force generation mechanism by using a sheet of paper and the airflow of the drone itself as a lightweight end-effector. The results of force measurement showed that perceptible force was successfully presented with the drone's airflow by the proposed method. In addition, the force was increased by the drone's airflow statistically. We confirmed the effectiveness of the our proposed device and the force generation mechanism for an encountered-type haptic display. The results of the subjective study of line drawing suggested that the haptic display was effective to support drawing a line in midair. Future work includes improving the drone's position control for more stable and accurate haptic feedback, and conducting further user studies involving more compli-

cated drawing tasks. Self localization of the drone by using the visual simultaneous localization and mapping (SLAM) methods will also be investigated which will eliminate the necessity of a dedicated tracking system.

Acknowledgments

This work was supported by JSPS KAKENHI Grant Numbers JP15K12082 and JP15K12083.

7. REFERENCES

[1] S. Kamuro, K. Minamizawa, N. Kawakami, and S. Tachi. An Ungrounded Pen-Shaped Kinesthetic Display: Device construction and Applications. In *Proceedings of the IEEE World Haptics*, pages 557–562, 2011.

[2] M. Hirose, K. Hirota, T. Ogi, N. Kakehi, M. Saito, and M. Nakashige. Hapticgear: the Development of a Wearable Force Display System for Immersive Projection Displays. In *Proceedings of the IEEE Virtual Reality Conference 2001*, pages 123–129, 2001.

[3] J. Rekimoto. Traxion: a Tactile Interaction Device with Virtual Force Sensation. In *Proceedings of the ACM SIGGRAPH 2014 Emerging Technologies*, page 25, 2014.

[4] H.Yano, M.Yoshie, and H.Iwata. Development of a Non-Grounded Haptic Interface Using the Gyro Effect. In *Proceedings of the 11th Symposium on Haptic Interfaces for Virtual Environment and Teleoperator Systems (HAPTICS '03)*, pages 32–39, 2003.

[5] T. Furukawa, K. Inoue, T. Takubo, and T. Arai. Encountered-type Visual Haptic Display Using Flexible Sheet. In *Proceedings of the IEEE International Conference on Robotics and Automation 2007*, pages 479–484, 2007.

[6] S. Nakagawara, H. Kajimoto, N. Kawakami, S. Tachi, and I. Kawabuchi. An Encounter-type Multi-Fingered Master Hand Using Circuitous Joints. In *Proceedings of the IEEE International Conference on Robotics and Automation 2005*, pages 2667–2672, 2005.

[7] Y. Yokokohji, N. Muramori, Y. Sato, and T. Yoshikawa. Designing an Encountered-type Haptic Display for Multiple Fingertip Contacts based on the Observation of Human Grasping Behaviors. In *Proceedings of the 12th International Symposium on Haptic Interfaces for Virtual Environment and Teleoperator Systems 2004 (HAPTICS '04)*, pages 66–73, March 2004.

[8] Y. Yokokohi, J. Kinoshita, and T. Yoshikawa. Path Planning for Encountered-type Haptic Devices That Render Multiple Objects in 3D Space. In *Proceedings of the IEEE Virtual Reality 2001*, pages 271–278, 2001.

[9] M. Yafune and Y. Yokokohji. Haptically Rendering Different Switches Arranged on a Virtual Control Panel by Using an Encountered-type Haptic Device. In *Proceedings of the IEEE World Haptics Conference (WHC) 2011*, pages 551–556, June 2011.

[10] H. Agrawal, S. Leigh, and P. Maes. L'evolved: Autonomous and Ubiquitous Utilities as Smart Agents. In *Proceedings of the ACM UbiComp 2015*, pages 487–491, 2015.

[11] M. Weise. RiftDrone. https://github.com/scopus777/RiftDrone. accessed 1 July 2016.

Enhancement of Motion Sensation by Pulling Clothes

Erika Oishi

The University of
Electro-Communications
1-5-1 Chofugaoka Chofu
Tokyo Japan
oishi@kaji-lab.jp

Masahiro Koge

The University of
Electro-Communications
1-5-1 Chofugaoka Chofu
Tokyo Japan
koge@kaji-lab.jp

Sugarragchaa
Khurelbaatar
The University of
Electro-Communications
1-5-1 Chofugaoka Chofu
Tokyo Japan
sura@kaji-lab.jp

Hiroyuki Kajimoto

The University of
Electro-Communications
1-5-1 Chofugaoka Chofu
Tokyo Japan
kajimoto@kaji-lab.jp

ABSTRACT

Stimulation of the vestibular and somatosensory systems has been proposed as a way to enhance motion sensation in combination with visual movement. However, such systems may be large with limited presentation areas. Here, we propose a method of enhancing motion sensation by pulling clothing. Our system uses DC motors and force sensors to present traction force and cause skin deformation. We investigated whether users perceived the presented sensation as acceleration, or another physical quantity, and found that they matched it with velocity. We also conducted a user study to see whether immersion of gaming contents could be improved by our clothes-pulling system.

Keywords

Haptic; Tactile; Clothes-pulling;

1. INTRODUCTION

In audiovisual content with self-motion, such as a racing game, successful presentation of the sense of motion is considered to be the key to realism. The sense of motion is a multisensory event, as it includes velocity information from the visual system and acceleration information from the vestibular and somatosensory systems. Various entertainment facilities incorporate stimulation of the vestibular and somatosensory systems by actually moving the user's body in accordance with the presented motion [7][12]. However, such devices tend to be bulky and expensive, which makes them difficult for home use.

One solution to this issue involves the use of somatosensory cues. For instance, several studies have investigated the effects of chairs that vibrate in accordance with visual contents [1][4][10]. Danieau [3] used haptic devices to shake the body parts of a user sitting on a seat. In addition, many haptic devices that present force feedback to the hands of users have been reported [2][5][9]. All of these devices succeeded in inducing the sense of motion, using only haptic sensations.

In this study, we tested a method of eliciting self-motion by pulling on the clothing of participants while they sat on a chair. Clothing generally touches a wide area of skin. Therefore, pulling

SUI '16, October 15-16, 2016, Tokyo, Japan
© 2016 ACM. ISBN 978-1-4503-4068-7/16/10$15.00
DOI: http://dx.doi.org/10.1145/2983310.2985749

on clothing may induce haptic and/or force sensations over a wide region of the body. Pulling on clothing is expected to produce traction force that could create the illusion of dramatic movement in the users' body. Furthermore, the shearing force between the skin and cloth could generate shearing skin deformation, which has been proposed as a cue for pseudo force [6][11]. Therefore, we hypothesized that these sensations could be used to enhance the perception of self-motion, for example, when a car is rapidly accelerated.

In this paper, we describe our clothes-pulling system, which uses DC motors and force sensors. We conducted a user study to assess whether users perceived the presented sensations as acceleration, or as another physical event. We also examined the overall influence of the clothes-pulling system on user experience.

2. SYSTEM

Figure 1 shows the clothes-pulling system. It is composed of a chair with a backrest, motors with a gear head (Maxon, 25 RE φ 25mm, 10W, 26 GP B φ26 mm, gear ratio 19:1), motor drivers (Okatech, JW-143-2), bobbins, guides, Kevlar string, clips, a microcontroller (NXP, mbed NXP LPC1768), load cells (A&D, LC-1205-K020) and amplifiers (A&D, AD-4532B).

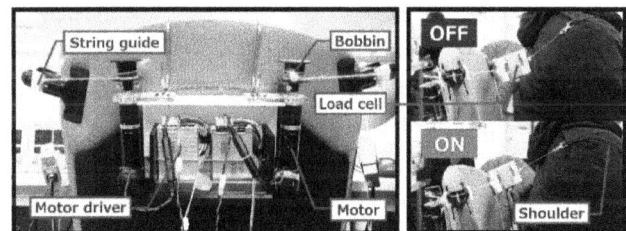

Figure 1. The clothes-pulling system

The clips with string are attached to the shoulder part of the user's clothes. By attaching the clips to the shoulder, the system can effectively pull the upper body backward. Using motors to reel in the string, the system pulls the clothing and presents a traction force. The motors are current-controlled by the microcontroller. The two motors correspond to the left and right shoulders, each of which can provide force of up to about 18N. In the initial state, traction of about 2N is presented to the body by weight of the load cell (0.3 kg). The traction force is measured by the load cells and controlled using proportional-derivative control (PD control).

3. HARDWARE EVALUATION

We considered that the device might not induce a traction force on the body based solely on the friction between the string and the guide. Thus, we directly measured the traction force using the load cells and controlled the force using a PD controller.

In Equation 1, I represents the electrical current delivered to the motor, k_P represents the coefficient for the proportional term, k_D represents the coefficient for the differential term, F_g represents the desired traction force, F represents the current traction force, and F_b represents the traction force of the previous frame.

$$I = k_P \times (F_g - F) - k_D \times (F - F_b) \qquad (1)$$

3.1 Motor Traction

Figure 2 shows the traction of one motor with and without PD feedback. The feedback loop was set to 1 kHz. When the feedback was not applied, the traction force was typically lower than the designated value, mainly because of friction. When the feedback was applied, the traction force was in agreement with the designated value.

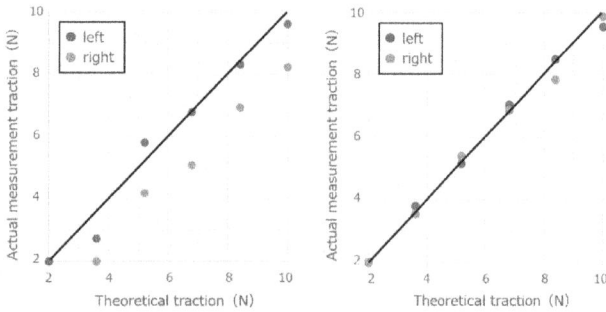

Figure 2. Traction of one motor without (left) and with PD feedback (right)

3.2 Motor Response

Figure 3 shows the response of one motor when we applied a 10 s step function with different designated values. The response time was about 0.16, 0.21, and 0.24 s when the designated traction force was 10, 14, and 18 N, respectively.

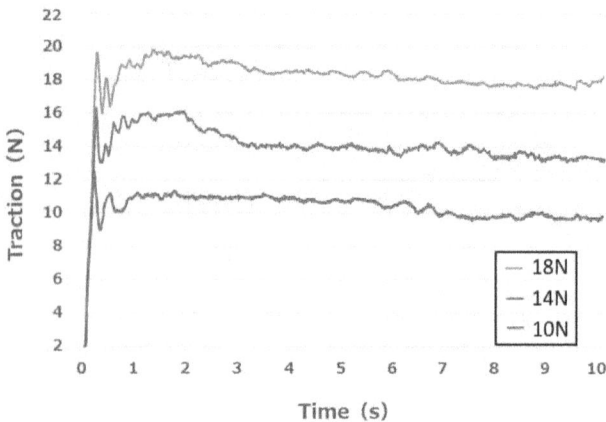

Figure 3. Response of one motor

4. EXPERIMENT 1: CORRESPONDENCE TO PHYSICAL QUANTITY

As the purpose of this study was to present the sense of motion, we found it necessary to consider the different types of motion. The physical quantity of motion has three aspects: position, velocity and acceleration. We wanted to identify the physical quantity that users felt or interpreted when our system presented as traction force.

Position, velocity, and acceleration are related by derivatives and integrals. If position is represented by a sine wave, then velocity and acceleration can also be represented as sine waves with phase differences of $1/2\pi$ and π relative to the sine wave of position. We used these properties to evaluate the subjective feeling elicited by our system.

4.1 Methods

Participants were exposed to an optical flow stimulus that moved forward and backward in a sinusoidal manner. Figure 4 shows the visual stimuli, which was rendered using Unity software (Unity Technologies, Inc.) and presented using a head-mounted display (HMD) (Oculus VR Inc., Oculus Rift Development Kit 2, resolution 1920 × 1080 (one eye 960 × 1080), horizontal angle of 90 °, diagonal angle of 110 °). To make the maximum speed of movement 60km/h, the point of view was moved back and forth according to a sine wave at 0.1 Hz. In addition, a fixation point was positioned in the center of the visual stimuli.

Figure 4. Visual stimuli (left: view of left eye, right: view of right eye)

We also presented a traction force, which changed according to a sinusoidal wave. However, the negative component of the wave could not be presented owing to system limitations. The sinusoidal traction force had a frequency of about 0.1 Hz, and ranged from about 2N (initial state) to about 18N, in accordance with the visual stimuli.

To control the clothing type and to facilitate the ease of attachment of the system clips, the participants all wore a hooded sweatshirt. They were instructed to sit on the chair that housed the clothes-pulling system, and to wear the HMD and noise canceling headphones (BOSE, QuietComfort15). We asked them to adjust the phase of the traction force to match the feeling between the visual motion and the traction force. If the phase difference between the sine wave of the visual stimuli and the sine wave of the traction force was close to 0, then the traction force was interpreted as positional displacement. If the phase difference was close to $1/2\pi$, then the force was interpreted as velocity. If it was close to π, then it was interpreted as acceleration (Figure 5). Twelve participants, 21–25 years of age, participated in this experiment. Five trials were carried out for each participant.

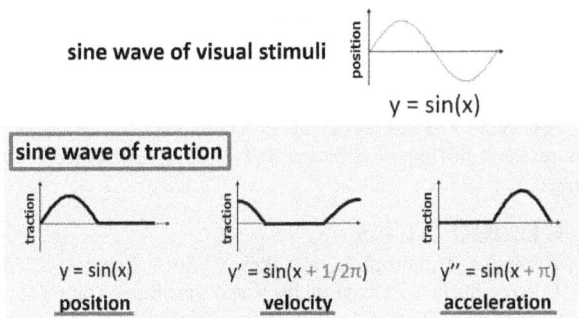

Figure 5. Three physical properties according to differences in sine wave phase

4.2 Results and Discussion

Figure 6 shows the sine wave phase difference between the visual stimuli and traction force. More than 80% of the participants answered that the difference in the sine wave phase between the visual stimuli and traction was approximately $1/2\pi$. This means that they felt that the traction was well matched with the visual stimuli when the traction force was proportional to the velocity of the visual stimuli.

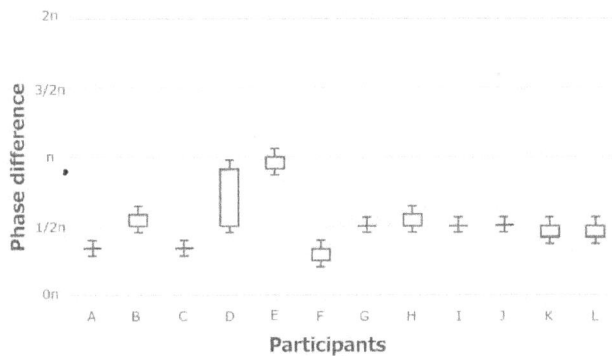

Figure 6. Difference in sine wave phase between visual stimuli and traction

According to basic physical properties, we hypothesized that the traction force produced by our system would be interpreted as acceleration ($F = ma$). However, most participants interpreted the traction force as velocity. It may be easier to perceive velocity, rather than acceleration, from visual stimuli. For example, when watching the scenery from the window of a moving car, it is possible to estimate the velocity at which one is travelling. However, estimating the acceleration is difficult in comparison. That the participants were able to adjust the traction force in accordance with visual stimuli may also have contributed to the tendency to interpret the traction force in our system as velocity.

5. EXPERIMENT 2: INFLUENCE ON USER EXPERIENCE

The result of Experiment 1 indicated that, for content with visual movement, the traction force should be presented in accordance with velocity. Based on this result, we investigated whether the immersion of content was improved by our system.

5.1 Methods

We prepared a simplified car driving simulation in which the point of view moved forwards when the user pedaled. Figure 7 shows the visual stimuli, which was rendered using Unity and presented via a HMD. In the visual stimuli, the height of the point of view was 1.2 m, and the road width was 4 m. Trees, 8 meters in

height, were positioned at 10 m intervals. The maximum velocity was 180km/h. The point of view was accelerated according to the amount of depression of a pedal (Logicool, Logicool® Driving Force™ GT).

Figure 7. Visual stimuli

We also presented a traction force in accordance with the velocity. As the velocity of the visual stimuli increased, the traction force became stronger in proportion. In this experiment, we used a simple clothes-pulling system without the load cells.

Each participant sat on the chair that housed the clothes-pulling system, wearing a hooded sweatshirt and the noise canceling headphones. We presented the visual stimuli twice for three minutes each, once with and once without the system (*Traction, No Traction*). The order of the two conditions was counterbalanced. After each condition, the participants answered questions on a 7-point Likert scale (1: very weak – 4: neutral – 7: very strong). They were asked to rate their feelings of movement, speed, acceleration, immersion, and enjoyment for each condition. We administered the Simulator Sickness Questionnaire (SSQ) [8] before and after each condition to measure the degree of motion sickness. The score after the trial was subtracted from the score before the trial, and the difference was used for analysis. Six naive participants, 20–24 years of age, participated in this experiment. Two trials, one trial for each condition, were carried out for each participant.

5.2 Results and Discussion

Figure 8 shows the average user feedback scores. The error bars show the standard error. Table 1 shows the result of a Wilcoxon signed-rank test. We found that traction trials were associated with significantly improved Acceleration (z=-2.23, p=0.026) and Enjoyment (z=-2.12, p=0.034) scores. Although we did not find significant differences for the other questions, we observed a consistent trend towards higher scores for trials with traction.

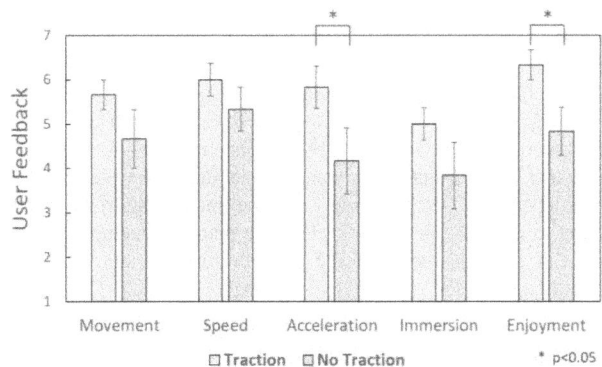

Figure 8. Average user feedback scores

Table 1. Results of Wilcoxon signed-rank test

	Traction		No Traction			
	M	SD	M	SD	z	p
Movement	5.67	0.33	4.67	0.67	-1.89	0.059
Speed	6.00	0.37	5.33	0.49	-0.96	0.34
Acceleration	5.83	0.48	4.17	0.75	-2.23	0.026
Immersion	5.00	0.37	3.83	0.75	-1.63	0.10
Enjoyment	6.33	0.33	4.83	0.54	-2.12	0.034

Figure 9 shows the average SSQ scores. The error bars show the standard error. Positive scores indicate an increase in motion sickness after a trial. A Wilcoxon signed-rank test revealed no significant differences between the two conditions.

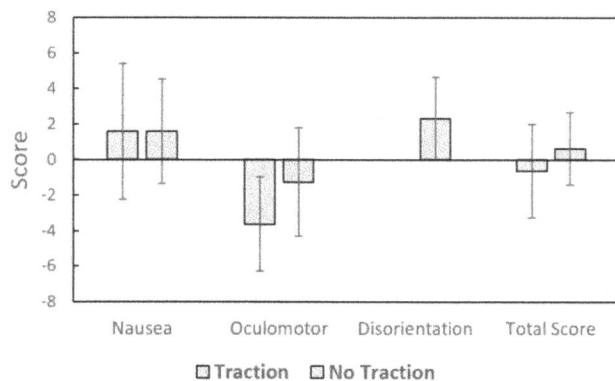

Figure 9. SSQ scores

We found that the clothes-pulling system improved the enjoyment of content score. Additionally, the feeling of acceleration was improved although the traction force was presented in accordance with velocity. However, most participants commented that the traction force was unnatural because it was not presented in accordance with acceleration. Indeed, this might explain the low immersion score. This was not consistent with the result from Experiment 1, in which users matched the traction force with velocity, not acceleration. One reason for this inconsistency might be that in Experiment 1, although the visual stimulus was sinusoidal (with positive and negative values), the force was presented only in the pulling direction. We intend to clarify this in future work by presenting forces in both directions.

The SSQ indicated a tendency towards decreased motion sickness with our traction system.

6. CONCLUSION

In this study, we tested a method for easily enhancing motion sensation via pulling on clothing. Experiment 1 indicated that the traction force should be presented in accordance with velocity. Experiment 2 revealed that enjoyment of content and the feeling of acceleration were improved by our system, but comments from the users implied that the traction force should be presented in accordance with acceleration. As this inconsistency is likely owing to a limitation of our system, we plan to develop a system that can present traction force in both forward and backward directions.

In our study, users wore hooded sweatshirts to facilitate the attachment of the clips to clothing. In the future, we plan to consider systems using seatbelts or harnesses. Additionally, attaching the system to a chair limits the chair in terms of size and shape. We plan to address this issue in future work.

7. ACKNOWLEDGMENTS
This research is supported by the JST-ACCEL Embodied Media Project.

8. REFERENCES
[1] Amemiya, T., Hirota, K., and Ikei, Y. 2011. Concave-Convex Surface Perception by Visuo-vestibular Stimuli for Five-Senses Theater. In *Proceedings of the 2011 international conference on Virtual and mixed reality*, 225–233.

[2] Buoguila, L., Cai, Y., and Sato, M. 1997. New Haptic Device For Human Scale Virtual Environment Scaleable – SPIDAR. In *Proceedings of ICAT'97*, 93–98.

[3] Danieau, F., Fleureau, J., Guillotel, P., Mollet, N., Lécuyer, A., and Christie, M. 2012. HapSeat: Producing Motion Sensation with Multiple Force-feedback Devices Embedded in a Seat. In *Proceedings of the 18th ACM symposium on Virtual Reality Software and Technology*, 69–76. DOI= http://doi.acm.org/10.1145/2407336.2407350

[4] Israr, A., and Poupyrev, I. 2011. Tactile Brush: Drawing on Skin with a Tactile Grid Display. In *CHI '11 Proceedings of the SIGCHI Conference on Human Factors in Computing Systems*. DOI= http://doi.acm.org/10.1145/1978942.1979235

[5] Ito, K., Okamoto, M., Akita, J., Ono, T., Gyobu, I., Takagi, T., Hoshi, T., and Mishima, Y. 2005. CyARM: an alternative aid device for blind persons. In *CHI '05 Proceedings of the SIGCHI Conference on Human Factors in Computing Systems*. DOI= http://doi.acm.org/10.1145/1056808.1056947

[6] Kuniyasu, Y., Sato, M., Fukushima,S., and Kajimoto, H. 2012. Transmission of Forearm Motion by Tangential Deformation of the Skin. In *Proceedings of the 3rd Augmented Human International Conference*. DOI= http://doi.acm.org/10.1145/2160125.2160141

[7] MediaMation. MX4D. http://www.mediamation.com/products_x4d.html

[8] Kennedy, S. R., Lane, E. N., Berbaum, S. K., and Lilienthal, G. M. 1993. Simulator Sickness Questionnaire: An Enhanced Method for Quantifying Simulator Sickness. *The International Journal of Aviation Psychology* Vol. 3, 203–220.

[9] Ouarti, N., Lecuyer, A., and Berthoz, A. 2014. Haptic motion: Improving sensation of self-motion in virtual worlds with force feedback. In *Proceedings of the Haptics Symposium 2014*, 167–174.

[10] Riecke, B. E., Schulte-Pelkum, J., Caniard, F., and Bülthoff, H. H. 2005. Towards Lean and Elegant Self-Motion Simulation in Virtual Reality. In *Proceedings of the 2005 IEEE Conference 2005 on Virtual Reality*, 131–138.

[11] Shikata, K., Makino, Y., and Shinoda, H. 2015. Inducing Elbow Joint Flexion by Shear Deformation of Arm Skin. In *Proceedings of World Haptics Conference 2015*.

[12] Simworx. 360° Rotating Flying Theatre. http://www.simworx.co.uk/360-flying-theatre/

Impact of Motorized Projection Guidance on Spatial Memory

Hind Gacem
Télécom ParisTech, CNRS
LTCI, France
gilles.bailly@telecom-paristech.fr

Gilles Bailly
Télécom ParisTech, CNRS
LTCI, France
gilles.bailly@telecom-paristech.fr

James Eagan
Télécom ParisTech, CNRS
LTCI, France
james.eagan@telecom-paristech.fr

Eric Lecolinet
Télécom ParisTech, CNRS
LTCI, France
eric.lecolinet@telecom-paristech.fr

ABSTRACT

Various guidance techniques have been proposed to help users to quickly and effectively locate objects in large and dense environments such as supermarkets, libraries, or control rooms. Little research, however, has focused on their impact on learning. These techniques generally transfer control from the user to the system, making the user more passive and reducing kinesthetic feedback. In this paper, we present an experiment that evaluates the impact of projection-based guidance techniques on spatial memorization. We investigate the roles of user (handheld) vs. system control (robotic arm) guidance and of kinesthetic feedback on memorization. Results show (1) higher recall rates with system-controlled guidance, (2) no significant influence of kinesthetic feedback on recall under system control, and (3) the visibility and noticeability of objects impact memorization.

Keywords

Guidance Technique; steerable projection; robotic; handheld; spatial memory.

Categories and Subject Descriptors

H.5.2. [**User Interfaces**]: Input devices and strategies

1. INTRODUCTION

Complex environments such as command and control rooms, warehouses, or libraries can contain thousands of objects, organized in a large physical space. Locating a given object in such environments can be difficult and time-consuming [25]. Saving even a few seconds off of this task can result in significant cumulative savings. Thus, many tasks, such as maintenance or control room operating, require memorizing the location of many objects to be performed efficiently. Moreover, being able to retrieve objects quickly is of crucial importance for safety-critical tasks. While an interactive guidance system would help, such a system may be only available for training, either because equipping production sites would be too costly or for security reasons, where the operator must be able to master the system in any situation. Operators must then learn the positions of objects so as to rapidly find controls and avoid costly – or even dramatic – errors.

Guidance techniques have been proposed to help users to quickly and accurately find a given target, including using maps [1], turn-by-turn instructions [1, 19], augmented-reality glasses [11] or steerable projectors [4, 9]. Previous studies have focused on how to help people more quickly find targets [9, 11, 12], but they have not explored the impact of such guidance on spatial memory (i. e., learning the positions of objects). Furthermore, findings about memorization in navigation studies cannot be extended to spatial memory, because of (1) differences in the nature of the task [23] and (2) the non convergence of results. For examples, some of these studies have shown a positive influence of active vs. passive exploration on memorization [16, 20], no effect [10, 28], or an inverse correlation [12].

In this paper, we study the impact on memorization of guidance techniques based on steerable or handheld projection. We focus on such techniques, as proposed in [4, 6, 9, 14, 17, 24], because steerable projection has been shown to be particularly effective at helping users to quickly locate targets [9].

More specifically, we investigate the role of (1) user versus system control of the guidance device and (2) kinesthetic feedback during object localization by comparing three techniques. The first technique transfers control to the system. It uses an implementation of Gacem et al.'s system-controlled robotic projection arm [9] which has been shown to help users quickly locate targets (Figure 1a). The second (Figure 1b) extends this approach to provide kinesthetic feedback by having users point at targets [26]. The third (Figure 1c) uses a handheld projector (similar to [24]) that guides the user to the target using directional hints and acts as a baseline.

SUI '16, October 15-16, 2016, Tokyo, Japan
© 2016 ACM. ISBN 978-1-4503-4068-7/16/10. . . $15.00
DOI: http://dx.doi.org/10.1145/2983310.2985751

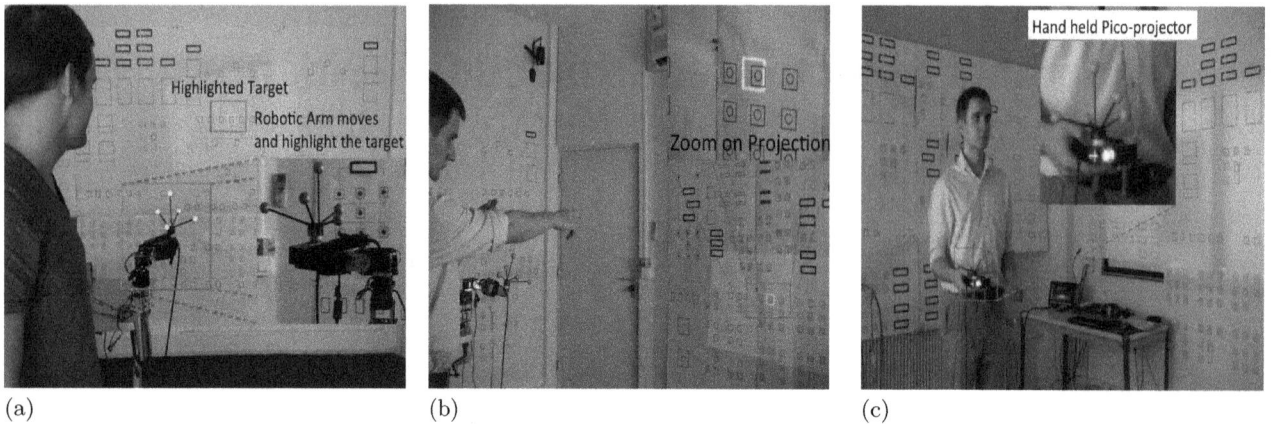

Figure 1: The three projection-based guidance techniques in the study: (a) an actuated pico-projector automatically highlights the target (system control), (b) an extension to the previous technique where the user adds kinesthetic feedback by pointing to the highlighted target, and (c) manual exploration with a hand-held pico-project that guides the user to the target.

Results show that (1) the system-controlled technique had a higher recall rate than the manual guidance technique, (2) kinesthetic feedback of pointing with the arm does not seem to have an effect on long-term memorization for the system controlled condition, and (3) the visibility and noticeability of objects impact memorization.

2. RELATED WORK

Various guidance systems have been proposed to help users find targets or navigate paths using a variety of different technologies, devices, and interaction styles. We focus primarily on projection-based guidance techniques (Section 2.1) and user control in guidance and memorization in navigation and spatial positioning tasks (Section 2.2).

2.1 Projection Systems

Projection-based guidance systems have been proposed either to expand the interaction space [5] or the display space [7, 21, 27] using motorized [21, 27] or handheld devices [5, 6, 7, 18]. These studies have considered such aspects as user acceptance [1], temporal performance [9], user preference of projector orientation [6], or spatial memory [13].

Butz et al.'s SearchLight [4] uses a ceiling-mounted steerable projector to help users find objects by shining a spotlight on them. Gacem et al. [9] extend this approach by mounting a pico-projector on a robotic arm within the user's field of view, finding that moving the projector within the user's field of view reduced search times by up to 24% [9].

Little work has studied the role of spatial memory while using projection based guidance. Kaufmann et al. [13] studied the effect on memory in map navigation of displaying a map on a smartphone vs. projected in the environment with a handheld projector, finding up to a 41% improvement to spatial memory when using the projector. They hypothesize that this difference may be due to the kinetic component of moving the projector. Fujimoto et al. [8] studied the effect of adding visual cues on targets to be memorized using an HMD system. They found that associating visual anotations with real world locations enhances the learning. To the best of our knowledge, no previous work has addressed the issue of spatial memory using motorized projection guidance. In

this paper, we investigate how transferring control from the user to the system impacts the memorization of object locations.

2.2 User vs. System Control

With user-controlled guidance systems, guidance provided by the system depends on the user's actions, whereas system-controlled techniques remove the user from much of the interaction loop. As such, system-controlled guidance (1) removes the kinesthetic feedback involved in moving the projector and (2) makes locating the object a more passive task. User-controlled guidance divides the user's attention between controlling the device and learning the target's location. Several studies have attempted to characterize the respective effects of user or system control in real or virtual navigation tasks, but we are not aware of such work on spatial positioning tasks.

Moreover, navigation studies in this area have not found conclusive results. Gaunet et al. [10] found no significant difference between exploring a virtual city with a joystick and passively observing the scene on estimating the direction of the starting points, reproducing the shape of paths, or on scene recognition. This result seems to echo those of Wilson [28], suggesting that active exploration does not benefit spatial memorization.

Other studies, however, have found that active participants, who also controlled their movement with a joystick, better recalled spatial layout (e.g., finding the shortest path, drawing a map of the environment, or identifying starting positions of a path) than passive participants [2, 3, 20]. In contrast, they did not find a significant effect on participants' recall of the correct locations of objects in the virtual environment.

Larrue et al. [16] and Ruddle et al. [22], on the other hand, found that user-controlled exploration yielded better memorization. Unlike the previous studies, however, these experiments involve richer body movement (e.g. body translation and rotation) and more complex environments. In particular, Larrue et al. found that controlling rotation with the head led to higher quality spatial representations [16]. Such kinesthetic feedback may play a role in spatial memorization, as Soechting & Flanders observed that short-term memory accuracy improved when users pointed toward targets with the arms, either actively or passively [26].

Together, these results show that kinesthetic feedback, that active or passive interaction, that divided attention, and that the complexity of the environment all may influence spatial memorization and may interact with each other. Moreover, such memorization may be different for paths and navigation than for learning the positions of objects [23].

We are not aware of prior work that explores the roles of kinesthetic feedback and of user vs. system control on spatial memorization of object positions in dense environments.

3. GUIDANCE SYSTEM

We consider three different projector-based guidance conditions in this study. We designed each of them to be similar enough to be comparable, yet provide distinct properties in terms of control and kinesthetic feedback.

Robotic Arm (RA). The robotic arm (RA) technique uses an improved implementation of Gacem et al.'s Projection-Augmented Robotic Arm technique [9] consisting of using a robotic arm with a pico-projector mounted on the end and attached to a small cart within the user's field of view (Figure 2). An ARTTRACK motion capture system and a predefined model of the environment are used for positioning the robotic arm towards the appropriate locations on the walls. The position of the highlight is computed by transforming the position of the target in the projection plane and applying a homographic transformation. The system described in [9] was improved by using better servo motors (MX-64T motors, with a precision of 0.089° instead of 0.35°) and the structure of the arm was modified in order to provide a 360° projection field.

The arm automatically moves in the direction of a target and highlights it with a spotlight. The amount of time needed for orienting the arm was between 228 and 3800 ms depending on the distance between the initial position and the final position of the arm. To locate a target, participants could see not only the spotlight but also the orientation of the arm, which is always visible (possibly in peripheral vision) (Figure 1a). The arm thus indicates to the user the general direction of the target, and the spotlight indicates its precise position.

Robotic Arm + Kinesthetic Feedback (RAK). This second technique combines RA with kinesthetic feedback. RAK is similar to the previous technique except that, when the robotic arm points and highlights the target, participants must point the target with their arm (Figure 1b). This kind of kinesthetic feedback is similar to that proposed by Soechting et al. [26].

Handheld Guidance (HG). The handheld guidance (HG) technique is inspired by Yee's Peephole interaction technique [30] and serves as a baseline guidance condition. The user holds a pico-projector (the same model as in the previous conditions) in his or her hand (Figure 3a). When the projector is far from the target, it displays an arrow in the direction of the target (Figure 3b). The participant moves the projector in the direction indicated by the arrow until the target is reached. The target is then highlighted, as in the previous techniques (Figure 3c).

These three techniques are each based on the same prin-

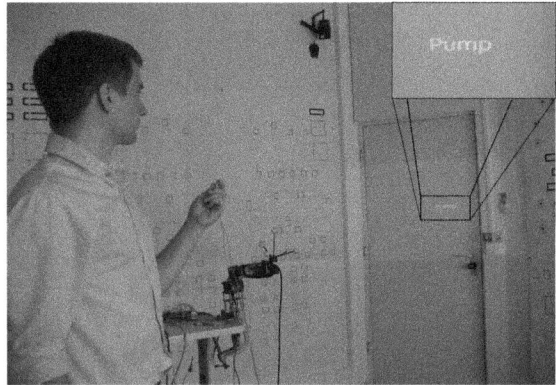

Figure 2: The Robotic Arm (RA) technique. The robotic arm is initially oriented towards the door and displays the name of the target.

ciple except that RA and RAK are system controlled while HG is user controlled. RA can be seen as HG performed by the robot instead of the user's arm. Transferring control to the robotic arm also removes kinesthetic feedback in the RA condition. The RAK technique reintroduces kinesthetic feedback through mid-air pointing by the user.

4. STUDY: USER VS. SYSTEM CONTROL

As previously explained, various guidance techniques transfer control from the user to the system, which results in an absence of kinesthetic feedback. While, in general, body movement seems to have positive impact on memorization, previous studies are somewhat inconclusive as results differ depending on the experimental setup. Indeed, the way control is performed, the level of embodiment, the resulting level of divided attention, and the complexity of the task seem to strongly impact results.

We thus further investigated whether motorized projection-based guidance would hinder spatial memorization by considering a task that is inspired by a real use case in which operators are trained to find controls rapidly. This experimental setup involves a complex environment with many objects laid out on the walls of a room, including behind the user. For this purpose, we compared the RA, RAK and HG conditions.

4.1 Hypotheses

Because the two conditions with robotic arm guidance (RA & RAK) reduce kinesthetic feedback, our hypotheses were that:

H1 Participants would (a) learn more targets (b) more quickly with handheld guidance (HG) than when transferring control to the robotic arm (RA & RAK).

H2 Adding kinesthetic feedback (RAK) when using the robotic arm (RA) should improve memorization because we expect "muscle memory" to play a positive role in learning. Pointing with the arm has been shown beneficial for spatial learning for simple localization [26].

H3 Regardless the guidance technique, memorization should be higher for targets located in front of the user, be-

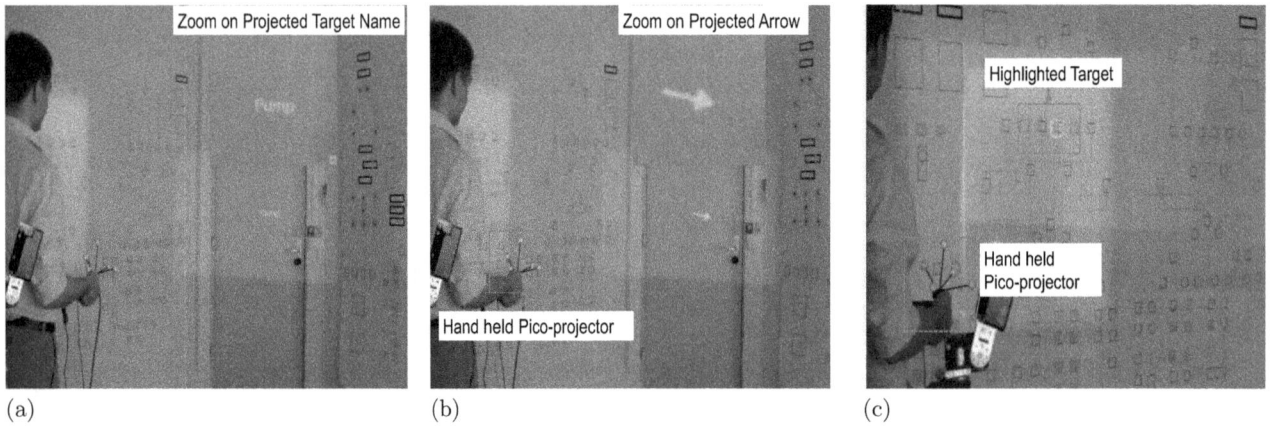

Figure 3: Handheld guidance (HG): (a) the participant points the projector at the starting position to reveal the name of the next target. (b) The participant presses a button to start the trial, showing an arrow that points toward the target. (c) When the user moves the projector near the target, it is highlighted. The user presses a button to end the trial.

cause building a mental model should be easier for targets that are always visible.

H4 Memorization should depend on the noticeability of targets (as explained below).

4.2 Experimental Design

4.2.1 Participants and Apparatus

Participants. 42 subjects (20 female), aged 21 to 34 (mean = 27.2, SD = 3.57), participated in the study. To avoid hidden confounds, we selected participants with a similar profile (engineering students from the same institution, with no HCI background) and controlled for gender across groups. We also performed a Guilford-Zimmerman test of spatial knowledge acquisition [15], which showed that the spatial abilities of participants were similar between groups (p=0.79). Participants were compensated with candies and, for each technique, the participant who memorized the most targets received a bonus box of chocolates.

Setting. The experiment took place on three walls of a room. Each wall measured approximately 2×5m (about 6.5×16.5 ft) and was located in front of, behind, or to the side of the participant (Figure 4). The room was under standard overhead fluorescent lighting with the curtains drawn so as to maintain consistent lighting conditions. Figure 4a shows a top view of the room with a participant at the starting position in the center of the room.

Projection. The projector's field of view was large enough to provide a sufficiently large peephole (about 1.2 m diagonal) to make framing a reasonable task and avoid disturbing participants.

Robotic Arm Speed. Previous findings have shown that guidance with a robotic arm reduces execution time [9]. To reduce a bias introduced by such timing differences, we set a slow movement speed on the projector in order to more closely align time on task for the RA, RAK, and HG conditions.

Targets. A set of 1143 targets were printed on paper posters affixed to the three walls (Figure 4b). They were equally distributed across the three walls, on a surface of 4.2×1.8 m for each wall. The design of the targets and their layout on the walls (Figure 5) was inspired from the control panels of an actual power plant. Their size ranged from 4×4 cm to 12×12 cm (more detail below) and the distance between their borders was variable.

While some distractors were only 5cm apart, all targets used during the experiment were at least at 8cm from their nearest neighbor in order to allow participants to unambiguously select targets and to let us focus on memorization rather than pointing accuracy.

Target labels were drawn from the industrial domain and consisted of simple words (e. g., Pump, Voltage, Engine, etc.). These labels were projected at the same place at the beginning of each trial to inform about the target (Figure 2). They were not printed on posters to avoid to bias the results of the experiment. Moreover, this situation mimics real conditions where labels are too small to be readable from a distance.

We took into account the position of targets, which were either in front, beside, or behind the user, which thus affected target visibility. We also distinguished two levels of *noticeability*. In contrast with other targets, those that were different from neighbors, isolated, or close to a landmark (like a door) were considered *easier-to-notice*. These targets made up 50% of those used in the experiment. We used this categorization to provide a rough approximation of the distinctiveness or noticeability of targets.

As detailed below, participants were instructed to learn a sequence of 12 targets, randomized between easy- or less-easy-to-notice targets and across the different walls (in front of, beside, or behind the user).

4.2.2 Method and Procedure

Because skill-transfer and interference is not well understood in such cases, memorization tasks commonly use between-subjects designs to avoid possible interaction effects (e.g. [2, 13, 16, 22]). In particular, our experiment involves two similar techniques (RA & RAK) and a third baseline (HG). Even counterbalancing the order would probably favor RA & RAK, so we used a between-subjects design with a relatively large number of participants (42) randomly assigned to three groups. Over the course of any given day, we ran one group (so as to counter-balance time-of-day effects such as post-lunch lethargy and to minimize possible interaction effects).

In summary, we evaluated the RA, RAK, and HG conditions in a between-subject test and the two characteristics of the targets (*position* and *noticeability*) in a within-subjects design. In total we had 6452 trials.

The experiment was divided into two sessions. The first session lasted approximately 30 minutes, and the second session lasted about 5 minutes. As shown in Figure 6, the first session involved four successive training and testing phases. The second session, performed 48 hours later, involved a single (long-term) memory test.

Training phase. During this phase, participants were asked to find, as quickly as possible, a sequence of 12 randomly ordered targets and to memorize their locations. The same list of targets was used along the experiment. For each technique, the same starting position was used, either through the system (RA & RAK) or by requiring the user to point the projector at the start position to reveal the stimulus (HG). The name of the desired target was then displayed by the projector (Figure 3a). The participant would then start the searching phase by clicking on a button, which would make the target name disappear.

In RA and RAK conditions, the robotic arm then started moving towards the direction of the target. In HG condition, a directional arrow appeared (Figure 3b) and the participant could start moving the handheld projector according to the direction of the arrow. In all cases, the target was highlighted when the projection window reached the target (Figure 3c and 1a). In the RAK condition, the participant also then pointed to the highlighted target with his or her arm. Participants could then take some time to memorize the target before moving on to the next trial.

Memory Test. Participants were instructed to find as accurately as possible the 12 targets they previously localized, but without any guidance. Twelve trials were performed in this phase (one for each target). Participants first had to point the projector on the same initial position to start a trial. As before, this caused the name of the target to be displayed. Participants were required to look at this name for one second before they could then click on the start button. This made the target name disappear and the projected cursor appear (Figure 5a). Participants could then move the projector to place the cursor on the target of their choice, then confirm by pressing again the same button. The system then provided feedback about whether the selected target correctly matched the stimulus (Figure 5b).

4.3 Results

4.3.1 Memorization

We used recall rate to evaluate memorization performance, that is the percentage of targets correctly identified by participants during the testing phases.

Memory Performance During Training. The training phase included four memory tests, as illustrated in Figure 6. We performed a two-way ANOVA test on the recall rates of these memory tests and found a statistically significant difference between the four testing blocks ($F_{3,117}=177$, p<0.01). Participants were increasingly accurate in correctly identifying targets as the experiment progressed (Figure 7). Recall rates increased by 39%, 13% and 6% between successive blocks for

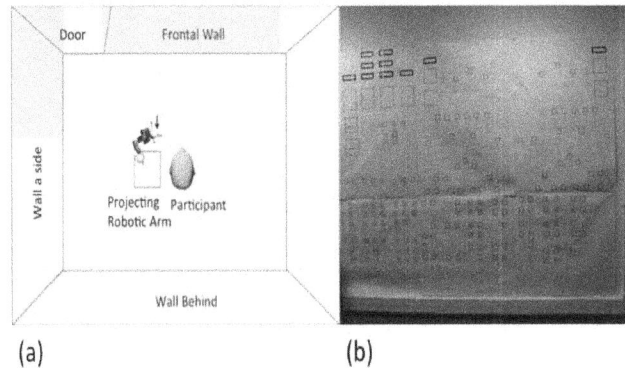

Figure 4: (a) The participant is standing at the center of the room. (b) A wall and objects in the room.

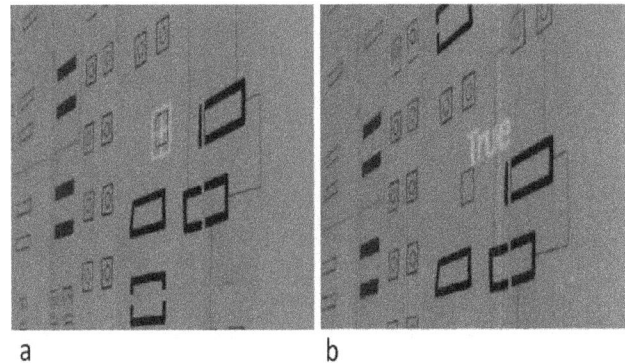

Figure 5: Memory test: (a) the hand-held pico-projector (HG) displays a cursor to the user. (b) A visual feedback (true or false) indicates if the selected item is correct.

RA, by 33%, 14% and 3.75% for RAK and by 29%, 19% and 19% for HG. Hence, the initial slope of the learning curve was quite high when using the robotic arm (RA and RAK), with more than two-thirds of the targets properly identified by the second test. In comparison, the learning curve was lower for the handheld technique (HG).

We also found a statistically significant difference in recall rate between techniques ($F_{2,39}=9.74$, p<0.01). Participants memorized targets more accurately when using the robotic arm (RA $F_{1,26}=16$, p<0.01 and RAK $F_{1,26}=13$, p<0.01) than with the handheld device (HG). There was no significant difference between RA and RAK.

During training, the interaction effect between techniques and blocks was statistically significant ($F_{6,117}=2.36$, p<0.05). A post-hoc Tukey test showed statistically significant results for the first three test blocks between RAK and HG and between RA and HG groups. RA Participants learned more than HG participants, and RAK participants learned more correct targets than HG. However, we found no statistically significant difference between techniques for the fourth block, probably because values were already quite high (Table 1).

Performance During the Retention Test. We performed a one-way ANOVA test on the recall rate over the final memory test, performed two days later. We found a statisti-

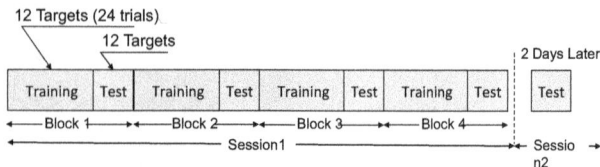

Figure 6: The experiment was performed over two sessions. The first session was composed of four successive training and testing blocks. The second session consisted in a memory test performed two days later.

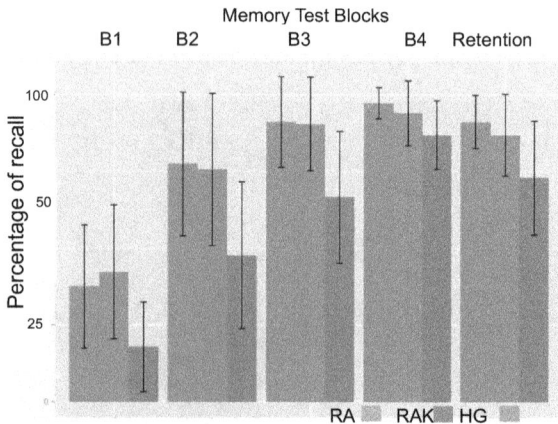

Figure 7: Mean recall rates. The first four groups correspond to the memory tests during the first session. The last group corresponds to the retention test in the second session, 48 hours later. 1: Robotic Arm (RA), 2: RA + Kinesthetic feedback (RAK), 3: Handheld Guidance (HG).

cally significant difference between techniques ($F_{2,39}$=6.4, p<0.05). Again, participants memorized targets more accurately when using RA ($F_{1,26}$=26.11, p<0.01) and when using RAK ($F_{1,26}$=5.21, p<0.01) versus HG. There was no significant difference between RA and RAK.

Target Position and Noticeability. We performed a three-way ANOVA test on the recall rates for block test, position, and noticeability of targets. We found a statistically significant difference between "easy-" and "less-noticeable" targets ($F_{1,156}$ = 7.77, p<0.01). Unsurprisingly, in the beginning of the experiment, recall rates were higher for "easy-to-notice" targets (36.1% vs. 28.1%) and this was still the case at the end of the experiment (94% vs. 81%). In the retention test, recall rates were also higher for "easy-to-notice" targets (87% vs. 80%).

Table 1: Percentage of memorized targets per technique and per memory testing block

Techniques	block1	block2	block3	block4	Retention
RA	37%	77%	91%	97%	91%
RAK	42%	75%	90%	94%	86%
HG	17%	47%	66%	86%	72%

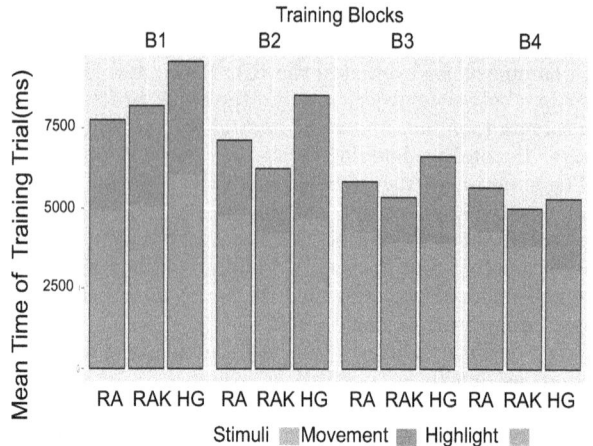

Figure 8: Trial exploration time for each block and technique.

Table 2: Trial Time in (s) for each technique and training block

Techniques	block1	block2	block3	block4	Total Mean
RA	7.7s	7.1s	5.8s	5.6s	6.5s
RAK	8.1s	6.2s	5.3s	5.0s	6.1s
HG	9.5s	8.5s	6.6s	5.3s	7.5s

We also found a statistically significant difference between targets located in front of and behind the participants ($F_{1,156}$ = 8.97, p<0.01). The recall rate of targets behind the user was lower in the beginning of the experiment (26.5% vs. 38.4%) but similar at the end (92% vs. 93%). No significant effect was found for the retention test.

4.3.2 Training Time

We performed a two-way ANOVA of the task time spent in each of the four training blocks, finding a statistically significant difference between blocks ($F_{3,117}$=34, p<0.001). Unsurprisingly, time decreased across blocks as illustrated in Figure 8.

We found no statistically significant difference on task time between techniques (p = 0.4), although the amount of time was slightly shorter on average for RA and RAK than for HG (Table 2).

As differences in performance did not seem related to global training time duration, we performed a deeper analysis by decomposing trials time into three parts: (a) *stimulus-time*, the duration in which the name of the target is displayed, (b) *movement-time*, the duration in which the projector moves towards the target (either automatically or by the user's movement), and (c) *highlight-time*, the amount of time spent by participants looking at the highlighted target before starting the next trial.

A two-way ANOVA of *highlight-time* showed a statistically significant difference between blocks ($F_{3,117}$= 18, p <0.001). Participants spent less time while advancing in the experiment for all techniques (Figure 8).

A two-way ANOVA of *highlight time* also showed a statistically significant difference between techniques ($F_{2,39}$ = 5.13, p <0.05). Participants from two robotic arm tech-

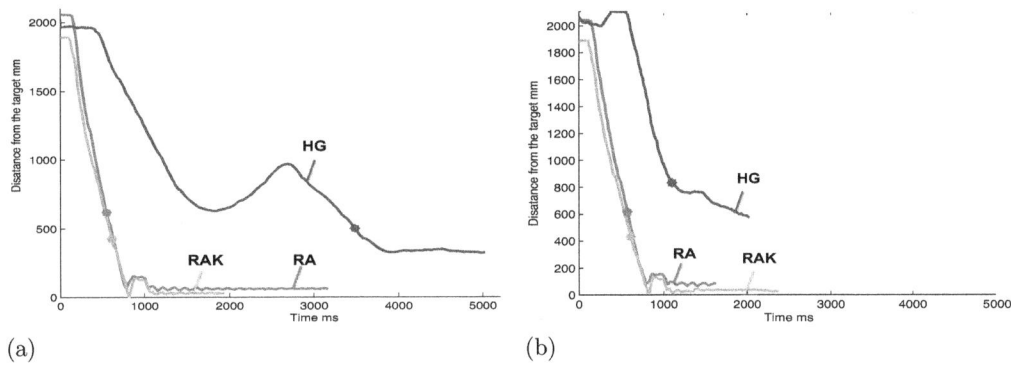

(a)   (b)

Figure 9: A sample training trial for one user (a) at the beginning the experiment (block 1) and (b) at the end of the experiment (block 4). The plots show the distance between the center of the projected area and the target. RA is shown in red, RAK in green, and HG in blue. The thick dot on each curve indicated the moment when the target was first highlighted.

niques spent less time (2 seconds for RA and 1.9s for RAK) looking at the highlighted target than those holding the projector (3s). Surprisingly, the group with lower memorization performance (HG) is thus the one that spent more time looking at the highlighted target.

4.3.3 Distance Curves

Figure 9 shows a sample training trial performed (a) at the beginning and (b) at the end of the experiment. Comparing the plots, we can see that training time considerably decreased at the end of the experiment, as each curve shifts left. The blue curve (HG) in Figure 9a shows an important fluctuation as the user overshoots the target. This fluctuation is highly attenuated at the end of the experiment.

The small oscillations at the end of the RA and RAK plots are the results of the abrupt stop of servomotors.

4.4 Discussion

User vs. system control (H1). Transferring control from the handheld guidance (HG) technique to the two robotic arm conditions makes the user more passive and reduces the time spent finding each target. As such, we expected participants to learn fewer target positions in the RA condition than in the HG condition, and that the benefits of kinesthetic feedback would put the RAK condition between the two.

The results show, however, that H1 did not hold: participants memorized more targets in less time (time spent looking for highlighted target) in the RA & RAK conditions than in the HG condition. We suspect that this difference may be the result of dividing the user's attention between controlling the device and locating the object, as is the case in [10, 28]. The *highlight-time* (Figure 8) is also higher for HG than for the two other conditions. This is a logical consequence of the fact that participants remembered less targets in the HG condition. Another factor is that a little longer time is needed until the highlighted location is stabilized in this condition. However, this increase in time is small, as can be seen on figure 9 (cf. the dot on the blue curve). Moreover, there was no difference in *highlight-time* for the first learning block, for which participants had not yet memorized any target location.

Observations of participants during training phases seem

to support this theory. Participants who explored the room manually (HG) seemed to be more concentrated on manipulating the projector before and while the target was highlighted. RA & RAK participants, however, tended to concentrate only on the highlighted target, more naturally and effortlessly locating the target.

Participants' subjective judgements also seem to support this hypothesis. At the end of the first session, we asked participants to rate cognitive effort, frustration, and subjective preference for each of the different guidance techniques on a 7-point Likert scale. We found no differences between techniques for frustration and preference, but participants found RA and RAK less cognitively demanding than HG (6.42 for RA, 6.5 for RAK and 5.57 for HG, higher scores are better). This difference may result from a higher level of divided attention.

Kinesthetic feedback and spatial memory (H2). Participants in the HG condition experience a kinesthetic feedback as they search for the target. We hypothesized that this feedback would reinforce memorization through some kind of "motor memory," echoing results by Kaufmann et al. [13]. In the RA condition, however, participants do not experience such kinesthetic feedback. We thus expected that kinesthetic feedback would lead to the same outcomes predicted by H1: HG would provide the strongest support for memorization, RA would underperform, and RAK would be between the two as it combines RA with a form of kinesthetic feedback. As described above, however, this kinesthetic feedback did not seem to have much impact when the robotic arm was used: RA and RAK produced similar results, both superior to HG. Thus, H2 does not hold.

This results contrasts with the findings of most previous studies on navigation tasks [20, 26, 29]. However, as indicated in Section 2, some other studies (e.g., [10, 28]) found no significant difference between exploring a virtual environment using a joystick and passively observing the scene. Hence, results may depend on various differences between studies, such as the kind of body movement, the complexity of the environment, the number of target objects, the inclusion of distractors, or the type of spatial memory involved. For example, in motor-based tasks (e.g., [16, 22]), it makes sense that motor feedback would enhance path or layout memorization.

57

That we observed no significant difference between RA & RAK conditions may be due to the fact that in complex localization tasks (e.g., learning 12 targets among 1200 objects), the task is primarily visual rather than motor-based and thus might not benefit as much from kinesthetic feedback. Moreover, in the RAK condition, kinesthetic feedback only occurred when the user was asked to point at the target, hence after the target was found. This constrasts with tasks where the user must continuously control a device during the whole search task.

Another possible explanation is that participants might got kinesthetic feedback through their mirror neuron system, which allows people to perceive kinetic movements outside of their bodies as their own movements. An additional experiment using a wide-angle projection system without motorized parts would be worth performing for examining this hypothesis.

These conflicting results for different kinds of spatial memory on different kinds of tasks and in different kinds of contexts call out the need for more work in this domain. Moreover, the fact that H1 & H2 did not hold suggests that more studies are needed to better understand the roles of, e.g., the complexity of the context and task, of divided attention and of types of kinesthetic feedback on spatial memorization. This work presents an important set of data points toward this understanding.

Lastly, that H1 & H2 were invalidated is encouraging for such guidance systems. It suggests that system-controlled guidance not only helps to more quickly identify the locations of targets, but also that users are better able to learn those positions than with a handheld, user-controlled guidance technique. In future work it may be interesting to compare such guidance to no guidance at all.

*Target characteristics (**H3** & **H4**).* As expected, targets that are easy to notice and that are always visible were memorized faster than those that were overloaded with distractors or those occasionally visualized. One possible explanation, is that permanent visibility of a target helps the development of a mental model of the environment and *easy-to-notice* targets provide enough hints to allow users to create a mental mapping of their positions.

5. CONCLUSIONS

People typically need to learn and memorize objects in training scenarios, to make them able to interact with (or maintain) complex environments such as plants or control rooms. The main motivation of this study was a real use case where operators are trained to rapidly find controls.

Guidance techniques help people to more quickly and more easily locate objects in complex environments, but their effect on learning is less well understood. In this paper, we compared guidance techniques in order to evaluate the impact of projection-based guidance techniques on spatial memorization. We compared two system-controlled guidance techniques that use a robotic projection arm and a user-controlled, projected peephole technique. A major difference between these two cases is that the first technique transfers control to the system, reducing the active involvement of the user, and is also likely to allow the user focusing on memorization.

We expected that the system-controlled guidance techniques, which help participants to more quickly and more easily identify the positions of targets, would hinder learn-

ing. Instead, we found that participants were able to learn the positions of more objects and more quickly with the robotic projection arm than with manual, handheld guidance. This suggests that such guidance techniques may be useful in training contexts, where learning is important and where merely finding objects is insufficient.

Our outcomes extend prior findings on spatial memory in positioning tasks, revealing that active control on its own is insufficient to improve memorization performance. We suspect that this result is due to the division of the user's attention between memorization and controlling the device. Similarly, we found that kinesthetic feedback does not necessarily improve spatial memory. Future work should study the the role of division of attention, task alignment, and more precisely identifying the role kinesthetic feedback can play in spatial memorization.

6. ACKNOWLEDGEMENTS

This research was supported by the French ANR/Investissement d'Avenir "Cluster Connexion" and by the EQUIPEX Digiscope ANR-10-EQPX-0026. We wish to thank the reviewers, the participants of the user studies, Catherine Devic and Bernard Nouailhas at EDF, and Patrick Bush and Gerard Mouret at Télécom ParisTech for the technical support.

7. REFERENCES

[1] K. Arning, M. Ziefle, M. Li, and L. Kobbelt. Insights into user experiences and acceptance of mobile indoor navigation devices. In *Mobile and Ubiquitous Multimedia*, pages 41:1–41:10. ACM, 2012.

[2] E. A. Attree, B. M. Brooks, F. D. Rose, T. K. Andrews, A. G. Leadbetter, and B. R. Clifford. Memory processes and virtual environments: I can't remember what was there, but i can remember how i got there. implications for people with disabilities. In *Proc. 1st Euro. Conf. Disability, Virtual Reality and Assoc. Tech.*, pages 123–132, 1996.

[3] B. M. Brooks. The specificity of memory enhancement during interaction with a virtual environment. *Memory*, 7(1):65–78, 1999.

[4] A. Butz, M. Schneider, and M. Spassova. Searchlight – a lightweight search function for pervasive environments. In PERVASIVE'04, pages 351–356. 2004.

[5] X. Cao, C. Forlines, and R. Balakrishnan. Multi-user interaction using handheld projectors. UIST '07, pages 43–52. ACM, 2007.

[6] J. R. Cauchard, M. Fraser, T. Han, and S. Subramanian. Steerable projection: exploring alignment in interactive mobile displays. *Personal and Ubiquitous Computing*, 16(1):27–37, 2012.

[7] J. R. Cauchard, M. Löchtefeld, P. Irani, J. Schoening, A. Krüger, M. Fraser, and S. Subramanian. Visual separation in mobile multi-display environments. UIST '11, pages 451–460. ACM, 2011.

[8] Y. Fujimoto, G. Yamamoto, H. Kato, and J. Miyazaki. Relation between location of information displayed by augmented reality and user's memorization. In *Proceedings of the 3rd Augmented Human International Conference*, AH '12, pages 7:1–7:8, New York, NY, USA, 2012. ACM.

[9] H. Gacem, G. Bailly, J. Eagan, and E. Lecolinet. Finding objects faster in dense environments using a projection augmented robotic arm. In *INTERACT 2015*, pages 221–238. Springer, 2015.

[10] F. Gaunet, M. Vidal, A. Kemeny, and A. Berthoz. Active, passive and snapshot exploration in a virtual environment: influence on scene memory, reorientation and path memory. In *Brain Res Cogn Brain Res*, volume 3, pages 409–429, 2001.

[11] S. J. Henderson and S. Feiner. Evaluating the benefits of augmented reality for task localization in maintenance of an armored personnel carrier turret. In *ISMAR 2009*, pages 135–144. IEEE, 2009.

[12] T. Ishikawa, H. Fujiwara, O. Imai, and A. Okabe. Wayfinding with a gps-based mobile navigation system: A comparison with maps and direct experience. *Journal of Environmental Psychology*, 28:74–82, 2008.

[13] B. Kaufmann and D. Ahlström. Studying spatial memory and map navigation performance on projector phones with peephole interaction. In *CHI '13*, CHI '13, pages 3173–3176. ACM, 2013.

[14] S. Kratz, M. Rohs, F. Reitberger, and J. Moldenhauer. Attjector: an attentionfollowing wearable projector. In *Kinect Workshop at Pervasive*, 2012.

[15] M. Kyritsis and S. Gulliver. Gilford zimmerman orientation survey: A validation. In *Information, Communications and Signal Processing*, pages 1–4. IEEE, 2009.

[16] F. Larrue, H. Sauzéon, D. Foloppe, G. Wallet, J.-R. Cazalets, C. Gross, M. Hachet, and B. N'Kaoua. Assessing the impact of automatic vs. controlled rotations on spatial transfer with a joystick and a walking interface in vr. In *INTERACT 2013*, pages 1–18. Springer, 2013.

[17] M. Löchtefeld, S. Gehring, J. Schöning, and A. Krüger. Shelftorchlight: Augmenting a shelf using a camera projector unit. In *UBIPROJECTION'10*, pages 20–23. Springer, 2010.

[18] M. Löchtefeld, J. Schöning, M. Rohs, and A. Krüger. Marauders light: replacing the wand with a mobile camera projector unit. Mobile and Ubiquitous Multimedia '09, page 19. ACM, 2009.

[19] A. Mulloni, H. Seichter, and D. Schmalstieg. Handheld augmented reality indoor navigation with activity-based instructions. Mobile HCI '11, pages 211–220. ACM, 2011.

[20] P. Peruch and F. Gaunet. Virtual environments as a promising tool for investigating human spatial cognition. In *Current Psychology of Cognition*, volume 17, 1998.

[21] C. Pinhanez, R. Kjeldsen, A. Levas, G. Pingali, M. Podlaseck, and N. Sukaviriya. Applications of steerable projector-camera systems. In *Workshop on Projector-Camera Systems at ICCV 2003*. Citeseer, 2003.

[22] R. A. Ruddle, E. Volkova, and H. H. Bülthoff. Walking improves your cognitive map in environments that are large-scale and large in extent. *TOCHI'11*, 18(2):10, 2011.

[23] J. Scarr, A. Cockburn, and C. Gutwin. Supporting and exploiting spatial memory in user interfaces. *Interaction*, 6(1):1–84, 2012.

[24] J. Schöning, M. Rohs, S. Kratz, M. Löchtefeld, and A. Krüger. Map torchlight: a mobile augmented reality camera projector unit. CHI EA '09, pages 3841–3846. ACM, 2009.

[25] A. D. Smith, I. D. Gilchrist, and B. M. Hood. Children's search behaviour in large-scale space: Developmental components of exploration. *PERCEPTION*, 34(10):1221, 2005.

[26] J. F. Soechting and M. Flanders. Sensorimotor representations for pointing to targets in three-dimensional space. *Journal of Neurophysiology*, 62(2):582–594, 1989.

[27] A. Wilson, H. Benko, S. Izadi, and O. Hilliges. Steerable augmented reality with the beamatron. UIST '12, pages 413–422. ACM, 2012.

[28] P. N. Wilson. Active exploration of a virtual environment does not promote orientation or memory for objects. *Environment and Behavior*, 31(6):752–763, 1999.

[29] M. Wraga. Thinking outside the body: an advantage for spatial updating during imagined versus physical self-rotation. In *Journal of Experimental Psychology: Learning, Memory and Cognition*, volume 29, pages 993–1005, 2003.

[30] K.-P. Yee. Peephole displays: pen interaction on spatially aware handheld computers. CHI '03, pages 1–8, 2003.

Inducing Body-Transfer Illusions in VR by Providing Brief Phases of Visual-Tactile Stimulation

Oscar Ariza, Jann Freiwald, Nadine Laage, Michaela Feist, Mariam Salloum,
Gerd Bruder, Frank Steinicke
Human-Computer Interaction, Department of Informatics, Universität Hamburg
{ariza,freiwald,5laage,0feist,0salloum,bruder,steinicke}@informatik.uni-hamburg.de

ABSTRACT

Current developments in the area of virtual reality (VR) allow numerous users to experience immersive virtual environments (VEs) in a broad range of application fields. In the same way, some research has shown novel advances in wearable devices to provide vibrotactile feedback which can be combined with low-cost technology for hand tracking and gestures recognition. The combination of these technologies can be used to investigate interesting psychological illusions. For instance, body-transfer illusions, such as the rubber-hand illusion or elongated-arm illusion, have shown that it is possible to give a person the persistent illusion of body transfer after only brief phases of synchronized visual-haptic stimulation.

The motivation of this paper is to induce such perceptual illusions by combining VR, vibrotactile and tracking technologies, offering an interesting way to create new spatial interaction experiences centered on the senses of sight and touch. We present a technology framework that includes a pair of self-made gloves featuring vibrotactile feedback that can be synchronized with audio-visual stimulation in order to reproduce body-transfer illusions in VR. We present in detail the implementation of the framework and show that the proposed technology setup is able to induce the elongated-arm illusion providing automatic tactile stimuli, instead of the traditional approach based on manually synchronized stimulation.

Categories and Subject Descriptors

H.5.2 [**Information Interfaces and Presentation**]: User Interfaces–Input Devices and Strategies, Evaluation / Methodology; I.3.7 [**Computer Graphics**]: Three-Dimensional Graphics and Realism–Virtual Reality

Keywords

Vibrotactile feedback; body-transfer illusions; 3D touch interaction; virtual environments; head-mounted display

1. INTRODUCTION

Most traditional immersive virtual environments (IVEs) are focused solely on the visual and auditory modalities, which often lim-

its the user's sense of body ownership and embodiment in virtual environments. However, by combining IVEs composed of head-mounted displays (HMDs) with head, hand and body tracking, with haptic feedback devices enables the creation of interactive experiences providing embodied visual, auditory and haptic feedback in response to user actions. In this way, it is possible to reproduce perceptual illusions involving tactile sensations, in which the stimulation of the sense of touch can be provided with an actuated device instead of using a real object, extending the interaction possibilities of the user, creating compelling illusions and, for instance, even creating the sense of having bigger, shorter or elongated limbs [1, 16, 31]. Additionally, current technology provides low-energy, wearable and wireless components to create ergonomic and low-latency vibrotactile devices, reliable enough to automate the creation of perceptual illusions in IVEs and possibly inducing effects similar to real-world demonstrators.

In this paper, we propose an approach to reproduce perceptual illusions, involving a hand-worn haptic device and an IVE with hand tracking to provide visually synchronized vibrotactile feedback on the fingers and the palm surface, offering freedom of movements and comfort for common hand-interaction tasks. Using the developed haptic gloves we show that we can reproduce a body-transfer illusion with brief phases of visual-tactile stimulation, thus offering an interesting way to create new spatial interaction experiences in virtual reality (VR). An implemented use case showed visual-motor and visual-tactile correlations in a perceptual experiment within a VR scenario, providing sight-and-touch sensory inputs in order to reproduce the illusion of an elongated arm.

2. RELATED WORK

In this section we summarize previous work related to vibrotactile devices and perceptual illusions.

2.1 Vibrotactile Devices

This work builds on research focused on wearable devices offering tactile sensations on the hand through on-skin vibrotactile stimuli eliciting the Panician Corpuscle receptors. Related research includes the work of Kramer et al. [17] involving prototypes of haptic hand-worn devices comprising vibrating actuators and bending sensors to test the effects of intensity and length of activation on the feeling of objects. Muramatsu et al. [21] developed a glove with vibration motors for perception experiments. More recent work, proposed vibrotactile gloves providing tactile sensations in order to evaluate texture discrimination [19] and shape recognition [9]. Martinez et al. [20] also developed a glove with 12 vibrators and optical tracking based on infrared LED markers. Other approaches are based on vibrotactile displays providing navigation cues in computer-aided surgery systems [12] and assistance in tele-

SUI '16, October 15-16, 2016, Tokyo, Japan
© 2016 ACM. ISBN 978-1-4503-4068-7/16/10. . . $15.00
DOI: `http://dx.doi.org/10.1145/2983310.2985760`

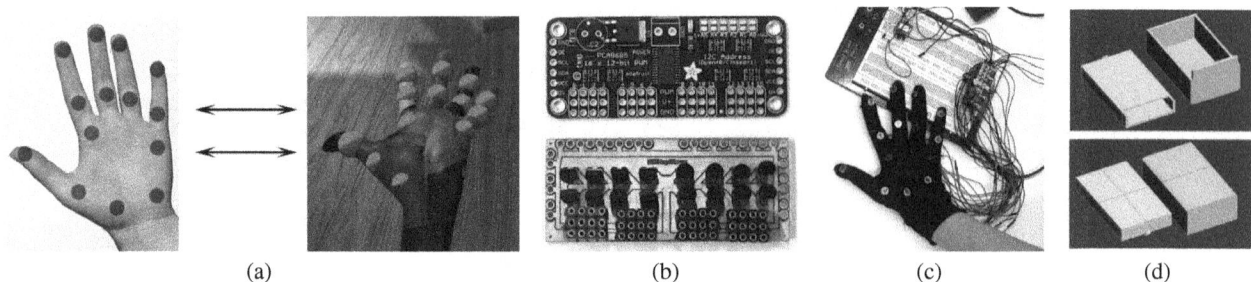

Figure 1: Arrangement and components of the vibrotactile display:(a) Distribution of the vibration actuators on the hand, (b) the PWM signal controller, (c) electronics testbed and (d) 3D-printed case.

operated assembly processes [7]. In contrast, recent research also based on haptic gloves [13] uses electro-tactile displays instead of vibration actuators to provide tactile feedback on grasping tasks in a VR environment, and other studies are focused on cutaneous and kinesthetic feedback with active thimbles [27].

The mentioned contributions and their foundations provide assessments and insights that are useful to design and create hand-worn vibrotactile devices which can be used on IVEs to facilitate the reproduction of body-transfer illusions. Our proposal integrated those insights to offer a wireless, low latency hand-worn pair of gloves, using materials to facilitate hand tracking with low-cost equipment, i.e. Leap Motion, and featuring easy integration with the graphics software in order to accurately activate the vibrotactile actuators when collisions are detected. In addition, our device architecture could be easily scaled to cover bigger body areas, enabling the creation of more complex vibrotactile wearables without a significant decrease on the current performance or latency.

2.2 Perceptual Illusions

Well-known perceptual illusions like the rubber-hand illusion, aiming to induce in the participant the sense of being touched on a fake arm behaving as if it would be part of their body [4] and the elongated-arm illusion [16], aiming to extend the body space by means of elongated virtual limbs, as well as the neural mechanisms which are responsible for perceptual illusions, in particular, the integration of tactile and visual feedback, are well-studied [6, 8, 10]. There have been discussions in the literature about how the fake limb should look like, in comparison with the real one. Prior research claims that there must be some correlation between the fake arm and the real one [31]. Newer investigations show that the illusion can be reproduced in VR and, in addition, it does not appear important whether the fake arm has the correct skin color or garments as the participant's arm and the illusion effect can even be achieved under controlled distortions between proprioceptive and visual information. However, the effect is negated when an abstract representation of the arm (such as an arrow) is displayed [33].

Further research shows that a perceptual illusion of body swapping can be induced for the whole body with an HMD showing stereoscopic real-time video imagery [22]. Investigations in HMD-based immersive virtual environments argued that a virtual body is a critical component and that it has a major effect on the users [11, 25], even for embodiment in body-representation illusions [29]. In investigations by Slater et al. [26] participants showed a higher sense of presence by using their virtual body to touch than by those who just pressed a button to confirm actions during experiments.

However, so far there are no conclusive results about the effects of replacing the traditional approach to provide the tactile feedback i.e. manual and synchronized tapping, with automatic vibrotactile

stimuli using a wearable device. Our proposed framework offer automatic stimuli in response to user interactions within the IVE, enabling the induction of body-transfer illusions without movement restrictions caused by tapping mechanisms or operators providing the tactile feedback.

3. VIBROTACTILE GLOVE DEVICE

We designed our device as a glove to recreate the sense of touch with vibrotactile feedback while the user is exposed to a VR visual stimulus involving body-transfer illusions. In this section, we detail the concepts and the implementation details of a pair of tactile devices (for bimanual interaction), which offer a wireless, lightweight and responsive tactile display solution, able to provide synchronized visual-tactile stimuli in VEs.

3.1 Vibrotactile Display

There is a wide range of methods to provide tactile feedback (i.e. temperature, vibration, pressure). Our approach is based on coin-type linear resonant actuators (LRAs), used to create vibrations by powering a voice coil, which moves a magnetic mass and vibrating at a resonant frequency in one dimension; in this case, the normal direction to the hand's palm surface.

The proposed glove consists of 14 PMC10-100 LRAs[1] distributed over the hand (see Figure 1a). The quantity of actuators was defined as a balance between device mobility and power usage while still offering a comfortable wearable device. The positions were chosen regarding neurological aspects; the density of actuators on individual parts of the hand depends on the size of the area in the somatosensory cortex. We concentrated on the fast adapting Pacini corpuscles (PC) described by Stark et al. [30] in the fingers and palm of the hand. The receptors are primarily reacting to vibration so it is easy to stimulate them with LRA actuators [5, 18]. The receptive fields of cortical neurons on the fingertips are smaller than the one on the palm. Therefore, each finger has two actuators, which are placed on the fingertip and above the metacarpophalangeal joints. The palm has only four actuators: Two on the ball of hand and two on the palmar surface, renouncing on placing one vibration motor in the middle of the palm, as it could not touch the skin under certain hand postures [9]. Israr and Poupyrev [14] proved with their tactile brush algorithm, that it is possible to create continuous, high-resolution tactile stimuli with a low-resolution grid of vibrating actuators by using the apparent motion and the phantom illusion.

For the resonance frequency Kuroki et al. chose 240 Hz for their mechanical feedback to stimulate the PC [18]. In general PC stimulate in an interval of 10 -500 Hz with a minimal threshold of 150-

---

[1]http://www.precisionmicrodrives.com/

300 Hz [5]. If the frequency is high, the localization of the single signal gets more difficult because the stimuli are propagated. After a test to detect stimuli overlapping, we set a frequency of 175 $\pm$5 Hz so the vibration is not too strong for sensitive people and keeping the source still distinguishable.

As a result, our grid of actuators can stimulate the hand in a detailed manner that is enough to provide the touch sensations required in perceptual illusions experiments, emitting vibration stimuli between the acceptable range [18]. The vibration motors are attached with a rubber band to a thin fabric glove. Previous prototypes of our device have shown that normal gloves do not create enough tension to produce the same vibration on different hand sizes. With regards to Choi and Kuchenbecker we included rubber bands to "ensure signal transmission" [5] and that the motors are nearly on constant places for a wide range of hand sizes.

3.2 Device Controller

The actuators are controlled by an Adafruit 16-channel 12-bit pulse width modulation (PWM) driver[2] and are powered by a 3.7V lithium polymer ion (LiPo) rechargeable battery. A self-made circuit board organizes the connections, provides signal enhancements (including amplifying, basic active breaking and basic overdriving) and fits directly onto the PWM driver (see Figure 1b). The driver is connected to an ARM Cortex System on a Chip (SoC)[3] via I2C. In addition, the SoC features Bluetooth Low Energy (BLE), which enables the wireless communication between the computer and the haptic gloves, decoupling the client PC which runs an UDP server sending activation commands to the vibrators according to the user actions. This UDP server is a standalone middleware that handles the BLE transmission of data to the gloves (See Figure 5). On the server side, low level BLE connections control the gloves independently, in this way was possible to optimize the data transmission, matching the processing threads with the wireless connections. To mount the circuitry around the arm, all the components are installed in a 3D printed case, which is attached to a neoprene arm belt (see Figure 2). The case also contains USB chargers for ease battery recharging and its dimensions are 108mm $\times$ 80mm $\times$ 39mm (see Figure 1d). The case is meant to be worn on the forearm, close to the elbow, pointing outside to keep the arms able to rest and interact freely in the personal space.

3.3 Tactile Control Points

When emitting signals to the vibration motors, we address the motor independently with values to define the intensity of vibration. Before emitting signals, we have to determine the intensity for each vibration motor. We do this by attaching Tactile Control Points (TCPs) to the avatar's hand bones at specific locations, which represent the real vibrators' locations on the gloves. Instead of using full vibration intensity when in contact with a surface, following an on-off approach, TCPs inherit an intensity value dependent on their distance to the nearest touchable collider in the scene. The used distance function is defined by $(1 - x/0.01)^4$ and returns values greater than zero for distances between zero and one centimeter, as shown in Figure 3. The "actual distance" refers to the size of the depicted hand, while the graph is only valid for the examined point on the surface at the coordinate (0,0). After determining the intensity for each TCP, all the data is collected and sorted by a central organizer unit. This unit puts all the intensities into an encoded-data packet and sends it to the UDP server (See Figure 5).

[2]https://www.adafruit.com/product/815

[3]https://www.nordicsemi.com/products/nRF51822

The choice to emit an intensity based on distance rather than contact, stems from the way the tracked hands interact with virtual objects. It is because of our inability to detain the user's real hands from moving when the correspondent virtual hands should, due to collisions. If we stopped the virtual hands from moving further in a direction because of an obstacle, we could not synchronize this behavior to the user's real hands, which are free to move in any direction at any time in our setup. Since it is a delicate task to maintain a hand position that actually provides tactile feedback while touching a static surface, we defined a certain range around the surface that would trigger a vibration on our glove. This eventually led to the implementation of the distance function to provide a more elaborate sensation.

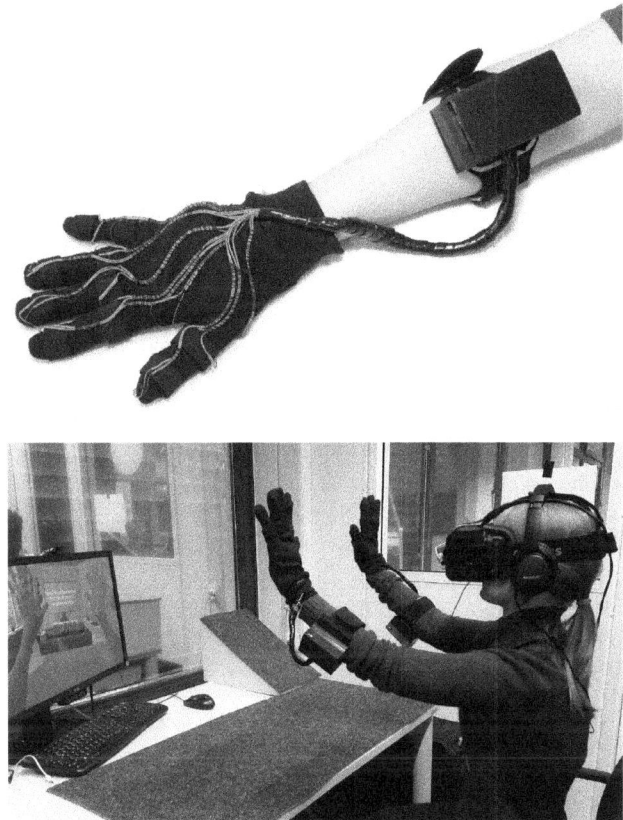

Figure 2: Images of (top) self-made glove with the electronic case attached to the forearm, and (bottom) participant interacting with the VR application, wearing the pair of gloves and the Oculus Rift DK2 with the Leap Motion attached in front to facilitate the hand tracking.

3.4 Device Latency

The glove's latency between the UDP server and the vibration actuators was measured with a high-speed camera at 240 frames per second. Each frame was analyzed to determine the time the signal was sent and the time the vibration actuators started swinging. The calculated latency is 25ms $\pm$4.166, which is near the "impact threshold" defined by Jay et al. [15]. This means the user's performance may decrease slightly, but the user stays unaware of the latency. The user would start noticing the latency when the system's latency exceeded the "perception threshold" at 50ms. There was no measurable difference in latency between driving one motor

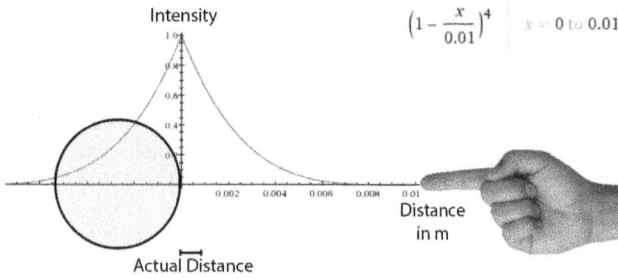

Figure 3: Curve depicting the signal to activate the vibrators and provide vibrotactile feedback as a function of the distance between the hand' representation and the virtual object.

and driving all motors at once because of the buffering settings in our embedded code and our multi-threaded approach on the client side. The presented value should be added to the latency between the hand tracking system and the UDP server to get the end-to-end latency, which makes a total of 43ms, which is still compatible with users' tolerance between sensations corresponding to visual and tactile modalities [24].

3.5 Integration

We integrated the vibrotactile glove into a VR setup using the Unity3D engine and an Oculus Rift DK2 head-mounted display with a Leap motion controller for hand tracking. The tracked pose of the glove can be used to induce vibrotactile feedback, for example, when collisions with virtual objects are detected. All the interaction between the VR software/hardware, the device controller and the vibrotactile device can be depicted in Figure 5.

4. EXPERIMENT

In this section we describe the within-subject experiment conducted to analyze whether the vibrotactile feedback condition, using our proposed device, can reach a similar effect strength as the traditional reference condition, in which tactile stimulation is applied manually with a real-world object as commonly used to induce the elongated-arm illusion in psychological experiments.

4.1 Setup

The virtual environment was designed with the Unity3D engine and deployed on an Intel computer with a Core i7 hexacore at 3.5 GHz CPU with 32 GB RAM and two Nvidia GeForce GTX 980 graphics cards in an SLI array. We used an Oculus Rift DK2 as a fully immersive display and a Leap Motion for hand tracking. In order to guarantee a reliable hand tracking for rested-forearm tasks and according to our experiences, the Leap Motion was tilted down by approximately 13 degrees using a 3D printed mount. Also, noise cancelling headphones were used to increase the immersion and filter out background noises.

As we wanted to make the experience as little irritating for the participants as possible, we chose to create a neutral environment in which a participant's avatar is seated in a desktop setup, looking from the avatar's point of view. This scene recreates the actual constellation of the participant to the chair, table and screen in the physical experimental setup. We ensured that sufficient free space was available between the participant and the screen in order to let them interact with their hands with virtual objects or interfaces 4.

A simple 3D user interface was included so that the participants could advance through the different experimental steps at their own pace. This was carried out via two hand panels, hovering above the table, which could be touched simultaneously to indicate that the participant was ready to be given the next instruction. The virtual room was refined by adding details in the form of furniture, windows, plants and decorative assets to reproduce the impression of the real place uses for the study.

4.2 Tasks

The experiment consisted of three phases. The first phase introduced the participant to the sensation of the vibrotactile feedback. This included being exposed to visual-haptic stimuli on the hands and recognizing basic shapes like a cube or a sphere. In the second phase, the participant's arm was stabilized in a comfortable position on a wedge of foam, and the participant was asked to hold the physical arm still while concentrating on the virtual arm, which was slowly elongated and after reaching twice-and-a-half of its original length was slowly retracted again to its normal length. While doing so, a virtual ball was bouncing on the virtual hand to attract the attention of the participant. The sensation of touch provided by the bouncing ball was assigned randomly and produced according to our two experiment conditions:

1. Through vibrotactile feedback activating the vibrating actuators in the gloves according to the collisions detected between the virtual hand and the virtual bouncing ball (further called *Vibrotactile Condition*).

2. Through a real ball which was bounced synchronously on the participant's real hand by a member of the team, tapping gently the real hand of the participant every time the virtual hand was touched by the virtual bouncing ball (further called *Tapping Condition*).

Once the second phase was finished, the participant was asked to answer a survey regarding the feeling and sensation of having an elongated arm. Also, the participant had to estimate the length of the perceived elongated arm. For the third phase, the participant had to repeat the same procedure as in phase two, but received feedback according to the remaining condition. Again the arm was elongated, but in contrast to phase two, it was threatened with a sudden event occurring when it was fully elongated, which consisted of a heavy object falling from the ceiling. Finally, the fourth phase gathered the same subjective data as the second phase.

4.3 Participants

In a time span of two weeks, 37 participants were recruited through academic mailing lists to test the experiment. All of them gave their informed consent and the study was approved by and conducted in accordance with the local Ethics Committee. The variety of age was between 10 and 54 years old ($M = 28.0$, $SD = 9.1$). The aspect of gender was distributed with 26 male and 11 female participants, mostly computer science students and IT professionals and all of them had normal or corrected vision. Two-thirds of the participants reported no prior experience with experiments involving vibrotactile devices. The mean time per subject, including questionnaires and instructions, was about fifty minutes. After removing a participant who failed the stereoscopic vision test, the analysis employed data of 36 remaining participants.

4.4 Procedure

The participation started with a demographic questionnaire and the Titmus test [28] for stereo-blindness assessment. The participants sat on a static chair in front of a table. Two computers were used for this experiment. The first one was only used for the testing environment and measuring the interpupillary distance (IPD). The

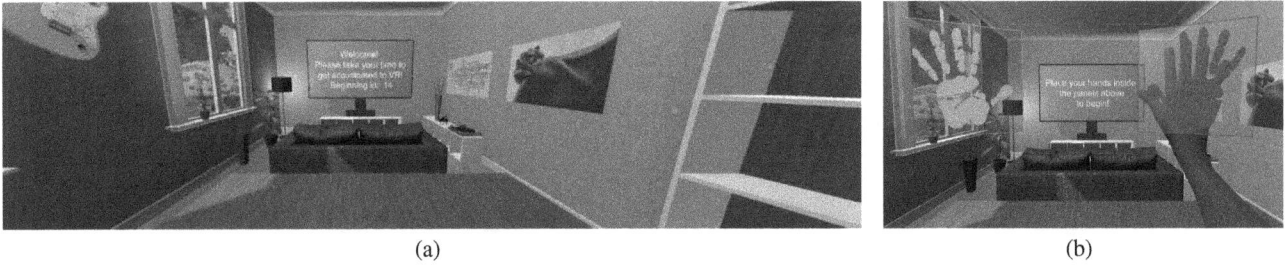

Figure 4: Virtual environment and visual stimuli: (a) Virtual room simulating the real-world environment of the experiment, and (b) view of the 3D user interface used to navigate through the experiment tasks.

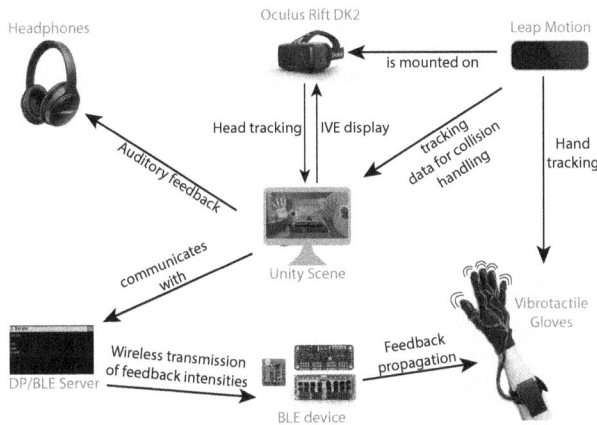

Figure 5: Interaction between the software and hardware components.

Variable	p-value	r	Z
Ownership	0.037	0.247	-2.094
Proprioception	0.007	0.348	-2.653
Comfort	0.300	0.127	-1.078
Variable	**p-value**	**Cohen's d**	**t(df)**
Perceived Length	0.043	0.350	t(35)=-2.101

Table 1: Results for the significance tests.

the evaluation was quantified according to predefined guidelines to score reactions like going back with their head and arms, twitching, faster breathing or comments made by the participants. Lastly, the participants were asked to judge their own feeling and reaction towards having his arm elongated and threatened by the sudden event. Directly after the elongated-arm stimuli (phase two and three), the participants were asked to answer different questions regarding their feeling of ownership of the virtual arm (scale 0 to 10 for the first three questions):

1. Please judge your sense of having an elongated arm.
2. Did the elongated arm feel like a part of your body?
3. How comfortable did you feel with an elongated arm?
4. How long do you think your elongated arm was (in %)?
5. Additional comments (I liked..., I didn't..., because...)

The four dependent variables, defined as *Ownership*, *Proprioception*, *Comfort* and *Perceived Length* from the first four questions, focus on the feeling of body ownership. If the corresponding answers show a trend towards high values, we can conclude that the elongated-arm illusion could be correctly induced [16]. The additional comments were used to comprehend and confirm the participant's answers.

5. RESULTS

The results of the experiment are shown in Figure 6[4]. For the analysis we ran comparative tests to measure the effects of the long-arm illusion induced with our vibrotactile condition in comparison with the traditional tapping condition. We ran a Wilcoxon Signed-Rank test at the 5% significance level for the *Ownership*, *Proprioception* and *Comfort* variables, and a paired t-test at the 5% significance level for the *Perceived Length* variable. Table 1 lists all the calculation details related to the following findings:

---

[4]RDI (raw data, description and inference) plot created with Yarr (github.com/ndphillips/yarr)

monitor was needed to synchronize the stimulation with the real ball at phases two and three. Unused devices (including keyboard, mouse, connector etc.) were moved away to not be a hindrance to the participant during the experiment. The second computer was used only for answering questionnaires. The table was covered with an infrared light absorbing material to support the tracking of the Leap Motion. For the experiment itself, the participants were asked to wear multiple devices: The Oculus Rift DK2 HMD with the attached Leap Motion sensor, the noise-cancelling headphones and the pair of HapGloves (see Figure 2).

For the stimulation with the real ball, a matching-size sphere was glued to a stick, so the member of the research team would not touch and distract the participant. In order to achieve higher accuracy in the *Tapping Condition*, the same experimenter performed all the tapping actions during the whole experiment. In addition, training sessions were conducted apriori to reduce the variance on timing and intensity, thus achieving a synchronous and believable movement comparable to the *Vibrotactile Condition* that consistently matches the visual feedback.

During and after the experiment, the results were collected in three different ways. First, a questionnaire was answered by the participant. As a second result, an attending member of the research team subjectively evaluated the reaction to the sudden event of a heavy object falling from the ceiling on a scale from 0 to 10 (being 10 the highest score), according to reflex reactions of the participant's body avoiding the threat and offering insights about the achieved sense of body ownership. To avoid experimenter bias,

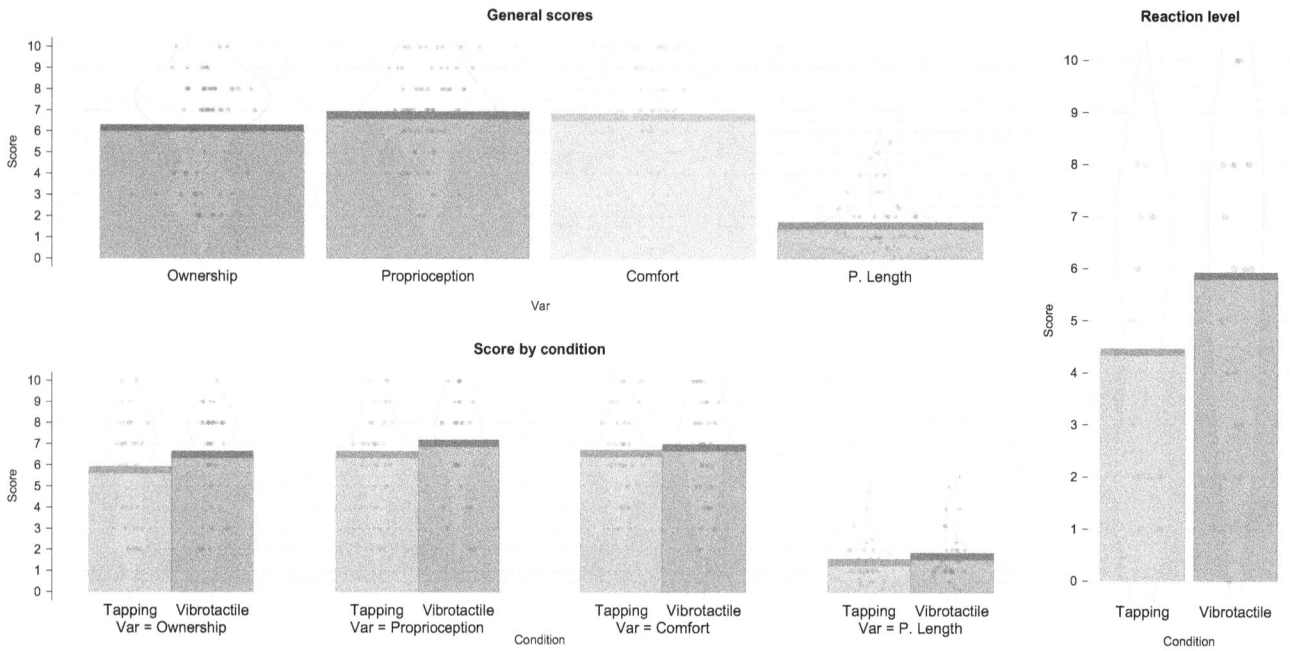

Figure 6: Plot corresponding to the dependent variables (ownership, proprioception, comfort and perceived length) showing (top) the general scores, (bottom) the scores ranked by experiment condition, and (right) the reaction levels.

- We found a significant influence of the elongated arm on **ownership** for the *Tapping Condition* (M=6.5, SD=2.171) and the *Vibrotactile Condition* (M=7.028, SD=2.210), reporting an effect of medium size (0.247).

- We found a significant influence of the elongated arm on **proprioception** for the *Tapping Condition* (M=5.778, SD=2.520) and the *Vibrotactile Condition* (M=6.50, SD=2.299), reporting an effect of medium size (0.348).

- We found no significant influence on the **comfort** variable for the *Tapping Condition* (M=6.555, SD=2.104) and the *Vibrotactile Condition* (M=6.833, SD=2.236).

- We found a significant effect of the elongated arm on the **perceived length** for the *Tapping Condition* (M=142%, SD=0.991) and the *Vibrotactile Condition* (M=170%, SD=1.267), the effect size is 0.350, with a standardized mean confidence interval of [-0.554; 0.010].

5.1 Subject Reaction

As described above, to draw further conclusions regarding the body ownership, a sudden event was presented to the participants at the end of the third phase. While doing the experiment, every participant (if previously agreed) was filmed to offer the possibility to recapture missed reactions during the study reviewing the video footage. The shown reactions were put into a scale from 0 to 10. If the participant did not show any signs of reaction, the value equals 0. If the participant showed a full reaction, like trying to protect his arm or showing full surprise reactions, like heavy breathing, then the value equals 10. The team did not only look at the twitching of the arm, but also included the surprise and fear reactions like laughing anxiously into the value. The presented reactions were noted as a comment to differentiate the values. The values of this subjective variable, indicate that almost 50% of the participants reacted

noticeably to the sudden event (M=5.25, SD=2.872), while the *Tapping Condition* (M=4.4, SD=2.746) presented a lower reaction level than the *Vibrotactile Condition* (M=5.857, SD=2.869).

5.2 Simulator Sickness

Although the participants kept a seated position during the experiment and were instructed to look forward avoiding fast head movements to reduce nausea among other simulator effects, we asked the participants to answer the Simulator Sickness Questionnaire (SSQ) [23] before and after the experiment. We analyzed the data with a non-parametric Wilcoxon Signed-Rank test at the 5% significance level. There are no significant increases in the condition of the participants between before (M=0.187, SD=0.143) and after the experiment (M=0.131, SD=0.065).

5.3 Presence

The participants had to judge their level of presence on the basis of the Slater-Usoh-Steed presence questionnaire [32] after the experiment (M=4.828, SD=0.259) indicating a good sense of presence in addition to positive comments from some participants about the quality of the VR experience.

6. DISCUSSION

The results of the study indicate that the elongated-arm illusion was produced under both experimental conditions, which shows that the brief phases of matching visual-vibrotactile feedback could induce a compelling illusion. Moreover, the results show significant differences for the variables *ownership*, *proprioception* and *perceived length* between the conditions (see Figure 6), slightly benefiting the *Vibrotactile Condition*. This effect is most noticeable on the *perceived length*, showing a higher value by approximately 20% in this condition (although, as the virtual arm was elongated to double the starting size, most participants underestimated the length of the elongated arm in both conditions). The same trend is also present in the subject reaction measurements, where the *Vibrotactile Condition* resulted in behavior more closely matching natural threat responses with high body ownership.

We believe that an explanation of these differences is that our low-latency vibrotactile stimulus could be presented with less sensory discrepancy than the manually synchronized tapping. Although several efforts were made to provide high accuracy in the manual stimulation, the higher scores on the *Vibrotactile Condition* might be attributed to this discrepancy. In order to remove this confounding factor in our next iteration, we will track the position of the physical ball (i.e. IR-LED marker tracking) and transfer this onto the virtual ball in our 3D scene. Going further, other question could also be addressed regarding the vibrotactile device: ¿Could non-realistic (in terms of intensity) or non-synchronous feedback still be effective to support the body-transfer illusion in VR?

It is an interesting finding that the vibrotactile feedback was not just comparable to haptic feedback with a real ball in terms of the body-transfer illusion in this experiment, but even supported the illusion. Moreover, the automatic contact detection and feedback generation in the Unity3D implementation allows us to induce or reinforce such body-transfer illusions with brief phases of synchronized visual-tactile feedback at any time during a VR experience, without the need for a trained operator standing by to provide manual tapping feedback. We believe that this will allow us to reach similar effects in other illusions as well, such as the rubber-hand illusion [4]. Informal preliminary testing being conducted at our laboratory seems to support this impression.

Regarding our device, we are considering different technologies and techniques to improve the feedback, like haptic cues or dynamic vibration patterns [2]. Although we had a shape-recognition task to familiarize the participants with our device, it is still necessary to integrate more sensors and actuators to enable the feeling of textures, weight and detailed shapes. For example, recent studies focused on electro-tactile devices [13] and reported good results in terms of precision and performance for grasping tasks using tactors, which could offer a good alternative to address some issues related to location acuity and location sensitivity in order to implement effective shape-recognition techniques. In the same way, our experiment relied on the hand tracking provided by the Leap Motion sensor, but an approach in combination with optical LED marker tracking might further improve the device.

7. CONCLUSION AND FUTURE WORK

In this paper, we presented a technology framework featuring a device able to provide brief phases of vibrotactile feedback synchronized at low latency with visual feedback for the goal to enable and simplify the process to induce and reinforce body-transfer illusions in VR. We provided details on the implementation of the system including the concept of TCPs for accurate feedback generation, and we provided evidence from an experiment showing that the automatic visual-vibrotactile feedback can be used to induce a similar elongated-arm illusion as that which traditionally requires an operator to be present in order to stimulate the user with synchronized visual-haptic tapping feedback. Our results suggest that the approach may be transferred to other body illusions as well, thus providing the means to improve VR experiences of users in a variety of application fields.

In future work, we plan to extend the capabilities of the Hap-Glove with independent haptic drivers[5] for the actuators to offer improved reactive tactile feedback and richer vibration patterns, migrating from the current LRA technology to piezo-electric ac-

tuators, which, among other benefits, will provide wide-range and simultaneous variations in frequency and amplitude. For the glove itself, we plan to test other materials, to support the contact between the skin and the actuators. Also, in order to sense subtle user reactions, we plan to measure skin conductance as a stress response [3], with the integration of galvanic skin response (GSR) sensors [33] and include fingertip heart rate monitors. The haptic device will be made available as an open-source solution, allowing the interested audience to integrate it into their own projects.

Finally, further work will be mainly focused in the integration of other perceptual illusions with the purpose of use the gained experience in the creation of perceptually inspired user interfaces for VR.

8. ACKNOWLEDGMENTS

This work was partly supported by grants from the Deutsche Forschungsgemeinschaft.

9. REFERENCES

[1] M. Achibet, A. Girard, A. Talvas, M. Marchal, and A. Lécuyer. Elastic-arm: Human-scale passive haptic feedback for augmenting interaction and perception in virtual environments. In *IEEE Virtual Reality (VR)*, pages 63–68, March 2015.

[2] O. Ariza, P. Lubos, F. Steinicke, and G. Bruder. Ring-shaped haptic device with vibrotactile feedback patterns to support natural spatial interaction. In *Proceedings of the 25th International Conference on Artificial Reality and Telexistence and 20th Eurographics Symposium on Virtual Environments*, ICAT - EGVE '15, pages 175–181, Aire-la-Ville, Switzerland, Switzerland, 2015. Eurographics Association.

[3] K. C. Armel and V. S. Ramachandran. Projecting sensations to external objects: evidence from skin conductance response. *Proceedings of the Royal Society of London B: Biological Sciences*, 270(1523):1499–1506, 2003.

[4] M. Botvinick and J. Cohen. Rubber hands 'feel' touch that eyes see. *Nature*, 391(6669):756–756, Feb. 1998.

[5] S. Choi and K. J. Kuchenbecker. Vibrotactile display: Perception, technology, and applications. *Proceedings of the IEEE*, 101(9):2093–2104, Sept 2013.

[6] C. Cruz-Neira, D. J. Sandin, T. A. DeFanti, R. V. Kenyon, and J. C. Hart. The cave: audio visual experience automatic virtual environment. *Communications of the ACM*, 35(6):64–73, 1992.

[7] T. Debus, T.-J. Jang, P. Dupont, and R. Howe. Multi-channel vibrotactile display for teleoperated assembly. In *Proceedings of the 2002 IEEE International Conference on Robotics and Automation*, pages 592–597, 2002.

[8] H. H. Ehrsson, C. Spence, and R. E. Passingham. That's my hand! activity in premotor cortex reflects feeling of ownership of a limb. *Science*, 305(5685):875–877, 2004.

[9] E. Giannopoulos, A. Pomés, and M. Slater. Touching the void: exploring virtual objects through a vibrotactile glove. *The International Journal of Virtual Reality*, 11(2):19–24, 2012.

[10] M. S. A. Graziano. Where is my arm? The relative role of vision and proprioception in the neuronal representation of limb position. *Proceedings of the National Academy of Sciences of the United States of America*, 96(18):10418–10421, Aug. 1999.

---

[5] http://www.ti.com/product/DRV2667

[11] C. Heeter. Reflections on real presence by a virtual person. *Presence: Teleoperators and Virtual Environments*, 12(4):335–345, 2003.

[12] A. Hein and M. Brell. contact - a vibrotactile display for computer aided surgery. In *Second Joint EuroHaptics Conference and Symposium on Haptic Interfaces for Virtual Environment and Teleoperator Systems (WHC'07)*, pages 531–536, March 2007.

[13] J. Hummel, J. Dodiya, L. Eckardt, R. Wolff, A. Gerndt, and T. Kuhlen. A lightweight electrotactile feedback device to improve grasping in immersive virtual environments. In *Proceedings of IEEE Virtual Reality Conference*, 2016.

[14] A. Israr and I. Poupyrev. Tactile brush: Drawing on skin with a tactile grid display. In *Proceedings of the SIGCHI Conference on Human Factors in Computing Systems*, CHI '11, pages 2019–2028, New York, NY, USA, 2011. ACM.

[15] C. Jay, M. Glencross, and R. Hubbold. Modeling the effects of delayed haptic and visual feedback in a collaborative virtual environment. *ACM Transaction Computer-Human Interaction*, 14(2):8, Aug. 2007.

[16] K. Kilteni, J.-M. Normand, M. V. Sanchez-Vives, and M. Slater. Extending body space in immersive virtual reality: A very long arm illusion. *PLoS ONE*, 7(7):1–15, 07 2012.

[17] J. Kramer. Force feedback and textures simulating interface device, Feb. 2 1993. US Patent 5,184,319.

[18] S. Kuroki, H. Kajimoto, H. Nii, N. Kawakami, and S. Tachi. Proposal for tactile sense presentation that combines electrical and mechanical stimulus. In *WHC*, pages 121–126, March 2007.

[19] J. Martínez, A. García, M. Oliver, J. P. Molina, and P. González. Identifying virtual 3d geometric shapes with a vibrotactile glove. *IEEE Computer Graphics and Applications*, 36(1):42–51, Jan 2016.

[20] J. Martínez, D. Martínez, J. P. Molina, P. González, and A. García. Comparison of force and vibrotactile feedback with direct stimulation for texture recognition. In *Cyberworlds (CW), International Conference on*, pages 62–68, Oct 2011.

[21] Y. Muramatsu, M. Niitsuma, and T. Thomessen. Perception of tactile sensation using vibrotactile glove interface. In *Cognitive Infocommunications (CogInfoCom), 2012 IEEE 3rd International Conference on*, pages 621–626, Dec 2012.

[22] V. I. Petkova and H. H. Ehrsson. If I Were You: Perceptual Illusion of Body Swapping. *PLoS ONE*, 3(12):1–9, 12 2008.

[23] K. Robert, L. Norman, B. Kevin, and L. Michael. Simulator Sickness Questionnaire: An Enhanced Method for Quantifying Simulator Sickness. *The International Journal of Aviation Psychology*, pages 203–220, 1993.

[24] Z. Shi, H. Zou, M. Rank, L. Chen, S. Hirche, and H. J. Muller. Effects of packet loss and latency on the temporal discrimination of visual-haptic events. *IEEE Transactions on Haptics*, pages 28–36, 2010.

[25] M. Slater and A. Steed. A Virtual Presence Counter. *Presence: Teleoperators and Virtual Environments*, 9(5):413–434, Oct. 2000.

[26] M. Slater, A. Steed, J. McCarthy, and F. Maringelli. The Influence of Body Movement on Subjective Presence in Virtual Environments. *Human Factors and Ergonomics Society*, 40(3):469–477, Sept. 1998.

[27] M. Solazzi, A. Frisoli, and M. Bergamasco. Design of a novel finger haptic interface for contact and orientation display. In *IEEE Haptics Symposium*, pages 129–132, March 2010.

[28] W. W. Somers and M. J. Hamilton. Estimation of the stereoscopic threshold utilizing perceived depth. *Ophthalmic and Physiological Optics*, 4(3):245–250, 1984.

[29] B. Spanlang, J.-M. Normand, D. Borland, K. Kilteni, E. Giannopoulos, A. Pomés, M. González-Franco, D. Pérez-Marcos, J. Arroyo-Palacios, X. N. Muncunill, and M. Slater. How to build an embodiment lab: Achieving body representation illusions in virtual reality. *Frontiers in Robotics and AI*, 1(9), 2014.

[30] B. Stark, T. Carlstedt, R. G. Hallin, and M. Risling. Distribution of human pacinian corpuscles in the hand: A cadaver study. *Journal of Hand Surgery (British and European Volume)*, 23(3):370–372, 1998.

[31] M. Tsakiris and P. Haggard. The rubber hand illusion revisited: visuotactile integration and self-attribution. *Journal of experimental psychology. Human perception and performance*, 31(1):80–91, Feb. 2005.

[32] M. Usoh, E. Catena, S. Arman, and M. Slater. Using presence questionnaires in reality. *Presence: Teleoperation Virtual Environments*, pages 497–503, 2000.

[33] Y. Yuan and A. Steed. Is the rubber hand illusion induced by immersive virtual reality? In *2010 IEEE Virtual Reality Conference (VR)*, pages 95–102, March 2010.

SHIFT-Sliding and DEPTH-POP for 3D Positioning

Junwei Sun, Wolfgang Stuerzlinger
School of Interactive Arts + Technology
Simon Fraser University, Vancouver, Canada
junweis@sfu.ca, http://ws.iat.sfu.ca

Dmitri Shuralyov
Department of EECS
York University, Toronto, Canada
shurcool@gmail.com

Figure 1. The left image rows illustrate SHIFT-Sliding. With this technique the user can lift an object off a surface to float (top row). The object reverts to sliding upon collision. Alternatively, the user can push the object into another (bottom). The object "pops" to the front to avoid being invisible. The middle image shows object height visualization during SHIFT-Sliding. The right image illustrates DEPTH-POP, with a *stationary* cursor. We can place the object into all four positions using up/down mouse wheel actions.

ABSTRACT

Moving objects is an important task in 3D user interfaces. We describe two new techniques for 3D positioning, designed for a mouse, but usable with other input devices. The techniques enable rapid, yet easy-to-use positioning of objects in 3D scenes. With sliding, the object follows the cursor and moves on the surfaces of the scene. Our techniques enable precise positioning of constrained objects. Sliding assumes that *by default* objects stay in contact with the scene's front surfaces, are always at least partially visible, and do not interpenetrate other objects. With our new SHIFT-Sliding method the user can override these default assumptions and lift objects into the air or make them collide with other objects. SHIFT-Sliding uses the local coordinate system of the surface that the object was last in contact with, which is a new form of context-dependent manipulation. We also present DEPTH-POP, which maps mouse wheel actions to all object positions along the mouse ray, where the object meets the default assumptions for sliding. For efficiency, both methods use frame buffer techniques. Two user studies show that the new techniques significantly speed up common 3D positioning tasks.

Keywords

3D object manipulation; constraints; frame buffer, layers.

1. INTRODUCTION

In 3D virtual environments, users often encounter the need to arrange a scene with numerous objects. Here we only deal with the

SUI '16, October 15 - 16, 2016, Tokyo, Japan
Copyright is held by the owner/author(s). Publication rights licensed to ACM.
ACM 978-1-4503-4068-7/16/10...$15.00
DOI: http://dx.doi.org/10.1145/2983310.2985748

3D manipulation of rigid objects. Posing a 3D rigid object, *i.e.*, manipulating the position and orientation of an object, is a basic task in 3D user interfaces. This task can be time-consuming as 6 degrees of freedom (6DOFs) have to be controlled: 3 DOFs for translation along three axes and 3 DOFs for rotation around three axes. Some techniques use 3- or 6DOF input devices for object manipulation, based on a one-to-one mapping of input and object movement. For such tasks, research has shown that 3DOF input devices outperform 2D devices in some contexts [18][26]. Yet, most users are more familiar with the mouse. Also, in some contexts 2D input is the better choice [5]. As evident by its pervasive use in 3D computer aided design (CAD) applications, the mouse has proven to be a reliable and accurate input device, despite the lack of the ability to directly manipulate a third DOF.

To compensate for this shortcoming, various mappings of 2D mouse input to 3D operations have been proposed. CAD user interfaces use a local coordinate system to assist object movement, typically via 3D widgets [34] controlled with the mouse. However, the orientation of this coordinate system is typically independent of other objects. Still, if one moves objects in the real world, their positions also depend on the surfaces of other objects. Sliding, *e.g.*, [7][28], links mouse movement directly to object movement and moves an object on the surface behind it, *i.e.*, uses the contact of the object with that surface. This effectively corresponds to manipulation in a *view* coordinate system, independent of the coordinate system of the object. Sliding typically assumes contact and non-collision for manipulated objects. With our enhanced SHIFT-Sliding method we break the contact/non-collision limitation of basic sliding and map manipulation based on the coordinate system of the surface that the object was last in contact with, which forms a new form of context-dependent manipulation.

When multiple surfaces are visible in the same area of a scene, there is an ambiguity in the mapping of 2D input to 3D position, *e.g.*, as the manipulated object could be placed on the table or the floor visible behind it. To address this ambiguity, we introduce a new DEPTH-POP method, which enables efficient control of object position in depth. For this, we map discrete mouse wheel actions to object movement in depth, which puts the object at all those positions along the mouse ray, where contact and non-collision assumptions are met.

We first review relevant previous object manipulation work. Then we discuss the overall design space and introduce our new interaction methods. In the following, we present implementation details and describe our user studies. Finally, we discuss the results and mention potential future work.

2. RELATED WORK

There has been substantial research in the field of object manipulation in 3D user interfaces.

Many mappings of 3- or 6DOF input device movements to object manipulation have been proposed. Ware *et al.* [41] introduced the bat, a 6DOF device with a natural one-to-one mapping. Hachet *et al.* [12] introduced the 6DOF Control Action Table, designed for immersive large display environments. The GlobeFish and GlobeMouse techniques [9] used a 3DOF trackball for 3D manipulation. Bérard *et al.* [5] compared the mouse with three 3DOF input devices in a 3D placement task and identified the mouse superior for accurate placement. Vuibert *et al.* [40] compared contactless mid-air manipulation with a Phantom and found mid-air manipulation faster but less accurate. Masliah *et al.* [25] studied the allocation of control in 6DOF docking and identified that rotational and translational DOFs are controlled separately. All techniques mentioned in this paragraph require 3D input devices, which currently do not afford the level of accuracy and precision of a modern mouse.

Many touch-based 3D manipulation techniques have been developed. Hancock *et al.*'s [13] multi-touch techniques provide 3D interaction within limited depth. Rotate' N Translate (RNT) [22] offers integrated control of translation and rotation through a single touch-point. Reisman *et al.* [30] presented a screen-space method that provides direct 2D and 3D control. Martinet *et al.* [23] proposed two multi-touch techniques. Users preferred the Z-technique, which permits depth positioning. A later improvement separated translation and rotation [24]. Herrlich *et al.* [16] presented two techniques that integrate translation and rotation. Au *et al.* [1] presented a set of multi-touch gestures for constrained 3D manipulation. In general, the input mappings for touch-based 3D methods require learning and do not support accurate manipulation.

Another approach to 3D manipulation is based on widgets [8][34], which encapsulate 3D geometry and behavior. Such widgets are now prevalent in 3D CAD software. Mine *et al.* [27] presented hand-held widgets, *i.e.*, 3D objects with geometry and behavior that appear in the user's virtual hand. Schmidt *et al.* [32] presented a system that automatically aligned widgets to axes and planes determined by a users' stroke.

Some 3D manipulation systems use 2D input devices, typically the mouse. Bier [6] proposed snap-dragging, which snaps the 3D cursor to object features close to the cursor using a gravity function. Van Emmerik [37] proposed a technique where the user can perform 3D transformations in a local coordinate system through control points. Venolia [38] presented "tail-dragging", where the user drags an object as it were attached to a rope. With a "snap-to" functionality, other objects also attract the manipulated object. Kitamura *et al.* [21] proposed a "magnetic metaphor" for object manipulation, which aims to simulate physical behaviors, including non-penetration. In most of these techniques, the local coordinate system for object movement must be explicitly controlled by the user.

Building on Object Associations [7], Oh *et al.* [28] presented a sliding algorithm, where the object follows the cursor position directly and slides on any surface behind it, *i.e.*, the moving object always stays attached to other objects. This form of sliding creates associations automatically, and these associations are not limited to predefined horizontally or vertically aligned surfaces. Compared to click-to-place methods, *e.g.*, [7], sliding provides better visual feedback as the result of a (potential) placement is continuously visible. For targets in contact, Oh *et al.* compared sliding with axis-widgets and found that sliding is significantly more efficient for novices. Yet, Oh *et al.*'s sliding method lacks direct access to object movement in the third DOF. The authors identified that for some tasks users have to slide an object on a sequence of surfaces to reach a desired "layer" in depth, which is not always easy to understand, see Figure 3.

2.1 Contributions

The main contributions we present here are:
- SHIFT-Sliding, which generalizes sliding to support floating and interpenetrating objects.
- A new method to map 2D input to 3D object translation based on the coordinate system of the surface that the object was last in contact with.
- A new DEPTH-POP interaction method that addresses the inherent depth ambiguity in sliding algorithms.
- Comparative evaluations of the new techniques.

3. SYSTEM AND INTERACTION DESIGN

In this section, we discuss the fundamental assumptions that our new object manipulation techniques build on. We target novice users without CAD knowledge. We focus on a desktop-based user interface with a mouse and a keyboard, as this provides high performance in both speed and accuracy. A mouse also helps to keep our system easy to learn and use by novices, as many are used to this interaction device. Yet, the interaction for DEPTH-POP and SHIFT-Sliding is so simple and direct, that it could even be applied to touchscreens, as mentioned in the discussion section.

3.1 Design Assumptions

We use a single perspective view, as this corresponds best to how novices are usually presented with 3D content [42]. We do not use stereo, as perspective and occlusion are usually sufficient to accurately judge an object's 3D position and visibility [39]. In our system, we assume that objects are *by default* in contact with other objects and do not interpenetrate them. Moreover, we choose not to enable manipulation of objects when they are invisible. Here, we detail the reasoning behind our design assumptions.

1) The manipulated object stays by default in contact with the rest of the scene. As recognized by Teather *et al.* [36] and Stuerzlinger *et al.* [35], floating objects are exceptional on our planet, as (almost) all objects are in contact with other objects in the real world. Also, the exact position of a floating object is harder to perceive accurately, as there are fewer references to judge against. Such objects are also harder to manipulate because more DOFs need to be controlled [20]. In the *default* sliding mode of our system, whenever an object would float, we automatically put the object back into contact with the first surface behind it. With our new SHIFT-Sliding method, we enable the user to override this. When there is nothing behind an object, it will slide parallel to the screen until something appears behind it.

2) The manipulated object does not interpenetrate the scene by default. In the real world, objects do not interpenetrate each other without explicit actions, such as drilling a hole. To avoid unwanted collisions, we choose to avoid interpenetration *by default*. When needed, we permit the user to force an object "into" another with SHIFT-Sliding.

3) The manipulated object is always at least partially visible to the user. Without other forms of feedback (such as haptics) an invisible object cannot be manipulated with precision with normal input devices. Moreover, a common issue in many 3D systems is that an object can become "lost" behind or inside other objects, which then forces the user to "find" it again through navigation. In our system and whenever an object would become completely invisible, we automatically bring the object to a position where it is visible.

When the user selects an object and manipulates it with standard sliding, the object will always remain in positions (and poses) where all three assumptions are met. Beyond the three scene-related assumptions above, we also assume that the scene is rendered as filled polygons. A wireframe representation of objects introduces ambiguities, as it does not explicitly define the enclosed surfaces. This is often difficult to understand for novices. Similarly, we also exclude volumetric content, such as a 3D brain scan.

3.2 Basic Sliding

Sliding [28] maps object movement so that the manipulated object moves along the surface behind it that it is currently in contact with. We use the normal vector at the contact point to determine the sliding plane. With this contact constraint, we can directly map 2D motions of the mouse cursor to 3D movement of the object. Figure 2 illustrates sliding. When the user selects an object (at position A), we record the intersection of the mouse ray on the object as the start point. We identify the normal vector at the contact point on surface 1 via the frame buffer. The start point and the normal vector define the sliding plane. The intersection of a new mouse ray and the sliding plane becomes the end point of the object translation. By moving the mouse cursor, the user then effectively translates the object parallel to the sliding plane. We examine the situation with multiple contacts in different planes in the discussion section.

When the user slides the object to position B in Figure 2, any further upwards movement would cause the object to float. Here, basic sliding snaps the object back to the next surface behind it, to position C on surface 2, while keeping the object under the mouse cursor. The new contact point provides a new normal vector for a new sliding plane. Then the user can slide the object on surface 2, to positions such as D. If the user now moves the mouse back down, the object can reach position E, where it is still partially visible from the camera. Yet, if the user slides the object from E further downwards, the object would become invisible to the user. Here, we *"pop" the object to the front, i.e.*, bring it to a position below (and a bit to the left of) B, in contact with surface 1. With this method we keep the mouse cursor at the same point on the object throughout, as an additional cue for object position, giving the user also a better understanding of the 3D object movement. To highlight the fact that the object is in contact, we render a semi-transparent rectangle at the contact surface.

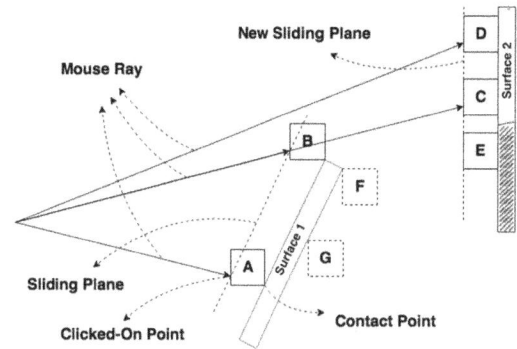

Figure 2. Illustration of sliding movements for an object across the front surfaces of two objects with an upwards mouse movement (positions A-D). The shaded part of surface 2 is occluded by surface 1. Position E can only be reached from C with a downwards mouse movement. Positions F and G cannot be reached from the current viewpoint, see text.

When dragging an object along a surface nearly aligned with the view direction close to the horizon, it can easily disappear into the distance, since a small mouse movement can cause a dramatic object movement in 3D. To deal with this, we perform an occlusion test for every frame and bring the object to the front whenever it becomes completely invisible — even if this causes the object to slide on another surface. When there is no surface behind the object, we keep the object sliding parallel to the screen and inside the camera frustum (even if the projection of the object is very small). With this, the user can never lose sight of the moving object.

In our system, the user can slide objects on invisible surfaces, such as a portion of the surface 2 in Figure 2 that is hidden by surface 1 (near E). To keep the interaction intuitive, we only permit sliding on surfaces facing the user. If we were to enable sliding on back-faces, this would create inappropriate mappings. Consider that the user slides from A to B with an *upwards* movement of the cursor along surface 1 in Figure 2. To reach position F, the cursor movement would then need to be mapped to a *downwards* motion of the mouse, which is indistinguishable from a movement back towards A. Thus, a better option is to snap the object to a position beyond surface 1 and slide the object on surface 2.

Object sliding maps mouse input to 3D object motions, which automatically defines an appropriate local movement plane. This also guarantees that the cursor and object always stay aligned, regardless of the surface involved. The new SHIFT-Sliding technique *generalizes* sliding to situations where objects float or interpenetrate. Our new DEPTH-POP technique gives the user discrete control over object depth relative to the camera with a contact assumption.

4. SHIFT-SLIDING

Basic sliding keeps the object in contact with the scene and automatically chooses the local sliding plane for the object. For some use cases, such as 3D game design or animation, there are scenarios where some objects are floating. Imagine a car in an action sequence or a bouncing ball in a 3D game. Basic sliding cannot deal with those situations effectively. With SHIFT-Sliding, users can break the assumptions of contact or non-collision. We still pop the object to front if it would become invisible to ensure accurate manipulation and for consistency.

While manipulating an object, the user can move the object *orthogonal* to the sliding plane by pressing the SHIFT key. If the user then "pulls" the object away from the surface, this will cause the object to float, see Figure 1. When the user releases the SHIFT key (with the mouse button still held down), the object will then keep sliding on a plane defined by the initial normal vector. In this state, the floating check is temporarily disabled. To provide feedback, we highlight the moving object in a different color in SHIFT mode. When the floating object collides, we transition the object back into sliding mode and start sliding on the collider surface.

If the user lifts an object up and releases the mouse button, the object floats and is highlighted accordingly. While the object is still highlighted, the user can later "re-capture" the object with a click, is then back in SHIFT-sliding mode, and can move the object on the previous sliding plane. If a floating object is no longer highlighted, it will snap back to a surface when clicked and then start sliding. Alternatively, with another SHIFT-click, the user can move the object up or down orthogonal to the sliding plane. This is an improvement over Object Associations [7], where breaking an association leads only to a three-axis manipulation mode.

If the user "pushes" the object into a surface while pressing the SHIFT key, the object will interpenetrate that surface. When the user releases the SHIFT key, the object will then keep sliding on the plane defined by the original normal vector, inside the surface, still maintaining the visibility assumption. We temporarily disable the collision check for objects pushed into a surface.

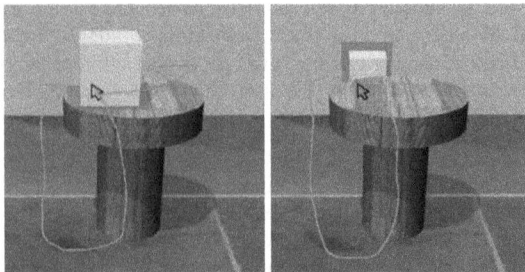

Figure 3. With sliding one can move between the two object positions by following one of the blue mouse paths. For the right path in the left image, the object snaps to the wall when leaving the table. With DEPTH-POP the user can directly transition with a *single* mouse-wheel action, without moving the cursor.

5. DEPTH-POP

Moving the object in the 3rd dimension with a 2D input device involves indirect mappings. With sliding, previous work has observed that users can move objects along the "shortest continuous path across visible surfaces," through long mouse motions [28]. For example, in Figure 3 and to move an object from the wall to the table top, novices will typically slide the object along the wall, the table leg and then onto the table surface [28]. With DEPTH-POP, the user can accomplish the same result with a *single* mouse wheel action, which makes manipulation more direct. To achieve the same result, Object Associations [7] or other "click-to-place" algorithms require the user to first move the object away and then into the right place, which requires a minimum of two move operations.

Hinckley *et al.* [17] used discrete cycling to select multiple objects along a mouse ray, but did not use this for positioning an object in 3D. LayerPaint [10] permits drawing continuous strokes even on occluded regions in multi-layer scenes through automatic depth determination. Igarashi *et al.* [19] presented layer swap, which allows the user to directly modify the depth order of the top two layers by clicking on a 3D layered object. They also presented

layer-aware dragging. While dragging an object, the user can toggle between drag-over and drag-under modes with the SHIFT key and the system will adjust the object's depth automatically.

Extending these works, we map the choice of 3D object position to scroll wheel actions, whenever the user is dragging/sliding an object with the left button. More specifically, with each wheel action our new DEPTH-POP technique selects the next, respectively previous, element from the set of 3D positions along the mouse ray that match our assumptions (contact, non-collision, visible). We map front and back movement of the mouse wheel to "push-to-back" respectively "pop-to-front". Together with sliding, this enables users to move objects in all three dimensions directly and independently.

5.1 Push-to-Back/Pop-to-Front

Moving the mouse wheel away from/towards the user triggers a push-to-back/pop-to-front event, *e.g.*, between position B and C in Figure 2. With push-to-back the object is moved to the next possible position further away from the camera that satisfies all three main design assumptions. For each pop-to-front event, the object is moved to the next position closer to the camera again maintaining the design assumptions. We also call pop-to-front whenever the object becomes completely occluded, *i.e.*, invisible.

5.2 Audio Feedback

For DEPTH-POP actions, we use different auditory cues to indicate a successful DEPTH-POP or a failed attempt to give the user feedback. Examples of infeasible actions are an object that is already the foremost visible object and thus cannot be pulled closer or an object to be pushed further away but with nothing behind it.

5.3 Orthographic vs. Perspective Projection

We display the 3D scene in perspective and use that camera also for visibility detection. After all, when all pixels of the selected object are invisible, the user cannot see and manipulate it with precision. If our system detects this situation, we call pop-to-front.

When we move the object along the mouse ray to bring an object closer or further away we use an orthographic camera in the DEPTH-POP algorithm. This design decision makes a functional difference for the user, as it guarantees that the point on the selected object remains stable underneath the mouse cursor at all times, which yields a better interaction mapping. After all, if the cursor position on the object shifts/changes during sliding, object movement becomes less predictable, and thus less precise. See Figure 4. The DEPTH-POP algorithm (see the appendix) computes a distance in depth, which corresponds to the distance that the object should move along the mouse ray. If we were to use a perspective camera, the minimum difference in depth occurs along various rays (a different one for each pixel), rather than a specific direction. Thus the smallest perspective depth difference is different from the mouse ray direction, which in turn would violate the static cursor property. Orthographic projection does not suffer from this ambiguity. Also, linear movements in orthographic projection correspond better to how an object moves in 3D. Thus, we set up an orthographic camera in the direction of the mouse ray and use the frame buffer of this camera for all computations and DEPTH-POP.

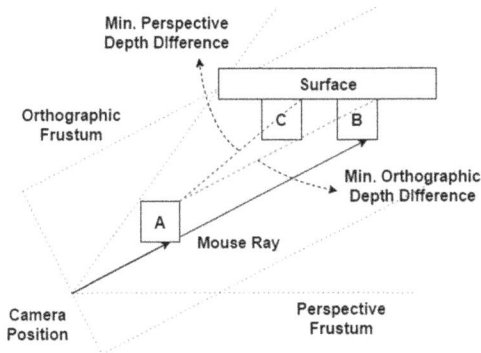

Figure 4. Perspective vs. orthographic projection. In orthographic projection, an object at position A will be popped to B where the minimum depth difference occurs (red dashed line), keeping the cursor stable. In perspective, the smallest depth difference (blue dashed line) would move the object to C, violating the static cursor property.

6. IMPLEMENTATION

Here we discuss implementation details of our system. We built our system in the Unity game engine. We use a desktop computer with 3.5 GHz i7 processor, 16 GB of memory, and two NVIDIA GeForce GTX 560 SLI graphics cards. We use a mouse and a keyboard as input devices.

6.1 Frame Buffer vs. Geometry

We exploit the computing power of GPUs and use the frame buffer for most of the computations. This also enables us to slide objects on more complex "surfaces", including even point clouds with normal vectors. Geometry-based methods would suffer from decreased performance with complex objects and surfaces. To support non-convex geometries, we use depth peeling [4] to compute all depth values for the hidden layers of the scene. With depth peeling, each unique depth layer in the scene is extracted, and the layers are enumerated in depth-sorted order. As in other systems, a left mouse down selects the closest object along the mouse ray. We highlight the selected object with a different color during sliding.

6.2 Floating and Collision Checks

When the user selects an object that is not in contact with a surface, or when an object slides off a surface, we need to push the object back to force it into contact with the scene. When the object collides with the scene, we pull the object front to resolve the collision.

After floating and/or collision is resolved, we slide the object as previously described. Our floating and collision checks guarantee that the object is always in contact with the scene, and that the sliding plane changes seamlessly.

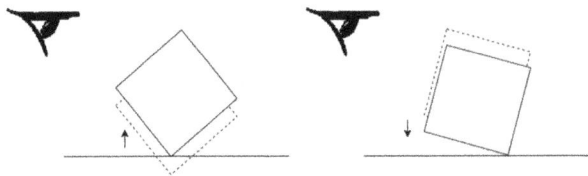

Figure 5. During rotation, an object is always kept in contact with the surface. To ensure contact, we move the object in the direction of the (contact) normal vector to resolve floating and collision situations.

6.3 Contact-Based Object Rotation

We map 3D rotation around the objects' center to the right mouse button with the two-axis valuator method [3] and wheel operation in this state to rotation in the 3rd dimension [33]. If the object is in contact at the start, we maintain all our design assumptions during rotation. If the object rotates to a pose where it would float or collide, we resolve it by moving the object in the direction of the normal vector of the (last known) contact. See Figure 5.

7. EVALUATION

We first evaluated the technical performance of our system. The system runs stably at 60 fps for scenes with almost a million polygons. The user can slide objects on various surfaces, including concave surfaces and point clouds. For the scenes shown on the right in Figure 6, a single DEPTH-POP operation takes less than 20 ms. We conducted two user studies to evaluate our new techniques.

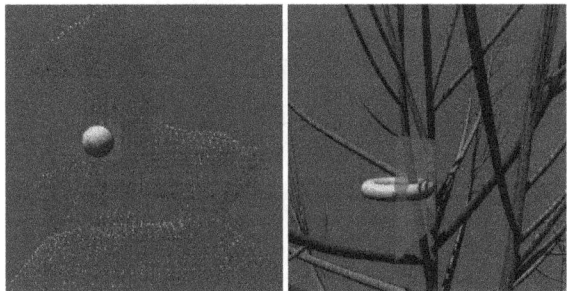

Figure 6. In the left image, the object slides on a point cloud. On the right, the torus can be placed on or around any branch of the tree (assuming enough space to avoid collisions).

7.1 Evaluation of SHIFT-Sliding

Oh *et al.* [28] had compared the Sliding algorithm against 3D widgets in an assembly task for in-contact conditions and found the sliding algorithm to be superior. Our new SHIFT-Sliding method extends basic sliding to support floating and colliding objects. We hypothesize that our new method will similarly outperform widget-based techniques for tasks where objects float or collide. To address a potential confound we *disabled camera navigation* in our study. To ensure internal validity, we also disabled object rotation and DEPTH-POP for this study.

In a pilot study we compared our sliding technique against widgets in various conditions, including single and four-view presentation. In the 3D widgets method, the user can drag either the three axes manipulators or the corresponding plane manipulators to move the object in one or two dimensions. For all situations where objects were in contact, we observed that our results matched the outcome of the previous evaluation of sliding [28]. Average sliding and widget times were significantly different ($F_{1,11} = 91.92, p < 0.001$) with 6.05 seconds, respectively 30.70, which matches the main result of Oh *et al.* [28]. Thus, we examine in our first user study only the manipulation of objects not in contact with the scene, *i.e.*, floating objects.

7.2 User Study 1

For floating objects, widget-based manipulation is easier if the local coordinate system of the object aligns with the world system. This can affect performance substantially. Thus we investigate coordinate system alignment through task subsets in our study.

7.2.1 Apparatus & Participants

We used the implementation described above to conduct this experiment. We recruited 12 (5 female) undergraduate and graduate students from the local university population. We did not screen participants for 3D/gaming experience. Our participants had varying game expertise, with 58% being regular gamers and 42% playing games only rarely. There was a 5-minute training session before the study, which introduced participants to the techniques in a playground environment, but did not include any version of the experimental tasks.

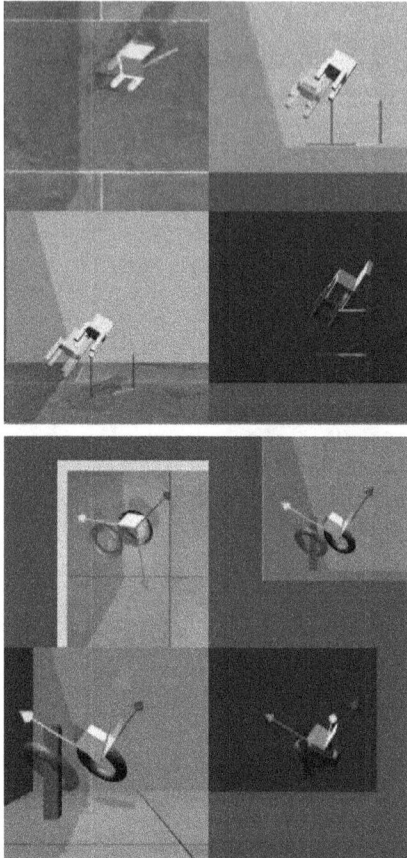

Figure 7. Top: The SHS condition with four views. The one-view condition uses only the bottom left view in full screen. The transparently shown target pose is floating above the floor. Bottom: The LCS condition with four views. The target position is around the pillar.

7.2.2 Experiment Design
We designed a 3D object positioning experiment and asked participants to move an object to a target position in various scenes. When the user positioned the object in the target, we measured the completion time and relative distance from the ideal target position. We recorded all actions of each user. The experiment had a 2 (techniques) x 2 (displays) x 2 (alignment) design. The order of technique, display, and alignment conditions was counter-balanced to avoid learning effects. The first technique uses a 3-axis widget aligned to the local coordinate system of the object. We call this technique LCS. With LCS, the user can drag either the three axes or the corresponding planes to move the object, as in most 3D editing software. The second technique is our new SHIFT-Sliding algorithm. We call this technique SHS here for brevity. The first display condition used four views (one perspective and three orthogonal views), corresponding to the standard user interface in 3D editing software. The second condition uses only a single perspective view. Figure 7 top shows the SHS condition with four views.

As discussed before, we designed our experiment to focus on floating objects. To investigate the effect of object alignment with the scene, the tasks were composed of two subsets, corresponding to aligned or rotated poses relative to the world coordinate system. The object orientations in the aligned condition were aligned with the three axes in the world coordinate systems. In the rotated condition, objects were rotated 45 degrees on all three axes relative to the world coordinate system. The effect of such object alignment had not been investigated in previous work. Each task condition had 5 trials, with different objects and scenes. The target positions were positioned so that movement along all three axes was necessary. On average the movement distance along each axis corresponded to a third of the viewport size (in the orthogonal views). Each user performed all trials in both two task conditions with all techniques and displays, corresponding to a total of 40 (5x2x4) trials for each user. We asked the participants to perform the tasks as quickly and as accurately as possible.

7.2.3 User Study Results
We used linear mixed models (with repeated measures) to incorporate subject variability. A critical value $\alpha = 0.05$ was used to assess significance. The results showed that SHS (M=33.31 seconds, SE=1.85) is significantly faster than the industry standard LCS (M=38.56, SE=1.88), OneView (M=31.37, SE=1.55) is significantly faster than FourView (M=40.50, SE=2.12), and the aligned condition (M=31.99, SE=1.71) is significantly faster than the rotated one (M=39.89, SE=2.00). See Table 1 and Figure 8.

In terms of completion time, all interactions were significant: SHS-OneView is faster than SHS-FourView and LCS-OneView. SHS-rotated and LCS-aligned are both faster than LCS-rotated. FourView-aligned and OneView-rotated are both faster than FourView-rotated.

A Tukey-Kramer's test shows that for *aligned* targets, SHS-OneView (M=25.58 seconds) is not significantly different from LCS-FourView (M=23.80). For rotated targets, SHS-OneView is significantly faster than all other combinations.

In terms of target distance, technique did not have a significant effect. FourView (M=0.065, SE=0.007) had a significantly smaller distance than OneView (M=0.220, SE=0.017). Alignment did not have a significant effect. There were no significant interactions on target distance.

Table 1. Linear mixed model analysis results for completion time and distance for study 1.

Source	$\chi^2(1)$ time	Sig	$\chi^2(1)$ distance	Sig
Tech	4.73	*	0.30	ns
View	14.32	***	19.24	*
Align	10.72	**	0.56	ns
Tech*View	4.41	*	1.30	ns
Tech*Align	17.33	***	0.01	ns
View*Align	6.44	*	1.25	ns
Tech*View*Align	15.60	***	0.11	ns

ns/ms = not/marginally sig., *,**,*** = p<0.05,0.01,0.001.

Nine of 12 participants found SHS easy to use. Eight participants prefer the SHS technique over LCS. Additionally, we got very positive feedback, see the discussion. Those who did not prefer SHS stated that the need to hold SHIFT down makes coordination slightly harder, but more practice might help.

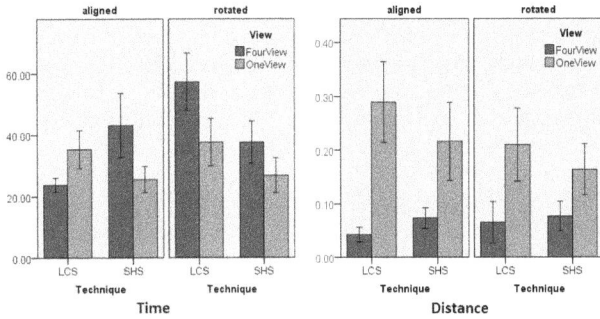

Figure 8. Time and distance for study 1. Error bars show 95% confidence intervals.

7.3 Evaluation of DEPTH-POP

We performed another pilot to compare basic sliding with DEPTH-POP. Several participants aborted the study due to frustration with basic sliding which made results hard to interpret. In scenes with simple geometry, such as Figure 3, sliding "around" works reasonably well, once users figure this out. Yet, in scenes with small thin features such as Figure 6 right, moving the torus between depth layers is challenging, as one cannot rely on the object becoming invisible to pop the object to the front. One viable strategy is to purposefully force a collision to pop the object to the front; yet then it becomes impossible to place the torus around the branch again. An alternative way for placing it around the branch is to slide an object from the tip of a branch inwards, but none of our participants were able to figure this out. Thus we concluded that basic sliding is not suited for such scenes and did not evaluate it.

7.4 User Study 2

In our second study we evaluated the DEPTH-POP algorithm in isolation, for objects in contact with the scene. We hypothesize that with DEPTH-POP users would be able to complete tasks quicker than with a widget-based technique.

7.4.1 Apparatus & Participants

We evaluated our implementation of DEPTH-POP in this experiment. We recruited 12 (5 female) different graduate and undergraduate students from the local university population. We did not screen participants for 3D/gaming experience. Our participants had varying game expertise, with 42% being regular gamers and 58% playing games only rarely. There was a five-minute training session before the study, which introduced participants to the techniques.

7.4.2 Experiment Design

Similar to the first study, the experiment had a 2 (techniques) x 2 (displays) x 2 (alignment) design. The order of technique, display, and alignment conditions was counter-balanced to avoid learning effects. We used LCS again as the first technique. The second technique was SHIFT-Sliding with DEPTH-POP enabled, which we call SDP here. The display conditions were again four views and a single view. We also looked again at tasks with aligned and rotated poses. All tasks involved only objects in contact and could be achieved with basic sliding and DEPTH-POP, *i.e.*, did not require SHIFT-Sliding. Still, we did not disable SHIFT-Sliding, as some tasks can indeed be completed with SHIFT-Sliding and the automatic collision response of our system. We had again 5 trials for each object alignment condition. Each user had to perform 40 (5x2x4) trials. Figure 7 bottom shows the LCS condition with four views.

Table 2. Linear mixed model analysis results for completion time and distance for study 2.

Source	$\chi^2(1)$ time	Sig	$\chi^2(1)$ distance	Sig
Tech	71.67	***	8.80	**
View	7.37	**	36.86	***
Align	56.83	***	0.58	ns
Tech*View	1.11	ns	9.55	**
Tech*Align	3.56	ms	0.03	ns
View*Align	13.16	***	1.77	ns
Tech*View* Align	7.68	**	0.20	ns

ns/ms = not/marginally sig., *,**,*** = p<0.05,0.01,0.001.

7.4.3 User Study Results

The results of a linear mixed model (with repeated measures) analysis showed that SDP (M=17.55 seconds, SE=1.18) is significantly faster than LCS (M=31.85, SE=1.57), OneView (M=22.41, SE=1.24) is significantly faster than FourView (M=27.00, SE=1.64), and the aligned condition (M=18.33, SE=0.97) is significantly faster than the rotated condition (M=31.07, SE=1.73). In terms of completion time, the interaction between views and rotation was significant: FourView-aligned and OneView-rotated are both faster than FourView-rotated. See Table 2 and Figure 9.

In terms of target distance, SDP (M=0.057, SE=0.007) had a significantly smaller distance than LCS (M=0.095, SE=0.012). Moreover, FourView (M=0.037, SE=0.003) had significantly smaller distance than OneView (M=0.115, SE=0.014). Alignment did not have a significant effect. The interaction of technique and view had a significant effect. Both LCS-FourView and SDP-OneView had a significantly smaller distance than LCS-OneView. The other interactions were not significant.

Seven participants found the SDP technique easy to use and relied solely on DEPTH-POP to complete the tasks. A few participants found it harder to understand when to use DEPTH-POP, so they performed *some* of the trials with SHIFT-Sliding. They stated that with more practice they would use it more frequently.

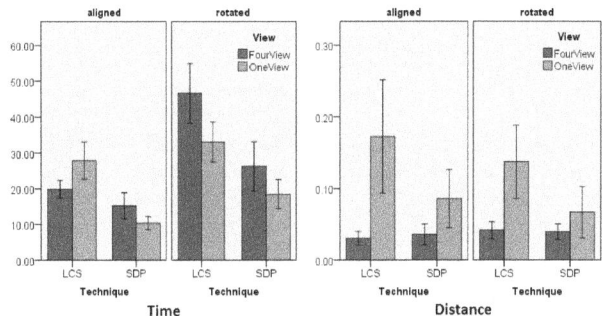

Figure 9. Time and distance for study 2. Error bars show 95% confidence intervals.

7.5 Improvements to 3D Object Position Visualization

Based on the feedback from the participants as well as our observations, we added some visualizations to our system to enhance the perception of 3D positions. Some users found it hard to judge the sliding plane and movement relative to the lift position in the floating state with SHIFT-Sliding. In DEPTH-POP, some users had issues with the idea that object movement is along the cursor ray. To address these issues, when an object is lifted up, we now draw a line with markers equal to the bounding box size (projected in the normal direction) to indicate height in SHIFT-Sliding, see Figure 1. When the user slides an object away from the initial lift position, we show additional lines in the local coordinate system that connect the object's current and lift position, see Figure 7 top. This provides strong perspective cues, which further help the user to better judge the object's position in 3D. To clearly indicate that an object floats, we replace the semi-transparent rectangle for contact visualization with a small circle. Unlike interactive shadows [15], this circle is not interactive. For push-to-back DEPTH-POP actions we also show (dark blue) guides to help the user understand the 3D movement better, see Figure 1.

8. DISCUSSION

Sliding keeps the manipulated object by default in contact with the remainder of the scene. The assumption is true for most scenes in the real world, and thus facilitates object movement in many scenes. SHIFT-Sliding adds the new ability to have objects float or interpenetrate. Moreover, SHIFT-Sliding *automatically* derives a local coordinate system from the last known contact surface, which makes it easy to position objects in space relative to other objects, without having to explicitly set a local coordinate system.

Results from the first study show that SHIFT-Sliding is easy to use and, for floating objects, 16% faster than the widget-based approach, the current industry standard. Together with Oh *et al.*'s results [28], this means that *SHIFT-Sliding* is globally faster than the widget-based method, regardless if the target position is in contact or not. Given the frequency of widget-based positioning in the 3D workflow, this means that *SHIFT-Sliding* can result in substantial time savings for practitioners. We got very positive feedback from the participants, where some even commented along the lines of: "*I wish I had this in 3DS Max*". Moreover, SHIFT-Sliding in a single perspective view is never significantly worse than the widget-based approach. With SHIFT-Sliding, users received enough depth cues to complete the tasks in the single perspective view. They found it easy to find an appropriate plane to start sliding with the SHIFT key, even for complex surfaces. In fact, we observed that it does not matter that much where in a given 3D movement task users start to use the SHIFT key to lift the object. For rotated target poses, SHIFT-Sliding was at least 29% faster than any widget-based condition. Widget-based manipulation also suffered with rotated targets, as dragging in the (rotated) widget coordinate system causes movement in more than one direction in the world coordinate system, which is harder to understand for users. Thus, SHIFT-Sliding effectively *merges the freedom of widget-based manipulation with the efficiency of sliding*. This fundamentally improves 3D object manipulation with 2D input devices.

The second study shows that SHIFT-Sliding with DEPTH-POP is more efficient, 81% faster, and 67% more accurate than the widget-based technique, as it *automatically* determines valid object positions in depth. The (seemingly) simple mapping to mouse-wheel actions together with our accelerated implementation greatly simplifies moving objects in depth and radically accelerates the associated tasks. DEPTH-POP facilitates even more challenging tasks, such as fitting a complex object around another one.

Results from both studies show that the OneView condition is on average more efficient than FourView, but less accurate. Based on our observations during the study, users might have tried to be more accurate with FourView display, at the expense of efficiency.

Also, with widget-based manipulation, FourView was faster for aligned targets, yet OneView faster for rotated targets. We are not certain that this last finding holds up, as in the orthogonal views of the FourView widget condition a *third* of the axis controllers did not always work correctly with rotated objects in the study. While users were able to complete the tasks, we recognize that the faulty controllers may have had a limited negative effect for this specific condition. Yet, participants had experienced this issue in the training session and thus learned to use the other views and/or controllers. Moreover, based on our observations during the study, we believe that the impact of this issue was overshadowed by the fact that users struggled (much) more with the challenges posed by a locally rotated 3D coordinate system.

In both studies, the participants commented that more practice would help. It would be interesting to measure the learnability of our new methods in a long term study. To address potential issues around having to hold the SHIFT key down during SHIFT-Sliding, one option would be to use the SHIFT key similar to a toggle [19].

8.1 Other Reflections

As there are only two interaction modes in our system, we can easily adapt our technique for a *touchscreen* interface. As is standard in most touch interfaces, the user can select and slide an object with a single finger. A second touch/hold can then serve as an activation event for SHIFT-Sliding to float an object. A *flick* of a second finger can be mapped to DEPTH-POP actions, depending on the direction of said flick. The second finger could be either a finger of the other hand or the same hand, as in recent work [31].

If the selected object has multiple contact points, the sliding behaviour depends on the contact points and their normal vectors. If the object slides across two identical table surfaces that are positioned side-by-side, the normal vectors and contact planes are the same. Thus the object can smoothly slide from one table to the other. If the object slides on a table surface towards a wall, the normal vector for the new contact will be different. In this case, the object would collide and we pop the object to the front (of the wall). Then, it will slide on the wall. Previous work, *e.g.*, [28], has already shown that multiple (compatible) contacts can be used to slide an object.

In our system users control translational and rotational DOFs separately during manipulation [25]. We choose to keep object orientation static during sliding. Alternatively, we could also dynamically change the objects' orientation with the normal vector of the sliding plane, thus keeping the same surface of the manipulated object in contact with the scene. This could be provided as a separated mode.

Ayatsuka *et al.* [2] already identified that manipulation via interactive shadows is unnatural, since three projections are needed. Yet, their penumbrae method [2] has also the drawback that penumbrae scale non-linearly with object height. The shadows in our system are not interactive. In the work of Glueck *et al.* [11], the shaded inner region of the base coarsely indicates the height of objects. Yet, as reported by Heer *et al.* [14], circular area judgments are not that accurate. The length of their "stalks" shows object heights directly – but is still perspectively foreshortened. We instead show markers at regular intervals to facilitate quick perception of object height.

As mentioned before, we disable back-face sliding. Yet, we could also temporarily enable such sliding in our system in some situations. One potential scenario is to permit the user to put an object in contact with a back surface with DEPTH-POP and slide along it. This would not cause the inappropriate mapping issue discussed before. Whenever the object loses contact, *i.e.*, starts floating or collides we would then transition to basic "front" sliding.

3D scanning a real scene yields point clouds. Converting such point clouds to geometry requires extra work. If the application scenario requires the user to place synthetic objects into a scanned scene, sliding can be used directly on the point clouds. For this, we only need normal vectors for each sample point. Then the contact point and sliding plane can potentially change at every frame during slides. SHIFT-Sliding also works on point clouds. However, DEPTH-POP only works if the samples form reasonably dense layers. With DEPTH-POP it is possible to place the object inside the "body" of a point cloud, *i.e.*, locations where the normal vector of the contact point is pointing away from the user. To avoid this, it is better to limit sliding only to front-facing points.

We accelerate most of the computations through the GPU. We use the frame buffer for most of the components in the system, including collision detection. For simplicity, we chose to use an image-based technique for identifying collisions, but any method, which provides information about the position, normal vector, and interpenetration distance where the collision occurs, suffices.

9. CONCLUSION

We presented two novel 3D positioning techniques that are efficient and easy to use. We extend basic sliding with the new SHIFT-Sliding and DEPTH-POP methods. The results of the user studies showed that for novice users the new methods are more efficient for 3D positioning compared to the standard widget-based approach. Both methods profoundly enhance the ease and efficiency of 3D manipulation with 2D input devices.

In the future, we plan to explore if rendering front layers transparent can aid the manipulation of invisible objects, based on previous work [10][29]. Also, we intend to look at new methods for manipulation with multiple constraints.

The current implementation of DEPTH-POP can slow down in scenes with high depth complexity on lower-end graphics hardware. In scenes with many hidden layers, the large amount of small fragments could lead to a huge amount of solutions. Many of those solutions might be meaningless for interaction. In the future, we will optimize the algorithm to deal better with such cases through appropriate pruning.

10. ACKNOWLEDGMENTS

We would like to thank all the participants.

11. REFERENCES

[1] Au, O.K.C., Tai, C.L. and Fu, H., 2012, May. Multitouch gestures for constrained transformation of 3d objects. In *Computer Graphics Forum* (Vol. 31, No. 2pt3, pp. 651-660). Blackwell Publishing Ltd.

[2] Ayatsuka, Y., Matsuoka, S. and Rekimoto, J., 1996, November. Penumbrae for 3D interactions. In *Proceedings of the 9th Annual ACM Symposium on User Interface Software and Technology* (pp. 165-166). ACM.

[3] Bade, R., Ritter, F. and Preim, B., 2005, August. Usability comparison of mouse-based interaction techniques for predictable 3d rotation. In *International Symposium on Smart Graphics* (pp. 138-150). Springer Berlin Heidelberg.

[4] Bavoil, L. and Myers, K., 2008. Order independent transparency with dual depth peeling. *NVIDIA OpenGL SDK*, pp.1-12.

[5] Bérard, F., Ip, J., Benovoy, M., El-Shimy, D., Blum, J.R. and Cooperstock, J.R., 2009, August. Did "Minority Report" get it wrong? Superiority of the mouse over 3D input devices in a 3D placement task. In *IFIP Conference on Human-Computer Interaction* (pp. 400-414). Springer Berlin Heidelberg.

[6] Bier, E.A., 1990. Snap-dragging in three dimensions. *ACM SIGGRAPH Computer Graphics*, 24(2), pp.193-204.

[7] Bukowski, R.W. and Séquin, C.H., 1995, April. Object associations: a simple and practical approach to virtual 3D manipulation. In *Proceedings of the 1995 Symposium on Interactive 3D graphics* (pp. 131-ff). ACM.

[8] Conner, B.D., Snibbe, S.S., Herndon, K.P., Robbins, D.C., Zeleznik, R.C. and Van Dam, A., 1992, June. Three-dimensional widgets. In *Proceedings of the 1992 Symposium on Interactive 3D Graphics* (pp. 183-188). ACM.

[9] Froehlich, B., Hochstrate, J., Skuk, V. and Huckauf, A., 2006, April. The globefish and the globemouse: two new six degree of freedom input devices for graphics applications. In *Proceedings of the SIGCHI Conference on Human Factors in Computing Systems* (pp. 191-199). ACM.

[10] Fu, C.W., Xia, J. and He, Y., 2010, April. Layerpaint: a multi-layer interactive 3D painting interface. In *Proceedings of the SIGCHI Conference on Human Factors in Computing Systems* (pp. 811-820). ACM.

[11] Glueck, M., Crane, K., Anderson, S., Rutnik, A. and Khan, A., 2009, February. Multiscale 3D reference visualization. In *Proceedings of the 2009 Symposium on Interactive 3D Graphics and Games* (pp. 225-232). ACM.

[12] Hachet, M., Guitton, P. and Reuter, P., 2003, October. The CAT for efficient 2D and 3D interaction as an alternative to mouse adaptations. In *Proceedings of the ACM Symposium on Virtual Reality Software and Technology* (pp. 225-112). ACM.

[13] Hancock, M., Carpendale, S. and Cockburn, A., 2007, April. Shallow-depth 3d interaction: design and evaluation of one-, two-and three-touch techniques. In *Proceedings of the SIGCHI Conference on Human Factors in Computing Systems* (pp. 1147-1156). ACM.

[14] Heer, J. and Bostock, M., 2010, April. Crowdsourcing graphical perception: using mechanical turk to assess visualization design. In *Proceedings of the SIGCHI Conference on Human Factors in Computing Systems* (pp. 203-212). ACM.

[15] Herndon, K.P., Zeleznik, R.C., Robbins, D.C., Conner, D.B., Snibbe, S.S. and Van Dam, A., 1992, December. Interactive shadows. In *Proceedings of the 5th Annual ACM Symposium on User Interface Software and Technology* (pp. 1-6). ACM.

[16] Herrlich, M., Walther-Franks, B. and Malaka, R., 2011, July. Integrated rotation and translation for 3D manipulation on multi-touch interactive surfaces. In *International Symposium on Smart Graphics* (pp. 146-154). Springer Berlin Heidelberg.

[17] Hinckley, K., Pausch, R., Goble, J.C. and Kassell, N.F., 1994, November. A survey of design issues in spatial input. In *Proceedings of the 7th Annual ACM Symposium on User Interface Software and Technology* (pp. 213-222). ACM.

[18] Hinckley, K., Tullio, J., Pausch, R., Proffitt, D. and Kassell, N., 1997, October. Usability analysis of 3D rotation techniques. In *Proceedings of the 10th Annual ACM Symposium on User Interface Software and Technology* (pp. 1-10). ACM.

[19] Igarashi, T. and Mitani, J., 2010, July. Apparent layer operations for the manipulation of deformable objects. In *ACM Transactions on Graphics (TOG)* (Vol. 29, No. 4, p. 110). ACM.

[20] Jacob, R.J., Sibert, L.E., McFarlane, D.C. and Mullen Jr, M.P., 1994. Integrality and separability of input devices. *ACM Transactions on Computer-Human Interaction (TOCHI)*, 1(1), pp.3-26.

[21] Kitamura, Y., Ogata, S. and Kishino, F., 2002, November. A manipulation environment of virtual and real objects using a magnetic metaphor. In *Proceedings of the ACM Symposium on Virtual Reality Software and Technology* (pp. 201-207). ACM.

[22] Kruger, R., Carpendale, S., Scott, S.D. and Tang, A., 2005, April. Fluid integration of rotation and translation. In *Proceedings of the SIGCHI Conference on Human Factors in Computing Systems* (pp. 601-610). ACM.

[23] Martinet, A., Casiez, G. and Grisoni, L., 2010, March. The design and evaluation of 3d positioning techniques for multi-touch displays. In *3D User Interfaces (3DUI), 2010 IEEE Symposium on* (pp. 115-118). IEEE.

[24] Martinet, A., Casiez, G. and Grisoni, L., 2010, November. The effect of DOF separation in 3D manipulation tasks with multi-touch displays. In *Proceedings of the 17th ACM Symposium on Virtual Reality Software and Technology* (pp. 111-118). ACM.

[25] Masliah, M.R. and Milgram, P., 2000, April. Measuring the allocation of control in a 6 degree-of-freedom docking experiment. In *Proceedings of the SIGCHI Conference on Human Factors in Computing Systems* (pp. 25-32). ACM.

[26] McMahan, R.P., Gorton, D., Gresock, J., McConnell, W. and Bowman, D.A., 2006, November. Separating the effects of level of immersion and 3D interaction techniques. In *Proceedings of the ACM Symposium on Virtual Reality Software and Technology* (pp. 108-111). ACM.

[27] Mine, M.R., Brooks Jr, F.P. and Sequin, C.H., 1997, August. Moving objects in space: exploiting proprioception in virtual-environment interaction. In *Proceedings of the 24th Annual Conference on Computer Graphics and Interactive Techniques* (pp. 19-26). ACM Press/Addison-Wesley Publishing Co.

[28] Oh, J.Y. and Stuerzlinger, W., 2005, May. Moving objects with 2D input devices in CAD systems and desktop virtual environments. In *Proceedings of Graphics Interface 2005* (pp. 195-202). Canadian Human-Computer Communications Society.

[29] Ortega, M. and Vincent, T., 2014, April. Direct drawing on 3D shapes with automated camera control. In *Proceedings*

of the SIGCHI Conference on Human Factors in Computing Systems (pp. 2047-2050). ACM.

[30] Reisman, J.L., Davidson, P.L. and Han, J.Y., 2009, October. A screen-space formulation for 2D and 3D direct manipulation. In *Proceedings of the 22nd Annual ACM Symposium on User Interface Software and Technology* (pp. 69-78). ACM.

[31] Scheurich, D. and Stuerzlinger, W., 2013, September. A One-Handed Multi-Touch Method for 3D Rotations. In *IFIP Conference on Human-Computer Interaction* (pp. 56-69). Springer Berlin Heidelberg.

[32] Schmidt, R., Singh, K. and Balakrishnan, R., 2008, April. Sketching and composing widgets for 3d manipulation. In *Computer Graphics Forum* (Vol. 27, No. 2, pp. 301-310). Blackwell Publishing Ltd.

[33] Shuralyov, D. and Stuerzlinger, W., 2011. A 3D desktop puzzle assembly system. In *Proceedings of the IEEE Symposium on 3D User Interfaces (3DUI)*, pp. 139-140. IEEE.

[34] Strauss, P.S. and Carey, R., 1992, July. An object-oriented 3D graphics toolkit. In *ACM SIGGRAPH Computer Graphics* (Vol. 26, No. 2, pp. 341-349). ACM.

[35] Stuerzlinger, W. and Wingrave, C.A., 2011. The value of constraints for 3D user interfaces. In *Virtual Realities* (pp. 203-223). Springer Vienna.

[36] Teather, R.J. and Stuerzlinger, W., 2007, November. Guidelines for 3D positioning techniques. In *Proceedings of the 2007 Conference on Future Play* (pp. 61-68). ACM.

[37] Van Emmerik, M.J., 1990, December. A direct manipulation technique for specifying 3D object transformations with a 2D input device. In *Computer Graphics Forum* (Vol. 9, No. 4, pp. 355-361). Blackwell Publishing Ltd.

[38] Venolia, D., 1993, May. Facile 3D direct manipulation. In *Proceedings of the INTERACT'93 and CHI'93 Conference on Human Factors in Computing Systems* (pp. 31-36). ACM.

[39] Vishton, P.M. and Cutting, J.E., 1995. Wayfinding, displacements, and mental maps: velocity fields are not typically used to determine one's aimpoint. *Journal of Experimental Psychology: Human Perception and Performance*, 21(5), p.978.

[40] Vuibert, V., Stuerzlinger, W. and Cooperstock, J.R., 2015, August. Evaluation of Docking Task Performance Using Mid-air Interaction Techniques. In *Proceedings of the 3rd ACM Symposium on Spatial User Interaction* (pp. 44-52). ACM.

[41] Ware, C. and Jessome, D.R., 1988. Using the bat: A six-dimensional mouse for object placement. *Computer Graphics and Applications, IEEE*, 8(6), pp.65-70.

[42] Wickens, C. and Hollands, J., 1999. Spatial displays. *Engineering Psychology and Human Performance, Prentice-Hall, 3.*

Preference Between Allocentric and Egocentric 3D Manipulation in a Locally Coupled Configuration

Paul Issartel
LIMSI-CNRS
Orsay, France
paul.issartel@limsi.fr

Lonni Besançon
INRIA
Saclay, France
lonni.besancon@inria.fr

Florimond Guéniat
LIMSI-CNRS
Orsay, France
contact@gueniat.fr

Tobias Isenberg
INRIA
Saclay, France
tobias.isenberg@inria.fr

Mehdi Ammi
LIMSI-CNRS
Orsay, France
mehdi.ammi@limsi.fr

ABSTRACT

We study user preference between allocentric and egocentric 3D manipulation on mobile devices, in a configuration where the motion of the device is applied to an object displayed on the device itself. We first evaluate this preference for translations and for rotations alone, then for full 6-DOF manipulation. We also investigate the role of contextual cues by performing this experiment in different 3D scenes. Finally, we look at the specific influence of each manipulation axis. Our results provide guidelines to help interface designers select an appropriate default mapping in this locally coupled configuration.

Keywords

3D Interaction; Control-Display mappings; Mobile devices

1. INTRODUCTION

With the rising availability of mobile devices and their increasing processing power, 3D applications are becoming more common on these devices. A fundamental part of interaction with such software is 3D manipulation [2], i.e. translations and rotations in 3D space. While most mobile devices rely on touch-based control, tactile input requires a 2D to 3D mapping for 3D manipulation. Several projects [10, 13] thus proposed to use the built-in motion sensors found in many mobile devices to provide full 3D input, by detecting the device's own motion and mapping it to virtual objects. Recently, the Tango tablet[1] provided a major technological step forward by combining gyroscopes, accelerometers, and visible/infrared cameras to fully track its translations and rotations relative to the surrounding environment. This mode of interaction is thus likely to become more widely used in the future.

A unique aspect of mobile devices is that they integrate input and display capabilities in the same device. This means

SUI '16, October 15–16, 2016, Tokyo, Japan

© 2016 Copyright held by the owner/author(s). Publication rights licensed to ACM.
ISBN 978-1-4503-4068-7/16/10...$15.00

DOI: http://dx.doi.org/10.1145/2983310.2985750

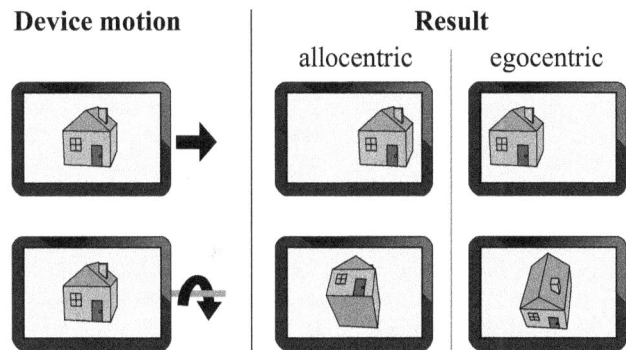

Figure 1: Illustration of an allocentric and an egocentric mapping. The object moves on the screen according to the device's motion (possibly scaled), but the *sense* of motion should be compatible with user expectations.

that users are holding both the input device and the display device in their hands—a "locally coupled" configuration. For this reason, using the motion of a mobile device for 3D input can be interpreted in two ways (see Figure 1):

- the mobile device could be seen as a "handle" to control 3D objects—the *allocentric* interpretation—or

- the mobile device could be seen as a "window" that moves around 3D objects—the *egocentric* interpretation.

In the allocentric interpretation, the manipulated 3D objects move in the *same* direction as the "handle" represented by the mobile device. In the egocentric interpretation, objects move in the *opposite* direction, as if the viewpoint itself was controlled through a handheld "window".[2]

Although either alternative can be obtained by simply reversing the direction of motion in the control-display mapping [10], the question remains of which mapping should be actually implemented. This is not only relevant if the interface does not offer a way to switch between the two alternatives, but it also affects first-time users. The concept

---

[1] http://www.google.com/atap/project-tango/

[2] In either case, the amount of motion may still be scaled by an arbitrary gain factor [10] but the distinction between allocentric and egocentric mappings remains unchanged.

of "compatibility" [4], originating from the ergonomics literature, states that a chosen mapping should correspond to the alternative *most often expected* among the population. Choosing a compatible mapping is thus essential for good usability and minimal fatigue [4], and to avoid errors such as accidental inversions [5]. Even after extensive training, evidence suggests that a non-compatible mapping still results in reduced user performance [4].

In this paper we thus examine which mapping users prefer in various situations, in order to help interface designers choose which mapping to implement in each case.

2. RELATED WORK

2.1 Allocentric and egocentric reference frames

Each interpretation of the locally coupled configuration is a matter of the cognitive relationship between the objects in space, called a *reference frame*. The literature on spatial cognition generally distinguishes between two fundamental reference frames [12]: allocentric (also called exocentric) and egocentric. However, most of this literature focuses on the relationship between the user and his or her surrounding objects. In our case, there is both a relation between the user and the mobile device, and a relation between the mobile device and the 3D objects displayed on it. We thus need to examine how we can apply these terms to this specific situation.

Klatzky [12] defines the two terms in the context of whole-body navigation: egocentric as being related to the "perspective of the perceiver," and allocentric as being related to an external, independent framework. Burgess et al. [3] studied these reference frames in a spatial updating task (judging the relative motion of objects between an initial and a final configuration), which has a certain degree of similarity with our situation. They define the allocentric frame as "the association of object locations to external landmarks" and the egocentric frame as being related to "self-motion." Poupyrev et al. [14] define these reference frames in the context of immersive environments: egocentric interaction techniques are those linked to the avatar's viewpoint, while "exocentric" (i.e. allocentric) techniques are those performed from an external location. In a study by Diaz and Sims [5] on accidental inversions, the egocentric condition was viewed from the operators' eyes and the allocentric condition was viewed from outside their body.

Overall, the egocentric term seems to be associated with the idea of the viewing perspective, and the allocentric term with the idea of a fixed, external reference point. In our case, when the manipulated object moves in the same direction as the mobile device, the object appears to be directly controlled by the device's motion and thus to move relative to the surrounding space. We therefore describe such mappings as "allocentric." When the manipulated object moves in the opposite direction, the mobile device appears to directly control the *perspective* on the object. We therefore call such mappings "egocentric."

2.2 Population stereotypes

The relationship between an input device's motion and the motion's result on a display has long been investigated in ergonomics. Although this relationship—or "mapping"—can take many forms, some of them better match the user's mental model. Such mappings are said to be *compatible* [7, 4]. An important goal for interactive systems design is thus to determine which mapping is most compatible with the target population.

When faced with several functionally equivalent alternatives such as the two mappings we study, the option which is most often expected among the population is called a *population stereotype* [6, 18]. Several population stereotypes have been identified in previous research. Warrick's principle [16, 18], for instance, states that the controlled display should move in the same direction as the side of the input device that is closest to it. The clockwise-to-increase principle [18] states that the controlled display should "increase" or "move up" when the input device is rotated clockwise. These principles, however, were established under the assumption that the input device is separated from the display. In our locally-coupled configuration, in contrast, they are both the same object: the mobile device. Existing population stereotypes thus cannot be applied unless they have been validated under a locally-coupled setting.

2.3 Preferred mapping in a locally-coupled configuration

Many interfaces have been proposed that use the motion of a mobile device to control objects on the device's screen. Only few of these works, however, explicitly mention the existence of two alternative mappings (direct/allocentric and inverted/egocentric) and the rationale behind the final choice.

Rekimoto [15] proposed a menu interface controlled by device tilt. Both mappings were discussed, but the chosen alternative (moving the menu behind a fixed cursor, equivalent to our egocentric interpretation) was selected for technical reasons rather than based on an user study. Weberg et al. [17] chose the opposite option (moving the cursor in a fixed menu, equivalent to our allocentric interpretation) in their tilt-based menu interface, on the basis that it "felt very intuitive and natural." Bartlett [1] mentioned the existence of two groups of users with different mental models, each expecting the controlled picture to move in an opposite direction when tilting the device. Hinckley and Song [9] also mentioned that slightly more than half of their users had an opposite mental model to others in their tilt-to-zoom technique. Although all this work was conducted in a locally-coupled configuration, it still does not provide sufficient evidence in favor of either the allocentric or the egocentric interpretation. In addition, the studies cited above were conducted on 1D or 2D interfaces, and may thus not be generalizable to 3D manipulation.

2.4 Preferred mapping for 3D manipulation

Kaminaka and Egli [11] investigated the preferred mapping to translate and rotate a cube through a lever. The lever was alternatively mapped to translations or rotations along each axis. Although this is an actual 3D manipulation task, the 1D input device and non locally-coupled configuration make the results of this study difficult to generalize to our case. Diaz and Sims [5] investigated "accidental inversions" of rotations, i.e. what happens when users encounter a mapping opposite to their expectation. Such inversions allow one to identify the actual population stereotypes for 3D rotations. However, the study used a 2D mouse as input device and an external display, which again makes the results difficult to apply to our case.

There appears to be a single study that is fully applicable to our case: Issartel et al. [10] studied the preferred mapping for 3D manipulation tasks on a locally-coupled mobile device. This work revealed some marked stereotypes in the studied population. However, the study was only preliminary and the number of participants (10) was relatively low for producing reliable results. Even though both translation and rotation mappings were considered, full 6-DOF mappings were not. Finally, the use of an external tracking marker in the environment could have created a bias toward the egocentric interpretation, a limitation mentioned in the study itself. We thus use Issartel et al.'s [10] work as a basis but greatly expand the experimental protocol, apparatus, and number of participants to produce broader, deeper, and more reliable results.

3. MEASURING USER EXPECTATION

It is challenging to determine the "expected" choice of allocentric or egocentric mapping: many experimental biases can affect a study such as prior exposure to the interface, learning effects, or even how the interaction is described to users. We considered several ways to determine this expected mapping.

The first one, inspired by previous work on population stereotypes [18] and spatial updating [3], would be to show participants a non-interactive description of a manipulation task: for instance, an image representing an object at an initial location, and another image of the same object at a target location. Then, participants would be asked which direction they would move the mobile device to obtain the target result. This protocol has the advantage of only providing the minimum amount of information needed to answer the question, thus avoiding many confounding factors. However, it also has an important drawback: participants never actually use the interaction technique. In our case, it might be difficult for participants to answer questions about this possibly unfamiliar mode of interaction without having experienced it beforehand.

Another way would be to ask participants to perform multiple 3D manipulations in both allocentric and egocentric modes, record the resulting trajectories, and analyze them to detect accidental inversions [5]. Such inversions can provide an objective indication that the mapping did not match the user's expectations. This protocol also gets the participants to actually use the interface, although there could be learning effects from prolonged use. It is challenging and error-prone, however, to reliably detect accidental inversions in full 3D trajectories as produced by untrained users. Participants may possibly be taught how to generate "clean" trajectories with extensive training, but this training may also distort their preference between the two mappings compared to the general population.

A third way would be to have participants perform object manipulation tasks in both allocentric and egocentric modes, then *rate* each mapping. Participants would rate a mapping depending on whether the manipulated object moves and rotates in the direction they expected (which we call the "naturalness" rating). Again, this protocol lets participants actually use the interface, but the actual evaluation now consists of a fully subjective assessment. Compared to the previous approach, this has the benefit of being practically feasible even with novice users, avoiding the biases associated with training. Furthermore, it is also possible that some participants may find both mappings acceptable—or reject both. By letting participants rate both mappings rather than simply choosing the "better" one, this protocol can provide a more detailed understanding of the actual user preference

between the two mappings. Therefore, we decided to use this last protocol in our experiment.

4. CONTEXTUAL CUES

Previous work [3, 5] has shown that the expected reference frame is not only a matter of personal interpretation, but can also be affected by cues from the environment, i.e. *contextual cues*. In our configuration, contextual cues would come from the *virtual environment* because we focus on what happens on the mobile device's screen. Since the virtual environment necessarily varies from one system to another, it is essential to determine whether and how the virtual scene visible on the screen can influence the expected mapping.

First, we can hypothesize that the nature of the manipulated virtual object itself may have an influence. If the object looks like it would be readily manipulable in the real world (e.g., a figurine or a fruit), users may expect to be able to move it directly, i.e. the allocentric interpretation. In contrast, if the object looks like it could be part of the scenery (e.g., a house or a landscape model), users may expect to move around it rather than manipulate it themselves—the egocentric interpretation.

Second, there could be an influence of the geometrical relationship between objects in the virtual scene. If the manipulated object visually moves on the screen whereas other objects in the scene remain fixed (relative to the device), then the surrounding objects may be perceived as an environment relative to which the manipulated object is moving, favoring an allocentric interpretation. If the manipulated object is viewed from inside, then the object is perceived as surrounding the mobile device, which may reinforce the interpretation that the mobile device is *moving inside* the object (egocentric interpretation) rather than moving the object (allocentric interpretation).

5. HYPOTHESES AND SETTINGS

Based on these thoughts we had the following hypotheses about which mapping would be expected in different situations:

- **H1**: When the manipulated object is viewed from inside, users expect an egocentric mapping;

- **H2**: When the manipulated object is moving within a fixed virtual environment, users expect an allocentric mapping;

- **H3**: When the manipulated object represents a typically static part of a virtual environment (e.g. a house), users expect an egocentric mapping.

Although Issartel et al. [10] seemingly disproved hypothesis **H2**, they suspected a bias caused by the presence of a fixed marker in the real environment, which could have led participants toward an egocentric mental model. We thus wanted to re-test **H2** in a markerless tracking setup without this bias.

In order to test the above hypotheses, we designed four different virtual scenes with different contextual cues (Figure 2):

1. a generic object (Stanford rabbit) on a black background, serving as the baseline scene;

2. an object more likely to be perceived as static (a house), on a black background;

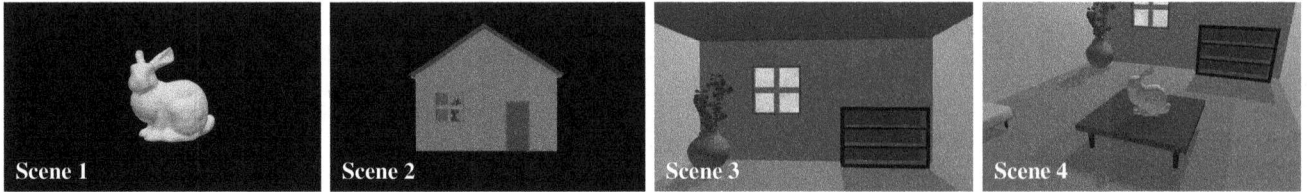

Figure 2: The four scenes used in the experiment. In Scene 3, the house model is controlled in the same way as in Scene 2 but the viewpoint is located inside the house. In Scene 4, only the object on the table is controlled by the user while the surrounding environment remains fixed.

3. the house seen from inside;

4. the same object as in Scene 1, surrounded by a fixed house environment.

Previous studies (e.g., [5, 10, 11]) often considered translations and rotations separately. The use of device motion as input modality, however, allows full 6-DOF manipulation. It is thus important to also consider both components simultaneously. To investigate the role of each component in 6-DOF manipulation tasks, we stated the following null hypothesis:

- **H4**: Having a "correct" mapping (which matches user expectations) is equally important for translations and for rotations, i.e. when performing translations and rotations simultaneously, the rating is equally affected by the choice of translation mapping as by the choice of rotation mapping.

Finally, some studies [5, 11] have revealed different user expectations between the axes of manipulation. We therefore hypothesized to find such differences in our configuration:

- **H5**: Some axes are more important than others in the perceived naturalness of the resulting mapping.

6. APPARATUS

The experiment was entirely self-contained in a single Tango tablet, providing display, input, and tracking capabilities. The virtual scene was displayed on the tablet's screen together with several tactile buttons to control the experiment. The tablet continuously tracked its own motion in the real world using its built-in sensors. There was thus no external marker in the environment. We captured positions and orientations relative to the fixed initial location where the software was started.

We used this tracking information to implement a relative position control mapping similar to Issartel et al. [10]. We chose this mapping for its directional compliance so that participants could focus on the *sense* of motion (allocentric or egocentric) without confusing it with with the *axis* of motion (which always matches device motion in a directional compliant mapping). We also added a clutching mechanism: the device motion was only applied to the manipulated object while a finger touched the tablet screen. Participants could thus interrupt manipulation to reposition the tablet during complex tasks.

Participants were seated on a chair during the experiment, holding the tablet in landscape mode with both hands. The chair stood in the middle of the room as the presence of nearby fixed objects (e.g., a desk) could have biased participants toward an egocentric interpretation. We used a non-swivel chair to encourage participants to rotate the mobile device itself during rotation tasks rather than rotating themselves on the chair.

7. PARTICIPANTS

To get more generalizable results than existing exploratory work [10], we used a larger and broader participant pool. We recruited 30 unpaid participants (12 females) whose age ranged from 20 to 53 (mean=30.3, SD=10.5). Among them, 22 had a university degree while 8 had a high-school degree or less. They all had normal or corrected-to-normal vision.

With this broader user sample it became possible to investigate an additional question: whether the familiarity with 3D software can influence the preference between allocentric and egocentric mappings. However, only 7 participants reported to have sufficient knowledge of 3D modeling software, which was too small to conduct such an analysis. On the other hand, 14 participants—nearly half of them—reported to regularly play 3D video games. We thus chose to focus on gaming experience as an indicator of familiarity with 3D software. Perhaps unsurprisingly, the group of video game players was largely correlated with younger age and male gender. Still, we assumed that the gaming experience itself would have more influence on this experiment than age or gender.

8. PROCEDURE AND TASK

We first presented participants with the tablet device and told them they would have to "perform translations and rotations in four different virtual environments." In our explanations we took great care to avoid terms such as "translating/rotating the object" or "moving in the virtual scene" since any such mention could have led participants toward an allocentric or egocentric interpretation. There was no prior training phase—we wanted to avoid biases associated with previous usage of the interface. Instead, we demonstrated how to perform translations/rotations by moving and rotating the tablet in front of the participant, and demonstrated the clutching mechanism by pressing and releasing a finger on the screen. The tablet's screen was blanked during this tutorial step.

Participants were then asked to conduct the experiment without further instructions. The experiment itself consisted of a series of *conditions*, in which two or more mappings were to be evaluated in a given virtual environment. On the bottom of the tablet's screen, several buttons labeled C1, C2, etc. represented the mappings, with the mappings randomly assigned to them. Pressing a button activated the corresponding mapping so participants could switch between mappings to rate them. Except for the third part of the experiment (see below), participants were free to change or go back and forth between mappings at any time during a condition.

To help them assess their own preference, participants were asked to perform 3D manipulation tasks under each mapping. These tasks consisted in translating/rotating a 3D object to a target location, i.e. a docking task. In a typical docking task, the target is normally visually represented in the virtual scene. However, we could not display this target in every condition since having a fixed object in the scene would have resulted in the situation mentioned in hypothesis **H2**. Moreover, we could not describe this task in terms of "moving an object to a target" as it would have biased participants toward an allocentric interpretation. We thus printed images of the target locations (Figure 2) on a physical sheet of paper, attached to the wall in front of the participants, and which they could consult any time wanted during the study. On each trial, the manipulated object started at a different position and/or orientation. Participants were asked to "try to obtain the same result" as in the images, by any means involving translations or rotations—thus without forcing them into an allocentric or egocentric interpretation. When the target location was reached, the manipulated object changed color to indicate success and was moved to a new location when the finger was released. Participants were encouraged to repeat this task several times to form an accurate opinion before rating a mapping.

When ready to give a rating, participants pressed a button on the tablet's screen and were presented a Likert scale ranging from "not natural" to "natural". We explained the meaning of "natural" to participants as "whether your actions produce translations/rotations in the direction you expected." Again, this definition was carefully worded to avoid any allocentric or egocentric formulation.

Since the Tango tracking system sometimes exhibits a small drift there was a risk that this could lead to unnatural ratings under the above definition. We thus also told participants that "if a slight continuous motion ever occurs without any action on your part, this is a technical limitation that you should ignore in your rating." When all mappings in a condition were rated, the next condition was automatically started.

8.1 Part 1: Translation and rotation

In the first part of the experiment, translations and rotations were evaluated separately. Therefore, the conditions consisted of translation-only tasks and rotation-only tasks in the four environments, under two mappings: allocentric and egocentric.

Scene 1—the most generic one—was always presented first to serve as a "baseline" with minimal learning biases. The first two conditions were thus translation tasks in Scene 1 and rotations tasks in Scene 1, presented in an alternate order between participants. The remaining conditions were the 6 combinations of translations and rotations with each of the three other scenes, presented in a random order. Ratings were given on a 4-point Likert scale. This scale was specifically selected to lack a "neutral" point and to encourage participants to decide whether they perceived a mapping as natural or not.

8.2 Part 2: Simultaneous translations/rotations

In a second part of the experiment, translations and rotations were performed concurrently (i.e., full 6-DOF manipulation) and each component was alternatively made allocentric

of egocentric. There were thus 4 mappings to be evaluated: the four combinations of allocentric or egocentric translations with allocentric or egocentric rotations. These mappings were evaluated within each virtual scene, themselves presented in a random order. We again used a 4-point Likert scale to establish comparisons with the results of the first part.

8.3 Part 3: Per-axis inversion

The third part was optional. Since the parts 1–2 already took approximately 30 min, we asked participants to continue voluntarily.

14 participants agreed to continue and with them we examined two conditions, one for translations and one for rotations, presented in random order. Both conditions were set up in Scene 1. In both conditions there were 8 different mappings, in which each manipulation axis (x, y, and z) was alternatively inverted. We then asked participants to rate the techniques on a 3-point Likert scale, thus turning the rating into a choice between "not natural," "neutral," and "natural". We deliberately reduced the rating scale and allowed a neutral point to not overwhelm participants, given the large number of mappings to compare and the small changes between them.

9. RESULTS AND DISCUSSION

In our analysis we focus on *effect sizes*—i.e., how much the ratings given to a mapping differ from the ratings given to another mapping—to investigate which mapping was preferred in each condition. The ratings obtained from Likert scales are *ordinal* data, so we used non-parametric statistical tests to quantify the effect sizes. For each condition we performed a Wilcoxon-Pratt signed-rank test on the ratings given to each mapping alternative. We then computed a normalized effect size r from the z statistic produced by this test, as per Fritz et al. [8].

Guidelines for the effect size [8] are that $r > 0.5$ is a large effect, $r > 0.3$ is a medium effect and $r > 0.1$ is a small effect, but these limits should not be seen as hard thresholds. We also report a bootstrapped standard error σ_r for each effect size.

9.1 Translations

Figure 3 summarizes the ratings given by participants to each mapping in the translation-only tasks.

Scene 1 was always presented first in order to minimize potential biases acquired during manipulation, and was meant as a neutral environment without any of the contextual cues present in the other scenes. Therefore, the ratings obtained from this scene should best approximate the participants' "baseline" mental model. Although the previous experiment by Issartel et al. [10] showed a strong preference for egocentric translations in such a neutral condition, there was a suspicion that this result could have been biased by the presence of a visible marker in the environment. Because we eliminated this marker in the present setup we had no reason anymore to expect that one mapping would be preferred over the other.

Nevertheless, translation ratings in Scene 1 revealed a small to medium preference in favor of egocentric translations ($r = 0.27$, $\sigma_r = 0.11$). While not as definite as in previous results [10], this preference nevertheless appears to remain true in our markerless setup. The distribution of answers shows that the egocentric mapping was indeed found natural by most participants, whereas the allocentric mapping led to mixed ratings. The egocentric mapping was thus clearly

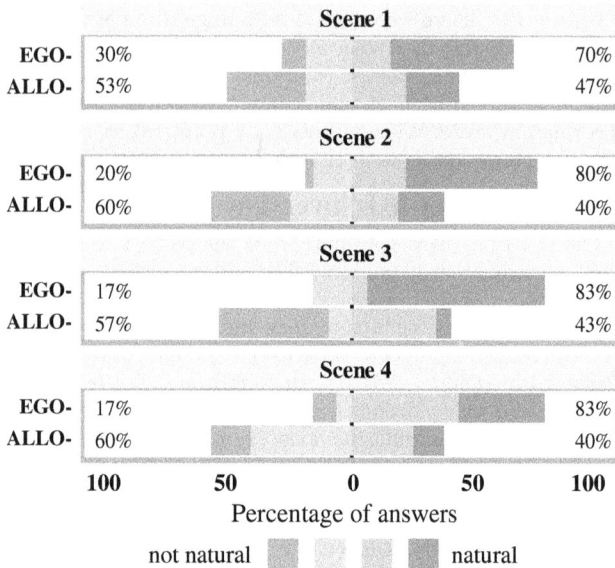

Figure 3: Participants' ratings for each mapping in the translation tasks.

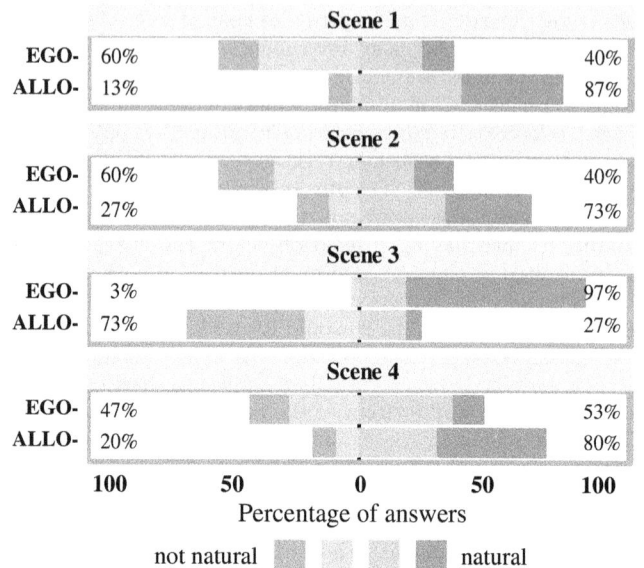

Figure 4: Participants's ratings for each mapping in the rotation tasks.

preferred by participants on this first approach to our interface, although the allocentric mapping was not completely rejected either.

Scene 2 showed a similar pattern to Scene 1, with egocentric translations being preferred over allocentric translations. The effect size was actually higher ($r=0.41$, $\sigma_r=0.09$), though the standard error makes this distinction not completely certain. This second scene was specifically designed to test hypothesis **H3** that a typically unmovable 3D object would favor an egocentric mapping. A stronger preference for egocentric translations would thus tend to support hypothesis **H3**. Yet, even if confirmed this effect appears to be quite small. In addition, since the "baseline" mapping for translations already seem to be egocentric (as demonstrated in Scene 1), an effect that reinforces the egocentric mapping would have little practical implications for the choice of a default translation mapping.

In Scene 3, the preference was strongly in favor of the egocentric mapping ($r=0.53$, $\sigma_r=0.05$), even more than in Scenes 1 and 2. There is thus strong evidence to support hypothesis **H1**, i.e., that translating an object viewed from inside is preferably accomplished with an egocentric mapping.

Scene 4 also showed an egocentric mapping preference ($r=0.30$, $\sigma_r=0.12$). This is surprising since we were expecting that manipulating an object within a fixed virtual environment would favor an allocentric mental model (hypothesis **H2**). When we noticed during the experiment that some participants gave unexpectedly high ratings to the egocentric mapping, we took the opportunity to ask them the reasons behind this choice at the end of the first session. Their comments suggested that they were mainly focused on performing the task and did not pay much attention to the fixed virtual scene. Indeed, since participants went through at least two other conditions before encountering Scene 4, it is believable that the task was beginning to become a "routine" at this point. In addition, since the scene was fixed in screen space it is plausible that some participants merely considered it as a background image and did not adopt the mental model that we expected them to do.

9.2 Rotations

Figure 4 summarizes participants' ratings for the rotation-only tasks. The "baseline" condition Scene 1 showed a medium effect ($r=0.37$, $\sigma_r=0.10$) in favor of allocentric rotations. Most participants rated the allocentric mapping as natural but gave mixed ratings to the egocentric mapping. This confirms the results of previous work [10] which also showed a preference for allocentric rotations in this condition.

The allocentric mapping was also preferred in Scene 2, but apparently less strongly ($r=0.24$, $\sigma_r=0.12$) than in Scene 1. Although the standard error again makes such a distinction uncertain, if confirmed this result would support hypothesis **H3** that a typically unmovable object favors an egocentric mental model. As with translations, however, this effect appears to be very small. Unlike translations though, this effect would lead people toward the *opposite* mapping compared to Scene 1. Yet, because of its small strength it does not seem to be sufficient to change the overall preference for allocentric rotations.

In contrast to the other scenes, Scene 3 showed a very marked preference for egocentric rotations ($r=0.57$, $\sigma_r=0.04$). This is again strong evidence for **H1** that manipulating an object viewed from inside is preferably accomplished egocentrically.

Scene 4 showed the same pattern as Scenes 1 and 2, i.e. we saw a preference for allocentric rotations ($r=0.28$, $\sigma_r=0.11$). Yet, egocentric rotations were still rated as natural by little more than half of the participants. Since the preferred mapping in Scene 1 was already allocentric, we cannot provide any particular support for **H2**. If anything, the smaller effect size compared to Scene 1 tends to disprove **H2** since the egocentric mapping was more readily accepted in this configuration.

9.3 Influence of gaming experience

We conducted a second analysis of the translation and rotation results by splitting participants into two groups: those with regular experience with 3D video games (*gamers* group, 14 participants), and those who reported to seldom

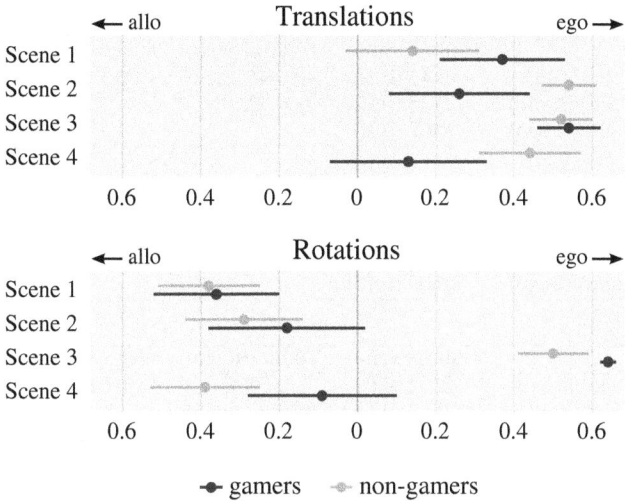

Figure 5: Effect sizes and standard error for the preferred mapping among the "gamers" and the "non-gamers" groups.

or never play such video games (*non-gamers* group, 16 participants). Although the preference for each mapping in each scene remained the same for both groups, in several cases the effect size was different—i.e. the preference was less marked for one group than for the other (Figure 5).

In Scene 1, non-gamers apparently had a weaker preference for egocentric translations ($r=0.14$, $\sigma_r=0.17$) compared to gamers ($r=0.37$, $\sigma_r=0.16$). Since Scene 1 can be considered as "baseline," we can thus observe that—with some reservations due to the standard error—non-gamers may not actually have a strong *a priori* preference for translations, and that gaming experience may create a bias for the egocentric mapping. Concerning rotations, the preference was nearly identical between gamers ($r=0.36$, $\sigma_r=0.16$) and non-gamers ($r=0.38$, $\sigma_r=0.13$). It thus appears that gaming experience does not produce any such bias for rotations.

In Scene 2, the gamers' preference for egocentric translations was of a comparable level to Scene 1 ($r=0.26$, $\sigma_r=0.18$). The non-gamers' preference, however, was much more marked than in Scene 1 ($r=0.54$, $\sigma_r=0.07$). Gamers thus seem to be less affected by a change of scene contents than non-gamers, possibly because their experience makes them more tolerant to using either mapping in various virtual environments—albeit with a persistent bias toward the egocentric mapping. The difference between the two groups was less clear for rotations, but still hinted at a similar trend (gamers: $r=0.18$, $\sigma_r=0.20$; non-gamers: $r=0.29$, $\sigma_r=0.15$). These results may thus support hypothesis **H3**, but only for non-gamers.

For Scene 3, the preference for egocentric translations was as strongly marked for gamers ($r=0.54$, $\sigma_r=0.08$) as it was for non-gamers ($r=0.52$, $\sigma_r=0.08$). We can thus infer that the conditions in Scene 3 (viewing the manipulated object from inside) had a strong enough effect to overcome the presumed tolerance of gamers for their non-preferred (allocentric) mapping. Rotations also showed a clear preference for the egocentric mapping among both groups (gamers: $r=0.64$, $\sigma_r=0.02$; non-gamers: $r=0.50$, $\sigma_r=0.09$), confirming hypothesis **H1**.

In Scene 4, like in Scene 2, non-gamers had a strong preference for egocentric translations ($r=0.44$, $\sigma_r=0.13$), while gamers were more tolerant of either mapping ($r=0.13$, $\sigma_r=0.20$). We observed the same pattern with rotations: non-gamers had a preference for allocentric rotations ($r=0.39$, $\sigma_r=0.14$), while gamers were more neutral ($r=0.09$, $\sigma_r=0.19$). Although these results still contradict **H2**, they are consistent with our above assumption that gamers may be more tolerant to using different mappings in various virtual environments.

9.4 Simultaneous translations/rotations

Figure 6 shows the ratings for each combination of allocentric and egocentric translations and rotations, in tasks involving full 6-DOF manipulation. For conciseness, we use the notation T(tmap)/R(rmap) in which "tmap" describes the translation mapping and "rmap" describes the rotation mapping. The results for Scenes 1 and 2 both present a similar pattern: pairwise differences in ratings were comparatively larger between T(ego) and T(allo) combinations (medium effect sizes) than between R(ego) and R(allo) combinations (small to zero effect sizes). It thus seems that, in these two scenes, the choice of translation mapping is more important than the rotation mapping when performing both simultaneously. This appears to disprove hypothesis **H4**.

As expected from the translation-only results, T(ego) combinations were rated higher than T(allo) combinations in all scenes except Scene 3. In these scenes, however, the T(ego)/R(ego) mapping was apparently preferred to the T(ego)/R(allo) mapping. This is surprising because our results for the first part of the experiment showed a preference for allocentric rotations in such scenes. Moreover, the T(allo)/R(allo) mapping also seems to be preferred to the T(allo)/R(ego) mapping in Scenes 1 and 4, with a tie in Scene 2. Although these differences are below the standard error, they nevertheless hint at a similar trend in each of these scenes. In addition to the dominance of the translation mapping, there might thus be a preference for having the same mapping for both translations and rotations.

Overall, the four combinations were given comparable ratings in Scenes 1 and 2, the differences between each combination were thus also comparable. These differences were, however, more uniform in Scene 2 than in Scene 1. This could be explained by the lower number of strongly negative ratings for the T(ego)/R(allo) and T(allo)/R(ego) combinations—i.e. two combinations that featured an egocentric mapping. This is consistent with the previously identified small possible effect that would slightly reinforce the preference for the egocentric mapping in Scene 2. It also provides additional (if small) evidence for hypothesis **H3**.

Scene 3 showed a strong difference between the fully egocentric (T(ego)/R(ego)) combination and the three other combinations. Almost all participants rated the former as natural, whereas the latter (not fully egocentric) three were largely rated as unnatural. Still, among these three lowest-rated combinations, T(allo)/R(ego)—the only one to feature egocentric rotations—was rated noticeably higher, despite consisting of two opposite mappings. We can hypothesize that this is due to the larger influence of rotations on visual flow when the manipulated object is viewed from inside. In such a situation, the positive effects of having rotations that match the preferred mapping (egocentric, as per our previous results) appear to noticeably alleviate the negative effects of a non-preferred (allocentric) translation mapping, even though the translation and rotation mappings are different. In any case, these results confirm again the importance of an

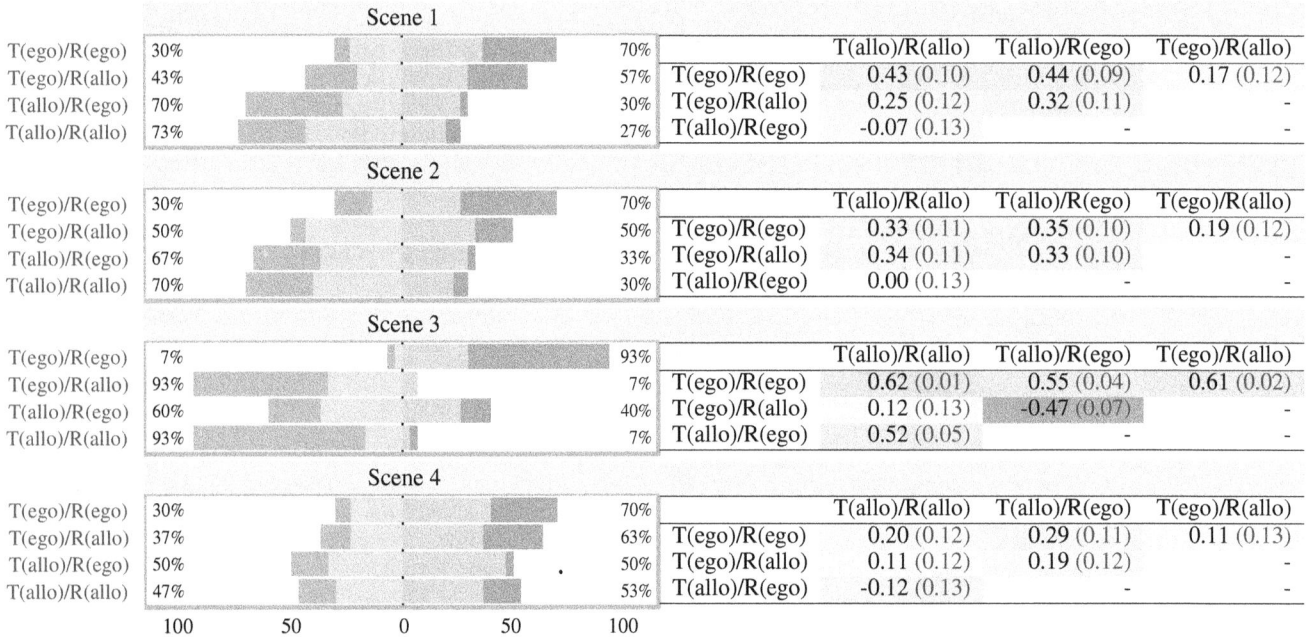

Scene 1

	100 → 0	0 → 100		T(allo)/R(allo)	T(allo)/R(ego)	T(ego)/R(allo)
T(ego)/R(ego)	30%	70%	T(ego)/R(ego)	0.43 (0.10)	0.44 (0.09)	0.17 (0.12)
T(ego)/R(allo)	43%	57%	T(ego)/R(allo)	0.25 (0.12)	0.32 (0.11)	-
T(allo)/R(ego)	70%	30%	T(allo)/R(ego)	-0.07 (0.13)	-	-
T(allo)/R(allo)	73%	27%				

Scene 2

				T(allo)/R(allo)	T(allo)/R(ego)	T(ego)/R(allo)
T(ego)/R(ego)	30%	70%	T(ego)/R(ego)	0.33 (0.11)	0.35 (0.10)	0.19 (0.12)
T(ego)/R(allo)	50%	50%	T(ego)/R(allo)	0.34 (0.11)	0.33 (0.10)	-
T(allo)/R(ego)	67%	33%	T(allo)/R(ego)	0.00 (0.13)	-	-
T(allo)/R(allo)	70%	30%				

Scene 3

				T(allo)/R(allo)	T(allo)/R(ego)	T(ego)/R(allo)
T(ego)/R(ego)	7%	93%	T(ego)/R(ego)	0.62 (0.01)	0.55 (0.04)	0.61 (0.02)
T(ego)/R(allo)	93%	7%	T(ego)/R(allo)	0.12 (0.13)	-0.47 (0.07)	-
T(allo)/R(ego)	60%	40%	T(allo)/R(ego)	0.52 (0.05)	-	-
T(allo)/R(allo)	93%	7%				

Scene 4

				T(allo)/R(allo)	T(allo)/R(ego)	T(ego)/R(allo)
T(ego)/R(ego)	30%	70%	T(ego)/R(ego)	0.20 (0.12)	0.29 (0.11)	0.11 (0.13)
T(ego)/R(allo)	37%	63%	T(ego)/R(allo)	0.11 (0.12)	0.19 (0.12)	-
T(allo)/R(ego)	50%	50%	T(allo)/R(ego)	-0.12 (0.13)	-	-
T(allo)/R(allo)	47%	53%				

100 50 0 50 100

Figure 6: Ratings in the full 6-DOF manipulation tasks (simultaneous translations/rotations), along with the pairwise effect sizes. The notation "T(tmap)/R(rmap)" refers to a translation mapping "tmap" and a rotation mapping "rmap".

egocentric mapping when the manipulated object is viewed from inside (hypothesis **H1**).

9.5 Per-axis inversion

Figure 7 shows the ratings given by participants in the third part of the experiment, in which the direction of motion along each manipulation axis was alternatively inverted. The x-axis ran along the left-right direction of the tablet's screen (which was itself held in landscape orientation), the y-axis was aligned with the top-down direction of the screen, and the z-axis was orthogonal to the screen plane. Unlike during the previous parts, we asked for ratings on a 3-point Likert scale.

For translations, one configuration was clearly preferred over the others: the fully egocentric mapping. This is consistent with the results of the previous parts that revealed a preference for egocentric translations in Scene 1. Given the strength of this effect (100% of participants rated this mapping as natural, far above the other configurations) there does not seem to be any advantage to gain from a mixed mapping for translations.

However, one question that still remains is whether some manipulation axes have more influence than others in the perceived naturalness of a mapping (hypothesis **H5**). One such pattern seems to be visible in the above results: configurations where the y-axis was inverted (i.e. egocentric) were consistently rated higher than the others—with the exception of the fully allocentric configuration. We thus conducted a further analysis by merging the ratings in egocentric and allocentric groups depending on the state (inverted or not) of each manipulation axis. The results indeed revealed a larger effect of the y-axis ($r=0.35$, $\sigma_r=0.07$), compared to the effects of the x-axis ($r=0.18$, $\sigma_r=0.09$) and the z-axis ($r=0.05$, $\sigma_r=0.10$). The reason why the fully allocentric was comparatively rated higher, despite its non-inverted y-axis, could be explained by a preference for a consistent mapping between

all axes—similar to the possible preference for a consistent mapping between translations and rotations discussed in the previous section. Nevertheless, the larger influence of the y-axis appears to validate our **H5** hypothesis for translations.

For rotations, no configuration was unanimously favored and the differences between each configuration were smaller overall than for translations. Merging the ratings into groups according to each manipulation axis confirmed that the influences of all axes were limited (x: $r=0.17$, $\sigma_r=0.09$; y: $r=0.00$, $\sigma_r=0.09$; and z: $r=0.11$, $\sigma_r=0.09$), which does not confirm **H5** for rotations. Yet, one configuration seems to have been strongly disliked compared to all the others: the allo-ego-allo (AEA) mapping. This result is unexpected, and we cannot find any reason that could explain such a sharp drop in ratings. This aspect would thus require further investigation.

10. CONCLUSION

The "baseline" preference, i.e. which alternative was found most natural with no prior exposure to the interface and minimal contextual cues, was *egocentric translations* and *allocentric rotations* among all users. In the gamers group, the baseline for translations was less marked than in the non-gamers group. However, the baseline for rotations was similar.

Regarding contextual cues, **H1** was strongly supported by our results: when a manipulated object is viewed from inside, the mapping should be egocentric for both translations and rotations. Surprisingly, **H2** was not supported. It appears that manipulating an object within a fixed virtual environment does not induce a preference for an allocentric mapping. There was limited support for **H3** that a typically static object should be manipulated with an egocentric mapping. The results hint at a possible weak effect, though not sufficient to overcome other factors (such as the baseline preference).

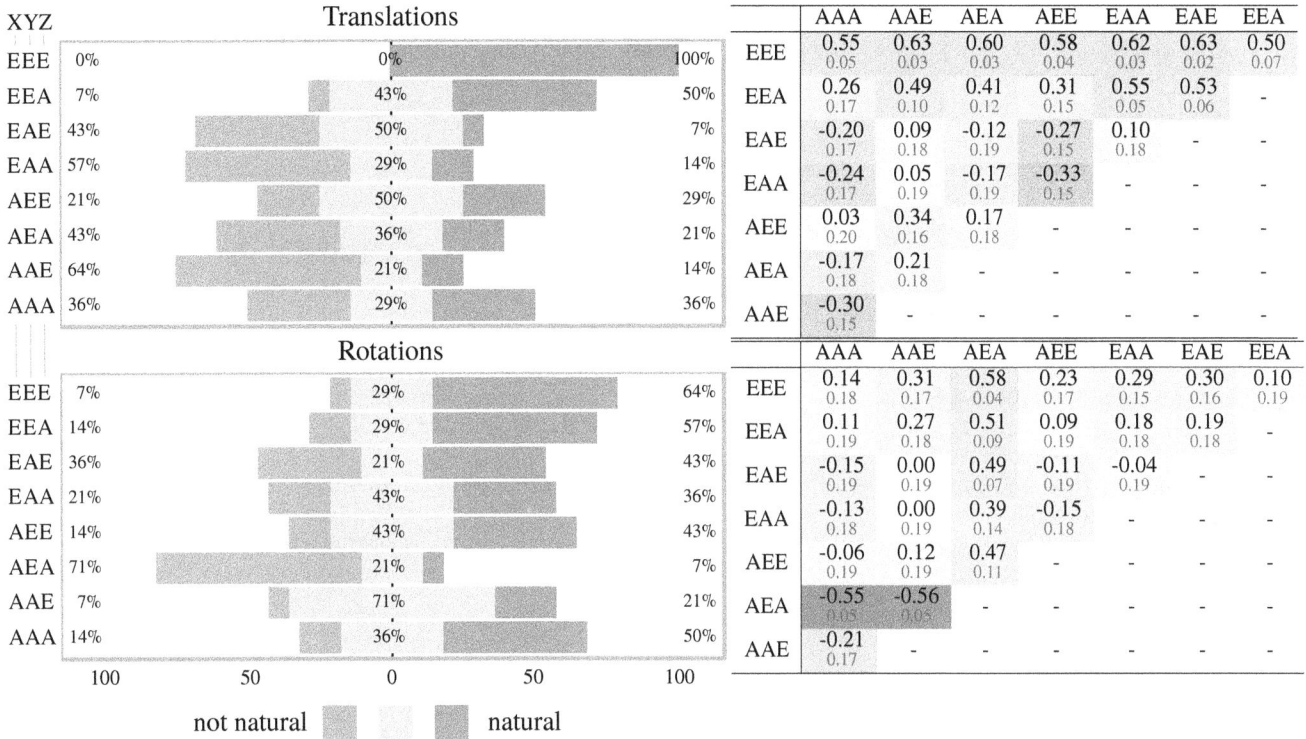

XYZ	Translations		
EEE	0%	0%	100%
EEA	7%	43%	50%
EAE	43%	50%	7%
EAA	57%	29%	14%
AEE	21%	50%	29%
AEA	43%	36%	21%
AAE	64%	21%	14%
AAA	36%	29%	36%

	AAA	AAE	AEA	AEE	EAA	EAE	EEA
EEE	0.55 (0.05)	0.63 (0.03)	0.60 (0.03)	0.58 (0.04)	0.62 (0.03)	0.63 (0.02)	0.50 (0.07)
EEA	0.26 (0.17)	0.49 (0.10)	0.41 (0.12)	0.31 (0.15)	0.55 (0.05)	0.53 (0.06)	-
EAE	-0.20 (0.17)	0.09 (0.18)	-0.12 (0.19)	-0.27 (0.15)	0.10 (0.18)	-	-
EAA	-0.24 (0.17)	0.05 (0.19)	-0.17 (0.19)	-0.33 (0.15)	-	-	-
AEE	0.03 (0.20)	0.34 (0.16)	0.17 (0.18)	-	-	-	-
AEA	-0.17 (0.18)	0.21 (0.18)	-	-	-	-	-
AAE	-0.30 (0.15)	-	-	-	-	-	-

XYZ	Rotations		
EEE	7%	29%	64%
EEA	14%	29%	57%
EAE	36%	21%	43%
EAA	21%	43%	36%
AEE	14%	43%	43%
AEA	71%	21%	7%
AAE	7%	71%	21%
AAA	14%	36%	50%

	AAA	AAE	AEA	AEE	EAA	EAE	EEA
EEE	0.14 (0.18)	0.31 (0.17)	0.58 (0.04)	0.23 (0.17)	0.29 (0.15)	0.30 (0.16)	0.10 (0.19)
EEA	0.11 (0.19)	0.27 (0.18)	0.51 (0.09)	0.09 (0.19)	0.18 (0.18)	0.19 (0.18)	-
EAE	-0.15 (0.19)	0.00 (0.19)	0.49 (0.07)	-0.11 (0.19)	-0.04 (0.19)	-	-
EAA	-0.13 (0.18)	0.00 (0.19)	0.39 (0.14)	-0.15 (0.18)	-	-	-
AEE	-0.06 (0.19)	0.12 (0.19)	0.47 (0.11)	-	-	-	-
AEA	-0.55 (0.05)	-0.56 (0.05)	-	-	-	-	-
AAE	-0.21 (0.17)	-	-	-	-	-	-

not natural ▨ ▨ natural

100 50 0 50 100

Figure 7: Ratings and pairwise effect sizes in the per-axis inversion part (labels are in the form "XYZ": A=allocentric, E=egocentric).

Gamers seem to be less influenced by the scene contents than non-gamers—except when the manipulated object was viewed from inside. This could mean that gamers are more tolerant to encountering various mappings in 3D applications. Yet, the overall preferred mappings were still the same in both groups. We recommend, therefore, that translations-only mappings should be made egocentric in all cases, and that rotation-only mappings should be made allocentric in all cases *except* when the manipulated object is viewed from inside—in which case it should be made egocentric.

In full 6-DOF mappings, where users perform both translations and rotations simultaneously, the choice of a "good" translation mapping (egocentric, according to the results of part 1) seems to be more important than the choice of rotation mapping, thus disproving the null hypothesis **H4**. However, when the manipulated object is viewed from inside, *both* mappings should be egocentric. In addition, there seems to be a positive effect of having the same mapping for translations and rotations. Therefore, we recommend that a 6-DOF manipulation mapping should be T(ego)/R(ego) (i.e. fully egocentric) in all cases.

We saw no benefit of a "mixed" mapping that selectively inverts some of the manipulation axes, compared to a "fully" egocentric or allocentric mapping. Yet, if such a mixed mapping must be implemented, the *y*-axis (along the vertical direction of the device's screen) appears to have more influence on the perceived naturalness of translations. This would support hypothesis **H5**, but only for translations. For reasons we have yet to explain, one mixed mapping for rotations (allo-ego-allo) was found much less natural than all the others.

11. REFERENCES

[1] J. Bartlett. Rock 'n' Scroll is here to stay. *IEEE Computer Graphics and Applications*, 20(3):40–45, May 2000.

[2] D. A. Bowman, E. Kruijff, J. J. LaViola, Jr., and I. Poupyrev. *3D User Interfaces: Theory and Practice*. Addison-Wesley, Boston, 2004.

[3] N. Burgess, H. J. Spiers, and E. Paleologou. Orientational manoeuvres in the dark: Dissociating allocentric and egocentric influences on spatial memory. *Cognition*, 94(2):149–166, 2004.

[4] A. H. S. Chan, V. W. Y. Shum, H. W. Law, and I. K. Hui. Precise effects of control position, indicator type, and scale side on human performance. *The International Journal of Advanced Manufacturing Technology*, 22(5–6):380–386, 2003.

[5] D. D. Diaz and V. K. Sims. Accidental inversion during three-dimensional orientational control. *Proceedings of the Human Factors and Ergonomics Society Annual Meeting*, 49(13):1248–1250, 2005.

[6] P. M. Fitts. Engineering psychology and equipment design. In S. S. Stevens, editor, *Handbook of experimental psychology*, pages 1287–1340. Wiley, 1951.

[7] P. M. Fitts and C. M. Seeger. SR compatibility: Spatial characteristics of stimulus and response codes. *Journal of Experimental Psychology*, 46(3):199–210, 1953.

[8] C. O. Fritz, P. E. Morris, and J. J. Richler. Effect size estimates: Current use, calculations, and interpretation. *Journal of Experimental Psychology: General*, 141(1):2–18, 2012.

[9] K. Hinckley and H. Song. Sensor synaesthesia: Touch in motion, and motion in touch. In *Proc. CHI*, pages 801–810, New York, 2011. ACM.

[10] P. Issartel, F. Guéniat, T. Isenberg, and M. Ammi. Analysis of locally coupled 3d manipulation mappings based on mobile device motion. arXiv preprint 1603.07462, Mar. 2016.

[11] M. S. Kaminaka and E. A. Egli. Lever controls on specialised farm equipment: Some control/response stereotypes. *Applied Ergonomics*, 16(3):193–199, 1985.

[12] R. L. Klatzky. Allocentric and egocentric spatial representations: Definitions, distinctions, and interconnections. In *Spatial Cognition*, pages 1–17. Springer, Berlin/Heidelberg, 1998.

[13] S. Neale, W. Chinthammit, C. Lueg, and P. Nixon. RelicPad: A hands-on, mobile approach to collaborative exploration of virtual museum artifacts. In *Proc. INTERACT*, pages 86–103, Berlin/Heidelberg, 2013. Springer.

[14] I. Poupyrev, T. Ichikawa, S. Weghorst, and M. Billinghurst. Egocentric object manipulation in virtual environments: Empirical evaluation of interaction techniques. *Computer Graphics Forum*, 17(3):41–52, 1998.

[15] J. Rekimoto. Tilting operations for small screen interfaces. In *Proc. UIST*, pages 167–168, New York, 1996. ACM.

[16] M. J. Warrick. Direction of movement in the use of control knobs to position visual indicators. *Psychological Research on Equipment Design*, pages 137–146, 1947.

[17] L. Weberg, T. Brange, and Å. Wendelbo-Hansson. A piece of butter on the PDA display. In *CHI Extended Abstracts*, pages 435–436, New York, 2001. ACM.

[18] J. Wiebe and K.-P. L. Vu. Application of population stereotypes to computerized tasks. In *Proc. Human Interface and the Management of Information*, pages 718–725. Springer, Berlin/Heidelberg, 2009.

Providing Assistance for Orienting 3D Objects Using Monocular Eyewear

Mengu Sukan   Carmine Elvezio   Steven Feiner
Dept. of Computer Science, Columbia University
New York, NY, 10027 USA
{mengu, carmine, feiner}@cs.columbia.edu

Barbara Tversky
Dept. of Human Dev., Teachers College
New York, NY, 10027 USA
btversky@stanford.edu

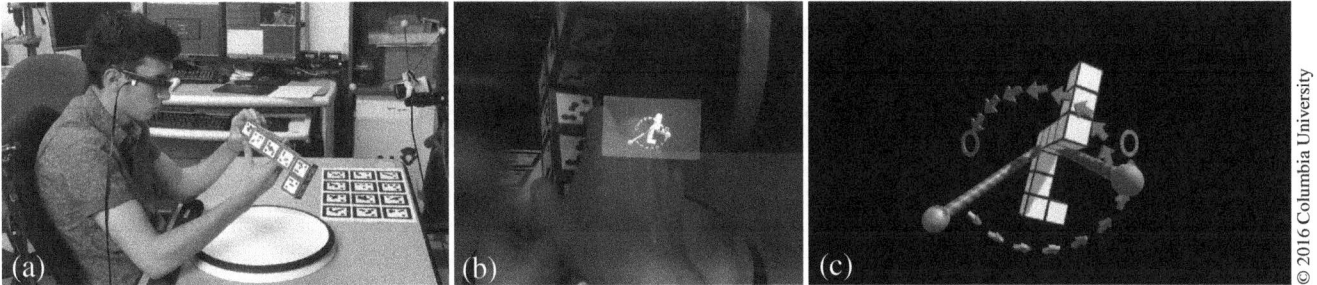

Figure 1: (a) Study participant manually orienting task object, guided by our system. (b) Participant's view of task and HANDLES visualization, photographed through Google Glass. (c) Screen capture of HANDLES visualization, rendered on Glass.

ABSTRACT

Many tasks require that a user rotate an object to match a specific orientation in an external coordinate system. This includes tasks in which one object must be oriented relative to a second prior to assembly and tasks in which objects must be held in specific ways to inspect them. Research has investigated guidance mechanisms for some 6DOF tasks, using wide–field-of-view, stereoscopic virtual and augmented reality head-worn displays (HWDs). However, there has been relatively little work directed toward smaller field-of-view lightweight monoscopic HWDs, such as Google Glass, which may remain more comfortable and less intrusive than stereoscopic HWDs in the near future. We have designed and implemented a novel visualization approach and three additional visualizations representing different paradigms for guiding unconstrained manual 3DOF rotation, targeting these monoscopic HWDs. We describe our exploration of these paradigms and present the results of a user study evaluating the relative performance of the visualizations and showing the advantages of our new approach.

CCS Concepts

•Computing methodologies → Mixed / augmented reality; Virtual reality; •Human-centered computing → *Graphics input devices; Interaction techniques; Interaction design theory, concepts and paradigms;* User interface design;

Keywords

Task assistance; Procedural task; 3D; UI; HWD.

SUI '16, October 15-16, 2016, Tokyo, Japan

© 2016 Copyright held by the owner/author(s). Publication rights licensed to ACM.
ISBN 978-1-4503-4068-7/16/10. . . $15.00

DOI: http://dx.doi.org/10.1145/2983310.2985764

1. INTRODUCTION

Many physical tasks require people to hold objects in specific orientations. In some cases, rotation tasks are simplified due to implicit physical constraints (e.g., a knob with discrete steps). However, numerous real-world situations, such as inspecting objects visually, or attaching one part to another, require unconstrained manual 3DOF rotation. Further, there are scenarios in which task objects or external references for alignment can be ambiguous; for example, a task object may be symmetric visually, but contain internal sensors, or a hand-held medical imaging device may need to be aligned with internal organs that are not seen directly. In these situations, providing guidance for rotating an object becomes a question of either conveying direction and magnitude explicitly, or annotating the environment to provide additional context for alignment.

Manuals, whether physical or virtual, often show different views of task objects and use annotations (e.g., connectors and arrows) to illustrate the required action [14]. However, these can be difficult to integrate, especially for complex, self-similar, or symmetric shapes, as mentioned above. Systems that present virtual instructions on a head-worn display (HWD) have been shown to help in transforming a rigid object to a predetermined position and orientation [12]. Such systems commonly employ basic virtual 3D UI elements such as arrows, animations, or clones of task objects as visual hints that guide users when performing manual operations (e.g., [8, 19, 15, 11, 17, 16, 6]). For example, based on this work, we can expect arrows to be suitable for showing a path of movement for a task object or body part. However, displaying paths as 3D arrows can be ambiguous for certain geometric projections, especially when viewed on monoscopic displays.

Even though these basic 3D UI elements have long been used in task guidance systems, we are not aware of any principled exploration of their effectiveness for real-time task assistance. In this paper, we begin to address this gap by presenting the design and comparative evaluation of a set of UI elements for a nontrivial rotation task, measuring their usability and effectiveness, and attempting to explain their relative effectiveness and trade-offs using cognitive science. In summary, we make four major contributions:

(1) We present HANDLES, a novel interaction and visualization approach to provide real-time guidance for unconstrained 3D rotation of hand-held objects (Figure 1). HANDLES was specifically developed to overcome shortcomings of existing approaches by providing persistent, clearly-visible alignment targets, and to work well on lightweight, monoscopic, small-FOV HWDs. (These devices, typified by Google Glass, Brother AiRScouter, and Vuzix M300, may remain more comfortable and less intrusive than wider-FOV stereoscopic HWDs in the near future.) We show that users guided by HANDLES perform a nontrivial orientation task significantly faster compared to other techniques and tend to prefer it over the other techniques.

(2) We describe three additional orientation-guidance approaches that are built using variants of common UI elements found in existing orientation-guidance systems (e.g., 3D arrows and animation) and detail how we carefully fine-tuned these approaches to improve their usability.

(3) For each approach, we outline our exploration of the design space and justify our design choices and visualization parameters, based on usability feedback from extensive pilot studies. We highlight advantages and trade-offs of each approach and discuss how we expect it to perform, based on principles of human cognition.

(4) We report results and analysis from a formal user study that compares these four approaches with an unaided side-by-side representation of the static target orientation and a dynamic virtual proxy of the tracked object, addressing speed of performance (both overall speed, and the breakdown into initial ballistic rotation and subsequent fine-tuning), preference, and task load.

We believe that our detailed and principled exploration of the design space and our findings are valuable for the 3D HCI community, as our approaches can be used as a foundation for future eye-worn guidance systems.

2. RELATED WORK

Our visualizations are inspired by elements from a large body of work exploring task assistance using augmented reality (AR). Instructional manuals have long used arrows to depict rigid body transformations [14]. This approach has been adopted in computer-based documentation systems, including ones targeting AR. For example, arrows can cyclically move in a direction in which an object is to be translated [8] or interactively change in size and color to indicate direction and magnitude of a 1-DOF rotation needed to align two tracked workpieces [12]. Ghosting is another common visualization technique used in real-time AR task guidance systems to visualize workpiece placement (e.g., [11]). Ghosting and animation have also been used to provide visual hints on how to move (e.g., reel or shake) hand-held props to activate gestures in an AR system [27].

AR interfaces have been developed to guide users in matching gestures and poses with parts of their body. Freeman et al. [9] assist users in learning multi-touch gestures on a touchscreen by showing a partial shadow of the user's hands on screen. Sodhi et al. [22] guide a user in translating a single hand using a 3D arrow, a 3D path, or colored regions indicating movement direction projected directly on the user's hand. Anderson et al. [1] guide a user in moving their body by displaying augmentations over a mirror image of the user. Their visualization includes both a simple skeletal representation of the user's current and target poses, and a ribbon indicating the path the user should follow to achieve the target pose. These systems focus on hand and body manipulation directly, whereas our system focuses on guiding users in rotating a hand-held shape to a target

orientation, allowing them to use their hands freely as they hold the tracked object.

We build on past work by focusing on a specific subtask—manual orientation of hand-held objects—aiming to improve upon existing techniques by providing users with continuous feedback designed to reduce cognitive load, facilitate corrective action, and provide confirmation once the target orientation is reached. Note that this is quite different from 3D applications on desktop systems that use separable rotation control widgets for one or more axes (e.g., [20]). Unlike those widgets, our techniques visualize the remaining rotation between a tracked object's current orientation and a target orientation. Further, our user is holding the tracked object with an unconstrained hand and cannot precisely manipulate the object to rotate only about a given axis as can be done with a desktop widget.

There is research on the standard mental rotation task, showing that people often spontaneously rotate a hand when solving the problem and that when they move their hand in the most efficient direction they perform better, but when forced to move their hand in the opposite direction they perform worse. That is, moving one's hands in a conceptually congruent way helps the user perform a mental transformation [4, 5, 25, 28]. This research inspired the design of the nontrivial rotation task underlying our user study.

Oda et al. [17] used an annotation-based solution to guide a user to match a 6DOF pose specified by a remote subject matter expert (SME). The 6DOF pose of a manipulatable object was constrained by the physical properties of a fixture on which the user placed the object. Two types of orientation guidance were presented. In both, annotations on the manipulatable object and on the fixture provided a complete 6DOF specification for how the manipulatable object should rest on the fixture. In one technique, this was augmented with a replica of the virtual representation of the manipulatable object that animated in conjunction with the remote SME's control of the manipulatable object's replica in their virtual environment. In their work, rotation guidance was handled completely through matching annotations, with no additional guidance.

In an earlier poster [6], we briefly described a set of unevaluated techniques to help users manually rotate a tracked object to an arbitrary 3DOF orientation, tailored to lightweight, monocular HWDs. Building on this work, we ran extensive pilot tests, leading to a number of significant modifications to improve user performance, and resulting in a novel visualization described below. Finally, we conducted a formal evaluation to compare the new designs.

3. IMPLEMENTATION

We implemented our work in Unity 3D. While our visualizations are device-agnostic (i.e., can be rendered on various screen sizes and modalities—head-worn, hand-held, or desktop; monoscopic or stereoscopic), we developed and tested them on Google Glass. Because the current generation of lightweight, monoscopic HWDs typically have FOVs that are small and off-center, we created a virtual proxy of the tracked object, so that annotations can be rendered and registered relative to it instead of the real object (Figure 1b). The virtual proxy and visualizations are rendered from the perspective of a stationary virtual camera located near the head of the user, who is assumed to be sitting in place, as we ensured in our user study (Section 5.4.4). Arbitrary viewpoints could be accommodated with minor changes if head-tracking were available.

3.1 Common Components

A number of our visualizations incorporate curved 3D arrows to communicate 3D rotations, whose design evolved as we prototyped and tested our visualizations. Initially, we used simple 3D cylindrical arrows (Figure 2a), with a cone for the arrow head and a curved

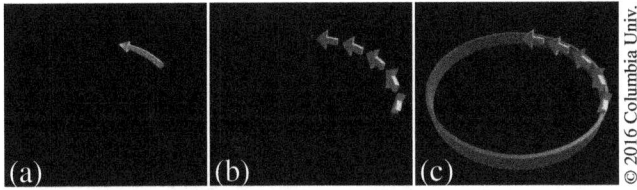

Figure 2: Arrow shape evolution. (a) A simple cylindrical, curved 3D arrow. (b) Repeating flattened 3D arrows increase amount of information encoded in arrow body. Walls facing towards the axis of rotation are colored differently to help disambiguate orientation. (c) Repeating flattened 3D arrows with semi-transparent ring to further clarify rotation axis.

cylinder for the body. During pilot studies, we noticed that the rotation axis implied by these arrows was often difficult to judge, especially when the magnitude of the arrow spanned less than 45°. To improve perceptibility, we switched to a flat, curved 3D arrow that had an extruded triangle for its head and an extruded rectangle for its body, which was essentially a curved version of commonly encountered 2D arrows, slightly thickened. This allowed us to provide more visual information about the implied rotation axis by increasing the width of the arrow. To further disambiguate the implied rotation axis, we applied a different color to the walls of the arrow that face towards the rotation axis, as opposed to one that face away from the rotation axis. The head of a flat 3D arrow can become indistinguishable from its body when the user is viewing the arrow from the side. Therefore, we made the arrow head into a pyramid with a single point at the tip and base that is wider than the cross-section of the body, to ensure that the head was distinguishable even when viewed from the side.

Even when the axis of rotation is clear, another issue we encountered was that in order to understand the direction of rotation, users had to constantly keep track of where the arrow head was. This problem was compounded when it was occluded by another object in the scene. To increase the amount of information encoded in the arrow body, we broke the single curved arrow into smaller ones along the same curve, analogous to a dashed line (Figure 2b).

Changing the length of the arrow body to represent the magnitude of remaining rotation created several issues. First, when the amount of the remaining rotation became small (i.e., the task was near completion), the amount of visual information available to the user was also lessened. This was counterproductive, since the user still needed as much information as possible to complete the fine-tuning stage. To address this problem, we added a ring (an extruded annulus) that contained the repeating arrows and did not disappear based on the magnitude of the remaining rotation. The ring is semi-transparent and has the same hue as the arrow (Figure 2c). We note that there is a trade-off here between cluttering the scene, especially when multiple arrows are present, and not providing enough information; however, based on our testing, we believe the ring to be worth the visual space it occupies.

Another problem we faced with dynamically sized arrows was in their implementation, where we decided not to recalculate the positions of vertices and modify the vertex buffer in each frame. Instead, we left the full arrow geometry (i.e., 360°, the end of the body touching the tip of the head) untouched and implemented a custom pixel shader that took the remaining angle as a parameter and painted only those pixels that were within that angle of the tip.

4. OUR APPROACHES

In our implementation, the virtual proxy turns green whenever the target orientation is matched within a certain threshold. This is particularly important in the user study we conducted, to indicate to users that they have followed the instructions correctly and can move on to the next trial.

4.1 SingleAxis Visualization

SINGLEAXIS (Figure 3) applies the improved components of Section 3.1 to the OptimalAxis technique described by Elvezio et al. [6]. The core of the technique is inspired by Euler's rotation theorem [7], which dictates that any sequence of one or more rotations of a rigid body in 3D space is equivalent to an optimal rotation about a single axis. (Note that this axis is the unique single axis about which the differential rotation can be performed and therefore cannot, in general, be aligned with a major axis of the shape.)

In this visualization, a ring with small repeating dynamic rectangular 3D arrows is rendered around the virtual proxy, perpendicular to the axis of optimal rotation. In addition, a large cylinder, tied to the axis of optimal rotation, pierces the center of the virtual proxy. As the user rotates the tracked object, the axis and ring update to reflect the new axis and direction for a rotation from the tracked object's current orientation to the target orientation (relative to the world). As the magnitude of rotation gets smaller, the number of arrows decreases (where a single arrow will collapse from head to tail as it disappears), starting from the arrow furthest from the camera, and ending at the arrow closest to the camera (Figure 3).

During pilot studies, we observed that while the visualization worked quite well for large ballistic rotations, it became difficult for users to manage as the tracked object neared the target orientation (i.e., the fine-tuning stage). This was due to the rotational error between the current and target orientations changing drastically in direction, even from small adjustments made by the user. Visually, this resulted in the axis and ring swinging wildly around, making it difficult for users to understand how to execute the remaining rotation. To address this issue, we piloted a version of SINGLEAXIS that applied motion smoothing to the cylinder that represents the axis. Surprisingly, we found that smoothing negatively impacted user performance, especially during fine-tuning, where subtle changes to the rotation axis were not immediately represented. As users frequently deviate from the instructed axis during fine-tuning, the smoothed instructions would usually lag behind the user. Thus, we decided not to smooth the visualization during the user study described below.

In another design iteration, we displayed a static version of the original optimal axis of rotation. When the user deviated from this optimal axis, instead of showing the updated axis for the remaining rotation, we displayed a set of arrows that highlighted how to bring their current axis of rotation back to line up with the original. However, this solution was also disliked by pilot users, who now had to mentally resolve two separate rotations, instead of focusing on the single remaining rotation of the original version.

4.2 Euler Visualization

Another common way to describe an orientation in 3D space is Euler angles: a sequence of three elemental rotations (rotations about the three axes of an object's local coordinate system). Many objects are easily understood in terms of a particular coordinate system, whose axes can be chosen for the rotations. For the object shown in Figures 1 and 3–7, we use axes perpendicular to the faces of the cubes from which the object is composed. Because this visualization decomposes the rotation into three steps, each associ-

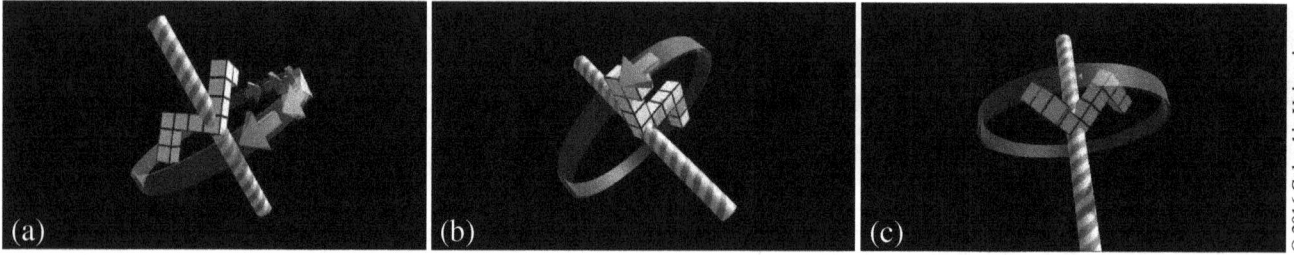

Figure 3: SINGLEAXIS. (a) The remaining rotation is represented by a cylinder showing the axis of rotation and a set of dynamic arrows indicating the direction and magnitude of the remaining rotation. (b) As the user follows the visualization, the axis and arrows update to reflect the current optimal rotation from the current pose of the object to the target pose. (c) As the user nears the target pose, the arrows collapse into their arrowheads.

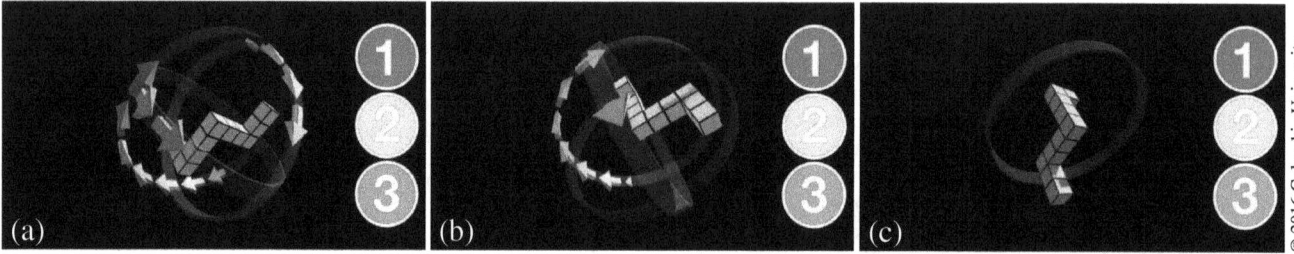

Figure 4: EULER. (a) The remaining rotation is represented by a set of three arrows showing the axes, direction, and magnitude of the remaining rotation. (b) As the user follows the visualization, in the order indicated by the colored numbered circles on the side, the arrows update to reflect the remaining rotation, per axis, from the current pose of the object to the target pose. (c) As the user nears the target pose, the arrows collapse into their arrowheads. If the user rotates away from the target about a particular axis, the arrows reappear.

ated with an easily recognizable axis, it might be easier to enact, especially by people with lower spatial ability (e.g., [24]).

Our EULER visualization (Figure 4) builds on the EulerAngles visualization [6]. In the previous EulerAngles, the axes of rotation were described by three cylindrical arrows, color-coded to represent the intended order of rotation based on the decomposition of the quaternion representing the remaining rotation. When pilot-testing this technique, we discovered that it was often difficult for participants to determine the direction of rotation about each axis, due to the fact that the user needed to search the cylinder that formed the shaft of the arrow for the arrow head. Additionally, it was possible that the virtual proxy itself would obscure the arrowhead, leading to situations where, with an untracked HWD such as Google Glass, it would be impossible to see the direction of the particular arrow without some initial trial and error.

To alleviate this, we used the improved components of Section 3.1 to introduce a number of new features. Instead of a single arrow per axis, we render a set of smaller arrows in a ring perpendicular to a particular principle axis. The smaller arrows disappear smoothly as described above. In addition, the front of the path is always anchored at the point on the ring closest to the virtual camera. The combination of these changes makes immediately clear, at all times, the intended direction of rotation per axis. Finally, upon nearing the completion threshold for a particular axis, the ring will disappear. It will return if the user breaks from the target orientation about a particular axis (Figure 4).

Since a sequence of 3D rotations is, in general, not commutative, there is a defined order for the axes about which the user should rotate the object when following the instructions. To remove the requirement that the user memorize the axis order, imposed in our previous work [6], we render three large icons on the screen showing the rotation order, represented by number and color.

4.3 Animate Visualization

Animation is a visualization technique frequently used to communicate motion or action. It became clear that animating the virtual proxy from its tracked (i.e., current) orientation to the target orientation was not ideal because the user had to wait until the animation finished and rewound to get feedback on current orientation. To provide feedback on both current orientation and desired motion simultaneously, our ANIMATE visualization (Figure 5) adds a second, animating copy of the virtual proxy to the scene. We quickly realized that the placement of this animating copy had a significant impact on user performance. Initially, since our task is rotation-only, the animating copy overlapped with the virtual proxy and made it difficult to distinguish one from the other. In our following iterations, we tried rendering the animating copy and the virtual proxy side-by-side, similar to our earlier work [6]. This proved to be suboptimal, especially in the fine-tuning stage, because it required users to detect differences between two objects that have similar orientations, but are spatially set apart. Going back to a co-located design, we addressed the occlusion and disambiguation issues caused by overlapping, by modifying the transparency of the animating replica to 50% and changing its outline from solid black lines to dashed grey lines (Figure 5). This faded visual is known as *ghosting*, an illustrative technique used in comics [13] where an object is rendered as semitransparent to represent its past or future state, and in previous visualizations (e.g., [27, 11]).

Another subtle, yet important, design decision was the timing and speed of the animation. We wanted to provide users with continuous feedback, so it was a natural decision to repeat the anima-

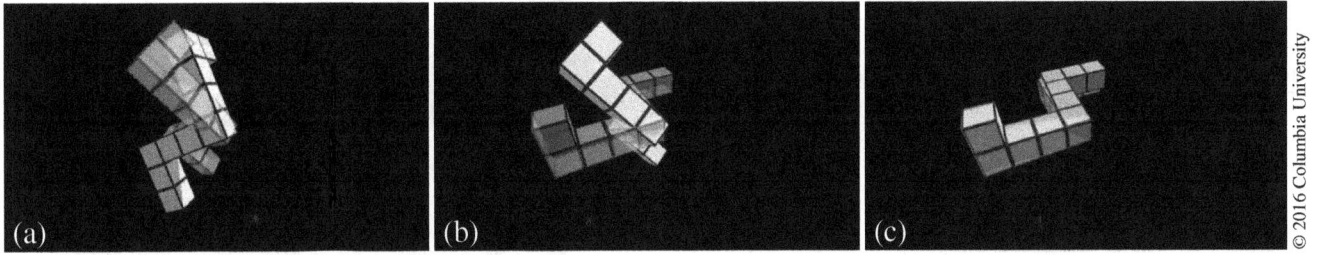

Figure 5: ANIMATE. (a) The remaining rotation is represented by an animating clone of the virtual proxy, which rotates from the current orientation of the tracked object, to the destination orientation. (b) As the user follows the visualization, the looping animation will begin from the latest orientation of the tracked object. (c) As the user nears the target pose, the frequency and speed of the animated object will increase, until the task is complete.

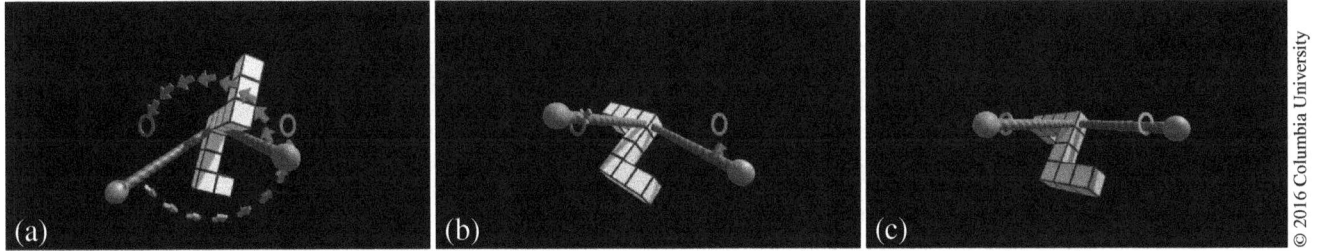

Figure 6: HANDLES. (a) The target orientation is directly represented by a set of two colored tori. Two colored poles extend from the center of the virtual proxy, and the user must try to align each pole with its matching torus. A set of arrows show the rotational path from each pole to its corresponding torus. (b) As the user nears the target pose, the arrows update to show the current rotational path from each pole to its corresponding torus. (c) Both handles have been aligned, the tori turn green, and the task is complete.

tion once the animating copy arrived at the target orientation by rewinding the animating copy to the tracked object's current orientation. We implemented an ease-in, ease-out interpolator to make the beginning and end of the animation less visually jarring and abrupt for the user. Setting the duration of each animation cycle to a constant value did not make much sense, since that would require the animating copy to move more slowly as the tracked object neared its target, which pilot users found frustrating.

Setting the speed of the animation seemed like a better idea and we found a rotational speed of 90° per second to be comfortable based on pilot tests. This ensured that when the tracked object was near its target orientation, the animation took less time and therefore repeated more frequently. However, when the frequency got too high, it became less helpful because it was hard to distinguish between the animation progressing forward and rewinding back to the current orientation. To address that issue, we introduced a 0.5 second gap between animations. Finally, we clamped the total animation duration to be between 0.2 and 2 seconds.

4.4 Handles Visualization

The HANDLES visualization (Figure 6) builds on the key insight that orientation in 3D space is commonly parametrized by two different directions (e.g., virtual cameras in computer graphics are often defined by specifying a non-collinear pair of vectors: look-at and up). In HANDLES, these non-collinear directions are represented by poles extending from the center of the virtual proxy, which look like physical handles. Each pole's target orientation is represented as a torus whose hole is just wide enough for its pole to go through. These tori are persistently placed in direct view of the user to avoid occlusion. Additionally, each pole is connected to its corresponding torus by a set of color-coded arrows to indicate

the direction of rotation necessary to achieve the target orientation (Figure 6).

The 2-Point visualization, developed in our earlier work [6], required the user to align a pair of points attached to the virtual proxy, represented by cones, with a pair of corresponding points that are fixed in space, represented by target spheres. In piloting an implementation of 2-Point, we found that it had shortcomings that severely limited its effectiveness. Users often tried to translate the shape so that a cone/sphere pair would align, even after being instructed that translation was not being tracked. The locations of the target spheres depended on the specific task in a seemingly arbitrary way. Additionally, users complained that the cones and spheres were too small, making it difficult to distinguish which way the cones were pointing, and the enveloping sphere made it difficult to see the cones and the virtual representation of the main object contained within.

Since we wanted to make the poles look like physical handles that are rigidly attached to the virtual proxy, we added a spherical knob to the end of each pole to (a) bolster the metaphor that the poles are handles that can be grabbed and moved, and (b) provide occlusion and perspective depth cues, which could be especially beneficial when the handles are near their targets (i.e., during the fine-tuning stage, which was an issue mentioned during pilot tests).

An important design question was where to attach handles to the virtual proxy. Initially, we attached them along the major axes of the shape, but for certain target orientations, this caused the tori to face away from the user, possibly occluded by the virtual proxy. Since the visibility of the tori is crucial for this task, especially in the fine-tuning stage, we wanted to guarantee that they are always front and center and clearly visible to the user.

To that end, we developed a heuristic in which we start with a vector connecting the centroid of the virtual proxy to the center of projection of the virtual camera, rotate it 30° about the virtual camera's up-vector (clockwise for the first torus, counterclockwise for the second), and pick the intersection of that rotated vector with a spherical hull that contained the virtual proxy (to ensure that the virtual proxy would never touch or occlude the tori in any orientation). Since we had a stationary virtual camera pointed directly at the virtual proxy, this heuristic gave us two locations that are projected to lie on the horizontal centerline of the screen. Picking where the tori end up first meant that the poles would have to be attached in different orientations relative to the virtual proxy for each new target pose, which was calculated during initialization by applying the inverse of the rotation between the current orientation to the target orientation, to the tori positions.

To provide users with a sense of which direction to move the object, we added arrows that connected each handle to its corresponding torus. Initially, we used the same curved arrows that we used in other visualizations, which depicted the shortest path along the sphere from handle location to torus location. During pilot tests, we noticed users getting frustrated when following the shortest rotation between one of the handles and its torus worsened the alignment between the other handle and its torus. To alleviate this frustration, we replaced the arrows that traced the shortest path for each individual handle with "cookie-crumb" arrows that trace the ideal path of the handles when both of them are moved towards their target simultaneously (i.e., by following the single-axis optimal rotation from the current orientation to the target orientation). Similar to our other visualizations, the trail of arrows gets shorter as the user rotates the object and the remaining angle gets smaller.

To provide visual feedback for when the alignment is complete, we relied on color. Specifically, when a handle enters its corresponding torus, that torus turns green to indicate proper alignment for that pair. Once one of the handle–torus pairs is aligned, the user needs to bring the second handle into its corresponding torus while holding the first handle in place, which can be achieved by executing a 1DOF rotation (Figure 6b–c).

5. USER STUDY

We conducted a formal user study to compare the performance of our new techniques, in addition to a control condition described below. For our task object, we created an abstract object similar to those used by Shepard and Metzler in research on mental rotation [21]. Our object consists of ten 1.75-inch wooden cubes attached face-to-face to form a rigid structure with three right-angled "elbows" (Figure 1a). This type of object is especially suited for rotation tasks because (a) it cannot be transformed into itself by any reflection or rotation (short of 360°) and (b) cognitive science research has shown that it is difficult to mentally rotate [21, 23].

We required that the accuracy with which the participant performed each trial be as close to the correct pose as possible for the trial to end; therefore, we compared only time, not accuracy. We settled on a threshold of 8° by incrementally loosening a tighter threshold until pilot users were able to satisfy it consistently. Tighter constraints were especially difficult for visualizations that provide little or no feedback during fine-tuning (e.g., STATIC).

5.1 Control Condition

To determine the effectiveness of the techniques described above, with respect to a simple baseline, we developed a fifth technique, STATIC, which showed only the static target orientation next to an updating representation of the virtual proxy's current orientation (Figure 7). The virtual proxy would update as the user rotated the shape. When the target orientation was achieved, the virtual proxy

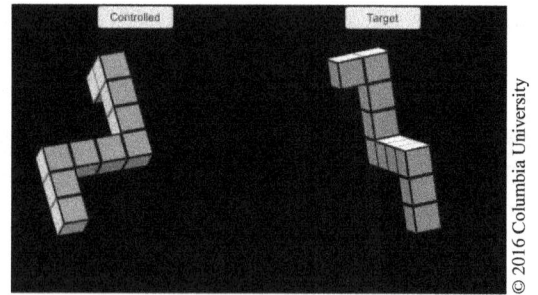

Figure 7: STATIC. Control Condition.

would turn green. This provided a simple control condition to use in the user study described below.

5.2 Pilot Studies

Pilot studies were instrumental in guiding the evolution of the techniques, as described above, and helped us refine study parameters. In particular, HANDLES was designed to overcome specific shortcomings of existing techniques by providing a persistent target and ensuring high visibility of landmarks and targets.

5.3 Hypotheses

Based on an analysis of the tasks and extensive design iterations informed by and tested in pilot studies, we formulated the following five hypotheses:

H1. HANDLES *will be the fastest technique.*

H2. HANDLES *will be the preferred technique.*

H3. SINGLEAXIS *and* STATIC *will be less preferred compared to* HANDLES, ANIMATE, *and* EULER.

H4. HANDLES *will be fastest for fine-tuning.*

H5. EULER *will be preferred by users with low spatial ability.*

5.3.1 Rationale

H1: In presenting the rotation instruction, HANDLES is the only visualization that presents both a persistent view of the target orientation (relative to the world coordinate system) and a view of the optimal transformation needed to get to the target orientation from the tracked object's current pose. ANIMATE shows the latter transformation, but to avoid cluttering the virtual scene with a third model of the virtual proxy, does not always show the target pose (besides the pause at the end of the animation loop). As a result, it is possible that the user will need to wait for a certain amount of time to comprehend the rotation instruction. SINGLEAXIS also shows the optimal path, but during pilot testing we found that due to limitations inherent to the small monoscopic display, it could be difficult to disambiguate certain rotation instructions, leading to situations where users would lose time trying to understand the direction of the instruction. EULER is similar to SINGLEAXIS, but breaks the transformation into three steps, further lengthening total trial time. Last, during pilot testing, we found that showing the target orientation at all times (and ensuring that the torii are placed at consistent locations relative to the user's line of sight), allowed the user to associate the destination target with a consistent position in the real world. In consideration of all four points above, we hypothesize that HANDLES will be the fastest condition in total completion time.

H2: Since the core components in HANDLES, the poles and tori, allow a user to easily determine the target orientation, and the connecting arrows show the remaining rotation, the user should be able to determine their next action by a short glance. A user may need to watch a few cycles of ANIMATE to completely understand the rotation instruction, potentially waiting for the animation to loop back to the beginning to follow along. SINGLEAXIS should work well with ballistic movements, but due to potentially radical motions of the axis in the fine-tuning stage, users may become frustrated as they try to complete a small rotation. EULER works consistently throughout a rotation task, but the required axis completion order makes acceleration difficult; thus, more skilled users could potentially be limited in performance. Consequently, we believe HANDLES would be the preferred condition.

H3: As the tracked object nears the target orientation, the axis-cylinder is highly sensitive to small movements that change the rotation axis. If the user is only a few degrees from the angular completion threshold, but drifts slightly in following the rotation instruction, it is possible that they stop progressing towards the goal as they try to adjust to the new rotation axis. As a result, users could potentially become confused and frustrated. Secondly, since STATIC provides no instruction (other than a visualization of the target orientation), users may struggle trying to match the pose in the given threshold, when fine-tuning. As the target object is positionally offset from the virtual proxy, and rendered on a small display, it may be difficult to discern the exact orientation difference between the tracked and target objects. As a result, we expect users will rate either SINGLEAXIS or STATIC as least preferred.

H4: In the fine-tuning stage, the remaining rotation is within 16° of the tracked object's current orientation, which for many of the visualizations may result in a very small or slight change. As explained in the rationale for H1, H2, and H3, HANDLES always shows both the target orientation and the remaining rotation. This gives users two forms of feedback to use in the fine-tuning stage. If one is not clear, the other may still provide enough information to discern the correct instruction. ANIMATE shows the exact motion needed to complete the task, but as the animated object is overlaid on the virtual proxy, and rendered on a small display, it is possible that a user simply may not be able to see the animated object clearly enough to discern the proper action. SINGLEAXIS has the issue of the fast-moving rotation axis cylinder, as described in H3. This makes completing the fine-tuning task potentially difficult. EULER shows the remaining rotation per axis clearly, but since breaking the completion status of a particular axis may require that a user recomplete it before continuing, it is possible that users spend a nontrivial amount of time in fine-tuning dealing with previously completed axes.

H5: Each of the visualizations require that a user be able to mentally map the instruction to a motor action in rotating the tracked object. For SINGLEAXIS, ANIMATE, and HANDLES, the instructed action may be a rotation about an axis that does not line up with a natural axis of the held object, and that may require an unintuitive motion. EULER instructs the user by presenting the rotation guidance through a set of three transformations about axes fixed to the virtual proxy. This allows the user to focus on one axis per motion, potentially rotating the shape to a more easily manipulated orientation before beginning. As EULER does not require the user to map the rotation axis to one not attached to the tracked object, we expect that users with low spatial ability who may struggle with this particular mapping to prefer EULER.

5.4 Methods

5.4.1 Participants

We recruited 17 participants from our institution (9 female), 19–32 years old (average 23), through email and posted flyers. Partic-

ipants attended a single-session experiment. Five participants had previous experience with AR, and none had any familiarity with our techniques.

5.4.2 Equipment

Participants wore a Google Glass Explorer Edition running Unity Remote 4. This Android app allows Glass to display visual output provided through USB 2.0 from our software running in Unity 5.3.3 on a computer powered by an Intel i7-3770k with 16GB of RAM and an Nvidia GeForce GTX 780. (Our software can also run in Unity directly on Glass, but causes it to overheat too quickly to complete the study.) The object held by the user was tracked using a Logitech c920 camera (visible at the right of Figure 1a), using tracking software in the Canon MREAL Platform, running on the same computer. The Logitech camera tracked both the held object and a fiducial array on the table where the user was seated, in order to ground the environment. The software running on Google Glass communicated to the MREAL Platform tracking application through a Unity application server, which ran on the same computer as the MREAL Platform software. Additionally, a foot-pedal was placed under the participant's table, and used to progress through the study.

5.4.3 Design

Since it was possible that certain rotations would be easier to maneuver than others, depending on how the user was holding the tracked object, the user study was designed to select from one of four possible rotations (80°, 100°, 120°, 140°) that would build on the target orientation in the preceding trial. There were an equal number of each of the possible rotation magnitudes across a single condition. Each trial would also generate a random rotation axis.

Trials were blocked by technique and randomized by rotation axis. Each block included four practice trials and 16 timed trials. The presentation order of the techniques was counterbalanced across participants to minimize bias due to learning.

5.4.4 Procedure

Participants were welcomed by the study coordinators and given the PseudoIsochromatic Plate (PIP) Color vision test to screen for color blindness, the Stereo Optical Co. Inc. Stereo Fly Test (SFT) to screen for stereo vision, and the Vandenberg–Kuse Mental Rotation Test (MRT) [23] to screen for spatial ability. All participants passed the PIP test. 12 participants passed the SFT, four had weak stereo vision, and one failed the test.

After completing the tests, the participant was seated in a chair pushed up to a table and instructed to rest their elbows on a gel wrist pad (1a) while holding the task object with both hands. These constraints ensured that their view of the virtual proxy was consistent with their view of the physical object. The participant was then introduced to the study and given an explanation of each of the techniques, with a small hands-on demonstration session for each technique (consisting of two practice rotations using the technique). Before the first condition, the participant was given a detailed explanation of each interaction technique.

At the start of each trial, the participant was shown the virtual proxy of the tracked object and the visual components of the current technique. The participant was instructed to match the 3DOF pose demonstrated using the current technique. The participant was instructed to press a button on a foot-pedal controller when the virtual proxy turned green, indicating that the target orientation had been met. The system prevented the user from completing the trial by pressing the button if the tracked object had not yet entered the acceptable range for the trial (as explained in Section 5). Once the trial was complete, the participant was instructed to hold their pose for 1.5 seconds as they entered the next trial. Throughout the study, the positions and orientations the tracked object were recorded.

Participants were asked to complete a three-part questionnaire before, during, and after the study, assessing the five techniques. The questionnaire included an unweighted NASA TLX, a request to rank the techniques from 1 ("Most Preferred") to 5 ("Least Preferred"), and room for free-form comments.

6. RESULTS

Each participant completed a total of 80 timed trials (5 conditions × 16 timed trials). We evaluated our hypotheses for significance using a Bonferroni-corrected α of 0.01 (0.05/5).

6.1 Task Duration

6.1.1 Outliers

We identified outliers in terms of task duration using Tukey's outlier filter. We chose a standard threshold (1.5 times IQR per user per condition), resulting in 5.0% (68 of 1360 trials: 13 ANIMATE, 13 EULER, 16 SINGLEAXIS, 15 STATIC, and 11 HANDLES) of our collected data being excluded from the rest of our analysis. Outliers resulted from occasional unstable tracking, connectivity issues, overheated HWD, or external issues (ringing cellphone, loose contact lens); in a few cases, users could not figure out the right answer and opted out, especially for STATIC.

6.1.2 Analysis

Our task completion metric is similar to reaction time (RT) data commonly analyzed in psychology experiments, in that we measure the time it takes users to react in response to a visual stimulus. Traditional analysis of variance (ANOVA) methods are generally not well-suited to RT data [26], because RT distributions are typically not Gaussian: they often have a long tail on the right, presumably due to confounding factors such as fatigue and external distractions. Before we began our analysis, we quickly confirmed that our task-completion data exhibited similar non-normality by fitting a linear model and visually inspecting the residual plots, which in fact showed obvious deviations from normality.

One widely adopted method for analyzing such heavily skewed RT data is to transform it into a reaction rate (analogous to speed) by taking the reciprocal ($1/x$) and then fit it with a linear-mixed-effects (LME) model to identify significant effects by adding and removing factors [2]. Using R [18] and its *lme4* package [3], we fit an LME model to our task-duration variable as a function of visualization condition (fixed effect) and participant (random effect). Compared to a base model with a random slope and participant as a random effect, a Kenward–Roger corrected F-test showed that visualization condition was significant as a fixed effect ($F_{(1,271)} = 119.16, p < .001$) (Figure 8a). A pairwise least-squares means comparison revealed that our participants were fastest using HANDLES, followed by ANIMATE, SINGLEAXIS, STATIC, and EULER, in that order, where all pairwise differences were statistically significant (Table 1). These findings validated H1.

6.1.3 Ballistic Approach vs. Fine-Tuning

In H4, we hypothesized that HANDLES would lead to faster task completion times compared to other techniques. Subdividing performance into a ballistic phase, followed by a visual feedback phase for "fine tuning" [10], We believed HANDLES would be faster because of its emphasis on providing visible, persistent feedback to help facilitate fine-tuning. In contrast to other techniques that rely on displaying the difference between current and target orientation,

Pairwise Comparison	t-statistic	p-value
HANDLES vs. ANIMATE	$t_{(1,271)} = 3.67$	$p < .001$
ANIMATE vs. SINGLEAXIS	$t_{(1,271)} = 4.98$	$p < .001$
SINGLEAXIS vs. STATIC	$t_{(1,271)} = 4.49$	$p < .001$
STATIC vs. EULER	$t_{(1,271)} = 6.34$	$p < .001$

Table 1: Task duration—Pairwise comparisons

in HANDLES the difference between current orientation and target orientation is small during fine-tuning.

To confirm this part of our hypothesis, we separated the overall completion time into two subtasks, as shown in Figure 8(a): ballistic approach and fine-tuning, following a simple distance thresholding heuristic. We counted the amount of time for each trial that was spent where the user-tracked object was more than a certain threshold away from the target orientation as *ballistic approach* and the rest of the time (i.e., when the tracked object's orientation was within that threshold) as *fine-tuning*. We chose $16°$ as our threshold for this analysis, which we arrived at by doubling our completion acceptance threshold of $8°$.

Similar to how we analyzed overall task duration, we fitted two separate LME models to model reciprocals of ballistic and fine-tuning durations (i.e., ballistic and fine-tuning rates) as a function of visualization condition (fixed effect) and participant (random effect).

Ballistic Approach: For the ballistic approach, compared to a base model with a random slope and participant as a random effect, a Kenward–Roger corrected F-test showed that visualization condition was significant as a fixed effect ($F_{(1,271)} = 111.73, p < .001$). A pairwise least-squares means comparison revealed that there were significant differences between all pairs except HANDLES–ANIMATE at $p < .01$. In other words, HANDLES and ANIMATE were fastest, followed by SINGLEAXIS, STATIC, and EULER, in that order.

Fine-Tuning: For fine-tuning, compared to a base model with a random slope and participant as a random effect, a Kenward–Roger corrected F-test showed that visualization condition was significant as a fixed effect ($F_{(1,271)} = 31.13, p < .001$). A pairwise least-squares means comparison revealed that there were significant differences between all pairs except ANIMATE–SINGLEAXIS, ANIMATE–EULER, and STATIC–EULER at $p < .01$. In other words, HANDLES was fastest for fine-tuning, followed by ANIMATE and SINGLEAXIS, followed by STATIC and EULER, which confirms H4.

6.2 User Feedback

6.2.1 Technique Rankings

A majority of participants (9, 53%) ranked HANDLES as their most preferred condition (Figure 8b), supporting H2. Three participants (18%) chose ANIMATE and EULER each, two participants (12%) chose STATIC, and none chose SINGLEAXIS as their favorite. On the opposite end of the spectrum, SINGLEAXIS was chosen as the least favorite 8 times (53%), followed by EULER with four times (24%). On average, HANDLES was ranked highest, followed by ANIMATE, SINGLEAXIS, STATIC, and EULER. A Friedman test confirmed that our participants' differential preference between techniques was statistically significant, $\chi^2_{(4)} = 17.459, p < .01$.

In H2, we hypothesized that HANDLES would be the most preferred technique. A post-hoc pairwise comparison using Nemenyi's procedure showed that the only statistically significant difference

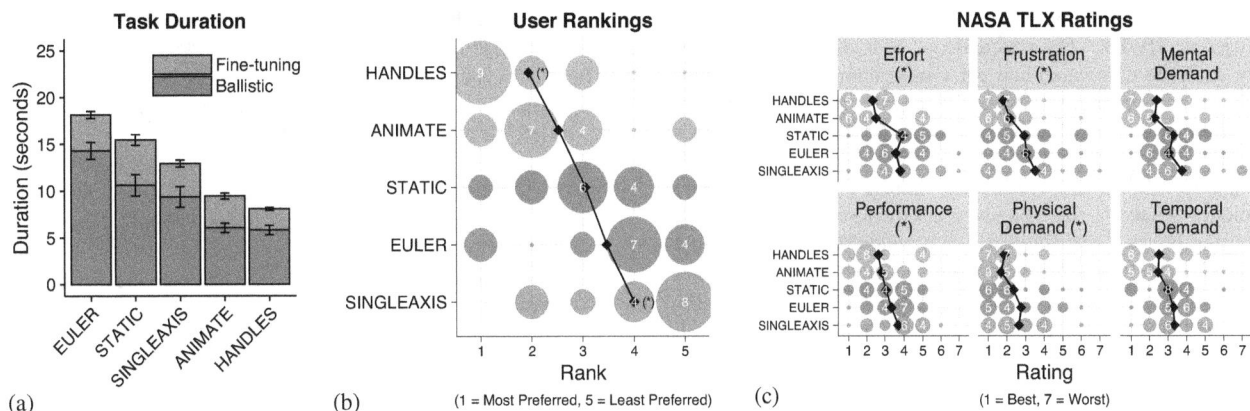

Figure 8: User Study: (a) Task duration per technique. (b) User rankings and (c) NASA TLX ratings per technique. Black diamonds shows average ranking/rating per technique. (*) denotes significance at $p < .01$.

in rankings was between HANDLES vs. SINGLEAXIS, $p < .01$. The differences between HANDLES vs. EULER and ANIMATE vs. SINGLEAXIS were nearly significant ($p = .039$ and $p = .052$, respectively), but above our Bonferroni-adjusted α of .01, supporting but not confirming H2.

Qualitative user feedback highlighted instances where participants found HANDLES to be generally more preferred for fine-tuning (e.g., "HANDLES was very accurate and didn't have changing parameters," "HANDLES was the best for putting the object in the exact position that the program wanted," "HANDLES is the best because it really helps with the small movements").

On the opposite end of the spectrum, SINGLEAXIS was generally rated as least preferred and participants reported frustration during fine-tuning (e.g., "SINGLEAXIS was frustrating, since the bar seemed to move very erratically with small movements, so it took a lot of concentration to do the fine movements near the target"). While the first part of H3 (i.e., SINGLEAXIS would be less preferred compared to HANDLES, ANIMATE, and EULER) was supported in our data, it was not confirmed because not all pairwise differences had $p < .01$.

In H3, we also hypothesized that STATIC would be less preferred compared to HANDLES, ANIMATE, and EULER. Surprisingly, STATIC was generally ranked higher than EULER in terms of overall preference, which meant that the second part of H3 should be rejected. Four participants (24%) ranked EULER as their least preferred technique and another six (35%) participants ranked it as their second least preferred.

In H5, we hypothesized that EULER would be preferred by participants with low spatial ability. The three users who ranked it as their most preferred technique had either above or close to average MRT scores of 8, 12, 14 (out of 20), failing to support H5.

To understand why many users found EULER challenging, we examined the questionnaire comments from participants who did not prefer EULER. Common themes were that the need to perform three sequential rotations along the major axes of the tracked object was onerous and having to track three arrows at once was challenging (e.g., "in aligning one axis, the other pre-aligned axes may drift and cause some confusion," "Too many rings, and too many changing rotations," "Holding the rotation in one axis constant while rotating the others was challenging. Also, following the order of rotation was not instinctual.").

6.2.2 NASA TLX

When we analyzed the results from the unweighted NASA TLX

questionnaire (Figure 8c), a Friedman test confirmed that technique was a significant factor for Mental Demand, Physical Demand, Effort, and Frustration at $p < .01$. (The p values for Temporal Demand and Performance were .081 and .051, respectively.)

Post-hoc pairwise comparison using Nemenyi's procedure indicated that SINGLEAXIS was rated as being significantly more mentally demanding compared to both HANDLES and ANIMATE ($p < .01$). HANDLES was perceived to require less effort than both STATIC and SINGLEAXIS, but the p values for the pairwise comparisons were just above our Bonferroni-adjusted $\alpha < .01$ ($p = .017$ in both cases). Similarly, HANDLES was rated as less frustrating compared to SINGLEAXIS and EULER, but that difference was also not significant ($p = .028$ and $p = .045$, respectively). There were no significant pairwise differences for Physical Demand.

7. CONCLUSIONS AND FUTURE WORK

We have described one new visualization (HANDLES) and three visualizations that improve upon existing approaches for guiding a user in rotating an object to match a specified 3DOF orientation. In addition, we have presented the results of a user study comparing the effectiveness of these visualizations, when viewed on Google Glass, a small field-of-view, monoscopic, off-center HWD. Our study found that HANDLES was significantly faster than and trended toward being preferred over the other techniques.

ANIMATE and STATIC include a representation of the object in the desired orientation, encouraging comparison of the current orientation of the object with the desired orientation. In contrast, SINGLEAXIS, EULER, and HANDLES provide virtual annotations as guidance (e.g., arrows, handles, and tori), requiring the user to attend only to those and shifting the task from spatial transformation to perceptual tracking. Despite this shift away from spatial thinking, HANDLES still provides a spatial representation of the final pose via its tori, which might explain why users were able to perform both ballistic and fine-tuning movements quickly. This was highlighted by several participants in their qualitative feedback (e.g., "Having the poles as a guide really helps. Don't have to think, can just get by with spatial intuition," "I just thought about how to put the sticks to the ring," "The two guides were very useful in determining the target position," "With HANDLES, I did not have to observe the orientation of the object I was holding to solve the trial").

While the visualizations were designed with small-FOV monoscopic HWDs in mind, they should also work well with wider-FOV stereoscopic HWDs. On a stereoscopic AR display, the virtual proxy could be eliminated and our visualizations could be registered with and rendered directly on the user's view of the task object. However, it is possible that relative performance among the visualizations may change with increased FOV and stereoscopy; for example, EULER might perform better relative to some of the other techniques, when not confined to a small monoscopic display. Further, using tracked, registered AR on a wider-FOV display might also result in different relative performance across the techniques. Thus, we believe it will be useful to run new studies to assess the relative performance of the techniques when used with different display technologies.

We would also like to build in color profiles that could be applied to accommodate users with color-vision deficiencies. (We note that while our current version of EULER would be problematic for users with red–green colorblindness, all of our study participants passed the PIP test.)

While this work focused on unconstrained 3DOF rotation, it is possible that a number of the visualizations may work when completing 6DOF transformation tasks. Similarly, looking at specific types of constrained rotations (e.g., camera-plane vs. horizontal or vertical planes; or roll vs. pitch or yaw) could reveal interesting differences between techniques. Thus, we would like to explore how our visualizations may be modified or combined with other visualizations to support translation and constrained rotations, allowing them to address a full range of rigid-body transformations.

8. ACKNOWLEDGMENTS

This research was funded in part by NSF Grants IIS-1514429 and IIS-1513841. We thank Google for the gift of Glass, Canon U.S.A. Inc. for loaning the MR Platform software suite, and Minhaz Palasara and Yujin Ariza for their contributions to our system.

9. REFERENCES

[1] F. Anderson, T. Grossman, J. Matejka, and G. Fitzmaurice. YouMove: Enhancing Movement Training with an Augmented Reality Mirror. In *Proc. ACM UIST*, pages 311–320, New York, NY, USA, 2013.

[2] R. H. Baayen and P. Milin. Analyzing reaction times. *Int. Jnl. Psych. Res.*, 3(2):12–28, 2015.

[3] D. Bates, M. Mächler, B. Bolker, and S. Walker. Fitting Linear Mixed-Effects Models Using lme4. *Journal of Statistical Software*, 67(1):1–48, 2015.

[4] M. Chu and S. Kita. Spontaneous gestures during mental rotation tasks: insights into the microdevelopment of the motor strategy. *Jnl Expr. Psych.: Gen.*, 137(4):706, 2008.

[5] M. Chu and S. Kita. The nature of gestures' beneficial role in spatial problem solving. *Journal of Experimental Psychology: General*, 140(1):102, 2011.

[6] C. Elvezio, M. Sukan, S. Feiner, and B. Tversky. [POSTER] Interactive Visualizations for Monoscopic Eyewear to Assist in Manually Orienting Objects in 3D. In *Proc. IEEE ISMAR*, pages 180–181, 2015.

[7] L. Euler. Formulae generales pro translatione quacunque corporum rigidorum. *Novi Acad. Sci. Petrop*, 20:189–207, 1775.

[8] S. Feiner, B. Macintyre, and D. Seligmann. Knowledge-based augmented reality. *Commun. ACM*, 36(7):53–62, 1993.

[9] D. Freeman, H. Benko, M. R. Morris, and D. Wigdor. ShadowGuides: Visualizations for In-situ Learning of Multi-touch and Whole-hand Gestures. In *Proc. ACM ITS*, pages 165–172, New York, NY, USA, 2009.

[10] K.-C. Gan and E. R. Hoffmann. Geometrical conditions for ballistic and visually controlled movements. *Ergonomics*, 31(5):829–839, 1988.

[11] A. Gupta, D. Fox, B. Curless, and M. Cohen. DuploTrack: A Real-time System for Authoring and Guiding Duplo Block Assembly. In *Proc. ACM UIST*, pages 389–402, New York, NY, USA, 2012.

[12] S. J. Henderson and S. K. Feiner. Augmented reality in the psychomotor phase of a procedural task. In *Proc. IEEE ISMAR*, pages 191–200, Los Alamitos, CA, USA, 2011.

[13] S. McCloud. *Understanding Comics: The Invisible Art*. William Morrow Paperbacks, New York, reprint edition edition, 1994.

[14] P. Mijksenaar and P. Westendorp. *Open here: the art of instructional design*. Joost Elffers Books, 1999.

[15] A. Miller, B. White, E. Charbonneau, Z. Kanzler, and J. J. LaViola Jr. Interactive 3D Model Acquisition and Tracking of Building Block Structures. *IEEE TVCG*, 18(4):651–659, 2012.

[16] P. Mohr, B. Kerbl, M. Donoser, D. Schmalstieg, and D. Kalkofen. Retargeting technical documentation to augmented reality. In *Proc. ACM CHI*, pages 3337–3346, 2015.

[17] O. Oda, C. Elvezio, M. Sukan, S. Feiner, and B. Tversky. Virtual Replicas for Remote Assistance in Virtual and Augmented Reality. In *Proc. ACM UIST*, pages 405–415, New York, NY, USA, 2015.

[18] R Core Team. *R: A Language and Environment for Statistical Computing*. R Foundation for Statistical Computing, 2015.

[19] C. M. Robertson, B. MacIntyre, and B. N. Walker. An evaluation of graphical context as a means for ameliorating the effects of registration error. *IEEE TVCG*, 15(2):179–192, 2009.

[20] R. Schmidt, K. Singh, and R. Balakrishnan. Sketching and Composing Widgets for 3D Manipulation. *Computer Graphics Forum*, 27(2):301–310, 2008.

[21] R. N. Shepard and J. Metzler. Mental Rotation of Three-Dimensional Objects. *Science*, 171(3972):701–703, 1971.

[22] R. Sodhi, H. Benko, and A. Wilson. Lightguide: projected visualizations for hand movement guidance. In *Proc. ACM CHI*, pages 179–188, 2012.

[23] S. G. Vandenberg and A. R. Kuse. Mental rotations, a group test of three-dimensional spatial visualization. *Perceptual and motor skills*, 47(2):599–604, 1978.

[24] D. Voyer, S. Voyer, and M. P. Bryden. Magnitude of sex differences in spatial abilities: a meta-analysis and consideration of critical variables. *Psychological Bulletin*, 117(2):250–270, 1995.

[25] M. Wexler, S. M. Kosslyn, and A. Berthoz. Motor processes in mental rotation. *Cognition*, 68(1):77–94, 1998.

[26] R. Whelan. Effective analysis of reaction time data. *The Psychological Record*, 58(3):475, 2008.

[27] S. White, L. Lister, and S. Feiner. Visual Hints for Tangible Gestures in Augmented Reality. In *Proc. IEEE ISMAR*, pages 47–50, 2007.

[28] A. Wohlschläger and A. Wohlschläger. Mental and manual rotation. *Journal of Experimental Psychology: Human Perception and Performance*, 24(2):397, 1998.

Combining Ring Input with Hand Tracking for Precise, Natural Interaction with Spatial Analytic Interfaces

Barrett Ens[1], Ahmad Byagowi[1], Teng Han[1], Juan David Hincapié-Ramos[2], Pourang Irani[1]

[1]University of Manitoba
Winnipeg, Canada
{bens, hanteng, irani}@cs.umanitoba.ca, byagowi@umanitoba.ca

[2]Lenovo R&T
Beijing, China
jramos4@lenovo.com

ABSTRACT

Current wearable interfaces are designed to support short-duration tasks known as micro-interactions. To support productive interfaces for everyday analytic tasks, designers can leverage natural input methods such as direct manipulation and pointing. Such natural methods are now available in virtual, mobile environments thanks to miniature depth cameras mounted on head-worn displays (HWDs). However, these techniques have drawbacks, such as fatigue and limited precision. To overcome these limitations, we explore combined input: hand tracking data from a head-mounted depth camera, and input from a small ring device. We demonstrate how a variety of input techniques can be implemented using this novel combination of devices. We harness these techniques for use with Spatial Analytic Interfaces: multi-application, spatial UIs for in-situ, analytic taskwork on wearable devices. This research demonstrates how combined input from multiple wearable devices holds promise for supporting high-precision, low-fatigue interaction techniques, to support Spatial Analytic Interfaces on HWDs.

Keywords

Head-worn display; HWD; HMD; naturalism; augmented reality; spatial interaction; analytic task; wearables

1. INTRODUCTION

Wearable technologies, such as watches, rings and head-worn displays (HWDs) are becoming commonplace, but their current interfaces are primarily designed to support micro-interactions: short bursts of activity, such as setting reminders or receiving notifications. *Spatial Analytic Interfaces* (SAIs) [4] have been proposed for moving beyond micro-interactions, to support *everyday analytic tasks* on HWDs. SAIs distribute information among multiple spatially situated information displays. These spatial layouts support efficient task switching via head motion [5], and their wearable platform allows tasks to be performed in-situ, when required for a particular situation. Supporting such everyday analytic tasks will require effective techniques for common operations such as selecting data and manipulating filter controls.

To support effective interaction in SAIs, we can draw from techniques developed for interacting in 3D and virtual environments [1, 16]. However, unlike in a lab setting where many such techniques are designed, a wearable interface must be made practical for mobile, *in-situ* use; users must not be encumbered by

SUI'16, October 15–16, 2016, Tokyo, Japan.
© 2016 ACM. ISBN 978-1-4503-4068-7/16/10...$15.00
DOI: http://dx.doi.org/10.1145/2983310.2985757

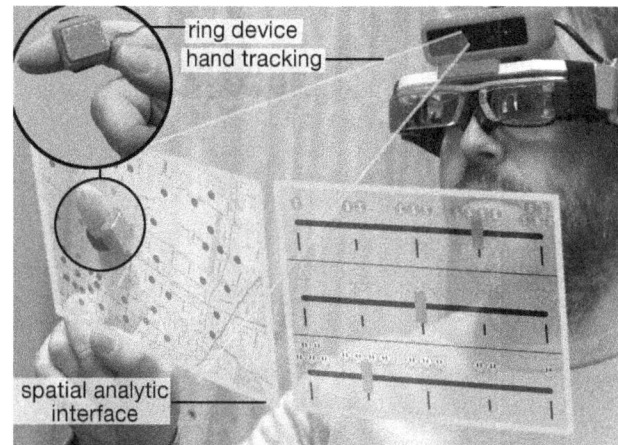

Figure 1. We combine input from a ring device with hand tracking by a head-worn depth camera to support interaction with Spatial Analytic Interfaces, which support everyday analytic tasks with multiple 2D views situated in 3D space.

bulky input devices. One option for eliminating hand-held devices is to track the user's hands using a depth camera embedded in the HWD [7], to detect intuitive grasping and pointing gestures. Such natural techniques have been shown to provide advantages in many tasks [2], but are also prone to fatigue [8] and lack of precision [17]. Another wearable form factor recently gaining attention is the ring device [3, 9, 14, 20]. Finger-worn devices can provide subtle and precise input, and may be used with the arm in a resting position to reduce fatigue, but these lack the naturalism of intuitive gestures that hand-tracking provides.

In this paper, we propose the combined use of wearable, optical hand tracking with input from a ring device to support in-situ interaction with SAIs (Figure 1). We show how the combined benefits of these input devices (Table 1) can be used to support naturalism, while also allowing precise selection and manipulation with reduced fatigue. We also aim to support *dual-tier* interaction for SAIs [4]. Dual-tier interaction supports two levels: manipulation of window layouts, for instance to place two views side-by-side for comparison, and interaction with window contents, such as selection of small data points. With both hand tracking and a ring device, users can seamlessly combine large, coarse gestures to manipulate multi-window layouts, with fine-grained input for

Table 1: A summary of the tradeoffs between hand tracking input and ring device input.

	benefits	drawbacks
hand tracking (grasping, pointing)	intuitive; fast, coarse motions	fatigue; limited precision
ring device-indirect (rotation, tapping, swiping)	precise; fast repetitions	requires device;

precise control of window contents. We envision this mixture of input methods to be used much like interaction with current hybrid, touchscreen laptops; direct input gestures may be used periodically for fast, convenient manipulation, while indirect input is applied over a longer duration, for precision and minimal fatigue.

2. HYBRID INTERACTION TECHNIQUES

Combining multiple input modes is a strategy that has been employed by researchers to overcome various difficulties in a number of interaction domains. For instance, conventional desktop input devices such as mice do not adapt well to large displays; moving the cursor over large distances requires either excessive clutching, or reduced precision due to high control-display (CD) gain [13]. HybridPointing [6] and ARC-Pad [8] use absolute, direct pointing to select a coarse region, followed by indirect, relative motion to acquire a target. An alternative technique, proposed by Nancel et al. [13], attempts to minimize mode-switching costs, by using head motion for coarse selection, followed by direct hand motion for precise interaction.

Hybrid techniques have also been applied in 3D environments. For example, to disambiguate the intended target of a raycast selection in dense 3D environments, the DepthRay and LockRay techniques [18] place a cursor at a discrete point on the ray, which can be controlled by moving the pointer along the ray axis. For the DepthRay technique, pointing and depth manipulations occur simultaneously, whereas the LockRay technique requires the pointer position to be 'locked' in place before the depth cursor can be manipulated. This temporal separation of the modes increases precision at a cost of time. Researchers have also explored techniques that combine natural hand gesture input with voice input [10, 15]. In virtual environments, the voice commands are a useful way to trigger mode switching, such as translation and rotation, while the hands are used for object manipulation.

These hybrid techniques, and many others, may described according to various dimensions, such as the number of input devices, and the nature of the different modalities (e.g. absolute vs. relative, direct vs. indirect, voice vs. hand). Another useful dimension to explore is the temporal relationship between modalities, as described in the framework of Vernier and Nigay [19]. Five potential relationships they described are shown in Figure 2. We use similar diagrams in the figures below to help depict the relationships of the various modalities used in our prototype implementations. Our goal is to show how a wide variety of rich interaction techniques can be created by combining ring device input with hand-tracking on a HWD. The techniques we demonstrate are aimed at providing natural input for use with SAIs, while improving precision and minimizing fatigue.

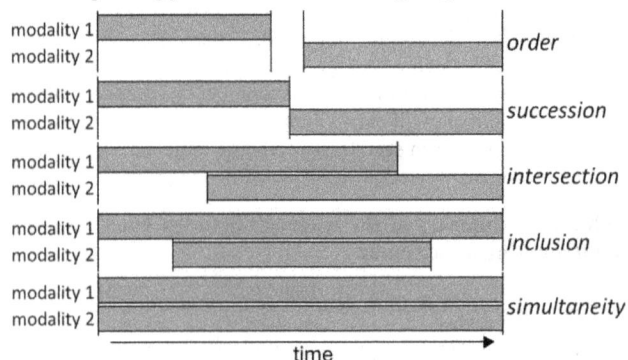

Figure 2. We apply the framework of Vernier and Nigay [19], which characterizes various ways to combine input modalities.

3. IMPLEMANTATION

To explore interactions that combine natural, direct input and precise, indirect input for SAIs, we built a prototype system that sends hand tracking and ring input data to a HWD. For hand tracking, we mounted a Softkinetic DS-325 depth camera on a Moverio BT-200 HWD (Figure 1). The camera input is processed by SoftKinetic's iisu middleware on a desktop computer, which connects to the Moverio via UDP. Transferred data include the hand centroid position, finger and thumb positions, pointing tip position, and hand state (open/closed). This setup is similar to upcoming commercial devices that contain depth cameras[1].

To supplement direct hand input, we use a small ring device (Figure 3) capable of basic and well-known touch gestures, such as tapping and flicking. The device contains a small capacitive touch sensor and a nine-axis inertial measurement unit (IMU). The capacitive touch sensor is composed of an array of capacitors arranged in a 3×4 grid on a surface measuring 12×16 mm. The capacitors are connected to a Microchip MTCH6102 controller, which sends position data with a resolution of 384×567, along with detected trackpad gestures. A Bosch BNO055 IMU module contains an Amtel ARM Cortex-M0 processor, and provides absolute pitch, roll and yaw. Both the touch control and IMU are interfaced using an I^2C bus, requiring only four wires for connection.

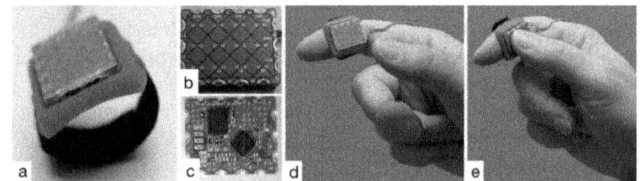

Figure 3: Our ring device (a) contains a miniature trackpad composed of an array of capacitive sensors (b) and a nine-axis IMU (c). When worn on the index finger (d), this small device supports simple techniques such as tapping (e) and swiping.

The unit is attached to a 3D-printed base, and affixed comfortably to the wearer's finger by a hook-and-loop fastener strip (Figure 3d). Data are relayed by Bluetooth to the HWD through a tethered Arduino microcontroller, worn on the wrist. Data filtering and all other processing are done onboard the Moverio unit, which runs Android 4.0. We developed the HWD program using Unity 3D.

4. SAI INTERACTIONS

We implemented several interaction techniques that leverage the benefits of direct and indirect input, drawn from a large body of available literature. We aim to show how these techniques can be supported in a wearable form factor to allow effective interaction with SAIs. We demonstrate these implementations using the novel combination of hand-tracking with a ring device, as described in the previous section.

For demonstration, we use a hotel search scenario as an example of an everyday analytic task. Imagine a traveler who arrives in a new city and needs to make a hotel booking. Given her immediate need for a room, she performs this search in-situ, while exploring the city centre. To assist in her search, she opens three windows containing a map, a filter panel, and a hotel preview panel. Viewing these through her HWD allows her to switch between views using head motion, more efficiently switching views on a smartphone. How might we also support effective dual-tier interaction with these multiple virtual window?

---

[1] For example, Microsoft HoloLens and Meta 2 track hand gestures:
http://www.microsoft.com/microsoft-hololens/en-us
http://www.metavision.com/

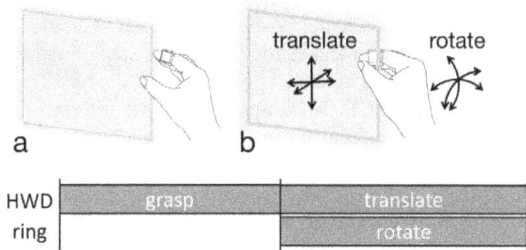

Figure 4. Direct manipulation is useful for infrequent, coarse-grained gestures. a) A user 'grabs' a window using a grasp gesture. b) Combining depth camera and ring IMU date allows the window to be translated and rotated freely in 6 DoF.

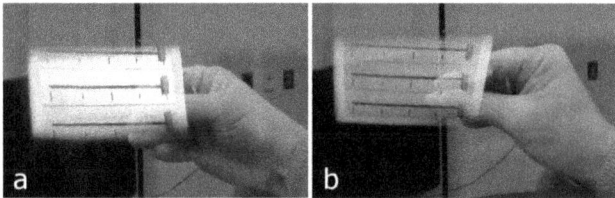

Figure 5. Our implementation, as viewed through the Moverio HWD showing direct manipulation of a window in 6 DoF.

4.1 6 DoF Direct Manipulation

Given a depth channel, human hands can be robustly segmented and the positions of centroids and fingertips are easily tracked. However, accurately measuring the absolute rotation of hands is more challenging, particularly if the hand is closed or fingers are otherwise occluded. Conversely, IMUs are capable of providing very accurate absolute orientation but cannot accurately track position. By combining the ring's IMU with the HWD's depth camera, we can enable tracking in 6 degrees of freedom (DoF).

In our implementation, this sensor combination allows windows to be freely manipulated in 3D space (Figure 4, Figure 5). After grabbing a window, by closing a hand around its virtual bezel, the user can position the window anywhere within reach.

4.2 Dual-Tier Selection

During an analytic task, users may apply various operations, such as moving windows to improve the layout, selecting data, or manipulating filter controls. Our implementation allows selection operations to be applied to both windows at layout level and to the contents at the container level. We provide two natural selection methods, for near and distant windows, respectively.

The first method uses absolute, direct input; the user simply 'taps' the window's virtual surface with an extended finger (Figure 6a, Figure 8a). The second method uses a virtual ray [12] projected from the user's hand. A tap on the ring enables the ray and a second tap selects a window (Figure 7a, Figure 8b), or disables the ray. With either technique, controls or objects closest to the point of intersection are selected. Once selected, either windows or contents can be used further by combining additional operations (Figure 6b, Figure 7b – see Control and Small Object Selection, below).

4.3 Control and Small Object Selection

Hand position tracking allows operation of virtual controls on a 2D interface; however, extended use of direct manipulation can quickly cause arm fatigue [2, 8]. Our system supports a combination of direct and indirect interaction methods. For instance, after selecting the filter panel, the user can cycle through

the vertically-aligned sliders by swiping up or down on the ring pad and move the selected slider by swiping left or right (Figure 6b).

Analytic tasks may also require the selection of data points on dense visualizations. Even assuming that current methods allow sufficient precision, research has shown that input precision suffers without a haptic surface [17]. After a coarse selection, we disable any points outside a defined threshold and allow refinement by cycling through the remaining points (Figure 7b).

4.4 Ray-Grabbing

When 6 DoF manipulation is not ideal, the ring's IMU allows alternate 3D interaction techniques [1, 16]. For example, a user can 'ray-grab' [1] a window with a tap-and-hold gesture on the ring (Figure 9a, Figure 10a). The grabbed window can then be repositioned by mapping ring rotation to window translation in 2 DoF on a body-centric sphere (Figure 9b, Figure 10b). Lifting the thumb from the ring pad releases the window. The window can then be shifted along the third axis (depth) [16] by swiping up or down on the ring pad (Figure 9c, Figure 10c).

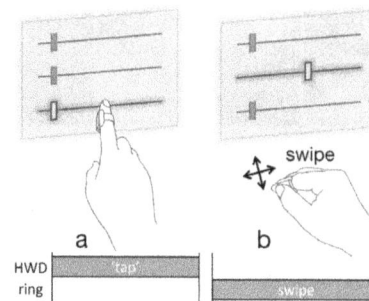

Figure 6: a) Selecting a virtual window with a 'tap' gesture also selects the nearest control within the window. b) Swiping gestures on the ring pad may be used to change the control selection and change the value of the selected control.

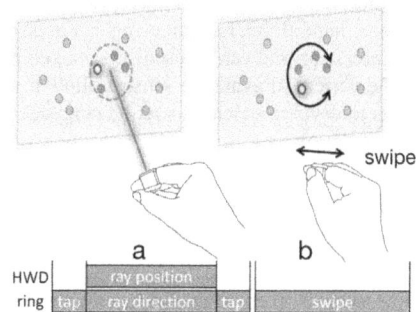

Figure 7. a) Items can also be selected with a virtual ray. Data points beyond a threshold distance from the ray selection point are disabled. b) Swiping the ring pad (horizontally or vertically) cycles through the enabled data points.

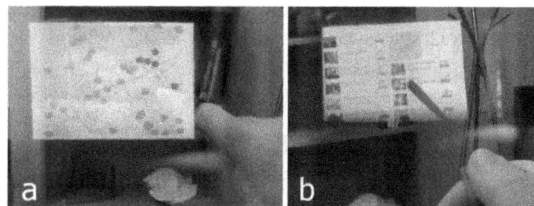

Figure 8. Our implementation uses the combined HWD and ring sensors to provide natural input methods. Users can select a window using a direct 'tap' gesture (a) on the virtual window surface, or by pointing a ray and tapping the ring pad (b).

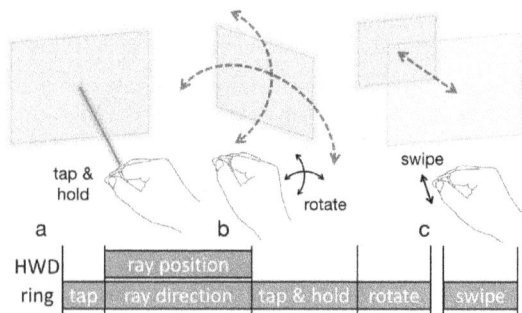

Figure 9. 'Ray-Grabbing' [1] constrains the window movement to two axis. a) The user taps and holds to select a window. b) Wrist rotation moves it along the surface of a body-centric sphere. c) The window's depth is manipulated using up and down swipes on the ring's touch pad.

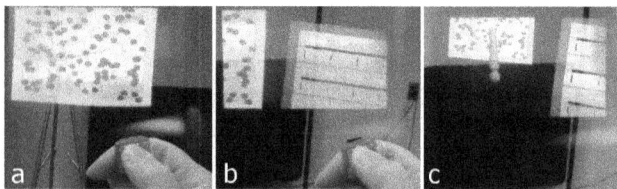

Figure 10. Raycasting is useful for interacting with windows that are out of reach. a) A user grabs a window (the ray is hidden, but stays connected), and places it beside another (b). c) The window is then moved in depth using swipe gestures.

5. CONCLUSION

We implemented a prototype system that combines ring device input with hand-tracking on a head-worn display. With this system, we demonstrate how a variety of interaction techniques can be created using various combinations of input values. These techniques are aimed at supporting natural interaction with SAIs, which require precise selection for everyday analytic tasks. Hand-tracking supports natural interaction using hand gestures. Ring input provides precision and can be used in a relaxed posture with low fatigue. The variety of available sensors allow a wide variety of combinations to develop a rich interaction language.

In future work we plan to develop a refined framework to describe hybrid interactions developed for SAIs, to help inspire new techniques. Further work will test these techniques in user studies, to determine which variations can best support seamless dual-tier control of both the window layout and content levels.

As we continue to develop an arsenal of techniques, we will apply these interactions effectively to analytic tasks. For example, we intend to develop features that help users switch their attention efficiently between coordinated views, and to design new controls for filtering and exploring data. These features must overcome the limitations of HWDs such as view size, and should be designed for in-situ use in mobile contexts. With this work, we hope to improve the usability of wearable systems and raise the bar beyond the productivity level of current mobile devices.

REFERENCES

[1] Bowman, D.A. and Hodges, L.F. 1997. An evaluation of techniques for grabbing and manipulating remote objects in immersive virtual environments. *Proc. I3D '97*, 35-ff.

[2] Bowman, D.A., McMahan, R.P. and Ragan, E.D. 2012. Questioning naturalism in 3D user interfaces. *Commun. ACM*. 55, 9 (Sep. 2012), 78–88.

[3] Chan, L., Liang, R.-H., Tsai, M.-C., Cheng, K.-Y., Su, C.-H., Chen, M.Y., Cheng, W.-H. and Chen, B.-Y. 2013. FingerPad: private and subtle interaction using fingertips. *Proc. UIST '13*, 255–260.

[4] Ens, B. and Irani, P. 2016. Spatial Analytic Interfaces: Spatial user interfaces for in-situ visual analytics. *IEEE Computer Graphics and Applications*, PP, 99 (Mar. 2016), 1-1.

[5] Ens, B.M., Finnegan, R. and Irani, P.P. 2014. The Personal Cockpit: A spatial interface for effective task switching on head-worn displays. *Proc. CHI '14*, 3171–3180.

[6] Forlines, C., Vogel, D. and Balakrishnan, R. 2006. HybridPointing: fluid switching between absolute and relative pointing with a direct input device. *Proc. UIST '06*, 211–220.

[7] Ha, T., Feiner, S. and Woo, W. 2014. WeARHand: Head-worn, RGB-D camera-based, bare-hand user interface with visually enhanced depth perception. *Proc. ISMAR '14*, 219–228.

[8] Hincapié-Ramos, J.D., Guo, X., Moghadasian, P. and Irani, P. 2014. Consumed Endurance: A metric to quantify arm fatigue of mid-air interactions. *Proc. CHI '14*, 1063–1072.

[9] Kienzle, W. and Hinckley, K. 2014. LightRing: always-available 2D input on any surface. *Proc. UIST '14*, 157–160.

[10] Lee, M., Billinghurst, M., Baek, W., Green, R. and Woo, W. 2013. A usability study of multimodal input in an augmented reality environment. *Virtual Reality*. 17, 4 (Nov. 2013), 293–305.

[11] McCallum, D.C. and Irani, P. 2009. ARC-Pad: Absolute+relative cursor positioning for large displays with a mobile touchscreen. *Proc. UIST '09*, 153–156.

[12] Mine, M.R. 1995. *Virtual Environment Interaction Techniques. UNC Chapel Hill computer science technical report TR95-018 (1995)*, 507248-2.

[13] Nancel, M., Chapuis, O., Pietriga, E., Yang, X.-D., Irani, P.P. and Beaudouin-Lafon, M. 2013. High-precision pointing on large wall displays using small handheld devices. *Proc. CHI '13*, 831–840.

[14] Ogata, M., Sugiura, Y., Osawa, H. and Imai, M. 2012. iRing: intelligent ring using infrared reflection. *Proc. UIST '12*, 131–136.

[15] Piumsomboon, T., Altimira, D., Kim, H., Clark, A., Lee, G. and Billinghurst, M. 2014. Grasp-Shell vs gesture-speech: A comparison of direct and indirect natural interaction techniques in augmented reality. *Proc. ISMAR '14*, 73–82.

[16] Poupyrev, I., Billinghurst, M., Weghorst, S. and Ichikawa, T. 1996. The Go-go interaction technique: Non-linear mapping for direct manipulation in VR. *Proc. UIST '96*, 79–80.

[17] Szalavári, Z. and Gervautz, M. 1997. The Personal Interaction Panel – A two-handed interface for augmented reality. *Computer Graphics Forum*. 16, 3 (Sep. 1997), C335–C346.

[18] Vanacken, L., Grossman, T. and Coninx, K. 2009. Multimodal selection techniques for dense and occluded 3D virtual environments. *International Journal of Human-Computer Studies*. 67, 3 (Mar. 2009), 237–255.

[19] Vernier, F. and Nigay, L. 2000. A framework for the combination and characterization of output modalities. *International Workshop on Design, Specification, and Verification of Interactive Systems* (2000), 35–50.

[20] Yang, X.-D., Grossman, T., Wigdor, D. and Fitzmaurice, G. 2012. Magic finger: always-available input through finger instrumentation. *Proc. UIST '12*, 147–156.

Thumbs-Up: 3D Spatial Thumb-Reachable Space for One-Handed Thumb Interaction on Smartphones

Khalad Hasan[1], Junhyeok Kim[1], David Ahlström[2], Pourang Irani[1]

[1]University of Manitoba
Winnipeg, Manitoba, Canada
{Khalad, kimj3415, Irani}@cs.umanitoba.ca

[2]Alpen-Adria-Universität Klagenfurt
Klagenfurt, Austria
david.ahlstroem@aau.at

ABSTRACT

People very often use mobile devices with one hand to free the second hand for other tasks. In such cases, the thumb of the hand holding the device is the only available input finger, making multi-touch interactions impossible. Complicating interaction further, the screen area that can be reached with the thumb while holding the device is limited, which makes distant on-screen areas inaccessible. Motivated by emerging portable object tracking technologies, we explore how spatial mid-air thumb-gestures could potentially be used in combination with on-screen touch input to facilitate one-handed interaction. From a user study we identify the 3D thumb-reachable space when holding a smartphone. We call this space 'Thumbs-Up'. This space extends up to 74 mm above the screen, making it possible to create interactions for the thumb of the hand holding the smartphone. We furthermore demonstrate how such Thumbs-Up techniques, when combined with on-screen interaction, can extend the input vocabulary in one-handed situations.

Keywords

One-Handed Spatial Interaction; Around-Device Interaction; Thumb Input; Reachability; Limited Multi-Touch Interaction; Occlusion.

1. INTRODUCTION

The majority of smartphone users interact with the touchscreen while holding the phone with one hand when the second hand is busy performing other tasks, such as holding a shopping bag or while clinging onto a handlebar in a bus [7, 8]. In such situations, the thumb is the only available finger to interact with touchscreen. Prior research has pointed out several limitations with one-handed thumb input on mobile devices. For example, the length of the thumb sets a significant limit to what screen areas can be reached [2, 8]. This is often referred to as a reachability issue. Furthermore, one-handed thumb input does not allow for multi-touch interactions that require more than one finger [3], and information on the screen easily gets occluded by the thumb [12].

Although numerous approaches to improve one-handed smartphone interaction have been proposed, very little is known about extending the input possibilities available to the thumb. A promising complement to standard touch input is to use the mid-air space surrounding the device for hand gestures [4, 6, 9, 10]. This form of interaction assumes that the smartphone's interaction plane extends beyond its physical boundaries and that users can access

SUI '16, October 15-16, 2016, Tokyo, Japan
© 2016 ACM. ISBN 978-1-4503-4068-7/16/10...$15.00
DOI: http://dx.doi.org/10.1145/2983310.2985755

on-device information by directly pointing above, below or around the device. For example, Kratz et al. [9] detect hand movements above the device using infrared proximity sensors and Song et al. [10] track hand gestures below the device using the device's built-in camera. Infrared sensors can also be used to detect multi-finger movements in the vicinity of a smartphone when it is placed on a surface [4]. These and similar projects clearly demonstrate the feasibility and social acceptability [1] of so-called around-device interaction.

Although around-device interaction has been widely explored, ways to leverage the void space just above the device which is reachable with the thumb of the hand holding the device is an unexplored interaction space. We present Thumbs-Up, the in-air space next to a smartphone that can be reached with the thumb on the hand holding the device. With Thumbs-Up, the in-air space could be used to access on-screen content by directly pointing with the thumb, as shown in Figure 1. Additionally, this surrounding space could be used in conjunction with current touch input to extend the input vocabulary.

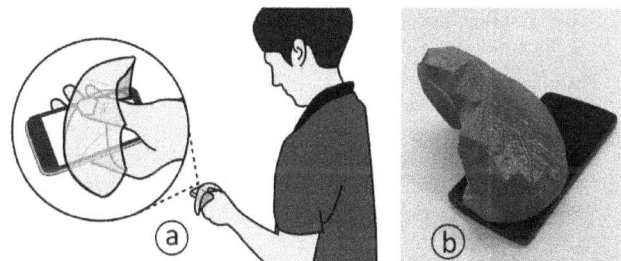

Figure 1. (a) Thumbs-Up interactions occur in the thumb-reachable in-air space around a smartphone. A 3D printed shape of this thumb-reachable space is shown in (b). During one-handed usage, users could utilize this space to overcome limitations of one-handed interaction.

We start with exploring the Thumbs-Up input range. Results reveal that study participants can reach a large in-air space (up to 74mm from the touchscreen) with their thumb. With a design workshop, we further elicit opinions from users about possible Thumbs-Up interactions to address commonly known limitations with one-handed smartphone usage. Workshop participants sketched a set of alternative designs that could potentially solve these limitations.

Our contributions include: (i) the definition of Thumbs-Up, the thumb-reachable in-air input space around a smartphone; and (ii) a set of interaction techniques that could be applied in Thumbs-Up to resolve concerns of reachability, limited multi-touch interaction, and thumb occlusion for one-handed smartphone input.

2. Thumbs-Up Input Range

We start with a study to identify the suitable thumb input range when the user holds the smartphone in the hand. Previous work [5] that has studied two-handed usage situations (where one hand holds the smartphone and the fingers on the other hand are used for on-screen input) shows that users frequently move or rest their input fingers in the air just above the screen between on-screen interactions. This observation motivated us to distinguish between: (i) *TouchSpace*: the space just above the screen (above screen-space) that people use to initiate or terminate touch gestures when these are performed with the thumb; and (ii) *Thumbs-Up space*: the in-air space around the device that is reachable with the thumb on the hand that is holding the device.

2.1 Participants and Apparatus

Twelve right-handed smartphone owners participated (three female, mean age 24.3 years, s.d. 5.8). All participants preferred to hold and interact with the phone in portrait mode. Participants' thumbs were on average 105mm long (from the carpometacarpal joint to the tip of the thumb). On average, their palm circumference, hand size (from tip of middle finger to bottom of the palm), and hand span measured 183mm, 184mm, and 200mm, respectively.

We used a Vicon MX system to track participants' thumb movements around a Samsung Mini S4 (screen size: 4.3", dimensions: 4.91×2.41×0.35"). We placed tracking markers on the smartphone and on a 3D-printed ring to track participants' thumbs (Figure 2). A Unity 5.0 application logged thumb movements in relation to the smartphone.

2.2 Tasks

Participants were instructed to hold the phone in their left/right hand with the left-bottom/right-bottom corner of the phone close to the centre of the palm (Figure 2). Participants performed two tasks:

(i) *Map navigation task*: We asked participants to navigate a map using flick gestures with their thumb. We showed participants two familiar locations in the city in the Google Maps application and asked them to navigate from the first to the second location. To perform this kind of task, a user has to repeatedly tap the screen and then flick to pan the map. After a panning action, the user needs to readjust the thumb to start the next panning action. We included this task to identify the *TouchSpace* zone above the screen – the in-air space where the thumb moves after an on-screen thumb-operation.

(ii) *Space filling task*: We asked participants to repeatedly move the thumb in mid-air, from left-to-right and right-to-left above the screen and thereby gradually increase the distance between the top of the thumb and the screen. We asked participants to do so until the top of the thumb had reached the maximum distance that could be managed without having to adjust the position of the device in the hand. These repetitive in-air movements generated a large thumb-reachable volume, which we refer to as *Thumbs-Up* space.

Figure 2. (a) Map navigation and (b) Space filling task.

Participants performed the tasks standing in a room equipped with the motion tracking system. We asked participants to imagine that one of their hands is holding a coffee mug and the other hand is available for on-screen interactions. All participants performed the two tasks with the right and with the left thumb. The tasks were performed three times with each thumb.

2.3 Results

TouchSpace: We found that during the map navigation task, participants moved the left thumb up to a maximum of 22mm above the screen (average 18mm, s.d. 2.7mm). The right thumb was moved to a maximum of 23mm above the screen (average 19mm, s.d. 2.3mm). Accordingly, we reserve this *TouchSpace* for completing or initiating on-screen gestures only.

Thumbs-Up space, height: The recordings from the space filling task revealed that participants could comfortably reach a maximum of 64mm above the screen with the left thumb (average 57mm, s.d. 5.8mm) and a maximum of 74mm (average 63mm, s.d. 9.6mm) with the right thumb. Accordingly, we can consider using this space (22 to 57mm above the screen for the left hand thumb and 23 to 63mm for the right hand thumb) for Thumbs-Up interactions.

Thumbs-Up space, width: When regarding the phone's bottom edge as the horizontal axis, participants moved the left thumb sideways within an arc spanning from 10° to 150°. With the right thumb, the movements were within an arc spanning from and 0° and 150°. With both thumbs, the corresponding arc length decreased as the thumb's height-distance from the screen increased.

Our results indicate that people can comfortably reach a relatively large in-air region above and beside the device with the thumbs. Figure 3 visualizes the corresponding accessible in-air space for the left and right thumbs.

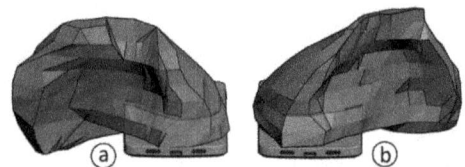

Figure 3. In-air thumb-reachable space with (a) the left and (b) the right thumb. The red areas indicate TouchSpace and the blue areas represent Thumbs-Up space.

We note that the in-air space for the right thumb is slightly larger than for the left thumb. On average it spans up to 64mm above the device with the left thumb and up to 74mm with the right thumb. We also observe that the region for the right thumb is larger in the horizontal direction than for the left thumb. We attribute these differences to the fact that all participants were right handed and frequently use their right thumb for one-handed smartphone interaction. This frequent usage provides them the flexibility to reach regions which are less intuitive/comfortable with the left thumb. A minor concern worth mentioning is the lack of significant diversity among our participant pool. However, we believe that more participants with balanced gender and handedness would further ascertain our findings.

3. Design Workshop

After having defined the accessible Thumbs-Up space, we explored how this space could be utilized in one-handed usage situations. We invited eight smartphone owners (all male, 22 to 29 years old, mean 24.9, s.d. 2.4) to participate in a design workshop. All participants were HCI students with significant interface design experience. We focused on three well-documented [2, 3, 8, 12] limitations of thumb-based interaction: i) *Reachability*: due to the bio-mechanical limits of the thumb it is difficult to access on-screen items located at the top region of the screen and in the lower corners of the screen; ii) *Limited multi-touch interaction*: as multi-touch gestures (such as zoom in/out a map) are difficult to perform with one finger (or a thumb), many of the touchscreen gestures are not available for one-handed thumb interaction; and iii) *Occlusion*: on-screen

Figure 4. Proxies for unreachable items could be placed inside Thumbs-Up space (a and b). An on-screen item could be highlighted based on the directions of thumb movements and the distance from the screen (c) or depending on the dwell time (d). A virtual joystick could be used to control the currently highlighted item (e). Unreachable items could be moved to the thumb reachable area using a gesture, such as bending the thumb (f) or a quick left-to-right movement (g).

interactions with the thumb (as with the index finger) occlude large parts of the screen and so covers on-screen information.

Our design workshop was structured as follows. We first familiarized the participants with one-handed interaction and discussed several common situations in which the user only has one hand free for interaction (e.g., when navigating a map while holding the smartphone in one hand and a shopping bag in the other hand, or when scrolling a list of contacts while clinging onto a handlebar in a shaky subway train). We also demonstrated and discussed how one-handed interaction limits multi-touch operations, and how it could lead to reachability and occlusion problems. After this introduction phase we introduced the idea of using the thumb in-air space for interaction on a smartphone. We demonstrated the Thumbs-Up space by placing a 3D-printed volume of the Thumbs-Up space – as defined through our earlier study – on top of a smartphone (Figure 1b). We then asked participants to familiarize themselves with thumb movements in the Thumbs-Up space while holding their own smartphones.

The next activity for our participants was to individually propose, sketch, and describe possible interactions that include the use of Thumbs-Up space. We instructed participants to focus on interactions targeted as solutions for the three key limitations of one-handed interaction. Each participant provided at least one Thumbs-Up interaction for each one of the three key limitations. We then discussed and refined the proposed interactions together with the participants. In the following sections we present the most promising interactions.

3.1 Limitation: Reachability

We collected a total of 26 sketches to tackle the reachability issue. We summarize the proposals under the following categories:

Placing items into the Thumbs-Up space: A common approach listed by the participants was to use the Thumbs-Up space to access unreachable screen items by placing virtual proxies in the Thumbs-Up space. An item would highlight on the screen based on the thumb position in Thumbs-Up space. Two variations are shown in Figure 4a and b, where the proxies are placed in the Thumbs-Up space or onto a bent surface inside the Thumbs-Up space.

Highlight an item based on the thumb position: Instead of placing proxies in Thumbs-Up space, this approach maps the thumb movement to the currently highlighted item. This mapping can be done in the following ways:

Direction+Height: In this style of interaction, the thumb of the hand holding the device acts as a ray-casting pointer and its height from the touchscreen defines the currently highlighted item in that direction (Figure 4c).

Direction+Dwell: Similar to Direction+Height, but a dwell-timer is used to define the currently highlighted. An item further away on the screen could be reached with a longer dwell time and a closer item could be attained with a shorter dwell time (Figure 4d).

Virtual joystick: An imaginary joystick is positioned centered above the screen and the thumb in Thumbs-Up space is used to control a screen cursor which highlights screen items according to thumb movements (Figure 4e).

Moving unreachable items to the thumb reachable space with a thumb gesture in Thumbs-Up space: Prior work has shown that items that are out of reach for the thumb require more effort to access as the user needs to readjust the way they hold the phone [2]. Moving such items to the thumb reachable on-screen region with a thumb gesture in Thumbs-Up space could be a potential solution to solve reachability issues. Many workshop participants suggested to use "micro-gestures", such as quickly bending or moving the thumb left-to-right (or opposite) inside Thumbs-Up space, to temporarily move unreachable screen items to a reachable screen area (Figure 4f and g).

3.2 Limitation: Multi-touch Interaction

Participants sketched a total of 19 designs to address the problem with limited multi-touch interaction for one finger/thumb situations. We summarize the design into the following categories:

Pie menu based approach: When the user moves the thumb into Thumbs-Up space an on-screen pie menu, which contains menu items to trigger any applicable multi-touch operations, appears on the screen (Figure 5a). The user can now move the thumb in Thumbs-Up space to invoke the desired operation from the menu.

Dual-gesture: This approach requires that the user performs two thumb gestures in Thumbs-Up space to complete a multi-touch operation. The gestures could be performed sequentially – e.g., a horizontal thumb movement immediately followed by a vertical movement – or in parallel – e.g., moving and bending the thumb simultaneously. For instance, bending while moving the thumb could be used to simultaneous pan and zoom a map, as visualized in Figure 5b.

Figure 5. (a) A pie menu with multi-touch functionalities is displayed when the thumb enters Thumbs-Up space; (b) sequential/parallel multiple thumb gestures are mapped with on-screen multi-touch gestures.

Continuous gestures: Many workshop participants suggested to map different continuous gestures to multi-touch operations. For example, a continuous clockwise or counterclockwise in-air movement could be used to zoom-in or -out (Figure 6a).

Touch+In-Air solution: Similar to prior work [5], some workshop participants suggested to interweave on-screen touches with in-air thumb gestures. In this approach, a gesture could start from the screen and end in the Thumbs-Up space, or vice versa (Figure 6b).

Additionally, these gestures can be directional (i.e., from a certain angle from mid-air to the touchscreen), complex (e.g., a lasso gesture in mid and then touch to the screen) or depend on a dwell-timer (e.g., 2 seconds inside the Thumbs-Up space and then a rapid touch on the screen to zoom in a map as shown in Figure 6b).

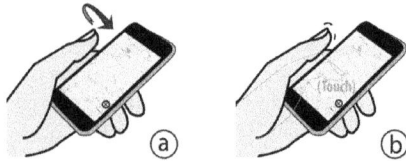

Figure 6. (a) A continuous clockwise movement inside Thumbs-Up space and (b) an in-air thumb gesture followed by a screen tap to zoom in a map.

3.3 Limitation: Occlusion

Workshop participants provided a total of 13 designs that could solve the occlusion problem. We summarize their proposals:

Use "Extended" Thumbs-Up space: The Thumbs-Up space could be divided into two areas: one area directly above the phone and the area other to the left of the phone (we called this area the Extended Thumbs-Up space), as shown in Figure 7a. Participants commonly suggested to use this Extended Thumbs-Up space to solve the occlusion problem.

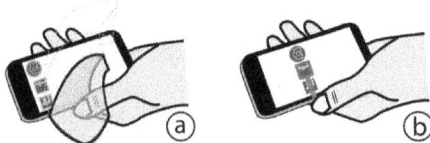

Figure 7. Occlusion problem could be resolved by using (a) the Extended Thumbs-Up space spatially located besides the phone's physical boundary, or by using (b) a "cursor" offset where the thumb highlights an object from its in-air position.

Bent surface: Participants suggested to use an imaginary bent plane inside the Thumbs-Up space for on-screen interaction, as shown in Figure 4b. Since the thumb accesses on-screen items on a plane vertical to the screen, screen occlusion may be reduced.

Shadow thumb: Instead of using a one-to-one mapping between finger and touch location, an offset could be introduced to overcome the occlusion issue (Figure 7b). Hovering the thumb in Thumbs-Up space would move the on screen cursor with an offset. Thus, the input thumb would never cover any on-screen items.

3.4 Challenges

Based on the above designs, we identify the following challenges:

Mid-Air thumb detection: The previously discussed designs rely on precise thumb movement detection in the Thumbs-Up space. Though current smartphones have the necessary capabilities to detect thumb movements in the air around the device, attaching external sensors (e.g., an omnidirectional mirror on top of the smartphone's camera [11] or wearing a magnetic ring on the thumb) could be used to track the thumb in Thumbs-Up space.

Initiate Thumbs-Up: Thumbs-Up interactions require a trigger mechanism to activate the Thumbs-Up space. A tap at the back of the smartphone (which produces a vibrational signal that is easily detected by the on-board accelerometer) or a quick swipe with the thumb back and forth across the screen bezel could be used.

Alternatively, a press on a physical button or a tap on a special screen button could activate/deactivate the Thumbs-Up space.

In-Air Selection: Thumbs-Up space allows the user to explore on-device items by moving the thumb. A selection is required when the user wants to invoke an item and put it into focus for more details. Specific finger movements such as a rapid thumb raise in Thumb-Up space could be used to trigger the selection.

4. Conclusion

We have defined Thumbs-Up space, the in-air space that is reachable with the thumb of the hand holding a smartphone. We have also presented several designs for interactions that rely on in-air thumb movements in Thumbs-Up space which could work as possible solutions to overcome three common problems encountered in one-handed smartphone interaction: limited reachability, limited multi-touch interaction, and occlusion issues. Our future work will include implementing these designs and to investigate how to incorporate them into current one-handed smartphone interactions. Additionally, further exploration is required to build self-contained smartphone approaches that can detect the thumb of the hand holding the device.

5. REFERENCES

[1] Ahlström, D., Hasan, K. and Irani, P. Are you comfortable doing that?: acceptance studies of around-device gestures in and for public settings. In *Proc. MobileHCI '14*, 193-202.

[2] Bergstrom-Lehtovirta, J. and Oulasvirta, A. 2014. Modeling the functional area of the thumb on mobile touchscreen surfaces. In *Proc. CHI '14*, ACM, 1991-2000.

[3] Boring, S., Ledo, D., Chen, X. A., Marquardt, N., Tang, A., and Greenberg, S. 2012. The fat thumb: using the thumb's contact size for single-handed mobile interaction. In *Proc. MobileHCI '12*, ACM, 207-208.

[4] Butler, A., Izadi, S., and Hodges, S. 2008. SideSight: multi-"touch" interaction around small devices. In *Proc. UIST '08*, ACM, 201-204.

[5] Chen, X. A., Schwarz, J., Harrison, C., Mankoff, J., and Hudson, S. E. 2014. Air+touch: interweaving touch & in-air gestures. In *Proc. UIST '14*, ACM, 519-525.

[6] Hasan, K., Ahlström, D., and Irani, P. 2013. Ad-binning: leveraging around device space for storing, browsing and retrieving mobile device content. In *Proc. CHI '13*, ACM, 899-908.

[7] How Do Users Really Hold Mobile Devices? http://www.uxmatters.com/mt/archives/2013/02/how-do-users-really-hold-mobile-devices.php, last access Aug. 2016.

[8] Karlson, A. K. and Bederson, B. B. 2007. ThumbSpace: generalized one-handed input for touchscreen-based mobile devices. In *Proc. INTERACT'07*, Springer-Verlag, 324-338.

[9] Kratz, S. and Rohs, M. 2009. HoverFlow: expanding the design space of around-device interaction. In *Proc. MobileHCI '09*, ACM, Article 4, 8 pages.

[10] Song, J., Sörös, G., Pece, F., Fanello, S. R., Izadi, S., Keskin, C., and Hilliges, O. 2014. In-air gestures around unmodified mobile devices. In *Proc. UIST '14*, ACM, 319-329.

[11] Yang, X. D., Hasan, K., Bruce, N., and Irani, P. 2013. Surround-see: enabling peripheral vision on smartphones during active use. In *Proc. UIST '13*, ACM, 291-300.

[12] Yatani, K., Partridge, K., Bern, M., and Newman, M. W. 2008. Escape: a target selection technique using visually-cued gestures. In *Proc. CHI '08*, ACM, 285-294.

Moving Ahead with Peephole Pointing: Modelling Object Selection with Head-Worn Display Field of View Limitations

Barrett Ens[1], David Ahlström[2], Pourang Irani[1]

[1]University of Manitoba
Winnipeg, Canada
{bens, irani}@cs.umanitoba.ca

[2]Alpen-Adria-Universität Klagenfurt
Klagenfurt, Austria
david.ahlstroem@aau.at

ABSTRACT

Head-worn displays (HWDs) are now becoming widely available, which will allow researchers to explore sophisticated interface designs that support rich user productivity features. In a large virtual workspace, the limited available field of view (FoV) may cause objects to be located outside of the available viewing area, requiring users to first locate an item using head motion before making a selection. However, FoV varies widely across different devices, with an unknown impact on interface usability. We present a user study to test two-step selection models previously proposed for 'peephole pointing' in large virtual workspaces on mobile devices. Using a CAVE environment to simulate the FoV restriction of stereoscopic HWDs, we compare two different input methods, direct pointing, and raycasting in a selection task with varying FoV width. We find a very strong fit in this context, comparable to the prediction accuracy in the original studies, and much more accurate than the traditional Fitts' law model. We detect an advantage of direct pointing over raycasting, particularly with small targets. Moreover, we find that this advantage of direct pointing diminishes with decreasing FoV.

Keywords

Head-worn display; HWD; HMD; field of view; FoV; peephole pointing; Fitts' law; modelling

1. INTRODUCTION

Head-worn display (HWD) technology has advanced rapidly over recent years, and powerful, self-contained systems such as Hololens[1] and Daqri[2] are now entering the market. Advanced sensing systems allow these devices to track their relative position, allowing rich and sophisticated user interfaces to be overlaid on the surrounding environment.

One limitation of current see-through HWD technology is the limited viewing region of the see-through display. Different devices use varying optical technologies that provide a field of view (FoV) ranging roughly from $20°$[3] to $90°$[4] in width. Researchers have found that FoV restrictions negatively influence spatial orientation and navigation [11], however little is known about the impact of FoV on object selection in spatial interfaces. Research has shown advantages of spatial interaction, using head and body motion, despite limitations on the available FoV [1, 3].

This research explores the effects of FoV size on virtual target selection. In a spatial user interface, any virtual objects that lie

SUI'16, October 15–16, 2016, Tokyo, Japan.
© 2016 ACM. ISBN 978-1-4503-4068-7/16/10. $15.00.
DOI: http://dx.doi.org/10.1145/2983310.2985756

outside of the available FoV are cropped from view. To select a hidden object, the user must first turn their head until the object enters the viewing region, and then proceed with the given pointing mechanism. This two-step selection process is analogous to "peephole pointing", a term used to describe target selection on spatially aware mobile devices. Models for two-step selection [2, 13] (Figure 1a), proposed in the context of peephole pointing, have been shown to predict selection time more accurately than Fitts' law [4]. Later work has independently verified these models in the similar context of a handheld projector [7].

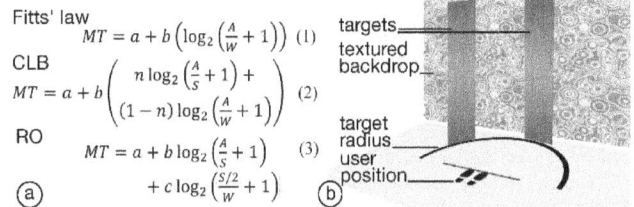

Figure 1. a) Equations for modelling pointing time, including two-component models created to model peephole pointing. b) The setup of our user study in a stereoscopic CAVE environment. Participants do a reciprocal pointing task between targets places on an imaginary arc.

We conduct a user study that emulates an HWD's FoV restriction in a CAVE environment (Figure 1b), to investigate whether these models retain their accuracy when head motion, rather than handheld device motion, is used to locate the target in the first step of the selection. We also intend to shed light on the effects of FoV width on target selection, to provide insights that may be useful for designing interfaces to work across a range of platforms with varying FoV widths. Unlike prior work with these models, we run our study using two different input techniques. We run a between-subjects study with raycasting and direct pointing, two potentially useful techniques for future HWD interfaces.

2. TWO-COMPONENT POINTING MODELS

Fitts' law [4] is an established model to estimate the average time required to select a target of width W at distance (amplitude) A. The movement time, MT, is predicted by the formula (1), as shown in Figure 1a, where a and b are experimentally determined constants. This model is commonly applied to 1D target selection tasks, but can be applied or adapted to selection in 3D virtual environments [5, 10, 15]. However, this model assumes that the target being selected is visible to the user. More recent models handle situations where the virtual workspace is larger than the available display space [8], such as with "peephole pointing" on a mobile device. Two similar models, shown in Figure 1a, were introduced

---

[1] http://www.microsoft.com/microsoft-hololens/en-us
[2] http://daqri.com/
[3] http://www.epson.com/MoverioBT200
[4] http://www.metavision.com/

independently: (2) by Cao, Li and Balakrishnan [2] (hereafter CLB), and (3) by Rohs and Oulasvirta [13] (hereafter RO).

Both models are derived from Fitts' law, but contain an additional parameter S, which represents the available screen size. Both models also give a sum of two components: the first component models the time required to search for an off-screen target until it becomes visible, and the second component represents the time needed to then select the target. In this paper, we generalize these using the term *two-component models*.

CLB tested their model by emulating a 1D peephole environment on a desktop computer, and found that targeting performance drops with a decrease in S. As S increases, the model converges to a standard Fitts' pointing task, however, their two-component model fits markedly better than Fitts' law when S is a variable.

RO tested their model using a spatially aware mobile device with a 2D selection task. Contrary to CLB, they only examined one value of S and found that Fitts' law is a good predictor in the "peephole" context, when the target exists only in the virtual workspace, but not for a "magic lens" context, when the actual target can be seen in the real world. Their model provided a good fit in both contexts.

Kaufmann and Ahlström [7] (hereafter KA) later revisited these models, in the context of a "spotlight" metaphor, where the virtual workspace is explored with a handheld projector. They verified both models, but found that they substantially outperform Fitts' law only when users do not have prior knowledge of the target location, and when S is sufficiently small. This explains to some extent the findings of RO, as they provided prior knowledge of the target layout. KA noted that Fitts' law is a good predictor within each individual value of S, and also found some interesting interaction effects, which we follow up on in our analysis.

Our study builds on these works by testing these models in a new context, where the search component is driven by head motion, independent of the selection technique. Head motion [6], direct pointing [17] and raycasting [9] have all been shown to follow Fitts' law, but it remains to be seen whether head motion combined with either selection technique can be predicted using existing two-component models. Beyond verifying these models, we also shed light on the effects of FoV limitation on target selection, and reveal how these effects vary between direct pointing and raycasting.

3. USER STUDY

We ran a study with 24 experienced computer users. All were males between 20 and 27 years old (mean 22.2, SD 1.7), and two were left-handed. Participants had varying previous experience with viewing 3D displays. Participation lasted approximately 1 hour.

We conducted our study in a CAVE environment to emulate the FoV limitation of a see-through HWD [3]. The CAVE combines a floor and wall display (Figure 1b) into a unified 3D image. Each stereo projector pair has a 1920×1080 resolution. Participants stood 1m from the wall, giving an apparent display width of roughly 130°. Textured targets were placed in front of a textured backdrop to assist stereo convergence [14]. Head and pointing motion were tracked using a high-precision, low-latency Vicon system.

Since HWD FoV is commonly measured in degrees, we designed our study to use model parameters A, W and S based on angles, measured in degrees of apparent width. Angular measures are commonly applied in immersive environments [12] and Fitts' law has been successfully expressed in terms of angular width [9]. Because the models are affected by the ratios between parameters, and not the absolute units, we expect that two-component models will predict angular units equally well to linear units.

3.1 Task, Selection Techniques & Study Design

Task: For purposes of comparison, we closely followed the study design of KA, and used a similar non-conventional, reciprocal 1D pointing task. Each sequence consists of two target selections, the first without prior knowledge of target location, and the second with. This knowledge is given by placing the second target in the same location as an initial starting target. Targets appear as bars the height of the display wall (Figure 1b). Targets of identical angular width W are placed at angular distance A (Figure 2a), however, each target appears only after the preceding target is selected to prevent accidental knowledge about their locations.

To begin a sequence, the start target must be located through the available viewing frusta (Figure 2a). The start target's placement to the left or right of centre informs the participant in which direction to search for the second target. This location is randomly chosen to be left or right, and is randomly offset to prevent predictability. The participant proceeds scanning until the first target is located, at which point they make a selection, then return to the initial start location to select the second target. Success is indicated with visual and audio feedback. Trials proceed whether or not a selection is successful, however, all targets must be selected successfully for a sequence to be valid. Invalid sequences are re-queued.

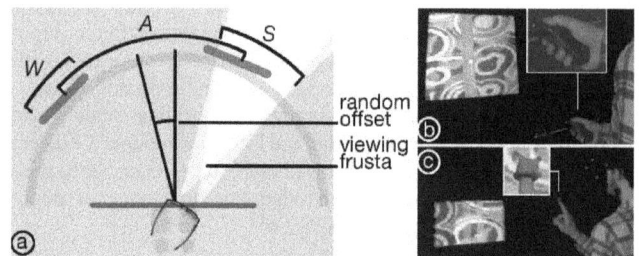

Figure 2. a) Our study layout, showing the relationships of the model parameters. A user making a selection using the b) raycast (*Ray*) and c) direct pointing (*Tap*) techniques.

Selection Techniques: We investigated two selection techniques for this study, raycasting (*Ray*) and direct pointing (*Tap*).

In the *Ray* technique, participants use a spatially tracked handheld mouse (Figure 2b). A virtual ray extends from the mouse and selection is trigger by pressing either top button. If the button is pressed when the ray is not intersecting the target area, then the selection is recorded as a miss.

In the *Tap* technique, the participant's dominant index finger is instrumented with tracking markers (Figure 2c). Selection is triggered when the finger crosses the target plane. If the finger crosses the plane outside of the target area, then the selection is recorded as a miss.

Targets are positioned 1m away from the participant for *Ray*, and 0.5m for *Tap*. This puts targets within reach for the *Tap* technique, but farther away in *Ray* to allow effective raycasting. In both techniques, the stereo frusta overlap at the target distance, so that any visible part of the target will be seen equally by both eyes.

Both of these techniques are "decoupled", in that pointing motion is independent from head motion. CLB's study compared a coupled cursor (fixed at the centre of the peephole) with a decoupled cursor (controlled by a secondary input device), and found the coupled technique to be faster. RO and KA studied coupled techniques only.

Study design:
We used a between-subjects design with four independent variables: target distance A (24, 48, 72, 96°), target width W (2, 4, 8, 16°), FoV width S (8, 16, 32, 64, 128°, SNR=No Restriction),

and prior knowledge of target position, *PK* (NoPK, PK). Each participant completed four blocks of 96 sequences. Each block contained one sequence for each *A-W-S* combination in a random order. Half of the participants used each technique (*Ray, Tap*). Participants were asked to select targets as quickly and accurately as possible, and were given adequate breaks between blocks. We collected data from a total of 10,242 sequences (20,484 selections).

3.2 Results

Errors: In 1,026 sequences, participants missed either one or both targets. In total 1,230 target misses were recorded (6% of all target selections). A Mann-Whitney U test showed that the number of missed selections did not differ between the two techniques (*Ray* 504, *Tap* 726; $U=52.0$, $p=.266$). As expected, and similar to what CLB and KA report, our analyses showed a significant effect of target width (Friedman test: $\chi^2_{(3,N=24)}=65.78$, $p<.001$) with an increasing number of misses as the target width decreases (*W16* 38, *W8* 95, *W4* 243, *W2* 854; Bonferroni adjusted post-hoc Wilcoxon Signed-Rank tests showed that all widths differed, all p's<.0083). Also in line with CLB and KA, we found no significant differences between the four amplitudes (*A24* 291, *A48* 306, *A72* 299, *A96* 334) or between selections with and without prior knowledge of the target location (*PK* 634, *NoPK* 596). Contrary to CLB and KA, who report significant effects of their peephole size, we did not find any significant effect of FoV width. However, we see similar trends to those reported by CLB and KA: fewer misses with smaller FoV widths and more misses with the two largest widths (*S8* 180, *S16* 177, *S32* 179, *S64* 172, *S128* 227, *SNR* 295). CLB speculate that with a small peephole the user is very careful, whereas with a large one the user may be too confident and relaxed, thus making more mistakes. Our data support this speculation and suggest that this may be the case in HWD-situations too.

Movement time: The following analyses are based on error free sequences only (18,432 selections in 9,216 sequences). The movement times (*MT*) were right skewed and we performed a logarithmic transformation (which resulted in distributions close to normal) before analyzing the data. A mixed ANOVA with *technique* as between-subject factor and *A, W, S,* and *PK* as within-subject factors showed the same significant main effects for *W* ($F_{3,66}=233.0$, $p<0.001$, $\eta^2=0.91$), *A* ($F_{3,66}=476.4$, $p<0.001$, $\eta^2=0.96$), *S* ($F_{5,110}=1064.9$, $p<0.001$, $\eta^2=0.98$) and *PK* ($F_{1,22}=29.5$, $p<0.001$, $\eta^2=0.57$) as CLB and KA report.

As expected from Fitts' law literature, and confirming CLB's and KA's results, we found that close targets took shorter time to select than targets further away: *A24* 1.09s, *A48* 1.31s, *A72* 1.50s, *A96* 1.72s (we use the geometric mean, i.e., the antilog of the mean of the log-transformed data to report time measures and we use Bonferroni adjustment for post-hoc tests. Post-hoc: all *A*s differed, all p's<0.0083). Likewise, small targets took longer time to select than larger targets: *W2* 1.72s, *W4* 1.50s, *W8* 1.29s, *W16* 1.11s (post-hoc: all *W*s differed, all p's<0.0083).

Our results regarding prior target location knowledge and influence of FoV width on target selection performance with head motion confirm CLB's and KA's peephole findings; We also found better performance in selections with prior knowledge than without (*PK* 1.29s, *NoPK* 1.49s) and that performance increased with increasing FoV width (*S8* 2.24s, *S16* 1.80s, *S32* 1.46s, *S64* 1.18s, *S128* 1.03s, *SNR* 0.99s, post-hoc: all *S*s differed, all p's<0.0033).

We did not find a main effect for *technique* (*Ray* 1.43s, *Tap* 1.34s) but did notice a significant *technique×W* interaction ($F_{3,66}=9.57$, $p<0.001$, $\eta^2=0.30$), plotted in Figure 3a. We attribute *Ray*'s low performance with small targets to the well-known jitteriness of raycasting techniques [14], which makes selecting small targets

difficult. Technique also interacted with *S* ($F_{5,110}=8.08$, $p<0.001$, $\eta^2=0.27$), as shown in Figure 3b. It seems *Tap* loses its advantage over *Ray* as FoV becomes more restricted. We suspect this is because participants were more careful with a narrower FoV, as noted by the decrease in errors. However, we are surprised to learn that *Ray* does not perform even worse with decreasing *S*, as the virtual ray becomes increasingly cropped by the view frusta.

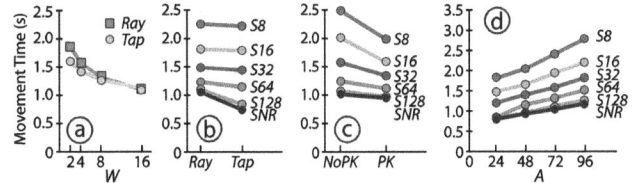

Figure 3. a) *MT×W*, b) *Technique×S*, c) *PK×S*, and d) *A×S* interactions found in our user study.

We observe a significant *PK×S* interaction ($F_{5,66}=9.57$, $p<0.001$, $\eta^2=0.30$) in Figure 3c, also reported by CLB and KA: the advantage of prior location knowledge is more beneficial with small FoV widths and almost disappears with large widths. A partial reason for this, as pointed out by KA, is that, with the largest FoV widths, some of the targets were visible from the onset of the movement selection (*A24* with *S64*, *S128* and *SNK*, *A48* with *S128* and *SNK*, and *A72* and *A96* with *SNR*). Intuitively, knowledge about target location is less important if the target is already visible.

Finally, we observed a significant *A×S* interaction ($F_{15,330}=16.21$, $p<0.001$, $\eta^2=0.42$), also reported by KA but not by CLB. This interaction is visualized in Figure 3d. With all FoV widths but *S64*, we see consistently increasing movement times as *A* increases. With *S64* we see a sudden increase between *A24* and *A48*. This mirrors the effect of having a target visible at onset: with *S64* targets at *A24* were visible, targets at *A48* were not.

Model fitting: We separately analyze the data from the two techniques, and data from *NoPK* and *PK* selections. We obtain the following R^2 values:

Ray+NoPK: CLB $R^2=.932$, RO $R^2=.877$, Fitts $R^2=.345$
Ray+PK: CLB $R^2=.950$, RO $R^2=.847$, Fitts $R^2=.483$
Tap+NoPK: CLB $R^2=.941$, RO $R^2=.916$, Fitts $R^2=.204$
Tap+PK: CLB $R^2=.944$, RO $R^2=.898$, Fitts $R^2=.272$

These results confirm KA's findings: when combining data from all six FoV widths, we find better fits with CLB's and RO's models than with the Fitts' law model. The reason is obvious in Figure 4, where we see how the regression lines for the separate *S* values are spread wide apart (the plots for *Ray+NoPK* and *Tap+NoPK* look similar but with larger intercept and slope parameters; the corresponding parameters can be obtained from Table 1).

Accordingly, we follow KA's analysis approach and look at model fits for separate FoV sizes (RO collected data from only one

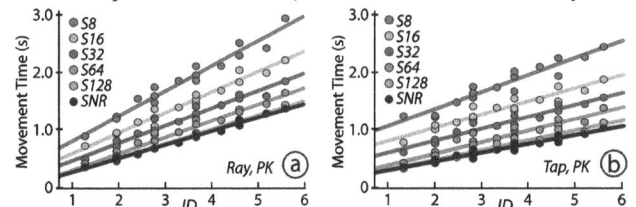

Figure 4. Fitts' regression plots for *Ray* and *Tap*, with *PK*.

peephole size, and CLB do not present separate analyses for their five peephole sizes). These modelling results represent realistic HWD interaction where the FoV width is kept constant during use. However, the two-component models may nonetheless be beneficial to designers, for instance to make an interface consistent across platforms with different FoV widths. There may also be situations where dynamically restricting the FoV is warranted, for example to encourage precise selection in critical instances.

Table 1 lists the regression results for CLB's and RO's models and the Fitts' law models for the different S values with the two selection techniques in trials with and without prior knowledge. As KA found in their model comparison, we also see strong fits with all three models in most cases. The R^2 values with the Fitts' model are slightly lower than those with the other models, particularly so in cases with no prior location knowledge. Nevertheless, in cases with many visible targets (SNR, or future HWDs with a very wide FoV) the comparably simple Fitts' law model shows to be a sufficiently good predictor of selection performance.

Table 1. Model fitting results for separate FoV widths.

		CLB model				RO model				Fitts' law		
		R^2	a	b	n	R^2	a	b	c	R^2	a	b
Ray + NoPK	S8	.905	.344	.690	.394	.898	-.232	.698	.860	.853	.872	.498
	S16	.929	.514	.509	.294	.926	.101	.570	.543	.903	.703	.398
	S32	.983	.219	.564	.451	.990	-.141	.705	.380	.937	.409	.362
	S64	.978	.107	.614	.568	.969	-.248	.882	.278	.915	.250	.317
	S128	.953	.327	.344	.348	.957	-.081	.814	.220	.948	.352	.236
	SNR	.961	.315	.461	.504	.960	-.571	4.25	.206	.960	.322	.233
Ray + PK	S8	.978	.340	.532	.275	.969	-.192	.540	.795	.956	.624	.429
	S16	.988	.293	.461	.321	.982	-.065	.514	.472	.959	.480	.351
	S32	.980	.306	.413	.347	.984	-.005	.536	.330	.958	.414	.299
	S64	.979	.179	.451	.437	.971	-.163	.709	.267	.955	.260	.284
	S128	.989	.240	.280	.128	.987	-.200	.792	.238	.989	.248	.248
	SNR	.987	.261	.237	.000	.969	-.655	3.94	.216	.987	.261	.237
Tap + NoPK	S8	.866	.569	.623	.547	.846	.195	.628	.546	.746	1.23	.383
	S16	.872	.745	.463	.422	.868	.493	.508	.403	.824	.991	.318
	S32	.966	.523	.490	.602	.976	.293	.579	.241	.845	.744	.256
	S64	.983	.209	.669	.737	.975	-.024	.847	.184	.817	.411	.249
	S128	.943	.329	.587	.762	.946	.076	.878	.137	.834	.423	.182
	SNR	.952	.463	1.04	.879	.963	-.023	3.25	.112	.916	.489	.141
Tap + PK	S8	.948	.732	.390	.342	.913	.392	.395	.512	.910	.991	.296
	S16	.949	.648	.325	.413	.944	.431	.357	.287	.900	.817	.225
	S32	.972	.493	.338	.484	.973	.292	.418	.213	.916	.615	.208
	S64	.977	.254	.517	.717	.973	.057	.665	.154	.831	.405	.201
	S128	.985	.269	.499	.725	.986	.020	.787	.135	.898	.345	.172
	SNR	.990	.356	1.36	.906	.988	-.139	3.58	.114	.938	.387	.149

4. CONCLUSION

We conducted a user study to test the prediction accuracy of two-component pointing models with a "peephole" controlled by head motion. Our study compared the performance of direct pointing and raycasting under these conditions.

Our results confirm that two-component (peephole pointing) models apply to target selection when the view is controlled by head motion, as with HWDs. We confirm previous findings from other contexts, that Fitts' law is a good predictor when targets are initially visible, and when S (display size, or in our case FoV width) is a known constant. Our comparison shows that direct pointing can be faster than raycasting with a sufficiently wide FoV. Raycasting is slow with small targets [16], however, we find the advantage of direct pointing is negated with reduced FoV.

Unlike prior research on two-component models, our user study focused on decoupled techniques, where head motion and target selection are controlled independently. In future work, we would like to further explore the degree of coupling between the user's hand and head motion during selections with these and other techniques, and to determine the role that FoV plays in coupling strength. We would also like to confirm our findings on various

HWD hardware platforms with 2D and 3D Fitts' pointing tasks. In further work, we would also like to explore design opportunities and benefits of HWD interfaces with dynamically changing FoV.

REFERENCES

[1] Ball, R. and North, C. 2008. The effects of peripheral vision and physical navigation on large scale visualization. *Proc. GI 2008*, 9–16.

[2] Cao, X., Li, J.J. and Balakrishnan, R. 2008. Peephole pointing: modeling acquisition of dynamically revealed targets. *Proc CHI '08*, 1699–1708.

[3] Ens, B.M., Finnegan, R. and Irani, P.P. 2014. The Personal Cockpit: A spatial interface for effective task switching on head-worn displays. *Proc. CHI '14*, 3171–3180.

[4] Fitts, P.M. 1954. The information capacity of the human motor system in controlling the amplitude of movement. *Journal of Experimental Psychology*. 47, 6 (Jun. 1954), 381–391.

[5] Grossman, T. and Balakrishnan, R. 2004. Pointing at trivariate targets in 3D environments. *Proc. CHI '04*, 447–454.

[6] Jagacinski, R.J. and Monk, D.L. 1985. Fitts' Law in two dimensions with hand and head movements. *Journal of Motor Behavior*. 17, 1 (Mar. 1985), 77–95.

[7] Kaufmann, B. and Ahlström, D. 2012. Revisiting peephole pointing: a study of target acquisition with a handheld projector. *Proc. MobileHCI '12*, 211–220.

[8] Kishishita, N., Kiyokawa, K., Orlosky, J., Mashita, T., Takemura, H. and Kruijff, E. 2014. Analysing the effects of a wide field of view augmented reality display on search performance in divided attention tasks. *Proc. ISMAR '14*, 177–186.

[9] Kopper, R. A human motor beh, Bowman, D.A., Silva, M.G. and McMahan, R.P. 2010. avior model for distal pointing tasks. *IJHCI*. 68, 10 (Oct. 2010), 603–615.

[10] MacKenzie, C.L., Marteniuk, R.G., Dugas, C., Liske, D. and Eickmeier, B. 1987. Three-dimensional movement trajectories in Fitts' task: Implications for control. *The Quarterly Journal of Experimental Psychology Section A*. 39, 4 (Nov. 1987), 629–647.

[11] Patterson, R., Winterbottom, M.D. and Pierce, B.J. 2006. Perceptual issues in the use of head-mounted visual displays. *Human Factors*. 48, 3, 555–573.

[12] Poupyrev, I., Weghorst, S., Billinghurst, M. and Ichikawa, T. 1997. A framework and testbed for studying manipulation techniques for immersive VR. *Proc. UIST '97*, 21–28.

[13] Rohs, M. and Oulasvirta, A. 2008. Target acquisition with camera phones when used as magic lenses. *Proc. CHI '08*, 1409–1418.

[14] Stuerzlinger, W. and Teather, R.J. 2014. Considerations for targets in 3D pointing experiments. *Proc. HCI Korea '14*, 162–168.

[15] Teather, R.J. and Stuerzlinger, W. 2011. Pointing at 3D targets in a stereo head-tracked virtual environment. *Proc. 3DUI '11*, 87–94.

[16] Vogel, D. and Balakrishnan, R. 2005. Distant freehand pointing and clicking on very large, high resolution displays. *Proc. UIST '05*, 33–42.

[17] Zeng, X., Hedge, A. and Guimbretiere, F. 2012. Fitts' law in 3D space with coordinated hand movements. *Proceedings of the Human Factors and Ergonomics Society Annual Meeting*. 56, 1 (Sep. 2012), 990–994.

Improving Interaction in HMD-Based Vehicle Simulators through Real Time Object Reconstruction

Michael Bottone
Department of Computer Science
University of Georgia
mbottone@uga.edu

Kyle Johnsen
College of Engineering
University of Georgia
kjohnsen@uga.edu

ABSTRACT

Bringing real objects into the virtual world has been shown to increase usability and presence in virtual reality applications. This paper presents a system to generate a real time virtual reconstruction of real world user interface elements for use in a head mounted display based driving simulator. Our system uses sensor fusion algorithms to combine data from depth and color cameras to generate an accurate, detailed, and fast rendering of the user's hands while using the simulator. We tested our system and show in our results that the inclusion of the participants real hands, the wheel, and the shifter in the virtual environment increases the immersion, presence, and usability of the simulation. Our system can also be used to bring other real objects into the virtual world, especially when accuracy, detail, and real time updates are desired.

Keywords

Virtual Reality; Sensor Fusion; Human Computer Interaction

1. INTRODUCTION

1.1 Background and Motivation

Bringing real objects into the virtual world has been shown to increase usability and presence in virtual reality (VR) applications. The goal of this paper is to create a system that combines the ideas of sensor fusion and object reconstruction, bringing real objects into the virtual environment (VE) and how that effects immersion, the impact of tactile user interfaces, and how all of this can be applied to a driving simulator that makes use of a head-mounted display (HMD).

Systems such as KinectFusion [1] and the work by Lok et. al. [4] [5] show how sensor fusion algorithms can be used to create reconstructions of objects in the real world, but these algorithms were applied to static environments or weren't suitable for real time updates. Google Tango [2] is a current research project that can dynamically map an environment

for use in augmented reality (AR), but is still used for the mapping of static environments. Lok went on in further work to apply the "visual hull" technique in a system that was able to update in real time [6]. We improve on this system by using modern hardware and software efficiency improvements.

Interacting with real objects in an HMD-based system is a difficult task without including the objects in the VE. The inclusion of real objects can improve the usability of interaction-intensive applications like typing or a driving simulator (McGill et. al.) [8]. Our application is an example of an interaction-intensive application due to the involvement needed from the user in order to operate the car. Lok investigated the impacts of bringing objects into the VE on usability [7]. This work showed than an exact reconstruction is not needed to achieve the usability improvements of using real objects in the VE and instead the idea of the "visual hull" can be used.

The use of real objects also brings a real tactile interface into the experience. Past systems have simulated touch using technology such as the Leap Motion and electro-tactile gloves [10] [9] [30] to achieve a tactile user interface, but using real objects removes the need to simulate the tactile feedback. Studies such as Mazalek et al. [19] show that usability of a system can be improved by including real tactile feedback since the objects the users interact with will feel and react like the user would expect. The gap between simulated and real tactile feedback is detrimental to system usability, and this gap is removed by using real objects.

Driving simulators have been a common VR application, but do not commonly make use of an HMD and instead use a triple monitor setup (TMS) or large, full-size hydraulic simulators with curved, collimated displays. Carlozzi et al. [11] performed a study that showed that HMD-based driving simulators are less usable and cause more simulator sickness than the TMS alternative. Due to the more immersive nature of HMD-based systems, matching what the users expect with motion cues and tactile feedback is important to reduce simulator sickness and improve usability. Kemeny et. al. [15] explored this idea of the user's perception being crucial in VR simulators. In order for an immersive simulator to be usable, the feedback (visual, tactile, motion, etc.) from the system needs to match the perception of the user as closely as possible.

1.2 System Goals

We built a system to bring real objects into the VE for use in a HMD-based driving simulator. We designed the system with the following goals:

1. **Low Latency Rendering** - In order for users to be able to interact with objects in the virtual world as they would in the real world, the reconstruction of the real objects should match the current locations and orientations of the real objects as closely as possible.

2. **HMD Rendering with Fast Updates** - The system should render at a high resolution to increase the immersion of the simulation. However, the simulation should also match the update rate of the HMD screen (75Hz) to prevent visual tearing and head tracking issues that could lower the user's immersion [13] [14].

3. **High Interaction Fidelity** - While the inclusion of real objects in the virtual environment increases the user's presence in the simulation [7] [8], the car, the physics of the car, and the user's perception of the world should follow what the user expects [15]. This improves the interaction fidelity [3] of the simulation.

4. **Improve System Usability** - Since the introduction of HMD-based systems in VR, shutting out the real world completely has caused issues with the usability and immersion of the system [8]. If the usability of an HMD based system is improved when user interaction is important, then various applications, including driving simulators, can fully explore the potential benefits of using a HMD.

1.3 Contributions

Due to consumer-grade HMDs becoming more widely available and increasingly capable of presenting a high-fidelity visual rendering, VR systems that traditionally did not use HMDs, either due to technical limitations or prohibitive system designs, are able to investigate the potential benefits of an HMD-based system. However, there are limitations of HMD-based systems that can make future research difficult, including the inability to include the real world. The immersion and usability of virtual reality systems are benefited by the inclusion of real objects in the virtual environment, particularly when the system involves spatial cognition related tasks. Systems that have not yet fully explored the potential benefits of HMDs are driving simulators. The lack of real world vision and motion cueing have made HMD-based driving simulators less desirable for use in research due to the increased simulator sickness and lack of immersion they bring. We show that a HMD-based driving simulator built with a high degree of interaction fidelity and inclusion of real-world objects can improve the usability and immersion of the simulation, allowing future research into HMD-based driving simulators and other applications to be more feasible.

Our contributions are as follows:

1. We show how real object reconstruction can be implemented for real-time updates, low latency, and performance for rendering to a high-definition HMD updating at 75 Hz.

2. We show how one of the current inhibitors of HMD-based systems can be mitigated by including real objects into the VE, which improves the usability and immersion of the simulation, and allows for more HMD-based system research in the future.

2. SYSTEM DESCRIPTION

2.1 Hardware

Our system consists of a depth camera, a color camera, a head-mounted display, a steering wheel and pedals, and a computer to run the simulation. For our system, we used the Microsoft Kinect for Xbox One for the depth and color cameras. The color camera reads RGB data at a resolution of 1920x1080 at an update rate of 30Hz while the depth camera reads a resolution of 512x424 also at a rate of 30Hz in a 70x60 degree field of view. This camera was mounted above the user to get a good perspective on the user's hands to better generate a reconstruction. We chose to mount the camera in a fixed position since our target is located in a fixed position. Also, if we mounted the camera to the HMD, there would be added latency to the system for the depth data to update for the user's new head position. A fixed camera can reconstruct objects the user isn't currently looking at, allowing the refresh rate of the HMD to be the only limiting factor as the user looks around.

For the head-mounted display, we used the Oculus Rift DK2 which renders at 960x1080 resolution for each eye and refreshes at 75Hz. The steering wheel we used is a Logitech G27 racing wheel. We designed and built a wooden rig (as seen in Figure 1) to mount the Kinect above the user facing the steering wheel to read the depth and color data of the user's hands, the steering wheel, and the shifter.

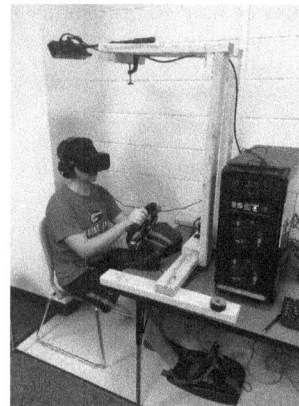

Figure 1: Hardware Setup

2.2 Software

The software for the system contains three main subsections: a native system plugin responsible for reading and processing the color and depth data from the Kinect in a multi-threaded environment, the reconstruction mesh rendering, and the simulation built in Unity.

2.2.1 Native Plugin

The native plugin is a C++ library that is accessed by Unity and run in a separate process in the operating system. We used a native plugin for independence from the simulation's update loop, and for data processing performance due to the lower-level language (C++) used. The native plugin is responsible for interfacing with the Kinect via the Kinect v2 API from Microsoft, reading the raw data stream, and processing the data for the simulation. The plugin needed to be accessible from the Unity simulation, and process both the color and depth data streams from the Kinect API. The data processing for the color and depth data frames is completely independent, so these two processes can be parallelized. We designed the plugin to have three components: the external interface, the color data thread (Thread A) and the depth data thread (Thread B).

The external interface is used by Unity to initialize the plugin. Unity sends over several pointers to memory for the plugin to write the data to. It sends a 3D data (x, y, z) array pointer to hold the mesh vertex data (which is initialized to a flat plane mesh), a 2D data (x, y) array to hold the mesh UV data, and a GPU texture pointer for the mesh texture. Once the pointers are set, the plugin initializes the Kinect API and gets the needed references to the sensor, color data frames, and depth data frames. Then, after the API is setup properly, the interface initializes the two worker threads and starts the update loops.

Thread A is responsible for the color data processing. The thread blocks execution until the API has a color frame ready. When the data is ready, the byte array of color data is copied from the API into local storage. Then, using DirectX3D 11, the byte array is written to the GPU texture pointer in RGBA format, which is the color format given by the Kinect API. This pointer is directly used by the rendering engine in Unity, so no other actions are needed to update the texture in the simulation. Thus, no additional computation is necessary in the update loop, which has a significant positive impact on performance.

Algorithm 1 Thread B Algorithm

$colorSpace \leftarrow array[depthReadings.length]$
$populateColorSpace(depthReadings, colorSpace)$
for $(x, y) \in depthReadings$ **do**
$\quad outputIndex \leftarrow (y * \frac{depthWidth}{2}) + x$
$\quad inputIndex \leftarrow ((y + \frac{depthHeight}{4}) * depthWidth) + (x + \frac{depthWidth}{4})$
$\quad vertexData[outputIndex].z \quad\quad\quad \leftarrow depthReadings[inputIndex] * scaleFactor$
$\quad$ **if** $vertexData[outputIndex].z < minValue$ **then**
$\quad\quad vertexData[outputIndex].z \leftarrow 0$
$\quad$ **end if**
end for

Thread B is responsible for the depth data processing. This thread also blocks execution until the API has a depth data frame ready. When the data becomes available, the array of unsigned 16-bit integers is copied from the API to local storage. Then, the API is queried for its color-to-depth mapping. This mapping allows us to create the UV mapping later. Once the API calls are finished, the depth points are iterated over, processed, and added to the output array. First, the vertex location in the input array may not be the same location in the output array, and in our application the output is offset to exclude points near the edges of the raw data. A mapping is created to map the vertex locations in the input array to the locations in the output array. Coordinates and distance in Unity do not have units, so the scale of the virtual objects used in the simulation may not match the size of the real objects. We mitigated this issue by scaling the depth data by a factor to match the size of the real steering wheel with the virtual steering wheel, which was a factor of 15%. The Kinect's depth accuracy

is most accurate between approximately 50cm and 300cm depending on lighting conditions. Points that fall outside this range become inaccurate.. For our system, the camera is pointed at the floor, so our filter focuses on points that are too close to the camera. To filter out these points, any depth values that are below a certain threshold are hidden by setting them to zero so the user will not be able to see them during the simulation. Once those points are filtered, the data is ready to be added to the mesh. The z-coordinate of the vertex at that point is updated with the scaled depth data. Once the data is set, then the UV mapping needs to be calculated.

The mesh is changing size every frame due to stretching from setting the vertex heights. This causes the depth data and the color texture to misalign. To fix this, the API provides a mapping from a 2D coordinate in color space to the corresponding 2D depth coordinate in the XY plane. This allows the plugin to then generate the UV data which assigns a 2D texture coordinate to each vertex in the mesh as an alignment guide. UV map coordinates are in the range $[0 \dots 1]$, so first, the corresponding color space point is retrieved from the mapping provided by the API. Then, the point's x and y coordinates are divided by the width and height of the color data, providing the floating point percentage values that we need for the UV data. This calculated UV value is then set to the shared UV data array. Once all the 3D data values are updated and the UV vectors are generated and saved to the shared pointers, the loop is finished and will wait for the next data frame to be ready.

All of the algorithms that read and process the data for Unity run in $O(n)$ time, where n is the resolution of the data (1920x1080 for color and 512x424 for depth). This time is required not only for processing the raw data points, but also for copying the data into the render engine.

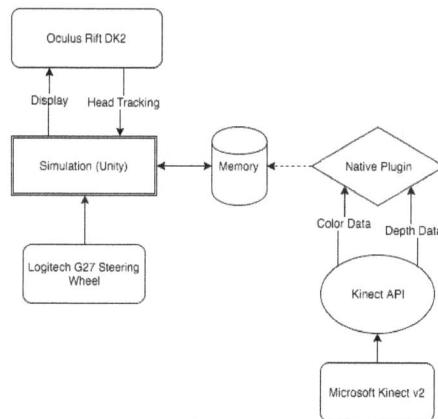

Figure 2: System Diagram

2.2.2 Reconstruction Mesh Rendering

Before the simulation begins, we generate a flat mesh with the desired vertex resolution in Unity. Each vertex is represented with a 3D data value that holds the x, y, and z values. The x and y values are preset to their location in the mesh. All of the z-values are set to 0 initially. These are the values that are set in the native plugin to match the depth readings. During development we started with a mesh that had enough vertices to cover the full resolution of the depth camera, however $512 * 424 = 217088$ vertices, which exceeds Unity's mesh vertex limit of 65535 vertices because each mesh indexes its vertices using a 16-bit integer. Although this is a limitation that was avoidable by selecting a different rendering engine, rendering meshes with over 65,000 vertices has a large performance impact, so we still wanted to avoid this setup. Our next idea was to create 4 meshes and arrange them in a rectangular pattern. We then give 25% of the data to each mesh, creating $\frac{512*424}{4} = 54272$ vertices per mesh, which fits into Unity's limit. This worked perfectly well, but then we realized that most of the data points near the edges were not needed for our application. So, we settled back on one mesh that instead contained the center portion of the data. This allows the mesh to still have full resolution detail, and includes a wide enough field of view for our real objects, ultimately letting us render only what we need.

To generate the mesh in Unity, the simulation first initializes the arrays of vertices and UV data that the native plugin writes to. The size of these arrays corresponds to the depth resolution that the simulation displays, which in our case is 256x212. Once the arrays are initialized, the full resolution is iterated through and a new vertex is added to the vertex array with a z-coordinate initially set to 0. Then, a blank UV is created and added to the UV data array. The UV data points are set later by the plugin, so there is no need to create them. Once the mesh is created, a blank texture is created and assigned to the mesh. The texture is also given an unlit shader so that the lights present in the 3D world will not affect the mesh. This is important because the objects being reconstructed are already lit by the real world and we didn't want to add additional lighting. Relighting objects is an area of active research and various relighting methods can be explored in future work. Once all of the assets that Unity needs to create are finished, the external API for the native plugin is called to set the pointers to the vertex data, the UV data, and the texture and start the update loop.

2.2.3   Driving Simulation

The driving simulation consists of three main parts: the car and the physics that are applied to it, handling the input from the user via the steering wheel, pedals, and shifter, and the world the user is instructed to drive through.

The car itself is a generic model that has been modified to fit the simulation better. The wheel is a separate mesh from the rest of the car allowing it to turn freely. This allows for the user to control the wheel orientation with their steering input. The Logitech G27 comes with a shifter that we use in the reconstruction, and we wanted the same shifter to be in the full virtual simulation as well. We created a static reconstruction of our shifter and added the model to the car. We then animated the shifter knob to move with user input so both the wheel and shifter moved to match user input in the full virtual simulation. For the real object simulation, the virtual steering wheel and shifter were removed to show the real steering wheel and shifter instead. To avoid confusing the user, we removed any objects from the virtual environment that the user could not interact with to avoid confusion. This put an emphasis on the real world objects that were being reconstructed, and allows the application to bring in whatever is needed to the virtual world. The only virtual elements that are left are the wheel and shifter that both update their orientations based on the current orientations of the actual wheel and shifter.

We added realistic physics to the car to further increase the immersion in the simulation. Our car physics system operates on a slightly modified version of the Unity car controller available in Unity 5. The car controller first sets the steering angle of the front wheels to ensure the car is pointing in the correct direction according to the user's input via the steering wheel. Then, the acceleration values are received from the user and the motor torque is calculated for the back wheel since the car is operating like a rear-wheel drive car. The brake values received are also used to calculate the amount of brake torque on each wheel. Once the proper torque is applied to each of the wheels, the overall speed is capped to allow for a normal top speed and to prevent the car from having a negative speed.

The user input is retrieved through the Logitech G27 steering wheel, the pedals, and the shifter in Unity directly using the input manager. The steering wheel values are represented in degrees from $[-450\ldots450]$. The gas and brake pedals both send values represented by a percentage from $[0.0\ldots1.0]$. Then, the values are translated into moving the car. The car's acceleration is set as $accel = (maxAccel * gas) - (maxBrake * brake)$. Then the speed is capped on both ends to include a top speed for the car and to prevent the car from accelerating backwards without being in reverse. The driving direction is simply set to the raw rotation multiplied by scale factor that was determined by testing the feel of the wheel compared to a real car.

Figure 3: Car Interior With Reconstruction

One of our system's goals is to have a high degree of interaction fidelity in our driving simulation. This ensures that the user's overall presence in the simulation is as high as possible. We implemented several features to accomplish this. First, the amount of acceleration and deceleration calculated form the pedal inputs was too high when the user only slightly pressed the pedals. We developed an algorithm that modified the scale of the pedals from a linear scaling to a polynomial one. This allowed the maximum and minimum acceleration to remain the same, but decreased the acceleration given when the user pressed the pedal partially. We did this simply by squaring the original values. Since the original range is $[0, 1]$, this gives us a new scaling with the same range, is more shallow in the beginning, and feels more like driving a real car. We also tested multiple steering ratios until the amount needed to steer to traverse a 90 degree turn matched that of an average sedan car. The car is also fitted audio features including engine noises and skidding effects. These audio features are included with Unity, but needed to be modified to fit our simulation. The audio system originally provided car engine sounds that scale their pitch with the engine load, but the volume and pitch scaling both sounded more like a race car than a sedan. We brought down the volume and reduced the scale factor of the pitch changes until they matched sounds that an average sedan would make.

3. USER TESTING

3.1 Study and Simulation Design

We developed a study that can show the usability benefits and increased immersion of this system as applied to an interaction-intensive application. We compared using the system with no real objects (referred to as the "full virtual environment (FVE)") versus an environment containing reconstructed real objects like the wheel, the shifter, and the user's hands (the "mixed-reality environment (MRE)"). The user's were asked to perform the same set of tasks in both versions of the simulation. The steps of the simulation were as follows (also seen in Figure 4):

1. The participant starts on a straight road and is asked to take the car out of park and follow the path of the road. The road starts out straight and then some gradual curves are introduced later.

2. Next, they have to stop at an intersection. After coming to a complete stop, they continue straight down the road.

3. They then stop at another intersection, turn into a parking lot, and are asked to pull into a space between two cars.

4. Once they are parked, they put the car in reverse, back out of the spot, and head back to the main road.

5. They then drive further down the main road before encountering a dead end. Here, they are asked to stop and finish the simulation.

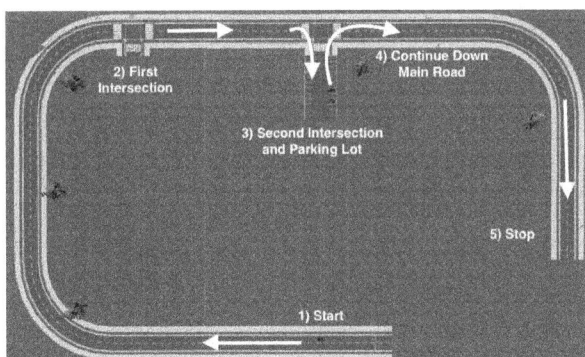

Figure 4: Simulation Instructions Overview

The simulation starts with the simple task of driving down the road. This step makes sure that the user understands the controls and can get to used to how the simulation is going to run. This step also requires the least amount of interaction with any other objects in the real world, showing little difference between the two simulations, and serves as a good baseline comparison. The next section brings in braking, as the user needs to stop at the stop sign. Not only does this section make sure the participant can find the pedals, but it also forces the user to be aware of the virtual world around them to know to stop at the stop sign. The next section the participants arrive at is the main comparison point. When the user pulls into the parking spot and puts the car in park, they have to reach out and find the gear shift from the wheel. Finding the gear shift in empty space was difficult without seeing their hands, and was easier once the reconstruction is enabled. Then, after they park they have to move their hands from the wheel back to the shifter to put the car in reverse. Since their hands are not on the shifter once stopped, they have to find the shifter for a second time. They also have to back out while making sure they do not run into the cars parked next to them, once again needing to be aware of their surroundings in the virtual environment.

Once the user completed the full simulation without hands, they were given a questionnaire about their experience in the simulation. Once the questionnaire was completed, they ran through the simulation again with the reconstruction turned on. Then, once the simulation was completed a second time, they answered a second questionnaire with questions more targeted to the benefits of being able to see their hands in the simulation. The participants were timed in both simulations to compare time improvement between the simulations.

Normally, for a user test that involves comparing two different variations, the starting order for the comparison is randomized from participant to participant. This approach presented some problems for our application. The most important difference between the simulations was observed when the participants have to grab the shifter. This task is greatly affected by being able to see their hands due to the difficulty of tracking one's hands in space. One way that people adapt to this issue is to use muscle memory to remember how to complete certain tasks. It can be an issue if the participants complete the real object simulation first, because they would be able to develop a memory of how to reach the shifter that participants who started on the full virtual experience would not have. Due to this issue, all participants started in the full virtual experience before completing the real object simulation. Having a comparison without a randomized order calls the validity of the completion time improvement as a usability metric into question. To mitigate this issue, some participants ran through the full virtual simulation twice to test for the average completion time improvement without the real objects. This will allowed us to isolate how much time improvement is due to the extra experience in the simulation during the second run through. We defined this group as our control group.

3.1.1 Data Collected

During our testing, the participants were given two different surveys. Survey 1 was given after completing the simulation without the reconstruction, and Survey 2 was given once the simulation with the real objects was complete. For some of the questions in the survey, we used a five-point Likert scale to obtain quantitative data from the participants. We gave each end point a label to indicate what the different levels correspond to. We chose a 5 point scale over other scales for its usability and use in the widely used System Usability Scale (SUS) [22] [23]. There was also an area for participants to indicate why they gave a specific rating.

Table 1: Survey 1

Question
1) How nauseated and/or disoriented did you feel during the simulation? (1 = No Feeling, 5 = Very Nauseous)
2) How easy did it feel to complete the simulation? (1 = Very Hard, 5 = Very Easy)
3) How similar to actually driving a car did the simulation feel? (1 = Nothing Alike, 5 = Very Similar)
4) What was the most difficult task during the simulation?
5) Do you have any additional comments?

Survey 1 consisted of the questions found in Table 1. Question 1 focused on the participant's sense of discomfort during the simulation. Simulator sickness is a very common phenomenon in VR, and it is important for usability to examine the system's potential to make the participants nauseous. Question 2 related to the ease with which the participant completes the simulation. Knowing how easy the simulation is without real objects was important to establish a baseline for comparison for the version of the system where the participants can see their hands. Question 3 asked for feedback on the interaction fidelity of the simulation to also established a baseline for comparison to see if adding hands to the simulation makes the overall experience feel more realistic. Question 4 clarified the rating provided in question 3 by narrowing down which task had the most impact on the feeling of difficulty in the simulation. All of these questions were repeated in the second survey to establish some comparisons with the MRE version of the simulation.

Table 2: Survey 2

Question
1) How nauseated and/or disoriented did you feel during the simulation? (1 = No Feeling, 5 = Very Nauseous)
2) How easy did it feel to complete the simulation? (1 = Very Hard, 5 = Very Easy)
3) How similar to actually driving a car did the simulation feel? (1 = Nothing Alike, 5 = Very Similar)
4) How helpful was being able to see your hands? (1 = No Help, 5 = Very Helpful)
5) How did seeing your hands, the wheel, and the shifter affect the overall simulation?
6) What was the most difficult task during this version of the simulation?
7) Do you have any additional comments?

Survey 2 consisted of the questions found in Table 2. Questions 1-3 were repeated questions from the first survey to allow us to compare their ratings to the first FVE simulation. Question 4 obtained the general feeling of the participant on how helpful the hands were to their experience.

One important aspect of usability testing is how helpful the user perceived the feature to be. Question 4 also contributed to this by asking how the hands, wheel, and shifter affected the overall simulation. Question 4 was the most important question during the study and helped show what the participants noticed about the impact of having real objects in the simulation with them. Question 5 repeated the question from the first survey asking for the most difficult task. If adding the real objects into the simulation helped the overall usability of the system, then the most difficult task from both versions of the simulation may differ.

3.2 Results and Discussion

3.2.1 Quantitative Data

Here we show the quantitative results collected during the course of the simulation. The statistics calculations and graphs were generated using R. Statistical significance tests were conducted using the Wilcoxon signed rank sum test. This test is functionally the same as a paired t-test, but does not assume the data sets are independent and follow a normal distribution. This was important because we knew our data sets were dependent and could not assume that the data would follow a normal distribution. We were able to test the system with 50 participants with only 2 participants stopping the simulation before giving data due to being too nauseated. 2 participants also could not complete the simulation due to lack of driving experience. Of the 46 participants that completed the simulation, 31 were in the study group and 15 were in the control group (the participants that completed a second run through of the simulation with no real objects).

Table 3: Average (Mean) Participant Ratings

Metric	Full Virtual	Mixed Reality	Δ	p-val
Sickness	2.42	2.19	−0.23	0.088
Easiness	4.45	4.61	+0.16	0.073
Interaction Fidelity	3.61	3.90	+0.29	**0.011**
Time	119.50s	110.69s	−8.81s	**0.003**
Helpfulness		3.48		**0.018**

As seen in Table 3, the rating for the overall helpfulness of the real objects had an average rating of 3.48, meaning that the average participant thought the hands were fairly helpful to the experience. We also see that nausea and discomfort ratings were fairly low for both simulations, with a small improvement from the first simulation to the second. Ease of completion and interaction fidelity ratings were both fairly high in both simulations with a minor improvement from the first simulation to the second. The helpfulness ratings, interaction fidelity ratings, and completion time differences were all statistically significant using $\alpha = 0.05$. Nausea/disorientation and ease of completion ratings were just above our significance alpha. Completion times averaged just under two minutes and show a moderate improvement from the first simulation to the next. We discuss all of the metrics in more detail and discuss their meanings in the following subsections.

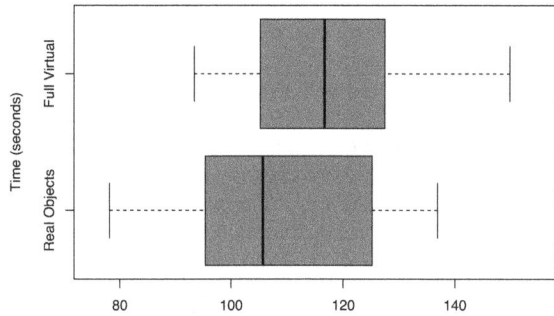

Figure 5: Completion Time Comparison

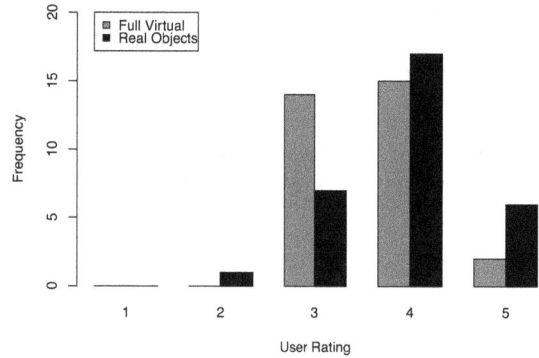

Figure 7: Interaction Fidelity Ratings

First we look at the distributions of the completion times for both simulations in Figure 5. Completion times for the second simulation show improvements in every quartile with the median completion time improving from 116.65s to 105.69s, showing a 9.4% improvement over the original full virtual experience simulation. The interquartile range of the data also increases, suggesting that the completion times become less consistent among the participants during the second simulation. Data from the first simulation is skewed slightly toward longer completion times, while the data for the second simulation shows a slight skew towards the shorter completion times.

both simulations with no participants indicating that the simulation didn't feel realistic at all in either simulation. 94% of users rated the first simulation at a 3 or 4 for the first simulation. However, the majority shifts for the real object simulation with 74% of participants reporting a 4 or 5 for interaction fidelity, indicating much higher realism of interaction when interacting with real objects. We also found that the improvement in interaction fidelity ratings for the MRE simulation was statistically significant.

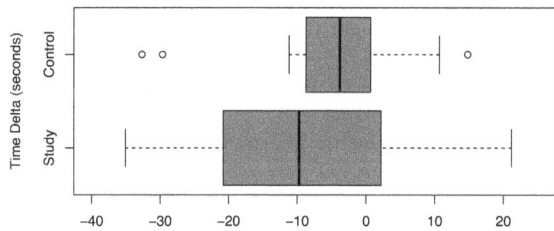

Figure 6: Completion TimeΔ

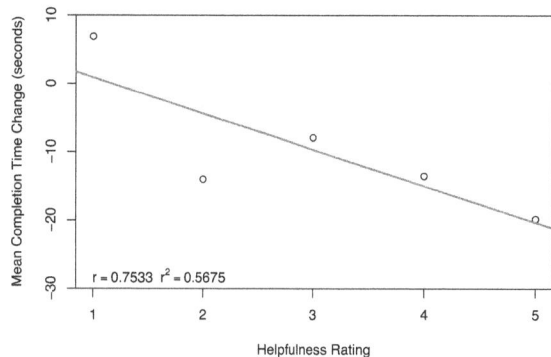

Figure 8: Helpfulness Ratings vs. Mean Completion Time Δ

In Figure 6, we examine the completion times further by showing the distribution of the time improvement from the full virtual simulation to the real object simulation and the distribution of the time improvement for the control group. The data shows a median time improvement of almost 10s with the study group, which confirms the data from the earlier charts, but this distribution also shows that 68% of the participants improved on their original time. Also, those who improved on their times had a greater time change on average than those who did worse on their second run. For the control group, the average time improvement was less than zero, but this is not statistically significant, meaning we did not have enough evidence to reject the null hypothesis that the time improvement was equal to zero.

We can see the participants' ratings on how realistic the simulation felt in Figure 7. The ratings were fairly high in

In Figure 8, we find a correlation between how the participants ranked the helpfulness of the real objects and how much faster they completed the simulation on average. With an R-value of .7533, there is a moderate correlation between these two metrics. However, there are only 2 responses that gave a helpfulness rating of both 1 and 2 with 87% of participants giving a rating of 3 or higher. When only the ratings above 3 are taken into account, there is an almost perfect correlation between these two metrics with a R-value of .99. Although the strength of both of these correlations is weakened by the relatively small sample size used in this study, there is enough here to say that there seems to be a significant correlation between how helpful the participant reported the real objects were to the simulation and how much their completion time improved.

The correlation also contributes to the validity of the completion time data. There is a concern we mentioned earlier about being able to differentiate between an improvement in completion time due to being able to see the real world or due to more experience in the simulation. This correlation helps show that at least some of the improvement is due to the inclusion of the real objects. If the time improvement from simulation to simulation was only due to more experience in the simulation, we believe there would be no correlation between how helpful the real objects seemed and the mean completion time deltas. If we assume the time improvement was only a direct result of more experience, we would see time improvements remain consistent across participants. Since the mean time improvement varies across participants, we can say there is another variable affecting the difference. This correlation has an r^2 value of .5675. This indicates that although the correlation is significant, other variables may also be affecting the mean improvement times as well. This correlation alone would not be enough to say the time improvement is, in some part, due to the inclusion of real objects. However, this correlation in conjunction with our control group data gives us enough to say that the mean time improvement was positively affected by the inclusion of real objects in the virtual environment.

3.2.2 Qualitative Data

Along with the quantitative ratings collected in the surveys, participants answered questions asking how they felt about certain aspects of the simulation. They were also asked to give feedback for the ratings that they gave.

The most common responses had to do with the lack of inertial feedback in the system. Participants gave comments like, "The lack of physical feedback was very disorienting. Things like inertia, acceleration were very missed for my experience.", and "Trying to resist the urge to lean into the turns. I kinda felt like I was rolling out of the chair." The most major difference between our simulator and most VR driving simulators is the use of the immersive HMD. A more immersive system brings more expectations of what the simulation should feel like, especially as it relates to inertial feedback. This isn't much of a problem in the standard three monitor setup because the user would not be expecting the feedback, but it is missing in an immersive version. Nearly every participant indicated feeling strange about either the acceleration, braking, or turning in the simulation. However, only about half of those participants indicated that it made them nauseous. The other half only mentioned the lack of feedback and that it felt a bit strange. This is probably due to each participant's predisposition to simulator sickness. Nearly everyone felt the lack of feedback, but it didn't necessarily make each person sick. We knew prior to the study that this would be the biggest source of disorientation in the simulation, so we took steps to try to mitigate this feeling. These feelings of disorientation arise from the disconnect between what the brain thinks the body should be feeling, and what it actually feels [24]. In this case, the brain expects to be pushed forward when braking and to be pushed to the outside of the car during a turn. According to the Sensory Conflict Theory, when the brain does not get that feedback, it gets disoriented. [25] We help these feelings by making the car accelerate and decelerate as slowly as possible while maintaining interaction fidelity. This gradual acceleration would come with much less force in a real car, so the brain expects much less feedback making the disconnect as small as possible and helps bring the levels of disorientation down. This idea of gradual acceleration is also applied to gradual turns present in the simulation.

The other most common responses related to being able to see the real objects and how that affected the overall simulation. Participants gave comments like, "It [Seeing the real objects] made it [The simulation] feel more like driving - especially because I could see my own hands.", and "It [The simulation] felt cozier and more natural. There was no thinking twice about, 'am I grabbing in the right place?'" Every participant commented on being able to see their hands and the other real objects because they were asked in the survey, but how they talked about them fell into a couple of categories. Five people mentioned that the hands didn't really seem to affect the difficulty of the simulation. These participants also gave the lowest scores in the quantitative subsection about the helpfulness of the hands. They all mentioned that it didn't help too much because they do not normally pay attention to their hands when driving. During the simulation they noticed that they ignored the fact that their hands were there and drove the same in both versions of the simulation. This is interesting because it helps confirm the interaction fidelity of the simulation since they fell into their normal driving habits, which involved not looking at their hands.

For the majority of participants, seeing their hands was helpful in some way to the simulation. Ten people indicated that seeing their hands directly made the simulation easier to complete. These participants also indicated that parking was very difficult. Many participants indicated that the tasks were not difficult to begin with, so the difficulty wasn't affected by the hands. The biggest way the hands helped the simulation had to do with the immersion and interaction fidelity of the simulation. Nearly half of the responses directly mentioned that driving felt more realistic, felt they had more control, felt they were more involved with the simulation, etc. Participants commented that, "It [Seeing the real objects] made it easier to understand how much my actions impacted the car movement." They mentioned that the first simulation felt fake while the second simulation with real objects felt more like driving. The biggest difference mentioned across all groups involves being able to grab the shifter. One participant mentioned, "It [Seeing the real objects] made it a bit easier to reach for the shifter." Participants felt it was difficult to find the shifter without seeing their hands but were able to find it extremely easily when they could see the real world.

All other responses are scattered among several topics. Two participants mentioned the lack of blinkers, one participant referenced the lack of mirrors, and one participant mentioned both. These were absent due to a combination of hardware limitations and performance bugs with the Oculus SDK but definitely should be added in the future to help improve overall interaction fidelity and presence. Once participant mentioned that the acceleration and deceleration were too slow, but this was done on purpose as mentioned earlier. The acceleration could be made more realistic if the lack of inertial feedback could be addressed. Two participants mentioned that the limited FOV of the HMD affected their disorientation in the system. [26] This is also due to hardware limitations with the Oculus Rift DK2. Other HMDs support a wider FOV than the Oculus, but are more expensive.

3.2.3 Other Observations

Among the recorded data from the surveys and simulation run times, we observed several interesting behaviors during the simulation. One major observation relates to how the participants fell into standard driving habits during the simulations. Specifically, once the participants had pulled out of the parking lot and were pulling back out on to the main road, 100% of participants were observed to check for traffic before continuing along the road. Before this point, they had driven through the world without any traffic for 5-10 minutes and completed most of the simulation as well. The participants would have had plenty of time to observe the fact that there was no traffic in the world with them, and yet, every single participant still checked for traffic before continuing along the road. Some participants also remarked on the fact that they were unsure why they were checking for traffic when they knew there wasn't any. This indicates a high level of presence in the simulation as well as a strong feeling of interaction fidelity in the simulation. The participants were falling into their normal driving habits because they were subconsciously convinced that they were driving an actual car. The quantitative data we collected also backs this up, as the majority of participants indicated a 3 or 4 and above for interaction fidelity during the simulations with the full virtual experience and using the real objects respectively.

Another interesting observation was how the participants reacted to the difficulty of grabbing the shifter when they were not able to see their hands. A very common way of dealing with this issue that around half of the participants used was to leave their hand on the shifter between uses. Participants that normally used two hands for driving would drive with one hand to allow for their other to rest on the shifter so they would not have to find it again. This behavior did not continue during the second simulation. Participants were able to drive with two hands like normal, because they were confident in their ability to find the shifter again when they needed it. The shifter was explicitly used in the simulations to provoke this type of response. Driving without seeing your hands is easy if they never have to leave the wheel, but becomes much harder if you have to find a specific item in the real world. One of the most common responses given related to feeling like the hands gave them more control and increased the presence of the simulation. If the participant is consciously having to keep their hand in a place they would not normally for a reason that explicitly relates to being in a simulation, they are going to be less present in the simulation. By removing this break in presence with the hands and other real objects, participants reported feeling much more present in the simulation.

4. FUTURE WORK

Our system could be improved further in the future by the inclusion of noise reduction algorithms [16] [17] or multiple cameras. Although the usability improvement of the system was not dependent on the noisiness of the reconstruction, the users' presence in the simulation could be further improved with a smoother looking reconstruction. The noise reduction algorithm used, however, would need to have very little performance impact as to not bring the update rate of the system below the 75 Hz required by the HMD. Multiple cameras could also be used to create more complete recon-structions of real objects by providing depth data from other viewing angles. Although this was not needed for our application, this approach would be helpful for a system where the user would be viewing an object from multiple angles.

5. CONCLUSIONS

We presented a system for bringing real time reconstructions of real objects into the virtual environment for use in interaction-intensive applications where low latency and accuracy are desired. We showed that, although there is much research into bringing real objects into the virtual world as well as reconstructing real objects using visual hulls, the systems have various limitations. Some systems created accurate reconstructions, but used algorithms not suitable for real-time updates. Other systems were unable to provide natural tactile feedback to the user because of the lack of real objects. Our motivation was to solve one of the limitations of HMD-based systems, the lack of real-world vision, by reconstructing real objects in the virtual environment. We showed in our system that we achieved our system goals of creating an accurate reconstruction with very low latency and high resolution. We were able to process the high definition color data and depth data to update a reconstructed mesh of real objects in real time. We brought together techniques from previous research into a system that has been shown to improve the usability, immersion, and presence of a driving simulator. Our user study showed how this kind of system can help improve an interaction-intensive application like driving. We tested our system with participants with metrics testing the disorientation caused by the system, the ease of completion, the usefulness of the real objects, and the degree of interaction fidelity in the simulation. We showed that there was a statistically significant improvement in the interaction fidelity of the simulation and the completion times by including the participants real hands, the wheel, and the shifter. We showed that the time improvement with the simulation that included the real objects was, in part, due to the real objects and not just more experience with the simulation. Our results showed that participants felt more present in the simulation, felt that the driving was more realistic, and felt more in control. Even though the participants had never used our simulation before, they were able to complete the simulation with ease using the driving experience they already had. This effect could be seen clearly when two participants with no driver's licensees were unable to complete the simulation.

Our research makes several contributions to the body of research. We show how to implement real object reconstruction for real-time updates, low latency, and performance for rendering to a high-definition HMD updating at 75 Hz. We also show how one of the current inhibitors of HMD-based systems can be mitigated by including real objects into the VE, which improves the usability and immersion of the simulation, and allows for more HMD-based system research in the future.

6. REFERENCES

[1] Newcombe, R. A., Davison, A. J., Izadi, S., Kohli, P., Hilliges, O., Shotton, J., . . . Fitzgibbon, A. (2011). KinectFusion: Real-time dense surface mapping and tracking. 2011 10th IEEE International Symposium on Mixed and Augmented Reality.

[2] Google Tango - https://get.google.com/tango/

[3] Mcmahan, R. P., Lai, C., & Pal, S. K. (2016). Interaction Fidelity: The Uncanny Valley of Virtual Reality Interactions. Lecture Notes in Computer Science Virtual, Augmented and Mixed Reality, 59-70. doi:10.1007/978-3-319-39907-2_6

[4] Lok, B. (2001). Online model reconstruction for interactive virtual environments. Proceedings of the 2001 Symposium on Interactive 3D Graphics - SI3D '01.

[5] Laurentini, A. (1994). The visual hull concept for silhouette-based image understanding. IEEE Transactions on Pattern Analysis and Machine Intelligence IEEE Trans. Pattern Anal. Machine Intell., 16(2), 150-162.

[6] Lok, B., Naik, S., Whitton, M., & Brooks, F. P. (2003). Incorporating dynamic real objects into immersive virtual environments. ACM SIGGRAPH 2003 Papers on - SIGGRAPH '03.

[7] Lok, B. C. (2004). Toward the merging of real and virtual spaces. Communications of the ACM Commun. ACM, 47(8), 48.

[8] Mcgill, M., Murray-Smith, R., Boland, D., & Brewster, S. A. (2015). A Dose of Reality. Proceedings of the 33rd Annual ACM Conference Extended Abstracts on Human Factors in Computing Systems - CHI EA '15.

[9] Scheggi, S., Meli, L., Pacchierotti, C., & Prattichizzo, D. (2015). Touch the virtual reality. ACM SIGGRAPH 2015 Posters on - SIGGRAPH '15.

[10] Pamungkas, D. S., & Ward, K. (2016). Electro-Tactile Feedback System to Enhance Virtual Reality Experience. IJCTE International Journal of Computer Theory and Engineering, 8(6), 465-470.

[11] Carlozzi, N. E., Gade, V., Rizzo, A., & Tulsky, D. S. (2012). Using virtual reality driving simulators in persons with spinal cord injury: Three screen display versus head mounted display. Disability and Rehabilitation: Assistive Technology, 8(2), 176-180.

[12] Schultheis, M. T., Rebimbas, J., Mourant, R., & Millis, S. R. (2007). Examining the Usability of a Virtual Reality Driving Simulator. Assistive Technology, 19(1), 1-10.

[13] Barfield, W., Baird, K. M., & Bjorneseth, O. J. (1998). Presence in virtual environments as a function of type of input device and display update rate. Displays, 19(2), 91-98.

[14] Hendrix, C., & Barfield, W. (1996). Presence within Virtual Environments as a Function of Visual Display Parameters. Presence: Teleoperators and Virtual Environments, 5(3), 274-289.

[15] Kemeny, A., & Panerai, F. (2003). Evaluating perception in driving simulation experiments. Trends in Cognitive Sciences, 7(1), 31-37.

[16] Smolka, B., Lukac, R., Chydzinski, A., Plataniotis, K., & Wojciechowski, W. (2003). Fast adaptive similarity based impulsive noise reduction filter. Real-Time Imaging, 9(4), 261-276.

[17] Wasenmüller, O., Bleser, G., & Stricker, D. (2015). Combined Bilateral Filter for Enhanced Real-time Upsampling of Depth Images. Proceedings of the 10th International Conference on Computer Vision Theory and Applications.

[18] Wu, A., Reilly, D., Tang, A., & Mazalek, A. (2011). Tangible navigation and object manipulation in virtual environments. Proceedings of the Fifth International Conference on Tangible, Embedded, and Embodied Interaction - TEI '11.

[19] Mazalek, A., & Nitsche, M. (2007). Tangible interfaces for real-time 3D virtual environments. Proceedings of the International Conference on Advances in Computer Entertainment Technology - ACE '07.

[20] Ladikos, A., & Navab, N. (2009). Real-Time 3D Reconstruction for Occlusion-Aware Interactions in Mixed Reality. Advances in Visual Computing Lecture Notes in Computer Science, 480-489.

[21] Reimer, B., D'Ambrosio, L. A., Coughlin, J. F., Kafrissen, M. E., & Biederman, J. (2006). Using self-reported data to assess the validity of driving simulation data. Behavior Research Methods, 38(2), 314-324.

[22] Dawes, John G., Do Data Characteristics Change According to the Number of Scale Points Used? An Experiment Using 5 Point, 7 Point and 10 Point Scales (February 29, 2012). International Journal of Market Research, Vol. 51, No. 1, 2008.

[23] Brooke, J. (1996). SUS: a "quick and dirty" usability scale. In P. W. Jordan, B. Thomas, B. A. Weeromeester & I. L. McClelland, Eds. Usability Evaluation in Industry, pp. 189-194. London: Taylor & Francis.

[24] Kolasinski, E. M. (1995). Simulator Sickness in Virtual Environments (No. ARI-TR-1027). ARMY RESEARCH INST FOR THE BEHAVIORAL AND SOCIAL SCIENCES ALEXANDRIA VA.

[25] Oman, C. M. (1990). Motion sickness: A synthesis and evaluation of the sensory conflict theory. Can. J. Physiol. Pharmacol. Canadian Journal of Physiology and Pharmacology, 68(2), 294-303. doi:10.1139/y90-044

[26] Arthur, K. (1996). Effects of field of view on task performance with head-mounted displays. Conference Companion on Human Factors in Computing Systems Common Ground - CHI '96. doi:10.1145/257089.257116

[27] Microsoft Kinect for Xbox One Specifications - http://image.slidesharecdn.com/ programmingwithkinectv2-150603164425-lva1-app6892/ 95/programming-with-kinect-v2-7-638.jpg?cb= 1433349971

[28] Oculus Rift DK2 Specifications - http://riftinfo.com/ oculus-rift-specs-dk1-vs-dk2-comparison

[29] Logitech G27 Racing Wheel Specifications - http://support.logitech.com/en_us/article/24832? product=a0qi00000069vCPAAY

[30] Leap Motion Specifications - https://www.leapmotion.com/product/desktop

Exploring Immersive Interfaces for Well Placement Optimization in Reservoir Models

Roberta C. Ramos Mota
University of Calgary
roberta.cabralmota@ucalgary.ca

Stephen Cartwright
University of Calgary
sgcartwr@ucalgary.ca

Ehud Sharlin
University of Calgary
ehud@cpsc.ucalgary.ca

Hamidreza Hamdi
University of Calgary
hhamdi@ucalgary.ca

Mario Costa Sousa
University of Calgary
mario@cpsc.ucalgary.ca

Zhangxin Chen
University of Calgary
zhachen@ucalgary.ca

ABSTRACT

As the oil and gas industry's ultimate goal is to uncover efficient and economic ways to produce oil and gas, well optimization studies are crucially important for reservoir engineers. Although this task has a major impact on reservoir productivity, it has been challenging for reservoir engineers to perform since it involves time-consuming flow simulations to search a large solution space for an optimal well plan. Our work aims to provide engineers a) an analytical method to perform static connectivity analysis as a proxy for flow simulation, b) an application to support well optimization using our method and c) an immersive experience that benefits engineers and supports their needs and preferences when performing the design and assessment of well trajectories. For the latter purpose, we explore our tool with three immersive environments: a CAVE with a tracked gamepad; a HMD with a tracked gamepad; and a HMD with a Leap Motion controller. This paper describes our application and its techniques in each of the different immersive environments. This paper also describes our findings from an exploratory evaluation conducted with six reservoir engineers, which provided insight into our application, and allowed us to discuss the potential benefits of immersion for the oil and gas domain.

CCS Concepts

• **Human-centered computing** → **Virtual reality;** Walkthrough evaluations; Scientific visualization; Gestural input; • **Computing methodologies** → **Virtual reality;**

Keywords

Virtual Reality; Immersion; Spatial User Interaction; Reservoir Engineering

1. INTRODUCTION

Oil and gas are naturally occurring hydrocarbons found in underground geological formations. Oil and gas reservoirs are subsurface pools of hydrocarbons encompassed by rock formations. The ultimate goal in the oil and gas industry is to explore these reservoirs and discover efficient and economic ways to produce oil and gas. However, as these petroleum products are trapped in reservoir rocks situated hundreds to thousands of meters underground, reservoir data acquisition is costly. For this reason only limited information is available from a variety of different sources such as seismic geophones, well logs, pressure transducers and core samples.

These different data sources are combined using complex geostatistical methods and expert judgment to develop a realistic three-dimensional reservoir model representing the structure and properties of the subsurface volume [5].

The structure of the 3D reservoir model is often represented by corner point cells, which are irregular hexagonal geometries arranged along three dimensions (i, j, k). Since corner points are not required to be regularly spaced nor spatially continuous, degenerated cells can be produced during the modeling phase, and some may also completely disappear, introducing connections between cells that were not initially neighbors. These properties of corner-point grids make it easy to introduce discontinuities across faces, and therefore include fractures and faults, which are a displacement within one or more rock layers as a result of earth movement.

A model typically consists of thousands to millions of cells, each of which is associated with various properties such as porosity, permeability, and oil saturation. Besides the cell data, reservoir models may also contain information about well trajectories within the reservoir.

Placement of wells in a reservoir has a major impact on the production and economics of the extraction scenario. However, optimal well placement is a challenging issue due to the many variables involved and the typical static and dynamic uncertainties. As a result, engineers must define and assess a number of different placement scenarios. This procedure is called well placement optimization.

The reservoir model is the context in which well placement scenarios are evaluated. To assess the scenarios, simulation techniques such as fluid flow simulations are performed in order to select the best scenario based on the predicted production performance. There are, however, limitations to the number of scenarios that can be assessed using dynamic simulation. The time required by dynamic simulation can be very high, and increases significantly with the complexity of the scenario, the fidelity of the simulation, or the size of the simulation.

Due to this, much research has been devoted to develop fast performance estimators as surrogates for flow simulation. These estimators do not aim to replace a full flow simulation; rather,

SUI '16, October 15-16, 2016, Tokyo, Japan
© 2016 ACM. ISBN 978-1-4503-4068-7/16/10...$15.00
DOI: http://dx.doi.org/10.1145/2983310.2985762

their value lies in rapidly determining parameter sensitivities and screening reservoir models or production scenarios. Hence, among the three contributions of our work, the first of them is an analytical method for performing static connectivity analysis. The second contribution is an application to support well optimization studies using our method as a surrogate for flow simulation.

Furthermore, as modern reservoir engineering and geoscience rely on 3D visual representations of petroleum reservoirs [24], there is increasing interest in using novel technologies to create better visualizations of the reservoirs and develop more intuitive ways to explore them [6] [25] [10]. In particular, as the design and assessment of well trajectories have an inherent 3D spatial nature, we believe immersive technologies may provide an improved medium to view and interact with three-dimensional structures such as reservoir models, wells, and flow behavior graphs. Immersion has been shown to provide real benefits that are useful for our specific demands, including increased spatial understanding and contextual information space, as well as more natural interactions [18] [19].

In order to utilize these benefits, we have developed an immersive application where individuals or groups can design well trajectories, evaluate them in a time efficient manner through static connectivity analysis, and use the learned knowledge to more effectively predict optimal well placements. The third contribution of our work is the exploration of different immersive interfaces to support more effective visualization and interactions in our application.

A primary goal of our application is to create an immersive system that fits engineers' needs and preferences for performing exploratory well placement analysis. However, we understand that we will only be able to achieve this if we meet the requirements of those that would be using the tool. For this reason, in this work we focused on interviewing subject matter experts about their requirements regarding well exploration techniques and immersive well exploration systems. We hope this will inform better design for our application and other such applications in the future.

This paper describes our analytical approach for performing static connectivity analysis. It then introduces our application and the techniques that were implemented for creation and assessment of well trajectories. Lastly, this paper describes an exploratory evaluation conducted with six petroleum engineers for two main purposes: to gather their thoughts regarding our techniques and brainstorm ideas for future development; and to collect their feedback and preferences regarding the immersive aspects of the application.

2. RELATED WORK
2.1 On Reservoir Engineering

As mentioned in [24], the development of three-dimensional visualization tools represented a real breakthrough in reservoir geosciences and engineering. Also, allowing real time manipulation greatly improves the understanding and eases analysis of the model [5]. Currently, several commercial software packages are available for reservoir simulation and visualization, and they have become integral to reservoir engineering. Among the available commercial solutions, GUI-based desktop systems such as CMG Suite [1] and Petrel [4] are the most common.

These solutions provide traditional visualization and interaction techniques for assessing reservoir models and monitoring oil and gas production. However, there has been a growing effort in some areas of reservoir engineering and geosciences to incorporate novel visualization techniques to improve the ease, speed and accuracy of visual analysis tasks. For instance, [6] proposed the use of a cutaway illustrative technique to improve the inspection and analysis of properties in reservoir models. This technique emphasizes important structures or parts of the model by selectively discarding occluding parts while keeping the contextual information in view.

Traditional desktop applications have clearly demonstrated value by improving the efficiency of reservoir modeling and analysis. However, desktop display systems provide a limited opportunity for collaboration between domain experts. It is widely acknowledged in the industry that collaboration is essential throughout the oil and gas exploration and production (E&P) life cycle [24]. To serve this need to perform group work and analysis and to showcase information, technologies have been developed to facilitate collaborative reservoir analysis and provide a shared awareness of the reservoir.

As an example, [25] proposed a set of techniques for supporting the visual exploration of reservoir simulation models in tabletops. The techniques included a method to probe individual cells and display property values; "splitting" and "peeling" gestures to view the inside of the reservoir while maintaining context; and a touch tap to select a well and to activate a cutaway view that removes cells occluding the chosen well path. As another example, [22] explored three techniques to create well paths in tabletops. One technique, called the 2D planes approach, allows the user to select a plane (xy, yz, or xz) and rotate it along its axis (x, y, and z, respectively) using a rotation widget. The user can then create a well path on the plane using a finger motion.

These approaches address the collaborative and interdisciplinary needs of an oil or gas development project. However, all face the fundamentally difficult problem of facilitating complex spatial tasks such as defining a three-dimensional well trajectory within a two-dimensional space such as a desktop screen or a touch surface.

By using an associative and spatial system for these 3D tasks, it is possible to present a 3D view that people are familiar with [15] and that is natural and intuitive when working with 3D geological datasets such as petroleum reservoir models. For this reason, there have been efforts that either explore tangible user interfaces (TUI) or immersive virtual environments (IVE) in reservoir geoscience and engineering.

Snakey [10] is a collaborative TUI to support designing and manipulating 3D well paths for reservoir engineering. ReservoirBench [23], is an interactive tangible workbench designed to teach basic geological science and engineering tasks, such as arranging seismic planes or creating vertical and horizontal wells.

The potential of immersive environments has also been investigated, including exploration of how immersive features can benefit the oil and gas domain [16] [18]. For example, the performance of different immersive environments for well path editing has been examined [19]. The authors compared task completion times and correctness between participants using an immersive CAVE-like environment and those using a desktop system. The immersive environment provided stereo and head-tracked viewing, and used a tracked wand for navigation and direct pointing. The desktop version of the application used a stereoscopic computer monitor with a mouse, keyboard, and virtual widgets to support interaction. Although this work found speed and accuracy improvements in the immersive environment when editing the path of a new well in a mature field, the differences in display or interaction techniques that may have caused the performance differences between the two conditions were not explored.

2.2 On Immersion

Given the inherent spatial nature of the tasks performed when designing and assessing well trajectories, we believe that some immersive technologies can provide improved visualization and interaction interfaces for these tasks. An important consideration however is that different immersive technologies may provide different benefits [20]. Some of these benefits may be particularly helpful for well planning in the oil and gas domain. These include enhanced spatial understanding, increased information space, and more natural interactions.

One major benefit of immersion is increased spatial understanding. As an example, [20] evaluated small-scale spatial judgments, which requires careful visual inspection of objects that are small relative to the scale of the environment. The authors evaluated the effects of field-of-regard, stereoscopy, and head-tracked rendering on the performance (time and number of errors) of the task of identification of collisions and gaps in complex underground cave systems. The results suggest that the addition of the higher fidelity system features support performance improvements in making precise spatial inspections of complex three-dimensional structures. Correctly making such judgments is important for well planning, which includes tasks such as evaluation of the geometry of objects, identification of object intersections, and determining whether different paths will cross each other or if open spaces exist between objects.

Studies have evaluated spatial understanding tasks that require participants to visually trace paths within three-dimensional graph structures [26]. In general, the findings suggest performance improvements in path-tracing tasks due to the addition of either stereo or head tracking, with the best performance achieved using a combination of both.

A second potential benefit of immersion relates to an increase in information space. Although large, high resolution desktop displays are becoming more common, the amount and variety of data that can be displayed and analyzed by a group of collaborators is limited. An immersive environment, in contrast, delivers increased field of view and field of regard which facilitates a larger information space so a larger amount of information and context may be considered at the same time.

Well planning should ideally integrate all of the available geophysical and geological data in the same visual environment. This data may include for example seismic data, horizons, faults, cell attributes, existing well paths and log data and often much more. Thus, immersive display systems have the potential to provide a common three-dimensional space to visualize and evaluate this often complex, multidisciplinary data in a clear fashion, so any inconsistencies or errors in the data, or in the geologic interpretation, are obvious and important insights may be more easily achieved.

Further to this, immersive features such as head tracking allow users to change the view using familiar physical movements such as walking, leaning, crouching, or turning, and provide the opportunity for more natural interactions with data, freeing the user to focus on the problem at hand rather than the tool.

3. WELL PLANNING

In reservoir engineering, well planning refers to the definition and evaluation of well placement. The placement of wells has a major impact in a development project. Optimal well placement improves the long-term and short-term performance of wells by maximizing hydrocarbon recovery, extending well life, and in cases of pressure support from injection, reducing water production.

However, optimal well placement is challenging to determine due to the many variables involved and the static and dynamic uncertainties. Variables include the location, trajectory, and perforations of the well, the type of the well, the flow rate of the well, and the type of enhanced oil recovery, if any. These many parameters interact with each other, often in complex ways, resulting in a large solution space that must be searched to find an optimal outcome.

For this reason, engineers must define and assess a number of different placement scenarios based on the expected reservoir response and production in order to select optimal scenarios. During optimization studies, the engineer changes parameters prior to simulation in search of an optimal scenario. Typical parameters that would be changed include the number of wells, the spacing between them, the locations and trajectories of the wells, the introduction or modification of injection fluids and possibly many others.

3.1 Using Dynamic Flow Simulation

Reservoir fluid flow simulation is commonly used to calculate the expected outcome of each placement scenario so that they may be evaluated. The scenarios are evaluated based on the economic production of petroleum products. After the simulation results are calculated, the engineer typically executes two analysis tasks: a) The production profile. This is a production x time graph showing how metrics such as oil production are expected to behave through time. b) The flow behavior. In existing reservoir simulation software, flow simulation results are typically represented through visualizations such as isosurfaces or streamlines (Figure 1). Typically, a slider widget is used to move between different time periods to observe how the oil flow changes through time. If there is a part of the reservoir where the flow does not reach, the engineer may try to understand why this happened by evaluating the geological features – e.g., "*is there a fault or fracture in this region preventing oil to flow?*", and the reservoir properties – e.g., "*is the permeability low in this region that is preventing the oil to flow?*".

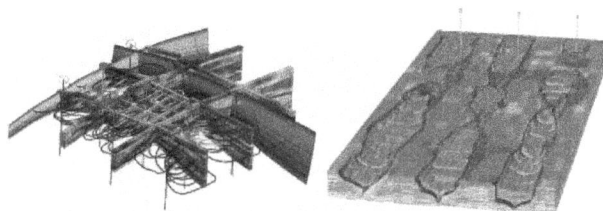

Figure 1: Isosurfaces (*right*) and streamlines (*left*) are commonly used to interpret flow simulation results.

Dynamic flow simulation may lead to accurate production predictions; however, the primary disadvantage is that this process is computationally expensive. Hours, days or even months may be required depending on the size of the model, the complexity of the model and the accuracy desired. This is a significant limitation for well optimization as the engineer is limited to run only a small number of flow simulations before choosing the "optimal" well placement scenario.

For this reason, alternative approaches are being investigated that use heuristics to find promising candidate well placement scenarios, and then run flow simulation on only the most promising scenarios. Typically, these approaches focus on using a combination of static geological reservoir properties to predict the approximate dynamic reservoir flow behavior. Despite a loss of accuracy due to the simplification relative to numerical simulation, this approach can provide very useful information relatively quickly. This is the approach taken in our application.

3.2 Using Static Connectivity Analysis

There is research showing that connectivity is a reservoir property that strongly correlates with the efficiency of hydrocarbon recovery [12]. In primary recovery, if a part of a reservoir is not connected to a producing well, then the hydrocarbon present in that region cannot be recovered. In secondary recovery, both producing and injecting wells need to be connected to the same reservoir geo-body in order to create sweep zones and, thus achieve better production efficiency [17].

A significant amount of research has been devoted to developing analytical methods that quantify reservoir connectivity using static geological properties [8] [11] [21]. This connectivity measure, in turn, is used as a fast reservoir performance estimator in different activities in oil and gas E&P such as well planning, comparison between finer and coarser models to evaluate whether structural and stratigraphic characteristics have been preserved during up-scaling, to rank different geological realizations for reservoir simulation, to name just a few possibilities.

Despite its relevance, to our knowledge, current geologic modeling and reservoir simulation software do not offer a means to assess connectivity in a way that is computationally efficient, interactive, and visual. Thus, our work proposes a novel application to support well optimization studies. Our application uses static connectivity analysis to serve as a proxy for flow simulation to provide performance estimation of well placements.

3.3 Our Approach

Our method to perform static connectivity analysis first converts the reservoir grid to a graph. The cells used in the reservoir model in which each cell has one or more properties, are converted to a node and edge-based representation.

In this representation, each node has the same cell properties; however, the edges are associated with new, additional properties related to the connection between nodes. One such edge property is transmissibility. The term transmissibility as used in reservoir simulation refers to a constant value characterizing the flow connection between two adjacent grid cells. The transmissibility between two nodes represents how readily fluid flows from one node to another. The inverse of transmissibility is also an edge property and referred to as the "edge resistance", or "edge cost".

Dijkstra's shortest path algorithm is then used on the graph to perform connectivity analysis for each well perforation along the well trajectory.

This gives the least resistive path from a perforation to a target node, taking into account the resistance of the edges along the path connecting the source to the target node. As illustrated in Figure 2, the method is applied in order to find the least resistive path between a perforation node and all other nodes that are reachable from the perforation. A node is not reachable when no transmissible path exists connecting the node to the perforation.

After running the shortest path method on a well perforation node, the output is: a) A "connectivity graph" that contains all nodes (cells) connected to the perforation. b) For each connected node, the least resistive path connecting it to the perforation, and the cumulative cost along this path – that is, the minimum cost to go from the perforation node to this node.

The minimum cost parameter associated with each connected node is referred to as "delta time". Not to be confused with absolute time, this measure represents relative time to reach a node. For the scenario illustrated in Figure 2, a perforation node w_p is connected to two nodes, n_1 and n_2, with respective delta times δ_1 and δ_2. If $\delta_1 > \delta_2$, it means that the path connecting w_p to n_1 is less transmissible than the one connecting w_p to n_2. Thus, the oil in n_2 would be produced before n_1.

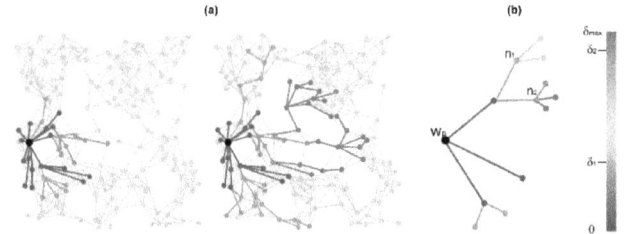

Figure 2: Shortest path calculation (a) along with minimum cost (delta time) parameter associated with nodes (b).

After running the shortest path in each well perforation, the user may then specify a threshold value, δ_{th}, to filter out connected nodes that are not connected strongly enough to be reached within the threshold delta time. The connectivity measure for a well perforation is calculated as the sum of the hydrocarbon pore volume (HCPV) of each connected cell, c, that has $\delta_c \leq \delta_{th}$. The overall connectivity measure of the well is the sum of the connectivity measures of all perforations in the well.

4. APPLICATION

Our work also involves the development of an application to support well optimization studies. This tool uses our method to perform static connectivity analysis as a proxy for flow simulation. Further to this, the application is tested in three immersive environments, as can be observed in Figure 3.

This section describes the software and hardware used for our application. We then describe the application features applied in each of the interaction interfaces: a gamepad and a leap motion controller.

Figure 3: Our application explores three immersive environments: a CAVE with a tracked gamepad (*left*), a HMD with a tracked gamepad (*center*), and a HMD with a leap motion device attached to it (*right*).

Figure 4: Illustrations of some of our techniques applied to the CAVE environment. From left to right: (1) vertical and (2) free-form well creation, (3) connectivity graph analysis, and (4) analysis of analytical tables of the connectivity.

4.1 Software Specifications

Our tool is a Unity application written in the C# programming language. A key consideration when selecting Unity was the relative ease with which cross platform applications may be developed.

Another consideration was the availability of MiddleVR [3], a library that makes it relatively simple to develop an application that works in different VR environments. MiddleVR provides an abstraction layer for different aspects of a VR application, such as display and interaction devices, stereoscopy, and clustering. These aspects may then be defined in a configuration file, simplifying deployment in different environments. Unity also integrates with the Hovercast VR toolkit [2], which provides a customizable menu interface for virtual reality applications.

4.2 Hardware Specifications

As illustrated in Figure 3, the application runs in three immersive environments. One is a CAVE with a tracked gamepad controller. The CAVE system consists of four screens powered by projectors each with a resolution of 1280x1024. The system supports active stereoscopy using Volfoni Edge VR 3D glasses. The gamepad controller is a Logitech F710. Tracking of both the stereo glasses and the gamepad is accomplished using eight Vicon T160 infrared cameras. The second environment consists of an Oculus Rift DK2 with a tracked gamepad. The same model of gamepad (Logitech F710) and the same Vicon system are used. The third environment consists of a Leap Motion controller along with the same Oculus Rift DK2.

4.3 Interactions Using Gamepad

4.3.1 System Control

When using the gamepad, the application uses a 1-DOF hierarchical graphical menu. This view-dependent menu appears when the user presses the *Y* button on the gamepad. The user can then select a menu item by hovering it and pressing the *A* button on the gamepad.

The menu is used to select tasks such as deletion or creation of a certain type of well trajectory, and to perform basic functions such as filtering cells based on property values or modifying properties displayed.

4.3.2 Basic Manipulations

The user may use the joystick on the gamepad to rotate, translate, or scale the reservoir. The left stick allows the user to translate the reservoir on the x- and z- axis; while the left and right bumpers translate on the y- axis. The left and right triggers allow the user to scale the reservoir model up or down. Finally, the right stick allows the user to rotate the reservoir around the x- and y- axis.

The user can also toggle transparency and visibility of the reservoir cells by using the start and back buttons, respectively. Setting the reservoir semi-transparent or invisible allows the user to view internal structures within the reservoir such as the well trajectories and their connected graphs. Semi-transparent mode allows a contextual view of the reservoir surface to be maintained.

4.3.3 Cell Probing

To be able to select a certain cell and view information only about that cell is a feature frequently used by reservoir engineers and geoscientists, and is common in commercial software. This feature is called cell probing and it allows a user to understand small scale data variations. This is an essential tool especially when inspecting grid cells to determine a candidate well trajectory. In our application, we provided a 3D, immersive version of this feature.

In order to probe cells, the user presses and holds the *A* button on the controller. This action activates a small, white probing cube close to the controller that mirrors its position and orientation. The probing cube acts as a three-dimensional cursor and whenever the cube collides with a cell, the grid cell is selected and rendered along with a small view-dependent window with information about the cell such as the i, j, k coordinates of the cell and properties related to flow efficiency such as permeability in i, j, k directions; porosity; and transmissibility in i, j, k directions.

A view-dependent, volumetric transparency lens appears around the cube in order to overcome the issue of surface occlusion when probing grid cells from outside of the reservoir surface. The lens allows the user to see into the reservoir and select internal cells. The lens removes grid cells surrounding the probing cube and only displays the reservoir's wireframe lines close to the cube and the cell being probed.

4.3.4 Well Trajectory Creation

As illustrated in Figure 4, there are two types of wells that may be created: vertical and free-form wells. For vertical wells, the user uses a ray attached to the gamepad to highlight cells on the surface of the reservoir. By pressing the *A* button on the gamepad, a vertical well is placed and a well perforation is created in each of the cells in the column below the currently highlighted grid cell.

When creating free-form wells, the user must select each of the perforations in the the free-form well. By holding down the *B* button on the gamepad, the probing technique is triggered and, whenever the button is released, the first well perforation is created on the currently selected cell. By repeating this process, other perforations are defined for the well. Re-selecting one of the perforations signals the completion of the well path.

4.3.5 Well Trajectory Analysis – Graph

As previously described, a connectivity graph is defined for each perforation along each well. In turn, each node included in a connectivity graph has an associated connectivity measure called "delta time". This measure indicates how strongly connected cells are, thus indicating the relative time that would be required for oil to flow from a cell to its associated well perforation.

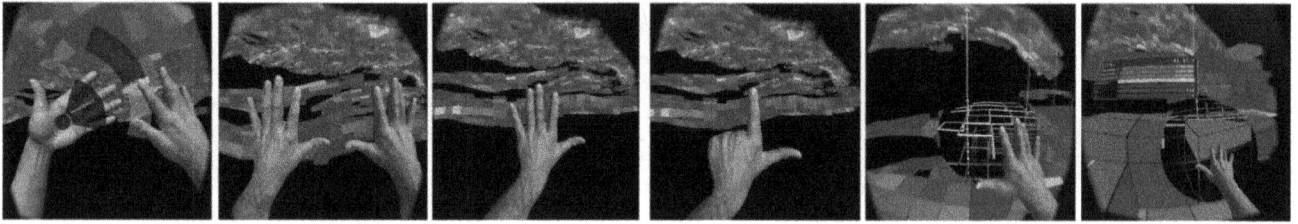

Figure 5: Illustrations of our interactions applied to a reservoir model while using gestures. From left to right: (1) property filtering through hand-menu; (2) scaling; (3) rotation; (4) translation; (5) alpha lens and (6) information window for probing.

A diverging color scheme is applied to the edges of the graph in order to encode "delta time" data. Edges with a deeper purple color have a lower delta time value and thus a stronger, more transmissible connection between the perforation and the cell. A brighter orange indicates a higher delta time value and thus a relatively low connection to the cell.

The graph is represented as a tube that radiates spatially from a perforation cell and connects the centroids of each pair of adjacent cells. In addition, the graph is rendered within the reservoir model as this facilitates the evaluation of the stratigraphic and geological factors influencing the connectivity between cells. For example, in a scenario where the connectivity changes abruptly, the user may use the transparency lens or set a semi-transparent reservoir in order to look for faults, fractures, or gaps on the cell geometries that may be acting as a barrier to the flow. The user may also probe cells along the edges of the graph where the connectivity suddenly changed in order to examine whether geological property values are negatively impacting the connectivity (see Figure 4).

Also, as previously mentioned, the user can define a delta-time threshold value in order to filter out cells not reached by flow at that time limit. The application uses a 1-DOF slider widget that ranges from zero to the maximum existing delta time. In order to define the threshold, the user places the ray pointer above the slider, holds the *A* button on the gamepad, and drags the ray along the slider. The spatial graph then changes accordingly to the user specified threshold.

Furthermore, as a reservoir model may contain multiple wells, and each well may have multiple graphs, the view may become cluttered. To help eliminate clutter, the user may press and release the *A* button on a well head. This selection causes only cells connected to the well to be displayed. Similarly, by selecting a specific well perforation, only cells connected to that perforation will be displayed.

4.3.6 Well Trajectory Analysis – Analytics

For each new well, along with the connectivity graphs, a tabular panel is created to display analytical connectivity data associated with the well (see Figure 4). The table contains four columns, and each row shows data associated with a well perforation. The last row shows cumulative data for the entire well.

The first column of the table shows the i, j, k coordinates of the perforations. The second column displays the total drainable hydrocarbon pore volume (HCPV) of all connected cells – that is, the cells associated with the nodes that compose the connectivity graph for the perforation. The third column shows the total HCPV of all connected cells that have arrival time below or equal to the currently selected time threshold. The last column shows the distribution of time for all connected cells.

The user may arrange each panel individually. Panels may be expanded or compressed so that they may be brought to the forefront of attention or minimized to reduce information clutter. To scale a panel up or down, the user hovers over it with the ray and presses the up or down buttons on the d-pad. Panels may be positioned anywhere in space, stacked on top of each other, sorted and organized according to the user's preference. To translate and to rotate a panel, the user places the ray on it and holds the *A* button on the gamepad in order to select the panel. Then the panel follows the movement of the tracked controller.

In order to decrease the physical effort of arranging panels, the mapping between the movement of the controller and the selected panel is not 1:1. When moved using the controller, the panel translates by a factor of 5:1 and rotates by a factor of 2:1 relative to the physical translations and rotations using the controller. These factors were empirically determined but we believe them to be effective in reducing physical workload while maintaining the required precision to efficiently perform the tasks.

4.4 Interactions Using Leap Motion

When using gestures as an interaction interface, the user has access to only a subset of features: setting a system control menu, manipulating the reservoir model, and probing the grid cells. This reduced feature set was implemented to collect initial feedback regarding gesture controls that could help designing the more complex features, such as the well trajectory creation.

4.4.1 System Control

When controlling the application with the leap motion device using the Oculus, the application uses a 1-DOF hierarchical graphical menu attached to the user's left hand. The arc-shaped menu appears whenever the user rotates the left palm towards the face. The user can then select the menu items using the index finger of the opposite hand. To select an item, the user moves a fingertip to the menu item and hovers briefly.

4.4.2 Basic Manipulations

When designing the rotation, translation, and scale operations, one important interaction design principle that we considered is that gesture-based interactions should be initiated with specific gestures that are rarely a part of casual movements. For this reason we devised initialization (or "trigger") motions from which an action may be initiated. After detecting a gesture pattern, the gesture-related action is triggered provided that the user performs a gesture motion above a certain speed threshold.

As depicted in Figure 5, to scale the reservoir model the user must put both hands up with all fingers extended and with palms facing outwards. In order to trigger the scaling operation, the user must then move either forward or backward fast enough to surpass a pre-defined speed threshold. If the movement is fast enough and is forward (that is, positive in the z-axis), the reservoir is scaled up equally in x-, y-, and z- axis; if the movement is fast enough and is backward (that is, negative in the z-axis), the reservoir is scaled down equally in all axes.

To rotate the reservoir the user must extend all fingers in the left hand with the palm facing outwards, while to translate the reservoir the user must extend the thumb and index fingers of the left hand with the palm facing outwards. When the operations are triggered, the hand motion is then performed per axis: given the hand motion vector $v = (vx, vy, vz)$, the filtered, per axis vector consists of the same vector with its two lowest values substituted to zero.

To toggle the transparency and visibility of the reservoir, the user uses the gesture based menu described earlier.

4.4.3 Cell Probing

As illustrated in Figure 5, the user extends all fingers in the right hand with the palm facing outwards to trigger the probing function. The user can then move the fully-opened hand to probe different cells. When using gestures, no small white cube is used as a cursor. Instead, the right index finger acts as the three-dimensional cursor. The right index is surrounded by the transparency lens and whenever it collides with a cell, this grid cell is selected, causing it to be rendered along with the data window.

5. EVALUATION

Our evaluation sessions were divided into two parts: an evaluation of the features of the application and an investigation into the suitability and preferences of engineers with regards to different immersive environments when performing the inherently exploratory tasks of the application. Throughout each session, we performed a series of standardized demos and interviews with each participant.

We conducted one pilot session with an expert reservoir engineer from our research group who was not involved in the design of the application. The other five sessions were with external reservoir engineering experts. Each of the six evaluation sessions lasted between 60 and 90 minutes.

Sessions started with a description of the goals of the evaluation session: feedback regarding the features of the prototype, as well as feedback regarding the different virtual reality mediums to be presented. Next, participants were asked to answer a questionnaire to understand their expertise, as well as their previous experience relevant to the domain.

5.1 On the Application

The features of the application were first demonstrated using the CAVE environment. Since most of the participants were new to virtual reality technology, we were aware that the lack of familiarity could create an unfavorable or intimidating experience. To reduce biased results and allow feedback without having to account for lack of training, each of the features were demonstrated by one of the two session facilitators. The facilitator used the tracked stereo glasses and thus had the optimal perspective and controlled the application using the gamepad. Participants used untracked stereo glasses and were requested to remain close to the facilitator to ensure their view perspective was not distorted.

Each of the implemented features were then introduced and explained in the same sequence presented in this paper: (1) basic manipulations, (2) cell probing, (3) vertical and free-form well trajectory creation, (4) well trajectory analysis using the connectivity graph, (5) well trajectory analysis using the connectivity analytics panels.

At the end of each of the five demo sections, participants were asked to provide their opinion on the feature they had been shown in that section, and to reflect on its usefulness, potential problems and suggestions for improvement. After all the five features were demonstrated, we asked them for suggestions for other potentially useful features, and then asked for additional comments if there were any. Sessions were video recorded for further qualitative analysis.

5.2 On the Immersive Mediums

After the demonstrations and interviews about the features of the application in the CAVE, a preliminary inquiry into other immersive display and other interaction devices were performed. The participants were exposed to the same application running in an Oculus Rift DK2 with the same tracked gamepad controller as used in the CAVE. Then, participants were asked to reflect upon the differences they noticed between their traditional desktops, the CAVE, and the Oculus; what advantages or disadvantages they noticed about each environment; which environments they preferred and why, as well as any general comments.

Following this, the participants were introduced to the same application using an Oculus Rift DK2 along with a Leap Motion controller. The participants were then asked similar questions to gather feedback comparing their traditional keyboard and mouse interface, the gamepad, and the Leap Motion controller.

5.3 Participants

Six individuals took part in this study: four males and two females. Their age ranged from 26 to 37 years old. All of them had undergraduate degrees and one or more graduate degrees in Petroleum Engineering. Five of them were enrolled in a Ph.D. Program in Petroleum Engineering and one was a post-doctoral scholar. Five of them had between one and seven years of professional experience as reservoir engineers. One of the participants was currently employed as a reservoir engineer and two others were currently working in a reservoir simulation software company.

6. RESULTS

6.1 On the Application

6.1.1 Cell Probing

When asked about the usefulness of probing, participants claimed the probe was one of the most common functions used – e.g. "*I probe all the time*". They appreciated the functionality of the transparency lens associated with the probe as it allowed them to efficiently see both the property values in the reservoir and the well configuration in 3D. When asked to compare with existing desktop software, participants commented that using existing tools it is required to either visualize the well path inside the reservoir across multiple 2D cross sections or view a transparent overview of the 3D reservoir model.

6.1.2 Well Trajectory Creation

When asked about the usefulness of the probing tool while selecting the well path, we received several different comments. One user commented that only seeing the selected cell is preferable. The main advantage of this, according to the user, is that the 3D geometry of the cell can be clearly observed to avoid the selection of shapes that could cause problems with the numerical simulation such as "pinch" cells. However, another participant commented it would be preferable to have more contextual information surrounding the selected cell. This user suggested an improvement would be to display the entire column or an adjustable number of cells neighboring the selected cell.

When asked about the well path creation tasks, participants requested to be able to remove well perforations – e.g. "*sometimes I already know which layers of the reservoir have oil, so I'll perforate only those layers*", "*the connectivity analysis shows me useless perforations, so I'd like to remove them*".

6.1.3 Well Trajectory Analysis – Graph

When questioned about the usefulness of the connectivity graph, we received positive comments – "*this is amazing. It's like I can see where the oil comes from*". Some participants praised the benefit of being able to quickly assess the region that can be covered by a well. They claimed that this would help them find locations that cover larger areas. They also commented that the connectivity graph would help with finding locations in the reservoir not covered by existing wells. Users claimed this analysis would help them evaluate how many wells might be needed to cover parts of a development field.

Other participants praised the ability to see the connected cells associated with each perforation, as this would help them more accurately design a perforation scheme that was efficient and without perforations that are not needed or even detrimental to recovery.

Some participants noted as a limitation of our application that a higher contrast color scheme should be used for the graph encoding to improve clarity.

When prompted for ideas for improvements, one participant suggested it would be useful to highlight locations where the connectivity changed abruptly so barriers to flow could be easily identified. Another participant mentioned that it would be interesting to also display a contour style visualization of the region connected to the well to provide a "*general trend*" or a "*big picture of the behavior of flow*" view as opposed to a "*detailed*" view using the connected graph.

Also, since wells are often associated with specific drainage areas, one participant requested a feature to filter the connectivity graph according to the distance from the well – "*when wells are producing, each well is associated with a drainage area. (...) it's important to see the volume connected to the well only in its share region*". One participant also mentioned that "*if we have two wells not too far away from each other, it's important to see the location and (delta) time when the regions connected to the wells start to interfere with each other*". This is because if two wells are producing, each one has an amount of recoverable oil volume associated with it. However, if there is interference, wells may not be recovering the expected oil production since they might only produce from the region up to where interference occurs.

The same participant also suggested it would be useful to display the shortest path between a user selected cell and the associated well along the spatial graph. According to this individual, this would provide a visual indication of permeable channel deposits or saturation fronts.

6.1.4 Well Trajectory Analysis – Analytics

The panels displaying analytical connectivity data were well received – e.g., "*this is very good as it gives a snapshot of the performance of each perforation and the entire well*". All participants felt it was very important to have both the visual and analytical data available so they could also access detailed information. Users appreciated the ability to move and organize the panels in three dimensional space, but some requested that

there be a way to help organize them, such as being able to set them to hover near their associated well, or automatically stack or sort based on user defined criteria.

One participant indicated it would be useful to be able to select ranges of the histogram in order to see the associated connected cells in the spatial graph. This action, in turn, would help define the coverage areas for different wells and the inter-well spacing between them – e.g., "*if two wells are producing and I see the connectivity graphs overlapping, I would need to decide how much to move one of them further away*".

6.1.5 Further Feedback

When asked about any additional comments or suggestions, most of the participants requested the ability to save well trajectory and perforation information to a file format that could be loaded in commercial reservoir simulation software. Requests for the tool to read in trajectories and perforation data from file formats commonly used by commercial reservoir simulation software were also common.

Some participants claimed it was important to edit well trajectories and perforations so that different well configurations could be easily evaluated. Further to this, one participant suggested a feature to support the comparison between two or more configurations of the same well. Another participant indicated it would be useful to be able to save and recall well configurations, so that a saved well configuration could be "pasted" into arbitrary locations in the reservoir as often as needed.

One participant suggested the current well connectivity analysis tool be extended to "*inter-well connectivity analysis*". The participant commented that for mature fields, engineers must commonly decide on the placement of injector wells based on the already existing producer wells. Thus, the evaluation of the connectivity between a pair of producer and injector wells would be even more helpful for this scenario.

6.2 On the Immersive Mediums

6.2.1 CAVE and Oculus

Following the interview regarding the application features, we captured each participant's impressions and preferences regarding two immersive environments, the CAVE and the Oculus Rift, using the same gamepad controller.

Participants claimed the visualization of the reservoir was clearer when using the Oculus Rift. They reported that the perception of details was better than in the CAVE. Most participants (five out of six) appreciated increased detail, relating that to the feeling of actually being immersed in the environment – e.g., "*it makes me feel more 'into it'; as if things are closer*".

One of the participants claimed that what they saw in the Oculus looked more familiar – "*things looked more aligned to what I know*". On the other hand, another participant argued that "*immersion on the Oculus is so high that it may complicate the analysis of the reservoir as a whole*". The participant was alluding to the fact that the field of view is narrower in the Oculus compared to the CAVE system and this was a hindrance to visualizing the reservoir – "*we are used to have a wider vision*".

When queried about the usefulness of both devices, most of the participants claimed they would prefer to work with the Oculus if they are working on their own; however, they would prefer to work with the CAVE if there are more individuals involved and the purpose is to collaborate with co-workers, to showcase projects, or to make joint decisions. The participants did claim they tend to work individually, but acknowledged that a device for collaborative work ("*which is common in industry*") is very important.

When queried about difficulties and limitations, one of the participants claimed they "*felt more in control with the Oculus when compared to the CAVE*". This participant pointed out that one of the shortcomings of the CAVE is that "*it shows things according to a particular person (...) this may be the reason why I have felt some eye fatigue*". Another difficulty mentioned by two participants was regarding comfort while using the Oculus Rift. One of them mentioned that "*technology may need to advance to be more practical*" after noting the heaviness of the Oculus compared to the glasses used in the CAVE.

As a suggestion for improvement, one participant claimed that it would be ideal if more users could "*control the environment*" when using the CAVE or "*share the environment*" when using the Oculus. This participant suggested that equal autonomy for users in the virtual environment would improve both the quality of the experience and the potential for collaboration.

6.2.2 Gamepad and Leap Motion

Finally, we captured impressions and feedback regarding experiences when using the Oculus Rift with two different interaction interfaces. Participants interacted with the application using a gamepad first, and then hand gestures.

All participants claimed that gestures were more natural and intuitive for them – e.g., "*your hands is part of you, so you know how to control it*"; "*(your hand) it's you. (...) with the gamepad, you have the buttons as an additional layer*". Nonetheless, they also claimed there was a learning curve and some period of adaption would be necessary – which they did not think was problematic however.

Although users agreed that gestures would feel more natural, they acknowledged that using a gamepad provided benefits that gestures did not. One of the participants noted that using gestures meant the hands were required to be "*fixed in a particular spot*" – that is, on the space covered by the gesture and motion sensor; whereas the gamepad allowed more flexibility. The same participant also noted that the use of gestures seemed to lead to some glitches during the interaction process; something the user did not notice when using the gamepad.

Another participant claimed that when probing, the gamepad allowed users to see and reach farther than hands and arms physically allow – "*most of the time, I probe multiple cells in different regions, so I don't want to be too close to a cell*". The user also claimed fatigue as another potential problem with using hands – "*probing is a feature that I use all the time, so having my arms resting on the chair is more convenient*". The participant suggested that an improvement would be to attach a cursor to the index finger in order to probe cells further away. In spite of the drawbacks mentioned, this participant claimed they would prefer to use gestures rather than the gamepad.

7. DISCUSSION

7.1 On the Application

There were several suggestions and many positive comments regarding our application. Many of them were related to the connectivity analysis. This shows that even though static connectivity analysis was a new approach for them, they understood its purpose and value. Not only were the participants

pleased with the connectivity technique, but they also claimed that the three dimensional perspective in both environments was superior to their traditional desktop environment. These results support our belief that immersion is indeed beneficial for our application.

Interestingly, several participants provided feedback that echo some of the challenges VR has historically faced in the field of oil and gas mentioned in [16]. For instance, many participants requested the ability to save and load well trajectories, fault information, and other data from a software familiar to them. During the feedback sessions, it was clear that it was important for participants to easily transfer data between their existing workflows and our tool. Lack of compatibility with software packages had been identified in [16] as a barrier to the use of VR in oil and gas.

For this reason, we chose to use VTK as our data format since it is widely used. Also, we created tools to convert reservoir data formats to the VTK format we use, increasing the ease of importing data into our tool. However, we have not yet built support for saving or loading well trajectories. This could be added relatively easily and clearly it is desirable to do so.

7.2 On the Immersive Mediums

Regarding immersive mediums, [16] noted the fact that accessing a large system that would require users to leave their desks would be a barrier to widespread use of VR in oil and gas. However, there are currently high quality virtual reality devices such as the Oculus Rift and the HTC Vive, and vendors are offering enterprise class VR workstations. Hence, it is now possible to affordably have a VR headset at a workstation for individual use or remote collaboration, and to move to an advanced visualization platform such as a CAVE or CAVE variant only for co-located collaboration, training, and demonstration to groups. Many participants mentioned they would prefer to use HMDs such as the Oculus Rift for individual work whereas they would rather use the CAVE when performing collaborative work. Our CAVE is relatively low resolution, but a high resolution system should address the concerns regarding clarity that were expressed.

Participants appreciated the ability to move between the head mounted display and the large scale immersive display, but were afraid that would require them to go through two types of training. There are many different display and input devices, and to provide a solution that has a consistent user experience on commodity HMDs and other immersive platforms is both a technical and a design challenge.

We used MiddleVR to mitigate the technical challenges of cross-platform VR applications. There are several important design considerations when developing cross platform VR applications however. It is essential to provide a consistent experience so that users are not confused when moving between platforms. Users should not require more than a trivial amount of training when moving between platforms, otherwise the effectiveness of moving between IVEs is compromised. For this reason, we sought to create spatial interactions that are intuitive and support working with our complex 3D datasets across different platforms.

8. CONCLUSION AND FUTURE WORK

Our efforts in this work were focused on three goals. The first was the design of an analytical method for performing static connectivity analysis as a proxy for numerical simulation. The second was the creation of an application that would help reservoir engineers perform well optimization tasks more effectively using this method. The third was to design this application to take advantage of the benefits of immersive environments. We performed interviews with six reservoir engineering subject matter experts to gather feedback regarding our method and application. Also, we demonstrated the application using three different immersive environments in order to explore the impressions of the reservoir engineering subject matter experts and gather the perceived benefits and drawbacks of each of the environments when it comes to performing well trajectory analyses.

We have presented the results and a discussion of our findings from the interviews. Even though this was an exploratory study, it has advanced our understanding of the needs and expectations of this tool, as well as how immersive environments may benefit reservoir engineers. We plan to improve the capabilities of our application using the suggestions provided by our participants. In the longer term, we plan to proceed with a larger task-oriented user evaluation and have interviews with a larger number of subject matter experts. We hope that our work will provide benefit for those designing immersive applications both in petroleum engineering and in other domains. Furthermore, we hope that our work elucidates how powerful and valid immersive environments are, and highlights their potential to transform the way we explore scientific data.

9. ACKNOWLEDGMENTS

We are very grateful to the Foundation CMG / Frank and Sarah Meyer Collaboration Centre for enabling our research.

10. REFERENCES

[1] CMG. http://www.cmgl.ca. Accessed: 2016-07-01.

[2] Hover vr interface kit. https://github.com/aestheticinteractive/Hover-VR-Interface-Kit. Accessed: 2016-07-01.

[3] Middlevr for Unity. http://www.middlevr.com/middlevr-for-unity. Accessed: 2016-07-01.

[4] Schlumberger petrel. http://www.software.slb.com/products/petrel. Accessed: 2016-07-01.

[5] R. Cossé. Basics of reservoir engineering: oil and gas field development techniques. Editions Technip, 1993.

[6] F. M. de Carvalho, E. V. Brazil, R. G. Marroquim, M. C. Sousa, and A. Oliveira. Interactive cutaways of oil reservoirs. Graphical Models, 84:1–14, 2016.

[7] D. Denney et al. 3d visualization: A common language for the drilling and subsurface communities. Journal of petroleum technology, 57(04):80–83, 2005.

[8] D. R. Fenik, A. Nouri, and C. Deutsch. Ranking realizations for sagd performance predictions. Published report http://www. ccgalberta.com/ccgresources/report11/2009-204 ranking realizations for sagd. pdf, 2009.

[9] R. Graves, J. Turley, B. Macon, et al. Educating for leadership, management and teamwork. In SPE Annual Technical Conference and Exhibition. Society of Petroleum Engineers, 1995

[10] J. Harris, J. Young, N. Sultanum, P. Lapides, E. Sharlin, and M. C. Sousa. Designing snakey: a tangible user interface supporting well path planning. In Interact 2011.

[11] K. Hird, O. Dubrule, et al. Quantification of reservoir connectivity for reservoir description applications. SPE Reservoir Evaluation & Engineering, 1(01):12–17, 1998.

[12] J. Hovadik and D. Larue. Stratigraphic and structural connectivity. Geological Society, London, Special Publications, 347(1):219–242, 2010.

[13] J. Hovadik and D. Larue. Predicting waterflood behavior by simulating earth models with no or limited dynamic data: From model ranking to simulating a billion-cell model. 2011.

[14] J. M. Hovadik and D. K. Larue. Static characterizations of reservoirs: refining the concepts of connectivity and continuity. Petroleum Geoscience, 13(3):195–211, 2007.

[15] H. Ishii and B. Ullmer. Tangible bits: towards seamless interfaces between people, bits and atoms. In Proceedings of the ACM SIGCHI Conference on Human factors in computing systems, pages 234–241. ACM, 1997.

[16] G. L. Kinsland and C. W. Borst. Visualization and interpretation of geologic data in 3d virtual reality. Interpretation, 3(3):SX13–SX20, 2015.

[17] D. K. Larue and J. Hovadik. Connectivity of channelized reservoirs: a modelling approach. Petroleum Geoscience, 12(4):291–308, 2006.

[18] E. M. Lidal, T. Langeland, C. Giertsen, J. Grimsgaard, and R. Helland. A decade of increased oil recovery in virtual reality. IEEE Computer Graphics and Applications, 27(6):94–97, 2007.

[19] K. Gruchalla. Immersive well-path editing: investigating the added value of immersion. In Virtual Reality, 2004. Proceedings. IEEE, pages 157–164. IEEE, 2004.

[20] E. D. Ragan, R. Kopper, P. Schuchardt, and D. A. Bowman. Studying the effects of stereo, head tracking, and field of regard on a small-scale spatial judgment task. IEEE Transactions on Visualization and Computer Graphics, 19(5):886–896, 2013.

[21] M. Sharifi, M. Kelkar, A. Bahar, T. Slettebo, et al. Dynamic ranking of multiple realizations by use of the fast-marching method. SPE Journal, 19(06):1–069, 2014.

[22] S. Somanath. Exploring tabletops as an interaction medium in the context of reservoir engineering. Master's thesis, University of Calgary, Citeseer, 2012.

[23] S. Somanath, A. Rocha, H. Hamdi, E. Sharlin, and M. C. Sousa. Reservoirbench: An interactive educational reservoir engineering workbench. In Human-Computer Interaction, pages 340–348. Springer, 2015.

[24] N. Sultanum, E. Sharlin, M. C. Sousa, D. N. Miranda-Filho, and R. Eastick. Touching the depths: introducing tabletop interaction to reservoir engineering. In ACM International Conference on Interactive Tabletops and Surfaces, pages 105–108. ACM, 2010.

[25] N. Sultanum, S. Somanath, E. Sharlin, and M. C. Sousa. Point it, split it, peel it, view it: techniques for interactive reservoir visualization on tabletops. In Proceedings of the ACM International Conference on Interactive Tabletops and Surfaces, pages 192–201. ACM, 2011.

[26] C. Ware and G. Franck. Evaluating stereo and motion cues for visualizing information nets in three dimensions. ACM Transactions on Graphics (TOG), 15(2):121–140, 1999.

A Metric for Short-Term Hand Comfort and Discomfort: Exploring Hand Posture Evaluation

Jonas Mayer
Technical University of Munich
Faculty of Informatics
Arcisstraße 21, Munich, Germany
jonas.a.mayer@tum.de

Nicholas Katzakis
Technical University of Munich
Faculty of Informatics
Arcisstraße 21, Munich, Germany
niko@tum.de

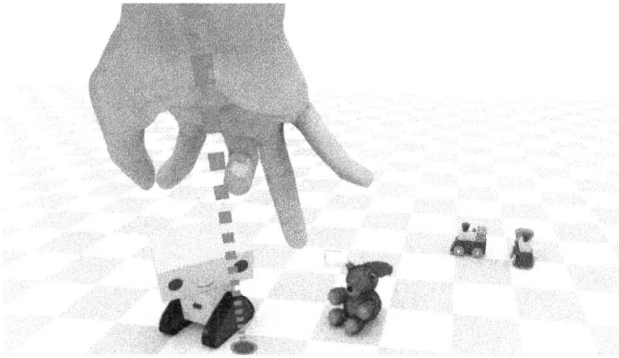

Figure 1: Controlling a Robot using Hand Postures

ABSTRACT

We propose a metric for quick short-term comfort and discomfort evaluation of non-resting hand postures. The metric is further improved using data from user studies. Comparing subjective user ratings with the metric indicates the metric to be a fitting model for perceived comfort and discomfort. Our results also indicate that there is an effect of hand comfort and discomfort on precision and performance in a 3D target pointing task.

Keywords

comfort; discomfort; hand; posture; control; gesture

1. INTRODUCTION

When using a traditional desktop computer users have access, through the keyboard, to a number of shortcuts and macros thanks to numerous keys and through the mouse, to a host of toolbars and context menus that allow for easily launching various commands.

The nature of virtual reality and human-robot interaction, however, does not allow for so many physical buttons or for mouse-level accuracy when accessing context menus.

SUI '16, October 15 - 16, 2016, Tokyo, Japan

© 2016 Copyright held by the owner/author(s). Publication rights licensed to ACM.
ISBN 978-1-4503-4068-7/16/10. . . $15.00

DOI: http://dx.doi.org/10.1145/2983310.2985752

In such contexts sometimes speech and hand gestures are employed. Nonetheless speech is limited when it comes to precise spatial designations, such as when commanding a robot to execute some household task (Figure 1). Pointing with the hands is much more efficient. Instead of menus and key macros, hand postures can be used to add additional expressiveness to pointing gestures. However, complicated hand postures might cause fatigue or discomfort and might limit user experience and precision [4]. Even though comfort and discomfort are often taken into consideration by designers, there are only a handful of evaluation methods [3].

In this work we propose a hand posture comfort/discomfort metric that allows for quick and objective hand posture evaluation. We combine state of the art comfort/discomfort models with hand anatomy and ergonomics knowledge to create models that can predict hand comfort and discomfort given a specific posture. Based on our model we created a *naive* metric. We improved this *naive* metric in a second step using data from a user study. Finally another user study was used to validate our metric and to show the impact of comfort and discomfort on performance in a hand pointing task.

2. HAND POSTURE COMFORT/ DISCOMFORT METRIC

The structure of the metric we propose is based on current ergonomics models [6]. These models define comfort as a *"pleasant state or relaxed feeling of a human being"* mostly caused by subjective impressions and expectations. Discomfort is defined as *"an unpleasant state of the human body"* resulting from physical stress. Using this information combined with knowledge of hand anatomy, we broke down hand comfort and discomfort in a non-resting hand into the following four components: deviation from Range of Rest Posture (RRP), inter-finger angles (IFA), finger hyperextension (HE) and finger abduction (FA). These components will be explained in the following sections.

For the computation of our metric we used a simplified 21 degree of freedom angle based hand model, similar to the model described by Su et al. [5], as it makes reading joint angles trivial. Furthermore, the 21 DOF angle based hand model was simply handled as a vector of 21 `float`s.

2.1 Deviation from Range of Rest Posture

Range of Rest Posture (RRP), as defined by Apostolico et al. [1], is a range of angles for an articular joint[1],

---

[1]The word "articular joint" refers to joints in the human

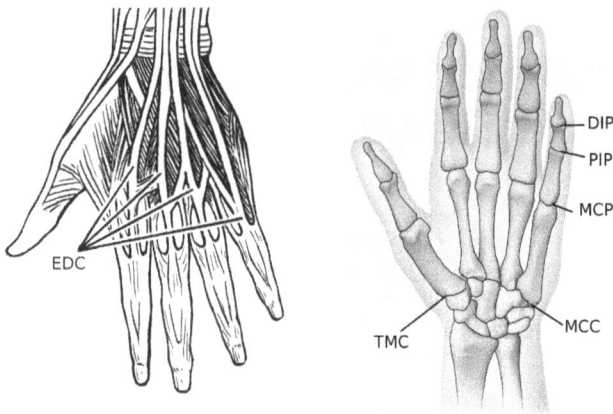

Figure 2: Hand Anatomy © Scott Foresman, Blausen.com

where the joint *"can be considered statistically in rest"*. The resulting relaxation of muscles and tendons creates maximum comfort in this particular joint. In our case, we considered the non-resting human hand to have a specific RRP for each finger joint, when the palm is facing downwards. Combining the RRPs of each finger joint for the entire hand results in a set of relaxed hand postures where comfort is maximized.

For articular joints perceived comfort decreases when deviating from the RRP and it minimizes at the bounds of the total range of motion. Applying this to the whole hand leads to the conclusion that hand posture comfort can be evaluated by adding up the individual joint angle distances to the RRP [3].

In our implementation the RRP was represented by a set of 50 relaxed hand postures recorded with the Leap Motion Controller. The metric **RRP(x)** was simply computed by calculating the minimum euclidean distance of a hand posture denoted as a multi-dimensional vector "x" to the RRP set. For simplicity we assumed comfort to linearly decrease with distance to the RRP.

2.2 The Inter-Finger Angles

The hand has a very compact and highly connected system of muscles and tendons that limits the individual movement of fingers (Figure 2). Aside from the thumb, fingers share *most* of their flexor and extendor muscles. Despite this, minor individual flexion and extension (Figure 3) of adjacent fingers is still possible due to finger tendons originating from different areas of the muscles. In the case of the EDC (*Extensor digitorum communis*) the finger tendons are even interconnected on the back of the hand (Figure 2).

Based on this, we expect hand postures with high bending differences of adjacent fingers to cause stress of tendons and muscles, resulting in discomfort.

The **inter-finger angle component IFA(x)** was computed by first adding up the flexion/extension angles of MCP (*metacarpophalangeal*), PIP(*proximal interphalangeal*) and DIP (*distal interphalangeal*) joints (Figure 2) for each finger. We then added up the differences in total bending of adjacent fingers (3 values). In order to compensate anatomical differences of the fingers, mostly affecting the ring finger, we added a ring finger bonus consisting of the difference of the ring finger's bending to both of its neighbors multiplied with an estimated weight coefficient. The importance of this body.

differentiation can be seen when the fist is closed. Extending the ring finger from a closed fist is much harder than extending the index finger.

2.3 Finger Hyperextension

As stated by LaViola, **hyperextension** (Figure 3) *"puts more strain on the [MCP] joints and tendons than the hand is accustomed to"* and therefore causes discomfort [2]. Even though this might seem redundant to the deviation from RRP on first sight, hyperextension takes an increased toll as it causes considerably more discomfort, compared to a full flexion of the fingers and compared to what the deviation from RRP would suggest.

For the **hyperextension** component **HE(x)** we simply added up the flexion/extension angles of the fingers' MCPs that had a negative angle and were therefore hyperextended.

2.4 Finger Abduction

Finger **abduction** (Figure 3) also causes stress on the MCP joint, the abduction muscles and tendons involved. Abduction was processed similar to hyperextension, as full abduction creates substantially more discomfort than full adduction (Figure 3). We computed the **abduction** component **FA(x)** by adding up the absolute abduction angle for the finger. This is possible as a fully adducted finger has an abduction angle of 0 in our model.

2.5 Naive Metric

After determining the single metric components, we designed the **naive metric** to combine these components. For this, we decided to add up the whole-hand component values $(RRP, IFA, ...)$ that are weighted with importance coefficients $(c_{RRP(x)}, c_{IFA(x)}, ...)$. These weighting coefficients were *empirically estimated* for the naive metric.

$$Naive(x) = c_{RRP} \cdot RRP(x) + c_{IFA} \cdot IFA(x)$$
$$+ \ c_{HE} \quad \cdot \ HE(x) \quad + \ c_{FA} \quad \cdot FA(x)$$

We hypothesize that the resulting metric will correlate with user perception, having the value 0 as maximum for comfort and minimum for discomfort.

2.6 Improved Metric

Even though the naive metric contains the causes of comfort and discomfort, it still lacks deeper consideration for the anatomical differences between the fingers. Our concept of improvement extends the thought process already used for inter-finger angles: instead of applying the metric to the whole hand, we consider the contributions from individual fingers and weight them with importance coefficients.

$$Improved(x) = c_{IFAindex} \cdot IFA(index(x)) + c_{IFAmiddle} \cdot \cdots$$

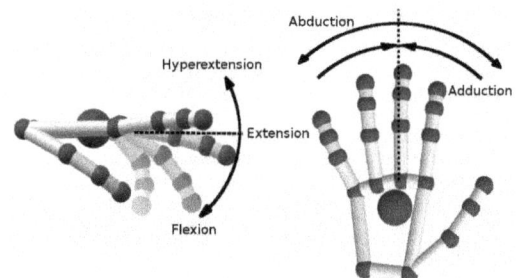

Figure 3: Hyperextension and Abduction

In our case we have five comfort values and a total of twelve discomfort values. However, the exact weighting coefficients are generally unknown and hard to estimate. To solve this problem, we reduced it to a curve fitting problem with 17 unknowns. We used data obtained from user studies to find the correct coefficients.

3. METHODOLOGY

For the collection of data, we created a test environment using **Unity 3D** with a total of two tasks.

In the first task (hand posture rating), the subject would be shown a randomly generated hand posture on screen. We used our naive metric to ensure a homogeneous distribution of expected comfort and discomfort. The subject was asked to mimic the hand posture with his or her dominant hand and then rate the posture. As we did not expect the subjects to be familiar with current comfort and discomfort models, we asked them to rate hand postures on an intuitive scale ranging from 0 (very uncomfortable) to 10 (very comfortable). This was chosen over a nominal or ordinal Likert scale because a numerical scale was needed for the metric's improvement and verification. Subjects were told to rate the hand posture with 0 points if they were unable to reproduce it. Before beginning the hand posture rating, subjects were asked to form two hand postures so that they have a comfort/discomfort reference. The first one was a completely relaxed posture, the second one was a randomly generated challenging posture (such as the posture in Figure 1).

The goal of the second task (target shooting) was to see, to what extent posture comfort and discomfort affects targeting performance. Again subjects had to mimic a random hand posture with their dominant hand and give it a rating from 0 to 10. After confirming their rating, subjects had to perform a target shooting task (Figure 4) with that specific posture. This specific task was chosen due to its similarity to real world tasks, where quick and precise spacial commands have to be issued. We tracked the subjects' dominant hand using an **ART Tracking Device**. The software showed subjects a minimalistic representation of their hand position and indicated the forward direction of their hand with a ray. Subjects were seated, with the elbow rested on a table. They had to use this ray to aim down a total of 12 targets, appearing in random order, and shoot them, by pressing a button with the off-hand. By recording the hand posture before the trial using a Leap, and checking the hand posture during the test, we made sure that the subject would not break the posture.

Table 1: Weighting Coefficients of the Improved Metric

	Thumb	Index	Middle	Ring	Pinky
RRP	0.631	-1.837	1.176	-3.021	1.288
IFA	-	0.547	0.216	1.670	-0.864
HE	-	-1.637	-2.685	10.401	-1.837
FA	-	-0.864	-3.857	0.0388	2.517

As a metric for performance, we measured the total time taken for the test. In order to have this affected by precision, we made the targets small and told the subjects to perform the test as quickly as possible.

We conducted a total of two user studies, a pilot study featuring multiple hand posture ratings only and the main study, where both target shooting and hand posture rating were tested multiple times. The studies were conducted with 12 (2 female) and 15 (5 female) participants respectively. The participants' mean age was 22 and 20. Subjects were informed about the aim of the study as well as their specific objectives beforehand.

For improving the metric the main goal was to fit the calculated metric values to the user ratings as closely as possible. For this, a least squares algorithm was used to find the optimal weighting coefficients based on the 250 data sets from the main study (training data). Afterwards, the metric was tested against the 60 data sets of the pilot study (test data).

4. RESULTS & DISCUSSION

For statistical analysis of the results, the Pearson correlation was used[2]. The results are displayed in Figure 5-8, with the single samples shown as dots and the line indicating the smoothed conditional mean, calculated by the `geom_smooth` function in R.

Unsurprisingly, the calculated values for the improved metric strongly affect the users comfort ratings, that were used to generate this metric (Figure 5). However, differences in anatomy and mindset of the participants and the limitation of hand posture ratings to 11 discrete steps introduced some noise to the data.

The computed weighting coefficients for the improved metric can be seen in Table 1. Due to the small number of participants, the coefficients are very noisy and don't seem to make much sense at first sight. It can also be seen that the IFA coefficients are generally less noisy than those of HE or FA. This indicates, that the different components are

---

[2]The effect size is determined by the correlation coefficient. A correlation is significant if $p < 0.01$

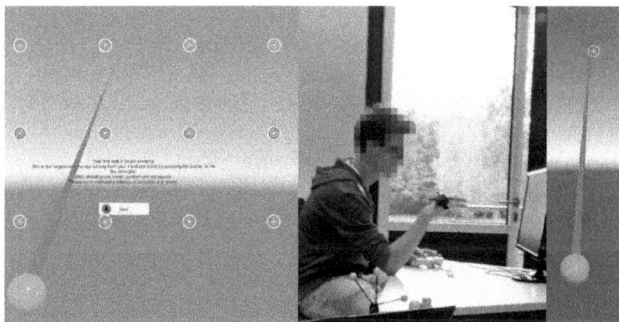

Figure 4: A Participant performing Target Shooting

Figure 5: Improved Metric and User Rating in Training Data. Correlation Coefficient: -0.645, p-value: < 2.2e-16

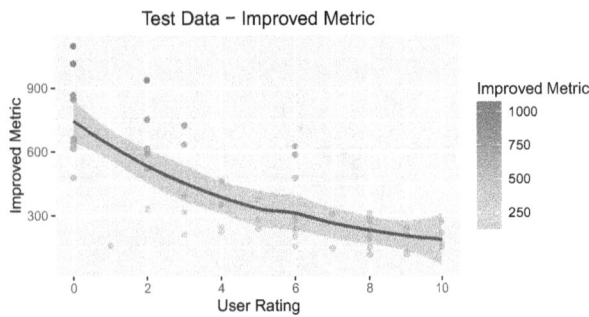

Figure 6: Improved Metric and User Rating in Test Data. Correlation Coefficient: -0.748, p-value: 5.89e-12

perceived differently and that the metric has room for improvement.

Despite the noise, the created metric also holds its large effect on the user ratings even when applied to the test data (Figure 6). This shows, that the improved metric is a valid extrapolation of the training data and can be used to predict the perceived user comfort and discomfort of a certain hand posture.

When looking at the naive metric, it can be seen that it predicts the user ratings in a similar way (Figure 7). However the improved metric creates a better prediction, as it reduces the metric values standard error.

The results from the target shooting task (Figure 8) shows that participants with harder hand postures generally took longer to finish. The large effect size is also confirmed by the Pearson correlation. This indicates that comfort and discomfort, as measured by our metric, significantly affect performance and precision in the context of hand postures. This strengthens the conclusion of Short et al. [4], that more comfortable postures generally create greater accuracy. However, the credibility of our results is limited by the relatively small number of participants. Further work is required before strong conclusions can be made.

5. CONCLUSION & FUTURE WORK

The main goal of this paper was to create a metric for quick and objective evaluation of hand posture comfort and discomfort. Furthermore we demonstrated the metric's relevance for design of hand postures, by proving its influence on precision and performance in a 3D pointing task. For the creation of the metrics we applied knowledge of hand anatomy and state of the art comfort and discomfort models and used data from a user study for improvements. Results from the testing user study suggest the improved metric to

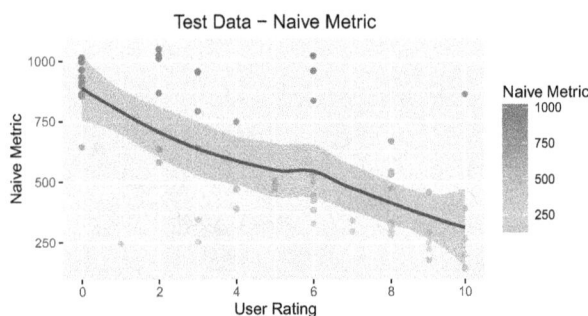

Figure 7: Naive Metric and User Rating in Test Data. Correlation Coefficient: -0.665, p-value: 6.73e-9

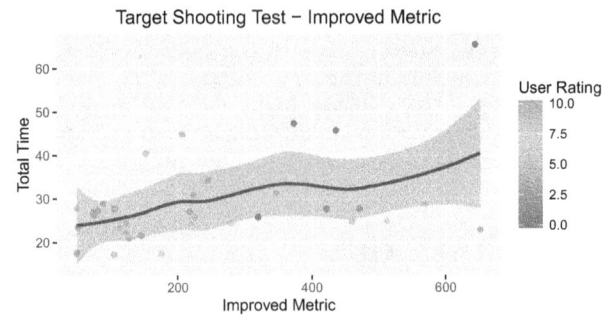

Figure 8: Improved Metric Value and Total Task Time in the Target Shooting Task. Correlation Coefficient: -0.665, p-value: 6.73e-9

be a valid extrapolation of the training data. In addition, the outcome of a small target shooting test indicate the existence of a correlation between comfort/discomfort and precision/performance, as already suggested for different contexts in other papers.

This work was only a first step for exploring hand posture comfort and discomfort. The metric created is still primitive and has some room for improvement. Furthermore only the short-term effects of comfort and discomfort combined were studied. Investigating the long- and short-term effects of comfort and discomfort separately in order to create more sophisticated models and metrics remains as future work.

6. ACKNOWLEDGEMENTS

Gudrun Klinker for the games lab space, Frieder Pankratz for the tracking setup. Figure 2 left ⓒⓒ Scott Foresman. Figure 2 right ⓒⓒ Blausen.com.

7. REFERENCES

[1] A. Apostolico, N. Cappetti, C. D'Oria, A. Naddeo, and M. Sestri. Postural comfort evaluation: experimental identification of range of rest posture for human articular joints. *International Journal on Interactive Design and Manufacturing (IJIDeM)*, 8(2):109–120, 2014.

[2] J. LaViola. A survey of hand posture and gesture recognition techniques and technology. *Brown University, Providence, RI*, 29, 1999.

[3] A. Naddeo, N. Cappetti, and C. D'Oria. Proposal of a new quantitative method for postural comfort evaluation. *International Journal of Industrial Ergonomics*, 48:25–35, 2015.

[4] M. W. Short and J. H. Cauraugh. Precision hypothesis and the end-state comfort effect. *Acta psychologica*, 100(3):243–252, 1999.

[5] S. A. Su and R. Furuta. A logical hand device in virtual environments. In *Proceedings of the ACM Conference on Virtual Reality Software and Technology (VRST'94)*, pages 33–42, 1994.

[6] P. Vink and S. Hallbeck. Editorial: Comfort and discomfort studies demonstrate the need for a new model. *Applied ergonomics*, 43(2):271–276, 2012.

Improving Gestural Interaction With Augmented Cursors

Ashley Dover,
G. Michael Poor
Baylor University
Waco, TX 76706, USA
ashley_therriault@baylor.edu
michael_poor@baylor.edu

Darren Guinness
University of Colorado Boulder
Boulder, CO 80309, USA
darren.guinness@colorado.edu

Alvin Jude
Ericsson Research
Santa Clara, CA, USA
alvinjude@acm.org

ABSTRACT

Gesture-based interaction has become more affordable and ubiquitous as an interaction style in recent years. One issue with gestural pointing is the lack of accuracy with smaller targets. In this paper we propose that the use of augmented cursors – which has been shown to improve small target acquisition with a standard mouse – also improves small target acquisition for gestural pointing. In our study we explored the use of Bubble Lens and Bubble Cursor as a means to improve acquisition of smaller targets, and compared it with interactions without them. Our study showed that both methods significantly improved target selection. As part of our study, we also identified the parameters in configuring Bubble Cursor for optimal results.

Keywords

Gestural Interaction; Augmented Cursor

1. INTRODUCTION

Over the last decade, the availability of affordable commercial off-the-shelf components for gestural interaction (i.e. the Xbox Kinect and Leap Motion) have opened the technology to the general public as an acceptable alternative for computer interaction. However, accuracy can be an issue when using mid-air gestures as cursor control or selection mechanisms [10]. The problem becomes increasingly difficult when the user's target is small or clustered with a number of other potential targets. For example, it has been noted that a target width of under 64px dramatically increases selection difficulty [5]. Given how ubiquitous cursor pointing and selection is in everyday computer usage, this problem is one that has been investigated for mouse interaction [12], with multiple methods showing improvement to the traditional interaction. By incorporating some of the more successful solutions with mid-air gestures, we will investigate whether or not the improvements seen when using the mouse can be applicable to this interaction.

SUI '16, October 15-16, 2016, Tokyo, Japan
© 2016 ACM. ISBN 978-1-4503-4068-7/16/10. . . $15.00
DOI: http://dx.doi.org/10.1145/2983310.2985765

In this paper, we describe a study to assess the performance (movement time and error rate) and usability (subjective workload) of gestural interaction enhanced with augmented cursors. Using mid-air gesture based interaction, we compared the standard Point Cursor with the Bubble Cursor, which is considered to be an improvement over the standard point cursor [4], and the Bubble Lens, which has been shown to be an improvement of the Bubble Cursor [9]. Once completed, we found that augmented cursors significantly improved the performance of gestural interaction, in both movement time and error rate.

2. RELATED WORK

Gestural Interaction, which has been studied for over 3 decades, leverages gestures from the body to interact with a computer. Various implementations are typically divided into two different types: (1) those that require the user to wear gloves, devices, or specific markers and (2) touchless gestural interaction. The latter leverages the "Come As You Are" design principle, which states that users should not be required to wear devices or specific markers to interact with a system [11].

Recent devices such as the Xbox Kinect, Leap Motion, and Myo Armband have gained popularity amongst researchers. These devices have demonstrated the potential use of gestural interfaces in medical professions that require sterile environments [11], as an accessibility device for those with impairments [1], and in mixed reality environments with head mounted displays [3]. Given the accuracy of this technology and the sensitive nature of usage, it is imperative to find a better form of selection when using this interaction.

Since graphical user interaction became the industry standard, the mouse was the default selection interaction mechanism. While this interaction has changed little over the years in regards to the default interaction, there have been improvements created for selection [12]. At this time, one of the fastest and well known general pointing techniques is the Bubble Cursor [4], in which a target-aware area cursor with a dynamically resizing activation area allows the cursor to always engulf the nearest target. Granted there have been some techniques that have equaled [2] or slightly improved upon [9] the Bubble Cursor's performance, none have surpassed it for general mouse pointing in all cases.

Though it has been shown to improve user interaction, the Bubble Cursor has some limitations. While it works well when a target is surrounded by empty space, the Bubble Cursor resorts to acting like a point cursor when the target is surrounded by other targets in a tight space [4].

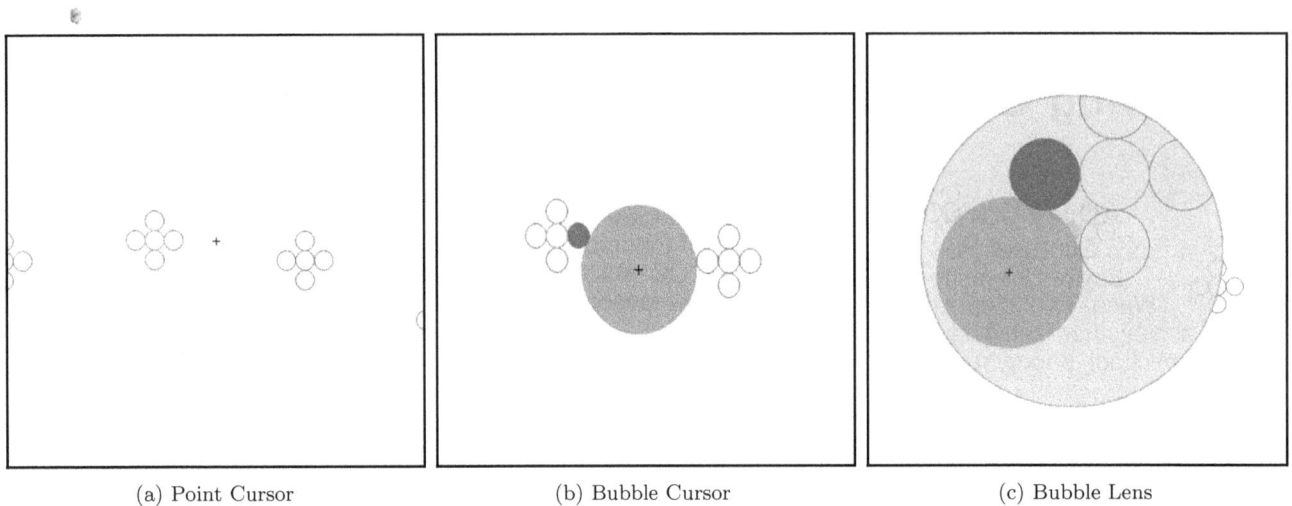

(a) Point Cursor   (b) Bubble Cursor   (c) Bubble Lens

Figure 1: Cropped screenshots of the task with each of the cursors (Point, Bubble, BubbleLens) showing the intended target in the center (orange outline) surrounded by distractor targets (green).

This type of interaction is very common in today's user interfaces (tool palettes, toolbars, etc). The Bubble Lens [9] was developed with the intention of addressing this limitation; when the target is closely surrounded by other targets, the Bubble Lens will automatically magnify nearby targets using a technique called kinematic triggering. Kinematic triggering is a technique that "continuously examines an unfolding velocity profile to trigger a mode change without explicit invocation [9]." In this work, the authors showed a significant improvement to the Bubble Cursor in both movement time and error rates. A different form of augmented cursors referred to as 'progressive refinement' has also been shown to work with in-air gestural interaction [8].

3. EXPERIMENT

This experiment follows the structure of a previous research [9], except the interaction in our experiment uses mid-air gestures instead of a mouse. The primary focus of this experiment was to assess whether augmented cursors can enhance gestural interaction, and improve performance and usability. Based on our observations of gestural interaction, we hypothesized that the threshold for what is considered a "small" and "dense" target may be different for gestural interaction than from interaction with a mouse. The Bubble Lens cursor uses this threshold to determine when to magnify a target. For mouse interaction this threshold was found to be 10 pixels [9]. We conducted an initial pilot study to determine whether the threshold should be different for gestural pointing, followed by a full study which compared the performance of different cursors with gestural interaction.

3.1 Myo Armband

The Myo Gesture Control Armband was used to recognize the arm's orientation in Euler angles (pitch, yaw, and roll) to control the cursor. In this experiment, we used a modeled interaction using spherical coordinates which has been shown to provide better performance, accuracy, and conformance to Fitts' law [6]. Interactions were performed in a seated position, with participants sitting approximately 3 feet from the monitor. Participants were allowed to per-

form the mid-air pointing either rested, with the elbow on the desk, or unrested but all participants finished the experiment from a rested position. Before each round, participants performed a calibration stage in which they positioned their arm at the desired angle for each corner of the screen. They were asked to recalibrate the interaction periodically and were allowed to pause and recalibrate if they experienced performance degradation.

3.2 Augmented Cursors

We used 3 different cursor types in our study. The Point Cursor (Figure 1a), used as a control has a single point of activation or hotspot as opposed to area cursors which have larger hotspots which vary in configuration[4]. The Bubble Cursor is a semi-transparent circular area cursor who's size varies to ensure that there is always exactly one target within its hotspot [4]. While the cursor works well when a target is surrounded by empty space, the Bubble Cursor (Figure 1b) resorts to acting like a point cursor when the target is closely surrounded by other targets [4]. The Bubble Lens [9] was developed with the intention of addressing the above limitation; when the target is closely surrounded by other targets, the Bubble Lens (Figure 1c) will automatically magnify nearby targets using a technique called kinematic triggering. Kinematic triggering is a technique that "continuously examines an unfolding velocity profile to trigger a mode change without explicit invocation [9]".

3.3 Experimental Design

Both the pilot and full study focused on comparing the performance of different cursors within gestural interaction used a $3 \times 3 \times 3$ within-subjects design which included 3 cursor types (Point Cursor, Bubble Cursor, Bubble Lens), 3 target widths (diameter of 4, 8, 16 pixels), and 3 spacing levels (zero spacing, half target-width spacing, full target-width spacing). Participants completed the 3 rounds in one of three orderings, based on the Latin cube ordering of interaction type and cursor type (Point, Bubble, Bubble Lens). Each round consisted of 16 trials, the first 3 counting as practice, for each of the 9 effective sizes. Participants completed a total of $3 \times 9 \times 13 = 351$ trials.

	MT (ms)		Error	
	mean	sd	mean	sd
Point Cursor	7570	4486	0.47	0.24
Bubble Cursor	5003	2543	0.32	0.23
Bubble Lens	3301	1084	0.13	0.14

Table 1: Overall means and standard deviation (sd) for movement time (MT) in milliseconds (ms), and error rates. Lower means are better for both.

3.4 Procedure

Each study consisted of one session lasting approximately 60 minutes. All testing was conducted in a lab setting on a 30-inch monitor with 2560 x 1600 resolution. Each study included 3 rounds of gestural interaction using all 3 cursors. Each round began with 3 practice trials, followed by a set of test trials. The task performed by the participants was adapted from that used in the original Bubble Lens study [9]: each trial required the participant to select an orange goal target from a set of gray distractor targets. In order to move on to the next trial, the goal target must be successfully selected. Target selection was done using the keyboard's space bar as the Myo's gestural recognition was found to be less reliable. Participants were told to select the target as quickly as possible while being as accurate as possible. They were also able to ask questions or provide feedback at any point during the experiment. After each round, participants were asked to fill out a Likert scale survey, and at the end of the experiment were asked to rank all rounds performed in order of preference.

3.5 Pilot Study

In order to understand what a small target meant within the context of gestural pointing, similar to previous research [9]. We conducted a pilot as described above with 7 Participants (6 male, 1 female) from a local university. The pilot showed that the Bubble Lens improved performance over the other cursors in both movement time and error rate for effective sizes 16 pixels or below. Thus we allowed the Bubble Lens to deploy for effective sizes 16 pixels or below.

3.6 Full Study

In order to better understand and validate the findings from the pilot we conducted a larger validation study with the same factors as above but with a larger sample size. The study was conducted to determine if the augmented cursor improvements held within a larger statistical sample, and to identify the situations in which the cursors did well.

3.6.1 Participants

Eighteen people participated in the study (12 male, 6 female) and all were university students. The age of participants ranged from 18 to 24, with an average age of 20.5. Fourteen of the participants indicated prior experience with a gestural input device.

3.6.2 Performance Results

Movement time (recorded from first cursor movement until target selection) and error rate (percentage of trials in which the goal target was not successfully selected on the first attempt) were recorded for and are shown in Table 1.

Given that the experiment was within-subjects, a repeated measures analysis of variance for both movement time and error rate were performed. The results for movement time were as followed: significant difference between cursor types (ggF (1.552, 26.383) = 110.933, $p < 0.001$, $\eta_p^2 = 0.867$), a significant difference between effective sizes (ggF (2.230, 37.909) = 76.508, $p < 0.001$, $\eta_p^2 = 0.818$), and a significant difference between effective sizes and cursor type (ggF (3.179, 54.044) = 14.303, $p < 0.001$, $\eta_p^2 = 0.457$). A post-hoc test with Fisher's LSD showed statistical significance between all pairs, with all pairs reporting p<.001. We therefore also measured effect size in Cohen's d with pooled variance to evaluate practical significance. An effect size below .2 is generally considered insignificant, .2 to .5 is considered small, .5 to .8 is considered medium, and d above .8 is considered large. We found an effect size of 0.70 between Point Cursor and Bubble Cursor, an effect size of 1.30 between Point Cursor and Bubble Lens, and an effect size of 0.87 between Bubble Cursor and Bubble Lens.

For error rate there was a significant difference between cursor types (ggF (1.959, 33.296) = 93.270, $p < 0.001$, $\eta_p^2 = 0.846$), a significant difference between effective sizes (ggF (5.265, 89.512) = 59.708, $p < 0.001$, $\eta_p^2 = 0.778$), and a significant difference between effective sizes and cursor type (ggF (7.274, 123.652) = 4.870, $p < 0.001$, $\eta_p^2 = 0.223$). post-hoc test with Fisher's LSD showed statistical significance between all pairs, with all pairs reporting p<.001. We likewise measured effect size in Cohen's d with pooled variance. This showed an effect size of 0.64 between Point Cursor and Bubble Cursor, an effect size of 1.76 between Point Cursor and Bubble Lens, and an effect size of 1.02 between Bubble Cursor and Bubble Lens.

3.6.3 User Feedback

	Point Cur.		Bubble Cur.		Bubble Lens	
	mean	sd	mean	sd	mean	sd
Mental	8.94	5.20	6.67	4.39	4.61	4.00
Physical	11.00	4.81	7.94	3.93	6.78	3.35
Temporal	8.17	5.66	6.56	4.53	7.11	5.32
Performance	10.17	4.68	6.89	3.51	5.72	3.34
Effort	14.56	4.12	10.94	4.17	8.83	4.46
Frustration	13.89	4.97	7.72	4.20	6.78	5.02

Table 2: Mean and standard deviations of workload ratings (NASA TLX) for each cursor. Lower is better for all.

After each round of the experiment, participants filled out a NASA TLX survey [7]. Workload was assessed using six scales for mental demand, physical demand, temporal demand, performance, effort, and frustration. The means and standard deviation of each feature is shown in table 2. From this table we see that, in general, participants rated Bubble Lens better than the Bubble Cursor, and the Bubble Cursor better than the Point Cursor. Friedman's tests for significance showed the following: mental demand ($\chi^2(2) = 7.62$, $p = 0.022$), physical demand ($\chi^2(2) = 13.0$, $p = 0.002$), temporal demand ($\chi^2(2) = 3.39$, $p = 0.184$), performance ($\chi^2(2) = 15.13$, $p < 0.001$), effort ($\chi^2(2) = 22.12, p < .001$), and frustration ($\chi^2(2) = 21.88, p < .001$). A pairwise test of significance was done with Dunn's test (Table 3). The Bubble Lens was rated significantly better than the Point Cursor in all aspects except temporal demand.

	PC - BC		PC - BL		BC - BL	
	Z	p	Z	p	Z	p
Mental	1.17	.120	2.86	**.002**	1.69	**.046**
Physical	1.84	**.033**	2.83	**.002**	1.00	.161
Temporal	0.78	.219	0.61	.271	-0.17	.435
Performance	2.17	.015	3.01	**.001**	0.84	.200
Effort	2.54	.006	3.81	**.000**	1.27	.103
Frustration	3.60	.000	3.91	**.000**	0.35	.363

Table 3: Pairwise significance testing with Dunn's test for all possible pairs of Point Cursor (PC), Bubble Cursor (BC) and Bubble Lens (BL). Z-statistic and p-values are shown, significance at ($p < .05$) is bolded

4. DISCUSSION

The results of our study showed that enhancing gestural interaction with augmented cursors improves performance, specifically the movement time used to select a target and the error rate. This is similar to previous research in mouse interaction[9]. The results also indicated that the Bubble Lens cursor improved performance more than the Bubble Cursor, as demonstrated with a high effect size. The magnification provided by the Bubble Lens may be a key factor in improving gestural interaction, which tends to be less accurate than mouse interaction, especially for small targets.

Subjective feedback from our participants showed that the augmented cursors did lead to better ratings for gestures, with nearly all workload measures significantly improved. Effort and frustration especially showed large differences between the Point Cursor and the two augmented cursors. The workload ratings show that augmented cursors can improve not only performance for gestural interaction, but also the users' experience, which may aid in making gestures a more practical form of daily computer interaction.

5. CONCLUSION

In this paper, our goal was to assess the performance and usability of gestural interaction that has been enhanced with augmented cursors. We compared the standard Point Cursor, Bubble Cursor, and Bubble Lens cursor. We found that the augmented cursors significantly improved both the movement time and error rate of gestural interaction, with the Bubble Lens cursor showing the best performance.

6. FUTURE WORK

This work has shown the effectiveness of augmented cursors in gestural interaction with small targets, but at what size does the augmented cursor stop being beneficial, if ever? By increasing the size of the targets over the course of experimentation, additional application and conclusion can be made about the potential of this interaction. Additionally the approach works with any device which can sense orientation (3+ DOF), potentially allowing for direct external display control using a smartphone or smartwatch. Future experiments might further investigate the power of magnification in improving gestural interaction. Some individuals, especially those with motor impairments, poor vision, or lower hand-eye coordination, may benefit from higher levels of magnification. The ability to automatically detect and adjust the magnification level may be helpful in such cases. Finally, our experiments were conducted in a desktop set-

ting, but it would make sense to perform a similar form of experiment in AR/VR setting where gestures are more prevalent.

7. REFERENCES

[1] G. Bailly, J. Müller, M. Rohs, D. Wigdor, and S. Kratz. Shoesense: a new perspective on gestural interaction and wearable applications. In *Proceedings of the SIGCHI Conference on Human Factors in Computing Systems*, pages 1239–1248. ACM, 2012.

[2] O. Chapuis, J.-B. Labrune, and E. Pietriga. Dynaspot: speed-dependent area cursor. In *Proceedings of the SIGCHI Conference on Human Factors in Computing Systems*, pages 1391–1400. ACM, 2009.

[3] B. Ens, J. D. Hincapié-Ramos, and P. Irani. Ethereal planes: a design framework for 2d information space in 3d mixed reality environments. In *Proceedings of the 2nd ACM symposium on Spatial user interaction*, pages 2–12. ACM, 2014.

[4] T. Grossman and R. Balakrishnan. The bubble cursor: enhancing target acquisition by dynamic resizing of the cursor's activation area. In *Proceedings of the SIGCHI conference on Human factors in computing systems*, pages 281–290. ACM, 2005.

[5] D. Guinness, A. Jude, G. M. Poor, and A. Dover. Models for rested touchless gestural interaction. In *Proceedings of the 3rd ACM Symposium on Spatial User Interaction*, pages 34–43. ACM, 2015.

[6] D. Guinness, A. Seung, A. Dover, G. M. Poor, and A. Jude. Modeling mid-air gestures with spherical coordinates. In *Proceedings of the 3rd ACM Symposium on Spatial User Interaction*, pages 133–133. ACM, 2015.

[7] S. G. Hart and L. E. Staveland. Development of nasa-tlx (task load index): Results of empirical and theoretical research. In P. A. Hancock and N. Meshkati, editors, *Human Mental Workload*, volume 52 of *Advances in Psychology*, pages 139 – 183. North-Holland, 1988.

[8] R. Kopper, F. Bacim, and D. A. Bowman. Rapid and accurate 3d selection by progressive refinement. In *3D User Interfaces (3DUI), 2011 IEEE Symposium on*, pages 67–74. IEEE, 2011.

[9] M. E. Mott and J. O. Wobbrock. Beating the bubble: using kinematic triggering in the bubble lens for acquiring small, dense targets. In *Proceedings of the SIGCHI Conference on Human Factors in Computing Systems*, pages 733–742. ACM, 2014.

[10] D. Vogel and R. Balakrishnan. Distant freehand pointing and clicking on very large, high resolution displays. In *Proceedings of the 18th annual ACM symposium on User interface software and technology*, pages 33–42. ACM, 2005.

[11] J. P. Wachs, M. Kölsch, H. Stern, and Y. Edan. Vision-based hand-gesture applications. *Communications of the ACM*, 54(2):60–71, 2011.

[12] J. O. Wobbrock, J. Fogarty, S.-Y. S. Liu, S. Kimuro, and S. Harada. The angle mouse: target-agnostic dynamic gain adjustment based on angular deviation. In *Proceedings of the SIGCHI Conference on Human Factors in Computing Systems*, pages 1401–1410. ACM, 2009.

Desktop Orbital Camera Motions Using Rotational Head Movements

Thibaut Jacob[1], Gilles Bailly[1], Eric Lecolinet[1], Géry Casiez[2], Marc Teyssier[1]
[1]LTCI, CNRS, Telecom ParisTech, France, [2]Université de Lille, France
{thibaut.jacob,gilles.bailly,eric.lecolinet,marc.teyssier}@telecom-paristech.fr,
gery.casiez@univ-lille1.fr

ABSTRACT

In this paper, we investigate how head movements can serve to change the viewpoint in 3D applications, especially when the viewpoint needs to be changed quickly and temporarily to disambiguate the view. We study how to use yaw and roll head movements to perform orbital camera control, i.e., to rotate the camera around a specific point in the scene. We report on four user studies. Study 1 evaluates the useful resolution of head movements. Study 2 informs about visual and physical comfort. Study 3 compares two interaction techniques, designed by taking into account the results of the two previous studies. Results show that head roll is more efficient than head yaw for orbital camera control when interacting with a screen. Finally, Study 4 compares head roll with a standard technique relying on the mouse and the keyboard. Moreover, users were allowed to use both techniques at their convenience in a second stage. Results show that users prefer and are faster (14.5%) with the head control technique.

Keywords

Head motion; 3D interaction; camera control; transfer function

1. INTRODUCTION

Manipulating 3D objects require designers to frequently change the viewpoint to avoid occlusion, see details, perceive depth or get a global view of the scene [6]. Interaction techniques using the mouse or the keyboard have been proposed to manipulate the viewpoint [6, 9], but this requires users to use the same modality (hand gestures) to control both what they see and manipulate. As a result, users must continuously switch between editing tasks and camera control, which interrupts their workflow, may impair their attention and increase execution time [6, 12, 28].

In the physical world, humans use head and eyes movements to control what they see and limbs movements to manipulate objects. Using head movements as an additional input channel to control camera motion may thus provide better comfort and increase the interaction bandwidth. This may be especially true when the viewpoint needs to be changed quickly and temporarily to disambiguate the view. A quick glance often suffices for this purpose, head interaction seem an efficient and natural way of performing to-and-fro temporary movements of the camera. Moreover, head-camera coupling may provide a more ecological visual perception of 3D scenes [18].

Head movement has been used in several studies to improve the feeling of immersion in Virtual Reality environments, either using head-mounted displays [32] or CAVEs [11]. But this approach has seldom been investigated for desktop workstations [20] although such an approach can be implemented at little cost as many computers have an integrated webcam.

In this paper, we investigate how to best define head-camera couplings to favor both comfort and efficiency [6]. We focus on *orbital control* because this type of camera motion is frequently used in 3D software (Blender, SketchUp), especially in 3D room-planning applications (IKEA Home Planner) or 3D sound interfaces. We focus on screen desktop environments because they are still the most used for 3D editing.

In this context, we report the findings of four user studies. Study 1 investigates the widest angles at which users can rotate the head on yaw and roll axes while maintaining a high level of physical and visual comfort. Results show that,

SUI '16, October 15-16, 2016, Tokyo, Japan
© 2016 ACM. ISBN 978-1-4503-4068-7/16/10. . . $15.00
DOI: http://dx.doi.org/10.1145/2983310.2985758

Figure 1: *Left.* Envisioned system: Yaw or roll rotations are captured with a webcam for orbital camera control. *Right.* Experimental setup: The head orientation is measured using a tree target attached to a cap.

when taking into account both criteria, larger head angles can be performed for roll ($35°$) than for yaw ($26°$).

Study 2 investigates the useful resolution [1] i.e. the smallest movements that can be willingly operated by users. Results show that (a) the useful resolution is $1°$ for a 95% success rate for both head yaw and roll and (b) that accuracy decreases with larger starting angles and with smaller amplitudes.

Building on these studies, we designed a transfer function for controlling orbital camera motion with the head. We derived two multimodal interaction techniques combining head movement (either roll or yaw) for controlling the camera and mouse input for selecting objects in a 3D scene. Study 3 compares the performance (success rate, time of completion) of these two techniques on a 3D task. Results show that participants performed better and preferred using roll than yaw.

Finally, Study 4 compares the technique using head roll with a standard technique relying on the mouse/keyboard. Results show that users are faster (14.5%) with our technique and they find it more comfortable.

2. RELATED WORK

2.1 Camera controls in 3D software

3D applications such as Unity Editor or Blender provide multiple camera controls (Table 1) that rely on the mouse and/or the keyboard. Camera *tilting* or *orbit control* (the camera rotates around a specific point in the scene, keeping this point in the center of the viewport) are generally performed by dragging the mouse or by pressing dedicated keys. Camera *translations* usually rely on arrow keys. The mouse wheel is typically used for *zooming*. Other camera controls (e.g., *fly mode* or roll motions) generally require using buttons on a toolbar.

As shown in Table 1, floor planning applications provide orbit control on two axes (yaw and pitch) so that the user can rotate around the scene both horizontally and vertically. Horizontal orbit control is especially useful for changing the viewpoint quickly. More generally, applications for 3D room planning, 3D sound editing or real-time strategy games (e.g. StarCraft) constrain camera motion and only provide a subset of camera controls. These applications tend to favor orbital camera control with a fixed height to obtain an isometric point of view, which is especially appropriate in this context.

Software	Orbit	Pan	Tilt
Blender, Maya	all axes	all axes	all axes
SketchUp	yaw, pitch	y, z	yaw, pitch
Google Earth	no	all axes	all axes
MeshLab	yaw, pitch, roll	x, y, z	no
IKEA Home Planner	yaw, pitch	x, z	no
floorplanner.com	yaw, pitch	x, z	no
RoomSketcher	yaw, pitch	z	yaw, pitch

Table 1: Camera controls commonly used in 3D applications

Numerous academic interaction techniques have been proposed for controlling the camera[38, 17, 39, 22, 3]. In this wide literature, we focus on head-camera coupling.

2.2 Head-camera coupling

Head-camera coupling has been investigated in different contexts such as desktop workstations [4], mobile devices [19, 10], tabletops [35] or CAVE systems [11], as well as different applications such as VR [22, 13], video-conferencing [20, 39], video games [23], teleoperation [29], accessibility [21] or surgery [33]. Therefore, different mappings were proposed:

Fishtank. Fishtank VR [38] is probably the most famous head-camera coupling. It enhances the perception of distance in 3D scenes with motion parallax. This technique couples the position of the camera to the position of the user's head. While it provides a sense of immersion in 3D scenes, this technique only allows relatively small displacements and cannot be used to inspect the different sides of an object.

Tilting. Tilting consists of rotating the camera around its own center. In VR [23], it is generally coupled to head yaw and pitch (e.g., in Occulus Rift games) but other mappings have been proposed in the literature [17, 39]. Some techniques combine multiple camera controls, such as [27] which combines Fishtank and tilting to extend the user's field of view.

Orbiting. In head-camera coupling systems, orbit control is performed around the vertical axis and coupled to the yaw rotation of the head [22]. In contrast, we aim at understanding which of yaw or roll rotations of the head is most appropriate for orbiting the camera.

2.3 Transfer function

Various transfer functions can be applied to transform head movements into camera motions. One approach consists in scaling head movements with a constant value (Control-Display gain or CD gain) [36, 24]. Teather et al. [36] considered gain values of 2, 3 and 5 to increase the amplitude of camera motion in a Fishtank system. Results showed no significant effect on time nor accuracy but participants preferred a 1:3 gain. Mulder et al. [27] amplified tilting rotations by a factor of 2 to extend the users' field of view. Poupyrev et al. [30] studied the performance of non-isomorphic rotations (1.8:1) against a 1:1 mapping. Results showed a 13% speed improvement for the latter for large amplitudes. Other amplification factors (1:1, 2:1, 3:1, 4:1) have been tested in [24], with a 15% speed improvement for a 3:1 gain without significant loss in accuracy compared to 1:1.

Non-linear gains have also been considered, as in [31] where, for 3D rotations, the gain remains constant to 1 under a certain threshold then becomes non-linear. PRISM [16] is a rotation technique where the rotation gain depends on the speed of the user. Offset recovery is provided in order to null the offset that is progressively accumulated. A drawback of this approach is its non nulling-compliance [30, 6].

3. DESIGN RATIONALE

We now describe the design rationale that motivated the studies and the techniques presented in this article.

3.1 Camera control and 3D editing

Editing a 3D virtual scene with a desktop application is a complex task involving many operations such as adding and removing objects, editing vertices position or modifying object properties, etc. Camera control is crucial to avoid occlusion, observe objects under different perspectives, explore the 3D scene or enhance depth perception through motion.

However, as mentioned in the introduction, camera control might interrupt the users' workflow, impair attention and increase completion time [6, 12, 28, 34].

As an example, let's consider a user who wants to move an object outside of the field of view of the camera. The user will have to 1) rotate and move the camera as far as possible while maintaining the object in the field of view; 2) drag the object in the direction of the desired location until reaching the border of the 3D scene; 3) repeat these operations until the object is close enough to the target location. Our objective is to reduce the cost of these interleave operations and to let users focus on their primary task, the edition of the 3D scene.

Using head movement to control the camera enables leaving the hands free for performing manipulation tasks, as in the physical world. This may be especially useful when the viewpoint needs to be temporarily changed, as when moving objects in the previous example, or if a quick to-and-fro movement of the camera is needed to disambiguate the view.

3D applications (Table 1) provide various types of camera motions, which availability depends on the application. However, interviews with CG artists and an analysis of 3D editing tools (Maya, Blender, MeshLab) and floor planning applications showed that orbit control is especially useful when editing a scene because it maintains the focus on the objects of interest, which allows users to easily rotate around them. Consequently, we chose to focus our study on this type of camera control.

While we focus on orbital control in this article, other head movements could also be used to control other camera movements such as zooming, panning etc. as will be discussed in the last section. However, controlling the camera with the head is probably mostly useful for camera controls that occur very frequently. Controlling many camera movements with the head might be ambiguous and hard to perform. Standard techniques relying on the mouse or the keyboard are probably more appropriate for camera controls that are seldom used.

3.2 Head movement

The head has six degrees of freedom (Figure 1) three degrees of rotation (yaw, roll, pitch) and three degrees of translation (T_x, T_y, T_z). However, they cannot be fully combined due to biomechanical constraints. We conducted a brainstorming session to find out which kind of input would be most suited for controlling orbital motion. We did not consider translations because they are difficult to perform while seating in a working chair. While the T_x translation seemed easier to perform, we observed that in fact participants tended to roll the head. We also withdrew pitch rotations because a pilot study revealed that participants did not spontaneously use such rotations for orbital control. We thus retained two types of head movements: *yaw* and *roll* rotations, which have a respective average amplitude of 70° and 40° in both directions [37].

In order to make the technique simple and mostly similar to what people do in the physical world, we decided to use position control and to limit the need of clutching. Hence, an appropriate rotation of the head produces an homothetic movement of the camera, according to the CD gain coefficient (which calculation is detailed below). Besides simplicity, another reason we chose position control rather than rate control is that the latter is more suitable for isomet-

ric or elastic devices (e.g. a joystick). Such devices feature a self-centering mechanism to return to their neutral state when released [8], which is not the case with the head. Finally, clutching tends to require additional movements, thus additional time [8, 14].

However, while head movement seems an efficient and natural way for performing temporary movements of the camera, it may not be appropriate for long editing sequences. Rotating the head is convenient if the user needs to hold her position for a limited amount of time, but a static posture may become unconfortable for longer periods. Head rotations may also be insufficient for covering long distances. For instance, a rotation of more than 360° would force users to go over (if even possible) their physiological limit. To alleviate this limitation, we made our technique *fully compatible* with existing mouse or keyboard camera controls. Hence, users can still use the mouse or the keyboard to change the default viewpoint. Once it is defined, head motion can be used for frequent and short camera movements.

3.3 CD gain

The CD gain is a unit-free coefficient which maps head movement to camera motion. With a CD gain of 1, the camera and the head are rotating by an identical amount. It turns proportionality farther and faster for a larger gain and covers less angular distance but offers higher precision for smaller values. A task can be characterized by the maximum camera angular distance A_{max}^{cam} and (depending on the smallest target size) the minimum angle W_{min}^{cam} needed to properly accomplish this task. The minimal CD gain is represented by the following formula:

$$CDgain_{min} = \frac{A_{max}^{cam}}{A_{max}^{head}} \quad (1)$$

where A_{max}^{head} is the widest angle users can perform during head rotations. This value might depend on the rotation axis (yaw vs. roll). Similarly, the maximal CD gain is:

$$CDgain_{max} = \frac{W_{min}^{cam}}{\hat{R}} \quad (2)$$

where $\hat{R}$ is the *useful resolution* of the device, i.e., the smallest movement users can willingly operate.

The task cannot be achieved if $CDgain_{min} > CDgain_{max}$ as, either the farthest target could not be reached or the smallest target could not be selected. Clutching is then necessary to move the camera over longer distances without impairing precision (see Discussion). The next sections present two user studies we conducted to estimate A_{max}^{head} and the useful resolution $\hat{R}$.

3.4 Resolution measurement

Device Resolution. While our technique is intended to work with non expensive equipment such as an embedded webcam (see the Discussion and the video), we used an ART motion capture system (www.ar-tracking.com/) for the sake of precision in the following experiments. The setup consisted of a cap with a mounted passive tree target (Figure 1).

We first conducted a pilot study to estimate R_{device}, the precision of our motion capture system. Due to environmental conditions (distance between the camera and the markers, lighting conditions, etc.) raw measurements are noisy even when the markers are perfectly stable. In order to get a better estimation of the device resolution, we used a method inspired by Bérard et al. that consists in positioning the input device at a fixed position and recording output during a given amount of time [5]. The estimated resolution then equals four times the standard deviation. We collected raw data for one hour with a passive tree target (ART TT3) fixed on a table. Results showed a R_{device} precision higher than 0.05° for all rotation axes, a value almost twenty times more precise than human head movements (as will be seen in Study 2).

Effective resolution of the head. We distinguish the useful resolution $\hat{R}$, which is the smallest movement users can willingly operate, and the *effective resolution* R_{eff}^{head} (or head noise) which represents the amount of movement users perform while remaining still because of uncontrolled tremor. This value is useful to ensure the stability of the interaction and avoid uncomfortable jitters. To estimate R_{eff}^{head}, we conducted a pilot study where participants were asked to remain still during 1 minute. A visual feedback (white cursor) represented the current orientations (yaw and roll) to guide participants. For each second interval we computed the range of movement, and obtained an average range of movement R_{eff}^{head} of 0.2°. This value is 4 times larger than the noise of the motion capture system we previously mentioned ($R_{device} = 0.05°$).

4. STUDY 1: COMFORT

The goal of this study was to estimate the widest angle users can perform during yaw and roll head rotations while maintaining a high level of *physical* and *visual* comfort. Biomechanic studies state that humans can perform larger yaw (70°) than roll rotations (40°) [37]. However, these studies focused on physiological amplitudes and did not consider the level of visual nor physical comfort when interacting with a screen.

4.1 Experimental design

Participants and Apparatus. 12 participants (3 females) aged 23 to 33 ($\bar{x} = 28; \sigma = 2.66$) were recruited from our institution via mailing lists and received a handful of candies for their participation. The setup (Figure 1) was a MacBook Pro laptop connected to an external 17-Inch screen, an external keyboard and a mouse. Participants controlled the keyboard using their non-dominant hand and the mouse using the other hand. The screen was at a distance of 50 cm from the participant. The seat could not be rotated.

Stimulus and task. Participants performed a visual search task. The stimulus was a 3-letter word [7] displayed on the top of the screen. Participants had to find this word in a 7×7 grid full of distractors as fast and accurately as possible.

Conditions. We both tested *Yaw* and *Roll* ROTATIONS. As said before, we withdrew pitch head movements because they were not spontaneously used by participants for this task in a pilot study. We also controlled the DIRECTION of the rotations (*Left* or *Right*).

Procedure. We first asked the participants to put their head in resting position and calibrated our tracking system to that the participants' resting positions corresponded to 0°. The system then indicated a rotation axis (Yaw or Roll) and a direction (Left or Right). Participants turned their head until reaching the largest amplitude ensuring (1) visual comfort (the screen remains in the field of view of the participant) and (2) physical comfort (no muscular tension

of the neck nor the eyes). Once they adopted the chosen posture, they pressed the space bar to start the visual search task. The trial finished as soon as the participant clicked on the target word.

Design. We used a within-participant design. The order of appearance of the conditions was counterbalanced between participants. Each condition was repeated seven times. The name and the location of the targets were randomly picked from a set of pre-defined values. For each trial, we measured the rotation angle when participants found the target word. In summary, the experimental design was: 12 Participants × 2 ROTATIONS (Yaw and Roll) × 2 DIRECTIONS (Left and Right) × 7 Repetitions = 336 selections.

4.2 Results and discussion

The results are summarized in Table 2. ANOVA revealed a significant effect for ROTATION on Angle ($F_{1,33} = 26.1, p < .0001$). A post Tukey test showed that users performed wider angles for *Roll* (35.3°) than *Yaw* (25.8°) rotations. No DIRECTION or ROTATION × DIRECTION effect was found on angles. ANOVA confirmed that the conditions had no effect on the visual search task (speed and accuracy).

Because bio-mechanic studies showed that humans can perform larger yaw than roll rotations [25], we expected "comfortable" rotations to be larger for yaw. Our results show an opposite effect because participants had to perform (1) comfortable head movements while (2) looking at the screen. Participants reported that yaw rotations quickly became visually uncomfortable because the screen shifted out of their field of view. This effect will be emphasized with larger screen as the user's field of view will cover less screen space. In contrast, participants' field of view remained unchanged during roll rotations.

Rotation	Direction (°)	Angle (°)	CI
Yaw	Left	25.0	3.7
	Right	26.5	3.2
Roll	Left	36.8	6.9
	Right	33.9	6.9

Table 2: Average and 95% confidence interval (CI) for the maximum comfortable angles for Rotation and Direction.

5. STUDY 2: USEFUL RESOLUTION

The objective of this experiment was to study the *useful resolution* of rotational head movements, i.e. the smallest movements that can be willingly operated by users.

5.1 Experimental design

Participants and Apparatus. We used the same participants and apparatus than in the previous study.

Method. We followed a methodology similar to Aceituno et al. [1] to find the useful resolution of the head. This method aims at defining the *smallest displacement users can reliably produce.* It differs from methods aiming at defining the smallest target size that users can acquire (such as [5]) because it focuses on controlling ballistic and corrective sub-movements users perform. This method has been successfully used to investigate human limits in small unidirectional mouse movements. In contrast, we apply this

Figure 2: Participants first move the handle with the head to reach the initial orientation. When the initial orientation is reached, the section becomes green. Participants then press the spacebar to start the trial.

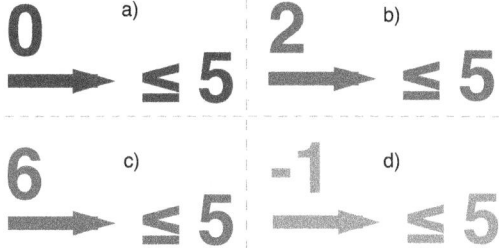

Figure 3: The different states of a trial are color coded: during trial (a), trial validated (b), trial failed (c), trial canceled (d).

method to find the human limits in small rotational (yaw and roll) head movements.

The main procedure of this method is the following: (1) choose a wide maximum amplitude (A) to test the resolution (R_A); (2) ask participants to perform a rotational head movement smaller than A. Repeat this action k times and compute the success rate (S_A); (3) choose a lower amplitude (A) and return to step 2; (4) the useful resolution $\hat{R}$ is the greatest R_A for which the success rate (S_A) $\geq 95\%$.

Factors. We controlled four factors: ROTATION was either *Yaw* or *Roll*. DIRECTION was either *Left* or *Right*. We also considered the INITIAL ORIENTATION of the head because we hypothesized it could influence the useful resolution of head rotations due to biomechanical constraints. We thus defined three different values of INITIAL ORIENTATION for each type of ROTATION: 0°, 10°, 20° for yaw and 0°, 20°, 30° for roll. These values are compatible with the findings of Study 1: (1) they are under the comfortable angles for each type of rotation; (2) initial rotations are larger for roll than for yaw. Finally, we controlled RESOLUTION, i.e. the maximal amplitude participants should not exceed. We chose the following values from pilot studies: 1°, 0.8°, 0.6°, 0.4°.

Task. Users performed a rotation of the head from an initial orientation along a specific direction with an amplitude inferior to a threshold value. A trial was divided into three steps as illustrated in Figure 2 and Figure 3 : (1) participants first rotated their head to an initial orientation by bringing the white vertical bar (handle) inside the corresponding interval (Figure 2 a). (2) Then, they pressed the space bar (Figure 2 b). (3) The system indicated the direction and the maximum amplitude they could rotate the head (Figure 3 a). Participants performed the corresponding movement. They were instructed to do their best to stay within this interval. The trial started with the first rotation of the head captured through the motion capture device and ended either when the movement exceeded the maximum amplitude

(failed trial, Figure 3 c) or the head *stopped moving* within the maximum amplitude (Figure 3 b) during 1 second [1]. Any movements reported in the opposite direction to the target canceled the current trial [1] (Figure 3 d). The participant would then repeat the trial until passing or failing it. A change in direction was detected when the amplitude exceeded one count unit.

Count unit. The count unit (*Count*) was estimated from the effective resolution of the head (head noise). This is a main difference with the protocol used in [1]. The reason is that hand noise is very small in comparison to head noise due to the stable position of the mouse on the table. In contrast, head tremor (0.2°) is larger than the resolution of the device (0.05°).

We thus decided to refine the definition of the count unit as:

$$Count = max(R_{device}, R_{eff}^{head}) = max(0.05, 0.2) = 0.2°$$
$$(3)$$

so that the amplitude of uncontrolled movements when users wanted to remain still would not be inferior to a count unit.

Design. We used a within subject experimental design. ROTATION, DIRECTION and INITIAL ORIENTATION were counterbalanced between participants. RESOLUTION was presented in descending order. In summary, the experimental design was: 12 participants $\times$ 2 ROTATIONS $\times$ 2 INITIAL ORIENTATIONS $\times$ 5 RESOLUTIONS $\times$ 10 repetitions = 2400 trials.

5.2 Results

The results are summarized in Figure 4. ANOVA confirmed a significant effect of RESOLUTION on accuracy ($F_{4,190} = 62.5, p < .0001$). However, no other significant effect was found. Results show that participants required at least 5 counts to successfully complete the task 95% of the time. From these results, we estimated the value of the useful resolution $\hat{R}$ for both yaw and roll rotations: $\hat{R} = 5 \times 0.2 = 1°$.

6. STUDY 3: TECHNIQUE COMPARISON

The goal of this study was to compare the impact of the rotation axes on both speed and accuracy on a task involv-

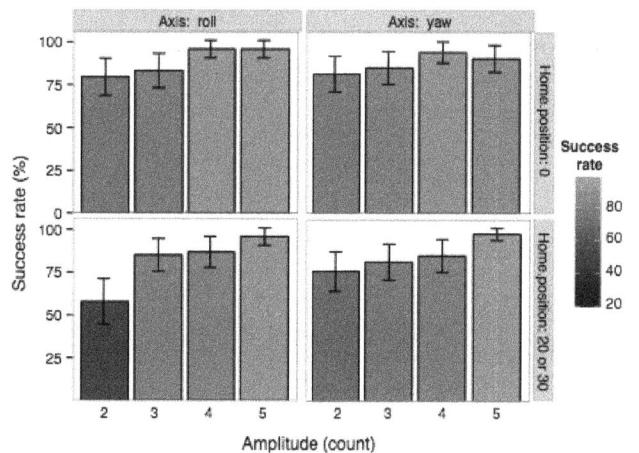

Figure 4: Success rates across all participants in percentage on both axes for both orientations and amplitudes. Amplitudes shown in counts.

ing head-camera coupling. To achieve this, we derived two interaction techniques.

Interaction Techniques. With both techniques, users perform orbital camera control with head movements while selecting and manipulating objects with the mouse. These techniques only differ in the movement controlling the camera: roll rotations in the first case, and yaw rotations in the second case.

We initially decided to compare our techniques to PRISM[16] because this technique provides an advanced transfer function designed for rotational motion. PRISM dynamically adjusts the control/display gain to provide increased control when moving slowly. However, it can accumulate an offset value representing the angular displacement between the head and the object being manipulated. PRISM provides offset recovery when the user exceeds a certain angular speed. But, pilot studies revealed that this technique does not work well for high gain values because the offset is quite important and it is difficult to predict when the offset recovery will occur. With a gain value of 6 or 7, the camera can turn 12 to $18°$ per iteration with the consequence that participants get lost in the 3D scene. We thus decided to discard this technique from our study.

6.1 Experimental design

Participants and Apparatus. Twelve participants (4 females) aged 23 to 36 ($\bar{x} = 27.4; \sigma = 3.8$) were recruited via mailing lists and word-of-mouth. They received a handful of candies for participation. 5 of the participants performed the study 1 or the study 2. We used the same apparatus as in the previous experiment.

Task. The task, which is inspired from floor planner tasks, involves the placement of a 3D object (a ball) in a target (a bowl on a shelf) in a 3D scene, as shown on Figure 5. This task combines both a head and mouse pointing task: (a) Participants first perform a pointing task with the mouse to select the ball in front of them; (b) They rotate the view (through roll or yaw head rotations depending of the technique) in the direction of the target, which is indicated by a green arrow on the floor of the 3D scene; (c) Once the head of the participants is aligned with the target, the target is highlighted in green; (d) participants then performs a pointing task with the mouse to align the mouse cursor (that carries the ball) with the bowl; (e) They can then throw the ball inside the bowl by pressing the mouse button and (f) return to the initial position to start the next trial. Feedback indicates whether the shoot is correct or missed. A missed shot can either be due to a misalignment between the camera and the target (head movement error) and/or between the cursor and the target (mouse pointing error).

Technique parameters. In this study, we wanted the participants to be able to perform a full orbital movement in each direction ($A_{max}^{cam} = \pm180$) in order to cover $360°$. Based on the findings of studies 1 and 2, we computed the CD gain for yaw and roll rotations as follows:

$$CDgain(yaw) = \frac{A_{max}^{cam}}{A_{max}^{head}(yaw)} = \frac{180}{26} = 6.9 \qquad (4)$$

$$CDgain(roll) = \frac{A_{max}^{cam}}{A_{max}^{head}(roll)} = \frac{180}{35} = 5.1 \qquad (5)$$

We could thus compute the theoretical smallest target width for yaw and roll rotations:

$$W_{min}^{cam}(yaw) = CDgain(yaw) \times \hat{R}(yaw) = 6.9 \times 1 = 6.9. \qquad (6)$$

$$W_{min}^{cam}(roll) = CDgain(roll) \times \hat{R}(roll) = 5.1 \times 1 = 5.1. \qquad (7)$$

Conditions. We controlled three factors in this study: (1) Target WIDTH defines the angular range for which the participant is aligned with the target. We chose four values in the vicinity of the CD gain of our techniques: $4°$, $5.1°$, $6°$ and $6.9°$; (2) Target DISTANCE: As we wanted to cover $2 \times 180°$, we chose both close and far targets: $28°$, $68°$, $113°$ and $158°$; (3) DIRECTION: The target was located either on the left or right side of the participant.

Procedure. The experimenter first explained the task. Participants then practiced the two techniques before starting the experiment. During this phase, they were free to change mouse sensitivity to their liking. Participants were generally satisfied with the default settings. They could also reverse the direction of the mapping toward positive or negative angles (i.e. rotating the head to the right would either rotate the camera to the right or to the left). Indeed, we noticed that some participants did not have the same mental model of the scene (11/12 used the default mapping on the roll axis, 8/12 on the yaw). Participants then performed the experiment during 1 hour. We invited them to take a break after each series of 5 trials. At the end of the experiment, participants were asked to answer a NASA TLX questionnaire to assess cognitive load, fatigue, strategies of use and ease of use for the various techniques.

Design. We used a repeated measures-within subject experimental design. Technique was counter-balanced between participants. WIDTH, DISTANCE and DIRECTION were countbalanced between techniques. For each condition, participants performed 5 trials. We measured completion time and success rate. In summary, the experimental design was : 12 participants $\times$ 2 ROTATIONS $\times$ 2 DIRECTIONS $\times$ 4 target WIDTHS $\times$ 4 target angular DISTANCES $\times$ 5 repetitions $= 3840$ trials.

6.2 Results

Accuracy. Repeated measures multi-way ANOVA reveals a significant effect for ROTATION on Accuracy ($F_{1,11} = 13.2, p < .001$). A post-hoc Tukey test shows that Roll (92%) is more accurate than Yaw (88%). ANOVA also reveals a significant effect for WIDTH on Accuracy ($F_{3,33} = 10.3, p < .0001$). A post-hoc Tukey test shows that the smallest target (4°: 85%)

Figure 5: The user must 1) pick up a ball on the floor using the mouse cursor; 2) rotate the view (using yaw or roll head movements depending on the condition) in the direction of the target (which is indicated by a green arrow on the floor); 3) Once the cursor is aligned with the target (highlighted in green), shoot the ball in the target by pressing the mouse button.

is significantly less accurate than the other targets (5.1°: 92%; 6°: 91%, 6.9°: 92%). ANOVA also reveals a significant effect for DIRECTION on Accuracy ($F_{1,11} = 7.2, p < .01$). A post-hoc Tukey test shows that Left (91%) is more accurate than Right (88%). No DISTANCE or interaction effects were found on accuracy.

Selection time. ANOVA reveals a significant effect for ROTATION on Selection time ($F_{1,11} = 61.8, p < .0001$). A post-hoc Tukey test shows that Roll (4.0s) is faster than Yaw (4.6s). ANOVA also reveals significant effects for DISTANCE ($F_{3,33} = 59.7, p < .0001$) and WIDTH ($F_{3,33} = 24.1, p < .0001$) on Selection time. Post-hoc Tukey tests confirm that selection time increases with distance and decreases with target width. No DIRECTION or interaction effects was found.

Return time. ANOVA reveals a significant effect for DISTANCE on Return time ($F_{3,33} = 78.3, p < .0001$). A post-hoc Tukey test confirmed the return time increases with distance. ANOVA also reveals a significant effect for DIRECTION ($F_{3,33} = 7.8, p < .01$). A post-hoc Tukey test shows that Left (1.5s) is faster than Right (1.6s). No ROTATION, WIDTH or interaction effect was found on return time.

Qualitative measures. Kruskal-Wallis tests reveal no effect for ROTATION on physical, temporal or mental demand. 8/12 participants preferred Roll and 10 participants found Roll faster than Yaw. 11 Participants reported that Yaw was too sensitive.

6.3 Modeling

We define the index of difficulty of the task, ID, as $\log(1 + \frac{D}{W})$ where D is the angular distance and W the angular width. A linear regression gives the following coefficients: T $= 1.7 + 0.6$ ID for roll ($R^2 = 0.96$) and T $= 2.5 + 0.5$ ID for yaw ($R^2 = 0.78$). While the model for roll is consistent with Fitts' law [15], it does not seem to be the case for yaw (Figure 6). One possible explanation is that some IDs are too high in the latter case. Another reason might be that, in the case of the yaw axis, the screen shifts out of user view more drastically.

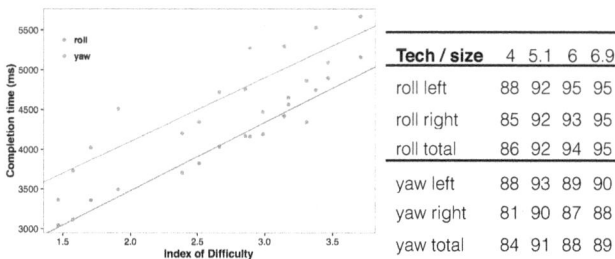

Tech / size	4	5.1	6	6.9
roll left	88	92	95	95
roll right	85	92	93	95
roll total	86	92	94	95
yaw left	88	93	89	90
yaw right	81	90	87	88
yaw total	84	91	88	89

Figure 6: Left: Linear regression model of roll and yaw rotations. Right: Average success rate for each technique, direction and target size.

7. STUDY 4: EXTERNAL VALIDITY

Finally, we performed a last experiment consisting of a 3D manipulating task to see how well our technique fares against a more mainstream approach.

7.1 Experimental design

Participants and Apparatus. Ten participants (2 females) aged 24 to 37 ($\bar{x} = 28.2; \sigma = 4.9$) were recruited. We used the same apparatus as the one used in the previous study.

Task. We chose a standard docking task that requires the user to place a sphere in a specific 3D position (Figure 7). This task is similar to the task of the previous study except that participants must move the ball into the target (Figure 7). The task thus combines *camera control* and *object displacement.*

Users performed orbital *camera control* either with roll head movements or with the mouse or the keyboard. Roll head movements allowed up to 180° of orbital motion in each direction, with the same gain (5.1) as in the previous experiment. Hysteresis was applied to roll movements to prevent jitter and increase stability. We reproduced the mouse and keyboard behavior of the Blender application to orbit the camera: Users had to press (and hold) the wheel button of the mouse to control the camera and the same gain of 2.5 was used. Alternately, users could also use dedicated keys (4 and 6 on the numerical pad). A single key press performed a rotation of 15°. Maintaining a key pressed allowed a continuous camera control with a speed of $360°/s$.

Users could *displace the object* in the camera plane by dragging the mouse (left button). They could also use a 3D helper (Figure 7) with 3 axes and 3 planes, which was attached to the object. This representation is commonly used in 3D applications to constrain the displacements of objects along one (axis) or two (plane) dimensions.

Conditions. We controlled three factors: (1) TECHNIQUE, which was either Head or Mouse/Keyboard, (2) Target DISTANCE, which had three values (68°, 113° and 158°) and DIRECTION, which was either on the left or right side.

Procedure and design. Participants performed several practice rounds for each technique before the experiment and could change angular mapping direction during this stage. Participants performed two sessions. In the first session, participants performed four consecutive blocks with each TECHNIQUE. The order of technique was counterbalanced between participants. Each block contained 6 trials corresponding to 3 DISTANCE × 2 DIRECTION. The order of trials was randomized between blocks and participants.

A second session was performed just after the first one. Participants were now free to choose to use the Head or Mouse/Keyboard *or both* during each trial. We conducted this second session to investigate users preference and whether participants would combine the two techniques. This "free" condition was not performed simultaneously with the previous ones to avoid probable order effect, i.e. participants would have been using these two techniques in a variable number of times depending on their preferences and on presentation order.

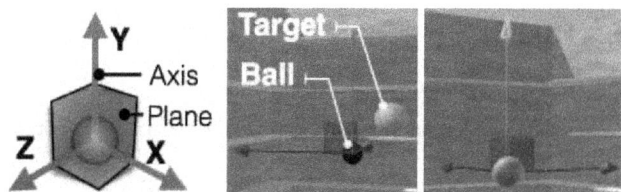

Figure 7: *Left.* **The ball can be displaced in the scene by pulling either on its axes or on its planes.** *Right.* **The participant had to displace the ball into the target using its axes or planes to validate the trial.**

Breaks were scheduled between each block, allowing participants to rest or give feedback. At the end of the experiment, they were asked to answer a NASA TLX questionnaire for the three techniques. The experiment lasted 45 minutes where users tested the different conditions. Overall, the experimental design was: 10 participants × 2+1 Techniques × 4 blocks × 2 Directions × 3 target angular Distances = 720 trials.

7.2 Results

We considered three different time measurements in this experiment: (1) Alignment time: the time taken to align the ball with the target (including the time needed to rotate the viewpoint); (2) Return time: the time needed to return to the home position after aligning the ball with the target; (3) Total time: the overall amount of time to complete the trial. Overall, Head Roll is faster than Mouse/Keyboard for Total (14.5%), Alignment (14.7%) and Return (13.4%) time. Repeated measures multi-way ANOVA reveals no effect (or interaction effect) for BLOCK or DIRECTION.

Total time. ANOVA reveals a significant effect for DISTANCE ($F_{2,18} = 20.2, p < 0.001$) and TECHNIQUE ($F_{1,9} = 9, p < 0.01$) on Total time. A post-hoc Tukey test shows that the largest distance (158°: 11.2s) takes more time than the two other distances (68°: 7.8s; 113°: 8.2s). A post-hoc Tukey test also reveals that Head Roll (8.3s) is faster than Mouse/Keyboard (9.8s).

Alignment time. ANOVA reveals a significant effect for DISTANCE on Alignment time ($F_{2,18} = 15.3, p < 0.001$) and Technique ($F_{1,9} = 7.1, p < 0.01$). A post-hoc Tukey test shows the largest distance (158°: 9.6s) takes more time than the two other distances (68°: 6.7s; 113°: 7s). A post-hoc Tukey test also reveals that Head Roll (7.1s) is faster than Mouse/Keyboard (8.4s).

Return time. ANOVA reveals a significant effect for DISTANCE ($F_{2,18} = 36.2, p < 0.001$) and TECHNIQUE ($F_{1,9} = 12, p < 0.001$) on Return time. A post-hoc Tukey test shows the largest distance (158°: 1.6s) takes more time than the two other distances (68°: 1.1s; 113°: 1.2s). A post-hoc Tukey test also reveals that Head Roll (1.2s) is faster than Mouse/Keyboard (1.4s).

Post-Experiment. During the "Free" condition, 8 participants used a technique involving Head Roll: 6 of them used Head Roll+Keyboard and 2 used Head Roll + Mouse. These participants reported that the combination of Head Roll with either mouse or keyboard was faster and more comfortable. Amongst those who did not use Head Roll, 1 used only the mouse and 1 used only the keyboard.

NASA TLX. Kruskall-Wallis tests revealed no effect for TECHNIQUE on cognitive load, fatigue and ease of use.

8. DISCUSSION

8.1 Human Factors

We investigated how to perform orbital camera control with rotational head movements. Study 1&2 helped to tune the transfer function. Study 3 compared techniques using roll or yaw head movements, and study 4 compared head roll interaction and mouse/keyboard interaction.

Head roll is an efficient input modality for head-camera coupling. Yaw might appear more appropriate for orbital camera control because (1) rotations are performed around the same axis for the head and for the camera, and (2) maximum yaw amplitude is larger than for roll. However, this study shows that participants are faster and more accurate with roll head movements and prefer them when interacting with a screen. Indeed, participants reported that yaw rotations are visually uncomfortable because the screen rapidly shifts out of their field of view. The comfortable range of movement for yaw (26°) is smaller than the range on the roll axis (35°). Most participants also reported that the technique using yaw was too sensitive, due to the high CD gain on this axis. This informs us that the range of "comfortable" yaw movement is too small for 360° camera control.

Direction is more intuitive with roll. Head control may introduce confusion about the direction of camera motion. Eleven out of 12 participants used the default mapping for roll but only 8 for yaw. One participant was not sure whether he should turn the head to the left or to the right.

Users are more accurate on the left side. During study 3, participants were slightly more accurate on the left side, possibly because of the *ocular dominance* effect (also called eye preference) [26] which is the tendency to prefer visual input from one eye to the other. A Miles test [26] revealed that 7 out of the 12 participants in Study 3 had a left dominant eye. A post analysis suggests that users are more accurate for the direction corresponding to their dominant eye (91.6%, $\sigma = 1.2$) than the other direction (88.6%, $\sigma = 1.8$). More participants would however be needed to validate this hypothesis.

Head roll motion and/or mouse/keyboard. Study 4 showed that Head Roll is faster than Mouse/Keyboard for Total completion time, Return time and Alignment time. When proposed to combine these techniques in the final "Free" condition, 8/10 participants chose to combine the head with either the mouse (2/10) or the keyboard (6/10). The Free condition was preferred by 80% of the participants and the total time was lower (7s) than for the Head Roll (8.3s) and Mouse/Keyboard conditions(9.8s). Note however that the Free condition cannot be statistically compared to the two other ones because it was performed in a second session for the reasons above explained. Some participants reported that "keyboard is useful for long distance, once Roll movements start being less comfortable" or to be "very fast by performing Head Roll and keyboard/Mouse movements at the same time".

8.2 Interaction technique

Head roll appears a promising modality to control orbital camera motion. However, an effective deployment requires considering additional factors which are task and platform dependent.

Controlling other camera movements. Even though we focus on orbital camera rotation in this article, other types of camera motions such as zooming, panning, other rotations, are needed in actual applications. Our goal was to make interaction faster and more comfortable when performing very common and frequent viewport manipulations in 3D applications. On the one hand, camera controls that are less often used can be performed using classical techniques that rely on the mouse, the keyboard or additional widgets located on the toolbar. On the other hand, head movement can also be used to control other camera motions without hampering the use of the proposed solution. For instance, yaw and pitch could be used for controlling other rotations and translations along the perpendicular axis of the screen for zooming in and out. We envision to evaluate to which extent these different movements can be performed independently in future work.

Activation. Some application might need a mechanism to specify when the technique is activated to avoid accidental camera viewpoint changes. One solution consists of using an explicit delimiter such as a key, but this would require using the hands. Another solution is to trigger the technique when the user performs a head movement larger than a certain amplitude. This value must be small enough to allow novice users to notice it, and large enough to avoid accidental activation. To determine this value, we recorded head movements of 4 participants over one hour in their usual desktop environment. Results revealed an average movement range on each side of $\pm 7.1°$ for yaw, $\pm 7.5°$ for pitch and only $\pm 5°$ for roll. Another solution enables the technique by default when a dedicated application is running (e.g. Floor planning). Interestingly, it is worth noticing that, no participant complained about potential undesired activation of the Head Roll technique in the Free condition. This can be explained by the fact that roll head movements seem pretty robust against undesirable activation. This may be a supplemental advantage of roll head movements over yaw head movements, which are more likely to be performed inadvertently.

9. APPLICATIONS

We developed three applications using the proposed interaction technique to illustrate its principle. While we used the ART motion capture system for the sake of precision in the previous experiments, we implemented the following application with a regular webcam and a commercial face tracking technology (http://visagetechnologies.com).

Hand-free interaction. Rough drawing allow users to give form to an idea and to evaluate it quickly. While easy in 2D applications, hand-free drawing or free manipulation of objects is more complex in 3D applications because it involves drawing or moving an object, which requires to constantly have the hand on the interaction device but also to manipulate the view. We implemented our technique in a room planner which allows users to focus on the drawing task without being disturbed by a physical hand movement to perform viewport manipulation (Figure 8) with the mouse or keyboard.

Figure 8: Hand-free interaction. User rotating the 3D scene with the head while drawing on a piece of paper.

3D editor. Moving an object in the 3D space generally requires multiple steps for manipulating the object and the camera. We implemented a script editor as an add-on for Unity, a real-time game engine widely used in the field, to check if our method was suitable on a daily basis by CG artists. The participants of our focus study, long-time users of this software, reported that they had the feeling to displace objects faster, thus be more productive for 3D manipulation tasks. It required them only a few minutes to adjust their workflow.

Immersion. Immersion is becoming preeminent in video games. Common solutions either rely on expensive hardware (*Oculus Rift, HTC Vive*) or are often limited to a Fish Tank effect [2]. To expand our technique within immersive environments, we created a First Person Shooter game. The main camera is overlapping the player's head, thus adding our orbital camera manipulation to basic FPS interactions (based on arrows keys to move the character and the mouse for a Mouse Look effect). Using a slight camera rotation, the player can perform subtle moves to reveal enemies behind obstacles while staying hidden. Our method requires less physical engagement from the player than traditional absolute mapping to achieve similar immersive effect.

These prototypes also show that this technique can be combined with other camera manipulations (scroll to zoom, pan) to provide a wider panel of interaction modalities. Moreover, as computing power is crucial for games and for 3D artists, it is worth noticing that it does not require much computing power, which makes it compatible with cpu-intensive and memory demanding tasks.

10. CONCLUSION AND FUTURE WORK

In this paper we reported how head movements can serve to efficiently change the viewpoint in 3D applications while letting the hands free to manipulate 3D objects with the mouse and the keyboard, a feature that seems especially useful when the viewpoint needs to be temporarily changed, as when moving objects in the 3D scene, or if a quick to-and-fro movement of the camera is needed to disambiguate the view. This research was focused on orbital camera control, the most common way to perform viewport rotations in 3D space. With four users studies, our findings are: 1) the useful resolution of the head is $\pm 1°$ for head yaw and roll, 2) head roll provides a wider comfortable amplitude than head yaw, 3) head roll is more efficient and precise than head yaw for 3D orbital control, 4) Head Roll is faster than common mouse or keyboard techniques for orbital camera control and let the hands free for additional input, 5) interaction combining Head Roll and Keyboard is preferred by users. Our findings gives designers of 3D software a solid basis to integrate head-based multi-modal interaction in their software. Future work is required to demonstrate (1) how this technique can be applied in various 3D applications; (2) how it can be applied to other camera controls and (3) what is the impact of the input device (motion capture system vs. webcam) on usability.

11. ACKNOWLEDGMENTS

This research work was supported by the Agence Nationale de la Recherche (ANR 13 CORD 008) and by the EQUIPEX Digiscope ANR-10-EQPX-0026.

12. REFERENCES

[1] J. Aceituno, G. Casiez, and N. Roussel. How low can you go?: Human limits in small unidirectional mouse movements. In *ACM CHI'13*, pages 1383–1386, 2013.

[2] K. W. Arthur, K. S. Booth, and C. Ware. Evaluating 3d task performance for fish tank virtual worlds. *ACM TOIS*, 11(3):239–265, 1993.

[3] R. Balakrishnan and G. Kurtenbach. Exploring bimanual camera control and object manipulation in 3d graphics interfaces. CHI '99, pages 56–62, 1999.

[4] F. Bérard. The Perceptual Window: Head Motion as a new Input Stream. *INTERACT*, pages 1–8, 2014.

[5] F. Bérard, G. Wang, and J. R. Cooperstock. On the limits of the human motor control precision: The search for a device's human resolution. In *INTERACT'11*, pages 107–122. Springer-Verlag, 2011.

[6] D. A. Bowman, E. Kruijff, J. J. LaViola, and I. Poupyrev. *3D User Interfaces: Theory and Practice.* Addison Wesley Longman Publishing Co., Inc., 2004.

[7] BSi. Visual acuity test types - part 1: Test charts for clinical determination of distance visual acuity - specification. BS 4274-1:2003, British Standards Institution, 2003.

[8] G. Casiez and D. Vogel. The effect of spring stiffness and control gain with an elastic rate control pointing device. ACM CHI '08, pages 1709–1718, 2008.

[9] M. Christie, P. Olivier, and J.-M. Normand. Camera control in computer graphics. *Computer Graphics Forum*, 27:2197–2218, 2008.

[10] A. Crossan, M. McGill, S. Brewster, and R. Murray-Smith. Head tilting for interaction in mobile contexts. In *ACM MobileHCI'09*, 2009.

[11] C. Cruz-Neira, D. J. Sandin, and T. A. DeFanti. Surround-screen projection-based virtual reality: The design and implementation of the cave. In *SIGGRAPH '93*, pages 135–142. ACM, 1993.

[12] L. D. Cutler, B. Fröhlich, and P. Hanrahan. Two-handed direct manipulation on the responsive workbench. In *ACM I3D '97*, pages 107–114, 1997.

[13] K. M. Fairchild, B. H. Lee, J. Loo, H. Ng, and L. Serra. The heaven and earth virtual reality: Designing applications for novice users. *IEEE VR*, pages 47–53, 1993.

[14] M. Fiorentino, A. E. Uva, M. Dellisanti Fabiano, and G. Monno. Improving bi-manual 3d input in cad modelling by part rotation optimisation. *Comput. Aided Des.*, 42(5):462–470, May 2010.

[15] P. M. Fitts. The information capacity of the human motor system in controlling the amplitude of movement. *Journal of Experimental Psychology*, 47(6):381, 1954.

[16] S. Frees, G. D. Kessler, and E. Kay. PRISM interaction for enhancing control in immersive virtual environments. *TOCHI*, 14(1), 2007.

[17] A. Fuhrmann, D. Schmalstieg, and M. Gervautz. Strolling Through Cyberspace With Your Hands In Your Pockets: Head Directed Navigation In Virtual Environments, 1998.

[18] E. J. Gibson, J. J. Gibson, O. W. Smith, and H. Flock. Motion parallax as a determinant of perceived depth. *Journal of Experimental Psychology*, pages 40–51, 1959.

[19] T. R. Hansen, E. Eriksson, and A. Lykke-Olesen. Use your head: Exploring face tracking for mobile interaction. In *ACM CHI EA'06*, pages 845–850, 2006.

[20] C. Harrison and A. K. Dey. Lean and zoom: Proximity-aware user interface and content magnification. In *ACM CHI'08*, pages 507–510, 2008.

[21] R. Jagacinski and D. Monk. Fitts' law in two dimensions with hand and head movements. *Journal of Motor Behavior*, 7:77–95, 1985.

[22] D. R. Koller, M. R. Mine, and S. E. Hudson. Head-tracked orbital viewing: an interaction technique for immersive virtual environments. In *ACM UIST '96*, pages 81–82, 1996.

[23] A. Kulshreshth, J. J. LaViola, and Jr. Evaluating performance benefits of head tracking in modern video games. In *SUI '13*, pages 53–60. ACM, 2013.

[24] J. Laviola and M. Katzourin. An Exploration of Non-Isomorphic 3D Rotation in Surround Screen Virtual Environments. In *IEEE 3DUI*, 2007.

[25] E. LoPresti, D. M. Brienza, J. Angelo, L. Gilbertson, and J. Sakai. Neck range of motion and use of computer head controls. In *ACM Assets '00*, pages 121–128, 2000.

[26] W. Miles. Ocular dominance in human adults. *Journal of General Psychology*, 3:412–429, 1930.

[27] J. D. Mulder and R. V. Liere. Enhancing fish tank vr. In *VR '00*, pages 91–. IEEE Computer Society, 2000.

[28] M. Ortega and T. Vincent. Direct drawing on 3d shapes with automated camera control. In *ACM CHI'14*, pages 2047–2050, 2014.

[29] C. Pittman, J. J. LaViola, and Jr. Exploring head tracked head mounted displays for first person robot teleoperation. In *ACM IUI'14*, pages 323–328, 2014.

[30] I. Poupyrev, S. Weghorst, and S. Fels. Non-isomorphic 3D rotational techniques. In *ACM CHI'00*, pages 540–547, 2000.

[31] I. Poupyrev, S. Weghorst, T. Otsuka, and T. Ichikawa. Amplifying spatial rotations in 3D interfaces. 1999.

[32] W. Qi, R. M. Taylor, II, C. G. Healey, and J.-B. Martens. A comparison of immersive hmd, fish tank vr and fish tank with haptics displays for volume visualization. In *APGV '06*, pages 51–58. ACM, 2006.

[33] R. Reilink, G. de Bruin, M. Franken, M. A. Mariani, S. Misra, and S. Stramigioli. Endoscopic camera control by head movements for thoracic surgery. In *BioRob*, pages 510–515. IEEE, 2010.

[34] A. L. Simeone, E. Velloso, J. Alexander, and H. Gellersen. Feet movement in desktop 3d interaction. In *IEEE 3DUI*, pages 71–74, 2014.

[35] M. Spindler, W. Büschel, and R. Dachselt. Use your head: Tangible windows for 3d information spaces in a tabletop environment. In *ACM ITS '12*, pages 245–254, 2012.

[36] R. J. Teather and W. Stuerzlinger. Exaggerated head motions for game viewpoint control. In *Future Play '08*, pages 240–243. ACM, 2008.

[37] G. Thibodeau and K. Patton. *Anatomy and Physiology Third Edition*. Mosby, 1996.

[38] C. Ware, K. Arthur, and K. S. Booth. Fish tank virtual reality. In *INTERACT and CHI '93*, pages 37–42, 1993.

[39] K. Yamaguchi, T. Komuro, and M. Ishikawa. Ptz control with head tracking for video chat. In *CHI EA '09*, pages 3919–3924, 2009.

On Your Feet! Enhancing Vection in Leaning-Based Interfaces through Multisensory Stimuli

Ernst Kruijff[1*], Alexander Marquardt[1], Christina Trepkowski[1], Robert W. Lindeman[2],
Andre Hinkenjann[1], Jens Maiero[1], Bernhard E. Riecke[3*]

[1]Bonn-Rhein-Sieg University of Applied Sciences, Grantham-Allee 20, 53757 Sankt Augustin, Germany,
[2]HIT Lab NZ, University of Canterbury, Christchurch 8140, New Zealand
[3] Simon Fraser University, 250 –13450 102 Avenue Surrey, BC, V3T 0A3, Canada
{ernst.kruijff, alexander.marquardt, christina.trepkowski, Andre.Hinkenjann, jens.maiero}@h-brs.de,
gogo@hitlabnz.org, b_r@sfu.ca

ABSTRACT

When navigating larger virtual environments and computer games, natural walking is often unfeasible. Here, we investigate how alternatives such as joystick- or leaning-based locomotion interfaces ("human joystick") can be enhanced by adding walking-related cues following a sensory substitution approach. Using a custom-designed foot haptics system and evaluating it in a multi-part study, we show that adding walking related auditory cues (footstep sounds), visual cues (simulating bobbing head-motions from walking), and vibrotactile cues (via vibrotactile transducers and bass-shakers under participants' feet) could all enhance participants' sensation of self-motion (vection) and involvement/presence. These benefits occurred similarly for seated joystick and standing leaning locomotion. Footstep sounds and vibrotactile cues also enhanced participants' self-reported ability to judge self-motion velocities and distances traveled. Compared to seated joystick control, standing leaning enhanced self-motion sensations. Combining standing leaning with a minimal walking-in-place procedure showed no benefits and reduced usability, though. Together, results highlight the potential of incorporating walking-related auditory, visual, and vibrotactile cues for improving user experience and self-motion perception in applications such as virtual reality, gaming, and tele-presence.

CCS Concepts

• **Information interfaces and presentation − multimedia information systems, artificial, augmented, and virtual realities;**

Keywords

Navigation interface; 3D user interface; leaning; VR; gaming; vibration; bass-shaker; whole-body interface; surface textures.

1. INTRODUCTION

While joysticks and gamepads are widely used methods for navigating games and virtual reality (VR), they offer hardly any of the self-motion cues accompanying real-world locomotion. Allowing for free-space walking while wearing a head-mounted display provides appropriate physical motion cues, but is often unfeasible because of restrictions in the tracked space, concerns of safety, cost, or technical complexity, or fatigue for longer exposures. Leaning-based navigation interfaces using the Wii balance board [20, 21, 57, 61] and other approaches [19, 34, 62] have been proposed and used as an alternative that allows for long-range locomotion without running into limitations of the tracked space. Compared to joystick and gamepad interfaces where the human body is mostly passive and vestibular/proprioceptive cues are largely lacking, leaning-based interfaces can improve navigation performance [21] and provide a more immersive and embodied experience as they allow for at least some full-body involvement and vestibular motion cueing, which can enhance self-motion perception (vection) [31, 40, 44]. Nevertheless, leaning-based interfaces still lack many of the self-motion cues experienced during real-world locomotion, such as full vestibular cues from translations and rotations, proprioceptive cues from walking, air moving by our ears, as well as haptic and auditory cues from our feet touching ground. We designed a multipart study to investigate if and how joystick- and leaning-based locomotion interfaces might be improved by adding different walking-related self-motion cues such as auditory cues (footstep sounds), visual cues (simulating bobbing head-motions from walking), vibrotactile cues (via vibrotactile transducers and shakers under participants' feet) and minimal walking-in-place.

While there is evidence that the visually-induced sensation of illusory self-motion ("vection") can be enhanced by adding matching auditory cues (e.g., dynamic sound fields) and vibrations/subsonics [24, 32, 40], it is largely unknown how they affect active locomotion conditions using seated joystick versus standing leaning interfaces. As self-motion sensations are typically enhanced by multisensory stimulation [32, 43–46], we do expect overall enhancement by providing additional self-motion related cues in the current studies. Similarly, we hypothesized additional benefits including improved speed and distance perception and overall performance and usability, especially in systems that require more precise navigation or wayfinding, or a higher level of user engagement through increased realism.

Some may consider the usage of walking-in-place (WIP) techniques [55] to overcome the caveat of lack of motion cues, as this technique does provide some proprioceptive cues by mimicking physical walking while not physically moving around. However, WIP can be tiring over time, which might lead to reduced usage. In addition, while WIP gestures are fairly natural for forward walking, they can be awkward for walking backwards or strafing,

SUI '16, October 15 - 16, 2016, Tokyo, Japan
Copyright is held by the owner/author(s). Publication rights licensed to ACM.
ACM 978-1-4503-4068-7/16/10...$15.00
DOI: http://dx.doi.org/10.1145/2983310.2985759

which are both common in the real world and computer games [51]. Furthermore, the physical motion rather resembles walking upstairs instead of natural forward motion.

In the approach presented in this paper, we follow a different direction. We present a system that can provide fine-grained multisensory cues for standing leaning-based interfaces, extending work by Marchal et al. [33] and Feng et al. [14] who focused on supporting seated users. The system provides audio-visual cues as well as foot-based stimuli ("foot haptics") that partly *substitute* real-world cues. Sensory substitution is a method in which sensory information is transferred from one kind of stimulus to another, both within or across the senses. For example, a popular method of substitution is the translation of kinaesthetic information into vibrotactile cues, being a substitution within the same (haptic) sensory system [29]. In our system, "foot haptics" are deployed by a dense grid of vibrotactors, a bass-shaker, and a loudspeaker under each foot. Cues are physically co-located similar to cues perceived during real-world walking.

The system design is guided by previous studies indicating that navigation techniques for synthetic environments can be enhanced by visual and non-visual cues such as head bobbing, step sounds, or plantar (foot-based) vibrotactile cues [10, 38, 45, 53, 56]. These cues can contribute to both the travel and wayfinding aspects of navigation, and have been reasonably well researched in the domain of physical walking interfaces. Yet, using additional cues for those users who are *not* moving around physically while navigating through an environment is still an open area of research. Exceptions include some studies that explore head bobbing, footsteps sounds, and vibration for seated stationary users [14, 53], and vestibular cues provided through motion platforms [26], showing positive effects on self-motion. Here, we investigate how adding different walking-related auditory, visual, and vibrotactile cues might affect standard joystick situations (with seated users) as well as standing leaning conditions, and if they might be differently affected by the added cues.

2. RELATED WORK

Navigation is one of the key tasks performed in both real and virtual environments, and encompasses both physical and psychological aspects. Physical navigation interfaces have been studied widely and can increase the overall usability and user experience of the system [6, 7, 41], enhance spatial perception and orientation important for a wide range of tasks [7], and reduce motion sickness [4]. In this section, we look more closely at related studies on leaning-based navigation interfaces, as well as feedback to support navigation interfaces.

Leaning-based locomotion interfaces. Our interface development and accompanying studies relate directly to leaning-based interfaces for travel in synthetic environments like games or virtual environments, including the use of the Wii balance board [20, 57, 61] and other types of leaning interfaces [19, 34, 62]. Leaning interfaces to some degree resemble other interfaces that keep the user physically at one location, such as WIP interfaces [51, 55], natural motion interfaces such as those supported by treadmills [12], or navigation systems for seated users. An overview of many techniques can be found in [7], while a focused overview of how in particular feet can be used for interaction purposes is described in [59].

Vection. Embodied self-motion illusions (e.g., vection) have long been studied and can be induced in stationary observers by moving visual flow fields, moving spatialized sounds, and biomechanical cues from walking on circular (but not linear) treadmills (see recent reviews in [24, 32, 44]). Visually-induced vection can be enhanced by adding simulated camera motions that mimic jitter [38] or head bobbing, the vertical and horizontal oscillatory motion of the head during natural walking [10], which can be communicated as a purely visual cue [52], as well as through physical movement of the user [26]. Researchers have also looked into the integration of visual and non-visual cues for self-motion perception [13, 23] and information storage thereof [2]. Some studies showed that minimal provision of vestibular cues can enhance self-motion [22, 27, 49], while also foot step sounds [42,53], wind [14], and tactile patterns associated with walking [44] or leaning in sideways directions [30] showed positive effects. Furthermore, body pitch affects self-motion [5, 8, 9]. Studies on actively tilting the body have shown that while horizontal (sideways left-right) vection was not affected by body tilt, vertical (a.k.a. elevator) vection was reduced for upright posture and increased to the level of horizontal vection as body tilt increased [35]. In contrast, static leaning has also been shown to positively affect self-motion for seated users [31].

Foot-based feedback. Foot-induced feedback for both physically moving and non-moving users has been approached from various directions. Not only the feet themselves, but also the legs have been stimulated [7], for example through moving foot pedals [28]. Furthermore, and a key instigator for our system, plantar cutaneous vibration feedback (the stimulation of the foot sole) can be sufficient to elicit a walking experience [54]. To achieve this, researchers have taken advantage of the high sensitivity of the foot sole [18]. Among others, researchers have looked into pressure distributions associated with heel and toe strike defining roll-off of the feet in natural motion by using a low-frequency loudspeaker [53]. Furthermore, non-directional tactile cues (e.g., floor vibrations) have been shown to provide some self-motion cues [13, 14, 53]. Some studies also looked specifically into navigational cues ("turn right") by deploying a dense grid of vibrotactors under the mid-foot [58]. Vibrotaction can also be used to elicit ground texture cues, partly also in combination with audio [36, 37, 39, 50] and has been shown to positively affect haptic surface compliance [60]. Finally, vibrotaction has been used for providing collision feedback [3]. With regards to auditory feedback, footstep sounds have been used to elicit self-motion sensations [14], as the frequency of steps provides some information about how fast the user is moving. Approaches partly include ground texture information, though it has been shown that perception can be biased through cross-modal effects [16]. Sometimes cues were displayed to the feet by mounting loudspeakers in close vicinity [39]. To some extent, vibration and audio cues have been studied in concert, and shown to improve vection [43]. This integration of audio and tactile cues also relates to recent studies looking specifically into the integration of various multisensory cues for rendering of walking [33], an area our system and user study also targets.

Gait. The physical aspect of locomotion can be defined by *gait*, the bipedal (forward) propulsion caused by the human limbs, which is affected by, for example, velocity and ground surface [15]. Gait is comprised of the different stride phases, in which the legs are moved, and the feet hit the ground (foot strike for each step). Stride phases differ in both frequency and length, depending on how fast the person moves. They include the stance phase (where a foot touches the ground) and swing phase (where the leg is moved and the foot is airborne); combined, they form one gait cycle. Thereby, ground contact of the foot is defined by a roll-off process of the human foot, affected by different force (pressure) phases underneath the foot sole (cf. Fig. 2). Furthermore, the amount of ground contact per roll-off (step) differs with velocity.

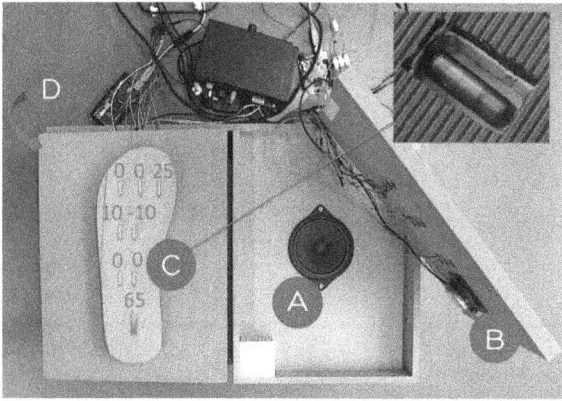

Figure 1. Hardware setup: Feedback to each foot consists of (A) a loudspeaker mounted in a solid case to provide air volume, (B) a bass-shaker, (C) eight vibrotactors mounted underneath the foot (overlaid in blue: seven small, one large vibrotactor, latter shown in close up from below foam sole), with PWM intensity control, and (D) the core frame of a Wii balance board.

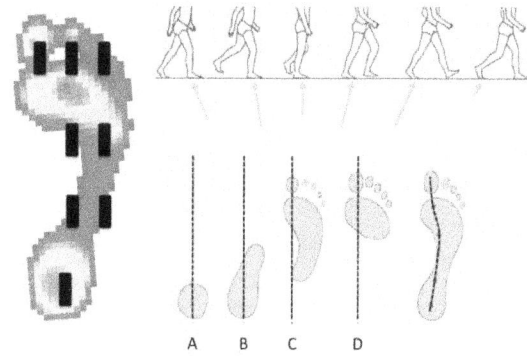

Figure 2. Left: Foot pressure distribution zones of a standing user (image Wikimedia commons) showing the vibrotactors locations. Right: gait analysis of half a gait cycle during normal walking showing (A) heel strike, (B) heel strike to foot flat, (C) foot flat to midstance, and (D) midstance to toe off (redrawn from [15]).

Foot strike can differ between different people, as for example runners commonly have either heel or mid-foot strike. In this article we mainly focus at heel strike roll-off patterns. Finally, as an effect of the stride phases and balance shifts, the human body will exhibit horizontal and vertical oscillatory motions, which are partly counterbalanced by the vestibular system [49]. The shift of balance can be noticed by human vision, as the human viewpoint shifts in a process commonly described as *head bobbing*.

3. SYSTEM DESIGN

The main research problem targeted in this paper is *how* to improve self-motion perception, usability, and user engagement in leaning- and joystick-based navigation through synthetic environments. To this end, we designed as system that combines multisensory feedback with sensors to detect the user's weight shifting, thus controlling the navigation.

3.1 System and Cue Overview

The overall system (Fig. 1) consists of various feedback components mounted underneath the feet, placed on top of the Wii balance board load sensors and electronics in a wooden (medium-density fiberboard) case. Cues are provided by actuators mounted underneath each foot: a loudspeaker (Fig. 1, A) mounted in a speaker case, a bass-shaker (exciter, Fig. 1, B), and a grid of vibrotactors (Fig. 1, C). Furthermore, additional visual cues are provided through the head-mounted display connected to the system, an Oculus Rift DK2. Stimuli for each foot are isolated by creating two boxes that are separated by 1cm thick solid foam insulation. As such, the feedback provided to one foot can hardly be noticed by the other foot. As a product of the various devices, the system can provide additional walking-related cues including **visual** (head bobbing), **auditory** (footstep sounds), and **vibrotactile** (foot roll-off pressure and ground impact) cues. The full system runs in real-time on a graphics workstation using Unity3D. The vibrotactors are controlled through pulse-width modulation (PWM) over two Arduino Mega boards triggered over Undoing, while the loudspeaker and bass-shaker are driven by two amplifiers. The system was designed to be compact and portable, and thus does not allow for full-body rotations or stepping away from the designated foot positions and vibrotactors.

3.2 Navigation Methods

Leaning-based locomotion uses the Wii balance board to allow the user to produce forward, backward, and sideways (strafing) motions, as well as turning during forward motion. We did not allow the user to turn around while not moving. The Wii measured users' leaning via center of pressure (COP) changes, which controlled translation velocities in the direction of the COP change. To allow for smooth control over both slow and faster locomotion speeds, we used an exponential velocity control ($velocity \sim COPdeflection^{2.7}$) based on pilot results. For the seated joystick conditions, we used a Microsoft X-Box gamepad with the same exponential velocity control scheme with a factor of 2.7. Velocities were limited to 3.7m/s for both interfaces.

3.3 Visual Head Movement

Largely following the specification of head bobbing by Grossmann et al. [17], a custom-built head-bobbing algorithm was implemented in Unity3D to simulate the horizontal and vertical oscillatory motion of the head during real-world walking. Iterative design and pretesting with several specialists was used to fine-tune the head-bobbing parameters to create a "flat 8" (infinity) motion pattern, synced with the user's speed of travel. To do so, two sine waves, one for each of the x- and y-axes, are instantiated, while the y-axis wave has double the frequency of the x-axis.

3.4 Audio

The design premise for the audio cues is the delivery of realistic walking sounds, which are presented using two loudspeakers (Visaton FR10 20W) mounted beneath the feet, driven by a single amplifier (Samson Servo 200). Sounds are thus collocated with the feet, similar to [39]. As such, added realism is achieved, as the walking sounds are spatially consistent with where they appear near the feet in real life. Walking sounds are defined by two main characteristics: the speed of walking and the ground surface over which the user walks. Based on the movement velocity, the step-sound duration is compressed to match the stride-phase duration and interrelated airborne phases where the feet do not touch the ground (see next section). Thus the sounds are always synchronized with the ground contact phases affected by the walking speed, starting when the heel hits the surface. We pre-selected a

Table 1. Walking and running phases and actuator / cue characteristics, inspired by literature, refined through iterative design

	Walking 5 km/h		Slow running 9 km/h		Fast running 13 km/h	
Stride frequency [1], also affecting bobbing frequency	120 strides / min Stride length: 0.7m 500 ms/ stride		128 strides / min Stride length: 1.17 m 470 ms/stride		159 strides / min Stride length: 1.35 m 380 ms/stride	
Foot roll-off: contact pressure [11,15,24]	*Vibrotactors*	*Bass-shaker*	*Vibrotactors*	*Bass-shaker*	*Vibrotactors*	*Bass-shaker*
	Base value	Volume 10%	Base value +10%	Volume 25%	Base value +20%	Volume 40%
Foot roll-off: ground contact [15]	570 ms ground contact / stride (10% double support period)		330 ms ground contact / stride (30% airborne phase)		220 ms ground contact / stride (40% airborne phase)	

solid (wood) and aggregates (gravel) to be representative of surfaces users normally can distinguish quite well [16].

3.5 Vibrotactile

Inspired by previous systems applying plantar vibration to improve self-motion perception [13, 14, 53] and navigation cues [58], we created a vibration system stimulating different parts of the foot soles. Vibrotactile cues are mainly used to *substitute* for light force cues that humans experience when striking the feet on ground surface, and are closely linked to the footstep sounds introduced in the previous section. As such, we perform sensory substitution within the somatosensory system, translating pressure cues into vibrotactile cues. We mainly focus on simulating the roll-off pressure distribution. The system deploys eight vibrotactors per foot: seven underneath the mid-foot and toes (Precision Microdrives Pico drive 5mm encapsulated vibration motors 304-116, maximum 15,000 RPM), and one underneath the heel (Precision Microdrives 9mm Pico drive 307-103 13,800 RPM) as illustrated in Figures 1 and 2. The vibrotactors are placed so that users with varying foot sizes can still perceive the stimuli. The vibrotactors are glued to a rubber surface, stretched over a solid foam sole, in which small holes are made to hold the vibrotactors. As such, each vibrotactor can vibrate well against the foot sole, instead of receiving a heavy load and dampening when users stand on them. This allows the feedback to be highly similar under different posture conditions, as postures (like standing or sitting) affect pressure on the soles differently. The vibrotactors are arranged to stimulate the key zones underneath the foot (Fig. 1), from heel to mid-foot and toes. The foot is in almost direct contact with the vibrotactors, as the leaning device is used without shoes, which would dampen the feedback unnecessarily. Users wear light socks for hygienic reasons. To strengthen heel impact on the ground surfaces, a bass-shaker (Visaton EX-60) is used. The bass-shaker is mounted on the foot-support plate underneath the heel, stimulating this part of the foot strongest during activation. While vibration cannot be isolated with the current design to solely target the heel, there is a noticeable fall-off of strength towards other parts of the foot, similar to the effect of ground impact during real-world walking. The vibrotactors and bass-shaker are synchronized to simulate the different **gait phases** during natural motion. Gait can be defined by stride phases and length, and differences in plantar pressure and duration (the "ground contact phase") experienced during the different stages of foot roll-off in a gait phase. Different motion speeds affect these characteristics to varying extents, as summarized in Table 1.

To mimic **foot roll-off behavior** during gait [15], we simulate plantar pressure by stimulating different zones of the foot sole over time. Fig. 2 (left) depicts the plantar pressure distribution of a standing user. The pressure distribution of different zones in terms of lower and higher pressure is roughly similar during walk-

ing. Yet, which zone receives pressure depends on the stage in the roll-off process. Roll-off can be divided into four phases (Fig. 2, right): namely (A) heel strike, (B) heel strike to foot flat, (C) foot flat to instance, and (D) instance to toe off [15]. Terziman et al. [53] simulated roll-off by using low-frequency loudspeakers mounted underneath the foot, allowing approximated roll-off feedback using contact models. In contrast, we make use of a dense grid of vibrotactors to fully simulate the pressure underneath the foot sole. This is also in contrast to other systems that only stimulate the heel and toes during physical motion [39, 50]. While the system by Velazquez et al. [58] makes use of a denser grid of vibrotactors, these only stimulate the mid-foot, and only provide directional cues for navigation. Notwithstanding, we assume that the roll-off procedure will also provide some motion cues, as the vibration pattern continuously "travels forward" when moving forward.

All vibrotactors are assigned different vibration profiles (Fig. 2) that mimics pressure changes during walking (the zones in Fig. 2, left). These patterns are affected by whether the user is walking, running slowly, or running fast, which defines the ground contact phase and duration. Based on the mentioned gait literature, we define three **walking profiles**. An increase in running speed affects stride parameters differently; either frequency or length [47] or both frequency and length [1] can increase. Within our system, we varied both frequency and length. Each of the three modes has different stride frequencies and lengths that we interpolate between (leaning adjusts speed continuously), while the pressure profile also changes. We based values on the background literature (Table 1), adjusting them accordingly through iterative design. During normal walking, either the left or right foot is always stimulated, with some overlap. With increasing velocity and a different swing phase associated with the motion of the limbs, the airborne phase increases [15], introducing phases in which none of the feet receives (vibrotactile) stimuli. These phases coincide with an increase in stride length, frequency, and ground contact [1], relative to a base PWM value defined by the surface material. Through design iteration and considering maximum PWM values, the base PWM for wood was selected at 156, while it is 130 for gravel. The base value is increased based on the aforementioned pressure profile, depicted in Fig. 2. Additionally, the **ground impact** increases with increasing speed of locomotion, though not equally over all parts of the sole [11, 25]. In particular the pressure under the heel increases more than all other points when the speed increases from walking to running slowly [25]. To adjust for this increase, we linearly increase the vibration with increasing speeds. Running slowly increases the base PWM of the vibrotactors by 10%, running fast by 20%. Thereby, we distribute the pressure simulation of the heel over both the vibrotactor and the bass-shaker mounted underneath the heel. In sync, the audio also gets louder. This is achieved by increasing the base volume; walk-

Table 2 – Procedure and design: overview of sessions of the experiment

	Session 1	Session 2	Session 3	Session 4	Session 5
Interfaces	Leaning, joystick	Leaning	Leaning, joystick	Leaning with/without WIP	Leaning
Cue conditions	[ON]: Audio, Vibrotactors, bass-shaker, head bobbing	[ON or OFF]: audio, vibrotactors, bass-shaker [ON]: head bobbing	[ON]: Either no foot stimuli, audio only or all cues (audio, vibrotactors and bass-shaker) [ON or OFF]: head bobbing	[ON]: Audio, vibrotactors, bass-shaker [OFF]: head-bobbing	[Either all ON or OFF]: Audio, vibrotactors and bass-shaker [ON]: head bobbing
Travel	Follow marker	Follow marker	Follow marker	Free movement	Free movement

ing has 10%, running slowly 25%, and running fast 40%. These values should be seen as relative, as the final loudness was defined at the amplifiers through calibration.

4. EXPERIMENTS

We performed a multipart study to create a better understanding of the potential effects and interaction of different multisensory cues provided by the system.

4.1 Method

Twelve participants (25-48 years old, mean age 29, one female) participated in the user study. Seven participants reported they played games daily or weekly, and the rest less frequently. All users had normal or corrected-to-normal vision. On average, the whole study took about one hour to complete.

4.1.1 Stimuli and Apparatus

For the various sessions of the experiment, we deployed the base system as described in Section 3. Participants were seated during all joystick conditions (cf. Fig. 3) to allow for testing effects of foot haptics on seated users and to match the most common (seated) posture during joystick usage. Participants were also seated when answering questions between studies. Simulated eye height was kept constant across seated and standing conditions to ensure comparable optic flow.

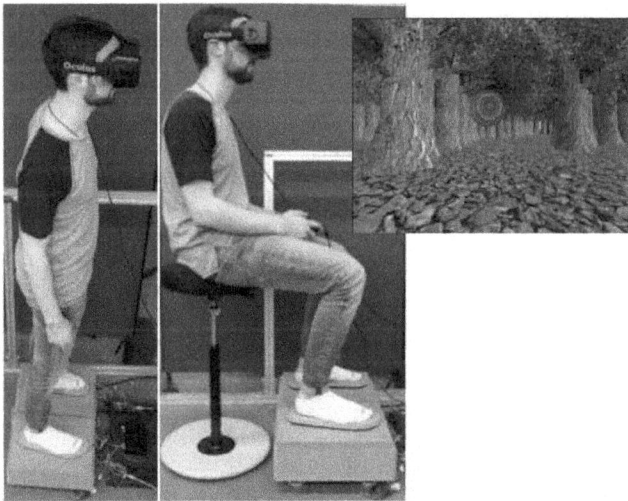

Figure 3. User in standing leaning (left) and seated (middle) pose. Right: Test environment with follow-me object.

4.1.2 Experimental Design and Procedure

The experiment was performed as a within-subjects study and consisted of five sessions as summarized in Table 2. As each session was designed to address different research questions and we

did not intend to compare absolute values across sessions, we did not counterbalance the order of sessions between participants but instead used the same order for everyone. Furthermore, the focus of this study was on participants' perception and user experience rather than task performance, so even if there was transfer of learning between the different sessions this should not critically affect observed results. Most sessions compared standing leaning against either seated joystick or standing leaning with added walking-in-place (WIP), deploying various combinations of cues provided through the feedback device. Before the first session, participants received oral instructions, signed informed consent, and answered demographics questions. We also checked for correct foot position on the vibrotactor surface by playing a test sequence over all vibrotactors and asking participants if all vibrotactors could be felt.

During the experiment, participants were asked to rate questions using a 11-Point Likert (0-10) scale, with 10 being in full agreement. After each trial in every session, users rated vection intensity ("I had a strong sensation of self-motion"), their ability to judge speed and travelled distance ("I could judge my velocity/distance travelled well"), the level of involvement (item INV2 from the IPQ questionnaire [48] "I was not aware of my real environment", also as a partial indicator of presence and user engagement), and level of motion sickness ("I feel sick or nauseous", only in Session 3). These questions where displayed within the HMD, rated orally, and noted down by the experimenter. After each session, the HMD was removed and participants answered post-session questions displayed in an online form on a desktop PC screen. Questions encompassed user comfort, the ability to concentrate on the task, perceived navigation performance, ease of learning, fun, the ability to use the interface for longer durations, vection intensity, and usability as detailed in Figure 6. After the first session, participants also rated the level of convincingness of walking on the two ground textures. We allowed participants to take a short break by removing the HMD when motion sickness was an issue. Before and After all the whole study participants reported if they were fresh and relaxed, as well as their level of motion sickness. In light of a previously performed study [31], we also asked if they thought leaning itself had positively affected self-motion.

The main task in all sessions was to navigate over a clearly visible curved path. We created six paths through a natural environment populated with trees at the border of each path (Fig. 3, right). All paths had the same curvature profile, as curves were basically mirrored. The trees were chosen to provide some motion cues in the peripheral visual field. The gravel path had the various non-visual cues adapted accordingly. To ensure similar velocity profiles despite active navigation, participants in Sessions 1-3 had to follow a marker (a clearly visible blue sphere, see Fig. 3 right) that was moving in front of them. In Sessions 4 and 5 participants were asked to move freely along the path and vary their speed dynamically. The marker was moved at different speeds starting with walking, followed by slow/fast or fast/slow running, changing every three seconds. The speeds were chosen to match walking, slow and fast running profiles (Table 1). Trials lasted about 10s. Pilot studies indicated that 10s is sufficient to experience vection and be able to experience and rate the different interfaces and cue combinations.

Before the main experiment, we performed a pilot study with three specialists. In this pilot, we calibrated the head bobbing to avoid motion sickness, and the strength of the vibrotactors and bass-shakers, resulting in the values shown in Table 1. Before starting a given session, the subject went through a vection calibration phase, in which they would lean forward and move through a star field simulation, providing strong vection cues. This served the purpose of providing the user with a sense of strong self-motion, forming the reference for the vection intensity rating requested after each trial. Thereafter, we performed the following five sessions.

Session 1: How well can different cues be associated with different ground surfaces? In this session, participants could practice the navigation interface, following the sphere marker for two trials each for both leaning and joystick interfaces, resulting in four trials. During navigation, we enabled all cues (vibrotactile, bass-shaker, audio, and head-bobbing). In contrast to Sessions 2-5, we separated the path into two zones (wooden planks and gravel) to get a first impression about how well users would rate the convincingness of walking on wood versus gravel.

Session 2: How do different audio-tactile cue combinations affect self-motion perception while leaning? In the second session, we focused specifically on the effects of different cues on the subjective rating of self-motion and involvement, employing a 2×2×2 factorial design. Each participant completed 16 trials, consisting of the factorial combination of two audio conditions (audio on, off), two bass-shaker conditions (bass-shaker on, off), and two vibrotactor conditions (vibrotactors on, off), and two repetitions per condition. Repetitions were blocked for all sessions, meaning that all cue conditions were finished before being repeated. Head bobbing was used during all conditions.

Session 3: What is the influence of leaning, head bobbing, and foot haptics when comparing joystick and leaning? In the next session, we focused on assessing the effect of the implemented cues on self-motion perception and involvement by comparing leaning (while standing) to the joystick (seated) interface, employing a 2×2×3 factorial design, using slightly different cue combinations from Session 2. Each participant completed 24 trials, consisting of the factorial combination of two navigation interfaces (leaning, joystick), two visual cue conditions (head bobbing on, off) and three foot-based stimuli conditions (no foot stimulation, audio only, and all audio, vibrotactor, and bass-shaker cues combined), with two repetitions per condition. Joystick and leaning conditions were grouped in counterbalanced order.

Session 4: Does minimal WIP enhance leaning locomotion? In this session, we explored the potential of adding minimal WIP while leaning to move forward. To prevent foot position from shifting away from the vibrotactors and to ensure that the vibrotactile stimuli could be continuously applied to the whole foot, we instructed participants to perform a "minimal" WIP where they moved the legs as when walking in place, yet without lifting the heel up from the foot interface. Pilot studies showed that this minimal WIP method only slightly affected leaning compared to normal WIP (where heels/feet may lift off the ground) where leaning could no longer have been used effectively. Participants were asked to freely move over the predefined path by leaning, either with or without added minimal WIP, repeated twice, totaling four trials. We allowed the participants to practice WIP once before starting the actual trials. Participants were encouraged to synchronize their WIP with the foot haptics and head bobbing stimuli.

Session 5: Does foot haptics affect perception during free locomotion? Finally, we specifically looked into the effect of multisensory cues during free exploration. We allowed the participants to freely move over a path, instructing them to vary their speed dynamically. The session only had two conditions, namely the presence or absence of all cues (vibrotactor, bass-shaker, and audio), repeated twice. As such, participants completed four trials. Although exploration time was not limited in Session 4 and 5, participants generally did not take more than 20s.

4.2 Results and Discussion

Generally, participants reported very positively on the overall usability and quality of stimuli, with an average of 7.25 (7.6 when excluding outliers in Session 4) on a 0-10 scale. Post-experiment questions showed average motion sickness scores of 3.92 on a 0-10 scale (SD: 2.64), with four of the 12 participants experiencing high levels (>5). Furthermore, confirming to some extent the results reported in [31], participants reported that leaning overall supported self-motion: eight users reported very positive (scores 8-10), and all but one reported scores of 4 or higher, leading to an average of 6.5 (SD = 2.40).

Session 1: How well can different cues be associated with different ground surfaces? Session 1 focused on allowing the participants to practice with the leaning and gamepad navigation techniques, while also looking into the perceptibility of different ground surfaces. The rated convincingness of walking on wood and gravel was overall fairly high (6.54 on a 0-10 scale) and showed no significant effects of surface type or locomotion mode (standing-leaning versus seated gamepad), although there was a trend towards higher ratings for the standing-leaning condition scores (wood M = 7.08, SD = 1.55, gravel M = 6.42, SD = 1.89) than the seated gamepad conditions (wood M = 6.75, SD = 1.01, gravel M = 5.92, SD = 2.04). Further per-trial analysis revealed no significant effects of surface or locomotion type on self-motion perception, speed and distance estimation, or involvement. In the post-session debriefing, participants stated that compared to the leaning interface, the joystick was easier to learn ($t(11) = 3.26$, $p = 0.008$), and allowed them to more easily concentrate on the task ($t(11) = 2.24$, $p = 0.046$) and more easily navigate and follow the guide object ($t(11) = 3.94$, $p = 0.002$), see Figure 4 (left). Joystick and leaning were rated similarly in terms of comfort (M = 8.21 on a 0-10 scale), enjoyment (8.63), self-motion sensation (8.08), overall usability (8.04) and long-term usage (8.25). This shows the potential and quality of foot haptics and leaning interfaces, even for prolonged usage, as gamepads are the quasi standard for travel in at least game environments.

Session 2: How do different audio-tactile cue combinations affect self-motion perception while leaning? ANOVA results showed increased sensations of self-motion (vection) both for adding audio ($F(1,11) = 16.89$, $p = 0.002$, $\eta^2 = 0.61$) and vibrations ($F(1,11) = 4.96$, $p = 0.048$, $\eta^2 = 0.311$), as depicted in Figure 4. Participants stated that they were better able to judge self-motion velocities with added audio ($F(1,11) = 10.01$, $p = 0.009$, $\eta^2 = 0.48$), vibrations ($F(1,11) = 5.13$, $p = 0.045$, $\eta^2 = 0.32$), and bass-shaker ($F(1,11) = 7.76$, $p = 0.018$, $\eta^2 = 0.41$). Participants further reported that they could judge traveled distances better with added auditory cues, $F(1,11) = 9.47$, $p = 0.011$, $\eta^2 = 0.46$. Finally, participants reported being less aware of the real envi-

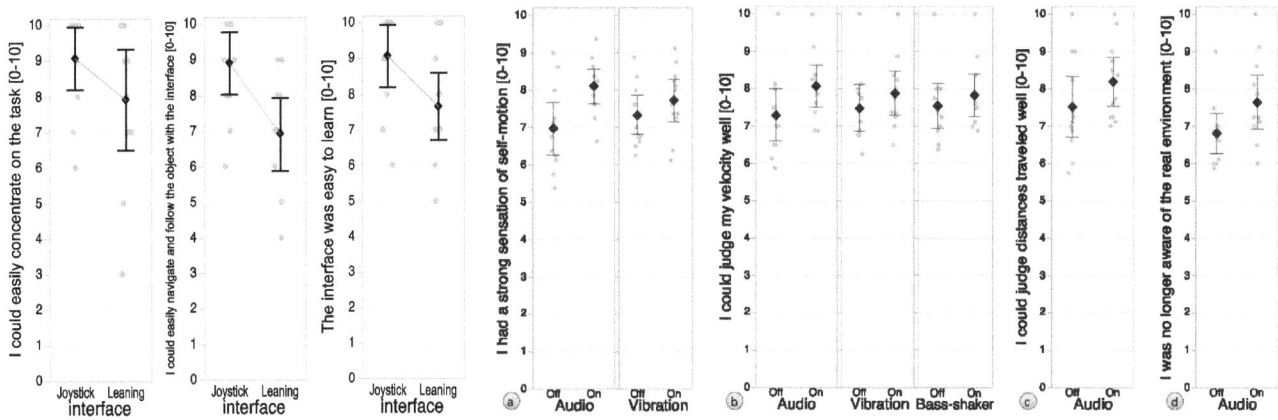

Figure 4: Data plots illustrating significant effects for Session 1 (left three plots) and Session 2. Diamonds and whiskers depict means and 95% confidence intervals; smaller dots depict mean individual participants' data.

ronment and thus more involved and present when auditory cues were added $F(1,11) = 5.87$, $p = 0.034$, $\eta^2 = 0.35$. None of the other main effect or interactions reached significance.

Session 3: What is the influence of leaning, head bobbing and foot haptics when comparing joystick and leaning? In Session 3, which took the longest, post-session ratings showed higher scores for the joystick versus leaning interface for comfort, concentration, ease of navigation, learnability, prolonged usage, and overall usability (see last six plots in Figure 5). While all ratings for the leaning interface were still fairly high (all above 6, most above 7), there is a clear need for improvement to bring them close to the joystick level. The per-trial ratings showed significant effects of the type of foot stimulation on participants' rating on vection ($F(1.15, 12.64) = 16.33$, $p = 0.001$, $\eta^2 = 0.60$), their stated ability to judge both self-motion velocities ($F(1.23, 13.55) = 8.93$, $p = 0.001$, $\eta^2 = 0.45$) and traveled distances ($F(1.13, 12.44) = 7.70$, $p = 0.003$ $\eta^2 = 0.41$) as well as involvement ($F(1.13, 12.44) = 7.98$, $p = 0.002$ $\eta^2 = 0.42$). As illustrated in Figure 5 (top), estimates were highest for the full stimulation using audio, vibrotactor, and bass-shaker cues combined, intermediate for the audio-only condition, and lowest for the condition without any foot or audio stimulation. Furthermore, vection was enhanced when adding head bobbing ($F(1,11) = 8.62$, $p = 0.014$ $\eta^2 = 0.44$) and when replacing the seated joystick interface with a leaning-based interface ($F(1,11) = 7.92$, $p = 0.017$, $\eta^2 = 0.42$). In particular, the significant effect of interface is interesting, as standing leaning improved the sensation of self-motion ($M = 7.11$, $SD = 1.48$) compared to the seated joystick usage ($M = 6.60$, $SD = 1.71$). This confirms and extends previous findings that found a positive effect of leaning while seated [31]. Finally, involvement ratings were increased when head bobbing was added, $F(1,11) = 5.92$, $p = 0.033$ $\eta^2 = 0.35$. Motion sickness was relatively low overall ($M = 2.43$, $SD = 2.05$ on a 0-10 scale) and did not show any significant effects of any of the independent measures.

Session 4: Does minimal WIP enhance leaning locomotion? Even though we were successfully able to use WIP during internal testing, all except two participants had major problems with WIP. This is reflected in significantly reduced scores for all measures including user comfort, the ability to concentrate on the task, perceived navigation ability, learnability, enjoyment, long-term-usage, vection, and usability as illustrated in Figure 6. As such, we conclude that combining leaning with the minimal WIP used (moving legs while keeping feet on the floor) is not a promising approach. A more pronounced WIP in which the heels could be

lifted might have led to other results, but would have disturbed the delivery of foot haptics to that part of the foot. Due to the low scores, we did not further analyze the per-trial results.

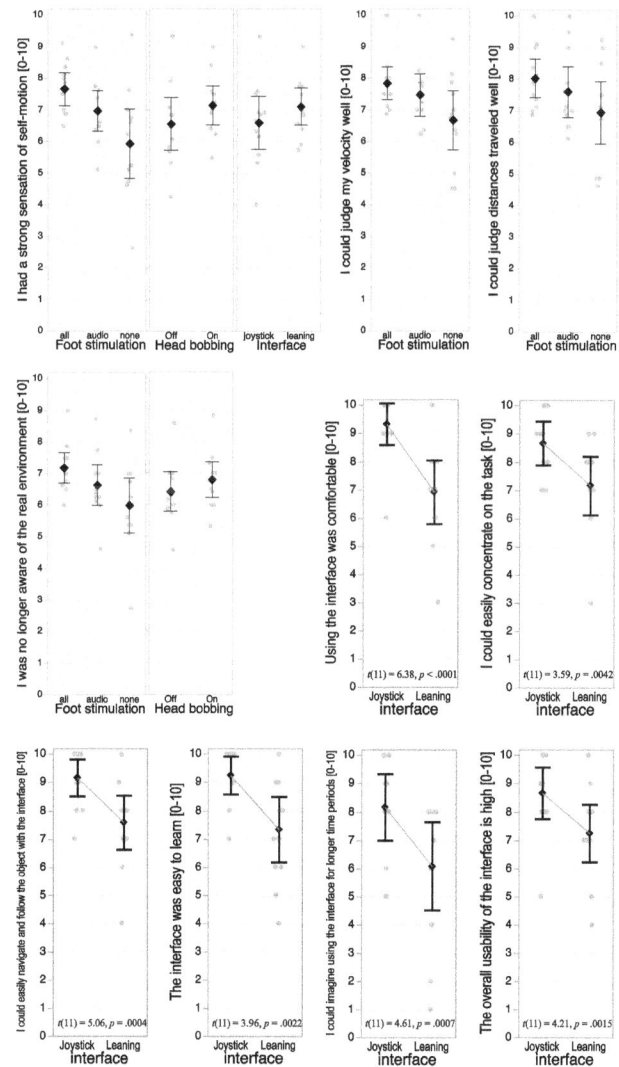

Figure 5: Data plots of significant effects in Session 3.

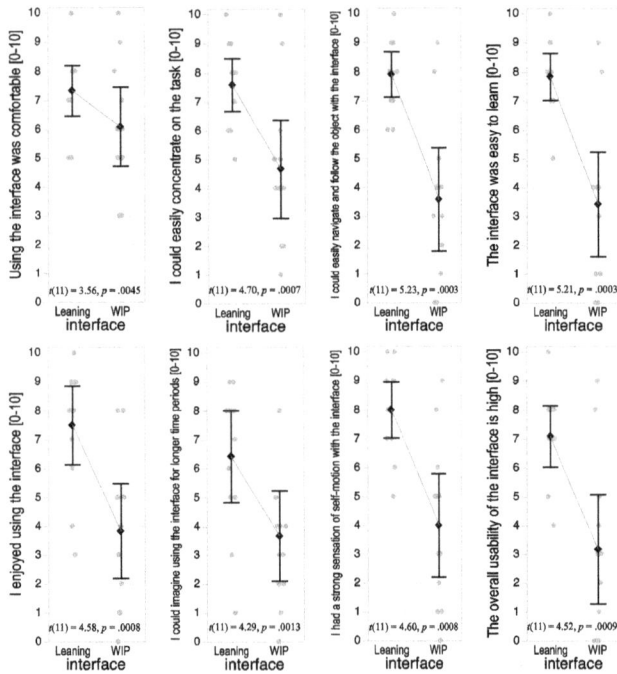

Figure 6: Data plots of significant effects in Session 4.

Session 5: Does foot haptics affect perception during free locomotion? The results were in line with the previous sessions: Adding combined audio, vibrotactor, and bass-shaker cues significantly enhanced all per-trial dependent measures (See Fig. 7). That is, when participants were provided with auditory and vibrotactile cues ("ON") compared to no such cues at all ("OFF") they reported significantly enhanced sensation of self-motion (vection: $t(11) = 3.88$, $p = 0.003$, OFF: M = 6.54, SD = 1.74, ON: M = 8.54, SD = 0.99), reported being better able to judge self-motion velocities ($t(11) = 2.96$, $p = 0.013$, OFF: M = 6.75, SD = 1.36, ON: M = 8.04, SD = 1.27), and travelled distances ($Z = -2.37$, $p = 0.018$, OFF: M = 7.20, SD = 1.53, ON: M = 8.33, SD = 1.29) and reported higher involvement ($Z = -2.67$, $p = 0.007$, OFF: M = 6.29, SD = 0.62, ON: M = 7.88, SD = 1.26). Overall, ratings were slightly higher than in the previous sessions. This is in alignment with participants' reporting in the post-session interview that they could better focus on the effects of the cues when they did not have to follow the moving object.

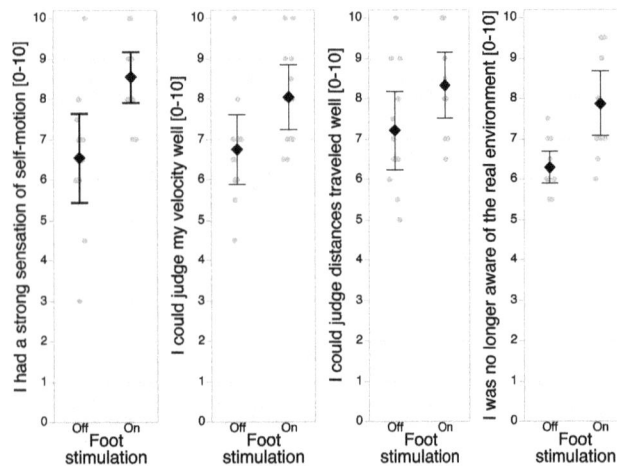

Figure 7: Data plots illustrating significant effects in Session 5.

5. CONCLUSIONS

In this article, we presented a novel system coupling leaning-based travel with foot-haptics mechanisms. Results showed that both self-motion perception (vection) and involvement/presence could be significantly enhanced by adding walking-related vibrotactile cues (via vibrotactile transducers and bass-shakers under participants' feet), auditory cues (footstep sounds), as well as visual cues (simulating bobbing head-motions from walking). Moreover, participants' self-reported ability to judge self-motion velocities and distances traveled was enhanced by adding footstep sounds and vibrotactile cues. Interestingly, all these observed benefits of adding walking-related cues occurred independently of whether participants controlled self-motion via joystick while seated or via leaning while standing. This suggests a more general benefit of adding walking-related cues that might generalize to further locomotion paradigms and interfaces, with many potential application areas.

Together, the outcomes support the assumption that haptic and proprioceptive cues experienced during natural walking can at least to some degree be substituted for by other feedback channels such as vibrotactile feedback, and can be further supported by audio-visual cues. This outcome is in line with previous studies, such as the system and study by Terziman et al. [53], showing similar effects for seated users.

A key finding in this paper is that leaning while standing improved self-motion perception significantly compared to seated users using a joystick, even though participants had extensive experience using joysticks but no experience using leaning-based interfaces. This extends prior work showing that passive (but not active) seated leaning on a manual gaming chair could enhance self-motion sensations [42].

Motion sickness was an issue for some users. While this might at least in part be attributed to the long duration of the experiment inside a head-mounted display, as even with breaks it took around one hour, further research is needed to investigate which factors might have contributed and how motion sickness could be reduced. Because of the marker-following procedure, we could only ask participants to introspectively rate their ability to judge velocities and distanced travelled. Future work is planned to investigate if this self-assessment also translates to improved behavioral measures of distance/velocity and more complex navigation behavior. Pilot data suggests that seated leaning can indeed reduce distance underestimation for VR locomotion. However, the current results suggest that compared to seated joystick usage, standing leaning interfaces, in particular when combined with minimal WIP might require additional cognitive/attentional resources, and would benefit from additional practice and further interface improvements.

In the future, we intend to extend the base system by looking into the potential of including limited haptic feedback to the feet, for example to provide collision feedback. We are also interested in the addition of other motion cues, such as wind and barely perceptible wind sounds that occur when someone is moving through the physical world. Furthermore, we will investigate how we can generalize the system to better include rotations, for example by using torso-directed locomotion [6].

Despite the need for further system improvements, the current results already highlight the potential of sensory substitution and incorporating walking-related auditory, visual, and vibrotactile cues for improving user experience and self-motion perception in applications ranging from virtual reality and gaming to telepresence and architectural walk-throughs.

6. ACKNOWLEDGMENTS

Our thanks go to all the people who volunteered to take part in the experiments presented in this paper.

7. REFERENCES

[1] Barreira, T.V., Rowe, D. and Kang, M. 2010. Parameters of walking and jogging in young adults. *International Journal of Exercise Science*. 3, 1, 4–13.

[2] Berthoz, A., Israël, I., Georges-François, P., Grasso, R. and Tsuzuku, T. 1995. Spatial memory of body linear displacement: what is being stored? *Science*. 269, 5220, 95–8.

[3] Blom, K.J. and Beckhaus, S. 2010. Virtual collision notification. *IEEE Symposium on 3D User Interfaces (3DUI)*, 35–38.

[4] Bos, J.E., Bles, W. and Groen, E.L. 2008. A theory on visually induced motion sickness. *Displays*. 29, 2, 47–57.

[5] Bourrelly, A., Vercher, J.-L. and Bringoux, L. 2010. Pitch body orientation influences the perception of self-motion direction induced by optic flow. *Neuroscience letters*. 482, 3, 193–7.

[6] Bowman, D., Koller, D. and Hodges, L. A Methodology for the Evaluation of Travel Techniques for Immersive Virtual Environments. *Virtual Reality: Research, Development, and Applications*. 3, 120–131.

[7] Bowman, D., Kruijff, E., LaViola, J. and Poupyrev, I. 2005. *3D user interfaces : theory and practice*. Addison-Wesley.

[8] Bringoux, L., Robic, G., Gauthier, G.M. and Vercher, J.L. 2008. Judging beforehand the possibility of passing under obstacles without motion: the influence of egocentric and geocentric frames of reference. *Experimental brain research*. 185, 4, 673–80.

[9] Bringoux, L., Tamura, K., Faldon, M., Gresty, M.A. and Bronstein, A.M. 2004. Influence of whole-body pitch tilt and kinesthetic cues on the perceived gravity-referenced eye level. *Experimental brain research*. 155, 3, 385–92.

[10] Bubka, A. and Bonato, F. 2010. Natural visual-field features enhance vection. *Perception*. 39, 5, 627–35.

[11] Cross, R. 1998. Standing, walking, running and jumping on a force plate. *American Journal of Physics*. 67, 4, 304–309.

[12] Darken, R., Cockayne, W. and Carmein, D. 1997. The Omni-Directional Treadmill: A Locomotion Device for Virtual Worlds. *Proceedings of the ACM Symposium on User Interface Software and Technology (UIST'97)*, 213–221.

[13] DeAngelis, G.C. and Angelaki, D.E. 2012. Visual–Vestibular Integration for Self-Motion Perception. CRC Press.

[14] Feng, M., Dey, A. and Lindeman, R.W. 2016. An initial exploration of a multi-sensory design space: Tactile support for walking in immersive virtual environments. *IEEE Symposium on 3D User Interfaces (3DUI)*, 95–104.

[15] Frowen, P. and Neale, D. 2010. *Neale's disorders of the foot*. Churchill Livingstone/Elsevier.

[16] Giordano, B.L., McAdams, S., Visell, Y., Cooperstock, J., Yao, H.-Y. and Hayward, V. 2008. Non-visual identification of walking grounds. *The Journal of the Acoustical Society of America*. 123, 5, 3412–3412.

[17] Grossman, G.E., Leigh, R.J., Abel, L.A., Lanska, D.J. and Thurston, S.E. 1988. Frequency and velocity of rotational head perturbations during locomotion. *Experimental brain research*. 70, 3, 470–6.

[18] Gu, C. and Griffin, M.J. 2011. Vibrotactile thresholds at the sole of the foot: effect of vibration frequency and contact location. *Somatosensory & motor research*. 28, 3-4, 86–93.

[19] Guy, E., Punpongsanon, P., Iwai, D., Sato, K. and Boubekeur, T. 2015. LazyNav: 3D ground navigation with non-critical body parts. *IEEE Symposium on 3D User Interfaces (3DUI)*, 43–50.

[20] de Haan, G., Griffith, E.J. and Post, F.H. 2008. Using the Wii Balance Board as a low-cost VR interaction device. *Proceedings of the ACM symposium on Virtual reality software and technology - VRST '08*, 289.

[21] Harris, A., Nguyen, K., Wilson, P.T., Jackoski, M. and Williams, B. 2014. Human Joystick: Wii-leaning to Translate in Large Virtual Environments. *VRCAI '14* (New York, NY, USA), 231–234.

[22] Harris, L., Jenkin, M. and Zikovitz, D. 1999. Vestibular Cues and Virtual environments: Choosing the Magnitude of the Vestibular Cue. *Proceedings of IEEE Virtual Reality '99*, 229–236.

[23] Harris, L.R., Jenkin, M. and Zikovitz, D.C. 2000. Visual and non-visual cues in the perception of linear self motion. *Experimental Brain Research*. 135, 1, 12–21.

[24] Hettinger, L.J., Schmidt, T., Jones, D.L. and Keshavarz, B. 2014. Illusory Self-motion in Virtual Environments. *Handbook of Virtual Environments*. K.S. Hale and K.M. Stanney, eds. CRC Press. 435 – 466.

[25] Ho, I.-J., Hou, Y.-Y., Yang, C.-H., Wu, W.-L., Chen, S.-K. and Guo, L.-Y. 2010. Comparison of Plantar Pressure Distribution between Different Speed and Incline During Treadmill Jogging. *Journal of sports science & medicine*. 9, 1, 154–60.

[26] Ikei, Y., Shimabukuro, S., Kato, S., Okuya, Y., Abe, K., Hirota, K. and Amemiya, T. 2014. Rendering of Virtual Walking Sensation by a Passive Body Motion. *Haptics: Neuroscience, Devices, Modeling, and Applications*. M. Auvray and C. Duriez, eds. Springer Berlin Heidelberg.

[27] Ivanenko, Y.P., Grasso, R., Israël, I. and Berthoz, A. 1997. The contribution of otoliths and semicircular canals to the perception of two-dimensional passive whole-body motion in humans. *The Journal of physiology*. 502, 1, 223–33.

[28] Iwata, H. 2001. GaitMaster: A Versatile Locomotion Interface for Uneven Virtual Terrain. *Proceedings of IEEE Virtual Reality*, 131–137.

[29] Kaczmarek, K.A., Webster, J.G., Bach-y-Rita, P. and Tompkins, W.J. 1991. Electrotactile and vibrotactile displays for sensory substitution systems. *IEEE transactions on biomedical engineering*. 38, 1, 1–16.

[30] Kruijff, E., Marquardt, A., Trepkowski, C., Schild, J. and Hinkenjann, A. 2015. Enhancing User Engagement in Immersive Games through Multisensory Cues. *In Proceedings of VS-GAMES*.

[31] Kruijff, E., Riecke, B., Trepkowski, C. and Kitson, A. 2015. Upper Body Leaning can affect Forward Self-Motion Perception in Virtual Environments. *Proceedings of the 3rd ACM Symposium on Spatial User Interaction - SUI '15*, 103–112.

[32] Lawson, B.D. and Riecke, B.E. 2014. The Perception of Body Motion. *Handbook of Virtual Environments: Design, Implementation, and Applications*. K.S. Hale and K.M. Stanney, eds. CRC Press. 163–195.

[33] Marchal, M., Cirio, G., Visell, Y., Fontana, F., Serafin, S., Cooperstock, J. and Lécuyer, A. 2013. Multimodal Rendering of Walking Over Virtual Grounds. *Human Walking in Virtual Environments*. F. Steinicke, Y. Visell, J. Campos, and A. Lécuyer, eds. Springer New York.

[34] Marchal, M., Pettre, J. and Lecuyer, A. 2011. Joyman: A human-scale joystick for navigating in virtual worlds. *2011 IEEE Symposium on 3D User Interfaces (3DUI)*, 19–26.

[35] Nakamura, S. and Shimojo, S. 1998. Orientation of selective effects of body tilt on visually induced perception of self-motion. *Perceptual and motor skills*. 87, 2, 667–72.

[36] Nilsson, N.C., Nordahl, R., Turchet, L. and Serafin, S. 2012. Audio-Haptic simulation of walking on virtual ground surfaces to enhance realism. *Proceedings of the 7th international conference on Haptic and Audio Interaction Design* (Berlin, Heidelberg), 61–70.

[37] Nordahl, R., Berrezag, A., Dimitrov, S., Turchet, L., Hayward, V. and Serafin, S. 2010. Preliminary Experiment Combining Virtual Reality Haptic Shoes and Audio Synthesis. Springer Berlin Heidelberg. 123–129.

[38] Palmisano, S., Allison, R.S., Kim, J. and Bonato, F. 2011. Simulated viewpoint jitter shakes sensory conflict accounts of vection. *Seeing and Perceiving*. 24, 2, 173–200.

[39] Papetti, S., Fontana, F., Civolani, M., Berrezag, A. and Hayward, V. 2010. Audio-tactile Display of Ground Properties Using Interactive Shoes. *Proceedings of the 5th International Workshop on Haptic and Audio Interaction Design* (Berlin, Heidelberg).

[40] Riecke, B.E. 2011. Compelling Self-Motion Through Virtual Environments Without Actual Self-Motion – Using Self-Motion Illusions ("Vection") to Improve User Experience in VR. In J. Kim (Ed.). *Virtual Reality*. J.-J. Kim, ed. InTech. 149–176.

[41] Riecke, B.E., Bodenheimer, B., McNamara, T.P., Williams, B., Peng, P. and Feuereissen, D. 2010. Do we need to walk for effective virtual reality navigation? physical rotations alone may suffice. *Proceedings of Spatial Cognition VII, International Conference on Spatial Cognition*, 234–247.

[42] Riecke, B.E. and Feuereissen, D. 2012. To Move or Not to Move: Can Active Control and User-Driven Motion Cueing Enhance Self-Motion Perception ("Vection") in Virtual Reality? *ACM Symposium on Applied Perception SAP* (Los Angeles, USA), 17–24.

[43] Riecke, B.E., Feuereissen, D. and Rieser, J.J. 2009. Auditory self-motion simulation is facilitated by haptic and vibrational cues suggesting the possibility of actual motion. *ACM Transactions on Applied Perception*. 6, 3, 1–22.

[44] Riecke, B.E. and Schulte-Pelkum, J. 2013. Perceptual and Cognitive Factors for Self-Motion Simulation in Virtual Environments: How Can Self-Motion Illusions ("Vection") Be Utilized? *Human Walking in Virtual Environments*. F. Steinicke, Y. Visell, J. Campos, and A. Lécuyer, eds. Springer New York. 27–54.

[45] Riecke, B.E., Väljamäe, A. and Schulte-Pelkum, J. 2009. Moving sounds enhance the visually-induced self-motion illusion (circular vection) in virtual reality. *ACM Transactions on Applied Perception*. 6, 2, 1–27.

[46] Rupert, A. and Kolev, O. 2008. The Use of Tactile Cues to Modify the Perception of Self-Motion. Technical report ADA505849

[47] Salo, A.I.T., Bezodis, I.N., Batterham, A.M. and Kerwin, D.G. 2011. Elite sprinting: are athletes individually step-frequency or step-length reliant? *Medicine and science in sports and exercise*. 43, 6, 1055–62.

[48] Schubert, T., Friedmann, F. and Regenbrecht, H. 2001. The experience of presence: Factor analytic insights. *Presence - Teleoperators and Virtual Environments*. 10, 3, 266–281.

[49] St George, R.J. and Fitzpatrick, R.C. 2011. The sense of self-motion, orientation and balance explored by vestibular stimulation. *The Journal of physiology*. 589, Pt 4, 807–13.

[50] Takeuchi, Y. 2010. Gilded gait: Reshaping the urban experience with augmented footsteps. *Proceedings of the 23nd annual ACM symposium on User interface software and technology - UIST '10* (New York, New York, USA, 185.

[51] Templeman, J.N., Denbrook, P.S. and Sibert, L.E. 1999. Virtual Locomotion: Walking in Place through Virtual Environments. *Presence: Teleoperators and Virtual Environments*. 8, 6, 598–617.

[52] Terziman, L., Marchal, M., Multon, F., Arnaldi, B. and Lécuyer, A. 2013. Personified and multistate camera motions for first-person navigation in desktop virtual reality. *IEEE transactions on visualization and computer graphics*. 19, 4, 652–61.

[53] Terziman, L., Marchal, M., Multon, F., Arnaldi, B. and Lecuyer, A. 2012. The King-Kong Effects: Improving sensation of walking in VR with visual and tactile vibrations at each step. *IEEE Symposium on 3D User Interfaces (3DUI)*, 19–26.

[54] Turchet, L., Burelli, P. and Serafin, S. 2013. Haptic feedback for enhancing realism of walking simulations. *IEEE transactions on haptics*. 6, 1, 35–45.

[55] Usoh, M., Arthur, K., Whitton, M.C., Bastos, R., Steed, A., Slater, M. and Brooks, F.P.J. 1999. Walking > Walking-in-Place > Flying in Virtual Environments. *Proceedings of SIGGRAPH '99*, 359–364.

[56] Väljamäe, A., Larsson, P., Västfjäll, D. and Kleiner, M. 2006. Vibrotactile Enhancement of Auditory-Induced Self-Motion and Spatial Presence. *Journal of the Audio Engineering Society*. 54, 10, 954–963.

[57] Valkov, D., Steinicke, F., Bruder, G. and Hinrichs, K. 2010. Traveling in 3D Virtual Environments with Foot Gestures and a Multi-Touch enabled WIM. *Proceedings of Virtual Reality International Conference (VRIC 2010)*, 171–180.

[58] Velazquez, R., Bazan, O., Varona, J., Delgado-Mata, C. and A., C. 2012. Insights into the Capabilities of Tactile-Foot Perception. *International Journal of Advanced Robotic Systems*, 1.

[59] Velloso, E., Schmidt, D., Alexander, J., Gellersen, H. and Bulling, A. 2015. The Feet in Human-Computer Interaction: A Survey of Foot-Based Interaction. *ACM Computing Surveys*. 48, 2, 1–35.

[60] Visell, Y., Giordano, B.L., Millet, G. and Cooperstock, J.R. 2011. Vibration influences haptic perception of surface compliance during walking. *PloS one*. 6, 3, e17697.

[61] Wang, J. and Lindeman, R. 2012. Leaning-based travel interfaces revisited: frontal versus sidewise stances for flying in 3D virtual spaces. *Proceedings of the 18th ACM symposium on Virtual reality software and technology - VRST '12* (New York, New York, USA, 121.

[62] Wang, J. and Lindeman, R.W. 2012. Comparing isometric and elastic surfboard interfaces for leaning-based travel in 3D virtual environments. *2012 IEEE Symposium on 3D User Interfaces (3DUI)*, 31–38.

Spatial User Interaction Panel

Hrvoje Benko
Microsoft Research
benko@microsoft.com

Katsuhiro Harada
Bandai Namco Entertainment
Katsuhiro_Harada@bandainamcoent.co.jp

Otmar Hilliges
ETH Zurich
otmar.hilliges@inf.ethz.ch

Alex Olwal
Google
MIT Media Lab
olwal@media.mit.edu

Aitor Rovira
Nara Institute of Science and
Technolgy
aitor@is.naist.jp

CCS Concepts

•Human-centered computing → Interaction paradigms; Interaction design; •Computer systems organization → *Embedded and cyber-physical systems;*

Keywords

Human-computer interaction; 3D interaction; Mixed Reality; Robotics

1. INTRODUCTION

In this panel, we will focus the discussion on the present and future of spatial user interfaces. The discussion will include both the technologies and their applications. We want to explore the current limitations, possible future solutions and how other fields such as artificial intelligence, body implants, or robotic-enhanced interactions will contribute to these interactions. New applications will also bring new possibilities, but they might also raise controversy, leading to a discussion about where the ethical limits are.

2. AITOR ROVIRA (MODERATOR)

Aitor Rovira is a postdoctoral researcher at the Nara Institute of Science and Technologies where he focuses his research in Augmented Reality and Haptics. He obtained his PhD for the University College London, supervised by Prof. Mel Slater. Before that, he obtained his MSc for the University of Girona (Spain), carrying out his thesis at the Louisiana Immersive Technologies Enterprise (Lafayette, LA, USA) as a visiting researcher.

His research interests include Virtual Reality, Augmented Reality, and Human-Computer Interaction, and how these technologies can contribute in other non-technological fields, with a special attention in Health Sciences, such as in Social Psychology and developing therapies. His interests also include Human Perception, Haptics, and Machine Learning in

SUI '16 October 15-16, 2016, Tokyo, Japan

© 2016 Copyright held by the owner/author(s).

ACM ISBN 978-1-4503-4068-7/16/10.

DOI: http://dx.doi.org/10.1145/2983310.2996295

order to deliver realistic experiences in Mixed Reality systems. http://imd.naist.jp/people/aitor-rovira/.

3. HRVOJE BENKO

Hrvoje Benko is a senior researcher at Microsoft Research. He explores novel interactive computing technologies and their impact on human-computer interaction. In particular, his research interests include augmented reality, computational illumination, surface computing, new input form factors and devices, as well as touch and freehand gestural input. He is fascinated by the intersection point where the digital technology world meets the curved, physical, 3D space we live in. Dr. Benko is the author of more than 30 scientific papers and journal articles. He served as General Chair (2014) and Program Chair (2012) of the ACM User Interface Systems and Technology conference. For his publications he received the best paper awards at both ACM UIST and ACM SIGCHI. His work has been featured in the mainstream media and on popular technology blogs. In 2010, he worked with Microsoft Hardware to turn one of his research projects into a product called Microsoft Touch Mouse. He received his Ph.D. in Computer Science from Columbia University in 2007 with prof. Steven Feiner. More detail can be found on his website: http://research.microsoft.com/~benko/.

4. KATSUHIRO HARADA

Katsuhiro Harada is a game director and producer at Bandai Namco Entertainment. He is best known for producing the Tekken video games series since the first installment of the series, until the present days, with Tekken 7 that will be released in the next months. He also produced the Soulcalibur series and the Pokken Tournament, and he also currently works on Summer Lesson, a title that will be released this Autumn along with Playstation VR. More details on http://tekken.wikia.com/wiki/Katsuhiro_Harada.

5. OTMAR HILLIGES

Otmar Hilliges is currently an Assistant Professor at ETH Zurich in the Computer Science Department where he leads the Advanced Interactive Technologies Lab. Previously he was a Researcher at Microsoft Research Cambridge and prior to that a post-doctoral researcher also at Microsoft Research. He was awarded a Diplom (equiv. MSc) in Computer Science from Technische Universitat Munchen, Germany (Summa Cum Laude 2004) and his doctoral degree in Computer Science from LMU Munchen, Germany (Summa Cum Laude

2009). His research interests are in Human Computer Interaction, interactive graphics and applied Machine Learning. He regularly publishes in the premier HCI conferences and his work has been awarded with multiple best paper awards at CHI, UIST, CSCW and ISMAR. He has recently received an ERC starting grant for his research on synthesis of interactive technologies. His group is also active in adjacent areas such as graphics, robotics and computer vision. He routinely serves on the program committees of several HCI conferences and reviews for many journals including ACM ToG, ACM ToCHI, IJHCS, IEEE ToSMC, IEEE JVR. Finally, his work has led to 23 patents (12 issued, 11 pending) in diverse topics ranging from input recognition algorithms to 3D reconstruction methods and interaction techniques. Website: http://ait.ethz.ch/people/hilliges/.

6. ALEX OLWAL

Alex Olwal (Ph.D., M.Sc.) is a Senior Research Scientist at Google, Affiliate Faculty at KTH, and Research Affiliate at the MIT Media Lab.

Alex designs and develops interactions and technologies that embrace digital and physical experiences. He is interested in tools, techniques and devices that enable new interaction concepts for the augmentation and empowerment of the human senses. Alex's research (www.olwal.com) includes augmented reality, spatially aware mobile devices, medical user interfaces, ubiquitous computing, touch screens, as well as novel interaction devices, sensors and displays.

He has previously worked with the development of new technologies for Human-Computer Interaction at MIT - Massachusetts Institute of Technology (Cambridge, MA), KTH - Royal Institute of Technology (Stockholm), Columbia University (New York, NY), University of California (Santa Barbara, CA) and Microsoft Research (Redmond, WA). He has also been a lecturer at Rhode Island School of Design (Providence, RI) and at Stanford University (Stanford, CA). Website: http://www.olwal.com/.

Sharpen Your Carving Skills in Mixed Reality Space

Maho Kawagoe[1], Mai Otsuki[2], Fumihisa Shibata[1], and Asako Kimura[1]

[1]Graduate School of Information Science and Engineering, Ritsumeikan University, Japan

[2]University of Tsukuba, Japan

kawagoe@rm.is.ritsumei.ac.jp

ABSTRACT

This paper proposes a virtual carving system using ToolDevice in a mixed reality (MR) space. By touching and moving the device over real objects, users can carve it virtually. Real-world wood carving with wood carving tools requires several steps such as carving a rough outline, shaping the wood, and carving patterns on its surface. In this paper, we focus on the step of carving patterns on a surface and implement it in our MR carving system.

Keywords

Carving system; Mixed Reality; ToolDevice

1. INTRODUCTION

We have developed ToolDevice, which is a set of interaction devices using the metaphor of existing tools familiar in everyday life and a mixed reality (MR) 3D modeling system that imitates real-life woodworking [1]. In this system, users can pick up and move virtual objects with the TweezersDevice, and cut and join virtual objects using the Knife/HammerDevice. By repeating these operations, users can build virtual wood models.

In the same way, we propose an MR carving system with an input device "CarvingToolDevice" which imitates actual carving tools for creating patterns on a 3D object in a manner similar to real-world carving (Figure 1). Using this system, users can understand the shape of the objects intuitively and change the carving strokes dynamically. In this paper, we focus on relief carving, a type of woodcarving in which patterns can be engraved on a flat wood panel.

2. CARVING MODEL

In real-world carving, the depth, width, and length of the carving footprint changes depending on the "pressure" and the "angle between the surface and carving tool." Similarly, in our carving model, users can change the virtual stroke based on the "pressure" and the "angle between the surface and device."

The carving depth is proportional to the pressure of the carving tool on the real object surface as well as the angle of the carving tool and the surface. As the angle of the tool becomes more vertical, the depth increases, because the tip of the carving tool cuts into the object surface more deeply. The width and length are proportional to the curve depth and angle of the device, respectively. The stroke becomes longer when the angle between the surface and the device is horizontal, because the pressure of the CarvingToolDevice disperses in the direction of the stroke (Figure 1).

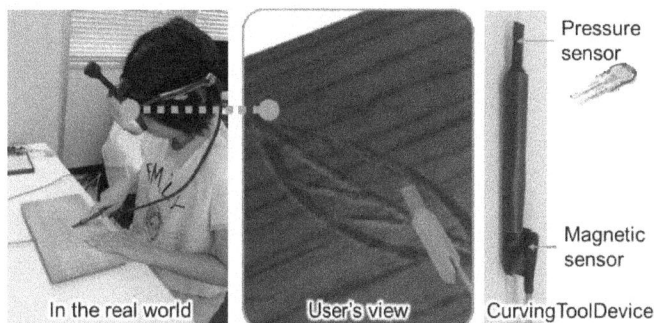

Figure 1: MR carving system

If users overlay a carving stroke, the system determines the overlapping part and increases the depth of that part.

3. MR CARVING SYSTEM

In the MR carving system, users wear a binocular see-through head-mounted display (HMD; Canon VH-2002), which enables them to perceive depth. The position and orientation of the HMD and the device are tracked using Polhemus LIBERTY, a six-degree-of-freedom tracking system equipped with magnetic sensors. We have developed the CarvingToolDevice. To detect the pressure of the carving tools on the real object, a pressure sensor (Interlink Electronics Inc., FSR400 SHORT) is attached to the tip of the device. To obtain the position and orientation of the device, a magnetic sensor is attached to the back end of the device. In addition, to provide tactile sensations, sandpaper is attached to the tip of the device.

4. CONCLUSION

In this paper, we proposed a virtual carving system that allows users to carve patterns virtually on the surface of a real object in an MR space, just as in real world carving. Using this system, users can change carving strokes with their actions (i.e., the pressure and angle of the device) in real time. For future work, we plan to extend the carving from a 2D plane to a 3D object and add more digital carving functions.

5. REFERENCES

[1] Arisandi, R., Otsuki, M., Kimura, A., Shibata, F., and Tamura, H.: Virtual Handcrafting: Building virtual wood models using ToolDevice, Proc. IEEE, Vol. 102, No.2, pp. 185 - 195 (2014)

Stickie: Mobile Device Supported Spatial Collaborations

Jaskirat S. Randhawa
Parsons School of Design
The New School, New York City
New York, USA
jaskiratr@newschool.edu

ABSTRACT

Stickie is an application that enables people to remotely perform sticky note collaborations over the Internet by utilizing two highly ubiquitous workplace devices – smartphones & TV screens. The phone acts as an interface between the tangible and digital space. Users can leave notes from their phones onto a TV screen by placing the phone itself on any ordinary non-touchscreen display. This research constructs a novel technique for sticky note brainstorming across the Internet. It extends the interaction spatially by incorporating cues of participants' physical expressions and activities.

Author Keywords

Mobile Interactions; Device supported collaborative work

ACM Classification Keywords

H.5.3 Group and Organization Interfaces: Computer-supported cooperative work

1. INTRODUCTION

Stickie focuses on virtual participatory experience and replication, of actual spatial interactions associated with sticky note collaborations. The interactions are designed to invite people to physically participate in virtual collaboration sessions. Users can create multimedia notes on a personal smartphone. They work with a TV screen that displays the shared workspace and physically place their phone on top of it at a point where they intend to *stick* the note. The note then gets transferred on the TV screen. To position the note correctly, a full-screen grid of uniquely colored cells is first generated on the TV screen. While the phone rests on the it, back-facing camera of the phone identifies the cell directly underneath by color. Then, a new grid is again generated within the detected cell. The camera identifies the color of the cell under it and so the process repeats. After consecutive iterations, the grid shrinks down to a few pixels and the center of the grid indicates the position of the phone on the TV screen. Through this process, the workspace locates the position of the phone without any additional hardware for its tracking.

2. SYSTEM DESIGN

Currently, Stickie is an open-source native application written in Java for Android devices. The web application stack

(http://stickie.space) is built with Node.js, MongoDB, Express and Jade. The phone application hosts several key features to draw freehand sketches. For example, the user can use the phone's touchscreen to draw notes, bring images from other phone applications, annotate them and post the content on the TV screen. When the workspace begins to exceed the field of view on TV screen, the user can use phone tilt function to pan around and navigate the limitless space. To move notes, a user can hover their phone over the note, hold the grab button and release at a point where the note needs to be relocated.

3. DEMONSTRATION

To initiate a session, the user logs in on the web application which generates a unique QR (Quick Response) code. The phone application has a QR reader integrated in it that reads the session code and pairs the user phone with it. Once the user has logged into the session, other people can be invited to join by sharing the session ID with them. The user can also suspend the session via a menu option in the phone application. The web application then opens up an analytics page, which shows the timeline of user activities since the start of the session.

Figure 1. User can physically interact with content on any ordinary non-touchscreen display through a personal smartphone.

4. TARGET AUDIENCE

Stickie is designed primarily for users like scrum masters, book writers, game designer and architects, for whom sticky notes are an integral part of teamwork, brainstorming and task management. Throughout this research several people from such professions tried and tested Stickie. The benefit to digitizing their work resonated strongly amongst every user test. In many cases, users found it very convenient to have the ability access and edit a session any time. It adds flexibility and accessibility in their core ideation processes.

5. ACKNOWLEDGEMENT

This work was supported by Parsons School of Design and Verizon Challenge, 2015 hosted by NYC Media Lab, New York.

SHIFT-Sliding and DEPTH-POP for 3D Positioning

Junwei Sun, Wolfgang Stuerzlinger
School of Interactive Arts + Technology
Simon Fraser University, Vancouver, Canada
junweis@sfu.ca, http://ws.iat.sfu.ca

Dmitri Shuralyov
Department of EECS
York University, Toronto, Canada
shurcool@gmail.com

1. INTRODUCTION

We introduce two new 3D positioning methods. The techniques enable rapid, yet easy-to-use positioning of objects in 3D scenes. With SHIFT-Sliding, the user can override the default assumption of contact and non-collision for sliding [1], and lift objects into the air or make them collide with other objects. DEPTH-POP maps mouse wheel actions to all object positions along the mouse ray, where the object meets the default assumptions for sliding. We will demonstrate the two methods in a desktop environment with the mouse and keyboard as interaction devices. Both methods use frame buffer techniques for efficiency.

With SHIFT-Sliding, users can move the object *orthogonal* to the sliding plane by pressing the SHIFT key. If the user then "pulls" the object away from the surface, this will cause the object to float. When the user releases the SHIFT key (with the mouse button still held down), the object will then keep sliding on a plane defined by the initial normal vector. When the floating object collides, we transition the object back into sliding mode and start sliding on the collider surface. If the user "pushes" the object into a surface while pressing the SHIFT key, the object will interpenetrate that surface. When the user releases the SHIFT key, the object will then keep sliding on the plane defined by the original normal vector, inside the surface, still maintaining the visibility assumption. SHIFT-Sliding *automatically* derives a local coordinate system from the last known contact surface, which makes it easy to position objects in space relative to other objects, without having to explicitly set a local coordinate system.

With DEPTH-POP, we map front and back movement of the mouse wheel to our new "push-to-back" respectively "pop-to-front" functionality. With push-to-back the object is moved to the next possible position further away from the camera that satisfies the assumptions of contact, non-collision and visible. For each pop-to-front event, the object is moved to the next position closer to the camera, again maintaining the same assumptions. DEPTH-POP addresses the inherent depth ambiguity in sliding algorithms.

2. SYSTEM

We built our system in the Unity game engine. The system works robustly and efficiently on many platforms. We will demonstrate the system on a Mac laptop. Figure 1 shows a person using the system on a PC. While holding the left SHIFT key she "lifts" the chair into the air. The system runs stably at 60 fps for scenes with up to almost a million polygons. The user can slide objects on

various surfaces, including concave surfaces and point clouds. While we demonstrate the system in a desktop environment, we point out that the methods work even in HMDs or CAVEs.

In our demonstration, users will have the chance to try the 3D positioning methods in various scenes. They will also be able to compare the SHIFT-Sliding and DEPTH-POP techniques with conventional 3D widgets. As shown in the user studies we performed, our two new methods significantly speed up common 3D positioning tasks.

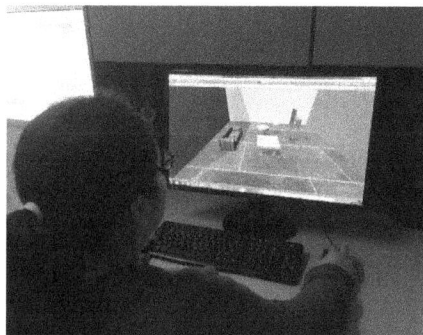

Figure 1. A participant using the system. The user uses the left SHIFT key to raise the chair highlighted in green into the air.

3. AUDIENCE

We designed the system for novice users without CAD knowledge. We focus on a desktop-based user interface with a mouse and a keyboard, as this provides high performance in both speed and accuracy. A mouse also helps to keep our system easy to learn and use by novices, as many are used to this interaction device.

4. BENEFITS

We presented two novel 3D positioning techniques that are efficient and easy to use. Both methods profoundly enhance the ease and efficiency of 3D manipulation with 2D input devices. As 3D editing and design tools are becoming more widely used, our methods will help designers to become more productive. Our work is of interest for the SUI community. The audience for our demo will gain first-hand experience with our system and understand the improvements of our new methods relative to the traditional, familiar 3D widgets.

5. RESEARCH LAB

Our research lab is located at Simon Fraser University, Surrey, BC. The research interests of our lab include 3D and Spatial User Interfaces, Virtual Reality, Human-Computer Interaction, Immersive Analytics and Visual Analytics.

6. REFERENCES

[1] Oh, J.Y. and Stuerzlinger, W., 2005, May. Moving objects with 2D input devices in CAD systems and desktop virtual environments. In *Graphics Interface 2005* (pp. 195-202).

SUI '16, October 15 - 16, 2016, Tokyo, Japan
ACM 978-1-4503-4068-7/16/10.
http://dx.doi.org/10.1145/2983310.2991067

Developing Interoperable Experiences with OpenUIX

Mikel Salazar
msalazar@augmentedinteraction.com

Carlos Laorden
claorden@augmentedinteraction.com

Augmented Interaction S.L. 48006, Bilbao, Spain

In recent years, the popularization of mobile platforms with advanced graphic rendering capabilities and heterogeneous sensor systems have enabled the development of new and more intuitive interactive experiences; from basic gyroscope-based VR visualizations in tourism apps to complex AR-based environments that cutting-edge smart-glasses allow. Nevertheless, current UI design tools and software distribution systems force developers to encapsulate their user experiences into closed interaction spaces (more commonly referred to as "apps"). A lack of interoperability that hinders the creation of workflows and, ultimately, relegates current mobile platforms to a secondary role.

Against this background, the framework we present in this demo aims to provide UI designers –and end-users– with a simple but powerful language with which easily create, modify and share advanced interaction spaces. A UI description language that takes into consideration the context of the users not only to adapt the contents of the SUI to their real needs and desires, but also to allow them to automatically discover new and meaningful experiences as they go about their daily lives.

Furthermore, while this open-source framework provides the necessary tools to –collaboratively– edit the different components of the interaction spaces (from the 3d representation of the virtual objects to the lighting conditions of the real environment or the physical presence of the users), what it sets it apart from other similar systems is its interoperability mechanisms. Beyond merely allowing the use of a predefined set of interaction techniques, the extension mechanisms built into the very own description language enables SUI designers to define and expand upon shared repositories of widgets behaviors and resources.

Nevertheless, to provide a level playing field for all users (while also protecting their privacy and copyright interets), the network model of the OpenUIX framework requires an entity that acts as an arbiter in the information exchange. This is where our research center, Augmented Interaction, rises to the challenge, providing the necessary network architecture to ensure the correct functioning of the whole model.

To properly showcase the different features of the OpenUIX framework, the presenters will provide SUI 2016 attendees with an AR browser created with it. This demo will be presented at the space granted by the organization of the event (on several VR/AR-enabled computer systems provided by the presenters), but to allow attendees to fully explore the possibilities of this technology, a version`of the AR browser will also be available to download for common mobile platforms (iOS and Android).

The presentation of the demo will be conducted in three scenarios, each of which focused on different interaction techniques and tracking technologies:

1. **Room-wide interaction:** At the table provided by the organization, attendees will be able to experiment with several use cases designed to allow them to familiarize with the features of the framework (enabling them to create new contents collaboratively and to play with several widgets that require interacting with both virtual and physical objects). After completing them, they will be asked to download the demo app on their own devices and use it to navigate through the room, cataloging other demo stands and posters (in a sort of "catch'em all" minigame).

2. **Venue-wide interaction:** To encourage the attendees to test the demo app, the presenters will create several user experiences across the conference venue. These experiences will range from a basic messaging system that enables organizers to place small texts and images on planar surfaces to guide the attendees to the different sessions and events, to a comment system that allows attendees to rate paper presentations and provide valuable feedback to the presenters.

3. **City-wide interaction:** Although the lack of a data plan for their devices might restrict the access to fully interactive, multi-user experiences, by taking advantage of geolocation technologies and ad hoc wireless communications, the demo presenters will provide conference attendees with several examples of the user interfaces that can be created with the OpenUIX framework. These include a navigation system for emergencies (guiding the users towards the nearest shelter in case of earthquake/tsunami), an AR-based firework display for the conference banquet and a 3D map of the venues of the Tokyo 2020 Olympics.

SUI '16 October 15-16, 2016, Tokyo, Japan

© 2016 Copyright held by the owner/author(s).

ACM ISBN 978-1-4503-4068-7/16/10.

DOI: http://dx.doi.org/10.1145/2983310.2989203

TickTockRay Demo: Smartwatch Raycasting for Mobile HMDs

Daniel Kharlamov
Game Research Lab
California State University
Monterey Bay
100 Campus Rd, Seaside,
California, USA
dakharlamov@csumb.edu

Krzysztof Pietroszek
Game Research Lab
California State University
Monterey Bay
100 Campus Rd, Seaside,
California, USA
kpietroszek@csumb.edu

Liudmila Tahai
School of Public Health and
Health Systems
University of Waterloo
200 University Ave West
Waterloo, Ontario, Canada
ltahai@uwaterloo.ca

ABSTRACT

We present a demo of TickTockRay, a smartwatch-based 3D pointing technique for smartphone-based immersive environments. Our work demonstrates that smartwatch-based raycasting may be a practical alternative to head-rotation-based pointing or specialized input devices. We demonstrate the technique in an example, virtual reality clone of the Minecraft game. We release TickTockRay to the research community as an open-source plugin for Unity.

CCS Concepts

•**Human-centered computing → Pointing;**

Keywords

raycasting, 3D pointing, smartwatch, virtual reality

1. INTRODUCTION

We demonstrate TickTockRay, an implementation of fixed-origin raycasting technique that utilizes a smartwatch as an input device. We show that a smartwatch-based raycasting is a good alternative to a head-rotation-controlled cursor or a specialized input device. TickTockRay implements fixed-origin raycasting with the ray originating from a fixed point, located, roughly, in the user's chest. The control-display (C/D) ratio of TickTockRay technique is set to 1, with exact correspondence between the ray and the smartwatch's rotation. Such C/D ratio enables a user to select targets in the entire virtual reality control space.

2. DEMO EXPERIENCE

We use TickTockRay to enable placement and destruction of blocks in an open source clone of Minecraft game[1].The demo experience consist of exploring the Minecraft VR world,

---

[1]https://github.com/gameresearchlab/TickTockCraft

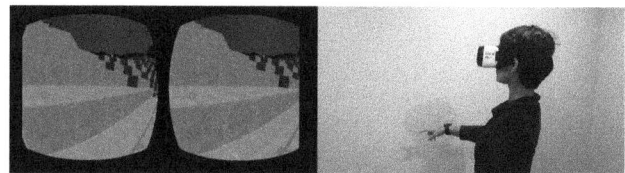

Figure 1: TickTockRay enables raycasting in a mobile VR using an off-the-shelf smartwatch.

destroying and placing blocks and building a simple block construction.

At the beginning of the demo the player is asked to put on the smartwatch and the smartphone-based head mounted display. Then, the player is instructed on how to position their elbow and arm, and is encouraged to move the cursor by moving only the forearm, while keeping their elbow close to the body. If needed, the player may reposition their entire body, instead of making wide movements with their shoulder joint, in order to reduce fatigue. For block creation (right click), the player may use a quick wrist twist by a minimum of 45° immediately followed by a return to the original position. Similarly, for a destruction of a block (left click), the wrist must be quickly twisted counterclockwise and back.

3. HARDWARE AND SOFTWARE

Our demo apparatus consists of Samsung Gear VR headset, Samsung Galaxy S7 smartphone and LG G smartwatch. In principle, the TickTockRay technique works on any modern smartphone + smartwatch + VR headset system. Because all the demo components are off-the-shelf, we also publish the demo app at https://www.gameresearchlab.com, so that the TickTockRay technique can be tested on the participant's devices.

4. ORGANIZATION

TickTockRay was developed in the Game Research Lab at the California State University Monterey Bay under the funding provided by the Undergraduate Research Opportunity Program. At the Game Research Lab, undergraduate students partake in gaming and virtual reality research, contributing to the fields of Human Computer Interaction, Graphics, and Machine Learning.

Mushi: A Generative Art Canvas for Kinect Based Tracking

Jennifer Weiler
School of Arts, Media & Engineering
Tempe, Arizona
jjweiler@asu.edu

Sudarshan Seshasayee
School of Arts, Media & Engineering
Tempe, Arizona
spseshas@asu.edu

ABSTRACT

Using modern technology in the form of body tracking and real-time image processing software, we propound to contextualize abstract art with an experiential system. Overall, our goal was to capture something as ethereal and transitory as movement and translate it into a painterly medium.

Keywords

Kinect; Processing; Programmable Art; Optical Flow; Histogram of oriented Gradients

1. INTRODUCTION

A key means to stimulate a person's interest is to present them with interactions that continually provide them with fresh, creative interaction based on a framework of inferable rules. By combining the artistic styles of Pollock and De Kooning with the interactive nature of performance art, we hope to channel the emerging technologies of body tracking and image processing software into an experience that can engage viewers.

2. RELATED WORK

The amount of power the user has over the installation can vary based on its design. However, this does limit the range of what the user can create within a range of pre-programmed responses [1].

There are several levels of interactivity that an installation can possess. Installations can be dynamic, interactive, and varying. While any type of movement in an installation changes how the viewers will perceive it, an installation that can respond varyingly can create an individual, unrepeatable experience for the user.

3. DEVELOPMENT

This phenomenon was derived from Chamfer matching [2] algorithm with Lukas Kanade filters. This approach is used for object detection and to specifically identify these feature points from a human pose [3]. It determines average distance to the nearest feature using the following equation:

SUI '16, October 15-16, 2016, Tokyo, Japan
ACM 978-1-4503-4068-7/16/10.
http://dx.doi.org/10.1145/2983310.2989179

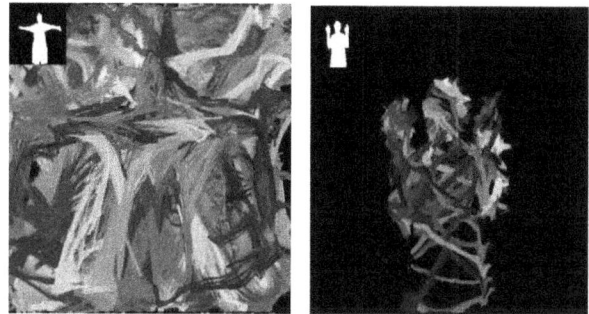

Figure 1. Abstract image modes being stretched and distorted in order to match silhouette of performer as seen by the Kinect

$$D_{chamfer}(T, I) = \frac{1}{|T|} \sum_{t}^{T} d_I(t)$$

where, T is a set of points that define the contour of the template, I is the image to search and d(t) is minimum distance for point t in some point in I. Any live feed is used as a template to these set of points and map a hierarchy of distance threshold. This information is juxtaposed with the brush strokes to give 2 modes as seen in Figure 1.

4. CONCLUSION

The plumages of color that our sketch generated attracted viewers before they even realized that it was an interactive piece. The piece contains a certain degree of abstraction, and this element of unknown helped prolong viewer engagement.

Going forward, we are interested in possible collaborations with dancers and other performance artists. There has already been some interest in combining the attributes of the Kinect with performance art in a Motion Capture stage.

5. REFERENCES

1. Francois, A., Schankler, I., and Chew, E. (2013). Mimi4x: an interactive audio-visual installation for high-level structural improvisation. *International Journal of Arts and Technology*, 6 (2).
2. Liu, Ming Yu, Tuzel, Oncel, Veeraraghavan, Ashok, Chellappa, Rama; Proceedings of the IEEE Computer Society Conference on Computer Vision and Pattern Recognition; 2010 p 1696-1703
3. Shotton, Jamie; Fitzgibbon, Andrew; Cook, Mat; Sharp, Toby; Finocchio, Mark; Moore, Richard; Kipman, Alex; Blake, Andrew, 2011, Real-time human pose recognition in parts from single depth images, CVPR, p. 1297-1304

AR Tabletop Interface Using an Optical See-Through HMD

Nozomi Sugiura
Saitama University
255 Shimo-okubo, Sakura-ku, Saitama
sugiura@is.ics.saitama-u.ac.jp

Takashi Komuro
Saitama University
255 Shimo-okubo, Sakura-ku, Saitama
komuro@mail.saitama-u.ac.jp

ABSTRACT

We propose a user interface that superimposes a virtual touch panel on a flat surface using an optical see-through head-mounted display and an RGB-D camera. The user can use the interface in a hands-free state, and can perform the operation with both hands. The interface performs markerless superimposition of virtual objects on a real scene. In addition, the interface can recognize three-dimensional information of the user's fingers, allowing the user to operate with the virtual touch panel. We developed some applications in which the user can perform various operations on the virtual touch panel.

Keywords

Augmented reality; head-mounted display; RGB-D camera; tabletop interface.

1. INTRODUCTION

User interfaces using small displays, such as smartphones and tablet computers, and those using large displays in conjunction with keyboards and mice, such as desktop PCs, are in widespread use. When comparing these interfaces in terms of usability and portability, these properties are generally in a trade-off relationship. New interfaces that are able to overcome the trade-off of existing interfaces are expected.

In this paper, we propose a user interface that superimposes a virtual touch panel on real space using a binocular optical see-through HMD and an RGB-D camera. Using the RGB-D camera, superimposition display of virtual objects is realized without markers using real scene information. User interfaces that superimpose virtual objects fixed on a real scene using an HMD have already been proposed [1,2], but there have been few user interfaces that use an HMD to provide a large operation space.

2. AR TABLETOP INTERFACE

A conceptual image of the interface we propose is shown in Fig. 1. A user uses the system in a seated position. The user can see images by wearing an HMD on the head. The operation space of the system is on the table that is common working environment in a seated position. The system displays a virtual touch panel on the HMD. The user cannot see an entire area of the virtual touch panel at a time because the field of view of the HMD is narrow. However, the user can extend the user's field of view by moving his or her head to look around the table. The touch panel looks fixed on a surface of the table even while the user is looking around the table.

SUI '16, October 15-16, 2016, Tokyo, Japan
ACM 978-1-4503-4068-7/16/10.
http://dx.doi.org/10.1145/2983310.2989180

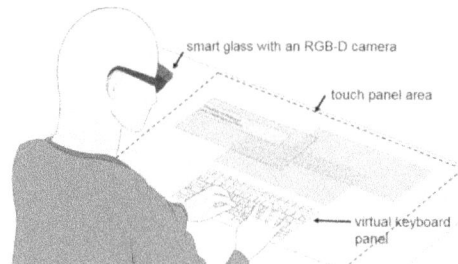

Figure 1. Proposed AR tabletop interface.

In addition, the system obtains three-dimensional information of the user's fingers and the table surface by using the RGB-D camera, allowing the user to operate with the virtual touch panel that is superimposed on the table surface. When the user touches the virtual touch panel, he or she can get physical feedback in the form of reactive force acting on his or her fingertips from the table, and stable operation of the touch panel is realized.

We developed an early prototype of the proposed interface. The system consists of an optical see-through HMD (STAR1200XLD), an RGB-D camera (DepthSense DS325) fixed on the HMD, and a desktop PC.

We implemented two applications to the developed system. One is a document editing application with a virtual keyboard panel with the QWERTY layout that allows users to type letters by touching the keys, as shown in Fig.2 (a). The second application is an image viewer. The user can drag one of the image thumbnails that are placed in the window and move it to outside the window, as shown in Fig.2 (b).

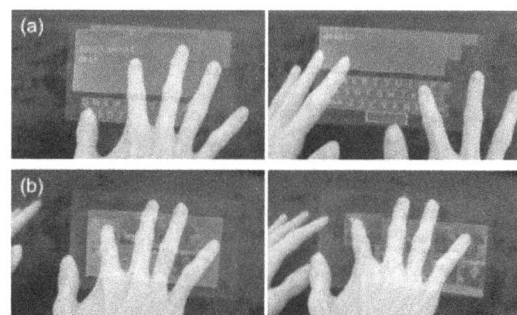

Figure 2. Application examples.

3. REFERENCES

[1] Kiyokawa, K., Billinghurst, M., Campbell, B., and Woods, E. An occlusion-capable optical see-through head mount display for supporting co-located collaboration. In *Proc. ISMAR 2003*, 133.

[2] Lee, G. A., Billinghurst, M., and Kim, G.J. Occlusion based interaction methods for tangible augmented reality environments. In *Proc. VRCAI 2004*, 419-426.

Coexistent Space: Collaborative Interaction in Shared 3D Space

Ji-Yong Lee, Joung-Huem Kwon, Sang-Hun Nam, Joong-Jae Lee, Bum-Jae You

Center of Human-centered Interaction for Coexistence, SEOUL, KOREA

ABSTRACT

It has long been a desire of human beings to coexist in a same space together with people in remote locations, communicate and interact with them in a natural way. There have been various proposed concepts to connect the real world with the remote world in 3D space [1, 2]. In the paper, the concept of *Coexistent Space* is proposed for collaborative interaction in shared 3D virtual space. *Coexistent Space* provides not only the feeling of coexistence as the sense of being with others, but also a shared virtual workspace for collaboration. Its main feature is that the users can share a virtual whiteboard for writing interaction and manipulate shared virtual objects with the bare hand touch interaction.

Keywords: 3D space; Collaborative Interaction; Spatial User Interface.

1. CONSTRUCTION of *Coexistent Space*

1.1 Devices and Coordinate Systems

Coexistent Space is constructed by using a video see-thru HMD system. The components are Oculus Rift DK1, RealSense Camera, OVRvision Camera, PTI VZ4050 MoCAP, and a haptic thimble. And, the comprehension of a few relationship is required: the relationship between hand and virtual eye coordinate system for spatial touch, between real and virtual coordinate system for human avatar control, and between remote and local coordinate system for shared space. The following Figure 1 shows the methods of calibration for the construction of *Coexistent Space*.

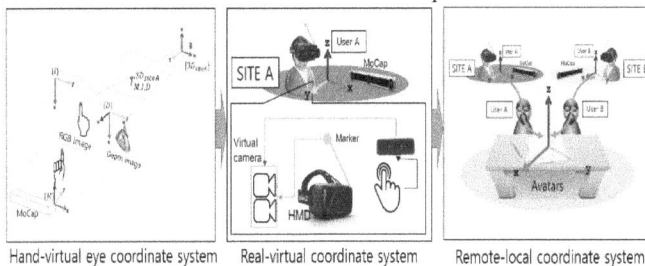

Figure 1. Coordinate systems

1.2 Spatial touch for interaction

For the collaboration in *Coexistent Space,* a haptic thimble was developed as a wearable user interface in a finger. The 3D position of thimble can be tracked by RGB-D sensor. Fingertips is detected

by three steps: hand segmentation, palm localization, and fingertip extraction using depth map and color information as shown in Figure 2. The haptic thimble provides a vibro-tactile feedback once the fingertip touches on a virtual object [3]. It is indicated that the feedback enhanced user's spatial perception. Moreover, user's real hand model is generated by 3D reconstruction of segmented hands.

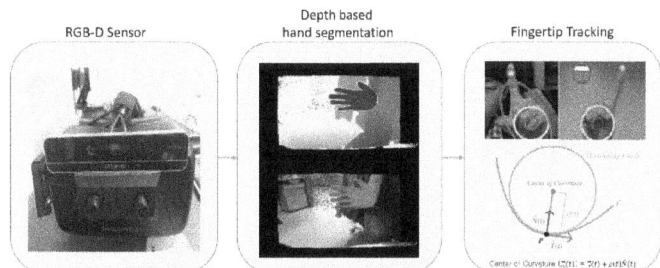

Figure 2. Spatial touch interface

1.3 Collaborative interaction

Two users (left and right images in Fig. 3) communicate and collaborate interpersonally by sharing a virtual whiteboard for spatial writing, by manipulating shared virtual objects thru spatial touch as shown in Fig. 3. The users for education write characters together on a same virtual whiteboard, and assemble components of drones on a virtual table and control drones in *Coexistent Space*.

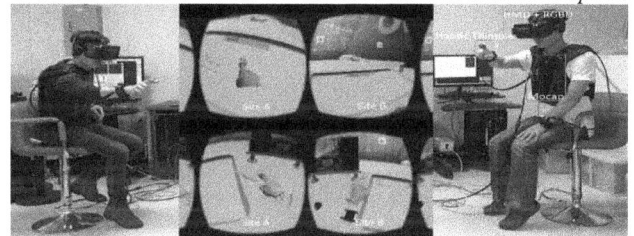

Figure 3. HMD based collaborative interaction

2. ACKNOWLEDGMENTS

This work was supported by the Global Frontier R&D Program on Human-centered Interaction for Coexistence funded by a National Research Foundation of Korea grant funded by the ministry of Science, ICT, and Future Planning in Korean Government (NRFM1AXA003-2011-0028374).

3. REFERENCES

[1] Stephan, B., Andre, A.K., and Frohlich, B. Immersive group-to-group telepresence. IEEE Transactions on Visualization and Computer Graphics 19, No.4, pp.616-625, 2013.

[2] Henry, F. and Bazin, J.C. Immersive 3D Telepresence. IEEE Magazine on Computer 47, No.7, pp.46-52, 2014.

[3] Yeom, K., Kwon, J., Maeng, J. and You, B.J. Haptic Ring Interface Enabling Air-Writing in Virtual Reality Environment. In Mixed and Augmented Reality (ISMAR), IEEE International Symposium on, pp. 124-127, 2015.

Development of a Toolkit for Creating Kinetic Garments Based on Smart Hair Technology

Mage Xue[1], Masaru Ohkubo[1], Miki Yamamura[2], Hiroko Uchiyama[2], Takuya Nojima[1], Yael Friedman[3]

[1] University of Electro-Communications
setsu@vogue.is.uec.ac.jp,
marchalloakbow@vogue.is.uec.ac.jp,
tnojima@nojilab.org

[2] Joshibi University of Art and Design
yamamura09014@venus.joshibi.jp,
uchiyama96022@venus.joshibi.jp

[3] Jewlery designer
yaelfriedman@gmail.com

ABSTRACT

Although there are many kinetic garment artworks and studies (ex [3]), installing kinetic elements into garments is often difficult for people in the field of textile. The reason for this issue comes from the complexity of kinetic elements to be handled by such people. Thus, simple technology is required to enable those people to create new kinetic garment easily. In this project, we propose a simple toolkit that enables installing kinetic function to textiles. This toolkit is composed of Smart Hair(s), a fine, light weighted bending actuator, and an Arduino based microcomputer. The basic design of the proposed toolkit will be described. Furthermore, we held a workshop in cooperation with students who major in fashion and textile to investigate the effect of this toolkit.

Keywords

Kinetic garment; shape changing interface; fashion design; toolkit; Smart Hair; Hairlytop Interface;

1. INTRODUCTION

In recent years, the concept of kinetic garments, garments that are capable of active motion, gains much more attention because of its potential to enrich the ways of expression. We believe that the combination of aesthetic expression and interactions will make kinetic garments an essential part of textile fashion. Unfortunately, most of the current fashion designers are not familiar with the way to implement such kinetic technology. Thus, designing kinetic garment usually takes long-lasting steps working with engineers. To solve this issue, simple toolkits that help designers to create kinetic garment easily will be required. Such toolkits will encourage more designers to participate in the kinetic garment designing filed.

2. TOOLKIT DEVELOPMENT

We propose using the soft hair-like bending actuator called Smart Hair (previously known as Hairlytop Interface [1]) to achieve this goal. The previous study shows that it has enough potential to be used in creating kinetic garments [2]. However, this actuator system is still too complex to be used by technology-unfamiliar users. We used Arduino based control circuit in this basic design of toolkit. Actuators' bending amount is related to the Joule heat. In

SUI '16, October 15-16, 2016, Tokyo, Japan
ACM 978-1-4503-4068-7/16/10.
http://dx.doi.org/10.1145/2983310.2989182

Figure 1. Left: Basic components of the toolkit, Right: A design sketch and the prototype made at the workshop

purpose of preventing overheating, remaining active, saving energy, the current need to be controlled difficultly. Give consideration to both usability and functionality, we choose only two parameters to control the motion of each Smart Hair, bending frequency, and the maximum electrical current can be interpreted as "frequency" and "force". Users can setup the two parameters for each Smart Hair independently. Also, several pre-configured motion patterns were installed in the program. The user can simply switch the patterns by pressing the key.

3. WORKSHOP AND DISCUSSION

A preliminary workshop was held to investigate the effort of this toolkit. Three students who major in fashion and textile participated. They learned how the toolkit works and draw dozens of design sketches about kinetic textile using this toolkit. Then after, they tried to develop the actual system based on their sketches. They succeeded composing two working kinetic textile. From our observation and participants' comments, the proposed toolkit have sufficient potential to enable a technology-unfamiliar person to create kinetic garments. One of the big issues is the difficulty in fixing the actuator onto flexible textile. Improvement about fixation method is strongly required. In addition, the control circuit of the proposed toolkit was still large when integrating the whole system into garments. Besides using surface mounted circuit, selecting the appropriate battery size depending on usage, split batteries are also considerable.

4. ACKNOWLEDGMENTS

This work was supported by JSPS KAKENHI Grant Number JP16K00268.

5. REFERENCES

[1] Nojima, T., Ooide, Y. and Kawaguchi, H. Hairlytop interface. In *Proc. WHC,* (2013), 431-435.

[2] Ohkubo, M., Yamamura, M., Uchiyama, H. and Nojima, T. Breathing clothes in *Proc. ACE,* (2014), Article No.39.

[3] Schiphorst, T., Chung, W., and Ip. E. Wo.Defy; in *Proc. TEI,* (2013), 319-322.

Large Scale Interactive AR Display Based on a Projector-Camera System

Chun Xie
Graduate School of System
and Information Engineering,
University of Tsukuba
s1520843@
u.tsukuba.ac.jp

Yoshinari Kameda
Center for Computational
Sciences,
University of Tsukuba
kameda@
iit.tsukuba.ac.jp

Kenji Suzuki
Faculty of Engineering,
Information and System,
University of Tsukuba
kenji@
iit.tsukuba.ac.jp

Itaru Kitahara
Center for Computational
Sciences,
University of Tsukuba
kitahara@
iit.tsukuba.ac.jp

ABSTRACT

School gymnasium, which has an important role in either physical or mental development of children, is a necessary facility for most schools. In recent years, considering the individual differences among students in terms of gender, age, developmental level or interest, many new forms of gymnasium activity have been developed to make physical education more flexible. In some cases, introducing new physical activity is accompanied by a requirement of drawing new contents on the floor of a gymnasium. Ordinary, this is done by using line-tape. However, contents created by line-tape need periodic maintenance that is costly and time-consuming. Moreover, overlapping lines for different purposes can make users confused. Furthermore, the most critical problem is that line-tape can represent only simple and static contents, thus, the variety of new physical education activity are greatly limited.

This paper proposes a projection-based AR system consisting of multiple projectors and cameras to deal with the problems described above. This system is aiming to provide extension functions to traditional school gymnasium by realizing not only representation of dynamic AR contents but also interactive display on the gymnasium floor.

Keywords

Augmented Reality; ProCam System; HCI; Gymnasium

1. LARGE SCALE PROJECTION-BASED AR

As shown in Figure1, our projection-based AR system is composed by multiple projectors and cameras (pro-cams). Each camera is installed on a projector. The pro-cams are installed on the ceiling of a gymnasium at regular intervals, and the orientation of the camera is adjusted to be approximately same as the corresponding projector. Although projections are aligned using a method similar to [1], multiple cameras, instead of a static one, are used so that the whole large projection area can be observed. Each pro-cam is calibrated by estimating three homography matrices: the homography H_{pc} between the 2D coordinate systems of camera and

Figure 1. Large scale projection-based AR system in a gymnasium

the projector, the homography H_{cf} between a camera and the floor and the homography H_{pf} between a projector and the floor.

We also developed an interactive interface basing on our large scale projection system which make user be able to create AR content on the floor easily. It is like sketch board application and can be run on a tablet pc with a stylus pen as the input device. Contents drawn on tablet are transmitted to system server and shown on the floor in real time. An example is shown in Figure 2.

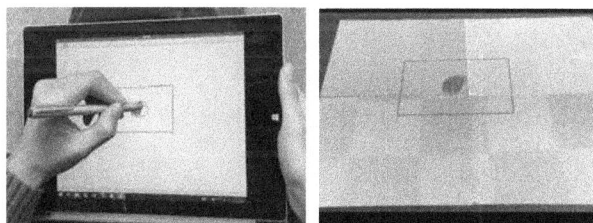

Figure 2. An interactive interface running on a tablet for creating contents(left), and the projection result(right)

Combing with other sensing technologies (e.g. video tracking), it is possible for our system to perform as a powerful education supporting facility. Contents that change interactively with students' actions can be projected on the floor around them. With the help of such a feature, it will be possible to develop AR-game-like physical education activities, and it can be expected that students will participate more enthusiastically.

2. REFERENCES

[1] Raskar, R., Baar, J.V., and Chai, J.X. 2002. A low-cost projector mosaic with fast registration. In *Proc. ACCV 2002*, pages 114-119,2002.

TickTockRay: Smartwatch Raycasting for Mobile HMDs

Krzysztof Pietroszek
Game Research Lab
School of Computing and Design
California State University Monterey Bay
100 Campus Rd, Seaside, California, USA
kpietroszek@csumb.edu

Daniel Kharlamov
Game Research Lab
School of Computing and Design
California State University Monterey Bay
100 Campus Rd, Seaside, California, USA
dakharlamov@csumb.edu

ABSTRACT

We present TickTockRay, a smartwatch-based 3D pointing technique for smartphone-based immersive environments. Our work demonstrates that smartwatch-based raycasting may be a practical alternative to head-rotation-based pointing or specialized input devices. We release TickTockRay as an open-source plugin for Unity and provide an example of its use in a virtual reality clone of the Minecraft game.

CCS Concepts

•Human-centered computing → Pointing;

Keywords

freehand pointing, 3D pointing, raycasting, virtual reality

1. INTRODUCTION

The promise of smartphone-based head-mounted displays (HMDs) is to democratize access to immersive 3D environments through a cost-effective alternative to specialized HMDs. However, today's smartphone-based HMDs provide limited interaction capabilities. We present TickTock-Ray, an implementation of fixed-origin raycasting[1] technique that utilizes a smartwatch as an input device. We believe that a smartwatch-based raycasting is a good alternative to a head-rotation-controlled cursor or a specialized input device, because both smartphones and smartwatches belong to the ecology of *everyday devices*, devices carried by a user at all times.

2. TICKTOCKRAY DESIGN

TickTockRay[1] implements fixed-origin raycasting using off-the-shelf smartwatch hardware. In the classic version of raycasting the ray originates in the tracking device. When the tracking device moves, the origin of the ray moves with

---

[1]Code at https://github.com/gameresearchlab/TickTockRay

SUI '16 October 15-16, 2016, Tokyo, Japan

ⓒ 2016 Copyright held by the owner/author(s).

ACM ISBN 978-1-4503-4068-7/16/10

DOI: http://dx.doi.org/10.1145/2983310.2989184

Figure 1: TickTockRay raycasting with smartwatch.

it. In contrast, our implementation relies upon the ray originating from a fixed point, located, roughly, in the user's chest, an approach that has been validated in the context of large screen pointing with smartphones. The C/D ratio (a coefficient that maps the physical movement of the pointing device to the resulting cursor movement in a system) of TickTockRay technique is set to 1, with exact correspondence between the ray and the smartwatch's rotation. Such C/D ratio enables a user to select targets in the entire virtual reality control space. For selection confirmation, we use a quick forearm twist by a minimum of $45°$, mapping the clockwise twist to the mouse-down event and the counterclockwise twist to the mouse-up event. If the clockwise twist is immediately followed by a return to the original position, the system registered a click, a command that confirms the target acquisition.

As an example application, we use TickTockRay to implement the placement, and the destruction of blocks in our version of Minecraft game[2]. In our testing, we used LG G Watch. The players are encouraged to interact by moving the forearm, keeping their elbow close to the body, and, if needed, reposition their entire body, instead of making wide movements with their shoulder joint, in order to reduce the gorilla arm effect. We plan to formally verify whether this approach results in a lower fatigue than using the whole arm.

3. CONCLUSION

TickTockRay demonstrates how off-the-shelf smartwatch hardware can effectively support raycasting interaction in smartphone-based immersive systems. Users do not need to carry specialized pointing devices or an additional mobile device – commercially available smartwatches are already able to support these interactions.

4. REFERENCES

[1] C. Wingrave and Bowman Doug A. Baseline factors for raycasting selection. In *Proc. of HCI Int.*, 2005.

---

[2]Code at https://github.com/gameresearchlab/TickTockCraft

3D Camera Pose History Visualization

Mayra Donaji Barrera Machuca, Wolfgang Stuerzlinger

SIAT, Simon Fraser University, Vancouver, Canada

{mbarrera, w.s}@sfu.ca

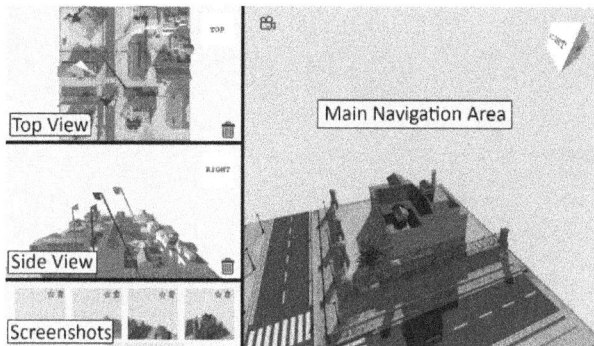

Figure 1: The current prototype for the camera pose history visualization system consists of the main navigation area, top and side views of the 3D world that let users identify saved camera poses and a list of saved cameras images taken from these poses.

Figure 2: A saved view from the study that shows three boxes (glow not shown in the study). Participants had to revisit this camera pose and then look for a single ball hidden inside one of these three boxes.

1. ABSTRACT

Navigating in 3D environments imposes a high cognitive load on users as control of 6 or more degrees of freedom for the camera is required. Most 3D interaction tools thus provide some form of assistance for 3D navigation. For example, some systems limit the DOF users can interact with [1], other systems utilize multiple views to help users navigate the environment [3]. A related problem is that revisiting a previous camera location and/or pose is also difficult. Our work enables users to recognize where they have been before by giving them the ability to revisit their navigation history. This improves 3D navigation as users can move more efficiently through the virtual environment by going back to previously visited places.

2. Camera History Visualization Tool

Our camera history visualization tool (figure 1) let users return to previous views without having to explicitly navigate to the corresponding camera pose using mouse and keyboard in a desktop workplace. The visualization also allows users to identify their position in relationship to previously visited views and the environment. This also help to identify unexplored areas of the environment. Each saved camera is shown as a pyramid icon with the corresponding saved pose. Color is used to classify cameras based on time spent in that view and the alpha channel is used to show the distance to the current camera.

Users save camera views by pressing the 'S' key. Each saved view has a heuristically determined zone of influence around its position, where only new changes in rotations can be saved. To return to a previous pose, users only need to click on the camera icon. If multiple views are saved for a given position, users can scroll through them. Other supported interactions include deleting cameras and views, favoring/bookmarking certain views and accessing favorite/bookmarked views using the function keys.

SUI '16, October 15-16, 2016, Tokyo, Japan

ACM 978-1-4503-4068-7/16/10.

http://dx.doi.org/10.1145/2983310.2989185

3. User Study

We conducted a study with 4 participants (M=1, F=3) to evaluate our new camera history visualization system. Our study was divided in two parts: first, participants were asked to navigate to four specific views and to save them to create a consistent history. Then, participants were asked to find four different balls hidden inside boxes. All the boxes were visible from the initial saved views (figure 2), but users needed to move the camera to see the inside of the box. Participants were free to save more views in this second part of the study. All users were able to complete the task within 15 minutes (avg. 10.5min). The results from a 7 point Likert scale (1-7) questionnaire are displayed below:

Questions	Mean	STD
Ease of interaction with top / side view	5.25	1.30
Ease of interaction with saved cameras view	5	0.71
Perceived speed of interaction when choosing a previous view images.	5.75	1.09
Perceived speed of interaction when choosing between views	5.25	1.30
Did you find the top/side view useful	6	0.71
Did you find the saved cameras view useful	5.5	1.12
Did you find go to favorite / bookmark view useful?	3.75	0.83

Most participants agreed that our tool is a useful and fast way to navigate to previous camera poses. Yet, limitations of our current prototype are that it can get difficult to find a specific view if users do not remember the pose and that the top / side views can get crowded with icons.

4. REFERENCES

[1] D. Scheurich and W. Stuerzlinger. 2013. A One-handed Multi-touch Mating Method for 3D Rotations. In *CHI '13* Extended Abstracts, 1623-1628.

[2] A. Khan, I. Mordatch, G. Fitzmaurice, J. Matejka, and G. Kurtenbach. 2008. ViewCube: A 3D Orientation Indicator and Controller. In *I3D '08*, 17-2

Social Spatial Mashup for Place and Object - based Information Sharing

Choonsung Shin, Youngmin Kim, Jisoo Hong, Sung-Hee Hong, Hoonjong Kang
Korea Electronics Technologies Institute
1599, Sangahm-dong, Mapo-gu
Seoul, Republic of Korea
+82-2-6388-6687
{cshin, rainmaker, jhong, shhong, hoonjongkang)@keti.re.kr

ABSTRACT
In this paper, we describe social spatial mashup for information sharing in public space. The proposed social spatial mashup is based on RGB-D SLAM and creates a 3D feature map and allows users to locate information and contents in a 3D space. It thus allows users intuitively and spatially share information among users based on real objects and 3D space. We also implemented and tested the mashup method with Google Project Tango.

Keywords
Social mashup; augmented reality; information sharing.

1. INTRODUCTION
With recent advances in mobile devices and technologies, it is very common and important to share information with other people in public spaces. For this purpose, previous works focused on placing information onto visual markers or GPS location. However the information connected to a physical space is still inaccurate for sharing information based on objects or places.

2. Social Spatial Mashup
In order to overcome the limitation of previous information sharing, we propose Social Spatial Mashup (SSM) for information sharing in a 3D pubic space. The proposed SSM allows users to create a 3D feature map and locate information in a 3D space.

For this purpose, SSM consists of mashup content, a user device and a content cloud. The mashup content represents the information resulted from mashup in a 3D space. The content includes 2D images, texts, 3D models, URLs, etc. These contents are also connected to a 3D space and users. The user device has two roles: mashup maker and mashup viewer. During map creation, the device builds SLAM (Simultaneous Localization and Mapping) map based on depth and RGB information [1]. The device then allows a user to place a content over the map created. For this purpose, the device estimates its pose by locating the device at the SLAM map by matching the features from current image and then visualizes appropriate UIs for content mashup.

Figure 1 shows the overall architecture of SSM. A user first needs to create the SLAM map of a 3D space and then locate information over the map. Afterward the information and map are stored at the

content cloud. Later another user matches his SLAM map to the content could. The user is then able to see the previous information.

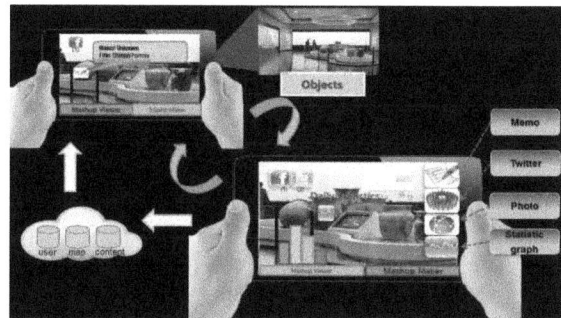

Figure 1. Social Spatial Mashup.

We also implemented the proposed SSM with Google Project Tango which has a RGB and a depth camera. Figure 2 show an example of SSM that locates an image in 3D space. The left of Figure 2 shows the initial status of a 3D object that has no contents. Later an image (a small logo) is located on the face of the 3D object after social spatial mashup as shown in the center of Figure 2. The

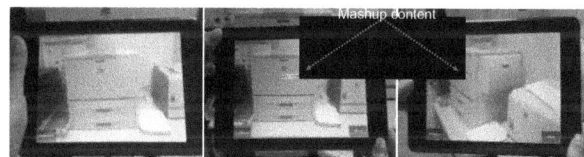

Figure 2. Preliminary example of SSM.

content is well registered on the object when the user device's location and orientation are changed (the right of Figure 2).

3. CONCLUSION AND FUTURE WORK
In this paper, we proposed Social Spatial Mashup for information sharing. This is ongoing work and thus should be improved in several aspects. We first would like to manage multiple SLAM maps to share among users. These multiple maps allow users to exploit veracious types of space for information sharing. We will also improve the UIs to allow users to intuitively place information in 3D space.

4. ACKNOWLEDGMENTS
This work was supported by the Ministry of Science, ICT and Future Planning (MSIP) (Cross-Ministry Giga Korea Project).

5. REFERENCES
[1] F. Endres, J. Hess, J. Sturm, D. Cremers, W. Burgard, Mapping with an RGB-D Camera", IEEE Transactions on Robotics, 2014.

Real-time Sign Language Recognition with Guided Deep Convolutional Neural Networks

Zhengzhe Liu[♭†], Fuyang Huang[♭†], Gladys Wai Lan Tang[†], Felix Yim Binh Sze[†],
Jing Qin[♮], Xiaogang Wang[†], Qiang Xu[†]
[†]The Chinese University of Hong Kong [♮]The Hong Kong Polytechnic University
{zzliu, fyhuang, qxu}@cse.cuhk.edu.hk

ABSTRACT

We develop a real-time, robust and accurate sign language recognition system leveraging deep convolutional neural networks(DCNN). Our framework is able to prevent common problems such as error accumulation of existing frameworks and it outperforms state-of-the-art frameworks in terms of accuracy, recognition time and usability.

Keywords

Sign language recognition, Convolutional Neural Networks

1. INTRODUCTION

The typical pipeline of sign language recognition system often contains several modules and inevitably results in error accumulation through the whole recognition procedure. There are also DCNN based systems taking raw video frames as input, which need a large amount of training data to get rid of unrelated elements in video. Our proposed end-to-end framework avoids error accumulation and parameter optimization problem in step-by-step frameworks, and improves the performance significantly. Also, we propose a training scheme called "training with guidance" to achieve good performance with limited training samples. Moreover, our system can be further applied in more interaction applications such as mid-air controlling.

2. DCNN DESIGN

Our guided end-to-end DCNN based system carries out feature extraction, feature ensemble and classification into a DCNN based framework so that all parameters involved can be jointly optimized during the training procedure. Also, the guided part including hand tracking, trajectory feature extraction and hyper class clustering helps DCNN focus on most discriminative elements such as hand regions.

---

[0]♭ means equal contribution

SUI 2016 15-16 October, Tokyo, Japan
© 2016 Copyright held by the owner/author(s).
ACM ISBN 978-1-4503-4068-7/16/10.
DOI: http://dx.doi.org/10.1145/2983310.2989187

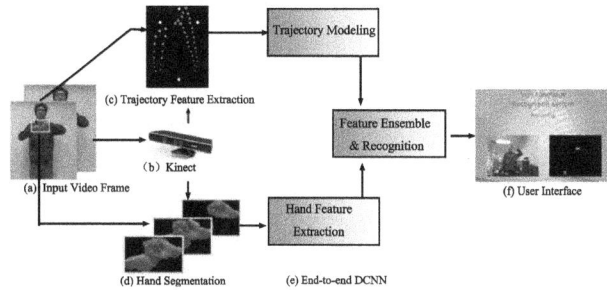

Figure 1: System overview.

Table 1: Comparison with state-of-the-art work

	GCN+SVM 2016[1]	Ours
Person dependent accuracy	88.23%	92.74%
Person independent accuracy	74.22%	79.54%
Time	291.85ms	29.85ms

3. EXPERIMENT AND CONCLUSION

There are 9 participants took part in the experiment. The experiment was conducted in two phases: firstly the participants signed the words one by one according to the tips shown on the screen to collect training data. After model training, a pair of participants signed in a dictation way as shown in our accompanying video. The dictator randomly chose a word from dictionary and read it, then the signer signed it and checked whether the recognition was correct.

We build two datasets to validate the performance of our system. For person dependent experiment, we collected 550 words, and each signed by one signer for three times. We use 2 samples for training and one for testing. For person independent experiment, we collected 300 daily words signed by 8 signers, and each word is signed for 23 times, in which 20 for training and 3 for testing. The result is shown in Table 1.

Our experiment demonstrated not only high recognition accuracy over state-of-the-art systems, but also dramatical improvements in terms of recognition time and usability.

4. REFERENCES

[1] H. Wang, X. Chai, X. Hong, G. Zhao, and X. Chen. Isolated sign language recognition with grassmann covariance matrices. *ACM Transactions on Accessible Computing (TACCESS)*, 8(4):14, 2016.

Window-Shaping: 3D Design Ideation in Mixed Reality

Ke Huo
Purdue University, USA
khuo@purdue.edu

Vinayak
Purdue University, USA
vinayak@purdue.edu

Karthik Ramani
Purdue University, USA
ramani@purdue.edu

ABSTRACT

We present, *Window-Shaping*, a mobile, markerless, mixed-reality (MR) interface for creative design ideation that allows for the direct creation of 3D shapes on and around physical objects. Using the *sketch-and-inflate* scheme, we present a design workflow where users can create dimensionally consistent and visually coherent 3D models by borrowing visual and dimensional attributes from existing physical objects.

Keywords

Design ideation; sketch-based 3D modeling; mixed reality

1. INTRODUCTION

The physical environment often serves as a means for inspiring, contextualizing, and guiding the designer's thought process for expressing creative ideas through early design objects are frequently used as references to explore the space of novel designs. Recent works have demonstrated that *see-through* augmented (AR) and mixed reality (MR) can play a vital role in *in-situ* geometric design by bridging the gap between physical and digital worlds [1, 2]. However, most of these approaches use the physical environment mainly as a dormant container of digital artifacts rather than a source of inspiration for facilitating quick digital prototyping for design ideation. We present *Window-Shaping*, an AR-based design workflow to explore the idea of re-purposing the physical environment as a reference, context, and sources of inspirations for quick ideation in early design.

2. WINDOW-SHAPING

Window-Shaping integrates sketch- and image-based 3D modeling approaches within a mixed-reality interface to develop a new design workflow (Figure 1). Using the Google Tango device, our approach leverages the RGB-XYZ representation of a scene allowing users to create planar curves on physical surfaces by directly drawing, placing curve template, and capturing contour of existing object. With the

SUI '16 October 15-16, 2016, Tokyo, Japan

© 2016 Copyright held by the owner/author(s).

ACM ISBN 978-1-4503-4068-7/16/10.

DOI: http://dx.doi.org/10.1145/2983310.2989189

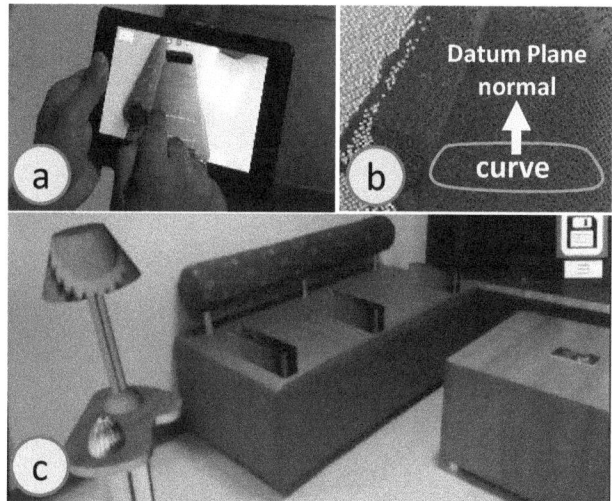

Figure 1: User draws a curve in the screen (a), that is mapped to a 3D planar curve using the point cloud (b). Using the inflation based scheme, *Window-Shaping* enables quick creation of virtual artifacts for augmenting the physical environment (c).

boundary and hole curves, the mesh is computed using constrained delaunay triangulation (CDT) and then *inflated* using certain distance functions. The multi-touch gestures on the screen such as 1-finger drawing, 2 and 3 finger pinching, 2 finger rotating, and tapping, etc., are unprojected on the physical environment and allow for 3D shape creation, editing, and manipulation. We further allow users to capture texture of existing shapes and re-purpose it in the new creations. These shapes can serve as geometric extensions to physical objects or can be completely new virtual assemblies created by re-purposing physical objects as spatial and visual references.

3. REFERENCES

[1] P. Paczkowski, M. H. Kim, Y. Morvan, J. Dorsey, H. E. Rushmeier, and C. O'Sullivan. Insitu: sketching architectural designs in context. *ACM Trans. Graph.*, 30(6):182, 2011.

[2] M. Xin, E. Sharlin, and M. C. Sousa. Napkin sketch: Handheld mixed reality 3d sketching. In *VRST '08*, pages 223–226, New York, NY, USA, 2008. ACM.

KnowWhat: Mid Field Sensemaking for the Visually Impaired

Sujeath Pareddy[*]
Department of CS&IS,
BITS Pilani,
Hyderabad, India

Abhay Agarwal
Microsoft Research,
#9 Lavelle Road,
Bengaluru, India

Manohar Swaminathan
Microsoft Research,
#9 Lavelle Road,
Bengaluru, India

{t-supare, t-abagar, manohar.swaminathan}@microsoft.com

ABSTRACT

KnowWhat is our solution to help speed up mid-field sense-making by visually impaired persons (VIPs). Our proto-type combines a spectacle mounted camera, passive fiducial marker based tagging of the environment and 3D spatial audio to build a novel interaction technique. We present qualitative results of experiments to evaluate our solution.

Keywords

3D sound; Accessibility; Sonification; Augmented Reality

1. INTRODUCTION

We use sensemaking in the broad sense of creating a mental model of the world that aids in dealing with it. Electronic Travel Aids (ETAs) can be categorized as dealing with near field (within a 1m radius of the person), mid-field (from 1m to several meters) or far field (beyond several meters). An example of mid-field sensemaking is that of learning to be comfortable with a new office lounge, knowing all the objects in the room and their positions in the room with sufficient confidence to be able to reach, for example, a coffee maker.

2. OUTLINE OF OUR SOLUTION

We augment the environment with passive fiducials (April-Tags [1]), attaching them to walls, doors and to all significant objects in the room. Each tag allows the localization of a camera's relative pose and position. Additionally, associated with each tag is metadata that is used to identify objects. We use semi-customized HRTFs selected from the LISTEN dataset through a user calibration step. Audio is delivered through in-ear earbuds. As the VIP enters the room, one or more tags come into the camera's view. The user then hears the names of the corresponding objects spoken out in a way that they appear to emanate from the objects' physical locations. The objects are named in the order of their relative position around the user's head. As the user moves around, objects enter and leave the field of view and the corresponding set of spatialized spoken names of objects is the primary cue for helping the VIP to orient and learn the space. We found that under experimental conditions, 6 cm x 6 cm tags were reliably detected at distances of upto 3 m and at angles upto 65° relative to the tag normal.

2.1 Experimental Setup

Two similar rooms with identical sets of furniture, but different layouts, were the sites of the experiment. All users were given the same task: enter the first room, learn the layout of the space using their preferred method. After they report that they have memorized the layout, we lead the subject out of the room and ask them to re-enter the room and to pick up a tagged cup from a table and sit down on a chair. We then repeat the above in the other room but using our device instead. The entire experiment is recorded and interviews are taken before and after the trials.

3. CONCLUSIONS

The qualitative results from early experiments with VIPs have been very positive (N=4). Firstly, the users felt that it can help them be more independent (P1: "This can help me work without other people's help... know the location of my stove, cot, table ...", P3: "This tells me about sofa, table...if it tells me about lorries, bus... if people are not there... I can travel without taking people's help"). There was delight in quickly moving in the direction and encountering the object described without having to feel their way around. Users also reported that they were quickly able to judge the nature of the space and conclude that they were present in a meeting room (presence of whiteboard and sofas) at a pace that they normally could not. Users were also interested in using this with a traditional cane (P3: "If the cane is my left eye, this can be my right eye... "). Our observations will feed into our design of interaction methods to enhance the effectiveness of our solution.

4. REFERENCES

[1] E. Olson. AprilTag: A robust and flexible visual fiducial system. In *Proceedings of the IEEE International Conference on Robotics and Automation (ICRA)*, pages 3400–3407. IEEE, May 2011.

---

[*]Work carried out during an internship at MSR India.

Spatial User Interaction 2016 Tokyo, Japan

© 2016 Copyright held by the owner/author(s).

ACM ISBN 978-1-4503-4068-7/16/10.

DOI: http://dx.doi.org/10.1145/2983310.2989190

Katsukazan: An Intuitive iOS App For Informing People About Volcanic Activity in Japan

Paul Haimes
Tokyo Metropolitan University
6-6 Asahigaoka, Hino
Tokyo, Japan
haimes@tmu.ac.jp

Tetsuaki Baba
Tokyo Metropolitan University
6-6 Asahigaoka, Hino
Tokyo, Japan
baba@tmu.ac.jp

ABSTRACT

Events in recent years have drawn attention to disaster risks related to volcanic activity in Japan. People having easy access to information regarding Japan's active volcanoes is of great importance — particularly as early work in our research indicated that visitors to Japan are unaware of these risks. Both disaster literature and interaction design theory emphasise considering the needs of users as part of the design process. Therefore, we are involving users at each step of the design process as we create an iOS application that allows people to explore and contextualise this information in a simple yet meaningful way.

CCS Concepts

•Information systems → Location based services; •Human-centered computing → Geographic visualization;

Keywords

mobile applications, spatial data, disaster management

1. BACKGROUND

Currently, digital information publicly available regarding volcanic activity lacks the kind of interactivity and relevancy that users expect from modern map apps, meaning it is not easily contextualised for a user's location or other points of interest. The Japan Meteorological Agency (JMA) website also states that its warnings regarding volcanic activity are "issued to residents via the media, prefectural offices and local municipalities" [3]. However, these avenues of communication may not be easily accessible or spatially contextualised for residents or visitors in Japan.

2. OUR APPLICATION

Using design guidelines from related research [2], our Katsukazan app uses data sourced from JMA via Japan's National Institute of Informatics. Information is available in both Japanese and English. The app was developed in Swift 2.0 [1], using Apple's Mapkit framework. Features such as search, geo-location (which shows user proximity to volcanoes), a standard map and satellite view (including a 3D 'fly-over' view on available devices), and zooming have been added to allow for easy spatial contextualisation of the information. We plan to release an Android version

SUI '16 October 15-16, 2016, Tokyo, Japan

© 2016 Copyright held by the owner/author(s).

ACM ISBN 978-1-4503-4068-7/16/10.

DOI: http://dx.doi.org/10.1145/2983310.2989191

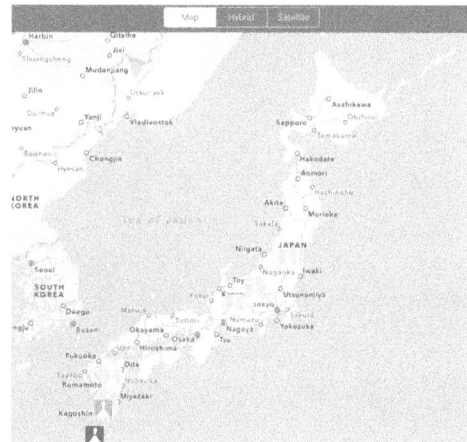

Figure 1: The map view of our Katsukazan app.

in the future. A web interface (http://hazards.jp) providing the same information is also available.

2.1 Initial user testing

Seven participants (Six residents of Japan, one visitor) undertook initial user testing of the app. 100% of users were confident using the app and no users felt that it was difficult to use. All users felt that the interface was consistent and was not complicated. The information itself was also considered useful by all users. Three users suggested adding user-sourced data (including photos) to the app, to supplement the official data.

3. CONCLUSION AND FUTURE WORK

Crowdsourcing will be added in the next iteration to gauge the usefulness of this feature in the context of volcano warnings. We may also create a VR/AR experience with the same data. However, using a design process inclusive of users — integral when presenting hazard information — means that only features driven by user input will be included in the next iteration of our app. [1]

4. REFERENCES

[1] Apple. Swift. A modern programming language that is safe, fast, and interactive., 2016. https://apple.com/swift.

[2] P. Haimes, T. Baba, and S. Medley. Mobile map applications and the democratisation of hazard information. In *SIGGRAPH Asia 2015 Mobile Graphics and Interactive Applications*, pages 1-4, 2015.

[3] Japan Meteorological Agency. Volcanic Warnings and Volcanic Alert Levels, 2016. http://www.data.jma.go.jp/svd/vois/data/tokyo/STOCK/kaisetsu/English/level.html.

[1] This work is supported by a Kakenhi research grant (15F15052) provided by the Japan Society for the Promotion of Science.

Empirical Method for Detecting Pointing Gestures in Recorded Lectures

Xiaojie Zha
Beijing University of Posts and Telecommunications
Xitucheng Road, Haidian District
Beijing 100876, China
+86 15210201807
charles_xjzha@yahoo.com

Marie-Luce Bourguet
Queen Mary University of London
Mile End Road
London E1 4NS, UK
+44 20 7882 3400
marie-luce.bourguet@qmul.ac.uk

ABSTRACT

Pointing gestures performed by lecturers are important because they seem to indicate pedagogical significance. In this extended abstract, we describe a simple empirical method for detecting pointing gestures in recorded lectures captured using a depth sensor (Kinect). We first analyse component gestures; second, we assign them weights; finally, we set a threshold on the aggregated weight in order to decide if a pointing gesture has been performed.

Keywords
Pointing gestures; Recorded lectures; Kinect; Body frame

1. INTRODUCTION

Recognising gestures from Kinect data has been attempted before. Methods proposed include geometric algorithms [1] and machine learning [2]. Our approach differs in that our aim is to simply detect the pointing gestures, and for doing so, a simple empirical method that consists in designing a filter to differentiate pointing from other gestures is adequate.

Four lectures from three English speaking lecturers were recorded using Kinect. For each 25 minute recording, the body frame data contains all the computed real-time tracking information about the lecturer. Kinect also automatically calculates the joints' position and orientation based on the depth frame information.

2. ANALYSING COMPONENT GESTURES

Through observing the recorded lecture videos, we found a limited number (nine in total) of simple component gestures that lecturers typically perform while delivering a lecture. The idea is that these component gestures (e.g. single arm stretch, body turn to screen, etc.) are very easily detected from the body frame data using straightforward calculations.

Observing our four lecture recordings, we calculated the frequency of the pointing gestures as well as of the simpler postures and movements that lecturers perform. As a result of these observations, an "indicator weight" was devised (see Equation below), to calculate in real time and for each detected posture and movement, the probability that it indicates that a pointing gesture is being performed. For convenience and to avoid decimal weights, the result of the division is arbitrarily multiplied by a factor 5.

$$Indicator\ Weight\ for\ a\ gesture\ G = \left[\frac{Times\ G\ acompanies\ a\ pointing\ gesture}{Total\ times\ G\ occurs} \right] \times 5$$

Some of the movements, such as "Single arm stretch", "Stretching to screen direction" and "Arm paused when stretching" are performed almost exclusively as part of a pointing gesture. Conversely, some other movements, such as "Both arm stretch" and "Hand closed", are never associated with screen-pointing. When detected, they are arbitrarily assigned a negative weight value. Table 1 shows examples of assigned weights.

Table 1. Assigned weights for the component gestures.

Component Gestures	Weights
Both arm stretch	-5
Single arm stretch	4
Stretching to screen direction	4
Arm waves back and forth	1
Arm stretch upward sloping	3
Arm paused when stretching	5
Body Turn to screen	1
Head turn to screen	3
Hand closed	-5

3. DETECTING POINTING

When several gestures are detected, their weights are added together. The higher the aggregated weight, the higher the probability that a pointing gesture is being performed. A pointing gesture is detected when the aggregated weight has reached a given threshold.

In order to evaluate the appropriate threshold, we recorded using the Kinect ten pointing gestures as well as a small number (five) of non-pointing gestures. The different variations of pointing included: pointing upwards, pointing horizontally, pointing while arm is folded, pointing while walking, etc. The non-pointing gestures included drinking water, head scratching, etc.

Different thresholds were then tried on this data, and the number of correct detections and wrong detections calculated. The best detection results were obtained with a threshold set to 8, which yielded the successful detection of 9 of the 10 pointing gestures, while rejecting all non-pointing gestures.

4. REFERENCES

[1] Boulabiar, M.I. & al. 2014. The Issues of 3D Hand Gesture and Posture Recognition using the Kinect. Vol. 8511 of the series Lecture Notes in Computer Science, pp 205-214.

[2] Van den Bergh, M. & al. 2011. Real-time 3D Hand Gesture Interaction with a Robot for Understanding Directions from Humans. In *Proceedings of* ROMAN 2011, pp 357-362

Arm-Hidden Private Area on an Interactive Tabletop System

Kai Li[1], Asako Kimura[1], and Fumihisa Shibata[1]

[1]Graduate School of Information Science and Engineering, Ritsumeikan University, Japan

kai@rm.is.ritsumei.ac.jp

ABSTRACT

Tabletop systems are used primarily in meetings or other activities wherein information is shared. However, when confidential input is needed, for example when entering a password, privacy becomes an issue. In this study, we use the shadowed area nearby the forearm when the user places their forearm on the tabletop. And our tabletop security system is using that hidden-area to show a confidential information window. We also introduce several potential applications for this hidden-area system.

Author Keywords

Forearm, Interaction techniques, Tabletop display, Shadow mapping, Privacy, Security.

ACM Classification Keywords

H.5.2. Information interfaces and presentation (e.g., HCI): User Interfaces – Interaction styles.

1. INTRODUCTION

Many solutions have been proposed for the security of tabletop systems. Isogawa et al. [1] used a three projector setup wherein the rear one projected a graphical image while the two front ones projected a complementary image. Anderson et al. [2] proposed an interface that prevents others noticing that the user is accessing or inputting information. However, in these studies, the concealed information could not be guaranteed to be hidden from the view of others. In this study, we proposed an interactive tabletop system that can present personal information within a personal space on the tabletop display that is inaccessible to other users.

2. METHOD

We based our approach on the gesture wherein a forearm is placed on the tabletop [3]. This allowed information to be hidden while adopting a natural posture. Using a shadow mapping technique, from the onlooker's point of view, the area behind the forearm is in shadow (Figure 1), and invisible to the onlooker. The principle underpinning this technique is that when viewing an object from a point at the source of the light, anything behind the object is invisible. Williams [4] introduced the concept as the mapping of a linear transformation of the X,Y,Z points as the X,Y,Z points in the observer's view. In our approach, the position of the onlooker was taken to be the source of light. Therefore, from the onlooker's point of view, the area behind the forearm is in shadow, and invisible to the onlooker.

The tabletop surface had a projection surface area of 1.52 m by

SUI '16, October 15-16, 2016, Tokyo, Japan
ACM 978-1-4503-4068-7/16/10.
DOI: http://dx.doi.org/10.1145/2983310.2989194.

Figure 1. Area hidden from co-worker

Figure 2. Applications using the hidden-area.(a) Input Password (b) Secret Photo Viewer (c) Urgent Information Checker.

0.82 m. A projector was placed beneath the tabletop. The positions of user's hands and onlookers are detected by a motion capture system.

3. APPLICATIONS

Input Password (Figure 2 (a)) is an application to conceal the users' password from other people working at the same table. When users place their forearm on the table, a keyboard with randomly arranged keys appears in the users' hidden-area. The Secret Photo Viewer (Figure 2 (b)) is another application to view pictures secretly or to select a picture without displaying a personal picture database to other people. The Urgent Information Checker application (Figure 2 (c)) is for the users checking the names and profiles of the meeting attendees secretly in the hidden area. It can also display a schedule and provide alerts for the users to subtly view their agenda.

4. CONCLUSIONS

This paper demonstrates an idea to manage privacy issues by taking advantage of a person's natural posture when working on a tabletop. When a user places a forearm on the tabletop, a display window will appear and information will be projected within the hidden-area.

5. REFERENCES

[1] Isogawa, M., Iwai, D., and Sato, K. 2014. Making graphical information visible in real shadows on interactive tabletops, IEEE Trans. Vis. Comput. Graph., vol. 20, no. 9, 1293 - 1302.
[2] Anderson, F., Grossman, T., Wigdor, D., and Fitzmaurice, G. 2015. Supporting subtlety with deceptive devices and illusory interactions. Proc. of CHI'15, 1489 - 1498.
[3] Koura, S., Suo, S., Kimura, A., Shibata, F. and Tamura, H. 2012. Amazing forearm as an innovative interaction device and data storage on tabletop display. Proc. of ITS'12, 383 - 386.
[4] L. Williams, "Casting curved shadows on curved surfaces," SIGGRAPH Com- put. Graph., vol. 12, pp. 270–274, Aug. 1978.

AnyOrbit: Fluid 6DOF Spatial Navigation of Virtual Environments using Orbital Motion

Benjamin I. Outram, Yun Suen Pai, Kevin Fan, Kouta Minamizawa, Kai Kunze
Keio University, 4-1-1 Hiyoshi, Yokohama
benjamin.outram@gmail.com

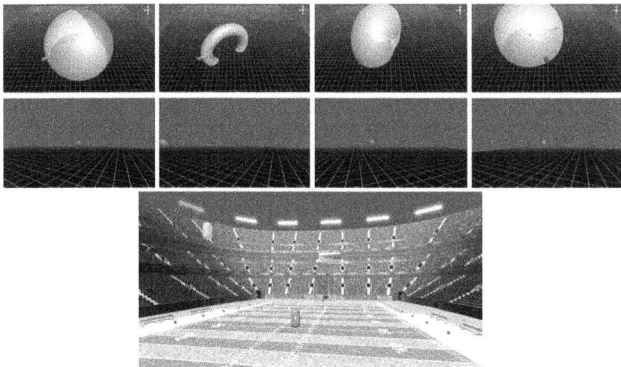

Figure 1: Left: Orbital motion on toroidal surface. Right: Virtual environment used for evaluation.

ABSTRACT

Emerging media technologies such as 3D film and head-mounted displays (HMDs) call for new types of spatial interaction. Here we describe and evaluate AnyOrbit: a novel orbital navigation technique that enables flexible and intuitive 3D spatial navigation in virtual environments (VEs). Unlike existing orbital methods, we exploit toroidal rather than spherical orbital surfaces, which allow independent control of orbital curvature in vertical and horizontal directions. This control enables intuitive and smooth orbital navigation between any desired orbital centers and between any vantage points within VEs. AnyOrbit leverages our proprioceptive sense of rotation to enable navigation in VEs without inconvenient external motion trackers. In user studies, we demonstrate that within a sports-spectating context, the technique allows smooth shifts in perspective at a rate comparable to broadcast sport, is fast to learn, and is without excessive simulator sickness in most users. The technique is widely applicable to gaming, computer-aided-design (CAD), data visualisation, and telepresence.

SUI '16, October 15–16, 2016, Tokyo, Japan.
© 2016 Copyright held by the owner/author(s).
ACM ISBN 978-1-4503-4068-7/16/10.
DOI: http://dx.doi.org/10.1145/2983310.2989195

1. PAST WORK AND IMPLEMENTATION

Orbital movement is ubiquitous in CAD software where it is instantly intuitive and suited to observational tasks [2]. Orbiting was first used with HMDs by Chung et al., where head orientation controls the angle, and the radius is fixed or controlled using an input [1]. Tan combined orbiting with flying and other 'modes' [3].

Previous techniques confine the user to a spherical surface, however, we position the user on the surface of a torus (figure 1), which allows the control of the horizontal and vertical radii of curvature individually, such that as the user rotates their head, they move on a spiral trajectory towards a spherical orbit about any chosen new point-of-interest (the red dot shown in figure 1).

2. EVALUATION

A study of 13 inexperienced users (9 male, age = 25.9 ± 3.2) evaluated AnyOrbit for simulator sickness and performance. Users were tasked with navigating between positions and facing directions in a VE (figure 1) representing camera angles typical of broadcast sport, in 3 trials of 5 minutes each. Users averaged 14 ± 8.6 seconds per task. In addition, an expert user completed tasks in 3.8 ± 1.2 seconds. This compares to 5 to 11 seconds for average shot lengths in sport broadcasts. There was a measurable increase in Simulator Sickness Questionnaire (SSQ) scores after the first 5 minute trial, but no significant increase on subsequent VE exposure.

3. CONCLUSION

We have presented an algorithm for allowing smooth navigation between orbital trajectories in VEs using HMDs, and 6DOF navigation and perspective selection. The technique is quick to learn and does not cause excessive simulator sickness in most users. The technique is well suited to future 3D sports media formats, storytelling in VEs, and spatial navigation tasks.

4. REFERENCES

[1] J. C.-M. Chung. *Intuitive Navigation in the Targeting of Radiation Therapy Treatment Beams*. PhD thesis, Chapel Hill, NC, USA, 1993.

[2] A. Khan et al. Hovercam: interactive 3D navigation for proximal object inspection. In *Proc. ACM I3D*, pages 73–80. ACM, 2005.

[3] D. S. Tan et al. Exploring 3D navigation: combining speed-coupled flying with orbiting. In *Proc. ACM CHI*, pages 418–425. ACM, 2001.

KnowHow: Contextual Audio-Assistance for the Visually Impaired in Performing Everyday Tasks

Abhay Agarwal
Microsoft Research,
#9 Lavelle Road,
Bengaluru, India

Sujeath Pareddy[*]
Department of CS&IS,
BITS Pilani,
Hyderabad, India

Swaminathan Manohar
Microsoft Research,
#9 Lavelle Road,
Bengaluru, India

{t-abagar, t-supare, manohar.swaminathan}@microsoft.com

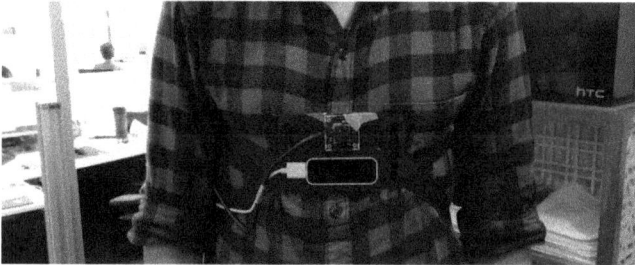

ABSTRACT

We present a device for visually impaired persons (VIPs) that delivers contextual audio assistance for physical objects and tasks. In initial observations, we found ubiquitous use of audio-assistance technologies by VIPs for interacting with computing devices, such as Android TalkBack. However, we also saw that devices without screens frequently lack accessibility features. Our solution allows a VIP to obtain audio assistance in the presence of an arbitrary physical interface or object through a chest-mounted device. On-board are camera sensors that point towards the user's personal front-facing grasping region. Upon detecting certain gestures such as picking up an object, the device provides helpful contextual audio information to the user. Textual interfaces can be read aloud by sliding a finger over the surface of the object, allowing the user to hear a document or receive audio guidance for non-assistively-enabled electronic devices. The user may provide questions verbally in order to refine their audio assistance, or to ask broad questions about their environment.

Our motivation is to provide sensemaking faculties that creatively approximate those of non-VIPs in tasks that make VIPs ineligible for common employment opportunities.

Keywords

Visual impairment; Accessibility; Multimodal Interface

*Work carried out during an internship at MSR India.

SUI '16 June 16–19, 2013, Tokyo, Japan

© 2016 Copyright held by the owner/author(s).

ACM ISBN 978-1-4503-4068-7/16/10.

DOI: http://dx.doi.org/10.1145/2983310.2989196

1. MULTIMODAL SENSEMAKING

We focus on sensemaking of objects within a user's physical near-field, or grasping distance, due to our qualitative background research of commonly inaccessible employment opportunities in India. Visual information is crucial in a variety near-field tasks from operating a microwave to identifying products in a store.

KnowHow comprises of a 160° Field-of-View (FOV) RGB camera, a 150° FOV dual-IR camera (Leap Motion^{TM}), an audio headset, and a hidden computation device (in this case a backpack-worn laptop). During the course of a user's everyday activity, the device interprets multimodal input from gestures, image, and verbal interlocution. Textual information is found by segmenting the image using Extremal Regions (ER)[1], then by utilizing the Tesseract character-recognition library on cropped segments. Based on the user's gestures, text detected by the device is either read out or an image is sent to the cloud where an object recognition API returns with detailed information. We compute offline any information that is highly time-dependent and critical to baseline functionality, thus a network connection is not required to read aloud text or recognize verbal commands.

2. FUTURE WORK AND APPLICATIONS

This research has yielded a theoretical framework for assistive technologies as well as a robust implementation of one such device. We are working with partner organizations to explore employment opportunities that can be opened up for VIPs by successful deployment of our device.

3. REFERENCES

[1] L. Neumann. Real-time scene text localization and recognition. In *Proceedings of the 2012 IEEE Conference on Computer Vision and Pattern Recognition (CVPR)*, CVPR '12, pages 3538–3545, Washington, DC, USA, 2012. IEEE Computer Society.

Effect of using Walk-In-Place Interface for Panoramic Video Play in VR

Azeem Syed Muhammad
Korea Institute of Science and Technology
Seoul, Korea
University of Science and Technology
Daejeon, Korea
s.azeem2004@gmail.com

Sang Chul Ahn
Korea Institute of Science and Technology
Seoul, Korea
University of Science and Technology,
Daejeon, Korea
asc@imrc.kist.re.kr

Jae In Hwang
Korea Institute of Science and Technology
Seoul, Korea
University of Science and Technology
Daejeon, Korea
hji@kist.re.kr

ABSTRACT

This paper describes the use of walk-in-place (WIP) interface to control the speed of 360-degree panoramic virtual reality (VR) video on a head-mounted display and through a pilot user study, the effect of using this interface with respect to the amount of simulator sickness and presence in the environment felt by the user is evaluated. The results are compared with traditional 360-degree VR video experience.

Author Keywords

Simulator sickness; 360-degree video; walk-in-place.

1. INTRODUCTION

Simulator sickness is a common problem when we watch a 360-degree VR video or navigate a VR environment using head-mounted display (HMD). In order to reduce simulator sickness, we evaluated walk in place interface for watching 360-degree VR videos. We implemented three different smartphone accelerometer based step detection algorithms for our WIP interface and conducted a user study to evaluate our WIP interface against traditional 360-degree VR video experience. We found that, in general, users felt less simulator sickness when they used WIP based interface as compared to when they watched a 360-degree VR video with traditional rotation only interface. Users also gave significantly high score to WIP interface for presence in the environment and usability of interface. Currently, our WIP interface works the best for 360 videos that are made by continuously moving the camera on a straight path.

2. OUR APPROACH

We implemented three approaches of step-detection for WIP interface and conducted a user study to find out that the method proposed by Zhao [3] gave the best real time step detection results. A user wore HMD and made WIP gestures, our system detected user steps using [3] and played a 360-degree VR video. The speed of the video play was directly proportional to stepping speed. We used Samsung Galaxy Note 4 smartphone and Samsung Gear VR HMD for implementation.

SUI '16, October 15-16, 2016, Tokyo, Japan
ACM 978-1-4503-4068-7/16/10.
http://dx.doi.org/10.1145/2983310.2989197

Our study consisted of 10 participants (3 females, 7 males) aged between 21 and 34. Each participant was asked to experience the

(Right) The scene of 360 panoramic video he is watching.

same 360-degree VR video (see Figure 1) both with rotation only and WIP interfaces and they could rotate their heads only. After each experience they filled survey forms for simulator sickness and usability & presence in the environment for each experience designed using [2] and [1] respectively.

From user study results we found that our WIP interface was significantly better in terms of presence in the environment while being slightly better in reducing simulator sickness. On a scale of 0 (no simulator sickness) to 3 (severe simulator sickness), the average user-rated score for WIP based method was 0.5 against 0.725 for rotation only interface.

3. CONCLUSION

We conclude that, with more user data, it can be proved that the use of walk-in-place interface causes significantly less amount of simulation sickness as compared to rotation only interface for watching 360-degree VR videos.

4. REFERENCES

[1] Ilias A, Daniel S. C, and Eelke F. Accuracy of Pedometry on a Head-mounted Display. Proceedings of the 33rd Annual Conference on Human Factors in Computing Systems, ACM, New York, NY, USA, 2153-2156.

[2] Kennedy, R. S., Lane, N.E., Berbaum, K. S. and Lilienthal, M.G. Simulator Sickness Questionnaire: An enhanced method for quantifying simulator sickness. International Journal of Aviation Psychology, 1993, 3(3): 203-220.

[3] Zhao, N. Full-featured pedometer design realized with 3-Axis digital accelerometer, Analog Dialogue 44, 06 (2010)

Using Area Learning in Spatially-Aware Ubiquitous Environments

Edwin Chan, Yuxi Wang, Teddy Seyed, Frank Maurer
University of Calgary
2500 University Drive NW, Calgary, Alberta, Canada
{chane, yuxwang, teddy.seyed, frank.maurer}@ucalgary.ca

ABSTRACT

We propose a framework using Google's Area Learning to create ubiquitous environments with cross-device proxemic interactions. We apply the framework to the domain of Emergency Response, and discuss the benefits and initial feedback of our framework.

Keywords

Sensors; Cross-device Interactions; Multi-surface; Area Learning; Ubiquitous Environments

1. INTRODUCTION

Ubiquitous environments have become increasingly common, as low-cost devices and sensors proliferate. Significant research has explored using these sensors to understand and interact with our surroundings. A recurring theme is to use proxemics, based on the relative positions of devices, to perform cross-device interactions. Existing frameworks for creating spatially-aware environments rely on strategically placed sensors, with many drawbacks. Camera sensors rely on line-of-sight, and run into the occlusion problem where moving users block each other from the sensors. If multiple sensors are used, they must be carefully calibrated to the same coordinate space. As the tracked space grows, the cost of expensive sensors also accumulates. We propose using the Area Learning tracking technology to enable spatially-aware ubiquitous environments, to overcome the aforementioned problems with existing frameworks and their sensors.

2. AREA LEARNING

Google's Area Learning (AL) is a spatial tracking methodology which maps an environment using mobile depth-sensing cameras [1]. The cameras are built into user devices, removing the need for external sensors. Each AL device is able to determine its own relative position accurately (± 0.1m) in 3D. By sharing the mapped environment, any number of devices can be integrated into a ubiquitous environment without any additional effort.

3. IMPLEMENTATION

SOD-Toolkit [3] is a flexible framework which can incorporate new sensors through its API. In addition to the existing Microsoft Kinect and Estimote iBeacon sensors, we used AL as a sensing technology. Mobile devices with AL capability are able to determine their own locations within the environment. Incompatible devices can still rely on other external sensors to

SUI '16, October 15-16, 2016, Tokyo, Japan
ACM 978-1-4503-4068-7/16/10.
http://dx.doi.org/10.1145/2983310.2989198

provide spatial information. All spatial information is plotted in the same coordinate space.

4. CASE STUDY

We used SOD-Toolkit with Area Learning within the Emergency Response domain, to design a spatially-aware Emergency Operations Centre [2]. Users were able to perform existing gestures from SOD-Toolkit, such as pouring data from a tablet onto a tabletop, with greater reliability using AL. In addition, users could interact in an augmented 3D space above the 2D tabletop, to interact with buildings on a map as well as their floorplans. The EOC prototype was demonstrated in several crowded environments, and required just minutes to setup at each location.

5. DISCUSSION & CONCLUSION

Previous versions of SOD-Toolkit required significant time and effort to setup, even by experienced users. The AL framework could be setup by anyone, and usually required under 10 minutes. For previous demos, we had to carefully consider the placement of devices while designating specific standing areas, as to not occlude sensors. In a recent demo, we had dozens of people standing side-by-side, and were able to reliably demonstrate cross-device proxemic interactions. We found AL to be highly robust, providing accurate spatial tracking at a relatively low cost. The ease of setup and flexibility to adapt spaces for different usages makes AL-enabled frameworks suitable for deploying spatially-aware ubiquitous environments in real-world scenarios.

6. REFERENCES

[1] Area Learning. Google Developers, 2016. https://developers.google.com/project-tango/overview/area-learning.

[2] Chan, E., Gonzalez, D. and Marbouti, M. et al. Multi-Surface Systems for the Emergency Operations Centre of the Future. In *CSCW 2016 Workshop on Collaboration and Decision Making in Crisis Situations - CADMICS*, (2016).

[3] Seyed, T., Azazi, A., Chan, E., Wang, Y. and Maurer, F. SoD-Toolkit. In *Proc of the 2015 International Conference on Interactive Tabletops & Surfaces (ITS '15)*. ACM, New York, NY, USA, 171-180.

MocaBit 2.0: A Gamified System to Examine Behavioral Patterns through Granger Causality

Sanghyun Yoo
School of Arts, Media and Engineering
Arizona State University
Tempe, Arizona
cooperyoo@asu.edu

Sudarshan Seshasayee
School of Arts, Media and Engineering
Arizona State University
Tempe, Arizona
spseshas@asu.edu

ABSTRACT

In this paper, we approach the study to shed light on the relationship between multi user's movement and influence through vision-based technology, gamification, and Granger Causality (GC). This research utilizes GC test in a gamified mo-cap system, named MocaBit, in order to figure out whether player's personal movement and influence affect each other with specific time-lag. As a result, it turned out that user's velocity and curvature have statistically affected other user's actions.

Keywords

Activity Tracking; Motion Capture; Gamification; Kinesiology; Measurement; Human Factors; Granger Causality

1. DESIGN AND IMPLEMENTATION

From a user experience standpoint, we implemented a sub-level architecture to explore the capability of our system.

1.1 Motion Capture

At the base of the hierarchy, our mo-cap system uses Motive an OptiTrack camera compatible software to obtain tracker data of the various subjects in the mo-cap stage. This then allowed a transmission of these objects in real time.

1.2 Visualization

Each user's position in localized space calculated their nearest neighbor, using the k-Nearest Neighbor (KNN) algorithm. As this computation constantly spews out a user index as they move around, a line is drawn between them and their Nearest Neighbor (NN).

1.3 Gamification

In order to obtain an optimum data set to test the capability of our system, we adapted the concepts of gamification. The NN users with a double connect racked up 1-5 points based on the time spent. This provided the users an incentive to move faster and more erratic.

1.4 Granger Causality

The mathematical definition of GC is considered a predictive analysis. [1] In this paper, this is done through F-tests. [2] Furthermore, we delve a step further by not just analysing the time series of x, y or z individually, but perform in 3 constraints. (i)

SUI '16, October 15-16, 2016, Tokyo, Japan
ACM 978-1-4503-4068-7/16/10.
http://dx.doi.org/10.1145/2983310.2989199

The original data compared with each user. (ii) The first partial derivative over time; ie. Velocity. (iii) The curvature of movement within a time window integral over the entire frame. This explores the various levels of abstraction obtained through movement.

Figure 1. Four user testers interacting with MocaBit.

2. RESULTS

After running a VAR model and deriving Fisher's information through the F-distribution model and normalized data, into the GC algorithm, the following F-ratio results are obtained.

Table 1. F-ratio Results

User	A	B	C	D
A	0	2.52695	5.94145	0.39935
B	7.45165	0	2.62565	2.21475
C	18.39745	18.6473	0	10.6941
D	1.2399	0.08663	12.21682	0

It is self explanatory that a user cannot GC themselves. Further, with 4 groups and from the data available, the closer its ratio to the critical value (~0.7) as obtained from the post-hoc analysis. The values under are rejected by null hypothesis.

3. CONCLUSION

This paper started with the simplicity of direction invariant single-point cloud data to determine the correlation between several user movement patterns. MocaBit localized motion-capture system and Granger Causality to figure out the relationship of user's movements.

Further, we can expand our approach in different scenarios such as larger space, larger crowd, and practical world examples in physical game environment, sports, public events, and traffic.

4. REFERENCES

[1] Granger, C. W. J. 1969 Investigating causal relations by econometric models and cross-spectral methods. Econometrica 37, 424-438.

[2] Berzuini, Carlo, Philip Dawid, and Luisa Bernardinell, eds. *Causality: Statistical perspectives and applications*. John Wiley & Sons, 2012.

Fast and Accurate 3D Selection using Proxy with Spatial Relationship for Immersive Virtual Environments

Jun Lee, JiHyung Park*
Center for Robotics, KIST
Hwarangno 14-gil 5, Seongbuk-gu
Seoul, Korea
82-10-2852-6450
junlee@kist.re.kr,

JuYoung Oh
University of Science and Technology
Hwarangno 14-gil 5, Seongbuk-gu
Seoul, Korea
82-10-2705-3497
dhwndud407@gmail.com

JoongHo Lee
Center of Human-centered Interaction
for Coexistence
Seongbuk-gu, Seoul, Korea
82-10-2875-3969
Yap153@naver.com

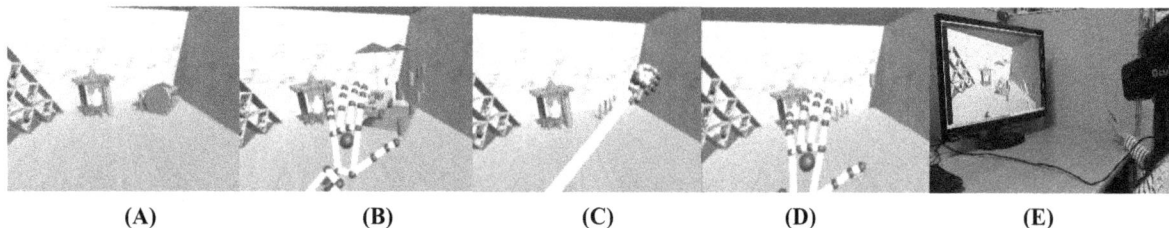

Figure 1 Concept design of the proposed selection method (A) A sphere is locating at a building with a car, (B) Proxies are visualized according to spatial relationships, (C) Users grasps a hand to select a virtual object, (D) Selected object is visualized, (E) Experimental environment with Oculus Rift DK2 and Leap Motion

ABSTRACT

In this paper, we propose a fast and accurate 3D selection method using visualization of proxies with spatial relationships. The proposed 3D selection method reduced selection errors and selection time comparing to conventional ray-casting method.

Keywords

3D object selection; Sphere-casting; Spatial Relationship; HMD.

1. INTRODUCTION

3D object selection is one of the fundamental tasks in immersive 3D virtual environments. 3D object selection is the ability of the user to specify an object for the subsequent manipulation in the immersive virtual environments. Since 3D object selection can increase the usability of 3D interactions, various research has been presented. Ray-casting extends a virtual ray from a user's body such as an arm or viewport, and the ray is used to select and manipulate objects. It is simple and general to select a virtual object. However, it is difficult to perform selection objects if they have a small visible area according to occlusions [1, 2]. SQUAD presented progressive refinement selection method [3]. When a user selects virtual objects using sphere-casting, a QUAD menu shows four classifications of virtual objects, and then a user selects the subset of objects until the target is finally selected. Although the selection performance was improved comparing to conventional ray-casting approach, spatial relationships among the selected objects are disappeared during the selection process. Therefore, a user may re-start the selection process when he/she lose awareness of the spatial presence of the highly occluded and cluttered objects.

We propose a fast and accurate selection method based on spatial relationships among the occluded objects. The proposed method uses sphere-casting with head tracking information through a HMD. Figure 1 shows examples of the proposed sphere-casting method with visualization

SUI '16, October 15-16, 2016, Tokyo, Japan
ACM 978-1-4503-4068-7/16/10.
http://dx.doi.org/10.1145/2983310.2989200

of spatial relationships. A user can move a sphere with rotating his/her head. The head tracking information matches to 3D position of the sphere as shown in Figure 1. (A). He/She then lifts a hand to select a virtual object. The proposed system calculates spatial relationships, and it visualizes proxies to avoid occlusion as shown in Figure 1.(B). In order to represent spatial relationships of the proxies, linked lines are visualized among the proxies. He/She then selects the target proxy with a grasping hand gesture as shown in Figure 1.(C). Finally, a selected object is visualized in Figure 1.(D). Figure 1.(E) shows the experimental environment.

2. CONCLUSIONS

We proposed a fast selection method which shows spatial relationships of occluded objects with visualization proxies. The proposed selection method reduced selection errors and task completion time comparing to ray-casting approach. In the future work, we will develop group-based sphere-casting method for 3D object selection among highly cluttered virtual objects such as a car engine and a molecular model.

3. ACKNOLEDGEMENT

JiHyung Park is a corresponding author.

This work was supported by the Global Frontier R&D Program on <Human-centered Interaction for Coexistence> funded by the National Research Foundation of Korea grant funded by the Korean Government(MSIP)(NRF-M1AXA003-2011-0031380).

4. REFERENCES

[1] Argelaguet, F. and Andujar, C. A survey of 3D object selection techniques for virtual environments. Computers & Graphics, 37 (3), 121-136, 2013.

[2] A. Steed and C. Parker. 3D selection strategies for head tracked and non-head tracked operation of spatially immersive displays. In 8th International Immersive Projection Technology Workshop, 13– 14, 2004.

[3] Kopper R. Bacim F. and Bowman D.A. Rapid and Accurate 3D Selection by Progressive Refinement, IEEE 3DUI 2011, 67-74, 2011

Haptic Exploration of Remote Environments with Gesture-based Collaborative Guidance

Seokyeol Kim
School of Computing, KAIST, Korea
sy.kim@kaist.ac.kr

Jinah Park
School of Computing, KAIST, Korea
jinahpark@kaist.ac.kr

ABSTRACT

We present a collaborative haptic interaction method for exploring a remote physical environment with guidance from a distant helper. Spatial information, which is represented by a point cloud, of the remote environment is directly rendered as a contact force without reconstruction of surfaces. On top of this, the helper can selectively exert an attractive force for reaching a target or a repulsive force for avoiding a forbidden region to the user by using free-hand gestures.

Keywords

Haptic interaction; telepresence; collaborative guidance

1. INTRODUCTION

Telepresence systems with pre-defined or autonomous guidance work well with typical tasks, but sometimes they still need a heuristic decision and manual guidance from a human assistant. To allow human guidance without hand-held-device-mediated interaction, we propose a collaborative haptic interaction method to explore a remotely located physical environment with hand-gesture-based guidance from a remote helper. An RGB-D camera captures the remote environment, and the image streams are transmitted to the client side in the form of a point cloud. If the user is in contact with real-world objects, a contact force is directly calculated from the overlapped points without reconstruction of surface meshes. At the same time, our method recognizes the hand of the helper from the image streams and exerts a proper guidance force according to the hand posture.

2. CONTACT AND GUIDANCE FORCES

For calculating a contact force without surface information, we directly measure proximity from a haptic interface point (HIP) to each point in the point cloud and estimate a surface normal by using a radial basis function [1]. During the contact, a surface contact point (SCP) remains on the estimated surface, and the contact force is proportional to the distance between the HIP and the SCP (Fig. 1-(a)).

To enable guidance of haptic exploration without a hand-held device, meanwhile, we adopt a hand recognition method based on skeletal tracking [2]. The detected hand position is considered as a pivot point, and the effective area of guidance is defined by a sphere around the pivot point. If the

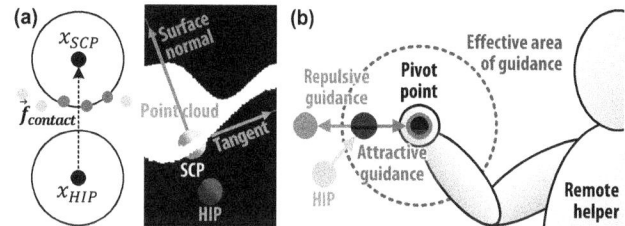

Figure 1: (a) Constrained motion of the SCP. (b) Collaborative haptic guidance from a remote helper.

HIP enters the effective area, an attractive guidance cue that helps the HIP reach a target or a repulsive guidance cue that makes the HIP avoid a forbidden region is selectively activated by the helper's decision (Fig. 1-(b)).

3. PROTOTYPE AND FUTURE WORK

The example situations that explain how guidance cues help the HIP reach a target object are shown in Fig. 2. A Microsoft Kinect camera captures both the physical objects and the helper in a remote environment, and the user can interact with the remote environment by manipulating a haptic device. In the future, we plan to support 6-DOF manipulation of the guidance cues by estimating the palm orientation and conduct a user study to evaluate the task performance and the usability of our approach.

Figure 2: Haptic exploration with the repulsive (top) and the attractive (bottom) guidance cue.

4. ACKNOWLEDGMENT

This research was supported by a grant from NRF funded by the Korea government (MSIP) (2010-0028631).

5. REFERENCES

[1] F. Rydén and H. J. Chizeck. A proxy method for real-time 3-DOF haptic rendering of streaming point cloud data. *IEEE Trans. Haptics*, 6(3):257–267, 2013.

[2] Z. Zhang. Microsoft Kinect sensor and its effect. *IEEE MultiMedia*, 19(2):4–10, 2012.

Subliminal Reorientation and Repositioning in Virtual Reality During Eye Blinks

Eike Langbehn
Human-Computer Interaction,
University of Hamburg
Vogt-Koelln-Str. 30
Hamburg, Germany
eike.langbehn@uni-
hamburg.de

Gerd Bruder
Human-Computer Interaction,
University of Hamburg
Vogt-Koelln-Str. 30
Hamburg, Germany
gerd.bruder@uni-
hamburg.de

Frank Steinicke
Human-Computer Interaction,
University of Hamburg
Vogt-Koelln-Str. 30
Hamburg, Germany
frank.steinicke@uni-
hamburg.de

ABSTRACT

Locomotion in Immersive Virtual Environments (IVEs) is one of the most basic interactions, while human walking is the most natural user-interface for this. Obviously, this technique is limited by the available physical space. Redirected Walking (RDW) wants to overcome this issue by subliminal redirection of the user inside the physical space. Traditional RDW algorithms need a circle with a radius of 22m to allow the user the exploration of an infinite virtual world [2]. Because this is still too large to fit in a room-scale setup, we have to optimize detection thresholds and algorithms.

Bolte et al. [1] already examined reorientation and repositioning during saccades and showed that a subtle manipulation is possible. In this poster we describe how we investigated reorientation and repositioning of the user in the virtual world during eye blinks. Furthermore, we present an experimental setup for evaluating detection thresholds of reorientation and repositioning during eye blinks. And we indicate first impressions of the perception and the usability.

Keywords

Virtual Reality; Redirection; Eye Blink

1. EXPERIMENTAL SETUP

We used a head-mounted display with an integrated eye-tracking device and showed a virtual replica of the real environment to the participants of the experiment. In a trial, the participant was asked to blink. During the detection of a blink the virtual world was rotated or translated. After that, we asked the participant to guess in which direction the world was rotated/translated and offered two possible answers (2-Alternatives-Forced-Choice-Task). We tested yaw, pitch, roll and translations on x, y, z axis with seven gains.

SUI '16 October 15-16, 2016, Tokyo, Japan

© 2016 Copyright held by the owner/author(s).

ACM ISBN 978-1-4503-4068-7/16/10.

DOI: http://dx.doi.org/10.1145/2983310.2989204

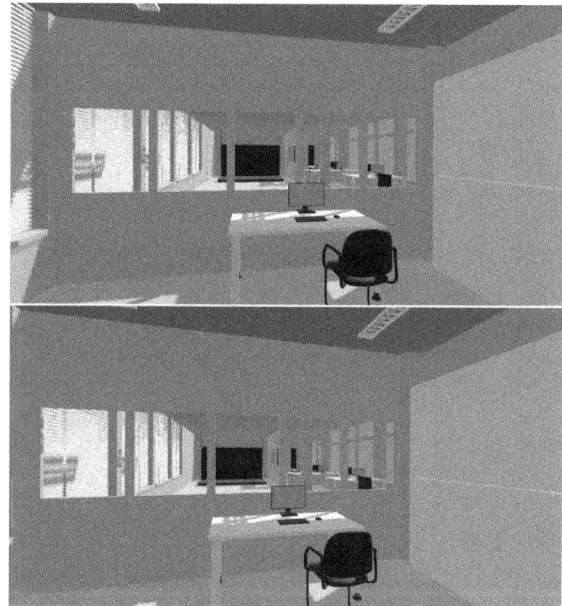

Figure 1: The virtual environment before and after an eye blink.

2. IMPRESSIONS

First impressions suggest that imperceptible reorientation and repositioning is possible during eye blinks. Moreover, initial feedback suggests that it could widen the known RDW detection thresholds.

3. REFERENCES

[1] B. Bolte and M. Lappe. Subliminal reorientation and repositioning in immersive virtual environments using saccadic suppression. *IEEE Transactions on Visualization and Computer Graphics (TVCG)*, 21(4):545–552, 2015.

[2] F. Steinicke, G. Bruder, J. Jerald, H. Fenz, and M. Lappe. Estimation of Detection Thresholds for Redirected Walking Techniques. *IEEE Transactions on Visualization and Computer Graphics (TVCG)*, pages 17–27, 2010.

Multimodal Embodied Interface for Levitation and Navigation in 3D Space

M. Perusquía-Hernández[1], T. Martins[2], T. Enomoto[1], M. Otsuki[1], H. Iwata[1], K. Suzuki[1]

[1]University of Tsukuba, [2]Universität für künstlerische und industrielle gestaltung Linz

monica@ai.iit.tsukuba.ac.jp, tiago.martins@ufg.at, takahisa@vrlab.esys.tsukuba.ac.jp,
otsuki@emp.tsukuba.ac.jp, iwata@kz.tsukuba.ac.jp, kenji@ieee.org

ABSTRACT

A multimodal embodied interface for 3D navigation was designed as a modular wearable. The user is suspended with a harness controlled by a mechanical Motion Base. This allows both physical and virtual displacement within an immersive virtual environment. Through a combination of passive and active modalities, users are enabled to fly at their own will.

Keywords

Embodiment; multimodal interaction; 3D space navigation

1. INTRODUCTION

As technology enables humans to experience individual flight, we propose to investigate what kind of techniques can be used to achieve embodied control navigation rather than vehicle-based fly control. Common approaches to embodied flight control are bird mimicking [2] or paragliding [3]. Additionally, the ability to fly using only our own body constitutes a completely new experience and thus, a design challenge. Furthermore, the perceived risk of falling is likely to cause unease. Our proposal addresses these challenges.

2. DESIGN AND USER EVALUATION

A wire-drive Motion Base (MB) allows three-axis flying movement. The MB is a carbon base connected to seven wires and seven pulleys that control wire length using a parallel link manipulator. A harness is attached to the MB, allowing deliberate user displacement (Fig. 1). Since body movements such as head and gaze orientation anticipate the direction of movement during gait [1], head orientation was chosen as passive modality for navigation. The active counterpart is pressure on the front, back, and sides of the harness. Additionally, electrophysiological signals were used for vertical navigation. While a calm user levitates, a stressed user stays on the ground. Electroencephalography (EEG) and Electromyography-based (EMG) jaw clenching detection indicate relaxation levels. The active equivalent for vertical movement is pressure on the harness bands, associated to the tendency of nervous, unaccustomed users to seek support by tightly holding on to these. The system consists of a modular wearable device that combines four flexible

Figure 1: Motion Base and wearable harness

textile pressure sensors attached to the harness; an Inertial Measurement Unit; and a 4-channel InteraXon Muse EEG head band. The movement speed was fixed to 20 cm/s. The sensor data was smoothed and mapped to positions corresponding to three states: (1) standing in the ground, (2) levitating, and (3) flying. Users always start on the ground, and need to first levitate before they can fly around.

A user evaluation was conducted to explore users' understanding of the proposed modalities. Seven participants (mean age=29 years, SD=3.69) were invited to explore different techniques to fly. No further instructions were provided. Whilst different strategies were used to control the interface, most users did try to relax and look up and down to move vertically, and tilt their bodies and heads to move forwards, backwards, and sidewards. The average agency was 3.71 (SD = 0.95, 1 = high agency, 5 = no agency). Although they reported enjoying the floating sensation (Net Promoter Score: 43%), most discomfort present was related to the movement limitations in the harness, and unresponsiveness of the device.

3. CONCLUSION AND FUTURE WORK

A multimodal embodied interface for 3D navigation was designed and evaluated. Although their satisfaction with the flying experience was fairly good, users perceived high system latency. Despite this, they explicitly reported having tried to look around in order to move. This points to the suitability of head orientation as a passive modality for 3D navigation.

4. REFERENCES

[1] Grasso, Bianchi, Lacquaniti, Owen, Cappellini, Ivanenko, Dominici, and Poppele. Motor Patterns for Human Gait: Backward Vs Forward Locomotion. *Journal of Neurophysiology*, pages 1868–1885, 1998.

[2] Rheiner. Birdly, an attempt to fly. In *ACM SIGGRAPH '14*, pages 1–1, 2014.

[3] Zepetzauer, Stefan, and Ritter. Humprey II, 2003. Accessed: 2016-06-30 URL: http://goo.gl/V0SFq0.

SUI '16 October 15-16, 2016, Tokyo, Japan

© 2016 Copyright held by the owner/author(s).

ACM ISBN 978-1-4503-4068-7/16/10.

DOI: http://dx.doi.org/10.1145/2983310.2989207

Acquario: A Tangible Spatially-Aware Tool for Information Interaction and Visualization

Sydney Pratte, Teddy Seyed, Frank Maurer
Department of Computer Science, University of Calgary
2500 University Dr. NW
{sapratte, teddy.seyed, frank.maurer}@ucalgary.ca

Figure 1. The Acquario interactive, spatially aware cubic display running a web-based demo application highlighting the proximity ranges of 'close' (b), 'near' (a) and 'far' (c).

ABSTRACT

Acquario is an interactive, spatially aware personal cubic display that can be used as an interaction tool for visualizations. Acquario uses the Pepper's ghost effect to transform a web-based visualization into a "holographic" visualization that can be interacted with using gestures, proximity or custom laser printed tangible objects with embedded NFC tags. The aim of Acquario is to enable proximity, tangible and gestural interactions for designers for keyboard and mouse based interactions, allowing users an innovative and "hands on" means.

CCS Concepts

• **Human-centered computing~Interactive systems and tools** • *Human-centered computing~Gestural input* • Human-centered computing~Ubiquitous and mobile computing design and evaluation methods

Keywords

Tangibles; spatial; gestures; information visualization;

1. INTRODUCTION

A significant amount of research has explored and continues to explore, novel and interesting ways to view and analyze datasets. Providing different means of exploration allows users to discover new and interesting insights from their data, which is only made possible with newer techniques of interaction [1]. More recent research focuses in information visualization are interaction techniques, as they allow users to "get their hands on the data" [1]. One interaction method with visualizations that has been explored in different contexts is proxemics. Similar to prior research, our research explores creating a tangible, spatial tool for interacting with information through gestures, tokens and proxemics. We introduce Acquario, which transforms web-based

visualization designs and allows users to manipulate and perform common information visualization tasks (e.g. comparison, selection, navigation) in a novel way.

2. ACQUARIO

The main goals of Acquario are (1) to provide designers of visualizations a means to enable proximity, tangible and gestural interactions, and (2) to allow users to explore visualizations in a manner that allows them to interact with data in a new way. The primary components of the system include a Samsung Galaxy Tab S2 8" tablet, a Spark Core development board, and laser-cut physical tokens with NFC tags. All components of *Acquario* are contained in a plexiglass cube (figure 1). The display of the tablet is reflected on a thin sheet of plexiglass inside the cube, at ~45° degree angle from the tablet's screen, creating the faux "hologram" that is projected onto the back surface of the cube. This technique (Pepper's ghost effect) makes digital information appear inside the cube, as seen in Figure 1.

Acquario detects when two cubes are within different proximic ranges. This can allow for individual versus collaborative information visualization. Proximity also allows users to interact with data in new ways; for example, compare data sets by bring them within a specified range. Acquario using NFC also recognizes tangible objects. When a user places a tangible object inside the cube from the left side, an event is triggered (e.g. query data). Additionally, depending on the design of a token, virtual information can be displayed on or around the token inside the cube.

3. CONCLUSION

In this work we present our early work on a tangible spatially aware tool, *Acquario*. Our research aim is to allow designers to explore data in a novel way using interaction techniques such as physical tokens, gestures and proxemics. In the next stages of this research, we will conduct further studies on usability and features that visualization designers could require from Acquario.

4. REFERENCES

[1] Sheelagh Carpendale. 2013. Innovations in visualization. In *Proceedings of Graphics Interface 2013* (GI '13). Canadian Information Processing Society, Toronto, Ont., Canada, Canada, 1-8.

Grasp, Grab or Pinch? Identifying User Preference for In-Air Gestural Manipulation

Alvin Jude
Ericsson Research
Santa Clara, CA, USA
alvinjude@acm.org

G. Michael Poor
Baylor University
Waco, TX, USA
Michael_Poor@baylor.edu

Darren Guinness
University of Colorado Boulder
Boulder, CO, USA
Darren.Guinness@colorado.edu

ABSTRACT

In-air gestural interactions can be used in desktop or other similar systems to perform cursor-based movements typically done with a mouse. One form of interaction that is required here is that of gestural manipulation, such as the ability to select a target and then move or rotate it, or any other forms of manipulation. In this paper, we implemented and evaluated 3 different gestures for users to manipulate objects on a screen, which we referred to as *"grasp"*, *"grab"* and *"pinch"*. We performed a usability study, which showed a strong preference for the *"grasp"* gesture.

Keywords

Gestural Input; Gestural Manipulation

1. INTRODUCTION

An important aspect of gestural interaction is manipulation. This is where users can select an item and manipulate it, analogous to a drag-and-drop action performed with a mouse. Such gestures have been introduced in the Leap Motion controller, including grab and pinch gestures [2]. In this paper we evaluate 3 gestures suitable for manipulation. We implemented versions of grab and pinch, and introduced one we call *grasp*. A user study was performed to evaluate user's preference of these gestures.

2. EXPERIMENT AND RESULTS

17 participants (F=7) between the ages of 18 to 22 were recruited for the study. A Leap Motion controller was used to recognise palm position and gestures. The cursor is moved based on palm position, while the users' elbow is rested on the table to reduce fatigue [1]. After the participants were comfortable with cursor movements, they were asked to perform 2 tasks. The first was to select and then rotate a 3D cube, and the second was to move an object from one part of the screen to another. All users performed both tasks with all 3 gestures. After the task, users were asked to rank the

gestures from first to last. We scored first choices with a 2, second choices with a 2 and final choices with a 0.

Of the 17 participants, 11 chose grasp as their first choice, while the remaining 6 chose pinch. The *grasp* had an average score of 1.58, the *grab* was 0.41 and *pinch* 1.00. None of the participants had used gestural manipulation before. They enjoyed its novelty and expressed interest in using it. None reported any fatigue during the experiment.

While it is clear that *grasp* was strongly preferred, more investigation is needed to understand why. We believe that this may be attributed to the ability to point at targets with the tip of their fingers using this gesture, making it a more natural gesture for a pointing-based manipulation task.

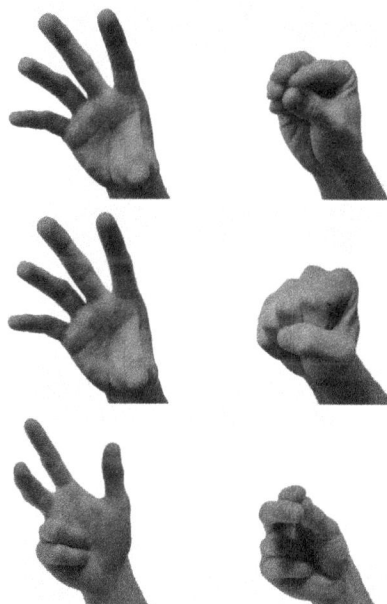

Figure 1: From top to bottom: the grasp, grab and pinch gestures respectively. Expected open hand position on the left; performed gesture on the right.

3. REFERENCES

[1] A. Jude, G. M. Poor, and D. Guinness. Personal space: user defined gesture space for gui interaction. In *Proceedings of the extended abstracts of the 32nd annual ACM conference on Human factors in computing systems*, pages 1615–1620. ACM, 2014.

[2] L. Motion. What's new with v2 tracking, 2014.

Author Index

Biometric Authentication Using the Motion of a Hand

Satoru Imura   Hiroshi Hosobe

Faculty of Computer and Information Sciences, Hosei University, Koganei-shi, Tokyo, Japan

satoru.imura@hosobe.cis.k.hosei.ac.jp   hosobe@acm.org

ABSTRACT

We propose a hand gesture-based spatial interaction method for biometric authentication. It supports 3D gestures that allow the user to move his/her hand without touching an input device. Using the motions of fingertips and joints as biometric data, the method improves the accuracy of authentication. We present the results of experiments, where subjects performed three types of gestures.

CCS Concepts

•**Human-centered computing** → **Gestural input;**
•**Security and privacy** → *Biometrics;* Multi-factor authentication;

Keywords

gesture-based spatial interaction, biometric authentication

1. PROPOSED METHOD

Our method performs authentication using the geometry and the 3D gestures of a hand, and adopts the Leap Motion controller (see Figure 1(a)). Previous work by Chan et al. [1] was focused on gestures for clicking and scrolling. By contrast, our method aims at using 3D gestures as an alternative to passwords. In the case of multi-touch devices, Sae-Bae et al. [2] studied the use of 2D gestures.

We studied three types of 3D gestures: fingertip, wrist, and complex. The fingertip type consists of two gestures: FCO (all fingertips close and then open); FBO (fingertips bend and extend one after another). The wrist type consists of four gestures: WUD (the wrist is bended up and down); WLR (the wrist is bended to the left and to the right; see Figure 1(b)); WCWY (the wrist is rotated clockwise along the vertical axis); WTR (the hand is turned over and back). The complex type consists of user-defined gestures: UDS (the user writes his/her signature in the air).

The method internally treats a gesture as a time-series data of multi-dimensional vectors. When it performs au-

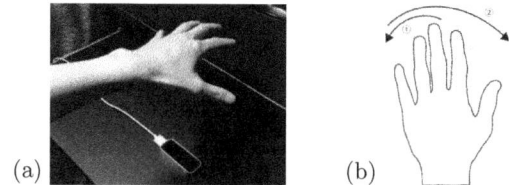

Figure 1: (a) The setting of the motion sensor for a hand; (b) a gesture called WLR.

Table 1: Results of the experiments.

Types	Gestures	Accuracy	EERs
Fingertip	FCO	90.4	3.8
	FBO	90.6	0.0
Wrist	WUD	94.0	2.4
	WLR	97.6	2.9
	WCWY	94.1	2.9
	WTR	93.0	2.3
Complex	UDS	100.0	0.0

thentication, it calculates the similarity of the input gesture with the templates in the database constructed beforehand.

2. EXPERIMENTS AND DISCUSSION

We conducted experiments on nine subjects. Table 1 shows the results of the accuracy and the equal error rates (EERs) of authentication. The EER is the rate at which false acceptance rate and the false rejection rate are equal [2].

These results indicate that, even if different subjects performed the same gestures, the method almost always distinguished their gestures. Therefore, it is difficult for users to imitate the gestures of other users, which is an ideal property for biometric authentication.

3. ACKNOWLEDGMENT

This work was supported by JSPS KAKENHI Grant Number 25540029.

4. REFERENCES

[1] A. Chan, T. Halevi, and N. D. Memon. Leap Motion controller for authentication via hand geometry and gestures. In *Proc. HAS*, volume 9190 of *LNCS*, pages 13–22, 2015.

[2] N. Sae-Bae, K. Ahmed, K. Isbister, and N. Memon. Biometric-rich gestures: A novel approach to authentication on multi-touch devices. In *Proc. ACM CHI*, pages 977–986, 2012.

Author Index